SOCIOLOGY: THE DISCIPLINE AND ITS DIRECTION

SOCIOLOGY: THE DISCIPLINE AND ITS DIRECTION

WILLIAM J. CHAMBLISS
University of California
Santa Barbara

THOMAS E. RYTHER
San Francisco State University

McGRAW-HILL BOOK COMPANY

New York   St. Louis   San Francisco   Auckland   Düsseldorf
Johannesburg   Kuala Lumpur   London   Mexico   Montreal   New Delhi
Panama   Paris   São Paulo   Singapore   Sydney   Tokyo   Toronto

For
Lou
and
Marta

SOCIOLOGY: THE DISCIPLINE AND ITS DIRECTION

Copyright © 1975 by McGraw-Hill, Inc. All rights reserved.
Printed in the United States of America. No part of this publication
may be reproduced, stored in a retrieval system, or transmitted, in any
form or by any means, electronic, mechanical, photocopying, recording, or
otherwise, without the prior written permission of the publisher.

1 2 3 4 5 6 7 8 9 0 M U R M 7 9 8 7 6 5

This book was set in Optima by Monotype Composition Company, Inc.
The editors were Lyle Linder, Helen Greenberg, and David Dunham; the
designer was Joseph Gillians; the production supervisor was Joe Campanella.
The drawings were done by Vantage Art, Inc.
The printer was The Murray Printing Company; the binder, Rand McNally &
Company.

Library of Congress Cataloging in Publication Data

Chambliss, William J.
    Sociology: the discipline and its direction.

    1. Sociology. I. Ryther, Thomas E., joint
author. II. Title.
HM 51.C42   301   74-17369
ISBN 0-07-010465-4

Acknowledgments

CHAPTER THREE
Selection 3-1 "Open Marriage: A Fantasy" by Ellen Wills. © 1973 Associated Press. Reprinted by permission.

CHAPTER FOUR
Selection 4-1 Colin M. Turnbull, *The Mountain People* (New York: Simon and Schuster, 1972), p. 141. © Simon and Schuster. Reprinted by permission.
Selection 4-2 Matsuyo Takizawa, "The Disintegration of the Old Family System," in George Dalton, *Tribal and Peasant Economies* (Garden City, N.Y.: Natural History Press, 1967), p. 357. © 1967 Natural History Press. Reprinted by permission.
Selection 4-3 Carl Sandburg, *Abraham Lincoln: The Prairie Years, Vol. I* (New York: Harcourt, Brace, 1926). © Harcourt Brace Jovanovich. Reprinted by permission.
Selection 4-4 "The CIA's Role in '64 Vote," *San Francisco Chronicle*, April 15, 1973. © Chronicle Publishing Co., 1973. Reprinted by permission.
Selection 4-5 "The Black Panther Party of Chicago," *New York Times*, Nov. 3, 1972, p. 40 and Nov. 5, 1972, p. 52. © 1973 by The New York Times Co. Reprinted by permission.
Selection 4-6 R. L. Caneiro, "A Theory of the Origin of the State," *Science*, vol. 169, 21 August, 1970, 733–738. © 1970 by the American Association for the Advancement of Science. Reprinted by permission.

CHAPTER FIVE
Selection 5-1 "Senator's Call for Institution Probe," *San Francisco Chronicle*, June 27, 1973, p. 50. © 1973 by Chronicle Publishing Co. Reprinted by permission.
Selection 5-2 "Bombs, Anonymous" by Joseph B. Treaster, *New York Times*. © 1973 by The New York Times Company. Reprinted by permission.
Selection 5-3 "The Uses of Vietspeak," *Time*, vol. 100, no. 6, 1972, p. 36. Reprinted by permission from TIME, The Weekly Newsmagazine. © Time, Inc.
Selection 5-4 "Moonshiners Caught in Electronic Traps." © United Press International. Reprinted by permission.
Selection 5-6 "Nixon Campaign Pledges: Funds Aiding Watergate Defense," *San Francisco Chronicle*, June 27, 1973, p. 50. © Chronicle Publishing Co., 1973. Reprinted by permission.

CHAPTER SIX
Selection 6-1 "The Victimized Mental Patients," by Margaret Hamilton, *San Francisco Chronicle*, Jan. 19, 1973, p. 1. © Chronicle Publishing Co., 1973. Reprinted by permission.
Selection 6-2 "The Public Loss of Confidence" by Mervin D. Field, *San Francisco Chronicle*, July 5, 1973, p. 8. © 1973 the California Poll-Field Research Corporation. Reprinted by permission.
Selection 6-3 "Coffee and the Heart: New Study," *San Francisco Chronicle*, July 14, 1973, p. 2. © 1973 The Associated Press. Reprinted by permission.

CHAPTER SEVEN

Selection 7-1   Carl Sandburg, *Abraham Lincoln: The War Years, Vol. II* (New York: Harcourt, Brace, 1926. © Harcourt Brace Jovanovich, Inc. Reprinted by permission.

Selection 7-2   "Woman of the House on Strike: Humane Treatment." © 1973 The Associated Press. Reprinted by permission.

Selection 7-3   "Women's Athletics at S. F. State" by Mary Ann Durney, *Phoenix,* vol. 12, no. 13, May 10, 1973, p. 2. © Journalism Department, San Francisco State University. Reprinted by permission.

Selection 7-4   "Early Working Conditions" from Carl Sandburg, *Abraham Lincoln: The Prairie Years* (abridged edition) (New York: Harcourt, Brace, 1926), p. 297. © Harcourt Brace Jovanovich. Reprinted by permission.

Selection 7-5   "Catholic Orders Shrinking" by George Cornell, *San Francisco Chronicle,* May 15, 1973, p. 8. © 1973 The Associated Press. Reprinted by permission.

Selection 7-6   "The City of God," *Newsweek,* Dec. 18, 1972, p. 81. © Newsweek, Inc., 1972. Reprinted by permission.

Selection 7-7   "Agrarian Reforms of Chile and Peru" by Jonathan Kendall, *San Francisco Chronicle, This Week,* March 6, 1973, p. 7. © 1973 by The New York Times Company. Reprinted by permission.

Selection 7-8   "Carmichael's New Ideology For Change," *San Francisco Chronicle,* January 27, 1973, p. 12. © Chronicle Publishing Co., 1973. Reprinted by permission.

Selection 7-9   "Great Revolutionary Effort Needed to Save the Nation," *Stanford Observer,* June 1973, p. 1. © Stanford Observer. Reprinted by permission.

Selection 7-10   "The Poor Rich: Tough Job of Making It on $30,000 a Year" by David Shaw, *Los Angeles Times,* Oct. 27, 1971, Part I, p. 1. © Los Angeles Times. Reprinted with permission Los Angeles Times/Washington Post News Service.

Selection 7-11   "The Americanization of Roseto" by Bud Richards. Copyright Washington Post. Reprinted with permission Los Angeles Times/Washington Post News Service.

CHAPTER EIGHT

Selection 8-2   "Tribal Life as Seen by a Native American in 1870" by John G. Neihardt, *Black Elk Speaks: Being the Life Story of a Holy Man of the Ogala Sioux* (Lincoln: University of Nebraska Press, 1961, pp. 152–154). © University of Nebraska Press. Reprinted by permission.

Selection 8-3   "Africa Massacre—the Elimination of a Tribal Class" by Stanley Meister, *Los Angeles Times,* April 4, 1973, Part 1, p. 1. © Los Angeles Times. Reprinted with permission Los Angeles Times/Washington Post News Service.

CHAPTER NINE

Selection 9-1   "They'd Rather Be Dead," *San Francisco Chronicle,* July 7, 1973, p. 14. © Reuters News Service. Reprinted by permission.

Selection 9-2   "Plight of the Gypsies" by Ronald Harker, *San Francisco Chronicle, This Week,* April 22, 1974, p. 24.

CHAPTER TEN

Selection 10-1   "The Folks Left Behind When the Young Move Away" by Ted Sell, *San Francisco Chronicle, Sunday Punch,* April 22, 1973, p. 4. © Los Angeles Times. Reprinted with permission Los Angeles Times/Washington Post News Service.

Selection 10-2   "When Our Resources Run Out," © Chronicle Publishing Co., 1974. Reprinted by permission.

Selection 10-3 "Rural Men Sing Out for Land Reform" by Lynn Ludlow. *San Francisco Examiner*, April 29, 1973. © 1974 San Francisco Examiner. Reprinted by permission.

CHAPTER ELEVEN

Selection 11-1 "Selfless Doctor Revealed—At Funeral," *San Francisco Chronicle*, June 22, 1973, p. 50. © Chronicle Publishing Co. Reprinted by permission.

Selection 11-2 "A Civil Rights Fight for the Mentally Ill" by Mildred Hamilton, *San Francisco Chronicle*, October 20, 1972, p. 27. © Chronicle Publishing Co., 1972. Reprinted by permission.

Selection 11-3 "Dying with Dignity: A God Given Right" by Louis Cassels, *The Salinas Californian*, Oct. 7, 1972, p. 7. © United Press International. Reprinted by permission.

Selection 11-5 "The Uneven Hand of Justice" by Leslie Oelsner, *San Francisco Chronicle, This Week*, Oct. 27, 1972. © 1972 by The New York Times Company. Reprinted by permission.

Selection 11-6 "Mexico City Smog: An Environmental Nightmare" by Allan Riding, *San Francisco Chronicle, This Week*, Jan. 28, 1973, p. 28. © 1973 Financial Times Service. Reprinted by permission.

CHAPTER TWELVE

Selection 12-1 "$4 Billion in Cash Just Sitting Around" by Milton Moskowitz, *San Francisco Chronicle*, March 9, 1974, p. 31. © Chronicle Publishing Co., 1974. Reprinted by permission.

Selection 12-2 "AMA Purchases of Drug Stocks Ok'd," *San Francisco Chronicle*, June 27, 1973, p. 6. © Chronicle Publishing Co., 1973. Reprinted by permission.

CHAPTER FOURTEEN

Selection 14-1 "CIA Chiefs Tell House of $8 Million Campaign Against Allende in '70–'73," by Seymour M. Hersh, *New York Times*, Sept. 8, 1974, p. 1. © 1974 by The New York Times Company. Reprinted by permission.

Selection 14-2 "FTC Report Fuel Shortage" by G. David Wallace, *San Francisco Examiner*, Section A, July 8, 1973, p. 1. © 1973 Associated Press. Reprinted by permission.

Selection 14-3 "The Role of the Giants in World Economy" by Milton Moskowitz, *San Francisco Chronicle*. © 1972 Chronicle Publishing Co. Reprinted by permission.

Selection 14-4 "The Shadowy World of ITT," *San Francisco Examiner*, July 8, 1973, Section A, p. 10. © 1973 Associated Press. Reprinted by permission.

Selection 14-5 "Boy Meets Co-Worker," *Time*, March 19, 1973. Reprinted by permission from *Time* The Weekly Newsmagazine. Copyright Time, Inc.

CHAPTER FIFTEEN

Selection 15-1 "Those Flying Follies of the Atomic Age" by H. Peter Metzger, *San Francisco Chronicle, Sunday Punch*, April 29, 1972, p. 2. © 1972 by The New York Times Company. Reprinted by permission.

Selection 15-2 "Bored People Build Bad Cars." © Saab-Scania of America, Inc. Reprinted by permission.

CHAPTER SIXTEEN

Selection 16-1 "The Saints and the Roughnecks" by William J. Chambliss. Reprinted by permission from *Society*, Nov.–Dec., 1973.

Selection 16-2 "The Chill of Mistaken Raids," *San Francisco Examiner*, June 26, 1973, p. 1. © Associated Press. Reprinted by permission.

Selection 16-3 "Computer, City Goof—He's Jailed" by Bill O'Brien, *San Francisco Examiner,* June 26, 1973, p. 1. © San Francisco Examiner, 1973. Reprinted by permission.

CHAPTER SEVENTEEN
Selection 17-1 "Low-Paid Farm Workers" by Richard Eder, *San Francisco Examiner,* December 22, 1972, p. 30. © 1972 by the New York Times Company. Reprinted by permission.
Selection 17-2 "At the Summit of the Affluent United States Society" by William Chapman, *International Herald Tribune,* March 18, 1971. © 1971 by World Press. Reprinted by permission.
Selection 17-3 "Rich Households Getting Richer," *Santa Barbara News Press,* 1973. © 1973 United Press International. Reprinted by permission.
Selection 17-4 "Chinese Universities Drop Entrance Examinations" by Lee Lescaze, *Washington Post,* Sept. 30, 1973. © Washington Post. Reprinted with permission Los Angeles Times/Washington Post News Service.
Selection 17-5 "The Postal Street Academy is Broke" by Ron Moskowitz, *San Francisco Chronicle,* July 7, 1973, p. 2. © Chronicle Publishing Co., 1973. Reprinted by permission.
Selection 17-6 "War on the Poor?" *Newsweek,* Jan. 18, 1971, p. 18. © Newsweek, Inc., 1971. Reprinted by permission.

CONTENTS

PART THREE   WHAT IS PUSHING US? THE HISTORICAL PROCESS

PART FOUR   SOCIAL RELATIONS IN THE MODERN ERA

INDEXES

PREFACE

The events of the 1960s made it impossible for sociologists to remain comfortable with the image of "society" which had dominated American sociology for the preceding decade. Several generations of sometimes careless textbook writing had not only represented society as an essentially healthy, self-correcting organism with a few minor illnesses ("social problems") and a few maladjusted individuals ("deviants"), but had reduced society to a contemporary phenomenon.

Sociological analysis based on a conflict perspective—that is, a perspective that assumes the centrality of conflict—was available, but it was out of favor with the discipline. Although social conflict was rampant in the 1960s, the treatment of conflict in sociology texts remained a psychological issue. But the events of the sixties were impossible to explain *without* some kind of conflict analysis, and practically no contemporary student would be guilty today of the bland self-assurance radiated by the sociological texts of the sixties. Our aim is to present a simplified, modernized version of the conflict perspective which can be used to introduce students to sociology.

At the same time that real events have been overtaking respectable sociologists, changes have been taking place among intellectuals in a variety of related fields. Thomas Kuhn's *The Structure of Scientific Revolutions* and, in sociology itself, Alvin Gouldner's *The Coming Crisis in Western Sociology* are widely read because they reflect a perspective which is useful in explaining contemporary events. The idea that our own social world represents a smooth evolution from primitive to industrial times has been challenged by respectable historians. In his book *At the Edge of History,* William Irwin Thompson says that people whose social worlds were more complex and sophisticated than our own probably inhabited corners of the earth twenty to thirty thousand years ago. And these social worlds did not die as part of a "moving equilibrium," a process through which functional theorists have explained away the ugly deaths of Athens and Rome. Decaying leaves may promote the growth of new saplings, but dead "civilizations" are not necessarily the underpinnings of a better future. Catastrophe, resulting from both human conflict and "natural" disaster, destroyed many social worlds which seemed to function quite well at their heights.

Immanuel Velikovsky, whose theories of catastrophe, drifting continents, tilting and shifting polar axes, and Noahlike floods were once mentioned only to provide a lighter side to geology classes, is being gingerly resurrected by some geologists. Evidence from physics challenges the whole idea of linear time and supports theories of precognition and mental manipulation of physical objects (psychokinesis). There exist strong currents of consciousness expansion, alchemy, a wide variety of mysticisms, and, in general, antirationalism. Change abounds in the intellectual world as it does in contemporary social relations.

A sociology based on a conflict perspective cannot respond to all these currents. But conflict-based sociology does provide a view of social relations which stresses the central importance of social conflict and change in shaping past, present, and future political, cultural, and social institutions.

This book is for those whose labor has made it possible: the printers, typesetters, truck drivers, lumbermen, editors, writers, and taxicab drivers. The labor of those closest to us is most appreciated. Especially we thank Lisa Stevens and Sylvia Warren who edited the entire manuscript. Not only did they rewrite substantial portions of the book, they made imaginative suggestions that were essential to its clarity and completeness. The selection of the photographs was a more demanding task than any of us anticipated. Lou Chambliss gave her endless energy and creative instinct to help us make the photographs both artistic and meaningful. Sharon Wiggins and Debbie Dewers typed, shuffled, and Xeroxed pages until they saw them in their sleep. Their good humor and encouragement were indispensable. Finally, we thank all the people whose written work has been the basis for our own writing. Footnotes do not adequately express our indebtedness to those who have adhered to the standards of freely expressed ideas and careful observation, often in the face of political oppression and academic complaisance.

William J. Chambliss
Thomas E. Ryther

INTRODUCTION

It is conventional when writing a text for introductory students to present the eternal truths of the discipline and to ignore the controversies, uncertainties, and conflicts that are in reality the moving forces behind any inquiry. We feel that although such a presentation may seduce students into a temporary belief in the purity of a particular discipline, it robs them of the deeper excitement to be had from truly disciplined inquiry and, in the long run, makes understanding more difficult. For these reasons we have tried first and foremost to convey the sense of controversy that surrounds sociological analysis. We have also tried to show how sociology itself reflects the social forces which shape the historical era in which it exists.

In presenting sociology as a moving, changing, controversial, *real-life* experience, we have admitted that not all sociologists share the same beliefs about human social behavior. We also admit that sociological analysis is not an esoteric, superscientific field which only an elite group can hope to pursue. We have stressed, instead, that everyone "does sociology" all the time. Sociology's only claim to uniqueness is the self-consciousness with which sociologists *ought* to go about constructing their version of reality.

Our commitment to "telling it like it is" and to avoiding the reification of sociology has led us to emphasize the following:

1   We have made it explicit that this introduction to sociology flows from the conflict perspective. We believe that books which do not state explicitly their theoretical perspective—that is, books in which the perspective is not clearly formulated and the underlying assumptions not spelled out—read more like mythology than an honest introduction to a discipline.

2   By making the parts of the perspective that underlie the book clear, we hope to encourage readers to begin to perform a disciplined analysis of that perspective—accepting, modifying, rejecting, recombining, and reformulating parts as they make observations and reflect upon their experiences in light of what they are learning.

3   We link the conflict perspective to the "social construction of reality" hypotheses which belong to the Weberian tradition in American sociology. Marx's version of conflict theory remains largely at the level of institutional analysis. However, as far as we can see, it contains no principles inconsistent with the idea that social structure is a special kind of reality constructed out of shared meanings. We have attempted to bridge the gap between economic determinism and social construction by positing the existence of an institutional "logic" whereby once a reality is constructed, several implications flow from it which shape and constrain it, putting limits on whatever additional social realities may be constructed. This is analogous to building a house in that additions to a house can be made, but are constrained by the materials and the shape of the original.

4   We have tried to focus on institutional analysis. We believe that analysis of the patterns through which people solve the big problems (economic survival) and distribute power (through wealth and violence)—that is, institutional patterns—is the key to conflict theory as it applies to sociology.

5   We do not accept the idea that conflict is the opposite of adjustment, which would mean that sociologists should emphasize the study of functioning, conflict-free social institutions. We leave social psychological questions (how are people's psychic organization affected by the use of social structures and cultures?) for other inquiries. Topics such as identity crisis, primary groups, socialization, and nature versus nurture are largely ignored in this book to avoid possible distraction from social structural issues, which are difficult enough in their own right.

6   We have given some space to methodological concerns in the belief that an introduction to sociology must communicate not only the

conclusions of sociology but also the process by which these conclusions have been reached. When to devote time to the methodology of sociology is a matter of great debate among teachers of introductory sociology. Some feel that methodology must be covered early so as to "set the stage"; others feel that an early presentation makes sociology appear too dry, too removed from everyday life, which is what students are most likely to find interesting. For the latter teachers, methodology, even a cursory view of it, must come after substantial issues and data have been presented so that the student is interested enough to want to understand *how* we know what we claim to know. A similar dilemma arises with regard to when we should teach the historical roots of contemporary society. Some teachers feel that today's world is most interesting to students and therefore we should begin there, saving a study of the historical processes that led to the modern world for a time when students can see clearly the relevance of delving into the past.

There is no way to resolve these problems, for there is clearly no single "best" way to teach introductory sociology. By dividing this book into parts, we allow teachers and students to follow their own preference with regard to sequence.

There is much understanding and enlightenment to be gained from the study of sociology. By providing a text that states explicitly the perspective from which the authors write, and which demystifies the process of doing sociology, we hope to give students tools which will enable them to better understand, live in, and change their world.

SOCIOLOGY: THE DISCIPLINE AND ITS DIRECTION

PART ONE

ON UNDERSTANDING SOCIAL LIFE:
THE SUBJECT MATTER
AND THEORETICAL PERSPECTIVE
OF SOCIOLOGY

The subject matter of sociology is human social behavior. The goal of the study of human behavior is to accurately describe and explain it. Put this way the enterprise seems simple and indeed in some ways it is. It is certainly true that most people believe it is quite easy to know and explain what is going on in the world. People's heads are full of descriptions that they assume are accurate and of theories they believe are true.

Between books, newspapers, magazines, parents, teachers, and friends filling us full of "truths" about human behavior, it is a wonder that we have any motivation left to explore other sources of "truth." Yet our interest in ourselves and our neighbors is practically unbounded. And the simple fact of the matter is that it is only by exploring a multitude of perspectives—that is, a variety of ways of analyzing human behavior—that we can hope to approach anything like an accurate picture of what is happening and why. Sociology is a particular way of making sense of the world—one additional tool for the understanding of human behavior—and cannot and should not stand as *the* path to truth about human behavior. Its value in the last analysis depends upon whether it helps us see and understand things that we did not discover elsewhere.

To introduce you to sociology we have tried to give a sense of the excitement of discovery inherent in the sociological effort. To accomplish this we have emphasized how theories and observations mutually influence one another and how both change over time. If there is a single underlying theme in the book it is the idea that sociology is a living enterprise which reflects the social realities in which it is being practiced. Today's truths are tomorrow's lies. Such a state of flux makes uneasy those who seek definite and final answers to all of life's questions. But this flux is also part of the excitement of sociology, for it means that we are all engaged all the time in the creative task of constructing a usable understanding of human social relations.

But what, exactly, do we mean by "human social relations"? Most generally we mean the way people relate to one another and to their world.

Sociologists are not, of course, the only ones engaged in describing or explaining human behavior. In the first chapter, as a way of introducing our study, we present a collection of glimpses into some of the varieties of human behavior that exist in the world today. For this we use relied upon descriptions by poets, historians, and anthropologists, as well as sociologists. Hopefully this provides a feeling for the variety of events that are the subject matter of sociology. Now with these descriptions in hand we move in Chapters 2, 3, and 4 to a discussion of how sociology tries to make sense of these varieties of human behavior.

ONE
Varieties of Human Experience

Today over 70 percent of the people in the world live in nonindustrialized nations. Most of these people live in small villages and depend upon agriculture, hunting, and fishing for their livelihood. Many live on the very brink of starvation, where every ounce of energy is devoted to the central problem of providing enough food for the next meal. The average life span is around forty years, as compared with a life expectancy of seventy years for people in the technologically advanced countries. The infant mortality rate (the proportion of children who die before the age of seven) is close to 50 percent. In the industrialized world, where medical facilities are more readily available, the infant mortality rate is much lower: in Sweden, for example, it is less than 13 deaths per 1,000 births and in the United States it is 22 deaths per 1,000 births.

Significantly, the proportion of people in urban areas in the nonindustrialized nations is rapidly increasing by leaps and bounds. In Latin America, for example, 80 percent of the people lived in rural areas in 1950; but today only 60 percent do so. In some nonindustrialized countries the proportion of people in cities now exceeds the proportion in the country. In the industrialized nations the bulk of the population has lived in urban areas for several decades.

What is life like in countries where the problem of survival is so overwhelmingly important?

In most cities of the less-developed world the problem of survival is no less acute than it is in the rural areas. In Calcutta, India, the problem is so overwhelming that carts go through the streets every morning and collect the dead bodies that have accumulated from the night before. In Africa, sanitation facilities are virtually unknown. Human and animal wastes abound on the roadsides. Large heaps of garbage collect in front of houses; with only goats, dogs, or sheep to eat some small portion of the garbage, the heaps grow larger year by year. Water is in desperately short supply. Animals are watered and people bathe in the same streams and ponds.

No wonder the life expectancy is short. No wonder that disease is rampant. No wonder that the population is vulnerable to the spread of any contagious disease. Children are malformed because of malnutrition and marked by skin diseases; ill health is so much a part of their lives that they do not know what it would be like to be free from sores and pains.

In the cities gainful work is difficult to come by. Children begin trading, hunting, and growing or gathering food at an early age in order to supplement the meager income of the family. Children may be abandoned frequently by parents too poor to feed them, or left alone because their parents are dead, ill, or have simply "disappeared." In most nations of the world there are no welfare agencies to care for children who have no parents. Some wander the streets stealing, begging, and starving. Others, the more fortunate, are cared for by strangers or relatives.

The governments of the less-developed countries, even the most humane ones, are powerless to alleviate all these problems. Available resources do not permit the massive expenditure needed to eliminate any one of the human problems that are the fate of most of the people in these countries. Aid from the industrialized world provides relief for but a very small proportion of those who live lives of desperation.

Either choice before residents of the less-developed nations—the city or the country —leaves much to be desired. Staying in the country means a life of twelve-hour days spent working on the land, and even that is no insurance against bad crops, drought, and starvation. Country people are also bound by the knowledge that the prospects of escaping the perpetual round of bare subsistence are practically nonexistent. Though most people still live in the country, the prospect of a better, less backbreaking, and potentially wealthier life increasingly attracts them to the city. With the minutest increase in industrialization in the less-developed world, there is a gigantic increase in the number of people who move near the industry in the hope of finding employment. Industrialization is occurring at a snail's pace while the demand for industry moves forward with the speed of a greyhound. Yet much of the increase in city populations in these countries occurs in the city itself. Many children are born for whom there are no jobs. They are in the city because they are born there, not because industrialization attracted them to new jobs.

Most of the more than 2 billion people who live in the relatively nonindustrialized countries are living in former colonies which gained their independence from England, France, Belgium, Germany, Spain, and other former colonial powers less than twenty years ago. As we will see in the chapters that follow, the condition of these former colonies is of profound importance to an understanding of life in every nation of the world. For it is one of the characteristics of the modern world that a shot fired in Abijan will resound throughout America, Japan, and beyond; a change of government in Thailand has implications far beyond the outskirts of the country; and a yellow fever epidemic in

India raises a specter in London as well as in Delhi.

A striking comparison is usually made between the hot, dusty, impoverished, agricultural life of most people in Africa, Latin America, India, and Southeast Asia and the life of people in industrialized nations. One slice of Western life in industrialized society was captured by poet Dylan Thomas when he described a moment of his childhood in a Welsh town:[1]

One Christmas was so much like another, in those years around the sea-town corner now and out of all sound except the distant speaking of the voices I sometimes hear a moment before sleep, that I can never remember whether it snowed for six days and six nights when I was twelve or whether it snowed for twelve days and twelve nights when I was six. All the Christmases roll down toward the two-tongued sea, like a cold and headlong moon bundling down the sky that was our street; and they stop at the rim of the ice-edged, fish-freezing waves, and I plunge my hands in the snow and bring out what wool-white bell-tongued ball of holidays resting at the rim of the carol-singing sea, and out come Mrs. Prothero and the firemen.

It was on the afternoon of the day of Christmas Eve, and I was in Mrs. Prothero's garden, waiting for cats, with her son Jim. It was snowing. It was always snowing at Christmas. December, in my memory, is white as Lapland, though there were no reindeers. But there were cats. Patient, cold and callous, our hands wrapped in socks, we waited to snowball the cats. Sleek and long as jaguars and horrible-whiskered, spitting and snarling, they would slink and sidle over the white back-garden walls, and the lynx-eyed hunters, Jim and I, fur-capped and moccasined trappers from Hudson Bay, off Mumbles Road, would hurl our deadly snowballs at the green of their eyes. The wise cats never appeared. We were so still, Eskimo-footed arctic marksmen in the muffling silence of the eternal snows—eternal ever since Wednesday—that we never heard Mrs. Prothero's first cry from her igloo at the bottom of the garden. Or, if we heard it at all, it was, to us, like a far-off challenge of our enemy and prey, the neighbour's polar cat. But soon the voice grew louder.

'Fire!'' cried Mrs. Prothero, and she beat the dinner-gong.

And we ran down the garden, with the snowballs in our arms, toward the house; and smoke, indeed, was pouring out of the dining-room, and the gong was bombilating, and Mrs. Prothero was announcing ruin like a town crier in Pompeii. This was better than all the cats in Wales standing on the wall in a row. We bounded into the house, laden with snowballs, and stopped at the open door of the smoke-filled room. Something was burning all right; perhaps it was Mr. Prothero, who always slept there after midday dinner with a newspaper over his face. But he was standing in the middle of the room, saying, "A fine Christmas!" and smacking at the smoke with a slipper.

"Call the fire brigade," cried Mrs. Prothero as she beat the gong.

"They won't be there," said Mr. Prothero, "it's Christmas."

There was no fire to be seen, only clouds of smoke and Mr. Prothero standing in the middle of them, waving his slipper as though he were conducting.

"Do something," he said.

And we threw all our snowballs into the smoke—I think we missed Mr. Prothero—and ran out of the house to the telephone box.

"Let's call the police as well," Jim said.

"And the ambulance."

"And Ernie Jenkins, he likes fires."

But we only called the fire brigade, and soon the fire engine came and three tall men in helmets brought a hose into the house and Mr. Prothero got out just in time before they turned it on. Nobody could have had a noisier Christmas Eve. And when the firemen turned off the hose and were standing in the wet, smoky room, Jim's aunt, Miss Prothero, came downstairs and peered in at them. Jim and I waited, very quietly, to hear what she would

[1] Dylan Thomas, *Quite Early One Morning* (New York: New Directions, 1960), pp. 20–32.

say to them. She said the right thing, always. She looked at the three tall firemen in their shining helmets, standing among the smoke and cinders and dissolving snowballs, and she said: "Would you like anything to read?" . . . And I remember that we went singing carols once, when there wasn't the shaving of a moon to light the flying streets. At the end of a long road was a drive that led to a large house, and we stumbled up the darkness of the drive that night, each one of us afraid, each one holding a stone in his hand in case, and all of us too brave to say a word. The wind through the trees made noises as of old and unpleasant and maybe webfooted men wheezing in caves. We reached the black bulk of the house.

"What shall we give them? Hark the Herald?"

"No," Jack said, "Good King Wenceslas. I'll count three."

One, two, three, and we began to sing, our voices high and seemingly distant in the snow-felted darkness round the house that was occupied by nobody we knew. We stood close together, near the dark door.

> Good King Wenceslas looked out
> On the Feast of Stephen . . .

And then a small, dry voice, like the voice of someone who has not spoken for a long time, joined our singing: a small, dry, eggshell voice from the other side of the door: a small dry voice through the keyhole. And when we stopped running we were outside *our* house; the front room was lovely; balloons floated under the hot-water-bottle-gulping gas; everything was good again and shone over the town.

"Perhaps it was a ghost," Jim said.

"Perhaps it was trolls," Dan said, who was always reading.

"Let's go in and see if there's any jelly left," Jack said. And we did that.

Always on Christmas night there was music. An uncle played the fiddle, a cousin sang "Cherry Ripe," and another uncle sang "Drake's Drum." It was very warm in the little house. Auntie Hannah, who had got on to the parsnip wine, sang a song about Bleeding

Hearts and Death, and then another in which she said her heart was like a Bird's Nest; and then everybody laughed again; and then I went to bed. Looking through my bedroom window, out into the moonlight and the unending smoke-colored snow, I could see the lights in the windows of all the other houses on our hill and hear the music rising from them up the long, steadily falling night. I turned the gas down, I got into bed. I said some words to the close and holy darkness, and then I slept.

These images, though touching a chord of memory for many of us, are caught through the eyes of a child and ignore the world of labor and toil that prevails as crushingly in industrialized countries as it does in nonindustrialized countries. A sense of the hardships that encompass that world is given by descriptions taken from the *Wall Street Journal* about some American men and the jobs they do.[2]

It was 1940 when Elmer Novak walked out of his sophomore year in high school and into the coal mines, just as his brothers had before him and his father before them.

Thirty-one years later, Elmer Novak has a mortgage, 10 kids and black lung. Looking back, he says he never would have gone down to the mines if he hadn't felt he had to. But there was not then—and there is not now—much else to do around Ebensburg, Pa., a tiny town on the western slopes of the Allegheny mountains. As a 100-pound 17-year-old, Elmer Novak started as a track layer's helper at $6.75 a day and graduated in a few months to pick-and-shovel miner at 65 cents a ton.

He quit the mine, once, in 1947, after his brother was crushed to death by a coal car, but in a few months he was back, for the money. Death in the mine can come fast, from a cave-in or an explosion, or slow, from the coal dust that causes black lung, and although Elmer Novak now is a man of 150 pounds he says

---

[2] "U.S. Workers: Sweat, Grime and Scars," *Wall Street Journal*, July 21, 1971.

"there's something about the air down there that makes the meat just fall off your bones." He recommends the mine to no one and is adamant in insisting that none of his six sons will ever go below the earth to bring back coal.

NO SAVINGS AND NO GOLF

Today Elmer Novak is a member of the rock crew at Number 32 mine of Bethlehem Mines Corp., where he timbers walls. He takes home $120 a week, often works in water up to his ankles, never has a coffee break, takes half an hour to eat lunch from a tin bucket and works

Much human work is exhausting and dangerous. In the United States, government depletion allowances, leasing of federal land, and tax subsidies for research support wasteful use of oil and coal, increase corporate profits, and help displace coal miners from their jobs as automated mining techniques are developed. (R. K. Fugate)

a rotating shift. After three decades, he is still not used to the danger or the coal dust or the chill in a mine shaft 1,000 feet underground. At home, he never talks about his job, and his wife never asks. He has never had a new car or a savings account, and he says there is "no way I could raise $100 in an emergency."

Elmer Novak has 14 years to go before he can retire on a union pension that currently is $150 a month—unless his illness worsens before that time and he can apply for black lung benefits. He is a pro-union man—"Nobody ever gave us something we didn't fight for"—but he hopes the United Mine Workers will improve pensions at the expense of wages in negotiations about to begin. He has given up golf because he can't afford the green's fees, but he says that's just as well—with black lung he doesn't have the wind to walk nine holes even if he had the money.

Why does Elmer Novak continue to work at a job that has cost him his health and paid him a wage that he had had to struggle on all his grown life? "There aren't many jobs around here for a high school dropout," he says. "I'd leave in a minute, but where would I go?"

That is the dilemma of millions of relatively unskilled manual laborers across the country. They mine coal, shovel steel slag, gut animal carcasses, sort mail, clean hotel rooms, bend over sewing machines and perform a thousand other grueling or mind-deadening tasks. They are by and large forgotten men and women in most discussions of the economy or of occupations. They are also, by and large, not young.

PRIDE BUT NOT HOPE

And when they are asked, as several dozen of them recently were by Wall Street Journal reporters, why they keep at it, most of them echo Elmer Novak: Where else would I go?

Most of them know they are not on the very bottom of the economic heap: they are not among the 17 million workers in the country—over 30% of the work force—who earn less than $5,000 a year. But for the privilege of escaping poverty they have paid the price of accepting labor that ranges from grinding to merely monotonous under conditions that range from uncomfortable to miserable.

Few of them hope any more for anything better. All of them say they learned long ago to simply stop thinking about the way things might have been. Most of them say they would never let their children follow them, but most of them are also bewildered or angered by younger workers who refuse jobs like theirs as demeaning or inhuman. Many of them hate every minute on the job. But a surprising number of them take a measure of pride in performing well jobs that can only be described as either backbreaking or deadly dull.

None of them works harder or under more miserable conditions than Alfred Hardy. Mr. Hardy is a foundry worker in Hamilton, Ohio, a suburb of Cincinnati. He tends the furnaces used to melt iron. He has done so for 20 years, and he hopes to do so another 16 years to retirement. From midnight each night until 10 a.m. or so, Mr. Hardy works in an inferno of heat, filth and noise. Part of the time he spends shoveling thousands of pounds of red-hot slag from beneath a furnace into large bins on wheels. Then he crawls inside the furace and chips away at hardened slag with a hammer and chisel. Then, with great globs of a thick, sticky black mud, he lines the furnace before it is fired up again.

SWEAT, GRIME AND SCARS

The temperature in Alfred Hardy's work area approaches 140 degrees. Flames shoot up from furnaces all around, and sparks the size of firecrackers spray into the air. Mr. Hardy must keep constant watch to dodge moving containers of molten iron that roll past his work area. With every breath, he inhales burnt resins and furnace smoke. He is surrounded by the constant staccato of air hammers, the roar of furnaces, and the whining and clatter of various machines. Once he finishes with one furnace, Mr. Hardy, bathed in sweat, covered with grime, scarred with the burn marks of 20 years, climbs out and starts shoveling the molten slag from beneath the next furnace.

In his two decades on the furnaces, Alfred Hardy has required medical treatment 104

times for some injury or another incurred on the job—50 times for burns, bruises and cuts, 54 times for injury caused by some foreign object, usually mud or iron, that has flown into his eyes. His work shirt and trousers become so filthy from mud and grease, he says, that "I don't bother to wash them. I just throw them away." Each week he buys a new outfit from Goodwill for about 70 cents. He points to grime ground into his palms and says there is no way to remove it short of peeling off the skin.

Alfred Hardy, unlike Elmer Novak, has made his peace with his job. Incredibly, over those 20 years, he has missed only 14 days of work— 10 because of injury, four for other reasons. His comment on every part of his job—the heat, the burns, the noise—is the same: "You get used to it." He says he prefers to work right through any sickness or injury that befalls him. "Alfred's from the old school," says a foundry official with approval. "He was brought up in an era when hard work was nothing to be ashamed of."

Mr. Hardy, in fact, seems surprised at the suggestion that he might grow weary of his work. "I've worked hard all my life," he shrugs. "Sure, I have a nasty, dirty job, but you have to do something to make a living. And once you get into it, it's just like anything else— you get used to it. Nobody likes to work, but you can't get by without it. There's only three choices—work, starve, or go to jail."

It's a good thing for Mr. Hardy that he is able to maintain that attitude, because officials at Hamilton Allied Corp. say little awaits him in the way of advancement, mainly because of his lack of a high school diploma.

16 YEARS TO GO

It's possible, in fact, that in a few years Mr. Hardy's job will be eliminated. If the foundry has to yield to federal pressure to lower pollution from the furnaces, it may install electric furnaces manned by skilled technicians. Then Alfred Hardy would become a laborer elsewhere in the plant.

Mr. Hardy says that after working, commuting and sleeping—he is exhausted after work—he has only about 2 hours a day for anything else, but he figures the job has been good to him. Last year, with overtime, he earned a little over $9,000—"a damn good year"—and he is proud that his four children have either completed or are attending college. As he sees it, he has come a long way from the days 25 years ago when he was a South Carolina dirt farmer share-cropping cotton, corn and greens. "I've done my best by my children," he says. "I don't want them to grow up like I did." His goal now: to last until retirement. There are 16 years to go, and Alfred Hardy says, "I can make it if my health holds out."

The kind of self-bred cheerfulness Alfred Hardy has learned to generate may be the best defense for a man with a grim, deadly job, but it also helps if a man can convince himself that his daily grind involves some small measure of skill or even bravado. That is something Marvin Conyers has never been able to believe. Mr. Conyers works the 3:30 to midnight shift on "the line"—the assembly line at Chrysler Corp. Jefferson Avenue plant in Detroit. Mr. Conyers, 34 years old and the father of five, has been on the line for seven years now, and he says bluntly and with considerable despair that it is brutal. Mr. Conyer's job involves physical effort and strain, but unlike Elmer Novak or Alfred Hardy, he doesn't lift heavy loads all day long. What he does is perform a job so monotonous and bleak that it drives him into a mental trance daily.

Marvin Conyers is a step up on many manual laborers—he has a high school diploma. Fifteen or so years ago, in fact, he even made a stab at attending a business college and working nights. But after one year, he dropped out "because of that depression they called a recession" and turned to the Chrysler assembly line for work. For eight years, he worked selling insurance or as a helper at his aunt's restaurant. He says he enjoyed that, but with a growing family he decided in 1964 to return to the line.

Mr. Conyers is better off now than he was then. At first, "I had to climb up into every car, put a seat brace in the back, then climb over into the trunk, weld in the back window, climb down, and get ready for the next car. I did that eight or nine hours a day about one car every fifty seconds." Later, he graduated to an easier job—welding steering wheel columns in place. Now, he is an "absentee pooler" —a worker who shifts from job to job to fill in for absent workers. The rotation of jobs is his only solace he says, but even with that, "I have a lot of days when I just don't want to go in, to stand there, doing the same thing over and over, once a minute, getting bored."

Mr. Conyers' day begins around noon. "I get up, go to the drugstore, get a paper, then come back home and maybe listen to records. It's the only time I have to meditate to myself." In a couple of hours, though, Marvin Conyers is headed to the plant and hating the thought of it. "It gets to you," he sighs. "It's so boring I could do it blindfolded—I've done 'em all." The biggest problem is fighting that boredom. "I think about everything, just everything, to keep my mind occupied. The day goes by real slow. It seems like 16 hours."

MONEY, BUT LITTLE ELSE

There is little camaraderie among workers on the line. Each man is relatively isolated, there are racial tensions and there is no mutual trust. Late at night, men leave the plant together in large groups to avoid being robbed in the parking lot. Alcohol and drugs are rampant, and Mr. Conyers admits he once or twice has been drunk on the job himself. Nearly 6% of the workers at the Jefferson plant don't show up on any given day, and nearly 30% of the work force turns over every year.

But for most, the alternatives are worse. Money brought them to the line, and it keeps them there. With the $9,000 Marvin Conyers makes each year and his wife's salary as a schoolteacher, he has been able to move to a neat, middle-class section of the city's northwest side. But the hours of the job have robbed him of home life. "I hardly ever see my family," he says. Nonetheless he avoids the day shift, for fear he couldn't be an absentee pooler; he says he "couldn't stand" the boredom of a single job.

PRIDE AND HORROR

"It all boils down to one thing, you can't afford not to do the job. Because they always find somebody to come out there and do it if you don't. If you think it's too bad a job to do, then there's some s.o.b. that'll come in and do it behind you."

That, of course, is the kicker. There are millions of men out there who would jump at a job—any job—that pays $8,600 a year.

For the working-class woman, life is not very different. The playwright Samuel Becket has said that life is a matter of choosing between boredom and despair. For some people the choice may be an unreal one, for having their lives seem filled with both. Such is the picture drawn by Polly Toynbee in an article from the *London Observer* (June 6, 1971) in which she relates her experiences working in a cake factory in England:

Outside the cake bakery the misty sun glances off the corrugated iron, the rusty fire-escapes, the rows of vans, the stacks of oil drums and the tarmac. Fork-lift trucks are at work already, shifting the piled-up cake containers. Service engineers lean against the doorways, smoking and laughing and whistling at the girls in white.

The cake bakery girls hurry across the 13-acre factory compound. It is 7:40 a.m., five minutes to clocking-in time. The girls don't look round at the men, but hurry down to the basement of their building, taking a last breath of fresh air, a last drag on the morning's first cigarette.

There is bustling and pushing at the clock. Then the machines start up, at exactly 7:45. The girls start the actions they will repeat thousands of times that day.

The noise is fearful, threatening and relentless. Like a horrible symphony orchestra, the sounds mix together in perfect rhythms, each bar repeated exactly over and over again. One sound is like the air-brakes of a lorry on a hill. Another is an old engine letting off steam at

the end of a long journey. Four packing machines are crashing huge hammers down on to metal plates very fast. The belts chug loudly and evenly, as the two slicers hiss. Overhead a line of clattering hangers circles the room, taking the finished cakes to the floor above. Somewhere in the background a loudspeaker is playing music, but only occasionally strains of it can be heard. When the machines stop, the music sounds loud, showing how noisy the machinery is. There is no conversation, only occasional shouted commands, often repeated several times before they can be understood.

From 7.45 until 4.15, apart from half an hour for lunch and two quarter-hour tea breaks, the girls worked down there for five days a week, doing one small action to every cake that came down the line—over and over, for a basic wage of what was then £10 12s. 4d. It has since gone up to £14.25, a remarkable rise of nearly 33 per cent. . . .

Anyone who has worked at all in a factory knows how deathly conveyor-belt work is. At first it is difficult to keep up, and when you're tired it is quite merciless. After a while, when you have become fairly used to it, the fact that you can't work faster is also infuriating. Sometimes, when things are going well, you feel that you could go fast for a while, and maybe slow up later when you were tired. But no, you must work at exactly the prescribed speed, making exactly the same movements, being careful to be as economical with energy as possible, learning not to put your back into it but to use only your arms, learning how to use the wrists the same way every day so the muscles are strengthened and don't go on aching. It looks so easy, and it is, but it's important to make it as easy as possible. One false move repeated 3,000 times is a painful mistake.[3]

Let us turn to a scene captured by an anthropologist, Elliott Liebow, who studied the black ghetto in Washington, D.C.

[3] "A Woman's Work: Opening a Personal Report by Polly Toynbee on Life at the Bottom of the Ladder," *Observer Review*, London, June 6, 1971.

On a thousand Tally's corners, the limited means of unneeded wage workers limit life. (Andrew Sacks from Editorial Photocolor Archives)

Liebow notes that a white truck driver going through the area sees the streets "filled" with black men standing around on street corners or in cafes, seemingly doing nothing even as someone is waiting on the corner to offer them work. In the eyes of the truck driver the black men are lazy and unwilling to work. Liebow goes beyond the superficial impression of the casual observer and in doing so describes an important aspect of life in the ghetto:[4]

> [S]ince at the moment [the men] are neither working or sleeping, and since they hate the depressing room or apartment they live in, or because there is nothing to do in there, or because they want to get away from their wives or anyone else living there, they are out on the street, indistinguishable from those who do not have jobs or do not want them. Some, like Boley, a member of a trash-collection crew in a suburban housing development, work Saturdays and are off on this weekday. Some, like Sweets, work nights cleaning up middle-class trash, dirt, dishes and garbage, and mopping the floors of the office buildings, hotels,

restaurants, toilets and other public places dirtied during the day. Some men work for retail businesses such as liquor stores which do not begin the day until 10 o'clock. Some laborers, like Tally, have already come back from the job because the ground was too wet for pick and shovel or because the weather was too cold for pouring concrete. Other employed men stayed off the job today for personal reasons: Clarence to go to a funeral at eleven this morning and Sea Cat to answer a subpoena as a witness in a criminal proceeding.

Also on the street, unwitting contributors to the impression taken away by the truck driver, are the halt and lame. The man on the cast-iron steps strokes one gnarled arthritic hand with the other and says he doesn't know whether or not he'll live long enough to be eligible for Social Security. He pauses, then adds matter-of-factly, "Most times, I don't care whether I do or don't." Stoopy's left leg was polio-withered in childhood. Raymond, who looks as if he could tear out a fire hydrant, coughs up blood if he bends or moves suddenly. The quiet man who hangs out in front of the Saratoga apartments has a steel hook strapped onto his left elbow. And had the man in the truck been able to look into the wine-

[4] Elliott Liebow, *Tally's Corner* (Boston: Little, Brown, 1967), pp. 31–36.

clouded eyes of the man in the green cap, he would have realized that the man did not even understand he was being offered a day's work.

Others, having had jobs and been laid off, are drawing unemployment compensation (up to $44 per week) and have nothing to gain in accepting work which pays little more than this and frequently less.

Still others, like Bumdoodle the numbers man, are working hard at illegal ways of making money, hustlers who are on the street to turn a dollar anyway they can; buying and selling sex, liquor, narcotics, stolen goods, or anything else that turns up.

Only a handful remains unaccounted for. There is Tonk, who cannot bring himself to take a job away from the corner, because, according to the other men, he suspects his wife will be unfaithful if given the opportunity. There is Stanton, who has not reported to work for four days now, not since Bernice disappeared. He bought a brand new knife against her return. She had done this twice before, he said, but not for so long and not without warning, and he had forgiven her. But this time, "I ain't got it in me to forgive her again." His rage and shame are there for all to see as he paces Carryout and the corner, day and night, hoping to catch a glimpse of her.

And finally, there are those like Arthur, able-bodied men who have no visible means of support, legal or illegal, who neither have jobs nor want them. The truck driver, among others, believes the Arthurs to be representative of all the men he sees idling on the street during his own working hours. They are not, but they cannot be dismissed simply because they are a small minority. It is not enough to explain them away as being lazy or irresponsible or both because an able-bodied man with responsibilities who refuses work is, by the truck driver's definition, lazy and irresponsible. Such an answer begs the question. It is descriptive of the facts; it does not explain them.

Moreover, despite their small numbers, the don't-work and don't-want-to-work minority is especially significant because they represent the strongest and clearest expression of those values and attitudes associated with making a

living which, to varying degrees, are found throughout the streetcorner world. These men differ from the others in degrees rather than in kind, the prinicipal difference being that they are carrying out the implications of their values and experiences to their logical, inevitable conclusions. In this sense, the others have yet to come to terms with themselves and the world they live in.

Putting aside, for the moment, what the men say and feel, and looking at what they actually do and the choices they make, getting a job, keeping a job, and doing well at it is clearly of low priority. Arthur will not take a job at all. Leroy is supposed to be on his job at 4:00 p.m. but it is already 4:10 and he still cannot bring himself to leave the free games he has accumulated on the pinball machine in the Carry-out. Tonk started a construction job on Wednesday, worked Thursday and Friday, then didn't go back again. On the same kind of job, Sea Cat quit in the second week. Sweets had been working three months as a busboy in a restaurant, then quit without notice, not sure himself why he did so. A real estate agent, saying he was more interested in getting a job done than in the cost, asked Richard to give him an estimate on repairing and painting the inside of a house, but Richard, after looking over the job, somehow never got around to submitting an estimate. During one period, Tonk would not leave the corner to take a job because his wife might prove unfaithful; Stanton would not take a job because his woman had been unfaithful. Thus, the man-job relationship is a tenuous one. At any given moment, a job may occupy a relatively low position on the streetcorner scale of real values. Getting a job may be subordinated to relations with women or to other non-job considerations; the commitment to a job one already has is frequently shallow and tentative.

The reasons are many. Some are objective and reside principally in the job; some are subjective and reside principally in the man. The line between them, however, is not a clear one. Behind the man's refusal to take a job or his decision to quit one is not a simple impulse or value choice but a complex combination of assessments of objective reality on the one hand, and values, attitudes and beliefs drawn from different levels of his experience on the other.

In America and most other industrialized nations wage-earning work forms a crucially important aspect of the social structure.

The effect joblessness has is only hinted at in the following description of life in the mountains of eastern Kentucky—the area known as the Cumberland Plateau—which takes in parts of West Virginia, Tennessee, and Kentucky.

In community after community one can visit a dozen houses in a row without finding a single man who is employed. Most are retired miners and their wives who live on social security and union pension checks. Hundreds of other houses are occupied by aged widows, some of whom have taken in a grandchild or other youngster for 'company' in their old age.

One row of camp houses has twenty-one residences. Seven are occupied by widows, the youngest of whom is fifty-two years of age and four of whom are more than seventy. Five are the homes of aged couples. Four shelter unemployed miners in their early fifties—men 'too old to get a job and too young to retire.' Three families draw state aid because the men are disabled from mining accidents. Only two houses are supported by men who still have jobs in a nearby mine.

One may walk the streets of camps and wander along winding creeks' roads for days and rarely find a young man or woman. For years the young and employable have turned their backs on the plateau. Each spring when warm weather begins to enliven the land the more energetic and ambitious of the young men and women develop a yen for a more hopeful region. One by one they slip away. A year after high school diplomas are distributed, it is hard to find more than 4 or 5% of the graduates in their home counties. In the autumn of 1960 one high-school principal assured me that not a single graduate of his

school in 1958, 1959 or 1960 was living in the county. A couple of dozens are in military or naval service, but 70% had found jobs (or at least lodgment) in Ohio, Indiana and Michigan. The others were scattered over New York, Illinois and California.[5]

Those who leave the hills to join the unskilled labor force in cities may not find jobs more plentiful; they may become part of a white ghetto much like the black ghetto described by Liebow. Those who stay in the hills, for whatever reasons, are likely to find that their lives include contact with "the authorities" whose rules do not take into account the way of life of the poor. Caudill describes a scene from one of eastern Kentucky's rural courts:

About 3:30 in the afternoon the county truant officer (known officially by the horrendous title of Director of Pupil Personnel) made his appearance. A warrant had been sworn out charging a father with failing to send his children to school. . . . The truant officer explained that the defendant was the father of six children, all of whom were of elementary school age. They had not been to school in the preceding month. The county attorney asked the Court to impose a fine or jail sentence. The father of the children was dressed in tattered overalls . . . and it was obvious from his stooped shoulders that he had spent many years under the low roof of a coal mine. He pleaded his defense with the eloquence of an able trial lawyer. With powerful conviction he said:

"I agree with everything that's been said. My children have not been going to school and nobody wants them to go any more than I do. I've been out of work now for four years. I've been all over this coalfield and over into Virginia and West Virginia looking for work. I've made trip after trip to Indiana, Ohio and Michigan and I couldn't find a day's work anywhere. I drawed out my unemployment com-

[5] Harry Caudill, *Night Comes to the Cumberlands* (Boston: Little, Brown, 1963), pp. 333–334.

pensation over three years ago and the only income I've had since has been just a day's work now and then doing farm work for somebody. I sold my old car, my shotgun, my radio and even my watch to get money to feed my family. And now I don't have a thing in the world left that anybody would want. I'm dead-broke and about ready to give up. I live over a mile from the schoolhouse on twenty acres of wore-out hillside land. Last spring the coal company that owns the coal augered it and teetotally destroyed the land. I couldn't sell the whole place for five hundred dollars if my life depended on it. Me and my oldest boy have one pair of shoes between us, and that's all. When he wears 'em I don't have any and when I wear 'em he don't have any. If it wasn't for these rations the govern'mint gives us, I guess the whole family would of been starved to death long afore now. If you want to fine me I ain't got a penny to pay it with and I'll have to lay it out in jail. If you think puttin' me in jail will help me young'uns any, then go ahead and do it and I'll be glad of it. If the county attorney or the truant officer will find me a job where I can work out something for me kids to weal I'll be much obliged to 'em as long as I live.[6]

Gerald Suttles describes yet another ghetto area, the Addams area of Chicago, an ethnically mixed collection of working-class city dwellers:

For someone first entering the Addams area, the most striking aspect is its street life . . . On the streets, age, sex, ethnic and territorial groups share boundaries that open them to mutual inspection, thus giving the occasion for transient interaction between groups, for gossip, and for interpretive observation . . . During the summer months the streets in the Addams area are thronged with children, young adults, and old people. Street life is especially active in the afternoon after school or work. The front steps are crowded with old people chatting back and forth between households while some occasionally bring out chairs

[6] Ibid., pp. 359–360.

when sitting space is scarce. Young girls stand in clusters a little distance from the 'stoop-sitters', giggling, squealing, and glancing at the passers-by. Young unmarried men seem to occupy every street corner or unused doorway. Small two- and three-year olds stumble, crawl, and toddle along the sidewalks in front of their homes.

On warm nights there is hardly a stoop, corner, alley, or doorway that has not been staked out by some of its regular habitués. The adults get the door stoops. The young girls stay close by, just out of earshot. The small children are given the run of the sidewalks in front of their mothers. The unmarried males are relegated to whatever little nooks or crannies are left . . .

Among Addams area residents . . . the home is essentially a place for sleeping, eating, protection against the weather, and ritual occasions . . .

Seemingly there is a distinct preference for encountering people on more neutral grounds than one's own household. Among teen-age boys this attachment to street life is especially great. After being arrested and released they do not speak of going home but of going 'back to the streets'.[7]

It is tempting to generalize from Liebow's Tally's corner and Suttles' Addams area that "the street" is the center of urban ghetto life. But, consistent with the diverse character of America, what is true of one ghetto is not true of another. In "the urban village" studied by Herbert J. Gans we find quite a different focus of social activities.

To the average Bostonian, the West End was one of the three slum areas that surround the city's central business district, little different in appearance and name from the North or the South End . . . To the superficial observer, armed with conventional images and a little imagination about the mysteries thought to lie behind the tenement entrances, the West End

[7] Gerald Suttles, The Social Order of the Slum: Ethnicity and Territory in the Inner City (Chicago: University of Chicago Press, 1968), pp. 73–75.

certainly had all the earmarks of a slum. Whether or not it actually was a slum is a matter that involves a number of technical housing and planning considerations and some value judgments. I felt that it was not . . . the West End can be described simply as an old, somewhat deteriorated, low-rent neighbourhood that housed a variety of people, most of them poor.

The basis of adult West End life is peer group sociability . . . a routinized gathering of a relatively unchanging peer group of family members and friends that takes place several times a week . . . the meetings of the group are at the vital center of West End life . . . they are the end for which other everyday activities are a means.

Membership in the group is based primarily on kinship . . . brothers, sisters and cousins of the husband and wife—and their spouses— are at the core . . . The peer group meets regularly in the kitchens and living rooms of innumerable West End apartments. There are no formal invitations or advance notifications; people arrive regularly one or more evenings a week. . . . The talk goes on for hours—often past midnight—even though the men have to be at work early the next morning. . . . The sexes remain separate most of the evening and, even when they gather around the kitchen table for coffee and cake, the men often sit at one end, the women at the other. Some people bring their children . . . [who] sit and listen until they become sleepy, and then are sent off to the bedrooms until their parents leave.

The peer group conversations cover a relatively small number of topics: accounts of the participants' activities since the last gathering; news of people they all know; plans for special events, such as weddings, showers, and other celebrations; current topics of interest; stories and anecdotes; and memories of younger days or highlights of the more recent past . . . a current happening will set off talk about the past, and people contribute stories of parallel events that took place earlier.[8]

[8] Herbert Gans, *The Urban Villagers: Group and Class in The Life of Italian Americans* (New York: Free Press of Glencoe, 1962), pp. 3–4, 74–77.

Urban slums produce their own peculiar style and form. One peculiarly American slum phenomenon is skid row:

Skid Row is a phenomenon peculiar to the United States. It is that run-down area in almost every American city where the homeless can and do live. It is that collection of saloons, pawn shops, cheap restaurants, second-hand shops, barber colleges, all-night movies, missions, flop houses, and dilapidated hotels which cater specially to the needs of the down-and-outer, the bum, the alcoholic the drifter . . . A few persons between the ages of fifteen and twenty-five are found in the skid rows of the West Coast, but virtually none in the Midwest and East. They have been replaced by the elderly, disabled, and retired who were caught in the squeeze between spiraling postwar inflation and a fixed pension or welfare benefits . . . Throughout the years (the skid rower) has remained both destitute and single. For the most part he claims no kith and kin. Outcast by all accepted standards, degraded and facing an ever-widening gulf between himself and society, the skid rower has nevertheless managed to survive . . . More than that, he has managed to evolve on his own behalf a community of sorts, a community which shelters, clothes, and feeds him and even keeps him supplied with drink. He asks for nothing more. . . .

It is not easy to become a model skid rower. . . . To be completely acculturated in skid row subculture is to be a drunk—since skid rowers place strong emphasis on group drinking and the acculturated person by definition is a conformist. The drunk has rejected every single one of society's established values and wholly conformed to the basic values of skid row subculture. Food, shelter, employment, appearance, health, and all other considerations are subordinated by the drunk to the group's need for alcohol. This group constitutes the drunk's total social world and it, in turn, bestows upon him any status, acceptance, or security he may possess. . . . As the only fully acculterated member of skid row subculture, the drunk—including the various sub-types, such as the wino, the lush, and the rubbydub—lives his life totally within the defiant community. He sacrifices everything to the drinking practices and needs of the group. The push of community condemnation and the pull of drinking companions, plus a habituated desire for drinking have combined to structure his life around alcohol—the point at which he has now arrived. In his own eyes as well as in the eyes of others, skid rowers and non-skid rowers alike, he has become a totally committed member of a deviant group. It has taken much more than a physiological craving, a personality type, an occupational history, destitution, and isolation to produce him—the skid row derelict. It has taken years of socialization en route to homelessness and a complex process of career commitment to produce this totally deviant individual.[9]

Moving out of the slums, one encounters what are known as the *tangential* slum occupants, for example, the "professional thief":

The professional thief lives in a world of whores, racketeers, corrupt policemen, judges and bail-bondsmen. It's a world where one day you are on top and pay two hundred and fifty dollars for a suit; blow nineteen thousand dollars in a weekend at Las Vegas or pay cash for a home for your current girl-friend. The next day you get busted and have to commit a caper (a robbery) in order to pay five thousand dollars to fix the case with the judge and the district attorney. And if you're the guy who is caught stealing when the bulls are getting a lot of heat to make an arrest for a "crime wave" that's probably just a fiction in some reporter's mind, then you're going to go to the joint—to the penitentiary.

In the thief's world "going to the joint" is just one of the facts of life. It's like you have to go to school to get a job in the bank; you don't go to school because you like it; you go because it gets you someplace you want to be. The thief's the same way. He doesn't like the

penitentiary sentence but he accepts it as one of the annoyances and inconveniences of his profession.[10]

The residents of the black ghetto, the rural slum, the streets of Chicago, the urban village, and the world of the professional thief represent some of the threads that make up the fabric of modern social life. Another part of the fabric is made up of those men who occupy positions in the ever-growing bureaucracies of business and government.

Among the multitude of jobs created by modern technology, the work of the bureaucrat accounts for an increasingly large percentage of work experience. That world has been described by the sociologist C. Wright Mills:

There are in the modern enterprise men who fulfill the bureaucratic formula; in brief, here is how they look and act:

They follow clearly defined lines of authority, each of which is related to other lines, and all related to the understood purposes of the enterprise as a going concern. Their activities and feelings are within delimited spheres of action, set by the obligations and requirements of their own 'expertise.' Their power is neatly seated in the office they occupy and derived on from that office; all their relations within the enterprise are thus impersonal and set by the formal hierarchical structure. Their expectations are on a thoroughly calculable basis, and are enforced by the going rules and explicit sanctions; their appointment is by examination, or, at least, on the basis of trained-for competencies; and they are vocationally secure, with expected life tenure, and a regularized promotion scheme. . . .

At the top of some hierarchies, one often notices personalities who are calm and sober and unhurried, but who betray a certain lack of confidence. . . . Liking the accoutrements of authority, they are always in line with the

---

[9] Samuel E. Wallace, *Skid Row as a Way of Life* (Totowa, N.J.: Bedminster Press, 1955), pp. 13–25, 179–188.

[10] Adapted from Harry King, as told to and edited by Bill Chambliss, *Boxman: A Professional Thief's Journey* (New York: Harper & Row, 1972).

aims of the employer and other higher ups; the ends of the organization become their private ends. For they are selected by and act for the owners or the political boss, as safe and sound men with moderate ambitions, carefully held within the feasible and calculable lines of the laid-out career. That is why they are at the top (of the bureaucracy) and that is the point to be made about them; they are cautiously selected to represent the formal interest of the enterprise and its organizational integrity; they serve that organization and, in doing so, they serve their own personal interests. Among all the apparatus, they sit cautiously, and after giving the appearance of weighty pondering usually say "NO".[11]

The world of the entrepreneur has some features in common with the bureaucrats, but the differences are impressive as well. Take the medical profession, traditionally one of the most independent enterprises in America:

The white-collar world of medicine is still presided over by the physician as enterpreneur. . . . Yet the self-sufficiency of the entrepreneurial physician has been undermined in all but its economic and ideological aspects by his dependence, on the one hand, upon informal organizations that secure and maintain his practice.

Medical technology has, of necessity, been centralized in hospital and clinic; the private practitioner must depend upon expensive equipment as well as upon specialists and technicians for diagnosis and treatment. He must also depend upon relations with other doctors, variously located in the medical hierarchy, to get started in practice and to keep up his clientele. . . .

Once through the medical school, the young doctors face the hospital, which they find also contains departments, hierarchies, and grades. One hospital administrator . . . told . . . how interns are selected: "the main qualification as

far as I can see is 'personality'." Now that is an intangible sort of thing. It means partly the ability to mix well, to be humble to older doctors in the correct degree, and to be able to assume the proper degree of superiority toward the patient. . . .

The inner core that abides in this code not only controls the key posts in the hospital, but virtually the practice of medicine in a city. . . .[12]

It is part of our contemporary mythology that something known vaguely as "the middle class" *is* America. The validity of this argument depends, of course, on what one defines as "middle class." There are many automobile workers and other wage earners who own little or no property who are in the middle of the income distribution. Of course, the middle-income group is by definition the largest single group. Among all those who earn wages, however, as distinguished from those whose income rests on management or profit, the white-collar workers view themselves as different from other wage earners. They call themselves "middle class." They try to lead different styles of life from other wage earners. What does the white-collar world look like? The preceding descriptions of the bureaucrat and the medical profession touch some features of middle-income life. Further insight is gained from studies of suburbia. Herbert Gans provides a description of life in a newly constructed middle-income suburb in New Jersey:

In October 1961, Levittown was three years old. As of that July 4200 homes had been built and occupied, the shopping center was half completed, most of the churches were either in their buildings or about to move in; new schools were still going up and a six-grade parochial school was in operation. Nearly a hundred organizations were functioning; government reorganization was about to take

---

[11] C. Wright Mills, *White Collar: The American Middle Classes* (New York: Oxford University Press, 1951), pp. 92–93.

[12] Ibid., pp. 119–121.

effect and a city manager was being hired. Levittown had become a community. . . .

The residents had at first associated almost exclusively with their neighbors, but some had sought more compatible people and activities outside the block and had thereby set in motion the founding of community-wide groups. . . .

The youthfulness of the community . . . affected the development of class and power structures . . . Without knowledge about people's income, with the absence of very poor and very rich neighbor's, and with the ever present fact that everyone lived in virtually the same house, it was difficult to base judgments on income. . . .

Occupation and education were more reliable indices of class position, and the professional received more deference than the factory worker, but many people had obtained some college education and the majority were white-collar workers. Finally, and perhaps most importantly, the intense need of community leaders and organizational participants in the early years temporarily set aside traditional class distinctions and allowed people of low status to become prestigious community figures. . . .

Conforming and copying occur more frequently than competition, mostly to secure the proper appearance of the block to impress strangers. A pervasive system of social control develops to enforce standards of appearance on the block, mainly concerning lawn care . . .

What people do inside their houses is considered their own affair, but loud parties, drunkenness, and any other noticeable activities that would give the block a bad reputation are criticized. So are parents who let their children run loose at all hours of the evening . . . Private deviant behavior is, of course, gossiped about with gusto, but only when it becomes visible, and repeatedly so, is gossip translated into overt criticism . . .

Many of Levittown's adolescents consider it a dull place to which they have been brought involuntarily by their parents . . . Specifically, adolescent malcontent stems from two sources:

Levittown was not designed for them, and adults are reluctant to provide the recreational facilities and gathering places they want. Like most suburban communities, Levittown was planned for families with young children. The bedrooms are too small to permit an adolescent to do anything but study or sleep; they lack privacy and soundproofing to allow him to invite his friends over . . . People's lives are changed somewhat by the move to suburbia, but their basic ways remain the same; they do not develop new life styles or ambitions for themselves and their children . . . Morale goes up, boredom and loneliness are reduced, family life becomes temporarily more cohesive, social and organizational activities multiply, and spare-time pursuits now concentrate on the house and yard.[13]

An outstanding characteristic of middle-class suburban communities such as Levittown is the universal drive for upward social mobility among their inhabitants. They not only aspire to higher status, more prestigious and better-paying jobs, but also fully expect that these advancements will occur. This, as well as many other features of middle-class life, contrasts sharply with the desires or at least the expectations of working-class suburbanites. As Berger reports from his study:

Very little, if any, social mobile attitudes are in evidence. Of the total sample (of persons interviewed in the suburb), 94 per cent reported that they thought of their jobs with Ford as 'permanent' jobs; only 3 per cent were keeping their eyes open for something better . . . these respondents are almost all hourly wage workers with relatively poor educations, and their apparent intent to stay with Ford does not indicate any real hope of rising in the company hierarchy.[14]

[13] Herbert J. Gans, The Levittowners: Ways of Life and Politics in a New Suburban Community (New York: Pantheon, 1967), excerpts from pp. 124, 131, 132, 176, 177, 206, 409.
[14] Bennett M. Berger, Working Class Suburb: A Study of Auto Workers in Suburbia (Berkeley: University of California Press, 1960), p. 76.

Blue-collar suburbanites differ in social participation in informal associations from their white-collar counterparts. Berger found

> no evidence that participation in formal association has increased since our respondents . . . moved to the suburb. Indeed, we find very little formal participation at all; 70 per cent of our respondents belong to no clubs, organizations, or associations at all; only 8 per cent belong to more than one.[15]

With respect to leisure time and especially interaction patterns among dwellers in the blue-collar suburb Berger discovered:

> Mutual visiting between friends and neighbors seems to be infrequent; on the other hand, participation in family activities seem to occur often . . . those more than 50 years old do very little visiting of any kind. The younger people, the well educated, the former home owners, and the foremen do slightly more visiting than comparable subgroups, but in no case are the figures very striking. . . . Television . . . gives us the answer to what they do with most of their spare time: they watch television. Almost half the sample spends more than 16 hours a week watching television. . . .[16]

Making yet another leap, we can glimpse at the way of life of the profit-managing class, first by a description of the life of the upper-income groups observed in a relatively small town in the southeastern United States.

> It is said that the urge for getting money is the spring upon which the enterprise system rests. I would contend that it also rests upon a concern for many other life values, but the money urge cannot be radically discounted. . . . In this regard . . . I shall now cite . . . as a case in point that of Mr. Cravitts. In viewing the man in full retrospect, it would seem that his personal bodily needs would have long since

been adequately met, yet his urge to get more money had not diminished. . . .

> The second most powerful man in Ivydale, next to the university president, is an insurance dealer, Wilfred Presley Cravitts, the son of a successful farmer. . . .

> Mr. Cravitts' integration into community affairs as the soft spoken symbol of local economic power stems from the fact that he has conducted a profitable insurance business in the community for nearly a half century. He is a part of Main Street. He is cautious; eager to gain. He is accepted by others as a person of hard business principle. Generally speaking, the latter characteristic is that of making a dollar as expediently as possible. He has access to the large economic opportunities that occasionally present themselves to the community.

> For several years, Mr. Cravitts has interested himself in local and state political affairs and through the contacts he has gained at political conventions of the county and state he has become recognized as a business and political contact in his own home town for others in other parts of the state . . . He was the leader of a political machine known locally as the Cravitts-Holloway machine. . . . The first Congressional District of Middle-State was made up of six counties, one of which was Ivydale county. While he held no political office, Mr. Cravitts was the acknowledged leader of the Ivydale delegation and, in turn, of the whole district. His second-in-command was another businessman . . . Jarvis Holloway . . . a real estate operator who, among other things, owned the largest office building in Lottsford and who was informally recognized as the liaison politician between the University of Middle-State and the state legislature. . . . These two men and their crony associates tightly controlled party politics in the district.[17]

The people who own and control the centers of America's industrial complex have their own way of life, which differs tremendously from the life-styles of Appalachia

---

[15] Ibid., p. 59.
[16] Ibid., p. 75.

[17] Floyd Hunter, *The Big Rich and the Little Rich* (Garden City, N.Y.: Doubleday, 1965), pp. 58–60.

and Levittown. For the very powerful, very wealthy "captains of industry," the "club" is a particularly important focus of attention:

It is when you go upstairs in the Duquesne (club) that you begin to enter the substratosphere of executive power. On the second floor there are no fewer than five dining rooms, including the main one; and in each of these, day after day, the same people sit at the same tables. As you enter the main dining room, the Gulf Oil table is across the way; Gulf's chairman, David Proctor, sits facing the door, surrounded by his senior vice presidents. In the corner over to the right is the Koppers table, populated by most of the top men in that company, and next to it is the U.S. Steel table, where sales vice presidents break bread together. In another smaller room nearby, Pittsburgh Coke and Chemical's president, chairman and vice presidents gather daily; in still another, Pittsburgh Plate Glass has a central spot, while Alcoa's executive committee chairman, Roy Hunt, holds forth in the corner —next to Jack Heinz's table.

If the Duquesne's second floor feeds the captains of industry, many of the field mar-

shalls are to be found on the fourth and fifth floors, where thirty-five suites are rented out by the year (at $12,000 and up) to such companies as U.S. Steel, Gulf Oil, Jones and Laughlin, Blaw-Knox and Alcoa, to name just a few. These attractively decorated apartments usually have a bedroom, living room and dining room; they are used by the companies' topmost brass for meetings and lunch almost every day, and for dinners perhaps two or three times a week, particularly when a visiting fireman, or rather fire chief, comes to town. . . .

In these company suites new products and mergers are planned, bargaining strategy for labor negotiations is hammered out, multi-million dollar financing arrangements are made. Here and in the public dining rooms below, the professionals of production get together and exchange ideas, day by day. There is a daily exposure of people to people who are all of the same mold or forced into the same mold. This tends, no doubt, to channel their interests and energies towards the mono-purpose goal of productions; and it may well be, as has been said, that Pittsburgh would not be the production marvel it is without the exchange of information, techniques and ideas

Entertainment and exploitation.
(Pictorial Parade/EPA)

that takes place every noontime at the Du-quesne.[18]

Of course the profit managers are not all cut from the same cloth, any more than the patterns of life among slumdwellers are all the same. E. Digby Baltzell makes this point well by citing different hiring practices and criteria in Boston, New York, and Phila-delphia:

It is said that an experienced employer once compared the social structures of New York, Boston and Philadelphia by citing three typical letters of introduction brought by young men seeking jobs in his firm; the letters from each city read somewhat as follows:

The Bostonian: Permit me to introduce Mr. Jones who graduated with highest honors in the classics and political economy at Harvard, and later took a degree at Berlin. He speaks and writes French and German, and if you employ him, I am sure his learning will make his services extremely valuable to you.

The New Yorker: The bearer, Mr. Brown, is the young fellow who took hold of Street & Company's Chicago branch a few years ago and built it up to one hundred thousand a year. He also made a great hit as Jackson & Company's representative in London. He's a hustler all right and you'll make no mistake if you take him on.

The Philadelphian: Sir, allow me to intro-duce Mr. Rittenhouse Palmer Penn. His grand-father on his mother's side was a colonel in the Revolution, and on his father's side he is connected with two of the most exclusive families in our city. He is related by marriage to the Philadelphia Lady who married Count Taugenichts, and his family has always lived on Walnut Street. If you should see fit to employ him, I feel certain that his very desirable social connections will render him of great value to you.[19]

[18] Osborn Elliott, *Men at the Top* (New York: Harper, 1959), pp. 166–167.
[19] E. Digby Baltzell, *Philadelphia Gentlemen: The Making of National Upper Class* (Glencoe, Ill.: Free Press, 1958), p. 31.

Another dimension along which people vary in America—and all other places—is represented by the cultural characteristics of different age groups. Young people do not live in the same world or have the same experiences as adults. What they do with their time and how they feel inside remain invisible to adults. Look, for example, at the following description of a middle-income juvenile gang which thrived (and in all likeli-hood a present-day equivalent still does) unknown to the parents, teachers, or officials in a middle-class American community:

As surely as night followed day you could rely on the boys who were members of the Saints to do what was right. At least that was what the people in Inglewood thought. These were the kinds of boys you could be proud of. They were always active in things at school: played on athletic teams, were in school plays and made good grades. Everyone liked them. They were never any trouble to anyone. Not that they were sissies, mind you. They would kick up their heels occasionally, especially when it was called for. But they were good boys, headed in the right direction. They were the boys who took seriously the commencement speaker's admonition that the future of the world was in their hands. Besides, they all came from good, solid, middle-class homes.

That, as I said, is how it looked to the resi-dents of Inglewood. The boys themselves be-lieved that this description was accurate. They knew they were a little wild at times; but it was "all good, clean fun and no one was ever really hurt, were they?" Miraculously, no one *was* ever really hurt, but this was no fault of the boys. The Saints certainly created ample opportunity for vast numbers of persons to be hurt—themselves included.

Among the most dangerous of the Saints' ongoing activities was driving. It was a fright-ening thing to watch them drive when they were sober; when they were drinking it was horrendous. And they 'were drinking' almost every Friday and Saturday night of the year. Over the two-year period that I observed this group, there were only eight weekends that they did not drive into "big town" (a large urban center near Inglewood) and get intoxicated. How intoxicated ranged from quite to thoroughly. Or, behavioristically, their intoxication ranged from being giddy to being unable to walk. The typical Friday and Saturday night drinking bout began when one of the boys would get into his car and go by and pick up the others. They would then drive, as they always did, at a speed well beyond that tolerated by the police, and head for big town. Once there, they would select a tavern, or, if they could afford it, a night club, and spend the next three or four hours drinking. By the end of that time they were quite pleased with themselves and the state of the world.

Sometimes they would precede their drinking with a number of innovative sporting events, but more often these 'pranks' were reserved for the hours following their drinking.

Probably the most frequent sporting event was vandalism. A choice piece of vandalism, from the boys' perspective, was to find construction work on the roads and to remove from the work site the lanterns and fences which had been placed there to warn traffic to stay away. If, in addition to getting these items for display the boys were still around when some unsuspecting motorist inadvertently drove into a hole in the road, then this added considerably to the enjoyment of the evening's activities.

But taking these items was not enough; the items pilfered had to be publicly displayed. On several occasions, the boys would run through the streets of the city waving the lanterns. Generally, these runs would end when a policeman was spotted or when someone 'thought' they saw a policeman, at which point the boys carrying the lanterns would 'ditch' them in an alley or a store-front. Fences ob-

Natural disasters strike hardest those least able to lose their homes. (Pictorial Parade/EPA)

tained from construction sites would be put up across a street somewhere, preferably at a curve where oncoming motorists would not see the fence until they were on top of it. Occasionally, the pilfered items would make their way to one of the boys' homes where he would put it in his bedroom. This, however, was more likely to happen to stop signs, curve signs, and the like, than with lanterns or construction fences. There was apparently a willingness on the part of the boys' parents to accept these additions to the home furnishings with little or no questioning since the boys did not hesitate to take them home if it struck their whimsy.

Other vandalisms consisted in breaking windows in houses; breaking into houses that were known to be vacant and destroying property. It was very rare that anything of any value was taken from the premises, but everything moveable was frequently destroyed in the spirit of the moment.[20]

Looking at these descriptions of various life patterns, one must ask, "Are these descriptions typical?" The answer is, of course, that they are *not*. That they are not is, in fact, the point. In a world of 3 billion people any broad category such as "youth" or "businessman" or "primitive" or "tribe" or "hippy" is typical only in the sense that each term stands for all the subgroups that fall in that general category. A full accounting of all the groups within each category can never be had. What we strive for in sociology is not complete description of every

possible category or group, but rather sufficient descriptions to enable us to make generalizations about the relationships among major groups. What we provide in this chapter, then, is evidence of the pluralistic nature of modern society. What we have *not* done is to provide a description of how these groups relate to each other.

SUMMARY

We must at the outset recognize that simply because we live in the same world—whether in England, Nigeria, Brazil, India, or Taiwan—we are not all part of "one big happy family," or, for that matter, of one big unhappy family. What we call tribes in non-industrialized societies exist everywhere, and "tribal" divisions along class, racial, and ethnic lines are found among all peoples. These are the assumptions that underlie the sociological investigation of human society.

This chapter has been a quick trip—an all too sketchy picture of the pieces and threads that are the human experience. We have covered only the smallest portion of the field, trying to convey a sense of the diversity and the drama of life. We must now move from this intuitive and impressionistic level to the more systematic and agonizing task of making sense of this array of experiences—to the sociological analysis of human behavior. We must not forget, however, that in the end it is the pieces and threads of human experience that we are seeking to pull together to describe and to explain.

[20] William J. Chambliss, "The Saints and the Roughnecks," *Society*, Nov.–Dec. 1973.

SUGGESTED READINGS

Harry M. Caudill, *Night Comes to the Cumberlands* (Boston: Little, Brown, 1967).

Thomas B. Cottle, *Time's Children: Impressions of Youth* (Boston: Little, Brown, 1971).

William Hinton, *Fanshen* (New York: Monthly Review Press, 1967).

Harry King, as told to and edited by Bill Chambliss, *Boxman: A Professional Thief's Journey* (New York: Harper Torchbooks, 1972).

Marie Korarovsky, *Blue-Collar Marriage* (New York: Random House, 1964).

Elliott Liebow, *Tally's Corner* (Boston: Little, Brown, 1967).

C. Wright Mills, "Work" from *White Collar: The American Middle Classes* (Available from MSS Modular Publications, reprint no. R139, MSS Modular Publications, 655 Madison Avenue, New York 10021).

Betty Roszak and Theodore Roszak (eds.), *Masculine-Feminine* (New York: Harper & Row, 1969).

Studs Terkel, *Working* (New York, Random House, 1974).

TWO
Sociological Analysis: What Is It?

Why?

Why do people not have shoes in the worked-over coalfields of Appalachia? Why do people go hungry? Why does the oldest woman resident of Wyoming live out her "golden years" on $75 a month? Why do a group of people in California ban together under the name of the Symbionese Liberation Army and declare war against American capitalism? Why do members of the Duquesne Club spend $12,000 a year to rent a private bed-lunch room for occasional use? Why do more people in the United States report to pollsters they are "happier" today than they were in 1950?

Asking "why" is the foundation of sociological analysis. Indeed, the central purpose of sociology is to ask questions about social life. The answers to these questions comprise sociological theory. The term *theory* is a useful one for it serves as a constant reminder that the answers to our questions and even the questions themselves are necessarily tentative. It is a reminder that sociological analysis is a process which is constantly in need of revision and change; a process that grows and develops out of the conflict of ideas.

In this chapter, analysis is defined and the skills of analysis are described. Behind all analysis is a problem. Starting with your own problems or with those that are real to you is often the best way to become skilled in doing analysis. Being real to you, the problems you choose will necessarily be engaging. On the other hand, because you are intimately involved in them, such problems often make analysis more difficult because of the difficulty that arises from trying to gain a perspective which is not merely self-serving.

In trying to understand acts of political espionage, such as Watergate, it is tempting and personally satisfying to simply blame the President, the Republicans, or the Democrats. But to do sociological analysis, you must seek connections between the economic system, the political system, and the acts of people in positions of power. To understand the shortcomings of education in the United States, sociological analysis means seeking the connections among the job market, the kinds of people who sit on school boards, and the ways high schools are run rather than blaming individuals or "the system." Questioning our penal system does not mean blaming the establishment but instead analyzing the connections among power, the way lawyers are trained and paid, the trial procedures, and who gets imprisoned and why. When faced with the observation that poor people get extremely bad health care in the United States, "common sense" may tell us "they deserve it," "give them some money," or "educate them." But analyzing such an observation might lead you to connect who the doctors are, how they are chosen, how they spend their time, and to question our concept of health and how tax money is spent on medicine. Doing sociological analysis means connecting job discrimination, the passive girl in children's books, low pay for females in many jobs, and government policy of fighting inflation by keeping unemployment high, while avoiding the satisfaction of blaming it solely on, say, "male chauvinism."

SOLVING PROBLEMS

People have problems. The people on Tally's corner have problems—finding steady work, staying healthy, feeling good about life. Growing up in the coal-mining economy of Wales presents problems: black lung and

fatherless children, trying to find a job, trying to figure out if the job is worth having, wanting all the things a job can buy. In the United States, trying to feed your children and drive to work when gasoline is $1 a gallon will be problems too.

Analysis is really consciousness expansion. It is simply seeing your problem as part of something bigger. If your car will not start and you become aware of the connection between the key, the starter, the starter motor, and the transmission, your consciousness has been expanded. Or consider the amoeba, a one-celled living creature common to drops of water. The amoeba has a problem when its little puddle begins to dry up. It lacks the simplest analytic skills—namely, a sense of time and space—needed to see the puddle as part of a bigger picture. Having no sense of the past, the amoeba does not even notice that the puddle is drying up. Having no sense of space, it does not notice a much larger puddle nearby to which its own little world is connected by a fast-drying canal. And so, the amoeba dies with its puddle.

Spaceflight allowed us a new perspective from which to see cloud patterns and other patterns in the processes which support life on earth. (NASA)

The most personal definition of analysis, then, is seeing how your problems are connected to other things. On a more complex level, if you have solved your problems, or are interested in looking beyond them, you may wish to see how the problems of others fit into the bigger picture.

For instance, if Elmer Novak's wife (see p. 9) must pay $1.25 per pound for hamburger and her husband's wages are fixed at $125 per week, her rent at $225 per month, and her medicine bills at $150 a month, then she has a problem. The question that must be asked is, "Of what larger patterns are the price of hamburger, her rent, her medicine bills, and her husband's wages a part?" Ms. Novak may suffer in silence and forego eating, but if she or you and I want to understand her hunger and the fact that she cannot afford to go to the doctor, we must do social analysis— that is, we must ask why the price of hamburger, the wages, the doctor bills, and the cost of rent are as they are. We expect to find the answer in some larger patterns of which the Novaks' problems are a part. In the same way we could understand a deer dying from thirst in the West as an event which reflects a larger pattern of destruction of range land by overgrazing and loss of the capacity of the soil to hold water.

My Problems and Their Problems

Ms. Novak is probably used to thinking of food prices as a personal problem—something that is connected only to the little world of her grocery store and her refrigerator. She may also think of the Watergate scandal as "their problem," something that does not really affect her own problems. But, in fact, Ms. Novak's own small puddle is intimately connected to the larger puddle called Watergate. She may not yet be hurt badly enough by food prices to look for a larger pattern. She may not get adequate information (observations of what ranchers and gov-

ernment officials are doing) to be able to do good analysis. But sociology is no more than people pooling their observations and ideas about big patterns to do better analysis.

The Skills of Social Analysis

Doing social analysis, then, requires vision of the kind the amoeba does not possess. This vision cannot be gotten in any easy way, but a good starting point is simply to imagine that there may be connections between things happening at home and those in faraway places; or connections between things happening now and things that happened in the past. *Vision* is an interesting word because it calls to mind a *whole* view of something—a look which shows you, dimly perhaps, some connections that you had never suspected.

Sensing a problem Simply to ask "why" is to start analysis. The word *problem* just means a question we wish to answer, not some big crisis in our lives. "Why do students take examinations?" or "Why do police officers wear uniforms?" are problems. Of course, some problems may raise your consciousness faster than others. If the amoeba had asked, "Why is this puddle drying up?" it would have been on the way toward a significant consciousness expansion.

Having a vision Knowing the right way to ask a question is a skill which speeds up the process of doing analysis. A vision, a general picture or model of what the world is like, is indispensable in helping us to ask the right questions. If Ms. Novak asks, "Why is my grocer so greedy that he is ripping me off every week, and why is my husband so incompetent that he can't make enough money for us to buy groceries?" then she will end with an explanation of her dilemma that links her grocery bill to the personal characteristics (like greed and laziness) of the grocer and her husband. Should Ms. Novak ask instead, "What is pushing the cost of living up so fast while wages rise so much more slowly?" then she will be led to see her problem as connected to the larger political and economic patterns in which she, her husband, *and* the grocer are enmeshed.

For scientific purposes a vision, a model or a perspective, is useful so long as it produces new insights, new ideas, and new ways of changing the world. A vision ceases to be useful if it produces stagnation and resignation. A college professor whose vision has stagnated runs the danger of being just like the amoeba. He may ask the same questions over and over again just to hear the answers, in spite of the fact that the questions are no longer related to the problems, and will not lead to their solution. A vision is useful if it is a tentative thing, gently suggesting connections to be explored. A vision is useless to analysis if it becomes the place where one settles rather than the place from which one goes forth to look.

A vision may be imparted to another person; people may share in doing analysis. *Perspective* is the term used throughout this book to describe a vision of the larger patterns behind events. A perspective is a vision which is public, written down, and spoken, so that others can see the connections it implies, and share in doing analysis.

The perspective which shapes this book is a vision of social relations which makes connections between the interests of the managers of corporate capitalism and the price of hamburger, and implies that in order to answer the question, "Why is the hamburger price pattern as it is?" one must examine the political and economic system.

Figuring out connections The third analytic skill is figuring out what should be true if the vision of the bigger picture is accurate. For example if the vision suggests that most of the patterns in the United States, including the price of hamburger, are shaped by the interests of the managers and owners of large corporations, then how do we know if we are right? To show exactly how rising hamburger prices would benefit the corpora-

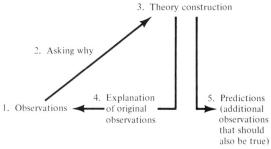

FIGURE 2-1   The steps in doing analysis.
1. Making observations—seeing, touching, hearing, smelling anything that other people could also sense in the same situation.
2. Asking why—that is, why do things happen this way?
3. Constructing theory, proposing a pattern of which the observation can be shown, by logical statements, to be a part.
4. Connecting theory to observations by logical steps.
5. Further testing the theory by predicting logically consistent observations.
Example:
1. Observation: The car doesn't start after the key is turned.
2. Asking why: Why did the key turn but the car not start?
3. Constructing theory: I think there's a pattern here. The key isn't just a random event; it is *part of a pattern.* The important pattern, I think, is an engine.
   If the key turns, then electric current moves from the live battery to the starter motor.
   If there is current in the starter motor, then the shaft turns.
   If the shaft turns, then there is a spark from the distributor and gas travels from the carburetor to the firing chamber.
   If a spark is produced and there is gas in the firing chamber, then combustion occurs.
4. Explaining original observation: If the battery is not live, then turning the key will not turn the starter motor, etc.
5. Testing theory: I could just stop here, having explained the failure of the car to start. I could also have logically explained why the car would not start by saying the squirrels that run on the treadmill moved over and the key didn't tickle them. Usefulness of analysis depends on testing the theory with new predictions.
Prediction: If I try a live battery, then the car will start.

tions is to make the connection between a specific problem and the bigger picture of which it is assumed to be a part.

One way to go about figuring out connections is to use models of familiar patterns. For example, if someone tells you that civilizations have a life cycle like humans, this means they believe that the pattern or process which connects the parts of civilizations is like the process of aging. You can then check out the idea, looking to see whether or not civilizations seem to have identifiable parts corresponding to birth, youth, maturity, old age, and death. The life-cycle model thus leads you quickly into the analysis of the parts and processes of historical change. Once there (that is, doing analyses), you can decide how useful the life-cycle analogy is for analyzing human history.

Analogies, such as one comparing culture and social structure to blueprints and houses, are useful as starters. They emphasize that organized social relations are like tools. Like tools, social structures are first "invented" or constructed, then justified and generalized; like tools, they are used *by* humans, rather than the other way around.

There we should stop. Organized social relations do not have many of the characteristics of houses. They are not physical, or capable of being touched, except in their indirect manifestations (lawbooks, Bibles, buildings). Rarely, except in cases of imprisonment, are people forced to use a certain house. But violent coercion to use certain social forms is commonplace in social life. Since a perfect match is impossible, analysis should make limited use of analogies such as that between social structures and a house. To stretch an analogy is to lose sight of the original patterns you are trying to discover and to get bogged down in a trivial matching game.

Looking to see   Knowing where and how to find out if the connections really exist is the fourth analytic skill. If we come up with the idea that hamburger prices rise because corporations are probably buying up cattle ranches and reducing competition in the raising and marketing of beef, we must test our theory. This means verifying who is buying cattle ranches, how much competition actually exists between ranchers, and how this is related to the price of hamburger. There are several skills involved, including knowing how to ask the right questions, where to find public information that is reliable, and whom to ask. Some of these skills are covered in more detail in Chapter 6, "Disciplined Analysis."

Improving the vision   The fifth analytic skill is making changes in the vision when you find it does not fit your observations. If we discover that there is tremendous competition in the cattle business, that most ranches are small operations, and that hamburger prices are connected to a disease that has made beef very scarce, then we must modify our perspective. It would appear that corporate managers have little control over or interest in the price of beef.

It might seem that a logical sixth step would be to do something about the price of hamburger. However, we are here talking about social analysis. The skills of social engineering—or how to do something meaningful about the connections you have discovered—are distinct from the skills of social analysis.

In summary, there are five skills involved in trying to solve social problems by looking for their causes in a bigger picture. If we were to study people who were *doing* social analysis, we would probably find that there is no linear progression; one can start with any one of these skills and go on to learn the others. Maybe learning to look is more interesting, comes first, and leads to the learning of the other skills. Maybe developing a vision comes first. Or, perhaps you can get into analysis only by starting with a problem of your own and trying to find its causes in a larger pattern.

Perspectives: Visions for All Seasons

Perspective: A sociological definition Because a perspective—a vision of the bigger forces which shape small events—is such an important part of the analysis, it deserves further definition and elaboration.

By adolescence, the majority of us are familiar with the most often used perspectives through which people analyze their world. All these perspectives taken together can be said to constitute public reality, or cultural reality. Public reality is what any set of people agree are the big forces and events shaping the world around them. "The seasons" is such a perspective; people have a vision of season change. Small events like the falling of leaves, increasingly cold weather, sprouting of leaves, and warm-smelling air can be understood, explained, and predicted as part of the larger pattern called "seasons." No one can see a season, but to have a vision of seasons is to make sense of a large and important part of the world.

Some people become specialists in developing perspectives with great complexity and logical coherence. For example, painters "see" a world of color and convey this perspective in paintings. Musicians develop a perspective on the world of sound. Ecologists "see" the cycle by which carbon dioxide is removed and oxygen returned to the atmosphere; the events of daily life for many organisms can be understood as being caused, in part, by this cycle.

Perspectives are tools used to make the small events of the world more understandable, predictable, and perhaps changeable. As tools, they are evaluated by their usefulness. New visions emerge frequently. If they prove useful in solving what seem to be pressing problems, they will be developed and taught to others. For example, in times past it would have been considered very strange to envision chairs, tables, walls, trees, and people as consisting of minute, constantly moving particles. But those people who came to be called atomic physicists, began to "see" the world as organized collections of atoms. This new perspective, or new reality, proved to be very useful. Many events that had not seemed connected before (chemical reactions, transformation of matter, release of energy) now could be understood by using the atomic perspective.

Learning to use new perspectives Many perspectives compete for attention, particularly in places like colleges, which are devoted to developing new perspectives and enlisting the help of each new generation in using them.

Learning a perspective involves developing two skills. First, one must learn the concepts or specific things one must "see" when looking at the world through the new perspective. For the perspective of atomic physics this involves two kinds of defining processes. Some of them are ideas, such as the idea that all matter is composed of small particles called atoms, and, further, that each atom consists of many other kinds of particles. Other defining processes consist of things to do—for example, developing and using machine to show the movements of atomic particles.

Second, one must learn how the parts of the perspective fit together. Using the perspective of seasons, for example, we have learned to expect winter to follow fall, which follows summer, which follows spring. The vision of atomic physics suggests that there are certain organized processes by which the various atomic particles are bound together.

Thus, seeing the world from a new perspective involves learning many new words and discovering how the things the words represent are thought to be connected.

Perspectives and problem solving Life would be very simple if each event could be easily understood using a single perspective. But consider: Is the northward flight of birds perfectly predictable from the perspective of seasonal change? Some observations indicate that birds may fly north at times which are not predictable from the seasonal cycle.

Or imagine that you have heard that people can develop ulcers in the stomach lining which are very painful. You decide that you would like to avoid getting an ulcer. Of what larger pattern is an ulcer a part? What perspective will help you to predict, understand, and hopefully control ulceration? To what kinds of things should you pay attention? If you were to look up "stomach ulcer" in the *Index Medicus*, which contains information on thousands of problems of health and illness, you would find there are many perspectives on human stomachs. One perspective sees the stomach as part of the nervous system, which is peculiarly vulnerable to emotional stress. From this perspective, you might conclude that trying to avoid emotional stress would prevent your having an ulcer. Another perspective sees the stomach as the expression of a genetic code passed on from parents to their children. From this perspective, you must have parents without ulcers. Still another perspective sees stomach ulcers as the expression of a poor diet. From this perspective, you could presumably avoid ulcers by eating the right foods.

Every so often someone promises us a single perspective which will make understandable all human problems, all human behavior, all human events (down to the slightest ulcer). Thus far, we have always been disappointed. It seems that for the present, solving specific problems will require familiarity with several perspectives. It does not follow, however, that it is better to have no perspective at all. By adjusting your diet and life-style, and by being especially careful because your mother had an ulcer, you may substantially reduce the possibility of having an ulcer.

In other words, if we are to go beyond conventional wisdom (what books and the supposedly "wise" tell us), we can only understand human problems through the use of many different perspectives. This should not surprise us, for the current cultural reality suggests that people are social, psychic, astral, physiological, anatomic, atomic, chemical, and indeed many other kinds of beings.

SOCIOLOGICAL ANALYSIS

Understanding events requires locating them in some larger pattern. Amoebas, for example, seem not to be able to develop perspectives on events and as a result are very much at the mercy of their environment. Humans *must* develop such perspectives for they seem to have few instinctual or nonthinking ways of solving specific problems. Analysis is the name given to the process of seeing how specific events are part of larger patterns. The skills of analysis include: sensing problems; developing perspectives; figuring out connections; looking to see if the events are connected; improving the perspective or vision. Social analysis involves placing the specific events of human social life in some larger pattern, and seeking the forces or processes which seem to be shaping the patterns through which humans relate to one another.

Increasingly over the past 200 years, humans have become more self-conscious about their social relations. New perspec-

A super performance is a predictable novelty in patterned play. (Mark Chester from Editorial Photocolor Archives)

tives have been developed, and logical connections among patterns of social life have been observed. Such a simple idea as the possibility that poverty is a result of class oppression rather than the stupidity of the poor might be the basis for a new way of understanding specific social events. The term "class oppression" might better describe the forces connecting many events than the conventional perspective of "stupidity."

Sociology refers to the logical perspectives being developed by people who devote much of their time to analyzing social life. Sociological analysis is distinct from social analysis, which is done all the time by most people, in that sociologists try to develop their perspectives on social life by giving more time and more energy than the "social" analyst to all the skills which make up the

analytic technique. There is no guarantee that sociological analysis will therefore be more useful to the understanding of human problems. Most sociologists hope, however, their analyses are useful and can better anticipate the social future and have implications for social change to a greater extent than perspectives which have not been so carefully and systematically developed.

SUMMARY

Sociological analysis is akin to the processes of reasoning which everyone engages in and, at the same time, is different from them. In solving personal problems and problems of curiosity, everyone engages in analysis: the attempt to find a source of the problem and an effort to tie a particular event to a larger pattern. Similarly, sociological analysis consists of trying to tie particular human events into larger patterns of social relations.

Sociological analysis begins, then, by asking "why" and attempting to find an answer in the patterns of social relations. Asking "why" leads to a vision, a model, that takes the form of a sociological perspective. In this chapter we have outlined the characteristic form of sociological analysis and the ways sociological analysis can be altered, checked, and developed. In the next chapter we will summarize the major "visions"—or, more accurately, perspectives—used by sociologists in their attempt to answer the "whys" of human social relations.

SUGGESTED READINGS

Charles H. Anderson, *Sociological Essays and Research,* rev. ed. (Homewood, Ill.: The Dorsey Press, 1974).

Peter Berger, *Invitation to Sociology: A Humanistic Approach* (New York: Doubleday, 1963).

Noam Chomsky, "The Fallacy of Richard Hernstein's I.Q.," *Social Policy,* 1972. (Available as an MSS Modular Reprint, no. R682. MSS Modular Publications, 655 Madison Ave., New York, N.Y. 10021).

Robert W. Friedrichs, *A Sociology of Sociology* (New York: The Free Press, 1970).

Gary L. Marx, *Muckraking Sociology: Research as Social Criticism* (New Brunswick, N.J.: Transaction Books, 1972).

THREE
The Ideas of Sociology

In some ways we are all like the amoeba: we live day by day in small-sized places and participate in small-sized events. For us, these day-by-day events are working, learning some things and ignoring others, eating, contemplating our problems, solving some problems and not others, making love or wanting to, watching images on a TV screen, or reading words in a book. For the amoeba, the small events are, presumably, the intake of food, changes in the condition of the surrounding water, and the relation of its environment to the wider world.

In the course of living our day-to-day lives, we develop ideas about the meaning, the importance, and the causes of our behavior. Human beings are different from amoebas in that they symbolize their actions in word pictures. In this symbolic process,

you have been doing analysis all your life. Sociologists add new dimensions to this analysis and attempt to systematically fit the day-to-day events into a big picture. Included in this big picture are ideas about what molds daily events and ideas about the kind of daily events which seem to reflect and corroborate the accuracy of the big picture.

We noted in Chapter 2 that the big picture constructed by sociologists may be seen as a type of vision and is usually referred to as a "perspective" or a "model" of human social relations. The newspaper article included here as Selection 3-1 is a good example of sociological analysis applied to the currently controversial issue of whether or not men and women should live in "open marriages." This analysis shows how the

SELECTION 3-1

OPEN MARRIAGE: A FANTASY

It's not news that marriages are becoming increasingly unstable, especially among younger people. When I broke up with my husband seven years ago, it was with some sense that my action was out of the ordinary.

I even felt a bit defensive about not having any melodramatic reason for leaving. Less than a decade later, it is the long-lasting marriage that seems, if not odd, at least worthy of comment.

With the rise in the divorce statistics has come a softening of the taboos on discussing one's marital problems in public. More and more people, married and divorced, are openly criticizing their marriages in a specific and personal way.

If marriage as we know it is breaking down, we had better find a replacement. The readiness of divorced people to remarry shows, if nothing else, that unhappy as they may be with marriage, they prefer it to being alone. Still, making the same mistake with different partners hardly qualifies as an alternative, and many people are actively promoting new possibilities, ranging from group sex to feminist marriage contracts.

Recently, we have been hearing a lot about something called "open" or "spontaneous" or sometimes just "new" marriage. Opinions differ on details (should it be open to outside sexual involvements?), but basically the phrase implies a union of two independent human beings. Participants do not try to possess or control each other: they respect each other's individuality and divide financial and domestic responsibilities on the basis of ability and interest.

It's an appealing fantasy—a nice, sensible, self-help approach. Unfortunately it also has very little application to life in the real world, for the assumption behind it—that marriages exist in a social vacuum—is false.

Whenever I read about open marriage, I feel I can picture the couples. Both have good educations, professional jobs they enjoy and at least an upper-middle-class income. They are childless or else they send their children to an expensive progressive day care center. They have

a housekeeper and can afford two cars, separate vacations, a large city apartment, a country farmhouse.

In short, they are able to buy their way out of most of the insecurities and frustrating compromises that cause trouble in the marriages of non-beautiful people.

The point is this: Marriage is an integral part of our social and economic system. The limitations of conventional marriage are further imposed by an intricate network of external rewards and punishments of obvious and subtle social pressures. Exhorting married couples to live up to their full human potential is a little like urging convicts to improve their sex lives.

For all their talk about the evils of sexual stereotyping, open marriage advocates seem to forget that we live in a male supremacist society.

As sole or chief wage-earner the husband is considered "head" of the household, even though his wife is doing an equally important job at home—and often working outside as well. It's pleasant, after all, to be served and catered to.

For a man to be an equal partner in an open marriage means relinquishing the prerogatives he takes for granted. I think it is unrealistic to expect many men to do this of their own free will. The average working man does not have an easy life; being king of his castle is at least some compensation for job tensions.

The average woman learns early that she had better catch a man if she wants to avoid a future of low-paying, dead-end jobs and the social stigma of being unmarried—a misfit. Every housewife knows that there are lots of younger, prettier woman around and that her residual secretarial skills from 20 years ago are worth zilch on the job market.

Is it surprising if she is possessive and jealous?

There is no way for a married couple to escape the pervasive effects of the sex-role system. For one thing, our entire economy is based on the premise that men should work and women should stay home.

A husband and wife may decide that they would really like to exchange roles—that she loves holding down a job, while he would rather take care of the children and garden. But if his job pays twice as much as any she could get, chances are they can't afford to switch.

Theoretically there is another alternative— each spouse can take a half-time job and stay home the other half, sharing paid work, domestic chores and child care. But again the economic reality is prohibitive: Most part-time jobs pay next to nothing and offer no fringe benefits, security or opportunity for promotion.

A further obstacle to a more flexible marriage relationship is this society's inhumane, doctrinaire approach to child-rearing, which decrees in essence that children should stay home with Mother and out of everybody else's way.

It makes no sense to preach open marriage to those caught in these all-too-typical binds. The proponents of open marriage are pushing a new version of an old familiar message: If you aren't happy in marriage, it's your fault.

Ten years ago women who couldn't adjust to the wife-mother role were considered neurotic: now women who can't transcend that role are put down as "unliberated."

It is not individual inadequacy that is to blame for marital breakdown, but the inadequacy of institutions that are failing to meet our needs.

The remedy is not for couples to embark on a futile struggle to create a free-marriage in an unfree society, but for the public to demand practical changes—an upgrading of part-time work, equal salaries and job opportunities for women, an end to the social segregation of mothers and children. Above all, institutionalized male dominance has got to go.

I am confidant that women, in the process of beginning to fight their second-class status, will eventually take the lead in redefining marriage—or maybe scrapping it for some other arrangement. But until there is genuine equality between the sexes, "open marriage" can be nothing but a cotton-candy slogan.

question of open marriages can best be understood by connecting it to a larger pattern —in this case, an economic pattern.

The explanations offered and the ideas suggested as important are, of course, bound by the perspectives we have in mind when we select certain features of the world as important while ignoring others. Although there have been almost as many perspectives from which to study human experience as there are varieties of experience, two very broad perspectives have dominated sociological analysis: the functional and the conflict perspectives.

Functional and Conflict Perspectives

Faced with the enormous variety of human experience, some people throw up their hands in despair and claim that any attempt to understand the diversity is fruitless. Yet the very existence of the social sciences testifies to the fact that many others continue to believe that understanding is possible. With

what perspective this understanding is to be attained is, of course, the subject of ongoing debate.

Bringing order to the variety of perspectives used by sociologists is no simple task. A convenient starting point, however, is to divide sociological orientation into the functional and conflict perspectives.[1] Of course, any particular sociologist may utilize some ideas from both perspectives, and some sociologists have even tried to construct a synthesis of the two points of view. For an understanding of what sociology is, however, there is no better way to begin than by grasping the fundamental issues on which the functional and conflict perspectives diverge.

1. In the functional view, there is a thing called "society." Society is a social system much like a machine or a living organism.

[1] Gerhard Lenski, *Power and Privilege: A Theory of Social Stratification* (New York: McGraw-Hill, 1966). The following discussion owes a heavy debt to this work.

This "thing" has various needs of its own which must be met if the needs and desires of its *members* are to be met. Conflict theories begin with the struggle of people to live. To the extent that people share solutions to problems, they share society. In the conflict view, this degree of sharing is to be discovered, not assumed. In most times and places, in this view, people are in conflict over how to solve major human problems. Conflict theory sees people as users of social structure, not as members of a thing called society. "Our society" is seen as a term used by the powerful to make the less powerful feel that they belong. But in this view, the term *society* has little analytic usefulness. Society itself does not cause events. They are caused by people, by the structures they create to solve their problems, and by the power they have to impose these structural solutions on others.

2. From the functional perspective, societies have governing bodies which "function" *for* society as value-neutral agencies within which various struggles take place. The conflict perspective sees the state as an agent consciously participating in the struggle on the part of one side or another. Conflict theories emphasize coercion (usually in the form of law- or war-making institutions) as the chief factor in maintaining social structures such as private property, slavery, and other institutions which give rise to unequal rights and privileges. In the functional view, it is argued that coercion plays only a minor role and that inequality arises as a necessary consequence of the fact that there is a general consensus within society on its most important values. Inequality, in this view, reflects the fact that some people are better off because they better live up to these universally held values.

3. In the conflict view, social inequality arises because of the operation of coercive institutions, which use force, fraud, and inheritance as the chief avenues for obtaining and maintaining rights and privileges. The

functional view has stressed such things as hard work, innate talent, and selection by merit as the reasons that economic advantages are obtained by some and not by others.

4. The conflict perspective sees social inequality as a chief source of social conflict. The functional perspective generally minimizes the existence of social conflict, and sees whatever conflict there is as stemming from human nature, not from the structured inequality of society.

5. In functional analysis, the concept of social class is regarded as a labeling device, calling attention to aggregations of people with certain common characteristics. In conflict analysis, it is useful to assume that there are social classes, collections of humans who have distinctive interests which inevitably bring them into conflict with classes having opposed interests.

6. Both functional and conflict theory seem to understand the effect particular social structures have on other social structures—for example, the effect of technology on family structure. The functionalist analysis generally stops when the consequences have been described. The conflict analysis goes on to ask which class of people benefits most from the established social relations that produce those events.

7. Whether studying war, social class, or deviant behavior, functional analysis typically asks, "What functions do these events serve?" The conflict approach asks, "How does war (or other social events) reflect class interests and arise out of class struggles?"

The importance of these various disagreements is best seen in the study of particular social phenomena. The specific models used, the questions asked, and the observations made to further test theory are all conditioned by the general model by which we shape our inquiry. The different perspectives emphasize different parts of specific social events or explain the same events differently.

The result is that for some problems, functional analysis asks the right questions. In other problems, only conflict analysis seems to serve. We believe conflict analysis deals best with some of our major current problems. We will show in the next few pages how conflict analysis raises questions and suggests answers for some of the most important problems facing the 3 billion human beings alive today. Social inequality, the relationship between industrialized and nonindustrialized peoples, bureaucratization, power, the quality of life, interests and human action, and social engineering. How might a functional analysis deal with these issues? A conflict analysis? After comparing the two modes of analysis here, we devote the remainder of the book to conflict analysis by taking up in greater detail some of the issues touched on in this chapter.

The Study of Social Inequality

According to the conflict model, social class and social inequality (that is, inequality in wealth, power, and privilege) are among the most important features to be studied if we are to understand society. The existence of social classes leads to inevitable conflicts, persistent tendencies to use force, and the emergence of laws and rules used to control threats to the established unequal relations. Although not accepting the dictum of Karl Marx that all of human history is but a reflection of class struggle, the conflict perspective nevertheless gives social class a prominent place in the analysis of human society.

The functionalist perspective, by contrast, either gives social class a very inconsequential role (as does Emile Durkheim)[2] or approaches it as a static characteristic of society that is "necessary and inevitable." For the functionalists, what makes social class necessary and inevitable comes down to two arguments, frequently joined but sometimes separated. The first argument is that inherent differences in ability make different individuals (and, collectively, different classes) mutually dependent on one another. The classic illustration of this notion of mutual dependence is Aristotle's analysis of the relationship between master and slave. Aristotle saw the master as providing the necessary intellect and guidance which slaves were incapable of providing for themselves. The slaves contributed the physical strength which was necessary for the master's well-being. Thus the master and the slave (or the wealthy and the poor), like the shark and the pilot fish, live in a symbiotic relationship of mutual benefit and harmony.

The second argument is that social inequality is necessary in order to motivate people to occupy more demanding positions. Davis and Moore have articulated this position most explicitly in laying down "some principles of stratification" to "explain in functional terms, the universal necessity which calls forth stratification in any social system."[3] The explanation offered by Davis and Moore is as follows:

> A society must somehow distribute its members in social positions and induce them to perform the duties of these positions. [Society] must thus concern itself with motivations at two different levels: to instill in the proper individuals the desire to fill certain positions and once in these positions, the desire to perform the duties attached to them. . . . Social inequality is thus an unconsciously evolved device by which societies insure that the most important positions are conscientiously filled by the most qualified persons.[4]

---

[2] Robert A. Nisbet, *The Sociological Tradition* (New York: Basic Books, 1966).

[3] Kingsley Davis and Wilber Moore, "Some Principles of Stratification," *American Sociological Review*, vol. 10, April 1945, pp. 242–249; Kingsley Davis, "A Conceptual Analysis of Stratification," *American Sociological Review*, vol. 7, June 1942, pp. 309–321; Kingsley Davis, *Human Society* (New York: Macmillan, 1949).

[4] Davis and Moore, op. cit., p. 242.

It follows from this that "those positions convey the best reward and hence the highest rank, which (a) have the greatest importance for the society and (b) require the greatest training or talent."[5]

This theory of social inequality derives quite logically from the assumption that whatever consequences we can impute to a social phenomenon must be the cause of its presence in society.[6] Thus since there *is* inequality, we need only "discover" (or imagine) what benefits inequality brings to society and we have laid bare its reason for being. Yet this logic, starting as it does in an assumption that there *is* such a thing as society, leads to erroneous conclusions.[7]

In Chapter 17 we will systematically evaluate the degree to which this functional theory of inequality is consistent with research findings. We conclude from the analysis that, in fact, inequality is not necessary to human social relations and, in fact, has many avoidable and unfortunate consequences. We will show, for example, that many of the "most important" positions receive the lowest economic and social rewards. Without sewage workers, garbage collectors, and coal miners the day-to-day life of cities and factories would simply come to a standstill. Yet these occupations receive the lowest rewards and, in the case of coal miners, carry a high risk of permanent physical impairment resulting from the work. Also, if "good for the most people" is a measure of deserving, many of the largest financial rewards go to the least deserving. Professional murderers, crooked businessmen, and large-scale con men make a great deal of money in the United States today. If there is a "society" which they benefit, it seems not to include the masses of people.

We will also show that a substantial body of research makes it clear that it is not essential for inequality to prevail in order to motivate people to perform the "most demanding tasks," if such tasks are defined as those requiring the highest amounts of education. Indeed, it seems probable that these demanding positions are sufficiently satisfying in and of themselves that there will always be more people willing to fill them than anyone can afford to pay. On the other hand, some of the least rewarding and most physically demanding positions, such as assembly-line jobs, where workers are plagued by boredom and physical fatigue, would doubtless go unfilled if not for the threat of economic deprivation facing those who refused such jobs. (This point was brought out by the description you read in Chapter 1.)

Following the tradition of Tocqueville and Durkheim, functional analysis tends to see those aspects of modern democratic societies which show increasing equality. The functionalist view is frequently linked to the emergence of a large white-collar class, which, in combination with strong labor movements in industrial societies, has greatly reduced economic differences among social classes. Lipset and Rogoff express this view as follows:

The assembly line and mass production, with the higher wages and more equal distribution of wealth that they make possible, are thus

[5] Ibid., p. 244.

[6] Walter Buckley has quite rightly pointed out that the Davis-Moore theory is a theory of inequality, not a theory of stratification. We therefore refer to it in this way rather than the more general term used by Davis and Moore. See Walter Buckley, "Social Stratification and the Functional Theory of Social Differentiation," *American Sociological Review*, vol. 23, August 1958, pp. 369–375.

[7] For detailed criticisms of the Davis-Moore theory see Buckley, op. cit.; Melvin Tumin, "Some Principles of Stratification: A Critical Analysis," *American Sociological Review*, vol. 18, August 1953, pp. 387–394; (Melvin Tumin, "Rewards of Task-Orientations," *American Sociological Review*, vol. 20, August 1955, pp. 424–430; and Richard L. Simpson, "A Modification of the Functional Theory of Social Stratification," *Social Forces*, vol. 35, December 1956, pp. 132–137. These articles are collected together in S. M. Lipset and R. Bendix, *Class, Status and Power* (New York).

probably more responsible for the development of the American "classless" society than
trends in social mobility.[8]

Significantly, these remarks are not derived
from empirical data, but rather from the
perspective which underlies Lipset and
Rogoff's view of society, a model which in-
corporates a belief that what *ought* to be
taking place in America is *in fact* taking
place. It remained for an historian, Gabriel
Kolko—who assumed conflict to be the de-
terminer of income rather than social function—to study the reality of income distribution.

> While the income share of the richest tenth
> has remained large and virtually constant over
> the past half century, the two lowest income-
> tenths have experienced a sharp decline. In
> 1910, the combined income shares of the two
> poorest income-tenths were about one-quarter
> that of the richest tenth; by 1959, their share
> had dropped to one-seventh. During this same
> period, the percentage of the next lowest tenth
> also decreased, while the fourth and fifth from
> the lowest tenths (the sixth- and seventh-rank-
> ing) neither gained nor lost ground appre-
> ciably. Together these five groups, which con-
> stitute the poorer half of the U.S. population,
> received 27 per cent of the national personal
> income in 1910, but only 23 per cent in 1959.
> Thus, for the only segments of the population
> in which a gain could indicate progress toward
> economic democracy, there has been no in-
> crease in the percentage share of the national
> income.[9]

A U.S. Census Bureau report shows that
in 1968 there were 900,000 American families whose income exceeded $50,000 and
that these 900,000 people accounted for 11

percent of the total national income. The
analysis, conducted by the chief of the U.S.
Census Bureau's population division, reveals
that in 1968 5 percent of the families controlled 22 percent of the total national income.[10]

The view that social inequality is functional is more an apologia for the status quo
than it is a sociologically useful model. As
Ossowski observed:

> Wherever there is a tendency to efface the dis-
> tinctness of social inequalities—whether this
> is motivated by a desire to deaden the sensi-
> tiveness of the oppressed classes or to appease
> the conscience of the privileged and reconcile
> the existing state of affairs with the theology
> which they profess—we find in the image of
> the social structure an inclination to give pri-
> ority to mutual dependence in the inter-class
> relationship.[11]

With the same sort of logic, functional
models are developed for "understanding"
war, deviance, and law. To argue that these
phenomena serve some "purpose" is useful
only if we ask the further question, "*Whose*
purposes do these social phenomena serve?"
Conflict theorists not only ask the question;
they suggest an answering hypothesis. Events
such as war serve the purpose of the ruling
classes, whose sons do not fight the wars but
whose way of life is protected as a result of
these wars;[12] whose children do not experience the sting of law enforcement or suffer
for their deviance;[13] and whose children do
not have to be taught to "defer gratifica-

[8] Seymour Martin Lipset and Natalie Rogoff, "Class and Opportunity in Europe and the United States." Reprinted from *Commentary*, p. 568, by permission: Copyright 1954 by the American Jewish Committee.
[9] Gabriel Kolko, *Wealth and Power in America* (New York: Praeger, 1962), p. 15.
[10] *International Herald Tribune*, March 16, 1971.
[11] Stanislau Ossowski, *Class Structure in the Social Consciousness* (New York: The Free Press of Glencoe, 1963), p. 90.
[12] Fred J. Cook, *The Warfare State* (New York: Macmillan, 1964); Tristram Coffin, *The Armed Society: Militarism in Modern America* (New York: Penguin, 1964).
[13] William J. Chambliss, "Two Gangs," unpublished manuscript summarized in William J. Chambliss and Robert B. Seidman, *Law, Order and Power* (Reading, Mass.: Addison-Wesley, 1971).

tion" in order for them to inherit their parents' position in society.[14]

The Relationship between Nonindustrialized and Industrialized Nations

The less-industrialized nations of the world are often referred to as the *third world*.[15] Viewing these societies in this way is indicative of the kinds of errors we can make when we fail to use the conflict perspective in analyzing events related to industrialization. The concept of a third world suggests implicitly (and inevitably leads to explicit theories) that: (1) the nonindustrialized nations form a social unit that has developed independently of the industrialized nations, and (2) such independence is true today. It also suggests that the nonindustrialized nations share certain unique characteristics (which the industrialized world has "outgrown" or "gone beyond") that allow them to remain autonomous.

Viewing nonindustrialized peoples as the third world leads us to look within those nations for the causes of nonindustrialization. It may lead us to look primarily at the *cultural* or *normative* characteristics of underdeveloped nations for an explanation of their nonindustrialized state. It even leads to the ludicrous view that underdevelopment stems from individual psychological traits. From such a perspective comes David McClelland's theory of *achievement motivation*, which states that a people with a generally high level of achievement will produce more energetic entrepreneurs who, in turn, produce more rapid economic development.

[14] Robert S. and Helen M. Lynd, *Middletown* (New York: Harcourt Brace, 1929).
[15] This discussion owes much to Andre Gunder Frank, "Sociology of Development and Underdevelopment of Sociology," *Catalyst*, Summer 1967. This article is also reprinted in Andre Gunder Frank, *Latin America: Underdevelopment or Revolution* (New York: Monthly Review Press, 1969); see also A. G. Frank, *Capitalism and Underdevelopment in Latin America* (New York: Monthly Review Press, 1967).

In Chapter 14 we will deal in some detail with these functional interpretations. Suffice it to say at this point that the conflict perspective avoids the error of concentrating exclusively on the characteristics of less-developed nations by focusing instead on (1) the historical development of capitalism and (2) the relationship between industrialized and nonindustrialized nations as the starting point for understanding the present-day dilemma of the nonindustrialized people.

Bureaucratization

Max Weber is rightly renowned for foreseeing the extremely important role bureaucracies and bureaucratization would play in indus-

Conflict analysis suggests that modern warfare is waged to protect the interests of the most powerful classes in the nation-state. The agonies of Vietnam were disproportionately borne by Vietnamese civilians and working-class Americans. The benefits of the war seem to have gone disproportionately to American corporations supplying military equipment. (United Press International)

trial society.[16] He, more than any other sociologist, devoted time and attention to the
characteristics of bureaucracy and its effects
on society. He provided us with a conceptual
framework for thinking about bureaucracies
which has dominated most thinking on the
subject since his initial observations were
made. For Weber the chief identifying characteristic of bureaucracy is that it has clearly
specified areas of jurisdiction which are
(usually) ordered by explicit rules—either
laws created by the state or regulations stipulated by administrative units. Concomitant
with this is the fact that the rules are enforced and lived up to by persons who occupy positions within the bureaucracy. These
persons gain their authority by virtue of the
positions they occupy in the organization.
They do not have authority because they
have inherited it (which would be traditional
rather than rational authority); nor do they
have authority because they are chosen as
leaders or because they can sway people to
follow them (which would be charismatic
authority). Their authority rests, according to
Weber, on the fact that they occupy a position with specified duties and obligations in
a bureaucratic structure. Their authority,
then, is neither traditional nor charismatic;
it is *legitimate*. Thus, legitimate authority becomes the defining characteristic of the positions that constitute the bureaucracy.

Nisbet has summed up other characteristics of bureaucracy that were of importance
to Weber:

> From the basic principle of fixed and official
> jurisdiction flow such vital practices and cri-
> teria as the regularization of channels of com-
> munication, authority, and appeal; the func-
> tional priority of the office to the person

occupying it; the emphasis upon written and
recorded orders in place of random, merely
personal commands or wishes; the sharp separation of official from personal identity in the
management of affairs and the superintending
of finances; the identification of, and provision
for, the training of "expertness" in a given
office or function; the rigorous priority of official to merely personal business in the governing of an enterprise; and finally, the conversion of as many activities and functions as
possible to clear and specifiable rules; rules
that, by their nature, have both perspective
and authoritarian significance.[17]

Weber's analysis is more than simply a
description of bureaucracy. The process of
bureaucratization is

> a powerful manifestation of the historical prin-
> ciple of rationalization. The growth of bureau-
> cracy in government, business, religion, and
> education is an aspect of the rationalization of
> culture that has also transformed the nature of
> art, drama, music and philosophy.[18]

Weber's followers have often translated "rational" as "good," in contrast to "irrational,"
which is "bad." Weber did not intend such an
interpretation. He saw the potential evils of
bureaucracy quite clearly:

> It is horrible to think that the world could one
> day be filled with nothing but those little cogs,
> little men clinging to little jobs and striving
> toward the bigger ones—a state of affairs
> which is to be seen once more playing an
> ever-increasing part in the spirit of our present
> administrative system.[19]

But our concern here is not with the consequences of bureaucratization. Our concern
is to point up the differences between conflict and functionalist approaches, and these

---

[16] Max Weber, "Bureaucracy," in Hans Gerth and C.
Wright Mills (eds.), *From Max Weber: Essays in Sociological Theory* (New York: Oxford University Press,
1946).

[17] Robert Nisbet, op. cit., p. 46.
[18] Ibid., p. 146.
[19] Ibid., pp. 292–293.

become clear when we try to explain *why* bureaucratization has taken place. Weber was concerned with describing the process of bureaucratization and with explaining why it has become so important in the West. Weber believed that the main cause for the spread of bureaucratization was the spirit of individualization promoted by Western religions. Weber emphasized religious ideology as the most important source of different types of social relations. Second, he stated that bureaucratization also spread because, in the modern world, organizations tended to be large; largeness, he argued, led to bureaucratization.

To see bureaucracy as a consequence of size is of questionable validity. As Gouldner has pointed out,

> Weber's emphasis on size as the crucial determinant of bureaucratic development is unsatisfactory for several reasons. First, there are historic examples of human efforts carried out on an enormous scale which were not bureaucratic in any serious sense of the term. The building of the Egyptian pyramids is an obvious example. Second, Weber never considers the possibility that it is not "large size" as such that disposes to bureaucracy; large size may be important only because it generates other social forces which, in their turn, generate bureaucratic patterns.[20]

The shortcomings of Weber's analysis are often magnified in the hands of less imaginative functional analysts. Talcott Parsons exemplifies this among contemporary sociologists:

> Technical advance almost always leads to increasingly elaborate division of labor and the concomitant requirement of increasingly elaborate organization. The fundamental reason for this is, of course, that with elaborate differentiation of functions the need for minute coordination of the different functions develops at the same time.[21]

Parson's argument is quite clear in this passage. Technological advance necessitates bureaucratization. Bureaucratization (like pollution), with all its faults, is a price we must pay for advancing technology.

Such an explanation leaves out more than it includes. The typical functional analysis (as the arguments of Weber and Parsons illustrate) ends precisely where the most compelling and challenging questions lie. For real insight into the process of bureaucratization, we must ask why the decision to bureaucratize is made by those responsible for the shape of the organization. We must also ask what meaning bureaucratization will have for the people at all levels of the organization. In short, a consideration of the dynamic process of bureaucratization must be a part of any responsible sociological analysis; it is simply not enough to point to the correlates of the process (technological advance and large-scale social pressures) and to suppose that we have thereby explained the process.

Furthermore, these alleged causes of bureaucratization do not hold up in the face of empirical data. As Weber himself recognized, bureaucratization occurs in organizations where technological "advance" is completely lacking—religious and charitable organizations, for example—and in agencies in contemporary Western societies which administer social services or enforce the law.

How might the process of bureaucratization be approached from the conflict perspective? A conflict theorist would immediately ask whose interests are served by the

---

[20] Alvin W. Gouldner, "Metaphysical Pathos and the Theory of Bureaucracy," *American Political Science Review*, vol. 49, 1955, pp. 496–507.

[21] Talcott Parsons, *The Social System* (Glencoe, Ill.: The Free Press, 1951), p. 507.

phenomenon of bureaucracy. Who benefits from the bureaucratization of industry and organizations? And how are the decisions to bureaucratize made? Who pays what price for bureaucratization, once established, and who is responsible for perpetuating it in the face of opposition? By asking such questions, much can be learned about the bureaucratic process that remains hidden if we accept too readily the superficial explanation that bureaucracies emerge with increased size; or that bureaucracies are necessary byproducts of advancing technology; or that bureaucracies simply reflect inevitable historical processes.

The fact is that bureaucracy does *not* represent "rational" organization in that it is not always the most sensible way of reaching the goals for which an organization ostensibly exists. For example, there is good reason to doubt that bureaucratization is the most efficient or, in Parsons' terminology, "functionally necessary" way to organize the production of material goods. Bureaucratization interferes basically with the process of education, as is becoming increasingly clear to everyone involved with today's high schools, colleges, and universities. And re-

cent analyses of the legal system have demonstrated how the bureaucratic demands of the law enforcement agencies tend to obstruct the goals of the law in democratic societies.[22] Indeed, it is not too much of an exaggeration to say that, in law enforcement, bureaucratization has been the principal cause of a breakdown in the legitimacy of law in the eyes of less powerful classes of people. In these cases, the separated functions of bureaucratic positions allow laws to be selectively enforced in favor of the powerful. Plea bargaining, in which an accused person pleads guilty to a lesser charge, may be an efficient way to rapidly obtain convictions, but it may also allow well-placed bureaucrats to use the law selectively. District attorneys may become very legalistic and rule-oriented with one defendant, very lenient with another. The privacy and specialization of bureaucratized roles, like that

[22] For examples of how bureaucratic goals come to replace the ostensible and agreed-upon goals of law enforcement agencies, see William J. Chambliss and Robert B. Seidman, *Law, Order and Power*, op. cit.; William J. Chambliss, *Crime and the Legal Process* (New York: McGraw-Hill, 1969), pp. 98–346; Jerome Skolnick, *Justice Without Trial* (New York: Wiley, 1966); Abraham S. Blumberg, "The Practice of Law as Confidence Game," *Law and Society*, vol. 1, June 1967, pp. 15–39.

Bureaucratized oppression. The German soldiers who starved and shot the Jews in the Warsaw ghetto in 1939 to 1940 claimed not to be responsible. They were following orders from above. (United Press International)

of district attorney, allow the resulting injustice to be partially hidden. But the public in general comes to believe that "It's not what you know, it's who you know." In short, bureaucratization has served to *lessen* the legitimacy of some social institutions—not to enhance it, as Weber would have us believe it should.

In the face of the high costs and inefficiencies of bureaucratic organization, can we now explain the continuation and expansion of bureaucracy? We must look for an explanation of this apparent paradox not in the lives of people who must cope with bureaucratic red tape, but rather in the needs of those in power to maintain their positions of power. And for this purpose, bureaucracies are very effective. In feudal times, traditional authority perpetuated the exploitation of the masses; bureaucratic organization serves that purpose in the modern world. The interests of the state and of the elite are served by bureaucracies, which claim to be (but in fact are not) impartial administrators of morality and justice.

Bureaucracies, in short, persist because they serve the interests of those in power. They do this by:

1. Blurring the lines of power so that those who benefit most are not so visible to those who benefit least

2. Claiming that their decisions are rational, universal, and fair, when they are in fact particularistic and consistently biased

3. Making the exploitation of those who get the least out of the available resources of society appear to be a consequence of the "organization" rather than of managers, capitalists, elites, or the "haves"

Holism

Although both the functional and conflict perspectives claim to be useful in understanding much of human social life, each ignore some large part. For example, in analyzing the relationship between industrial and nonindustrial societies, the functionalist approach is to look at each nation-state (a geographical entity) as though it is a self-contained unit whose people generally agree about how to do things (thus leading to such explanations of developmental rates as achievement motivation, amount of particularism, etc.). The conflict perspective, starting from an analysis of the *relationship* between nonindustrial areas and areas dominated by industrial technologies, looks at *all* countries as comprising the unit of analysis. The conflict perspective has led some theorists to see the underdeveloped nations as satellites of the developed (European and North American) nations and, further, to see this satellite relationship as one root of the power of the industrialized countries.

This basic difference in approach is also clear in evaluating one of the propositions of Marxian theory.[23] Marx asserted that one of the characteristics of capitalism is to force increasingly large proportions of people out of self-employment into wage-earning. One consequence, he argued, is increasing misery for the masses. In attempting to deny that this has occurred, those who use functional analysis claim that within the United States (or Great Britain, West Germany, and France), although fewer are self-employed, wage earners are relatively well off. Yet if one looks at the entire world and not just at particular societies, Marx's assertion is not so easily dismissed. For Latin America, Africa, India, and most of Asia, the prophecy has proved quite true: there has been an increasing proletarianization (forcing people into wage earning) and increasing misery for the vast majority. The capitalist economic system has created precisely the kind of conditions for most people that Marx saw as in-

[23] William Appleman Williams, *The Great Evasion* (Chicago: Quadrangle Books, 1964).

evitable, given the structure of capitalism. Only if our view is restricted to looking at *one* "society" and not at the relationships between all peoples can we sustain the argument that Marx was in this instance wrong.

On Power

The different interpretations of power by the conflict model and the functional model parallel rather closely points made in the discussion of social class and social inequality. Two further differences, however, deserve special mention. In general, the conflict perspective emphasizes the cohesiveness and unity of interests of the profit-managing upper classes in industrial nations. It sees these upper classes as comprising a ruling class. The functional perspective, in contrast, emphasizes the divisions within the upper classes and their supposedly conflicting interests.

The conflict perspective also gives primacy to the role of money and wealth in the determination of social power. The functionalists' view is more eclectic and emphasizes a variety of types and sources of power. This difference between functional and conflict models comes out clearly in a comparison of Marx's conflict approach and Weber's functionalist perspective.

> Max Weber, who was the first to present a comprehensive alternative to Marx's theory, did so by distinguishing, in the first place, between different modes of stratification which coexisted in modern societies: class stratification with which Marx had been primarily concerned, and stratification by social prestige or honor. He also treated as an independent phenomenon the distribution of political power in society, which Marx had viewed almost exclusively as the product of class stratification.[24]

[24] Robert Nisbet, op. cit., p. 214.

Functional analyses, following Weber, tend to analyze power, if at all, as a problem of how different types of power are diffused throughout a society. Conflict theorists, following Marx, tend to concentrate on those groups that control the "big decisions." The title of C. Wright Mills' best-known book, *The Power Elite*, points up an essential difference between conflict and functionalist models in this regard.[25] Not only would someone working with a functional model avoid such a title, he or she would not, in all likelihood, be led even to research the question of whether there is a ruling elite, unless to disprove the assertions of critics. Instead, functional analysis assumes that power is diffuse and that the appropriate study of power should concentrate on who wields power in what particular situation over what particular group.

In part, these different conceptions of power go back to different conceptions of the unit of study. Conflict theory starts not from "society" but from economic power as it arises from the way people organize economies. From this it is a natural step to view other institutional patterns (the family, courts, education, religion) as reflecting the wholly pervasive effects of conflicts in economic interest. These effects, of course, cut across national boundaries. The functionalists' unit of study, by contrast, is a "society." Functional analysis tends to focus on how power differences might function to hold together a particular way of doing things. Conflict analysis, whose unit of study is the social relations between individuals, is not distracted by the issue of what is supposedly good for the abstraction "society." We can focus on the oppressive effects of concentrated power on individuals and on classes of individuals.

[25] C. Wright Mills, *The Power Elite* (New York: Oxford University Press, 1956).

Some answers to issues raised here concerning power are contained in the chapter to follow. At this point, however, it may be well to quote the argument of Bottomore in support of the conflict approach to the study of power.

> If power is really so widely dispersed (as the functionalists would have it) how are we to account for the fact that the owners of property—the upper class in Marx's sense—still predominate so remarkably in government and administration, and in other *elite* positions; or that there has been so little redistribution of wealth and income, in spite of the strenuous and sustained effort of the labour movement to bring it about? Is it not reasonable to conclude . . . that notwithstanding political democracy, and despite the limited conflicts of interest which occur between *elite* groups in different spheres, the upper class in capitalist societies is still a distinctive and largely self-perpetuating social group, and still occupies the vital positions of power? Its power may be less commanding, and it is certainly less arrogantly exercised, than in an earlier period, because it encounters an organized opposition and the test of elections, and because other classes have gained a limited access to the *elites;* but the power which it has retained enables it to defend successfully its most important economic interests.[26]

The Quality of Life

In keeping with their general orientations, the conflict and functionalist perspectives take quite different positions with regard to the quality of life. In general, the conflict theorist investigates and emphasizes the disruptive, inherently contradictory features of modern civilization.[27]

The general conclusion that humanity faces ecological disaster is a viewpoint increasingly voiced by politicians and scholars alike. It is, indeed, becoming so apparent that the environment is being spoiled irretrievably by human action that even the functionalists can be expected to begin paying some attention to this problem in the near future. Predictably, however, they will not stress the fact that the interests of some segments of society conflict with those of others; rather, their focus will doubtless be on the tendency of "people" (not the business elite or the political power holders) to exploit "cheap resources," or to litter, and thereby to despoil the environment. The clear advantage of the conflict model is that it leads one to ask questions about the misuse of the environment before it becomes a popular political and moral issue, and it focuses attention on those who are responsible for the real despoliation. To link the leaving of paper on roadsides with the dumping of pollutants into air and water is to completely distort the problem and to foster impotence in the face of necessity for change.

The problem of modern peoples' estrangement from the world is also an integral part of the conflict model. Karl Marx put the point succinctly in writing about the workers in capitalist societies:

> In what does the alienation of labor consist? First, that the work is external to the worker, that it is not a part of his nature, that consequently he does not fulfil himself in his work but denies himself, has a feeling of misery, not of well-being . . . the worker therefore feels himself at home only during his leisure, whereas at work he feels homeless.[28]

Elsewhere in his writings, Marx extends this notion of alienation (or "estrangement") to apply to all of modern humanity. He sees not only the worker but also the profit-managing (bourgeois or capitalist) class as

---

[26] T. B. Bottomore, *Classes in Modern Society* (London: Allen and Unwin), pp. 63–64.

[27] Karl Marx, *Economic and Political Manuscripts*, translated and edited by T. B. Bottomore in *Karl Marx's Early Writings* (New York: McGraw-Hill, 1964), p. 127.

[28] *Reports on Happiness*, National Opinion Research Center, Chicago, 1962.

suffering estrangement from the forces that shape their lives and from fellow humans. In addition to accepting the broad application of the prevalence of estrangement, modern conflict theories also apply Marx's ideas of alienation to all people dominated by industrialized economic forms.

The functionalist perspective, although not uniformly arguing that people are content and finding the quality of life satisfactory, does tend to see the quality of life as generally high in modern industrialized society. The emphasis is on the cohesive nature of existing norms and the meaning given to life by the belief systems which prevail.

There is little empirical evidence to test these theories except what people *say* about how happy they are. Social science techniques have proved grossly inadequate to the task of assessing the quality of life. The results of questionnaire attempts to assess objectively the presence or absence of "alienation" among workers or other groups have been contradictory.[29]

Those who generally use the conflict perspective point to such things as the amount of crime, the high suicide and alcoholism rates, and the disappointment of adults with youth and vice versa as indications of a general state of unhappiness and estrangement.[30] On the other side, rising wages, presumed high rates of social mobility, and an improvement in the standard of living for more and more people are viewed as indications that social institutions function to improve the quality of life and that alienation has declined.

The fact that students and many adults are deeply concerned about the meaninglessness of life—are vocally and overtly expressing estrangement from modern times (the

gang described in Chapter I is but one example)—is perhaps ample support for the conflict position. Conflict analysis gives voice to the lives of people who have been most exploited by the modern system—women, the rural poor, small farmers, black people, native Americans, Spanish-speaking Americans, and a host of others—who share an intense dissatisfaction with the modern world. The silent voice of this majority, a sociology dominated by functional analysis from 1930 to 1960, speaks for the validity of this perspective. Even the better-off working class (the "hard hats") and the supposedly "silent" middle-management class find much wrong.

Interests and Human Action

Marx once noted that "history is nothing but the actions of men in pursuit of their ends."[31] The implications of this point of view have not been traced very systematically, although some of the writings included in Part 4 of this volume touch on it. The focus among conflict theorists after Marx has been on the role of collections of people who are acting in their own interests; and, consistent with their model, the emphasis has been on groups which grow out of economic divisions of society into social classes.

The contrast with functionalist thinking is striking. Where a conflict theorist emphasizes the clash of interest in people's use of economic strategies, functionalism emphasizes the mutuality of interest. Where conflict analysis emphasizes the role of the state in supporting the interests of particular groups (especially the elites), functionalism tends to see the state as a value-neutral setting in which interest groups share a more or less equal footing—some form of balance or homeostasis is reached through the state.[32]

[29] Ely Chinoy, *Automobile Workers and the American Dream* (Boston: Beacon Press, 1965); Richard Hamilton, *Affluence and the French Worker in the Fourth Republic* (Princeton: Princeton University Press, 1967).
[30] William A. Williams, op. cit.

[31] Karl Marx, "The Holy Family," in Lloyd Easton and Kurt Guddat (eds.), *Writings of Young Marx on Philosophy and Society* (New York: Doubleday-Anchor), 1967.
[32] William J. Chambliss and Robert B. Seidman, op. cit.

In the abstract either point of view may appear equally defensible. The important task for the beginning uses of sociological analysis is to isolate those issues or problems for which one or the other model is most useful. As we have suggested thus far, many of the problems and issues of industrialization seem more usefully understood through conflict analysis. In the section of this text which deals with industrialization (Chapters 12 through 16), we will trace a number of issues related to industrialization, and it will become clear from these analyses how the conflict model approaches the problem.

At this point it may be useful to discuss one illustrative case before leaving the issue. For some time now certain sociologists have been proclaiming the explanatory utility of the *theory of status inconsistency*. The crux of this "theory" is that people who have roles involving conflicting statuses (such as having a good deal of education but a poor-paying job) are less content than the average person with their lives and with the political order. According to the status-inconsistency argument, they are thus susceptible to extreme political viewpoints such as those of the John Birch Society or the Communist party.

This view has a good deal to recommend it from the functionalists' point of view. It reinforces the idea that it is disharmony (a lack of status consistency), and not poverty, lack of power, or conflicts inherent in dominating economic patterns, that leads men to take something other than the "rational" or "normal" course of nonradical political views.

The evidence in support of the theory of status inconsistency is conflicting, but one attempt to assess the theory's utility concludes that

comparisons between the relative ability of social class membership and status inconsistency to predict political attitudes quite clearly demonstrate the superiority of social class as a predictor. . . . Social class membership and minority group status appear to be far superior explanatory concepts. These concepts may be time-worn and smack of Marxism. But if they are in fact the kinds of sociological variables that determine the behavior of men then we should use them. Concepts like status consistency . . . unquestionably have a more sophisticated sound to them. But if we sacrifice substantial usefulness for sophisticated appearance, then our contribution to knowledge will be meager indeed.[33]

This investigation and a number of others have suggested that the notion of social classes acting according to their own interests is a far more useful predictor of political predispositions than is status inconsistency.

The Relative Importance of Culture and Social Structure

Within each sociological perspective it is analytically useful to distinguish between culture and social structure. Culture refers to the prevailing ideas of right and wrong, the belief systems, and the rules for interacting with other people and institutions. Culture also includes the tools with which people adjust, drop out of, or attempt to change established relationships. Language, technological know-how, religious dogma, and legal rules are among the most important elements of culture.

Social structure refers to the structured (that is, predictable, patterned) behavior expected for solutions to specific problems. An example is the whole set of specific ways people are expected to relate to private property: who can use it and how. The general belief in private property, and the various technologies that can be combined in

[33] K. Dennis Kelley and William J. Chambliss, "Status Consistency and Political Attitudes," *American Sociological Review*, vol. 31, no. 3, June 1966, p. 382.

many ways to create a structured relationship to private property, may be analyzed separately and called by a different name— culture. But the fact that individuals own private property and that this ownership determines their day-to-day patterned relations with others is social structure, just as the fact that the world of large corporations exists and dominates the decision-making processes in contemporary Western societies is part of that social structure. The fact that the Western world controls 60 percent of the world's natural resources and uses them to support its way of life is also part of that structure.

Both the functional and conflict perspectives use the concepts of culture and social structure. The difference is that functional analysis leads to an emphasis on culture in shaping social structure, whereas conflict analysis emphasizes the primacy of social structure in shaping culture. Marx's view of religion as "the opiate of the masses"—that is, his view that religion derives from the established exploitive relationship between those with property and those who live by labor—places religious beliefs (part of the culture) in the context of established economic relationships (the social structure). This contrasts dramatically with Durkheim's contention that the religious beliefs that developed through the centuries were the "glue," the foundation of society. To be sure, Durkheim talked about and emphasized structural characteristics, just as Marx and conflict theorists after him have talked about and emphasized culture. As we have

pointed out, the difference lies in the relative importance placed on these different facets of social life. Which view is more useful can be judged only by the questions, explanations, and researches each produces. Time and a willingness to look open-mindedly at the merits of both positions will lead to a judgment of the relative merits of each in the understanding and solution of specific problems.

SUMMARY

Sociology is in some respects like a three-ring circus—not because it is particularly entertaining, but because there are so many acts going on at once that it is difficult to see them all as part of the same show. Until recently, however, American sociology did possess one unifying characteristic—a strong urge to avoid at all costs any interpretation of the United States which emphasized class conflict.[34] The inability of conventional, inherently conservative, functional theory to account for, predict, or make sense of the myriad of violent and unanticipated events in America in the sixties, however, has breathed new life into the conflict perspective. What the historian William Appleman Williams has aptly called "the great evasion" of American intellectuals has, at long last, begun to break down.

[34] See the excellent treatment of this in Robert W. Fredericks, A Sociology of Sociology (Glencoe, Ill.: The Fress Press, 1970). See also Alvin W. Gouldner, The Coming Crisis in Western Sociology (New York: Basic Books, 1970).

SUGGESTED READINGS

William J. Chambliss (ed.), Sociological Readings in the Conflict Perspective, Part I (Reading, Mass.: Addison-Wesley, 1973).

Andre Gunder Frank, "The Sociology of Development and the Underdevelopment of Sociology," Catalyst, 1967 (available as MSS Modular Reprint no. R164).

C. Wright Mills, *The Sociological Imagination* (New York: Oxford University Press, 1959).

C. Wright Mills, "The Promise," in *The Sociological Imagination*, 1959 (available as MSS Modular Reprint no. R140).

John Rex, *Key Problems of Sociological Theory* (London: Routledge and Kegan Paul, 1961).

Pierre L. Van den Berghe, "Dialectic and Functionalism: Toward a Theoretical Synthesis," *American Sociological Review*, 1963 (available as MSS Modular Reprint no. R763).

FOUR
The Conflict Perspective

In the preceding chapters, we tried to do several things:

1. Indicate the great variation in people's experiences as they move with, work with, communicate with, and struggle against nature and one another.

2. Convey some of the urgency of understanding people's social relations in a world where consciousness of war, oppression, and pollution seems to spread faster than the awareness that it is possible to live without hunger and violence, and with self-respect, human fulfillment, and self-determination.

3. Ask why *these* problems—wars which have killed millions of civilians in the past fifty years, oppression on a scale never imagined, hunger and disease, threats to the very processes which sustain all life on earth —and not others are the problems of our time.

4. Suggest that at present we find the most useful and most accurate theoretical explanations to be those which derive from the conflict perspective. The conflict perspective is a way of looking at human social life. It focuses upon the social relations among people which stem from the way people in a particular historical period transform the material conditions of their existence into ways of surviving.

5. Show the importance of learning how to analyze old problems and new ones by developing and testing perspectives most people do not yet use in everyday problem solving.

A full appreciation and understanding of the conflict perspective can be gained only by reading and studying extensively the rich body of literature concerning this tradition which has developed over the centuries. However, it will help to grasp the important features of the conflict perspective if we present a much compressed version of the ideas that are central to it.

In Chapter 2 we spelled out some of the essential differences between the functional and conflict perspectives. In this chapter we will elaborate the major ideas contained in the conflict perspective, which may be summarized as follows:

1. People struggle to meet their perceived or fundamental needs and desires. Perceived needs include such things as the need for prestige and status; fundamental needs are such things as food and shelter. This struggle to meet needs produces patterned ways of solving the problem of survival. Particular patterns may be shared by many or few people. The patterns favorable to some may be imposed on others.

2. Coercion of one group by another is a basic feature of most historical periods. Coercion inevitably leads to conflicts between those who are coercing and those who are being coerced.

3. The struggle of those who are coerced and exploited is a moving force behind the historical development of contemporary social relations.

4. Social inequality is a fundamental feature of modern times as well as the past.

These machines harvesting wheat reflect the complex organization achieved within a capitalist industrial form. (United Press International)

Inequalities of wealth, power, prestige, and living conditions give rise to conflict between those who have and those who do not. The struggle between those who own and control more of the resources and those who own or control less of the resources is the single most important shaper of social relations in any community.

5. The state and the law are instruments by which those who control the resources attempt to reduce the power of those who do not.

6. Social classes emerge in historical periods that have an economic surplus; the surplus is utilized by certain groups to maintain their interests, and these interests, relative to the economy, are different from those of other groups. Membership in a particular social class then shapes other interests of the people in it, and the interests in turn determine how groups of people will relate to one another, both in and out of conflict situations.

7. To understand human social relations we must understand what social classes benefit from established social relations and in what ways.

It will help to think of these preceding points as comprising the basic framework of the conflict perspective. But the conflict perspective is more than these seven propositions. It is in fact a thoroughgoing theory of social relations which uses this basic framework as a stepping stone for building a more detailed explanatory model. With this in mind, we can now develop a set of general principles and some corollary propositions derived from the conflict perspective. Those social relationships which derive from the need to survive provide the most convenient foundation upon which to build the principles of the conflict perspective. The relationships which are used to ensure food and shelter, the essentials of survival, are then

the first processes to be understood. Many of the problems for which people may organize a solution (settling disputes, allocating scarce resources, teaching how to survive) are problems produced by how people construct their economic system in the first place. Put another way, we assume people will invest the most energy in preserving whatever individual advantages they have in the organized ways they relate to others to produce material survival out of raw materials. These organized, predictable ways of turning the physical environment into usable things for humans are economic institutions, or economic forms.

As we summarize the main points of conflict theory, we will present selections from others' written descriptions of human life. The intent of these selections is to give real-life examples of situations that could easily be analyzed using conflict theory. Each selection, although not originally written to support a conflict view, does, in fact, support and illustrate one or more of the principles of conflict theory.

THE PRINCIPLES OF CONFLICT THEORY
Principle One
Economic forms shape other institutional forms.

There are other problems in human survival than economic ones. People must solve the problems of childrearing, learning the patterns of predictability (education), protection (policing and military defense), settling disputes (courts, arbitrators), making decisions about the use of scarce resources (politics), figuring out why they are doing all this and relating to other realities (religion, philosophy), clarifying or muddying communication (media), staying alive and healthy (medicine). People may produce predictable ways

SELECTION 4-1: An illustration of the economic priority principle.

HOW THE LOSS OF AN ECONOMY DESTROYED OTHER PARTS OF A WAY OF LIFE

The Ik are a people who traditionally hunted in the northwest part of what is now Uganda. It is their misfortune to have collided head on with the needs of the new state of Uganda to preserve the game herds and to prevent people from fighting over hunting grounds. As a result, the Ik have been prevented from hunting and have been confined to what was only a small part of their former hunting range. In his study of the Ik, Colin Turnbull describes how the entire structure of social life disintegrates as a people are no longer able to produce, in the old ways, enough food to benefit from each other. The life of the Ik today supports the theory that an economy, a way of producing usable resources, is a necessary precondition of and shaper of the other social patterns. In the following brief passage from Turnbull's account, we observe the impact of the loss of economic structure on the rest of social life.

So communal hunts, either by netting or by beating, were ruled out, and hunting, like other activities, became an individual affair. It was common to hear and sometimes see men coming back after dark laden with meat that they could not consume on the spot, risking a brief night with it in or near the village, then off before dawn to sell it to the Police Post without as much as a bite for a wife or child. I remember that once Lomer, Yakuma's oldest son, came back from several weeks' absence hunting on and beyond Zulia. It was the height of the famine and Yakuma himself was away scavenging for himself, but Matsui and the other children were there, all starving except Lokwam. The two beautiful girls had nobody to sell themselves to, Ngorok was ill, and little Naduie was the weakest member of the junior age band. Their oldest brother came back so fat, not just plump, that I hardly recognized him. His face was like a balloon, his arms and legs were fleshy and his stomach was obscene. He brought nothing with him except three gourds of honey, all of which he took straight to the Police Post for sale.

of solving these problems, but we assume that other institutional patterns will be shaped by people's wishes to protect their basic economic system and to make other social relationships support their predictable chances to get food and shelter. This principle logically implies that people will fight hardest to protect or gain an economic advantage, and that the hardest fighting will result when resources are scarcest. It also suggests that other institutional patterns will tend to support the economic interests of the dominant class.

Noneconomic forces may shape the patterns of childrearing, politics, medicine, policing, and settling disputes, but all these processes will be under strong pressure to conform to the dominant economic relationships. Conversely, if the economic form changes, we can expect people to change their other institutional forms. A case which reflects this principle is the recent history of the people called the Ik, which is detailed in Selection 4-1. In this case, as with the other selections describing principles of conflict theory, we have chosen material from people who have observed social life from very different perspectives.

SELECTION 4-2: An illustration of the principle of population limits as a structural contradiction.

THE SITUATION OF THE PEASANTRY OF JAPAN IN THE 16TH–17TH CENTURIES AD

As successful peasants produced more sons than could farm the land, feudal Japan began to face the problem of large numbers of people who could not be integrated into the village economy of feudalism.

Filial piety, family solidarity and family co-operation, then, were the categorical imperatives of family life, which were destined to hold a firm grip upon the consciences of every person born into a family group during the feudal period. But even this time-honored family system began to show signs of disintegration in the later Tokugawa period. The legislators and moral philosophers of the time thought it an unpardonable sin for the people to slight or disturb the order of the family, which was the sacred heritage of their ancestors. Their des-perate efforts, however, to preserve the family system were of little avail against the great forces that were transforming the whole eco-nomic and social system.

In commercial towns, which were rapidly de-veloping, the demand for labor was limitless. The poor agricultural people, who were finding it harder and harder to support large families, began to send their children to be apprentices or servants in the houses of thriving mer-chants . . . All the day laborers were required to receive a license at the office and were placed at various temporary tasks such as transporta-tion and road repairing. Although the wages of these unskilled laborers are not known at pres-ent, the fact that they could pay the thank-money of twenty-four mon (later thirty mon) of copper money per month to their employ-ment office shows that they could get along comfortably on their wages except at times when there was a sudden jump in the price of rice. Thus masses of young people in the vil-lages were driven into the towns. They no more regretted breaking away from their families than throwing away old shoes, as Dazai Shundai expressed it . . . As more and more avenues of work opened up for those who left their village homes, the family became less significant as an economic unit.

Principle Two

A particular economic form or mode of pro-duction tends to dominate a given time or place.

Energy and resources devoted to one way of surviving, say hunting, are not available for use in another economic mode, say farming. In one place and time people will tend to be hunters but not farmers because each strategy has its own implications for every part of an individual's life. It is hard to have the politics of a farmer and the religion of a hunter. Analysis of the buffalo-hunting econ-omy of native Americans, or Indians, after the white conquest clearly shows how this way of gathering food shaped other parts of the lives of the Indians. Of course, in the same time and place different people may be using several economies or modes of production, but *one* will usually dominate.

Principle Two   Corollary one:

If a *community form* is defined as the logic of a particular economic form plus the insti-tutions and cultural patterns shaped by eco-nomic forces, then there are a limited number of community forms.

In any given time or place there is a limited set of dominant institutional patterns— shaped by the logic of a particular way of surviving, whether hunting, farming, or man-ufacturing. Although people may be using a variety of forms, the greatest amounts of

SELECTION 4-3: An illustration of the principle of class conflict as a structural contradiction.

ABRAHAM LINCOLN ON CLASS CONFLICT

When Abraham Lincoln campaigned for Congress in 1848, he was sensitive to a great issue of his times: the tendency of the small landholders or small businessperson to be forced into wage labor. His analysis led him to conclude that a proper function of government was to protect individuals from having the value of their labor expropriated by a class which did not labor.

In the early days of our race, the Almighty said to the first of our race, "In the sweat of thy face shalt thou eat bread"; and since then, if we except the light and the air of heaven, no good thing has been or can be enjoyed by us without having first cost labor. It follows that all such things of right belong to those whose labor has produced them. But it has so happened, in all ages of the world, that some have labored and others have without labor enjoyed a large proportion of the fruits. This is wrong and should not continue. To secure to each laborer the whole product of his labor, or as nearly as possible, is a worthy object of any good government.

Karl Marx made the same observation at about the same time. His analysis of the contradictions in one economic form, the capitalist form, is much more detailed and, being more detailed, suggests more specifically what a government might do to achieve that "worthy object" of which Lincoln spoke: the assurance of the fruits to each laborer. Oversimplifying Marx's analysis, the most important contradiction in a capitalist economy is that to increase wages means to decrease profits, while to increase profits means to decrease wages. Marx deduces from this contradiction three important conclusions: (1) that to the extent some people are wage earners and others are profit makers, there are social classes consisting of wage earners and profit managers; (2) that all other classes and class conflicts in capitalist society will be drawn into this conflict and into these two classes (the wage earners and the profit managers); and (3) that the conflict between these two classes will shape the other parts of these people's lives and the other institutions they are using.

energy and resources will be tied up in the dominant community form, or *survival kit*.

Principle Three

Each economic form has inherent contradictions which produce classes, and class conflict, and which may produce its own destruction.

Principle Three   Corollary one:

There is a contradiction between successful use of an economic form and population growth.

Any economic form, and its resultant community forms, can support only a limited number of people. When the form is used well enough to produce surplus food and when that surplus is enough to keep additional people alive, then there will come a point when there are more people than can comfortably use the form. The form itself will become less usable, less effective, as population surpluses increase. If, in addition, the available country and resources are filled up with users of this form, and the problem cannot be solved by the extra people leaving to replicate the old community form somewhere else, then the existing form will experience a contradiction. In this case, the contradiction is between the success of the community form and the surplus (ultimately unabsorbable people) made possible by that success.

Principle Three   Corollary two:
Each economic form has its own internal contradictions.

A social contradiction occurs when the use of a social structure leads to the attainment of some goals at the expense of others. When people use complex social structures (like family, economic, political, and other institutions) in order to get certain things done, to achieve certain goals, it begins to appear, *as the particular structure is used*, that getting some things done prevents getting other things done. This is a structural contradiction.

Principle Three   Corollary three:
Social classes and class consciousness are produced by contradictions.

A social class is defined by the relationship of people to the means of production—the tools, whether money, machinery, or animals, in a particular economic form. The most important class division is between those who own and control the means of production and those who do not. In complex economies there are often classes represented by groups who manage but do not own the resources, and classes that do not own, manage, or work within the productive forces of the society.

To the extent that people try to achieve goals through social forms containing structural contradictions (for example, in capitalist structures, the higher the wages, generally the lower the profits), to that extent

will separate classes form. To the extent that people become *aware* that their goals are in conflict with those of other classes will they become *class conscious*. To the extent the goals are in conflict, and to the extent that class consciousness develops, people will be engaged in class conflict.

Classes come in pairs and reflect different and conflicting interests resulting from a contradiction within a social structure. There are many such class pairs in a social structure, even many class pairs relative to a specific economic structure. For example, men-women, consumers-producers, workers-managers, town dwellers-city dwellers, and farmers-manufacturers are class pairs; as they use a capitalist economy they find their goals are in conflict *within that structure*. Class conflict shapes institutional patterns and leads to social change. An important question for understanding any particular historical period is, "Which are the most powerful class conflicts, powerful in the sense of having most impact on the social lives of the people involved?"

Classes should not be confused with social strata: social strata are aggregations of people who have similar amounts of job prestige. Functional theorists often use *social class* to mean upper class, middle class, or lower class. Such groupings may be interesting for statistical comparisons, but they are of minor significance to the issue of how institutional patterns are changed because social strata generate no force like the clash of interests which results from contradictions in economic structure.

Principle Three   Corollary four:
The most powerful classes, and the most important class conflicts, are those resulting from contradictions in the economic structure.

Principle 1 states that people value their economic relations—their means of physical survival—above all other relations. If we further assume that the basic resources out of which power differences arise are economic resources (money, raw materials, finished products or services, and knowledge of economic processes), then we can say more about the importance of class conflict. We can say that when these basic resources and means of livelihood are threatened by classes of people with opposing economic interests, people will neglect other values and other life problems to defend their economic interests and resources. From this, we can conclude that as conflicting interests exist and as people become conscious of them, economic classes and economic class conflicts will be the most powerful social forces, reflecting as they do the most valued and powerful social relations.

Principle Three   Corollary five:

The most important classes and class conflicts result from contradictory relationships with the means of production; specifically, when one class has an interest in the production of surplus value (converting raw materials into something more than just enough food to stay alive) and another has an interest in the distribution of surplus value, the resulting conflict is the most powerful of social forces.

There may be many contradictions in the way economic activity is structured. For example, there are ways of producing goods or services that benefit producers while hurting consumers; or that benefit urban dwellers while hurting farmers; or that benefit big business while hurting small business. But because surplus value, the value added to raw materials by labor, is the fundamental source of economic power, conflicting interests in the distribution of surplus value will produce the most important classes. These classes will be the most important because they are created by the most fundamental opposition of interests. Because the basic source of power is the issue, the conflict between these classes will be the most powerful social force shaping other parts of one's way of life. For example, if an economy is structured in such a way that some people manage the distribution of surplus value (which they call profit) and others work for wages, these two classes have contradictory interests in the economy. These contradictory interests result from structuring the

Many Americans are on "welfare" because they cannot use the work roles available within the dominant economic institutional form—industrial capitalism. (EPA Newsphoto)

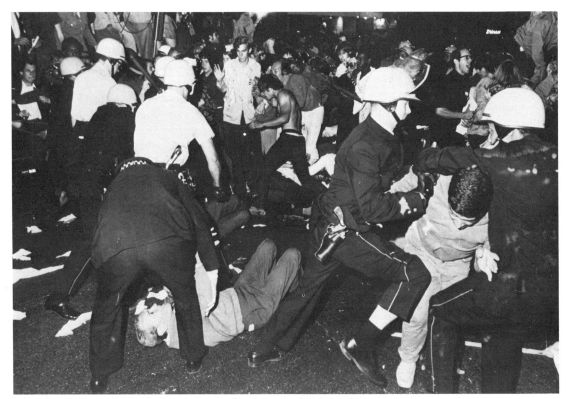

Police break up a Yippie demonstration at the Democratic National Convention in
Chicago, 1968. Threats to dominant institutional forms provoke violent police reaction.
(United Press International)

economy in such a way that profits generally
rise by keeping wages down and that wages
generally rise by reducing profits. Classes
created by this conflict of interest will try
to protect their own goals or interests in the
economy, one class struggling to protect
profit, the other wages. These classes will
attempt to shape other elements of life—
ways of educating people, making political
decisions, ordering family life, indeed all of
social life—so as to protect their own interests and increase their share of surplus value.

Principle Four

Class conflict shapes other social institutions.

Class conflict will shape noneconomic institutions (patterned or predictable solutions

to the problems of childrearing, decision
making, judging, health defense, policing),
and the more powerful classes will be better
able to shape these institutions to serve their
own interests.

A Definition: Power

Power lies in the relationship between classes
or individuals, not in the classes or individuals themselves. If power is defined as
the ability of class a to get class b to do
something for class a at less cost in energy
to class a than to class b, then potential
power will be a function of the resources
of class a as they fit or do not fit the needs
of class b and the resources of class b as
they do or do not fit the needs of class a. This

SELECTION 4-4: An illustration of the principle of class-shaped institutional patterns.

THE CIA'S ROLE IN 1964 CHILEAN ELECTIONS

Class conflict shapes basic institutional patterns so that ways of doing things best support the interests of the more powerful class. As a patterned way of solving political issues, government should reflect the interests of the more powerful class. Foreign policy would be expected to benefit the interests of the profit managers of powerful corporations, if indeed they are the most powerful class. The interference of the U.S. Central Intelligence Agency in Chilean elections seems to reflect the operation of this principle.

Previously the committee (Senate Foreign Relations Committee investigating corporate influence in American foreign policy) had been shocked at disclosures that International Telephone and Telegraph had pledged $1 million toward the defeat of Salvador Allende in his race for the Presidency of Chile in 1970. The Central Intelligence Agency had declined the offer at that time, testimony indicated, and Allende had gone on to win the election and bring in the first democratically elected Marxist regime in the Western Hemisphere.

Six years before, however, Allende's run for the Presidency had been squelched. And a former U.S. intelligence official who had been involved in that election said American support of Christian Democrat Eduardo Frei in 1964 made the 1970 effort look like a "tea party" by comparison. "U.S. Government intervention in Chile in 1964 was blatant and almost obscene," said another former intelligence agent. "We were shipping people off right and left, mainly state department but also CIA with all sorts of covers."

suggests that the power relationship between two classes, groups, or individuals can be changed by changing *any one of four factors:* the resources of *a*, the needs of *b*, the needs of *a*, or the resources of *b*.

We can look for evidence of the workings of principle 4, the principle that class conflict shapes institutions. Any state is faced with the political problem of distributing scarce resources. These resources may be distributed so as to do the maximum good. However, if class conflict and class power shape political action, we would expect the more powerful classes to influence the distribution of scarce resources to serve their interests and not the interests of the less powerful.

Principle Five

Class conflict leads to institutional compromise, failure, and experiment.

As the needs of the less powerful classes are met less and less through the dominant institutional patterns, forces for social change arise.

Principle Five   Corollary one:

Attempts will be made to compromise needs so as to make the use of institutional structures more satisfying.

For example, workers may be conscious that much of the value they add to a piece of iron ore by converting it to a steel girder is not paid them in wages. They may become conscious that this added or surplus value is used by management not to pay higher wages, or for research or investment in equipment, but to influence government officials, as in the recent ITT and dairy industry contributions to the 1970 election campaigns. Although conscious of this alienation of their power, the turning of the value they added to the iron ore against their interests, workers may feel too weak to do anything about it. They may decide to do without truly representative government.

The ruins of Macchu Pichu, a city of the Inca people in what is now called Peru. The Incas had finally integrated an agricultural economy just 100 years before being destroyed by the Spanish, users of a more advanced economic form. (Alain Keler from Editorial Photocolor Archives)

Principle Five   Corollary two:

The less powerful, more oppressed, and alienated people may experiment with new institutional patterns.

Alternative institutional patterns should be expected to the degree that people are: (1) conscious of class manipulation of the dominant patterns and/or (2) totally denied even the use of those class-dominated institutions. In short, the conscious and the truly down-and-out may develop other ways of getting food, staying healthy, raising children, getting sexual satisfaction, protecting themselves.

Principle Five   Corollary three:

Insofar as they conflict with the interests of the more powerful class, parallel or alternative forms will be suppressed.

From the conflict perspective, institutions do not change as a result of the needs of history, the needs of God, or the needs of an abstraction called society. Institutions are shaped by human needs, human conflicts, and human action. Institutional patterns are attacked and abandoned when people become conscious that such patterns do not work for them. Neighborhood food con-

spiracies (described in Selection 4-5) are alternatives to the supermarket. Free schools appear. Parallel medical institutions of many kinds, such as poor people's neighborhood

The Chinese Revolution of 1946 climaxed a long period of economic breakdown in China. (Eastfoto)

SELECTION 4-5: An illustration of the principle of institutional failure and experiment.

THE FOOD CONSPIRACY

As inflation raised food prices in the early 1970s, some people responded by not shopping at supermarkets and trying to create their own solution to the problem of food distribution.

Our system is the result of a good deal of experimentation. After making the decision to buy the food collectively, we faced the question of what to buy. We thought it would be best to separate our collective diet into several groups: produce (fruits and vegetables), grains, canned goods and non-perishables, meat. Wholesalers usually specialize in one of these categories. We decided to begin buying in one category in order to see if our system would work, to deal with problems which we knew would come up, and to discover what new problems would arise that we had not foreseen. . . . By going through this process we are bypassing a couple of middlemen who push prices up along the way. As with all other prices, food prices are very inflated. We have thus been able to save money . . . As important as these savings is the fact of our establishing a new way to meet our needs. We are sharing and cooperating in a group effort to satisfy our food needs where we were isolated before. . . . The food coops which institutionalized decentralization have been able to engage in more community dinners, writing newsletters, and have begun to engage in "skill sharing" (furniture making, weaving, repairs, child care, cooking, carpentry).

clinics, are developed. Changes in diet and life-style become alternatives to doctors. The family structure of black and other non-Caucasian people in the United States can be better understood as an alternative to institutions that do not work for them. Even private armies and vigilante groups emerge from time to time.

When such emergency patterns are perceived by the powerful as threatening their interests, active attempts at suppression are to be expected. Suppression is likely to be most violent where oppression is long-standing and class hatred and guilt have built up. Such is the case with racism.

Principle Six
Contradictions lead to radical transformation.

New economic structures emerge and are adopted because they resolve some of the contradictions of older economic forms or because they are imposed on people by powerful outsiders (colonialism, imperialism, enslavement). We have stated the assumption that economic forms and the related institutional patterns have a coherence and logic of their own. Economic forms are systems, just as fire is a system. Fire is a combination of fuel, heat, and oxygen, which, once combined in certain proportions, will persist until interfered with from the outside or exhausted by its own internal processes. In this sense, we can say that social relations are like a functioning system. However, while this notion of system is central to the functionalists, conflict theorists emphasize two things as more important than the system-forming tendency. These are: (1) the class inequality in power, and (2) the tendency of a social system so structured to produce oppression, thereby destroying, rather than transforming, itself. Fire cannot transform itself into water. In the same way, the conflict perspective assumes that a feudalistic economy, like an unusable building, cannot transform itself into something new. Feudalism is a way of life—a logic, a strategy through which humans can survive—but its very use generates conflicts which increasingly prevent the people within the system from continuing to use it. In Europe, at least, alongside the ravaged shell of feudalistic economies, those merchants and traders who came to be called bourgeois were building

SELECTION 4-6: An illustration of the principle of suppression of alternative institutional patterns.

THE BLACK PANTHER PARTY OF CHICAGO: POLICE ATTACK

Before dawn on a December morning in 1972, Chicago police broke into an upstairs apartment, shooting as they came. Subsequently two black men, Fred Hampton and Mark Clark, were killed, seven others including a pregnant woman, Deborah Johnson, were wounded. All were black people. All were members of the Black Panther Party. No immediate outcry over these killings was heard, although it might be instructive to imagine what would have been the situation had the leading political figures in a local unit of the Democratic or Republican parties been invaded and shot up by police. Finally in 1973 a Commission on Inquiry Into Black Panthers and Law Enforcement, headed by former U.S. Attorney General Ramsey Clark and Roy Wilkins, Executive Director of the NAACP, and including thirty prominent civil rights, law, political, and business figures, released findings on the killings of Hampton and Clark. They found that law officials, including States Attorney E. V. Hanrahan and thirteen others, "acted with wanton disregard for human and legal rights of American citizens and charged them with conspiring to obstruct justice in the raid on the Black Panther headquarters."

Hanrahan and the others were subsequently acquitted of these charges. Here is how the raid seemed to someone who was in it, Deborah Johnson, one of those sleeping in the apartment when the doors were shot open:

Someone came into the room, started shaking the chairman, said, "chairman, chairman, wake up—the Pigs are vamping." Still half asleep, I looked up and saw bullets coming from, it looked like the front of the apartment from the kitchen area. They were . . . the Pigs were just shootin'. And about this time, I jumped on top of the chairman. He looked up . . . looked like all the Pigs just converged at the entrance way to the bedroom area. The mattress was just going. You could feel the bullets going into it. I just knew we would all be dead, everybody in there. (Hampton, shot, lay on the bed from which he had never gotten up). The Pigs kept on shootin'. So I kept on hollerin' out. Finally they stopped. They pushed me and the other brother by the kitchen door and told us to face the wall. I heard a Pig say, "He's barely alive, he'll barely make it." I assumed they were talkin' about Chairman Fred. So then they started shootin', the Pigs started shootin', shootin' again. I heard a sister scream. They stopped shootin'. The Pig said, "He's good and dead now." The Pigs ran around laughing, they was really happy, you know . . . talking about Chairman Fred is dead. I never saw Chairman Fred again.

SELECTION 4-7: An illustration of the principle of radical transformation.

THE ORIGINS OF PERUVIAN FEUDALISM

When a way of life no longer works for masses of people, two forms of radical transformation seem to reoccur throughout history. They are (1) imposition of a new economic form by powerful outsiders or (2) creation of a radically new economic form by the people themselves. The discussion of the origins of Peruvian feudalism seems to hint at both kinds of transformation.

Since autonomous villages are likely to fission as they grow, as long as land is available for the settlement of splinter communities, these villages undoubtedly split from time to time . . . until all the readily arable land in the valley was being farmed. At this point . . . cultivation was intensified and new, previously unusable land was brought under cultivation by means of terracing and irrigation. Yet the rate at which new arable land was created failed to keep pace with the increasing demand for it . . . villages were undoubtedly already fighting one another over land . . . Once this stage was reached, a Peruvian village that lost a war faced consequences very different from those faced by a defeated village in Amazonia. There, as we have seen, the vanquished could flee to a new locale, subsisting there about as well as they had subsisted before, and retaining their independence. In Peru, however, this alternative was no longer open to the inhabitants of defeated villages. The mountains, the desert, and the sea, to say nothing of neighboring villages—blocked escape in every direction . . . subordination (which resulted for the losers) sometimes involved a further loss of autonomy (in addition to paying tribute)—incorporation into the political unit dominated by the victor.

a new economic system. The logic of capitalism radically transformed European institutional patterns and has dominated and shaped them for nearly 500 years.

Principle Six   Corollary one:

Economic surplus produces two kinds of contradiction, or conflict. Surplus may drive people outside an economic form if the form works well only when used by certain people (principle 3-1). Surplus may also produce classes which have conflicting interests with regard to the distribution of the surplus (principle 3-2).

Principle Six   Corollary two:

Transformation of economic and political systems occurs through conflict between real people. If we assume that no autonomous people, that is, people in control of their own economic form, ever give up their autonomy without the application of external force, we can deduce the following: When contradictions (3-1 and 3-2) make an economic form unusable for a particular people, the move to a new form will be a period of intense conflict (6-1) and radical transformation in the sense that not only the economic form, but also the political, judicial, educational, childrearing, military, and all other institutional patterns, will be simultaneously undergoing transformation (2-1).

SUMMARY

The conflict perspective has been presented in simplified form through six principles. The aims of such a presentation are to provoke questioning and discussion of the issues raised by the conflict perspective. Argument should lead to observation and observation to analysis. Analysis is a judgment of how well a perspective or theory answers the question "why." What could we expect to see happening in the United States and the world if the conflict perspective is a useful way of understanding human social behavior and of predicting directions of change? In what ways can the conflict perspective be modified, clarified, added to, or changed to help us better understand the institutional patterns through which people attempt to solve their problems?

In summary form, the principles of the conflict perspective are:

Principle 1: Economic forms shape other institutional forms.

Principle 2: Usable economic strategies are limited in number.

Principle 3: Each economic form has inherent contradictions which produce classes, and class conflict, and which may produce its own destruction.

Principle 4: Class-shaped institutions:

class conflict will shape noneconomic institutions, and the more powerful classes will be better able to manipulate these institutions to serve their own interests.

Principle 5: When the needs of the weaker classes are met less and less through the dominant institutional patterns, forces of social change arise.

Principle 6: Contradictions lead to radical transformation.

SUGGESTED READINGS

C. H. Anderson, *Toward a New Sociology* (Homewood, Ill.: The Dorsey Press, 1974).

C. H. Anderson, *Sociological Essays and Research*, rev. ed. (Homewood, Ill.: The Dorsey Press, 1974).

T. B. Bottomore, *Classes in Modern Society* (New York: Pantheon Books, 1966).

G. D. H. Cole, *The Meaning of Marxism* (Ann Arbor, Mich.: University of Michigan Press, 1966).

Ralf Dahrendorf, "Out of Utopia: Toward a Reorientation of Sociological Theory," *American Journal of Sociology* (available as a Bobbs-Merrill Reprint).

Erich Fromm, *The Sane Society* (Greenwood, Conn.: Fawcett, 1955).

PART TWO

DOING SOCIOLOGICAL ANALYSIS: THE METHODOLOGY OF SOCIOLOGY

Section One was meant to convey some feeling for the broad outlines of the subject matter and the major theoretical perspectives of sociology. This section is concerned with the *methodology* of sociology— how sociologists systematically apply their perspective in doing socio- logical analysis.

Chapter 5 gives us some useful definitions and discussions of terms frequently used in sociology. Phenomena important to both the func- tional and the conflict perspectives are dealt with. Any analysis requires communicating to others the concepts with which one is dealing, and in disciplined analysis it is particularly important to clearly present all definitions, procedures, and values. Therefore, this chapter is a logical starting point for the methodology of social science.

Chapter 6 is primarily concerned with the techniques of developing and testing theories and perspectives through disciplined analysis. The "rules" of disciplined analysis are preceded by observations about why some perspectives are more likely to be used than others, and the attempt to define analytic techniques is placed in a larger picture. This chapter raises the possibility, inherent in sociological analysis, that the forces shaping social life also shape the search for knowledge and the analysis of social life. Insofar as that search for knowledge is itself social, what we know is limited by social forces, just as other things we do are limited by them.

FIVE
Patterns in Human Social Life

Using a sociological perspective does not mean *denying* the uniqueness of each person. Rather, a sociological perspective requires that we deemphasize uniqueness, and seek patterns of social relations among people. Every blade of grass, every vegetable, every bit of dirt is unique. Some tomato plants are tall, some short; some leaves are dark green, some light; some bits of dirt are square, others round. But dealing with the world of vegetables and soil requires learning to ignore individual differences and focusing attention upon *patterns*. So it is with sociology: to do sociological analysis we must focus on the patterns that recur. To accomplish this we must know something about *how* to look for patterns (which we discussed in Chapter 2), and we must also learn some of the *language* we use to communicate the patterns we think are worth reporting. In this chapter we focus on developing a useful vocabulary and clarifying some important definitions of words often used in analysis.

SOCIAL STRUCTURE

The simplest view of social structure is to see it as a great net for the trapping of energy, the resource on which all life depends. Both functional and conflict views of social structure assume that individuals and species better their chances of survival by exhibiting *predictable* rather than *random* behavior toward others of their kind. The behavior of bees, for example, in performing predictable dances telling other bees where to find pollen, is an example of a structured way of saving energy through social predictability.

Almost all living species show structured —that is, predictable, patterned—social behavior. Even the seemingly random behavior of persons called schizophrenics has been found in many cases to be the result of rational reactions to a particular environment. In nonhumans, much of social behavior seems the result of genetic codes passed from one generation to the next. In humans, predictable structured relations are learned and therefore more flexible over time than nonhuman social relations. Thus social structure in humans is a continually changing set of predictable behaviors.

Human social structure is in large part dependent on language, that is, words which produce approximately the same images in different people's minds, and which people use to predict the behavior of others and to make their own behavior predictable to others. In this way it is like a net for trapping scarce energy by getting others' help.

On the foregoing general outline, conflict and functional perspectives agree. Here, however, they diverge. Conflict analysis emphasizes that the patterns used are often imposed by one group on others and that energy savings in a particular structured relationship may benefit one user or class of users far more than another. In short, conflict analysis goes a step beyond functionalism by asking "functional for whom?"

Sociologists must get some idea of the patterns people are using as they relate to

FIGURE 5-1 The process of conceptualizing (imagining) structured human relations and using these imagined structures as part of a theory to explain and predict human social behavior.

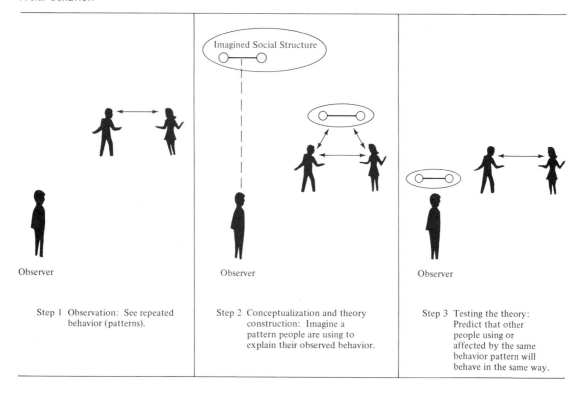

Observer

Step 1 Observation: See repeated behavior (patterns).

Observer

Step 2 Conceptualization and theory construction: Imagine a pattern people are using to explain their observed behavior.

Observer

Step 3 Testing the theory: Predict that other people using or affected by the same behavior pattern will behave in the same way.

each other. We hope to explain past behavior and predict future behavior from this imagined reconstruction of social structural and cultural elements. This process of imagining, or conceptualizing, social structural and cultural patterns is illustrated in Figure 5-1.

Institutional Patterns

An institution is a pattern through which a collection of people solves a basic problem of human survival. Giving names to those patterns which are primarily oriented toward the solution of one big problem of survival, we speak of the family institution (the problem of raising children), the medical institution (health), or the judicial institution (settling disputes). By these we do not mean the houses, hospitals, or court buildings within which the attempted problem solving takes place, but the patterns people use to relate to one another. In popular use, parts of the economic institutional pattern are themselves called institutions. Selection 5-1 illustrates how manipulation of group structures and assets can intensify class conflict by concentrating wealth in the hands of a single class of investors.

Conflict analysis often uses institutions as a stepping off point for analysis in this way: Start with a real human problem; next go to the institutional pattern within which that problem is usually solved; next look for

FIGURE 5-2 The use of analysis in everyday life. Analysis is useful if it leads toward solutions to problems, toward questions which increase understanding.

1. Observing — "My throat hurts."

2. Asking why — "Why does my throat hurt?"

3. Constructing a theory — "I must have smog throat."

4. Explaining — "If there are particles in the air, they will make my throat hurt."

5. Predicting — If I have smog throat, I should not have a fever.

6. Testing predictions — "I have a fever."

Since this theory didn't work, either revise it or make another theory.

7. **Further observing** — "I have a fever and sore throat."

8. Asking why — "Why do I have a fever and sore throat?"

9. Constructing a theory — "I have the flu."

10. Explaining — "Germs cause the body temperature to rise."

11. Predicting — "I should find germs in my throat. I should get better if I drink liquid and rest."

12. Testing predictions — "I have germs. I feel better after I drink liquid and rest."

some larger pattern or force which is causing difficulties within that institution; finally, look to see if the same force is at work in other institutional patterns, and if the same force is reflected in similar problems between the two institutions.

Figures 5-2 and 5-3 show how such analysis is done. For example, suppose your "human problem" is that some people are having trouble with college. They find it boring, irrelevant, hard on their sense of self-respect, and not producing relevant learning. Doing conflict analysis you might use the following steps.

1. Look at the patterns through which people are educated in your time and place —the institution of education—in terms of how important parts of that institution (patterns of taxpaying, administrating, trusteeing, teaching, and studenting) are structured.

2. Look at how these patterns may reflect larger forces. (Remember that the conflict perspective proposes that these larger forces are economic arrangements, and the resultant contradictions, class conflict, and exercise of power in the interests of certain economic classes.)

3. Analyze the specifics, the patterns through which individual students relate to individual teachers, or to people in administrative roles, to see if these patterns are understandable in terms of the larger forces.

To say that a pattern is *institutionalized* means that it has been a recognized set of relations which has endured. One pattern

FIGURE 5-3 Sociological analysis is like everyday analysis. To do it, use sociological concepts (like social class, contradictions, social structure) and systematic observations of human behavior.

1. Observing	2. Asking why	3. Constructing a theory	4. Explaining	5. Testing theory by predicting observations
"College is boring, and I'm not learning."	"Why do I feel bored, and why am I not learning?"	"The social structure of the classroom includes competition for grades."	"I feel bored because when I compete for grades I don't learn."	"In noncompetitive classrooms, there should be less boredom and more learning."

Continuing analysis

6. Observing	7. Asking why	8. Constructing a theory	9. Explaining	10. Testing theory by predicting observations
"Some classrooms are noncompetitive; some are competitive."	"Why are some classrooms noncompetitive?"	"Class conflict shapes institutional patterns."	"The profit-managing class benefits by encouraging competitive attitudes between potential wage earners."	"The profit-managing class should be seen as controlling decisions about competition and grading."

SELECTION 5-1: An analysis of a part of the economic institution.

SENATOR'S CALL FOR INSTITUTION PROBE

Washington—Senator Lloyd M. Bentsen asked yesterday for a congressional probe of what he called the potentially disastrous domination of the stock market by a handful of banks and other large institutional investors.

He said the small investor, who has been the backbone of the country's economic system, has been abandoning Wall Street in rapidly increasing numbers.

Part of the reason, Bentsen told a news conference, is what he termed manipulation of the market by about 50 huge banks, mutual funds, and insurance companies which puts individual investors at a disadvantage.

The Texas Democrat asked both the Senate Finance Committee and the Joint Economic Committee to investigate the influence of bank trusts on the stock market.

For a long time, he said, the system of selling an equity share in business has worked remarkably well for millions of individual investors and thousands of companies.

"In 1960 individuals held over 40 per cent of the value of stocks of the New York Stock Exchange, while institutions held less than 40 per cent," he said. "By 1971 individuals held slightly over 30 per cent while institutions had increased their share to 68 per cent."

repeated in classrooms by the thousands is teacher and student—or instructor and instructee. This pattern can be better understood if we see it as an institutionalized pattern of education, by virtue of the fact that it is in evidence wherever education, the institution, exists.

Group Structure

A *group structure* is a set of patterned relationships, shared understandings, or habits which connects ways of doing specific tasks. These tasks are subproblems, or parts, of the larger problems which help us to define institutions. Why are the people described in Selection 5-2 dropping bombs? The answer can be given by analyzing what they are doing as a part of a group structure, which involves connected roles like pilot, bombardier, navigator, commanding officer. The existence of the roles student and teacher is an institutionalized pattern. The ways students and teachers relate to each other is part of a group structure, the tasks of which are the learning of skills. Among the relationships expected to occur between these two roles are: person using teacher role should talk; person using learner role should listen; person using learner role should raise hand when wishing to speak; person using learner role should expect to be evaluated by person using teacher role. In turn, this group structure is part of the institution of education, because mastery of those skills is intimately tied to assignments of credit toward degrees or certificates from an educational institute.

There are three analytic problems related to "seeing" group structure:

1. What *is* group structure, the group patterns through which people relate to each other for the solution of a problem which is part of a larger human survival (institutional) problem?

2. What are the forces which shape and change this structure?

3. How well does this particular structure solve the problem whose solution is sought by the people using it?

The English word *group* is habitually used to signify a collection of people. This is unfortunate for the beginning sociology student, for in sociological analysis the word *group* generally refers to the patterns people use in relating to one another. A theologian put this simply when he said the important thing in the I-Thou relationship is the hyphen. To study the hyphen in the I-Thou

SELECTION 5-2: Group structure. The observation of behavior of Air Force officers can be analyzed in terms of roles and inter-role relations.

BOMBS ANONYMOUS

By Joseph B. Treaster

Andersen Air Force Base, Guam—Six hours and 14 minutes after taking off from this Pacific island base, Captain Terry Jennings' B-52 shuddered and 32,000 pounds of high-explosive bombs plummeted toward South Vietnam.

A few seconds later a ground controller radioed, "good job"—the bombs were right on target.

There was not a flicker of reaction from any of the six crewmen—no sign of satisfaction or any trace of excitement.

For the crewmen, sitting in their air-conditioned compartments more than five miles above the steamy jungle of South Vietnam, the bomb run had been merely another familiar technical exercise. The crew knew virtually nothing about their target and they showed no curiosity.

Only the radar-navigator, who in earlier wars would have been called the bombardier, saw the bombs exploding, and those distant flashes gave no hint of the awesome eruption of flames and steel on the ground. No one in the plane, including this correspondent, heard the deafening blast.

* * *

In many ways, Jennings and his men are typical of the scores of crews that have been sent to Guam since February in a mammoth build-up that has brought the number of B-52's bombing Indochina to about four hundred in the theater at the close of last year. Some of the big bombers are based at Utapao, Thailand.

They are intelligent, steady family men doing a job they've been told to do. Major Orbert Marrs, the radio-navigator or bombardier, is 42 years old and has a family in Welch, W. Va. Captain Mark Wiley, the co-pilot, of Concord, N.H., and the navigator from Cleveland, are both 26. Working in a bubble on the end of the aircraft is the tail-gunner, Master Sergeant Clyde (Ed) Edwin Going, from Shreveport, La.

Because they are professionals, they take pride in doing their work well. But neither Jennings' crew nor any of the numerous other pilots and crewmen interviewed displayed the kind of enthusiasm for their assignment that bubbles through conversations with fighter pilots. "It's a job," the bomber men often say.

* * *

The huge, eight-engine planes that they fly are dropping more bombs in South Vietnam than any other kind of aircraft and they have been credited with having played a major role in blunting the North Vietnamese offensive.

On the ground a B-52 strike—or "Arclight," as they are commonly called—is a chilling spectacular event, sometimes electric with excitement. Tremendous clouds of smoke and dust boil up and a thunder of kettle drums splits the ears. People in the "impact" area are killed or sent reeling in shock. South Vietnamese troops sometimes cheer or just sigh in amazement.

But none of this feeling reaches the B-52 crew. "We're so far away," said Captain Gordon Crook, the 34-year-old electronic-warfare officer on Jennings' bomber. "It's an impersonal war for us."

The crewmen are highly skilled technicians trained primarily for missions with nuclear weapons. What they are doing in Vietnam demands precision, but only a fraction of their skill. The routine seldom varies and they say they are bored.

* * *

On most raids, clouds or darkness make it impossible for anyone in the plane to see South Vietnam. The people are always invisible. There is no anti-aircraft fire in South Vietnam that threatens the high-flying B-52's and so far none of the bombers has been reported lost to surface-to-air missiles or enemy fighter planes in the North.

The U. S. Military Assistance Command in Vietnam selects B-52 targets, takes responsibility for insuring that they are clear of civilians and decides how many planes are needed and what combination of bombs they should carry. So the big bombers, their crews and commanders on the ground here are all part of a highly specialized delivery system.

* * *

Whether the war is right or wrong is not an issue with the crew they say. They have been trained to operate the machinery of the B-52 and that is what they do. Where they put the bombs is someone else's responsibility, they feel.

"As far as losing any sleep over what we're doing, how many people we kill . . . we never get to see the damage," said Crook, whose home is in Memphis, Tenn.

At another point he said, "If we're killing anybody down there with our bombs I have to think we were bombing the enemy and not civilians. I'm quite sure about our targeting."

* * *

The missions themselves are exhausting. Jennings and his crew began studying their mission plan one day recently at 7:35 a.m. and dragged through their final debriefing nearly 17 hours later at 12 a.m. the next day.

They laugh when you ask if they volunteered to fly B-52's. No one seems to like the plane. It is an unmaneuverable monster and the last choice of flight-school graduates. B-52's are uncomfortable to ride and some crewmen say they are afraid of serious mechanical or structural failure in the complicated, nearly 20-year-old planes.

relationship is to study what is *between* I and thou, what is between *us*.

It will help your consciousness of social

structure if you will discipline yourself to say *group structure* when referring to the patterns people use in relating, and *group* only when referring to collections of people. Sociologists have added to the confusion by using *group* sloppily, as in "groups of students," "groups of cops," or "political groups."

Unfortunately, this is more than just sloppy thinking; it is politically oppressive. How people use terms for role and group structures is a social pattern in itself. Some of the people using roles of political authority refer to "criminals," or "groups of students," or "groups of hippies," implying that certain people—the people disliked by those in authority—are not humans, using roles, they *are* roles or groups.

A conflict analysis insists that you start from the assumption that people are more than the roles and group structures and institutional patterns they use. A conflict analysis insists that you can effectively study the patterns people use in social relations only if you discipline yourself to focus attention on finding the actual patterns, and not assuming that those patterns most commonly

We use patterned ways to express loneliness and tiredness, as well as other feelings. (Michelle Stone from Editorial Photocolor Archives)

accepted are, in fact, operational. We insist that unless you stop referring to "our society," "American society," "political groups," "student groups," you will see only what other people want you to see. These "others" benefit from unexamined assumptions that all Americans agree about social life, and that all unliked people are deviant.

Role Structure

A *role* is a set of patterned habits or understandings through which individuals try to accomplish a specific task or solve a specific problem within a group structure. Within the institution called the family there are many group structures, and hence many roles. Examples are cook–food eaters, garbage makers–garbage carrier-outers, money earner–money budgeter, lover–lover, discipliner–recipient of discipline. Each of these group structures is developed by people as an attempt to solve one of the subproblems of the larger problems of childrearing and procreation. Each of the specific tasks which people think helps to solve this subproblem defines a role. So if people think eating can be accomplished better by separating cooking from appreciating, people will become cooks, or appreciators, in ways that will be predictable to one another, forming a pattern useful to solving the problem of eating.

Analysis of single roles is nearly impossible. It requires looking at behavior while avoiding preconceptions about the patterns that may or may not be found there. Unfortunately, the detachment necessary to accomplish this is precluded by the fact that as a sociologist you, too, are occupying a role and burdened by that role's perception. Observational data are also biased because people may be unaware of the patterns they are using or unable to describe them in words, or they may be trying to hide them.

Particularly in role analysis it is sloppy to accept certain widely used terms as descriptive of actual roles. For example, we could only talk about the *husband role* or the *wife role* if *everybody* understood the specific tasks performed by all men using the husband role, and all women using the wife role. In actuality, however, most people do not divide up tasks among males and females the same way, or at least we should look to see whether they do rather than assume they do. Further, because these terms do not focus on definite tasks, they turn attention away from the group structure. *Husband* and *wife* are words used by people to describe a general relationship and to produce a favorable image. But they are not analytic terms because they provide no clue to how specific people really relate to one another, or any start for *analysis* of how people really relate to one another. Talking about husband and wife roles may be politically advantageous for people who benefit from present chauvinistic family patterns precisely because these terms obscure real patterns of relationship rather than helping to analyze them.

For more successful analysis of how people relate at the level of roles, try to say, "She is using the secretary role," or "He is using the cop role," rather than "She is a secretary," or "He is a cop." To go further and say this is *how* she uses the teacher role focuses attention on the social structure, which is what sociological analysis should analyze.

CULTURE

Culture is the collection of general habits, ideas, and shared understandings which justifies social structure or specific solutions to specific problems. People using culture create, sustain, repair, give excuses or rationalizations for, or in some instances destroy social structure. Without culture people would have to create unique and separate solutions for every problem they face. Having culture means having a ready-made set of tools, words, ideas, gestures, implements from which solutions to new problems can be created. For example, people feeling the injustice of the ways in which migrant farm workers are treated in the United States can use the cultural idea of *union organizing*, gestures like waving picket signs, and technological devices like mimeograph machines in order to create a new structural solution, a migrant worker's union, to the problem of migrants' working conditions.

Cultures are not abstract ideas that float around in the atmosphere somewhere like Plato's New Republic. Culture is in people. The parts of culture may be artificially disconnected for purposes of analysis, but a living person sees culture in the lives of other people. All the words, ideas, gestures, and implements flow together as part of everyday life. The lives of wise old street persons or professional thieves are living survival kits for those who care to watch.

The following sections discuss two major components of culture: language and ideas. Idea culture is subdivided into two categories: ideas about nonhuman objects, or technology, and belief systems.

Language: The Smallest Parts of Culture

The English word *language* comes from the Latin word for tongue (*lengua*). Your tongue can be used to help the other parts of your mouth, throat, and lungs shape a variety of separate sounds, which can be combined to make many separate meanings, or words. Tongues can also be used to stick out. Sticking one's tongue out at another person has many meanings in many places and even different meanings in the same place depending on precisely how one sticks it out.

Why make sounds or gestures? Predictability seems a big part of the answer. People make their social structures partly by producing pictures in other people's heads. If two or more people have the same picture in their heads, the behavior of any one can be predicted by the other(s). If I say "chair" and the sound of the word produces the same picture in your head as in mine, and if I further say, "You be the chair-getter," and you get the chair, we have created a role structure, the beginning of social structure.

Social structure is possible without verbal, or word, language. Gestures can be used to produce the same picture in two or more heads. Almost every species has social structure, and many species do not seem to have word language. These species seem to rely on gestures which produce instinctual responses, such as the dance by which bees communicate the direction of a new pollen supply.

Human beings use *both* word language and gestural language. Word language allows humans to create new social structures rapidly, by combining new words and thus new social patterns from combinations of old. New patterns for the solution of problems can then be rapidly communicated to other human beings.

Word language makes social structure learnable, and it makes the continuation of structured social life possible even though specific individuals may drop out, leave, or die. Human social structure is thus neither so rigid and unchanging as the inherited patterns of the bees, nor does it disappear with the deaths, sicknesses, or disenchantments of individual human beings.

Humans also use a wide variety of *gestures*, which are cultural in the sense of being generally understood patterns useful in creating, sustaining, and destroying specific patterns of social interaction. The wave of the hand, which in times past showed another that one had no weapon, evolved into a gesture by which one simply conveyed friendliness, thereby often initiating interaction. People share understandings about the meaning of different ways of using the eyes or holding the body, how near or how far one person stands from another, or tone of voice. Such gestures can be described as *interaction cues*. Some cues signify to the person "receiving" them that the person using the cues is ready, willing, and able to carry on social interaction. On the other hand, someone who stares off into space, stands very far away, turns slightly away from you, talks in a listless tone of voice, or does not bother to make sense when conversing with you can by any one of these gestures cue you to his or her lack of interest in interaction, or unwillingness or inability to engage in interaction.

Physical objects may become extensions of the self, gestures by which interaction may be started, kept going, or stopped regardless of the specific roles being used. The wearing of certain types of clothing is an example. "Hippie clothing" can get people started relating to each other through a variety of specific role structures, for example, driver-hitchhiker, merchant-buyer, householder-crasher. Of course some gestures —for example, the quarterback putting his hand on the buttocks of the center in American football, or the stethoscope hanging unused from the doctor's pocket—are specific to specific roles. Those gestures which are part of culture are the ones whose meanings are so general that they can be used in many situations and for many roles.

Incorrect use of gestures can stop interaction. Spilling the soup into the guest's lap, or walking into a classroom with unzipped pants, are gestures which may result in embarrassment, and interfere with interaction. Failing to make sense when you talk may so upset people that not only will they refuse to interact with you but they may consider locking you up so that you cannot use any roles at all except the role of crazy person. This is true even when interaction is so routinized, as in a factory, that it really does not affect the work roles whether one talks sense or not.

Analysis of the words people use and the images those words convey is believed very important by some sociological theorists who call their approach *symbolic interaction theory*. They argue that because predictable human social interaction depends on shared meaning, then the most revealing clues to human behavior are found in the meanings themselves.

A different approach to language is taken by some anthropologists who feel that language is like a logically connected web which creates a reality by "telling" humans what to see. Further, this web limits and constrains the kinds of social relations humans might have. For example, in contemporary English the only word which describes a long-term attachment between adults is *family*. If *family* implies only adult male, adult female, and their biological offspring, then people will be limited to that pattern. They will create few other patterns as long as they use a culture whose language makes real only the kind of family attachments described above.

The anthrolinguists Benjamin Whorf and David Sapir (see Suggested Readings) have pointed out that some languages are so different in structure from ours as to create very different "realities" or views of the world in the minds of the users. The Hopi language, for example, does not emphasize the noun-verb difference as does English. Hopi people speak of "raining" rather than saying "it rains" or "coming" rather than "she comes." Whorf and Sapir believed the social structure of people is largely determined by the structure of their language. The Hopi language is not rich in nouns and makes little of one thing causing another. Every sentence in English implies one thing *doing* something or causing something to happen to another. Whorf and Sapir felt that a people using a noun-verb-dominated language will be limited to a social structure which emphasizes causes, change, action, and power. They felt that people using a language like the Hopi's will be more accepting of life, less concerned about changing things.

From the conflict perspective, historical analysis should reveal that language patterns, like other cultural patterns, are the results of two processes: (1) cultural imperialism or the attempts of one people to impose their view of the world on another; or (2) conflicts between economic classes resulting from contradictions in the social structures people are using. An example which shows both processes at work can be found in contemporary English. Consider the following list of words:

beef	cow
mutton	sheep
venison	deer
pork	pig

Why should English have two different words, one for the live animal and another for the animal when prepared as food? Is there any other difference between the two sets of words—some larger patterns of which the two lists are a part? There is. The words on the left are all of French origin; the words on the right are all Germanic. The contemporary English language reflects a long struggle between people for control of England. In 1066 A.D. the Normans conquered the island, and for some time after 1066, the ruling nobility spoke the French language of the Norman conquerors. The Anglo-Saxon peasants, who spoke a Germanic language, did the dirty work of caring for the animals. Their words came to signify the live animal. The French-speaking nobility ate the animals. Their words came to signify the animal as food. Embedded into contemporary English we can see the traces of an old struggle between social classes which was in turn the result of cultural imperialism, the attempt of the Normans to impose their ways on the Anglo-Saxons.[1]

Why in everyday usage does the word *culture* often stand for Italian-language opera, paintings owned by large museums, and the music of the elite classes of eighteenth- and nineteenth-century Europe? Why does use of the word *ain't* set up a certain kind of relationship between a teacher who does not use the word and a student who does? What is the meaning of the phrase "terminate with extreme prejudice"? If it actually means to kill Vietnamese civilians suspected of spying on the United States Army, why not use the word "kill"? Why are children who use street language or ghetto English labeled ignorant, and, if they refuse to learn classroom English, unteachable? Selection 5-3 is an example of uses of language which have the result of blurring, obscuring, or diverting attention from one reality.

Conflict analysis suggests that the single process which connects all these observable bits of language behavior is the attempt of advantaged classes to retain their advantage. Language is a tool which can be put to whatever purpose humans wish, and manipulation of language culture seems to be one of

[1] Albert C. Baugh, *A History of the English Language* (New York: Appleton-Century-Crofts, 1957), pp. 217–218. Professor Baugh takes it further. Which of the following words do you think are of French origin, which of Germanic or Anglo-Saxon origin? House-mansion; ask-demand; veal-calf; shun-avoid; private-general?

SELECTION 5-3: Language may be used to obscure as well as clarify meaning. Language is simply a tool that can be used for many different purposes.

THE USES OF VIETSPEAK

Q: When is a war not a war? A: The fighting in Viet Nam is referred to as an "international armed conflict," according to the Judge Advocate General's Office.
—Army Digest, April, 1968

Every war makes its peculiar contributions to the language. There was still a sense of heroics in the neologisms of World War I: over the top into no man's land. World War II created a new terminology of mass death: fission, fire storm, and the final solution. From Korea, the first confrontation with Asian Communism, we acquired the widespread use of gooks and brainwashing.

The most vividly iconoclastic new words generally come from the G.I.'s and so, in Viet Nam, the grunts spoke of slants and slopes, of Charley (Viet Cong) and Yards (Montagnard tribesmen) and White Mice (white-uniformed local police). Where they were was "the boonies of Nam"; everything else was "the world." Officials spoke windily of "winning hearts and minds," but the G.I.s shortened that to WHAM. To the airmen, the jungle was Indian Country, where you might end up either in the Hanoi Hilton (prison camp) or Buying the Farm (dead).

Killing was the reality for which the G.I. invented the largest number of euphemisms: zapping, fragging, offing, greasing, waxing, hosing down a village (or using a Zippo Squad to set it afire). When Lieut. William Calley testified that he had been ordered to attack My Lai, he did not say that he had been told to kill but to "waste" everyone in sight.

In devising such brusque euphemisms, however, the G.I.s hardly matched the ornate creations of their superior at headquarters. Specimens:

▶ Air raid—Limited duration protective reaction strike
▶ Artillery fire—H & I (harassment and interdiction)
▶ Murder of an enemy spy—Termination with extreme prejudice
▶ Defoliation—Resources control program
▶ Refugee camp—New life hamlet

"War does things to the language," New York *Times* Columnist Russell Baker once wrote, "and the language in revenge refuses to cooperate in helping us to understand what we are talking about." In Viet Nam, it was all too unpleasant to "understand what we are talking about," so even when the U.S. finally decided to start withdrawing its troops it created a new word to disguise reality one last time. It called the process Vietnamization.

---

the processes through which elites attempt to retain privilege.

Idea Culture

If words are single bits of meaning given by humans to the phenomena of the world in which they live, then ideas are connected words or connected meanings. The idea of *family* is associated with a whole series of meanings—mother, father, feelings like love, anger, security. The culture that lives in our own heads is not disconnected words, but sets of words or ideas. The analysis of culture is a powerful tool. Just as we can understand much about houses and can predict the kinds of houses people will build if we see the plans from which they are building, so can we understand much and predict much about the specific social structures people will use if we know both the kinds of building material (language) used and the kinds of plans (ideas) which are their "right way" to build houses. Culture is experienced as the "right way to do things."

It is useful to divide idea culture into two categories: (1) technology, or ideas about nonhuman objects, and (2) belief systems, or connected ideas about humans and human actions.

Technology *Technology* is the set of meanings, created by humans, applied to nonhuman objects. The meanings are general in the sense that any one of the ideas and the objects they are connected with can be used in more than one role, group structure, or even institutional pattern. For example a *chair* is an object, the implied meaning of which is *to sit*. A chair can be used in any social structure in which sitting helps solve specific problems.

When we are fully immersed in our own culture, we forget that objects do not have their *own* purposes and meanings. The purposes of these objects, their meanings as we know them, are created by us. These meanings that *we* create become so accepted that to some of us technology is experienced as the only "real" part of culture. Yet technology is no more real than any other part of culture.

Users of institutional patterns, group structures, and roles can rearrange existing technological "meanings" to make new meanings. *Computer* is a new arrangement of the meanings attached to bits of metal (wire), bits of glass (windows), and bits of oil (plastic tape). People who need to solve a problem where computing will help do not have to develop a totally unique way of computing. If they know the meanings of computer and if they have the power to control one, they can create many roles around its use. This may include the use of computers by people trying to increase population control through the magical legitimacy of "scientifically" stored information. Or it may include the use of computers by people doing radical political analysis to get information on the actual ownership of the largest business corporations. Technology encompasses these and the many other uses or meanings which have been attached to the computer.

Some sociologists see technology as the major determinant of social structure. William Ogburn, for example, theorized that technology is continually changing, while the rest of culture, and by implication the social structure, lags behind and is constantly trying to catch up with the new technology. This kind of analysis might argue that

The windows of city buildings reflect the horizontal and vertical role patterns of bureaucracies; each role is both isolated and linked by authority communication and limited responsibility. (Jan Lucas from Editorial Photocolor Archives)

changes in family structure are connected to a larger pattern of social change resulting from the invention of television. It seems to us that the problem with such an approach is that it ignores the question, "Why should technology change at all?" It seems to suggest a kind of universal urge toward technological change and to forget that *human beings* supply the meanings for objects.

Using this analysis, it is hard to explain why some people have used the same technologies for thousands of years. If the rate of technological change is very fast in some places and very slow in others, it seems that factors other than a simple technological drive are at work. So basic a meaning as "land" is part of the technology of a people. It is that set of ideas about how to use land or how to relate to it. These ideas are an important part of peoples' technological survival kits.

The Kiowa, native people of the Great Plains of North America, resisted strongly the push toward improvement of farming technology which the white people seemed to assume was necessary:

You say [the farmers] want to work the land. That's all wrong. Land doesn't work. Land doesn't want to be worked. Land gives you what you need if you're smart enough to take it. We know how to take what it gives us. It takes care of us. We don't want these people working this land. That's the way to kill it, if you try to take things out of it. When they work the land, they drive the buffalo off it. The buffalo go away. Then we haven't anything to eat. We live off the buffalo. Buffalo are smart. They know you can't work the land.[2]

An alternative to Ogburn's technological determinism is offered by conflict analysis:

[2] Alice Marriott, *The Ten Grandmothers* (Norman, Okla.: University of Oklahoma Press, 1945), pp. 119–120.

A given time and place will be dominated by an overall set of ideas about nonhuman objects which is determined by the dominant economic pattern. The Kiowas, who were hunters and gatherers, saw the land as a living thing. The whites who displaced them used an extractive economy and were more likely to see the land and all its products as separate materials to be combined and recombined in whatever ways they wished. Conflict analysis also predicts that the technological ideas that dominate a time and place will be those ideas which most benefit the more powerful economic classes. Or they will be the ideas that the more powerful class *think* will most benefit what they *think* are their interests.

Selection 5-4 can be analyzed as a reflection of the development and use of new technologies which work to support the interests of economic elites. The moonshiners seem to be getting the short end of the new stick.

Belief systems Belief systems are connected sets of ideas about human beings and human activities. The ideas may be about specific technologies, or about "useless" technology, that part of the nonhuman world believed not to have any specific uses for human activities. Belief systems are much more. They give meaning and purpose to specific human actions by suggesting values, both good and evil; and by suggesting those enterprises that should be sought and those that should be avoided.

What is an example of a belief system? One set of ideas that is expressed frequently in the United States is represented by the term *human dignity*. This belief seems to consist of several connected ideas. One of these ideas is that all people should have equal opportunity for self-expression, and another seems to be that self-expression helps people to feel proud of themselves.

SELECTION 5-4

MOONSHINERS CAUGHT IN ELECTRONIC TRAPS

Washington—(UPI) The "revenooers" are going after the moonshiners with devices and techniques perfected in the Vietnam war—infrared scanning and detecting.

The infrared search concentrates on a 40,000 square mile area of the states of Alabama, Georgia, North Carolina, and Tennessee. A federal official said moonshining still goes on in those areas, partly because some of them are "dry" areas and partly because moonshine is cheaper than heavily taxed liquor in some areas. Some people also prefer moonshine.

Several years ago, the Alcohol, Tobacco and Firearms Division of the Internal Revenue Service started thinking about using infrared scanners to discover moonshine operations.

Wallace Hay, enforcement coordinator for ATF, said the technique involved putting an infrared scanner in an airplane for flights over suspected moonshine territory.

Infrared rays are those between visible and radio waves. They manifest themselves thermally—that is, one can detect them as differences in temperature. So, in effect, the infrared scanner can record what things on the ground are cold and what things are hot.

Flying at about 10,000 feet above the ground in a slow aircraft in the early morning hours, the agents can scan a stretch of ground with the infrared device and record the results on film. The agents then go over the film with a magnifier and pick out the "hot spots."

A related belief is that one needs to feel dignity to be fully human. You may be able to think of other ideas which are connected by many people to the three we have listed. Individuals use this set of beliefs, this idea system, to create specific roles, group structures, and institutional patterns. People using family roles may find it destroys dignity to restrict the household dirty work to only one person. Using their beliefs about dignity as a guide, people may change the family role and group structure they are using, so that the dirty work is shared by all.

Beliefs may be rationalizations or justifications for things that people want to do or must do because the social structures they are using limit their choices, or they may actually be guiding forces in human behavior. One reason for studying beliefs is that people seem to emphasize them so much. The amount of attention people give to beliefs suggests to most sociologists and anthropologists that humans want to view their own social behavior as reflecting something more than an efficient means of survival. Belief systems give a common thread of meaning to many separate patterns of human interaction. As individuals we may analyze such different acts as driving to school, drinking coffee, getting stoned or drunk with friends, flattering professors, flirting with fellow classmates, reading in the library many hours, or cramming for examinations as all having in common a greater meaning, a greater goal, a greater good—*education*, or developing one's mind. We each seem to analyze our own behavior to some degree by linking specific acts to a larger pattern, whether it is God's pattern, ideas about human nature, or beliefs about universal human values (dignity, freedom, justice). If we were to look through a glass window in the roof at a factory assembly line, what would we see? Would we see only a confusing mass of humans moving randomly around some large pieces of metal which emit tremendous noise? Or could we discern some pattern which would help us in understanding all the confusing movements?

We might analyze what the people are doing as evolving from their belief system. Maybe the workers believe that the most efficient way to work is to divide up the work into very small tasks, like moving a punch-press pedal twenty times a minute. Maybe they work this way because they believe they can live better doing repetitive movements with a machine. Maybe they believe that the better, more efficient workers will get promoted to easier jobs. This belief might explain why there are some people who simply walk around in white shirts. What kinds of systematic observations might help us decide if the belief system we imagine is indeed the larger pattern which causes what is happening in the factory?

Still looking through the glass window in the factory roof, let us approach our analysis from the conflict point of view, which starts from the principle of classes and class-shaped institutional patterns. The idea is that the economic pattern that the factory is part of has produced at least two collections of people who have conflicting interests. What is good for one class, and what it wants, will not necessarily be good for the other class, and may oppose what that class wants. Perhaps the people in the white shirts have certain interests or goals with respect to all the machinery, and perhaps the people in blue shirts are interested in other things. Maybe the repetitive work is efficient for the interests of those in the white shirts, but not for the interests of those in blue shirts. Maybe the people in the blue shirts do the repetitive work because they have less power relative to the people in the white shirts. Could this be a better analysis of the factory? If the workers in blue shirts believe that the more efficient will become workers in white shirts, *why* do they believe this? A very important question raised by a conflict analysis is, "Why are some people seemingly not conscious that their belief system is oppressive, that they are not alone in their desire for change?"

Selection 5-5 is a quotation from a governor of California. It can be analyzed as re-flecting a general belief that whatever violations of criminal law are committed by members of the economic elite are not *really* criminal acts. Further, it *implies* a belief that poor people who violate criminal law *are* criminals. That is, the people whose class interests are close to the governor's are the people he is concerned about. Poor people are seen from a distance, and always in their worst roles. Such belief systems are understandable as expressions of class interest—looking out for "one's own kind."

"SOCIETY" AND "COMMUNITY"

For several reasons, we think the meanings of the words *society* and *community*, terms used often in most sociology texts, have become obscure. The words themselves have been used to mislead rather than to help analyze. Some elitists who disdain sociological analysis nevertheless talk at length about "our society" and "American society." They imply that everyone living in the United States believes in, uses, and supports the same institutional patterns, the same ideas. A whole generation of sociology textbooks has led students into the same trap. Once in the trap, the student sees conflict only as what happens to a few nuts on the fringes of "our society." The amount of agreement on institutional patterns is precisely what sociologists ought to be analyzing rather than taking for granted. The term *nation state* or *state* is often what people really mean when they say society. It is incorrect to substitute the term *society* for the interests of the government or for the dominant political power in a particular geographical area. The word *society*, as in *our society*, keeps people from thinking about the possibility of real conflicts of interest by creating the image of a big, blurry, together *thing*. It obscures the facts that the state (national government) is just one part of people's

SELECTION 5-5: Class influence on belief structure.

Ronald Reagan
GOVERNOR OF CALIFORNIA

I think the tragedy of this (Watergate) is that men who are not criminals at heart and certainly not engaged in criminal activities committed a criminal or illegal act and now must bear the consequences. The venality that has been assigned to this could destroy some lives now and the futures of some men.

lives, and that the state may be so designed as to protect the interests of a few, supporting the interests of the weak only when it is in the interest of the powerful to do so.

Community is a word often used in the same way as *society*, only to convey a more cozy feeling. Community is intended to convey a sense of closeness, of brotherhood and love, of empathy, as in "the black community," "our community," etc.

A definition of community consistent with the logic of social structure and culture is: shared social structure and culture sufficient for the solution of all the major human survival problems into the second generation.

Deciding whether or not there is community in this sense in a particular place is a matter of systematic observation of the degree to which the people involved do share the ideas and institutional patterns they need to survive and rear a new generation. In very few parts of the world today are there collections of people living in a small geographical area who completely share a culture. Thus community today is usually a matter of more or less. In some places people share more ideas about how to survive together. In other places people may live side by side and not share much of anything except the local shopping center.

The term *community form* is more useful to conflict analysis. It describes a set of abstract ideas which may dominate a particular time or place and which may exercise a powerful effect in shaping dominant institutions. Community form does *not* refer to a collection of people. Rather it refers to one of several general plans for human survival to which people in many different times and places may refer. Later we will refer to the specific community forms of *familism, tribalism, feudalism,* and *capitalism.*

SOCIAL CHANGE

The concepts social structure and culture describe existing patterns in human relationships. These ideas alone tell us nothing about why there is such great diversity and change in the patterns people use. To focus attention entirely on social structure and culture might lead to the conclusion that there *is* no significant change, and that whatever social structures and cultures are presently noticed by sociologists are those which are desirable, or have a useful purpose or function.

The dominant culture in the United States today seems to locate the sources of change in people's changing beliefs. For example, in popular understanding the Revolution of the American Colonies was the struggle of new good ideas to overcome old bad ideas. Once the new ideas won, popular culture seems to say, a new social structure, a constitution, and free enterprise emerged.

Human perversity, boredom, and curiosity are also widely believed to be sources of social change. We have mentioned Ogburn's "cultural lag" theory, which views social change as the attempts of people to adjust their relations with one another to their changing relationships with machines. Various other evolutionary theories find support in the current dominance of evolutionary ideas in biology and the related life sciences, and to some extent in physical sciences such as geology and astronomy. Some propose a continuous evolution of human consciousness as the driving force in social change. Life-cycle theorists, accepting the idea of *society*, propose that societies have a birth, youth, maturity, old age, and death much as do individual organisms. It is supposed that there is no linear evolution, but rather a back-and-forth alternation as first one society dominates and dies, then another.

A conflict analysis of social change assumes two sources of change: (1) cultural imperialism, the attempt by people to impose on others a new way of life by force and violence; (2) contradiction, the tendency of people to strive for ends which are in conflict with each other within a particular social structure.

Conflict analysis assumes that people do not change their social structures and cultures except when forced by other people to do so or when the structures they are using become unworkable, as a result of contradictions within the structures.

Contradiction

Contradiction is an effect, a result, of the use of specific social structures. It is an effect which is implicit in the structure itself in much the same way as death is implicit in the beginnings of life. The result of contradictions is the achievement of some goals, values, or political/economic formations at the expense or defeat of others. It is important to note that whichever survive may or may not be those people *sought* to achieve through the use of that particular social structure.

For example, United States cities are structured socially in certain ways. They rely on property taxes to support a publicly elected mayor and council who have certain powers to make laws and the right to use tax-sup-

ported violence to enforce those laws. People using the city and its dominant social arrangements discover that using this structure achieves some goals and prevents the achievement of others.

One of the effects of the use of the nuclear-family pattern (one male, one female, and biological offspring living under the same roof separate from other kin) may be fewer children—a lower birthrate. This does not constitute a contradiction unless: (1) having fewer children is a goal only for some people; or (2) having fewer children results in failure to achieve some other goal, something else that people want, for example, female decision-making power. Some effects of the use of specific social structures are not contradictory.

If, however, use of the nuclear-family pattern produces self-centered, and self-confident, children but the parents become worn out and sick, a contradiction exists. The self-confidence of the children might be achieved at the expense of the health of the parents, a result of the use of a particular social structure. Use of a different structure, or family pattern, might have no effect at all on either self-confidence in children or on parental health. But it is unlikely that it would not exhibit contradictions of its own in other areas.

Selection 5-6 can be analyzed as the emergence of a contradiction. The Nixon administration was pursuing a goal of trying to get power in negotiations with the North Vietnamese. It used a secret organization within the White House called the Plumbers to fabricate a TV poll showing several thousand false phone calls recorded as favoring the President's mining of Haiphong harbor. The Plumbers' structure may have given the President additional power, but at the expense of what *other* goals?

Another example of inherent contradiction is found within the public school pat-

SELECTION 5-6: There seems to be a contradiction between honest polling of public opinion and political leaders' views of what was good for the country. What is the social structure that produces this contradiction?

NIXON CAMPAIGN PLEDGES: FUNDS AIDING WATERGATE DEFENSE

Money still coming in to the Committee to Reelect the President is being used for legal defense of committee members tangled in the Watergate affair, a spokesman for the committee revealed in Palo Alto yesterday.

DeVan Shumway, director of communications for President Nixon's re-election campaign, told a luncheon of local editors that the money is from pledges still outstanding and that it is being used for legal defense only of those so far not indicted in the Watergate burglary.

Shumway declined to say how much money was involved or to specify for whose legal defense it is being used, although he indicated it is for attorneys representing witnesses called to testify either before a federal grand jury or the U.S. Senate committee.

The former Sacramento bureau chief for United Press International conceded to the 100 editors at the luncheon in Rickey's Hyatt House that "I'm afraid I wasn't much help" to reporters seeking Watergate details during the campaign.

"I never felt any information I gave out was false," Shumway said. "I was not told all the truth all the time. I based my statements on facts given to me by people I believed were telling the truth."

Up until two months ago, he said, "I felt fully convinced the whole thing began and ended with Gordon Liddy."

Even now, Shumway added, "It is my sincere belief that the President had no foreknowledge of the Watergate affair and clearly had no knowledge of the coverup."

Shumway also revealed that he felt the rigging of a television poll to show support for the administration's decision to mine Haiphong harbor last year was "morally justified" because the administration was at the time involved in touchy negotiations to end the Vietnam conflict.

tern in the United States. In many places, high schools have been used to keep large numbers of young people forcibly *in* school, and hence *out* of the labor force, already too large. Large amounts of money are spent to prevent people from dropping out, whether or not they benefit from high school. Truancy laws are vigorously enforced. Young people who have no desire to attend can be forced to be physically in the classroom, but cannot be forced to use the teacher-student roles required by the authorities, and their presence may lead the teacher to spend more time on discipline and less on teaching. The result may be less learning by all students. An analysis of structural contradictions would suggest that the goal of keeping students out of the labor force is contradictory to the goal of learning when pursued through the existing social structure of the United States public high schools.

Social Classes

Social classes are collections of people who stand in conflicting relationship to one another because of their relationship to contradictions in the social structures they are using. Let's suppose, for example, that as United States public schools get better at keeping ever-larger numbers of students sitting quietly in school all day, less and less learning takes place. Now if some people identified strongly with the goals of discipline and order, and others strongly advocated the goal of more learning, the two groups would gradually become social classes. We would have the basis for class conflict.

From conflict theory, we can deduce that the most important social classes are those classes produced by contradictions in the dominant economic patterns, that is, those made up of people who have contradictory and hence conflicting interests in the dominant economic structure, who stand in different relationships to the means of production.

Remember it is the process of *using* social structures which makes the inherent contradictions apparent. It is the process of *using* social structures which makes people conscious that one set of goals is achieved at the expense of another set of goals. It is the conflict between classes which is the driving force, the shaping power, behind changes in institutional patterns and culture.

Thus Marx argued that the use of a capitalist economic structure would reveal a contradictory relationship between wages and profits, as well as a growing consciousness of that contradiction. People whose relationship to the economy is the earning of wages should become increasingly aware that as profits go up their wages and buying power either remain the same or decline. Conversely, people whose relationship to the economy is the making of profits should become increasingly aware that their profits can increase when wages are held down. Marx gave the names *proletariat* (from *proletarius*, Latin for citizen of the lowest class in early Rome) and *bourgeoisie* (from *bourgeois*, French for middle class) to the classes which emerged out of this contradiction.

In conflict analysis, the patterns of class consciousness and class conflict are of equal importance with the patterns of social structure and culture—they are part of the big picture. The events of everyday life, price changes, court decisions, legislative changes, new technologies, government economic

policies will be more undertandable if we can "see" classes, class interests, and class conflict.

Some methods of conflict resolution are reflections of attempts to reconcile contradictions built into the social structure. These attempts at compromise may occupy much of people's social energy. The complex patterns of union-management bargaining are an example. In this case each side seeks to avoid a possibly destructive test of power by appearing to compromise on vital goals. However, if the compromises do not change institutional patterns, the contradictions remain and sustain class conflict. Over time, one class may become powerful enough to make the institutional patterns largely unusable for the other. This happened in feudal systems where the peasantry was ruined because the land-hungry nobility took the peasant's land away.

SUMMARY

Sociology is like truck-driving, professional theft, journalism, and physics in that it has its own special language for looking at the world. This chapter has summarized the most important concepts of sociology and has shown how they are used to describe and explain the social relations most important to a sociological understanding.

Three concepts are outstanding to the extent that sociologists of many different persuasions rely upon them—social structure, culture, and social class. Closely related to social structure are the concepts of institution, role, and group structure. From the whole set of ideas, beliefs, and ways of doing things that constitute culture, we have singled out language, ideas, technology, and belief systems as the most important features. Social class is not used by all sociologists to refer to the same thing, but it is probably true that in one form or another social-class analysis are ideas about contrast in sociology. Closely connected with social-class analysis are ideas about contradictions and social change.

This, then, is the basic vocabulary one must have to do sociology. The vocabulary is no more or no less than a set of tools designed to help us see human relations. Next we explore the logic behind using this language in a disciplined, systematic way.

SUGGESTED READINGS

Role and Group Structure Analysis

Erving Goffman, *The Presentation of Self in Everyday Life* (New York: Doubleday, 1959).

Erving Goffman, *Behavior in Public Places* (New York: Free Press, 1963).

Gerald Gordon, *Role Theory and Illness* (New Haven, Conn.: College and University Press, 1966).

Institutional Analysis

Barbara Ehrenreich and John Ehrenreich, *The American Health Empire* (New York: Random House, 1970).

Edward C. Hayes, *Power Structure and Urban Policy* (New York: McGraw-Hill, 1970).

Seymour Melman, *Pentagon Capitalism: The Political Economy of War* (New York: McGraw-Hill, 1970).

Language Analysis

Noam Chomsky, *Syntactic Structures* (The Hague: Mouton, 1957).

E. T. Hall, *The Silent Language* (Garden City, N.Y.: Doubleday, 1959).

Harry Joijer, "The Relation of Language to Culture," in A. L. Kroeber (ed.), *Anthropology Today* (Chicago: University of Chicago Press, 1953), pp. 555–573.

Edward Sapir, *Language* (New York: Harcourt, Brace, 1921).

Benjamin L. Whorf, *Language, Thought, and Reality*, edited by J. B. Carroll (Cambridge, Mass.: M.I.T. Press, 1956).

Sociological Analysis of Technology

Robert Blauner, *Alienation and Freedom* (Chicago: University of Chicago Press, 1964).

William F. Ogburn, *The Social Effects of Aviation* (Boston: Houghton Mifflin, 1946).

Alvin Gouldner and Richard Peterson, *Technology and the Moral Order* (Indianapolis: Bobbs-Merrill, 1962).

Belief System Analysis

Karl Mannheim, *Ideology and Utopia* (New York: Harcourt, 1936).

Max Weber, *The Protestant Ethic and the Spirit of Capitalism*, trans. by Talcott Parsons (London: George Allen & Unwin, 1930).

SIX
Disciplined Analysis: Improving the Tools of Sociological Analysis

Seeing patterns and connecting events to these patterns is analysis. In Chapters 3 and 4 we discuss the importance of a perspective in doing analysis. In Chapter 5 we provide some definitions for the sociological terms you may need to communicate your analysis to others. Now, in this chapter, we are concerned with how to improve the tools of sociological analysis, in other words methodology. The chapter asks the questions, "Have we found any techniques, any regular ways of doing analysis, which seem to improve our understanding and expand our consciousness; or are we all so wrapped up in our roles, social groups, and positions in the social structure that we cannot see beyond them?" Also, "Are there ways to test the validity of the analysis so that it may be not only interesting but legitimately useful?"

The answers to these questions are to be found in the tools of disciplined analysis. The rules of disciplined analysis are the framework within which it is possible to convey new ideas in a way that others can understand. Such analysis is not simply science. The word *science* has come to be synonymous with laboratories and white coats. Disciplined analysis can be, and is, done anywhere by people who wish to seek the truth together through a single framework of ideas. Thus the aims of this chapter are twofold. The first aim is to show that the search for truth is a social pursuit and, therefore, determined in part by the social forces of contradiction, class, and class conflict. The second aim is to show that even within these constraints it is possible to do a good or a bad job of seeking the truth. It is possible either to seek the truth blindly and haphazardly or to seek the truth in a logical manner, using methods that others may evaluate and repeat.

THE SOCIAL CONSTRUCTION OF REALITY

It is possible that there is some larger truth of which we are either unaware or only partially aware, or of which some are aware and others are not. Let us let the phrase "God's truth" stand for the possibility of a *separate reality*—separate in the sense of not being knowable through the social senses, but available only through private knowing. In subsequent chapters we will say something about the ways in which the pursuit of a separate reality, such as God's truth, has become institutionalized, that is, how people have developed patterns through which they support each other in the search for this essentially private reality. But if there *is* a separate, nonmaterial reality, it has not, as yet, been publicly demonstrated. Reality for most of us is a combination of what we have been told and have accepted, and what we have learned from our own experience. That portion which is accepted rather than learned is by far the most extensive part of our reality. It is composed largely of conceptual designs we learned as part of our culture. These conceptual designs are ways of looking at the world which orient our attention to some things and help us to ignore others. Consider yourself as you lay in bed this morning. Imagine for a moment that you had attended to every single stimulus that came your way. That would mean that every sight, sound, touch, taste, and smell would capture your attention. The infinite complexity of patterns of light on the ceiling, the infinite complexity of sounds from inside and outside the room, the infinite complexity of smells—all would together or in turn attract you. If this were not enough to fully occupy you, your memories, an infinity of past stimulations, could also capture your attention. We would literally never get out of bed if we had to attend to every stimulus which touched us.

Through the conceptual designs learned as part of culture we learn to ignore things. To conceptualize is to be able to get out of bed because you can ignore about 99 percent of the things happening around you. Most of what we know as truth and reality are those designs or concepts we share with large numbers of people, concepts such as what constitutes art and music, justice, and success.

The rest of our reality is a product of the mysterious workings of us as individuals and how we make sense of our small world of experiences. Some individuals may have experiences that negate the realities they have been led to accept. A black youth from Watts, for instance, who is sentenced to a year in jail for the same offense for which his white peer got a warning, may find the public concept of justice quite obscure.

Another individual's experience may lead him to ignore altogether the conventional definitions of reality and consider himself the reincarnation of Christopher Columbus. These individuals become so occupied with their private vision that they withdraw from the use of social structures and culture to a large degree. Depending on how noticeable this is to others, there is a likelihood that such a person will be labeled as deviant. From a sociological point of view, all this means is that such people are not desirous of using social structures that other people wish them to use, are incapable of using these social structures, or more likely, in view of recent research, are excluded from using public social structures.

MAKING NEW VISIONS INTO PUBLIC REALITIES

This is not to say that reality is a constant. New perspectives do become accepted, but social processes carefully control their development and translation into public reality. This phenomenon can be seen in many areas of social life. There are "schools" of painting, for example. This implies a recognized process by which one's painted vision of reality is judged acceptable. Galleries, museums, and art schools all act to create institutionalized patterns by which the innovations of any individual artist come to be accepted. The same seems true of music. People were privately playing combinations of rhythm and blues and country music long before the recording and personal-appearance industries began to give public recognition to rock, the "new" vision.

This is consistent with a conflict analysis of social processes, for it seems clear that the interests of those people in powerful positions are served by slowing the incorporation of innovations into the social structure and by the restraining expansion of consciousness within the less powerful classes.

Despite the fact that the search for knowledge is, in these ways, tethered by the social forces of contradictions, class and class conflict, the pursuit of new perspectives and the furthering of understanding is essential. To give you some idea about how to pursue these goals, we turn now to an examination of disciplined analysis.

DISCIPLINED THEORY CONSTRUCTION

The essential idea behind disciplined analysis is to develop some methodology by which new realities, new perspectives, and theories may be developed, evaluated, tested, and communicated by anyone interested in understanding and improving the world one lives in.

Freud, Darwin, Marx, Einstein, and Curie are alike in that each stated a radically new theory of the nature of the world. They are also alike in that once they stated their theory they began to work within the frame-

work of disciplined analysis to make public their vision.

The work of these people exemplifies the two basic features of disciplined analysis: attraction of followers and adherence to rules of analysis.

Many perspectives languish because they fail to attract the right followers: individuals in powerful positions willing to develop the logic of a perspective, observe the world to see if events fit the predicted pattern, and to implement the changes implied. The contradiction in committing onself to a perspective is that the strength of one's argument often becomes proportional to one's blindness to contradictory evidence. Because a perspective directs the focus, we are likely to overlook facts which might prove us to be wrong. To correct against this tendency, people committed to disciplined analysis should remember to keep all their ideas and evidence public, so that others may check their work. Thus disciplined analysis is primarily a *social* approach to the problem of relating new perspectives to the old ideas.[1]

Through its social nature, the construction of theory through disciplined analysis makes the benefits of testing easier to achieve in several ways. For example, people can be taught how to do analysis in large numbers, in high school "science" courses, say. Disciplined analysis can, by attracting large numbers of followers, tremendously increase the speed with which the usefulness of a perspective is tested. "Many minds are better than one" expresses the possibility of more frequent intuitive or logical improvements in an idea when the effort is collective.

However there are difficulties in using disciplined analysis, not the least of which is the fact that to attract adherents and support, a new set of ideas must be noticed. If existing elites are threatened by certain

[1] For further exploration of these ideas see Thomas S. Kuhn, *The Structure of Scientific Revolutions* (Chicago: University of Chicago Press, 1962).

ways of interpreting the world, they may withhold financial support, and use propaganda or state-legitimized violence to suppress the advocates of these ideas. Thus only certain kinds of visions may become part of the process of disciplined analysis in a way that leads to their testing and rapid incorporation into public reality. The time span between the vision of the atomic bomb and the first atomic test was incredibly short when compared with the time span between the vision of Karl Marx and any serious considerations of his ideas in American academia, or even the freedom from persecution of his followers.

The contradiction in publicly supported disciplined analysis flows from the constant tension between elites and others whose interests are threatened by a new truth and those who wish to get tax money to support their pursuit of the truth.

Disciplined analysis does not require tax money.

The principles of disciplined analysis can be used by anyone who has a problem to solve and a new vision with which to solve it. In fact, people with problems use the rules of disciplined analysis all the time when they are really committed to the finding of truth. James M. Henslin, in a participation-based analysis of the relationship between taxi drivers and their fares, found that taxi drivers have very well-developed theories about the kinds of customers likely to tip well as well as about those likely to rob them. The drivers were very careful to constantly test these theories in an objective way. Their analysis is disciplined in two ways. They get help from other drivers in testing their ideas, and they are very careful in honestly using observation to change ideas not supported by experience.[2]

As we will see in the remainder of this chapter, the use of disciplined analysis imposes restraints on us which we are not used to experiencing in our everyday analyses of the world. It requires humility about our own ideas and constant openness to the possibility that these ideas are wrong. It requires continuous attempts to see objectively by devising new techniques of observation and a commitment to checking whether or not the kinds of events our perspective leads us to expect do, in fact, occur. This discipline involves a commitment to communicate our findings to others as well as a constant awareness of the possibility that the vision may be or is being used for the wrong purposes.

For these reasons disciplined analysis is more demanding than informal analysis. But there can be great rewards. To compensate for the exposure of one's ideas to the *criticisms* of others is the possibility of extending one's own senses, including thought processes and observations, through the help of those committed to the same disciplined enterprise.

The goal that should always be kept in mind was elucidated by the fifth-century Greek philosopher Socrates:

> Surely we are not now simply contending in order that my view or yours may prevail, but I presume that we ought both of us to be fighting for the truth.[3]

Socrates worked for a world in which everyone would be committed to the nonviolent examination of one's own and other's ideas. Whether the inherent contradictions in such a world would make it a social impossibility would depend in part on how the idea was translated into social structure. To struggle with such issues is food to the academic but it is certainly premature to take up discussion of such a possibility at this point in our development of conflict analysis. Instead we

[2] James M. Henslin, "Trust and the Cab Driver," in Marcello Truzzi (ed.), *Sociology and Everyday Life* (Englewood Cliffs, N.J.: Prentice-Hall, 1968), pp. 138–160.

[3] Socrates, in *The Dialogues* of Plato.

continue, having established our altruistic goal of truth, with a more concrete outline of the rules of disciplined analysis.

The rules which those using disciplined analysis try to follow are of two types: (1) rules for construction of theory and (2) rules for making observations to test theory.

RULES FOR CONSTRUCTION OF THEORY

The first set of rules for disciplined analysis lists the ways in which theories may be made more open, more social, and more rational.

Disciplined Analysis as a Social Activity

THE RULE: Concepts must be defined in a way such that *other* persons are able to make the observations which test the theory.

If *others* cannot look at what your theory claims to be true, then your theory will remain private. However true it is, you will be unable to get others to help you extend it, to help you see where else and in what new ways it is true.

Disciplined analysis *must* be social because it is so easy to fool ourselves. Think about singing to yourself. When you sing to yourself (silently) you are always musical—

right pitch, right tune, smooth flow. Singing aloud is another thing. Somehow it does not come out just right without practice. It is the same with theory. Theorizing alone to yourself always seems to work out just right— you know what you mean by *love* or *lower class*. It is only when you have to explain to someone else that things get difficult.

You have been conceptualizing (using concepts) since you were a baby. One-year-old infants increase their power over the world when they conceptualize *mama*. Out of all the large, two-legged, two-armed, hair-topped, constantly noise-making shapes around, babies abstract a few qualities (maybe tone of voice, quality of touch). The word *mama* is associated with these qualities. Infants can now call mama and change their world.

The *concept* is the smallest part of theory. In disciplined analysis a concept must be made concrete. This means one must be able to tell others what they can *do* to "see" that part of the world which the concept suggests is "there." As part of his theory of class struggle, Karl Marx suggested the concept of social classes. According to Marx's analysis the basic contradiction in capitalist economics is that between profit making and

Patterns in mud cracks. Disciplined analysis starts with the capacity to conceptualize or see repeated or patterned events. (R. K. Fugate)

wage earning. To make his concept concrete Marx said we could learn to see social classes by finding out who owns the means of production, that is, who derives most of their income from investments in capital, and who does the direct work on raw materials. Those who work for a wage are, according to Marx's operational definition, the proletarian class. Those who own the means of production are the bourgeois class. Now we can "see" a social class in Marx's terms. By contrast, a person engaging in undisciplined analysis might be purposefully vague in defining concepts. "High-class people work harder," says the undisciplined arguer. "But," you say, "I have evidence here that poor people put out more work for less salary than rich people do." "That's not what I meant by work." "But I have evidence here that poor people pay more taxes than the rich." "That's not what I meant by class." This argument is undisciplined because the arguer is unwilling to define the concept *work* or the concept *class* by presenting an operation by which anyone could see whether or not there is a patterned relationship between class and work. Thus, a theory cannot be tested unless the concepts it involves are defined by stated ways in which any observer may look to see such things as classes, atoms, work. Perhaps there are so few disciplined arguments about love because a definition of love which can be used by others to make observations has yet to be proposed. Theories which define love in terms of how long couples stay married seem insufficient and boring because many see this as a trivial aspect of love.

Joining Concepts

THE RULE: Concepts must be linked to other concepts.

The purpose of this rule is to build theory, which is a major task of analysis. Remember,

analysis tries to answer the question "why" Theory is the proposed "why" of an event. It is suggested by the perspective, or larger pattern, we are using. Theory involves identifying several concepts between which connections are assumed. For example, using the conflict perspective, four concepts are linked to describe a conflict theory of inequality: economic structure, contradiction, social class, and conflict. A perspective then suggests the broadest concepts of a theory and may be thought of in this sense as sort of a supertheory.

Using Logic

THE RULE: The rules of logic must be followed in linking principles to make theory.

The purpose of this rule is to allow others to see how you reached your conclusions.

Here is an example of a violation of the rules of logic. "There is a sale on at the store, so I'm going to save some money." The problem is that there are no statements which logically relate spending money at the sale to saving money. If it is your money that is about to be "saved," you may spot the logical fallacy right away. Another example of *missing logical connectives* can be seen in the theoretical statement, "Putting persons convicted of crimes in prison will deter others from committing crime and will make the person locked up less likely to violate the law again when released." Many people seem to agree with this theoretical statement although much direct observation indicates that it is not true. Yet we cannot test *why* it is untrue because there are no concepts, propositions, or reasons given which show *why* imprisonment should lead to deterrence or rehabilitation. What is missing from this theory is the full disclosure of the ideas about how one pattern (putting people in prison) leads to another pattern (reducing further convictions of the same persons).

Without such statements the theory cannot be taken apart to see which of its ideas are useful, which partially useful, and which useless. As it stands, the statement is less a theory than a justification or rationale for our penal system.

Another common violation of the rules of logic is the use of circular reasoning, technically called *tautological* reasoning by logicians. An example of circular reasoning is the following: "If a person is a juvenile delinquent, then he or she is psychologically disturbed." "How do we know he or she is psychologically disturbed?" "Because doing delinquent things is crazy." The problem here is that there is no way to test the theory. Each half of the theory "proves" the other half. It is a closed system. "I'm locked up here because I'm crazy." "How do I know I'm crazy?" "Because I'm locked up." This argument is not disciplined analysis because it violates one of the basic rules of logic.

Thus use of the rules of logic allows others to deduce (figure out) events that ought to occur, observations that might be made, if the theory is correct. If the big ideas or principles are valid, then many small events logically consistent with the principles should also be valid.

A testable conclusion derived from a theory by the use of the rules of logic is called an *hypothesis*. For example, if one concludes from Marx's theory about capitalist economics that societies with capitalist economic structures will make war on undeveloped countries, one must be able to show the reasoning by which this prediction was reached. If the connection between Marx's theory and this hypothesis is a logical one, then the test of this hypothesis will be also a test of Marx's theory. If the hypothesis is observed to be correct, our confidence in Marx's theory is increased. If we observe that many capitalist countries do not make war to gain economic markets, then we will want

to modify that part of Marx's theory from which the hypothesis was derived.

Causal Analysis

THE RULE: The types of causal relationships between concepts should be specified.

This rule is an extension of the use of logic. It implies building into a theory clear statements about the several logically possible relationships between patterns. Causal analysis makes clearer the *kind* of relationships between patterns.

"People with beards are radicals" is a statement which confuses rather than analyzes. It does not tell us whether radicalism causes beards, whether beards cause radicalism, whether all radicals wear beards or all beard wearers are radicals, or whether there is simply an accidental joint occurrence of the two things.

Through analysis we try to answer "why" —to get an understanding of the patterns of events that lead to specific other events. We call such patterns *causes*.

There are at least four ways in which concepts may be related:

1. *Association.* Two concepts may simply appear together without one causing the other. Thus, although long hair and radicalism are often found together, neither causes the other.

2. *Necessary cause.* If one thing or pattern is absent, then the other cannot occur. If long hair were a necessary cause of radicalism, whenever long hair was absent (short hair or bald) then the person would not be radical. If long hair is a necessary cause of radicalism, then long hair *must* be present in order for a person to become radical. This does not imply that when long hair is present, the person will always be radical. A germ may be a necessary cause for the common cold, but apparently it is not sufficient. People can carry germs but not show the symptoms of a cold.

3. *Sufficient cause.* If one pattern is present, than the other pattern will always be present. If long hair is present, then the person will always be radical. This does not imply that long hair is the only cause of radicalism; there may be others. However, you are sure to become radical if you let your hair grow. If the germ was a sufficient cause of having a cold, one would always show cold symptoms if one had germs. But getting rid of germs would not necessarily get rid of colds; there might be *other* sufficient causes of colds.

4. *Necessary and sufficient cause.* If one pattern is present then the other pattern will be present, *and* if the first pattern is absent then the other will also be absent. Wearing long hair always causes radicalism (sufficient cause) *and* is the only cause of radicalism, since if one does not wear one's hair long, one will not be radical (necessary cause). If the germ was a necessary and sufficient cause of the common cold, we would get a cold every time we had contact with germs (sufficient cause) and would never get a cold in the absence of contact with germs (necessary cause).

As a test of your understanding of the rule of causal analysis, try this. Specify what you think is the causal relationship between smoking marijuana and shooting heroin.

One recent example of failure to specify the *kind* of causal relationship in a theory can be found in a statement made by a Vice President of the United States to the effect that parents' reading of a particular child-care book caused the children of these parents to become radical. Perhaps the two events *are* associated—careful observation is needed. But the theorizer fails to tell us whether the parents' reading habits were necessary or sufficient causes of radicalism, or the logic by which reading the book is connected to raising radical children. If he had, we might be able to see how much of the theory is correct, or up to *what point* it is correct and where it is false. As presently stated the theory is a statement made to move people, not to increase understanding through analysis.

One of the best ways to check for the presence and type of causal relationship between two concepts is to construct a little table or picture, called a *fourfold table* because it shows four possible relationships between the two concepts. For example, we could check the theory of childrearing just mentioned by constructing the following table:

	Radical children	Nonradical children
Parents read "permissive" book	Cell 1 ? %	Cell 2 ? %
Parents did not read "permissive" book	Cell 3 ? %	Cell 4 ? %

Try filling in this table. What percentage of the children whose parents read the "permissive" book do you think would become radical? What percentage would not? How about the children of parents who did not read the permissive book? Observations of the frequency of occurrence of the different behavior patterns described in cell 1, cell 2, cell 3, or cell 4 would tell us a lot about the kind of causal relationship between reading the book and becoming radical. If most children of parents who read the permissive book could be placed in cell 1, it would seem that the theory is true that reading the book is a sufficient cause of rearing radical children. If, in addition, most of the children of parents who did *not* read the book were observed to be "not radical" (cell 4), it would support the theory that reading the book is both a sufficient *and* necessary cause of radical children.

Practice making up these tables for any statement that implies a causal relationship between two concepts, such as "Germs cause colds," "Smoking causes lung cancer," "Welfare causes people to be lazy," or "People are happier in a free enterprise system." You are confronted with theoretical statements implying a causal relationship many times a day. Try testing each one with a fourfold table. You will have a powerful tool for measuring the degree of accuracy in a particular analysis.

The next example is taken from a statement in a sociology textbook. The author said, "Crime [is] an inevitable consequence of the kind of competitive and alienating institutions inherent in capitalist societies."[4] Although the author did not do a causal analysis, his statement implies that capitalism *causes* crime. But what *kind* of cause is it? Using imaginary data we can show three possible causal relationships.[5]

1. Capitalism is a *sufficient* cause of high crime rates:

	High crime rates	Low crime rates
Capitalist countries	100%	0%
Noncapitalist countries	50%	50%

2. Capitalism is a *necessary* cause of high crime rates:

	High crime rates	Low crime rates
Capitalist countries	50%	50%
Noncapitalist countries	0%	100%

[4] David Gordon, *Problems in Political Economy* (New York: Heath, 1970), p. 276.

[5] Those are imaginary data. No such study has ever been done to our knowledge. Obviously one of the problems of knowing the type of causal relationship is that accurate observations must be made of *how many* or *what percent* of cases fall into each of the four cells of the table. Rules for disciplined observation are presented later in this chapter.

3. Capitalism is a *necessary and sufficient* cause of high crime rates:

	High crime rates	Low crime rates
Capitalist countries	100%	0%
Noncapitalist countries	0%	100%

The importance of specifying the type of causal relationship is increased if you want to *do something* about the phenomenon you are studying. Using the example above, we can make the following statements.

1. If there is an association but no causal relation between capitalism and crime, changing capitalism will have no effect on crime rates.

2. If capitalism is a necessary cause of high crime rates, then by abolishing capitalism we will abolish high crime rates.

3. If capitalism is a sufficient cause of high crime rates, then by abolishing capitalism we will be sure to get rid of *one* of the causes of high crime rates.

Falsifiability

THE RULE: The propositions and hypotheses of a disciplined theory must be stated in such a way that they can be proved false.

The purpose of this rule is simply to encourage honesty—to encourage the theorizer to state publicly the specific conditions under which he or she would agree to change their ideas. This is perhaps the most demanding rule of disciplined argument. Most of us say most of the time, "Well, I'll change my theory next week or next month if more evidence comes in, not now." A recent United States President questioned findings of a pornography commission he had created, saying he did not care how many studies showed that there was no relationship between pornography and deviant sexual behavior. He *knew* pornography made sexual deviants. This is an extreme example of undisciplined analysis.

You might think it would make more sense to have a rule stating how a proposition can be proved true. But the spirit of disciplined argument is the assumption that anything may be proved false at any time. So this rule implies that we will accept a theory as true as long as the evidence supports it, but be ready with a definite commitment that if certain contradictory evidence turns up we will abandon the theory, change it, or use it taking into account its limitations. In fact, in all the organized disciplines there is evidence available which is inconsistent with some of the aspects of the dominant theoretical perspectives in those disciplines. Disciplined analysis requires stating that a theory is false at the points relevant to these observations which refute it.

This is a difficult rule to follow, especially for those caught up in the spirit of a particularly powerful perspective. Apparently one biologist was driven to suicide in the 1920s because his colleagues violated this rule. He produced repeated evidence for the possibility, in amphibians, of the inheritance of acquired, that is, environmentally induced, characteristics. These observations contradicted what is still the dominant perspective in the discipline of genetics—that only genetic characteristics may be inherited—and the biologist was accused of falsifying his experiments. Recent restudy of his data shows he was very careful and probably correct.[6]

Stating the evidence that will prove a theory false is easier said than done. It is easy with a theoretical statement like, "If the earth does turn, then we will see the sun tomorrow." If the earth does turn, but we do not see the sun, we know something is wrong with our theory, although we might

[6] Arthur Koestler, *The Case of the Midwife Toad* (New York: Random House, 1971).

at first wish to doubt our eyesight rather than the theory.

You may begin to see why the word *discipline* is used so much. Seeing all the ways in which our ideas may be wrong, or our observations may be deluding us, is discouraging. To pursue ideas and observation in the face of such difficulties is as good a definition of discipline as any.

One of the most common ways in which people avoid disciplining their own ideas is by refusing to state, even within loose limits, the kinds of evidence they would accept as requiring change in their ideas. Tune in on an analysis being done by two people in the form of an argument. Person A is arguing that all white people are narrow-minded bigots. Person B says that he knows a lot of white people who are not narrow-minded bigots. Person A then replies that person B does not *really* know these white people (challenges B's observations). Person B then says that a recent Gallup poll showed that 66 percent of white Americans feel that the United States has discriminated against black people for too long. Person A replies that these people just talk unbigotedly but act bigotedly (challenges B's definition of concept). A's theory may be either true or false. But A and B will get nowhere toward convincing each other without *criteria of falsification*—an agreement on the kind of evidence that would require A's theory to be modified or discarded. Until then B and A will simply play the game of rejecting each other's evidence. In fact, it seems that they will need to agree first on how to define *bigotry*, by specifying the kinds of observations to make to test the relationship between whiteness and bigotry, before they can agree on criteria of falsification.

This rule seems to be the one which most clearly distinguishes open systems of ideas (open to change) from closed systems. *Religion* is a word which describes sets of ideas which are usually not open to being proved false. One who sets out to test the truth of a closed idea system will discover that there are excuses or explanations for every piece of evidence which contradicts the theory. Sometimes it is argued, tautologically, that one's lack of faith or belief caused the test to turn out wrong. Some religions maintain, for example, that illness is the result of not being "at one with God." If someone enjoys unusually good health, or someone whom doctors have pronounced incurable is cured, it is seen as evidence that the person *is* at one with God. On the other hand, if someone becomes ill or dies from a disease, it is explained as resulting from that person's lack of belief. This kind of reasoning makes it logically impossible to ever obtain evidence which would prove the stated ideas false. All evidence is seen as support for the theory. This view of religion does not say that religion and other closed idea systems are "bad." It simply implies that ideas without criteria of falsification have other aims and purposes than the collective attempt to approach truth through public evidence which is the aim of disciplined analysis.

Disciplined Analysis and Social Change

THE RULE: A theory or perspective that derives from disciplined analysis must be judged according to whether or not it suggests avenues of change in line with stated values.

This requirement is a controversial one among social scientists but not, interestingly, among physical and biological scientists.

Sociology is a policy-oriented discipline. Sociologists study human relations and social institutions, and whatever conclusions they come to necessarily have implications for social action. We cannot study racial prejudice, social evolution, or legal systems without having our analysis imply something

about how we might change or alter the present set of circumstances. Specifying the direction of change toward which we want to strive requires that we specify our values —for example, universal health, oppression of the masses, equality of opportunity, rule by an intellectual elite. Whatever we take as good, we are bound to produce facts and ideas which bear upon the end result we or someone else wishes to achieve.

The best arguments are those that provide us with clear avenues for changing the conditions we do not like and for maintaining those aspects of the current social order which we do like. We must be willing to specify our likes and dislikes, and we must also be willing to submit these points of view to disciplined analysis. It is by submitting our values to disciplined analysis that we gain some semblance of being "value free." This does not mean that we can do our work without having our values involved, but only that we articulate our values so that others can criticize and confront them. That is, the implications for social change evolving from a particular perspective—its assumptions and values as well as its formal theories—must be subject to the scrutiny of others if they are to be products of disciplined analysis.

DISCIPLINED OBSERVATION

There is nothing mysterious about the existence of patterns. If in every large room you enter on a college campus, one person is standing in the front of the room and others are sitting toward the rear, there is a pattern. The same person does not stand in front of an empty room, and hence the pattern is interpersonal—it seems to happen only when people are *together*. If in addition the person in front is usually a white male, this is evidence of another pattern within the same social situation. Disciplined observa-

This man, woman, and child have more in common than merely using the same car. They are probably also linked by a pattern of relationships called the "nuclear family." (R. K. Fugate)

tion of these patterns helps suggest to us theories which are more specific than our perspective. Once we pose a theory, using disciplined observation to test it is also extremely important; or, the appeal of the theory may be so powerful that it goes unchallenged.

For example, Lewis Mumford has suggested that the theory of "natural" science in the West has caused people to look only at what can be defined by numbers. He claims that because natural science defined its concepts by numbers and was so successful in manipulating parts of reality in terms of number, a "halo" effect occurred. People did not question or observe carefully the limits within which numbers were useful and came instead to believe that only that which could be measured by numbers (inches, pounds, dollars) was real and worth paying attention to.[7]

[7] Lewis Mumford, "Quality in the Control of Quantity," in S. V. Ciriacy-Wantrup and James J. Parsons (eds.), *Natural Resources: Quality and Quantity* (Berkeley, Calif.: University of California Press, 1967), pp. 7–18.

We learn very early to use the concepts which make up the public reality used by people around us. Influenced by the success of natural science, Americans teach their children to conceptualize length by numerical measurements. (Marion Bernstein from Editorial Photocolor Archives)

To help us learn disciplined observation, it is first helpful to discuss some major ways to go about observing and then to develop some rules of discipline to be used while we observe.

Public observation There are many places in which people relate openly and naturally with one another. Park benches, streets and sidewalks, waiting rooms, and public buildings are among the many public places in which people relate. Systematic observation of, say, a courtroom may reveal patterns in the way judges and lawyers relate to each other and to defendants. There may be patterned differences in gestures, language, and orders used by judges and lawyers toward different classes of defendants. The participants may be so used to these patterns that they do not even see them. An observer looking for regularities of any kind can discover and systematically record a variety of these patterns.

Participant observation Many events of great importance to our understanding of the large forces shaping social life are not public. For example, what goes on *outside* the courtroom among district attorneys, lawyers, and judges—what goes on in private—may be more important to the patterns of justice than what can be seen *in* the courtroom. The only people who know what goes on in private are the participants. Participant observation is potentially the most useful kind of systematic observation, but also the most difficult. To obtain observations of natural behavior, the participant observer must be or appear to be a real insider. If an observer is known as "that sociologist" rather than "one of us," people may not use their normal patterns. But if the observer solves this problem by concealing the fact that systematic observations are being made, ethical problems are created.

The rights of privacy, whatever they are today in the United States, would be further destroyed by sociologists who "spy." Those being observed have no control over how the observations of their private behavior may be used unless the observer agrees at the end of the period of observation to allow those observed to pass judgment on what should be revealed. According to testimony taken in recent United States hearings, police spies have been used on United States campuses for years. There is no more guarantee to people being observed by participant-observers who are sociologists that the findings will not be used against them than there is a guarantee that legitimate students can control the uses made of information gathered by police officers posing as students. Balanced against these ethical difficulties are the tremendous potential benefits of participant observation. Studies of insane asylums by sociologists who had themselves committed were the only means of uncovering what could not be seen in public—namely, that inmates were systematically abused, stripped of humanity, and "taught" to be crazy.

Experimental observation Experimentation is the preferred method of systematic observation for people using chemical, physical, biological, or geological perspectives.

An experiment often is neither a private nor a public event, but a *constructed* situation. The experimenter creates a situation in which physical patterns (chemical action, for example) can be manipulated. He or she varies one pattern in order to see what effects that has on other patterns, and explores connections among patterns.

An experimental approach to the question, "Is there patterned bias in the treatment of defendants by judges?" might involve organizing two courtrooms in such a way that the only difference between the two was the skin color of defendants. We could determine the effect of skin color on sentencing if we could ensure that the two courtroom situations were the same in all other respects —offenses involved, economic status of defendants, kind of legal aid, etc. If the experiment demonstrated that black defendants got shorter jail terms than white, we could be quite confident that the pattern of jail terms was connected to a pattern of antiwhite prejudice because skin color of defendants was the only difference between the two courtrooms.

It is rare that such an experiment can be carried out. Sociologists with humanist values are aware that human privacy, dignity, and security have often been violated in psychological experiments. Such researchers know that if an experiment is significant (i.e., deals with large areas of human behavior), then individual humans involved will lose control over a correspondingly large area of their lives insofar as the experiment must control patterns in order to study them.

There are "natural" experiments in which much can be learned from observation of public behavior in situations where some important patterns are controlled, but not by sociologists. For example we might compare courtrooms in socialist states with courtrooms in capitalist states to see if there exist discernibly different patterns of judicial decisions, assuming that economic patterns are the only significant "controlled" difference between the two countries and that other "uncontrolled" differences are not important. This is an experiment in the sense that patterns are controlled, and systematic observations of the effects of these patterns are made. It is "natural" in that the patterns were not arranged by a sociologist.

Real studies often combine observation techniques. The study described in Selection 6-1 combines participant observation (the

observers had themselves confined as inmates in a mental hospital), public observation (watching nurses, doctors, and patients in public places), and experimental observation (controlling the behavior of the "pseudo-patients"). (See also Wiseman and Aron's *Field Projects for Sociology Students.*)

Asking People to Describe Social Patterns

All people are observers of social behavior. We all know something of the patterns others use. It is possible to collect large numbers of observations of the patterns of social life simply by asking people what are the ways they usually relate to others.

For example, if we are trying to find whether there is systematic injustice in courtroom patterns, we might ask lawyers, defendants, and judges what usually happens in courtrooms. There are two techniques for asking people to report social patterns: the interview and the questionnaire.

The Interview An interviewer obtains spoken answers to questions. For example, judges might be asked the question, "Do defendants get fair treatment in your courtroom?" Judges' answers to this question are equivalent to observations of the verbal behavior patterns of judges. They might tell us whether or not most judges verbalize a belief that their courts are just for all defendants.

Interviews may be more or less *structured,* that is, consist of more or less predetermined questions. Whether or not the questions are predetermined, the interviewer has the advantage of being able to make sure the respondent understands the question, and clarifies or elaborates his answer.

Most public opinion polls are done by interview. In Selection 6-2 a sample of California residents was asked about their confidence in several "basic institutions." Their answers are observations of cultural patterns

SELECTION 6-1: A study which combines features of participant observation with experiment.

THE VICTIMIZED MENTAL PATIENTS

by David Parlman

Stripped of his personal individuality, powerless, neglected, and shorn of dignity, the patient in a mental hospital is a leper who carries his stigma forever.

He bears the label of crazy whether he is truly insane or not; no matter how rationally he behaves, his hospital guardians distort their view of his behavior as proof of his illness.

The diagnosis of his mental disease may be grossly in error, but the doctors and staff of mental hospitals will not admit their error. At best they may find their patient "in remission" —temporarily improved.

Yet the mental hospital itself may be far more "bizarre" than the patients in it. Violence and "inappropriate hostility" may mark the actions of some staff members. Doctors, nurses and attendants may display aloofness, suspicion and dread toward their patients. Who are the irrational here? Who are paranoid?

Implicit

These questions are implicit in a remarkable first-hand study of diagnosis and treatment inside psychiatric hospitals that was published today in Science, the journal of the American Association for the Advancement of Science. Titled "On Being Sane in Insane Places," it is based on a three-year series of unique experiments led by Dr. David L. Rosenhan, Professor of Psychology and Law at Stanford University.

Rosenhan and seven colleagues secretly had themselves admitted to a total of 12 typical mental hospitals, and by giving only a few false clues to psychiatrists at the beginning, all were promptly diagnosed as insane. Seven were tagged as schizophrenics and one was labeled more hopefully as a victim of "maniac-depressive psychosis." They were kept in the hospitals for periods ranging from seven to 53 days before being released as "in remission."

According to Rosenhan, no such lengthy detailed inside study of psychiatric confinement has ever been reported by professional and presumably sane investigators before. ("But maybe we all had to be insane even to undertake the experiment," Rosenhan remarked in a conversation with The Chronicle.)

Labels

Although the eight "pseudopatients" were "paragons of cooperation" and rationality during their investigation, Rosenhan said, their diagnostic labels stuck to them throughout confinement.

"Indeed the label is so powerful," Rosenhan reported, "that many of the pseudopatients' normal behaviors were overlooked entirely, if not profoundly misinterpreted" by the hospital staffs. One pseudopatient, who reported a happy family life with few marital disputes and minimal punishment of his children, was recorded in his hospital case summary as prone to "angry outbursts," emotional instability and ambivalence.

A pseudopatient calmly pacing a corridor was asked by an anxious but kindly nurse, "nervous, Mr. X?" He eased her mind. "No," he replied, "just bored."

Investigators taking notes on their hospital confinement were interpreted by the staff as displaying compulsive "writing behavior."

And the same gross misinterpretation of behavior marked staff observations of real patients, no matter how rational their actions.

Syndrome

One group of patients, for example, was seen waiting outside the hospital cafeteria a half-hour before lunch. This, said a psychiatrist instructing a group of physician-students, illustrated the "oral-acquisitive nature of the syndrome."

Rosenhan had a simpler explanation: "It seemed not to occur to him," he commented, "that there were very few things to anticipate in a psychiatric hospital besides eating."

In all the real patients, Rosenhan observed, the diagnosis of mental illness served as a self-fulfilling prophecy: "eventually the patient himself accepts the diagnosis and behaves accordingly."

Dehumanization is a disease characteristic of mental institutions both good and bad, Rosenhan reported. Patients are most often ignored; doctors and nurses almost never make contact with them. The experimenters counted the times the psychiatrists emerged from their glass-enclosed staff "cages" on the wards to move among the patients; it took ten minutes each time.

Analysis

They also analyzed their own contacts with staff members. They stopped staff members a total of nearly 1500 separate times to ask brief, perfectly rational questions. In 71 percent of these incidents the doctors simply hurried by quickly, eyes averted; only 6 percent of the questions elicited a pause or answer. Nurses were worse, fewer than 3 percent paused or talked when questioned.

Rosenhan cited one "bizarre" response by a psychiatrist: "Pardon me, doctor," asked a pseudopatient in the hall, "could you tell me when I'm eligible for grounds privileges?" "Good morning, Dave," was the doctor's reply. "How are you today?" Then the physician hurried off, without waiting for an answer to his own question.

Violence was frequent during the confinement of the investigators—but it was mainly violence by staff, Rosenhan reported.

"I have records of patients who were beaten by the staff for the sin of initiating verbal 'contact,'" he said. And Rosenhan himself says an attendant beat a patient who merely walked up to say, "I like you."

Awakening

Violent language is also common. Morning attendants often wake patients, Rosenhan reported, "with 'come on, you m—f—s!'"

As for psychotherapy there was little indeed, although there were pills-a-plenty for everyone. The eight investigators recorded their own therapeutic encounters with doctors and psychologists; they averaged 6.8 minutes a day during their entire confinement.

And they counted their pills: the pseudopatients were given a total of 210 powerful tranquilizer doses—Elavil, Steiszine, Compasine and Thorazine—although their behavior was consistently tranquil and rational. They threw their pills away in the toilets—and observed that many real patients were doing the same regularly.

—of verbalized beliefs about institutions—although the answers tell us little about how people *use* these institutional patterns. It is interesting to note that the least-liked institutions—food stores—are probably the most often used.

The Questionnaire Another way to observe systematically people's reports of the social patterns they use is the questionnaire.

Use of the questionnaire can generate large numbers of observations with a minimum expenditure of time and energy. Thousands of questionnaires may be given to potential respondents, and their written or checked answers can be summarized by automatic data-processing machines. Weaknesses of the questionnaire are the inability of the observer to know whether respon-

dents understood the questions and what, exactly, respondents understood their answers to mean.

A problem with the use of both interview and questionnaire observations is that what people *say* may be very different from what they *do*. In fact systematic observation of the relationship between words and deeds shows little positive correlation between the patterns people say they use and the ones seen in their behavior. Self-reported observations are useful as long as it is remembered that they are not predictors of actual behavior, other than the response itself.

Observations of the material parts of social patterns *Artifact* is a term used to describe the physical traces of social life. Artifacts in-

SELECTION 6-2: An example of structured interview as a means of observing people's attitudes toward institutional patterns.

THE PUBLIC LOSS OF CONFIDENCE

By Mervin D. Field

On the 197th anniversary of this country's birth of independence, the California public's confidence in many of our society's basic institutions appears to be less than strong.

In a survey completed in May of this year, a representative cross-section of 541 California adults was asked to express what degree of confidence it had in a range of basic institutions, ranging from the medical profession, to Congress, universities, organized religion, manufacturing companies, and so on. In all, a list of nineteen entities was tested.

"Research scientists," law enforcement agencies, such as the "local police department" and the FBI score relatively high, as does the medical profession. Relatively low levels of public confidence are found for food companies, for manufacturing corporations, for financial institutions, and for organized labor.

The public expresses marked lack of confidence in the public school system, in organized religion and in the Presidency.

For this survey, a representative cross-section of 541 adults was asked this question: "Now, I would like to find out how you feel about some of our governmental, business, and social institutions. For each group listed on this card, I'd like you to tell me how much confidence you, personally, have in it."

Here are the results.

LEVEL OF CONFIDENCE—
ALL ADULTS STATEWIDE

	A lot percent	Some percent	Not much percent	No opinion percent
Research scientists	58	34	5	3
Local police department	51	40	7	2
The medical profession	43	44	13	*
The F.B.I.	43	40	13	4
Consumer protection groups and organizations	37	42	14	7
The President of the United States	34	34	31	1
Public utilities (such as gas, electricity, telephone)	33	48	17	2
The Supreme Court	31	45	21	3
Congress	30	53	15	2
Environmental protection groups and organizations	30	48	17	5
The news media (such as newspapers, television news, and news-magazines)	27	55	18	2
Universities and colleges	25	62	11	2
Organized religions and churches	24	46	28	2
Public school system	23	51	25	1
Financial institutions (banks, insurance companies)	22	51	25	2
Organized labor	13	50	34	3
The State Legislature	12	67	16	5
Manufacturing corporations	9	55	30	6
Food companies	9	52	35	4

* Less than one-half of one percent.

clude the entire range of physical objects that people use in their relations with one another: books, pictures, foods, furniture, clothing, paper, buildings, weapons, tools. The advantages of the use of artifacts are their availability and abundance (except for distant places and the distant past), and the fact that their use does not create the ethical problems, or involve the language confusions, surrounding other types of systematic observation. On the other hand, interpretation of the patterns of social life implied by a particular artifact are uncertain because the people themselves are not there to tell us or show us how the artifact was actually used.

Among the most important artifacts are those that are descriptive of human life. These may be divided into two categories: (1) descriptions (diaries, stories, legends, histories); art objects (pictures, sculpture, music); and audio-visual records (films, tapes, and phonograph records); and (2) proscriptions, which record the ways people are *supposed* to relate to one another in a particular time and place (organization charts, lists of rules, lawbooks).

Those materials people use in their dealings with one another and with the physical environment can reveal much about social life, both by their relative abundance and by their shapes. Imaginative reconstructions of social life have been made from systematic observations of a few artifacts. For example, the growth in the relative frequency with which the bones of very young and of female wild cattle were found in ruins of 50,000-year-old villages was used as evidence for the emergence of the use of domestic animals as an economic pattern.

RULES FOR DISCIPLINED OBSERVATION

To make the kinds of observations discussed above requires the discipline of looking without prejudice and prejudgment. Like construction of disciplined theory, disciplined analysis is as much an art, or an attitude, as it is a routine which can be described by rules. Reading the rules will not get you there, but once you are there the rules may help you to organize your observation and save yourself a little time.

This is a little like learning to ski or to ride a motorcycle, when you must unlearn some old and usually very helpful ways of dealing with gravity. We are not used to observing

without prejudice, without making judgments. In undisciplined observation, when our first look confirms our prejudice or judgment, we tend to stop looking. Disciplined observation requires looking first and judging later. It requires looking carefully, and continuing to look even when we think we have the answer. You no doubt use the skills of disciplined observation often in your everyday life. The reason for turning these skills into rules is so you can apply them to new situations. If you drive a car a lot, but lack the money to fix it, you learn to observe it carefully and without prejudice. Careful observation made to test your theories about why it is or is not working will save you time and energy. Sociological observation is done by people who need to know about human social relations with the same intensity the poverty-stricken drivers of cars need to know about their automobiles.

Most of our lives are so fragmented that we can patiently observe only a few things. Also, we are so well encased in already provided answers about social life that we rarely feel a need for new ones. Yet when one does arrive at the point of need and willingness to observe carefully, a few reminders of past insights into the art of disciplined observation of human social life may be helpful.

Don't Observe Randomly

THE RULE: Observe those things suggested by the theory and carefully define what you are looking for.

True random observation is probably impossible. Given this, it is necessary to be as explicit as possible about the conceptual "lenses" through which we are looking at the world, to be specific about what we are seeing. One of the ways to be more sure about what we are seeing is to be specific about what we are looking for. What we are looking for is suggested to us by ideas we have about what is important. And what theory does is to suggest to us what is important.

Think for a moment about the people you pass on the street. There are a variety of things you could notice about these people: the size and weight of every part of their body; the colors, angles, and planes of every skin surface; the number of hairs. Yet you look at just a few things—a few lines in the face, the expression of the eyes, a few of the ways in which the person carries his or her body, a few details of clothing. Why are these the things you "see" about the person? You see these things and not others because you have a theory which suggests that in "knowing" people, it is more important to observe expression, carriage, and dress than minute physical details. Yet unless you are explicit about what you are looking for, how can others see how right your ideas are?

The first rule of disciplined observation, then, is to make sure that you are observing through conceptual lenses that others can look through—concepts defined so that others can repeat your observations. For example, if you are testing the theoretical idea that poor people do not get equal justice in American courts, you must be sure that you carefully define *poor* and *justice*, as well as present ways of looking at behavior that are known or can be made known to other people who would be interested in the relationship between being poor and getting justice. Or imagine that you have been tutoring schoolchildren who are "slow readers." You think you observe that you can increase reading skill by having the children watch TV shows and then try to read the script. For these observations to be useful to others you must carefully define *TV script* (what type of show, etc.) and *reading skill* (measured by their ability to later read

other things). When you proceed in a disciplined way, defining your terms and your methods of observation, then your observations will do one of two things. They will test your theoretical ideas about the relationship between poverty and justice, or that between a particular use of TV scripts and building reading skills; or they will serve as observations on which later theory can be built.

Definitions help us to extend our view. They make it possible for others to help us make observations when we cannot do the looking ourselves. If a concept is defined carefully, others will be looking for the same things we are.

Don't Close Your Eyes

THE RULE: Observe every possible test of the theory.

It is possible to prove anything by carefully observing only those events which support our theory. We see this frequently in everyday life. A person who believes growing a beard leads to political radicalism may only read about or "see" those beard wearers who are political radicals, thus "proving" his theory.

The trick of disciplined observation is to force yourself to look at *every* instance by which a theory can be tested. Do not settle for a single method of observation or a single illustrative example. Look at every event which is a smaller part of the big picture suggested by your theory.

A SUBRULE: Use sampling techniques.

There is a technical term for all the events which are part of a bigger pattern. The word is *universe*. The universe of beard wearers is *all* beard wearers.

We can deduce from conflict theory that criminal court decisions under a capitalist economy will favor the interests of the owner class over the interests of the working class. To test this theory we should look at the universe of criminal court decisions in countries dominated by a capitalist economic structure. The universe of criminal court decisions is *all* decisions during the time period our theory is supposed to apply. Obviously, it would take years to study and observe all criminal court decisions, even if we looked only at United States courts. One way to honestly observe all tests of our theory without the expense in time and energy of looking at the entire universe is to take a *sample*. If it is impossible or very difficult to observe the universe of events or objects which test a theory, the next best thing is to look at a sample of these events or objects.

A sample is a small part of a universe chosen in such a way that this part of the universe will be representative of the universe, only smaller and easier to observe. *Random sampling* means to choose events or objects from a universe in such a way that each event or object in the universe has an equal chance of becoming a part of the sample. A random-sampling process should produce a sample that is reasonably representative of the universe being studied. The sample, or miniature version of the universe, is the set of objects which are actually observed in order to test the theory about the universe. Sometimes, *stratified samples* are used. A stratified sample is one in which the observer decides which important subgroups in the universe must be represented in order to give a weight to their opinions or actions that is in proportion to their actual frequency in the total universe. This makes certain that some hard-to-interview people like working women will be represented when random sampling might allow an interviewer

to just keep picking until a person in some other category came up.

The techniques of sampling are best known to the public through opinion polls. For example, authors of one opinion poll claimed that "60 percent of Americans believe they would vote for a qualified black man for president."[8] This finding, however, represents the opinion of 1,682 Americans who are a stratified sample of the total population.

Sampling protects the observer against the tendency to talk to only those people who will confirm the hypothesis being tested, or to observe only those events which support the theory. Sampling is used in all the types of observation we are considering.

A SUBRULE: Do not generalize beyond the universe from which the sample is drawn.

Do be sure to define the universe being sampled and the universe to which the theory applies. A common way of cheating at arguing is to generalize beyond the universe sampled. If you spend a lot of time in San Francisco you might conclude that *everyone* under thirty is a pacifist. It might be true that a large majority under thirty are pacifists in San Francisco, but if your theory presumes to apply to everyone in the United States, then everyone in the United States should have an equal chance to state his or her opinion about war.

A SUBRULE: Do not draw a biased sample.

Be sure that every event, every person about which your theory is concerned, has an equal chance to be heard or observed. If you theorize that prejudiced attitudes are the cause of discrimination against minority

[8] Quoted in Richard M. Scammon and Ben J. Wattenberg, *The Real Majority* (New York: Coward-McCann, 1970).

people in American hiring practices, then you must give every act of hiring an equal chance of being observed. It may be easier to observe only those instances of hiring where employers are willing to talk with you. But this would constitute a biased sample if there is any possible relationship between willingness to talk with you and prejudiced or nonprejudiced hiring.

Minimize the Effects of Observing

THE RULE: Attempt to discover and minimize the effects of the act of observing on the observations.

One of the difficulties of studying people's social behavior is that asking people questions and watching them do things may affect their behavior. This is a problem not only for sociologists, but for people who study insects, atoms, or stars. Recently some atomic physicists have reported systematic observations of the effects of mental states of observers on observed behavior of subatomic particles. Although long ridiculed, the supposition that people affect plant behavior is now supported by extensive systematic observation.

The important task is to try to list and be aware of the ways in which your own act of observing might affect what you are observing. For example, the way in which questions are worded has a great effect on how people answer them. Questioners want to assume that the words used in the question will have the same meaning to all who hear or read the question, that the question will be the same stimulus to behavior for each person questioned. Disciplined questioning requires testing the questions to be used to be sure they will mean the same to all who answer them.

Each type of observation has its own spe-

cial and possible effects on behavior. In some cases it is possible to cause the very behavior which confirms the theory being tested.

The dress, age, color of skin, and tone of voice of the questioner all have been shown to affect the kinds of responses people make to interview questions.

The honest researcher constantly tries to know what are the effects of the act of observing so that he or she may either control these effects or do away with obtrusive measures.

In many ways we are all obtrusive observers. We observe others, and ask countless questions, all with the aim of building theory to help understand and predict others' behavior. It is when observational activity becomes organized that people feel threatened by it, and well they should, given some of the snooping that goes on in the name of sociology. Perhaps this is a contradiction in the socially organized study of social life: the more valid and efficient are the ways of observation, the more they interfere with the behavior being observed and the more they offend people.

Make Observations for Full Causal Analysis

THE RULE: Try to look at all the logically possible relationships between variables you suspect are causally related.

This is a difficult rule to follow when a theory suggests that six or eight concepts (variables) are related to each other (and why it takes so long to analyze a faulty car or a crying baby). Yet the rule is so frequently violated in the interest of bulldozing someone else into belief that it should be applied as a test to any claim that a theory has been checked by observation. Smoking causes lung cancer, right? Well, maybe. A sloppy test of this idea looks only at the percentages of smokers who have lung cancer. For example, suppose we find that 60 percent of cigarette smokers have lung cancer and 40 percent do not.[9] This does not represent a disciplined test of the theory. We also have to look at nonsmokers. If our observations of nonsmokers show the same thing, namely that 60 percent of nonsmokers have lung cancer and 40 per cent do not, then we will draw very different conclusions about the relationship between smoking and cancer than we did when we looked only at the figures regarding smokers. The general rule, then, is to ask for observations of all four possible relations between two kinds of events as a test of any statement that one event or pattern causes another.

The news story about a sociocultural behavior, coffee drinking, and heart attack (Selection 6-3) exemplifies the difficulties of causal analysis and sampling. How were the analysis and sampling described in this article carried out?

DESCRIPTIVE SOCIOLOGY

Although it is true that every conceptual filter through which we view the world has behind it a theoretical idea which suggests why it is important to see that part of the world, there is much of value in sociology which is purely descriptive and which does not self-consciously aim at testing theory. There is a problem here in that the more one describes the world in terms of well-known concepts (for example, population sizes, composition of social classes, distributions of power, distributions of belief systems, etc.), the more one provides implicit support for the theories by suggesting that these are the important concepts to use in viewing human social behavior. On the other

hand, certain areas are so important that almost everyone wants descriptions of them. It seems necessary to know such things as who has the most money, who gets arrested most often, who is most likely to be punished, who is having the most babies, or whether the marriage rate, or the divorce rate, is rising or falling, *whether or not* descriptions of such things will later be used in testing new theories.

Some observations are believed to be so important that everyone should know about them. These observations are believed important because presently the most accepted theories of social structure suggest that they can predict a lot about future human behavior.[10] The observation that the United States, with 6 percent of the world's population, presently uses about 49 percent of the world's available nonrenewable resources is a tremendously important social fact. We feel that it is important because we suspect that the rest of the world is not forever going to put up with American economic imperialism and pollution. Yet someone not distracted by a conceptual framework suggesting that population size and resources used are the keys to the future might want to cite a different observation as important, and might, as a result, do a better job of predicting how other people will behave toward the United States. The point is that what is seen as an important fact or description is always a result of what your theory tells you is important.

Some theories have been around for so

---

[9] Imaginary observations and numbers.

[10] Kenneth Boulding, the economist, has his own list. "We need to know something about the order of magnitude of the factual world; that in this country agriculture is only 5% of the gross national product . . . that the world war industry is equal to the total income of the poorest half of the human race. . . . Even in universities there is an incredible ignorance about the orders of magnitude of the world." From Irving Morrissett and W. W. Stevens, Jr. (eds.), *Social Science in the Schools: A Search for Rationale* (New York: Holt, Rinehart and Winston, 1970).

SELECTION 6-3: Problems in causal analysis and sampling.

COFFEE AND THE HEART— NEW STUDY

Boston—Researchers who first indicated a possible link between heavy coffee drinking and heart attacks say their findings are supported by a second study.

The coffee industry attacks this interpretation of the new study as "simplistic."

The researchers say their latest study backs up the findings of a study published last year that suggested that persons who drank one to five cups of coffee a day had a 60 per cent greater chance of heart attack than noncoffee drinkers. Those drinking six or more cups a day incur 120 per cent greater risk of this type of heart disease, researchers said.

A heart attack, or acute myocardial infarction, is a form of heart disease in which heart muscle is damaged or destroyed.

Caution

In the new study, published Thursday in the New England Journal of Medicine, researchers of the Boston Collaborative Drug Surveillance Program of Boston University Medical Center cautioned that it was too early to conclude that coffee caused heart attacks.

However, Dr. Hershel Jick, head of the research team added, "The possibility that coffee contributes to the risk of myocardial infarction cannot be ignored."

The Coffee Information Institute said a "simplistic interpretation" of the Boston studies could lead many to conclude prematurely that coffee drinking causes heart attacks.

In a statement, the institute claimed there were weaknesses in the Boston studies and cited other research reports that found no association between coffee drinking and any type of heart disease in the normal population.

Scope

The research by Jick and his team involved an eight month study of 12,759 patients hospitalized in 24 Boston area hospitals. The researchers compared coffee drinking habits of the 440 patients hospitalized for diagnosed heart attack with those treated for other ailments.

Results of the first study, which involved a similar but smaller sampling, were published in the June 1972 edition of the Journal.

In an editorial, accompanying the new article, doctors of the Framingham Heart Study cautioned that more evidence is needed before a definite coffee-heart attack link is established.

They said no evidence has been found in their project, a long term survey of heart disease in 5000 persons, in a community outside Boston, to support a coffee-heart attack connection.

Similarity

The coffee institute cited similar negative results from a study by Dr. Siegfried Heyden of Duke University.

The coffee institute noted that heart attacks normally kill more than 60 per cent of their victims before they reach a hospital but the Boston study focused on survivors. The institute said the fact that they drank more coffee "might conceivably be interpreted as evidence of coffee-drinking individuals' ability to survive heart attack."

long that people are constantly updating the observations that are relevant to these theories. Observations on education, occupation, and income, for example, are important because these are the factors used by many sociologists to differentiate among social strata. Most theories of social behavior assume that people in different social strata behave differently. Because occupation, income, and education are related to social power in many societies, it is easy to see why descriptions of changes in these factors are watched so carefully.

EMPHATHETIC SOCIOLOGY

Another kind of sociology involves the attempt to describe how social life looks through the eyes of different groups of people. The uses of such sociology are varied.

For example, knowing that many of our present institutions and ways of doing things came to us out of the ruins of feudal society, we may attempt to see the social world of the peasantry of England, China, or Africa through the eyes of the people of those "middle ages." Empathetic sociology is a new kind of history, an alternative to learning only about the wives of kings and the battles of the nobility.

It is the inability to see the world through the eyes of others which makes us prisoners in our own small social worlds—bound in, threatened on all sides, bored, and restless. One aim of authors of novels, poems, or plays is to let us see the world through others' eyes. Beginning with the traveling anthropologists who studied "primitive" peoples, there has been a parallel tradition in the systematic study of social life. The anthropological term *ethnography* is most often used to describe the systematic or disciplined methods by which one takes an empathetic look at how distinguishable groups see or construct their social world. There can be and are ethnographies of juvenile gangs, of middle-strata families, of homosexuals, of surfers, of upper-strata nursemaids, of professional thieves. The list is growing all the time.

Narrowmindedness and provincialism are all too common, and are often not recognized for what they are, especially by the people who exhibit these qualities. Take, for example, a national TV magazine's description of a special on some white explorers' "discovery" of the sources of the Nile, of their journeys through "largely unknown areas of Africa."[11] There are white and black racism, male and female chauvinism, young and old generationism—blinding and constricting attitudes which feed on each other. None stands up very well to the willingness

to study the struggle of humans around the world to make meaning of absurdity. It seems right to assume that unless we are willing to try and experience the ways in which people make their lives meaningful—through *their* eyes—we will probably not understand them.

So this is one starting point for doing sociology. It is only through experience that we learn, but our experiences are not like pebbles falling into an empty canyon. We all carry around filters and lenses with which we see people, social life, and patterned social relations. The lens of the sociologist includes a commitment to disciplined analysis and observation. But this commitment is only the beginning. Sociologists also rely upon general perspectives and theoretical models to decide what are the important things to look for. These perspectives must be changed only on the basis of honest observation and straight reporting of what people are doing, however limited by conceptual blinders these may be.

SUMMARY

In this chapter we have described how sociological analysis may be improved. Sociological analysis is a social act aimed at obtaining others' help in discovering patterns which help us explain, predict, and control human social behavior. Improvement of the tools of analysis therefore requires a collective agreement, or discipline, about how to best develop, use, and extend sociological analysis.

All of culture may be seen as a social construct, a set of tools created by people to provide an instant and widely accepted analysis of the nature of social reality. For many, the dominant culture of their time is the only sociological analysis they need or want to know.

New visions of reality do emerge. How these visions are transformed into publicly

[11] *TV Guide*, February 5, 1972, p. 6.

used reality is the central concern of this chapter. Prophecy, or individualized and cultish visions, does transform public reality. In the Western world, however, the use of reason as a major disciplinary or shaping force for new visions has been a social fact since at least 400 B.C. Disciplined analysis remains an ideal because its objects of study, it adherents, the use of its findings, even the logic which is its defining quality are all subject in varying degrees to control by the interests of powerful individuals and social classes.

Disciplined analysis can be studied as two processes: disciplined theory construction and disciplined observation. The rules of disciplined theory construction are based mainly on the careful use of logic in defining the patterns and stating connections between the patterns which constitute a new vision or theory.

Disciplined observation consists of knowing the appropriate use of and improving the tools of observation developed by sociolo-gists. These tools include ways of (1) directly observing human social behavior; (2) asking people what kinds of patterns they use in relating to others; and (3) observing the material aspects, or artifacts, connected with human social behavior. In addition, there are rules of disciplined observation primarily involved with ensuring that one knows and can communicate what one is looking for and that one knows how to ensure, through careful sampling, that one does not unintentionally bias one's observations.

There are many paths to truth. Those who are aware of the social forces shaping knowledge are not so bold as to discuss out-of-hand searches which do not fit precisely the prescription we feel is best. Thus there is clearly a place for such things as empathetic and descriptive sociology. At present, however, most sociologists adhere to the belief that disciplined theory and disciplined observation are the most appropriate ways to pursue sociological inquiry.

SUGGESTED READINGS

Norwood Russell Hanson, *Patterns of Discovery* (London: Cambridge University Press, 1958).

Thomas Kuhn, *The Structure of Scientific Revolutions* (Chicago: University of Chicago Press, 1962).

Karl Popper, *The Logic of Scientific Discovery* (New York: Basic Books, 1959).

John Rex, *Key Problems of Sociological Theory* (London: Routledge and Kegan Paul, 1970).

PART THREE

WHAT IS PUSHING US?
THE HISTORICAL PROCESS

From the functionalist perspective society is a *thing* which exists in a state of moving equilibrium, the parts of which are constantly adjusting to one another. For a functional analysis, the history of this *thing*—society—is irrelevant. One need only know the present parts of society and how they are presently adjusted to one another. Change is believed to be independent of the past nature of society and relative to the fit between the parts at any given moment.

The public acceptance of this functionalist view can be seen in the public utterances of United States politicians. Since the 1930s no United States president has talked much about historical processes at work within the United States. Rather the image of the United States conveyed by presidents, including F. D. Roosevelt, Truman, Eisenhower, Kennedy, Johnson, and Nixon, is of a giant machine which only requires occasional tinkering as the parts get out of adjustment.

In the culture which dominates the United States, a historical view seems to be of interest only when it shows the progress of the machine which is "society." Most history being taught assumes that United States "society" has gotten progressively better all the time.

A view which suggests that long-term historical processes, both positive and negative, are at work on the social tools used by Americans is viewed with suspicion if not outrightly persecuted. One columnist recently said a certain way of teaching history was as bad as the Watergate scandal. He referred to history which showed the cold war between the United States and the Soviet Union as part of an historical process rather than a crusade of good against evil.

In contrast to this view, which tends to ignore history, conflict analysis implies a continuing historical process involving movement, contradiction, and conflict. The movement is not necessarily seen as progress, but simply as solutions of problems created by the use of present social arrangements.

If you have been thinking about analysis of the present and have understood the principles of conflict theory, you might already have figured out why and how history is important.

Conflict theory stresses that presently used social structures are the results of past internal contradictions, development of social classes, and class conflict. To understand the present requires knowing which contradictions and classes developed, and how their conflicts were and are being resolved. Understanding the future requires a picture of the past process because it is expected that this process will continue to develop in the future.

Actually there is nothing new to most people about historical analysis. Most of us are not antihistory in our more personal analyses of how to solve our day-to-day problems. Ask people why they do almost anything and they will answer with variations on the theme that they do it because *in the past* they got pleasure from it; or in the past they found it was connected to something from which they got pleasure; or someone told them in the past that if they did it, it would lead to something pleasurable. In short we are all used to analyzing the cause of our own behavior as part of our personal histories. If as individuals we say "history is dead" we are implicitly saying that usable history began when we were born. Unusable, or dead, history is all that occurred before we were born. This seems lacking in consciousness about connections between our lives and the lives of others.

If some students are indeed turned off to history, it is because, like the amoeba, they see no relationship between their particular puddle and the puddles historians talk about. The larger perspective of conflict analysis tries to make clear how historical patterns are related to the everyday events of each of our lives. It assumes that the past before we were born can be as real and useful to us as our personal histories. The problem, of course, is knowing what *parts* of history are useful.

The purpose of a conflict theory is to suggest just what parts of history *should* be observed by suggesting what the important patterns are. Obviously no one can look at the whole of past human history. Whatever analytic framework is chosen, the test is whether the parts of the past on which it throws a spotlight are useful in helping us understand the present and change the future.

Within this section we seek to develop the idea that there are great forces at work within the structures and cultures humans use. Once people take up a way of life they begin immediately to learn the kinds of problems inherent in that way of life—they begin to experience specific times, places, and ways of life as *forces*. These forces create classes, class consciousness, and conflict. They direct human emotion toward very fundamental issues, which do not go away after a local war or a local fight or even after great disasters. Economic disaster, war, or natural disaster seem to only temporarily affect these forces, which persist over long periods of time. The idea of the persistence of the influence of basic forces is a fundamental principle of conflict anlysis.

Thus the chapters of this section are concerned with four issues: (1) different ways of life and the forces of change generated within them; (2) how individuals and collections of people are related to and participate in these forces; (3) the kinds of evidence to be found in histories of specific peoples for these forces or historical processes; (4) how the dominant economic structure and culture of the United States today can be understood to be developing out of the contradictions and conflicts of past social structures and cultures.

SEVEN
Social Change: Evolution, Revolution, and Social Movements

INTRODUCTION

The purpose of this chapter is to develop a general analysis of historical events such that we can see the pattern of forces from the past which are still shaping and pushing the social structures and cultures in use today. In subsequent chapters we will show some of the historical evidence which supports a conflict analysis of the forces shaping the social present.

We have stated and restated our belief that we must start with some ideas about the patterns for which to look. Without a perspective the present as well as the past is experienced as an infinite series of unrelated events. Such a series may be pleasant to see. But seeing in this way makes us passive, prisoners of each event. Action requires a theory. A perspective suggests what the im-

portant patterns in history are—what *kinds* of events we ought to study. It further suggests how these events ought to have occurred if indeed the supposed pattern is at work shaping these events. If events do not or did not occur as our perspective or theory suggests they will or should have, we must, if following the rules of disciplined analysis, begin to change our ideas or theories about the patterns. The new theory should be more consistent with what we can observe of past events.

Are there patterns in what we know of the history of human social relations? Patterns are types of events or clusters of events which are *repeated*. Because they are repeated, knowledge of them allows us to act. The problem is to know not only what the different patterns are but when specific events are examples of a particular pattern.

If there are patterns in history, they may take hundreds or thousands of years to unfold. Imagine you are looking for a pattern in a rug but the rug maker has made the pattern so large that you must unroll 100 yards of rug in order to see those figures which repeat to form the pattern. The first 20 feet you look at show only bits and pieces which do not repeat themselves at all.

Just as it takes 100 yards of rug to see a pattern, so it may take a very long view of human history to see what kinds of things seem to occur over and over. And, like the amoeba, our consciousness is often limited to our own puddle.

In Chapter 4 we listed the patterns which together make up the conflict perspective. In this chapter we will move on to apply this perspective to human social history. First, we will describe in more detail what a conflict analysis suggests are the patterns to be seen in human history; we list the different survival kits, or economic structures, which seem to have been developed throughout known human history; and we illustrate the patterned use of economic forms, and of the process of radical transformation from one form to another. Each economic form generates its own social structure and culture, and contradictions, classes, and class conflict. Subsequently each economic form is destroyed by its own contradictions.

The second aim of this chapter is to discuss the ways in which individuals relate to social change. A typology of social-change behaviors is developed which includes: individual compatible change; unorganized class conflict; and four types of social movement (reactionary movement, compatible movement, communitarian movement, and revolutionary movement).

ECONOMIC FORMS AND SOCIAL CHANGE

Three of the principles of conflict analysis together state the theory that economic patterns generate the most powerful forces shaping other institutional and cultural patterns. These principles, repeated from Chapter 4, are:

PRINCIPLE 1: The priority of economics principle. Economic forms shape other institutional forms.
PRINCIPLE 2: Survival-kit principle. Usable economic strategies are limited in number.
COROLLARY 1: A particular economic form or mode of production tends to dominate a particular time and place.
COROLLARY 2: If a *community form* is defined as the logic of a particular economic form plus the institutions and cultural patterns shaped by economic forces, then there are a limited number of community forms.
PRINCIPLE 3: The contradiction principle. Each economic form has inherent contradictions which produce classes and class conflict, and which may lead to its own destruction.

These ideas are the essence of conflict analysis. Can sociologists, historians, and others use these ideas to make sense of past or present social life? These ideas have come from the work of people who have spent years trying as objectively as possible to see how others live and of what they construct their social lives. Some people who have done conflict analysis have devoted themselves to searching out obscure or even suppressed observations of social events.

The story which follows is a recounting of some features of human history as reconstructed by these people. It is told in such a way as to show the measures and events which brought people to acknowledge the idea that there are such forces at work as economic strategies, contradiction, class, and class conflict.

The Story of Human Social Tools

Social structure and culture are tools that human beings have developed to help them survive, both as individuals and as a species.

From the perspective of conflict analysis the story of the use of these tools reveals patterns, which are processes of development and changes in the social tools themselves. Having discovered the flexible, wondrous devices of social structure and culture, humans have discovered that these tools seem to transform themselves in their hands, or to wear out in surprising ways as they use them.

The story of human social life seems to have three themes that run throughout it:

1. There are a limited number of social tools that can be used for survival.

2. When people "pick up" one of these social tools and begin to use it, the tool reveals a logic of its own. This logic limits and therefore shapes other parts of life, even though these other parts may be not directly related to physical survival.

3. The paradoxes and contradictions within the tool itself constitute a social force which ultimately makes that particular tool unworkable. This process leads to the abandonment of the old tool and the taking up of a new one.

A limited number of strategies for human survival Human history reveals only a few distinctly different ways in which people have turned the earth into food, shelter, warmth, and energy.

Gathering wild foods, mainly vegetation, is one. Hunting wild animals is another. Agriculture, or controlling the growth and reproduction of plants and animals, is a third. Manufacturing, or artificially producing food and energy directly from more basic chemical and physical materials as well as indirectly from plant and animal materials, is a fourth.

The activities involved in each of the four economic strategies are very different, and each of the four is associated with very different ways of life. Hence we say these four economies are basic. Some sociologists consider fishing and herding unique enough to be considered as separate economic forms. This is possible. Whether there are four or six basic human survival strategies is not so important. The important question really is whether most people using hunting economies use institutional patterns more like those used by other hunting peoples and less like those used by agricultural peoples. This question is critical because if the theory is useful it should predict how other parts of life will be limited by the particular economic strategy used. The number of discrete economic strategies is not as important as whether the theory fits historical and contemporary evidence.

Are there a limited number of basically different economic strategies viable at a particular time in history? It seems logical that there should be a limited number if one starts with two assumptions. The first is that humans are limited by their biology: an economic mode based on teleportation or individual self-propelled flight or sending down roots into the soil is out of the question for people. Secondly, knowledge of possible alternatives is always limited by our past history, the most important being a particular epoch in the immediate past. In this way, for example, some of the ideas used in manufacturing economies grew out of agricultural modes of thought.

In sum it seems to fit our observations of human history that a limited number of economic strategies have actually been used.

Forces within the tools themselves Structured, predictable ways that people can relate together to produce food, shelter, warmth, and energy are what we mean by economic tools, or strategies. The story of people using these tools is the story of sequential abandonment of one economic structure after another. In parts of the world where we can see, through archaeological reconstruction, a fairly uninterrupted sequence of physical cultural remains, one sequence occurs over and over. In the Yellow River valley, in the valley of the Tigris and Euphrates, in the Nile valley, in the fertile lowlands of Yucatan—the story is the same. People first gathered the native plant products—the fruits, nuts, roots, flowers, and other edible parts—as part of a gathering economy. Later, people must have switched to a hunting economy, for the remains of large animals are found with increasing frequency in the places of human habitation. Later yet, remains of wild plants and wild animals are increasingly replaced with the remains of domesticated plants and animals—with grains, such as wheat, barley, rye, and with cattle, sheep, and goats. More recently these remains are in turn overwhelmed by the debris of industrial societies, from tin cans to tires.

Was it inevitable progress, curiosity, or the hand of God which led people to abandon old economic strategies for new ones?

None of these, says conflict analysis. From conflict analysis we conclude that humans never willingly give up a way of life that allows them to survive. Some force other than inevitable progress, curiosity, or the hand of God must have caused the abandonment of economic strategies.

The nature of the force toward change is understood as the paradoxes and contradictions arising from the use of the economic tool and working toward its ultimate unusability. The force generated by the use of the tool itself has three manifestations: (1) the *logical* use of the tool, which refines and makes the tool more efficient; (2) the *contradictory force*, the tendency of the tool to produce classes and class conflict; and (3) the *exclusion force*, the tendency of the use of the economic strategy to allow survival of more people than can efficiently work together using the particular economic tool.

In speaking of a *force*, we have no intention of making this a mysterious, unknow-able thing. If the theory is any good, you should be able to see and experience the process in your own life although you may never have thought to see it in precisely the context offered here. There is nothing mysterious about the force of contradiction, for example, to someone who has ever felt deeply in love. Being in love often leads to spending more and more time alone with, even in bed with, the person you love. But doing this makes it less and less possible to be intimately involved with others. In the general language we have been developing, your love is a tool for your survival with one other person. But the development and elaboration of this tool, if you really get into it, excludes all other people but you and the one you love. Not a very good way to survive. Over the long haul, it seems very hard for collections of humans to avoid taking their survival strategies—such as that for the survival of love—to extremes. Love has been described as dangerous throughout literature. It is a tool which, once picked up, may come to possess the user. Fiction, as in the stories of Romeo and Juliet, Tristan and Isolde, Faust, indeed of most great lovers, repeats this theme again and again. A variation of the same theme is the core of the recent United States film *2001: A Space Odyssey*. Man-apes are portrayed getting the idea of tools from a monolith-machine. The man-apes possess the tools, but the viewer experiences a growing feeling that the tools also possess the man-apes. As the tools are developed to their logical extension, they seem to lead the man-apes in a certain direction.

Now how is this idea of a force inherent in economic strategies reflected in the human story?

A logic One of the forces generated by the choice of a particular economic strategy is well described by the word *logic*. The force is a logic in the sense that once people start living by hunting, for example, it is only logical to do a lot of related things in a certain way—logical in the sense of easy, efficient, not getting in the way of, in fact helping, the hunting. For example, it is logical to make houses that are small and easily transportable, the better to follow the animals. It is logical to involve all the hunters in making political decisions, since all must eventually carry them out. If it is true that each way of life is logically connected to a specific economic strategy, then certain things should be true of the historical record. People who are hunters should be more like one another in their way of life then they are like people who use some other economic strategy.

Exclusion A second social force generated by each economic strategy becomes apparent only when the strategy is working well. The idea of a logic is that each economic strategy requires a certain kind of organization to carry it out. For example, gathering wild plant products needs only a small, simply constructed group, while hunting requires more organization—more bodies either hunting or developing new weapons. But the plant gatherers did not become hunters because they had a "progress" mentality—an innate drive toward complexity. As people developed better the relationships with others needed to carry out a plant-gathering economy, they began to live a better life. This life was better in the sense of being more secure; the people were better fed. One of the consequences of doing better is that more children survive to raise their own children. However this creates a problem. The family structure through which all this plant gathering is being accomplished "has room for" (that is, can be successfully used by) only a limited number of people. The new generation, products of a better life, must go elsewhere. The most likely thing to do is to go somewhere else

where plant foods are equally available, to recreate the plant-gathering family structure in the new place.

Thus the successful use of an economic strategy creates population problems *for that strategy*. Note carefully that we are not talking about population problems relative to scarce resources or destruction of the environment, but population problems of a *social* nature. There are too many people to use the existing dominant economic strategy. As an example in contemporary life, we should ask if there is a maximum number of people who can use an industrialized economic strategy. If more people survive than this maximum, will they be able to find jobs, have rights to consumership, and have ready access to the use of institutional patterns?

At some times and in many places, just moving away and recreating the old forms could work no longer. The surplus people of one generation may have run into people expanding from another direction, from another center of human habitation. Maybe people moving up the Yellow River valley of China encountered people moving down the river. Or perhaps these extra people reached the limits of rich vegetation—perhaps they came to the edge of the mountains or the desert or the ocean. At this point, when people could no longer simply recreate the old strategy, they might either perish, as many undoubtedly did, or develop a new strategy for surviving. Their environment would be harsher at either the geographical limits, the desert's edge, or at the people limits, where they were contesting gathering grounds with strangers. They would no longer be able to live well within the shield provided by the previously efficient, small, extended family grouping. They may have flowed together in larger groups, attempting to preserve the extended family, somehow relating at the same time to people outside their families. Some must have figured out ways to get survival from these larger numbers through changing from a plant-gathering strategy to a hunting strategy. At some point, successful hunters must have turned back to destroy and take the land of those still using the gathering economy, in order to create hunting grounds.

This story fits well enough what we know of some parts of the world to think it might be a universal pattern. It surely did not happen everywhere at the same time. It could have happened in some places more than a million years ago among people we might not even consent to call human. In some parts of the world, this exclusionary force developed early. In some parts it developed late. In some places today, people are still essentially gatherers, living within extended family groupings.

The force of exclusion is proportional to the richness of any area in the resources most in demand by a particular economy. It creates conflict between new and old in the lives of specific individuals excluded from the use of the old economic form by its very success. The exclusionary force is a special kind of contradiction. In a perverse way, success seems to produce failure, particularly if the physical environment is a kindly one, containing much of the resources needed within a particular economic strategy.

Contradiction A third force generated by the use of a particular economic strategy comes from the problems created by structural or internal contradictions. Like the exclusionary force, the force from classes and class conflicts created by contradictions is felt most when an economic logic has been fully developed and worked out.

Imagine, if you will, the merchants who began to appear in numbers once again in medieval Europe (the loss of Roman arms to protect the roads had made merchanting very dangerous) in the ninth and tenth centuries A.D. A big part of the logic of manufacturing goods and selling them as we understand the process is a *contract*, which is a guarantee of exchange of goods and services, the more binding when backed by force. We take so for granted that laws and the power of the state ensure the validity of contracts that it is hard to imagine a time when such was not the case. In the ninth and tenth centuries, however, people largely settled issues by appeals to force of arms, to customs, and to loyalties to one's caste, noble or peasant. In short, there was no court of law to which a merchant might turn if he had been cheated. This made doing business difficult, to say the least. The merchants began to entrench themselves in towns and to develop a new economic strategy or logic which required contracts, the essence of which were bits of work and bits of business exchange. This new economic strategy took a long time, and several violent revolutions, to develop. Its emergence as the dominant logic required the failure of the old economy.

The development of a contractual economic strategy illustrates the working out of a logic. Also, when the essence of an economic strategy begins to penetrate institutional patterns of all kinds, then its contradictions begin to be more apparent. For example, as used as we are to contractual logic, we are not surprised to find the state wanting to write into law contracts which would protect children from their parents.

But use of a family structure wrapped around by contracts (laws) which restrict parents' behavior toward children may achieve the goal of protecting children from physical abuse, but may also make it very unappealing, perhaps even dangerous, for adults to get involved with children at all. This is a *contradiction* in the merchant-manufacturing type of structure.

Conflict theory suggests that contradictions may appear in any social structure as it is used, and that the greatest social forces are those generated by contradictions in the economic structure. Of these economic contradictions the ones which are located in the mode of production itself will produce the greatest pressure toward antagonistic social classes and class conflict.

The forces flowing from contradiction are not mysterious—they are expressed in the acts of people fighting for their own interests as they pereceive them. The struggle for class interests is not mysterious either, nor is it necessarily a conspiracy of rich against poor. It is the struggle of individuals to achieve what they think are *their own* interests. The force of contradiction is important to social history simply because while trying to achieve their own interests, people are in the process of destroying the interests of others. A struggle created by a contradiction is precisely one in which the use of a particular social structure leads to the achievement of some goals at the expense of others. Thus, whether people conspire or not is immaterial to the idea of contradiction and class conflict. For example, if in the United State today the higher wages are the lower profits are, then there is a contradiction—a struggle between people who earn wages and people who are rewarded by high profits. Whether people who are wage earners want to be or consider themselves part of a "class," they will find that every time they stop struggling, saying "to hell with these union wages" or "to hell with all this bargaining," their interests suffer. Each class may honestly believe that it is indispensable to the other and therefore should be allowed to achieve its own goals. Profit makers are quite convinced that the economy would go to pieces if they were not able to make a profit for reinvestment and "creation" of new jobs. Wage earners are equally convinced there would be no economy without someone to do the work. The force of contradiction lies not in bad

will or in conspiracy, but simply in the tendencies for use of any economic structure to lead to achieving certain goals at the expense of others.

In the late stages of the use of an economic structure attempts to compromise between the contradictory interests will fail with increasing frequency. There was a long period in European history from the tenth to the sixteenth centuries during which attempts were made in France, England, and Germany to resolve some of the conflicts of interests between the nobles and the peasants within an agricultural economy. Each time the compromises, or temporary repairs of noble-peasant relations, failed, the basic antagonism between noble and peasant returned, and each time with greater difficulty to both classes. Ultimately the system became unworkable for both peasant and noble and was replaced by a new economic strategy, bourgeois capitalism. (See Chapter 10, on feudalism, for a more detailed explanation.)

It is important to understand how temporary repairs are made in a deteriorating social structure, even if one knows that in the long run the repairs cannot fix the fundamental rot. One should not forget that temporary repairs, the ending of a depression, for example, mean life or death for thousands. To better understand the repair process—the nature and failure of compromise or contradiction—is one of the great unfinished tasks of conflict analysis, even though the conflict view of history is that in the long run these repairs must fail.

Evolution and Revolution

Evolution is a term whose meaning has been most fixed in the biological-analysis disciplines. There it has come to mean a process by which there is a continuous disappearance of those characteristics of species and individuals, and those species, which do not change in response to environmental changes. In both the popular and academic cultures, this idea has been applied to human social life as well. It is a particularly satisfying idea in that it implies that whatever is present now in the way of human social structures is the most highly evolved, and therefore the best fit to survive. It has also been extremely congenial to those who benefit most from present social arrangements.

Conflict analysis of the type presented here does *not* imply inevitable progress, nor that the present social arrangements are those best fitted to the "environment," whatever that is. In these senses of the word, conflict theory is not an evolutionary theory.

It is possible, in fact, that people who use a hunting or a gathering way of life are better adapted to their environment than some people using an agricultural or industrial strategy. We might try to evaluate what "better adapted" means. We do have standards by which one can judge social arrangements. Do people eat better? Do they live longer? Are they happier? But no one at present seriously tries to add up all these things for each of the people who inhabit human history to arrive at even an approximation of the "betterness" of present social arrangements. Even if we did this, it would be a long way short of assessing whether present arrangements are better adapted in terms of survival of the species, which is the criterion biologists use and the criterion implied by the term *evolution*. Some might argue that we are today, through the use of industrial technologies, much closer to extinction as a species than our ancestors were.

Conflict analysis does imply the following constants in the change of human social structures and cultures.

1. The longer economic strategies are used, the less usable they become.

2. As economic strategies become unworkable *by human standards,* they are abandoned.

3. There seems a tendency for later economic strategies to be organized to be used by larger numbers of people.

Economic strategies do not fall apart or become unusable all at once. In the examples we have given thus far, it is suggested that the problems created by exclusion and class conflict in some cases developed over hundreds, even thousands, of years. In the last part of this chapter we will ask how individuals relate to this long historical process. Here we simply want to point out that for some individuals the dominant economic forms worked quite well, and for others at the same time they worked poorly or not at all. Among those for whom the forms did not work well, the majority must have died or suffered in silence. The leap to a new economic strategy is conceived as a struggle by a few for a new way. These few *have no other choice.*

Further, the new economic strategy does not spring into existence fullblown, with solutions to all the major problems of human survival. There are transition periods as well as carry-overs from older forms. In fact, each new economic strategy seems to build on the foundation of the institutional pattern most highly elaborated by the users of the previous economic strategy. Hunters built their tribes around the family-kinship groupings used by gathering peoples; agricultural peoples built their caste system around the religious institutions developed by tribalists; industrialists built their economy around the professions, an institutional pattern which emerged in feudal agriculture as the guild system. Each of these institutional patterns seems ultimately to "wither away" as it gets farther and farther away from the times in which it originated. Conflict analysis predicts the eventual disappearance of old family, religious, professional, and institutional patterns as people move farther away from the economic strategies to which these patterns were centrally important. Karl Marx, the earliest developer of a coherent conflict analysis of history, predicted that the modern state, an institutional pattern central to industrial capitalism, will also wither away.

In conflict analysis, *revolution* is an organized movement (a social structure) through which people move toward the end of introducing a new economic strategy and the institutional patterns implied by that new economic strategy.

The place of revolution in the solution of the agonies of unworkable economic strategies is not clear. There is a need for a careful analysis of history to more precisely work out when and how revolutions have occurred, which ones have failed, which ones have succeeded, and why.

The word *revolution* has several uses in popular culture which should be carefully differentiated from the definition used above. For example, a revolution is not necessarily violent, although enemies of social change have in many times and places succeeded in equating revolution with violence in the popular mind. They may hope thus to deter people from working out new solutions to their problems by causing them to fear the violence supposed to accompany radical, or revolutionary, change. Further, conflict theory does not say revolution necessarily comes from the dispossessed, those for whom the dominant economic strategy is proving least workable. These may also be the people most brutalized and most oppressed, and least likely to organize. Revolutions may in fact come from, or at least be tried by, the elites. For example, the vast and organized movement to develop a technology for the invasion of privacy (telephone bugs, microphones, computer storage of personal data, numbers for names, etc.) may

in the long run prove revolutionary. That is, it may end up totally restructuring the economy and most of the institutional patterns through which people live. Such a revolution may also be violent; notice that our definition does not *rule out* violence as part of the technique of revolutionary organization.

A CONFLICT VIEW OF HISTORY: SUCCESSIVE ECONOMIC STRATEGIES

Figure 7-1 is our present view of four distinct economic strategies that can be found in human history, and their relationship to one another in terms of patterns of contradiction and breakdown, and simultaneous emergence of new economic strategies.

The conflict view of the natural history of economic strategies proposes that three processes go on at the same time and place: experimentation, coherence, and disintegration. On the left side of the diagram are listed peoples essentially under the dominance of old economic strategies, who are nevertheless experimenting with new ones. The diagram implies that these people may be outcasts or people who for some reason cannot make it so well within the dominant economic strategy. Across the top are listed some of the processes of coherence by which the logic of a particular economic strategy emerges. These include making the economic activity itself into a structural unit by means of a bonding principle, or social "glue." For example, hunting peoples made the hunting of animals into a structural unit —the tribe—by means of tribal morality (see Chapter 8). What finally emerges is a fully coherent way of life—a hunting economy with all that implies for ways of rearing children, building shelter, settling disputes, and making political decisions. At the same time, disintegration processes are at work, as depicted along the right-hand side of the chart. These reflect contradictions within the economic strategy and structure, and the re-

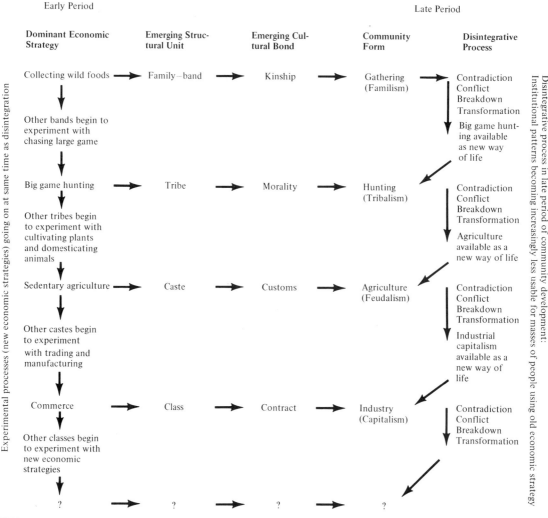

FIGURE 7-1 Outline of conflict-evolutionary theory of development of community forms. Parallel processes of experiment, with new forms on right side of chart and disintegration of old on left side of chart.

sultant way of life. Those economic experiments which successfully resolve the contradictions of the old economic strategy will be available as a new way of life when the old way becomes unusable.

People never totally abandon a way of life, except in some cases of imperialistic imposition of a new way. Bits and pieces of old forms are always brought along and woven into new ways of life. Historical evi-

dence supports the idea that each economic form has a particular institutional area which is most fully developed as a complement to the economic institutional pattern. In the gathering economy, the family institutional pattern is developed in great complexity. People who use a hunting economy seem to fully develop the religious institutional patterns, while retaining, in diminished form, the family as an important institutional pattern. People using a caste-based agricultural economy seem to most fully develop the institutional pattern of professions—priestly professions, alchemic professions, legal professions, medical professions. The state, a pattern within which political decision mak-

ing is raised to its most elaborate and complex level, seems to dominate the institutional architecture of people using industrial economic strategies. Figure 7-2 illustrates the idea of dominant institutional patterns, and the "withering" of institutions as formerly

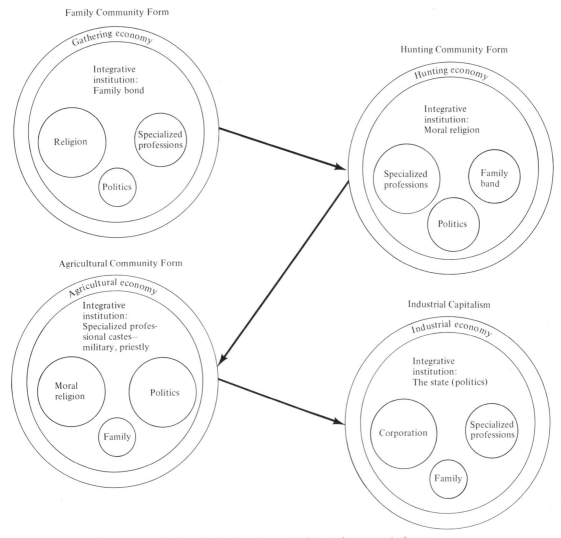

FIGURE 7-2 "Withering away" of institutional patterns. Within each economic form, economic patterns shape other institutional patterns. Within each economic form is found an integrative institutional pattern (family for gatherers, moral religion for hunters, specialized castes for agricultural peoples, the state in industrial capitalist and state socialist economies). This integrative institutional pattern tends to become less important as people take up new economic strategies. Thus family, moral religion, castes, and the state tend to "wither away."

dominant patterns become less important. It shows also the carry-over of bits and pieces of institutional patterns from old to new community forms.

According to conflict theory, the primary features of the historical process, as observed in the lives of people and in the reflections of peoples' lives which are the historical record—the fragmentary glimpses we have through artifacts, folklore, legends, art, the stories of travelers—are the following.

1. The tension and conflict which reflect contradictions in social institutions, and, most importantly, contradictions in the economic strategy, are the *dialectic* of history.

2. In different times and places in human history, people have had to deal with four great crises. These crises reflect the disintegration of the economic strategies of gathering, hunting, agriculture, and industry, and the social forms that correspond to them—familism, tribalism, feudalism, and capitalism.

3. The four great crises have been resolved through experiments in new economic strategies, carried on at the edges of a dominant economic strategy.

The Limits of Conflict Analysis of History

Every human individual participates in some ways in the drama of human history. To keep the question of the place of the individual in perspective, one caution is in order. We should remind ourselves that there is often more to being human than the use of human social tools. While it appears necessary to use human social tools to be fully human (at least as social-tool-using humans define *humanity*), there is much more to human activity.

This further implies there are many histories—biological, cosmic, astrologic, geologic—and many kinds of analysis are necessary to the understanding of these histories. Conflict analysis is a framework for understanding a specialized kind of history.

Conflict analysis poses some specific questions about the history of changes in human institutional patterns. There is much work yet to be done before we begin to have the evidence necessary to tell us how useful this perspective is even for understanding the limited kind of history involving human social tools. Remember that until the past few years American academicians could hardly ask the questions raised by conflict analysis without losing their jobs. The official ideology was, and to some extent still is, that the United States is a classless society. To try to see how useful it is to understand United States history in terms of class struggle was, to say the least, unpopular.

In the recent past, sociology students have been told that conflict analysis is a waste of time because it is based on the obviously absurd idea that economics is the total of human life. To say there is more to life than economics is to say something every human knows. Changes in human consciousness, human physical development, human relations with the land, human relations with other life (terrestrial or extraterrestrial, germs or elephants), all might proceed more or less independently of the changes occurring in human social institutions. To use the fact that humans do more than survive as an argument to discredit conflict analysis or as a reason for not testing conflict analysis is foolish. It is very much like saying the theory of the internal-combustion engine (or the knowledge of how to fix cars) is no good because there is more to life than cars. A conflict analysis of the historical process does not attempt to account for all of human history—only for the patterns that we may see or might discover in the changes in human institutional structures.

THE INDIVIDUAL AND SOCIAL ORDER

A specific person is involved in the process of transforming economic strategies and in-

SELECTION 7-1

LINCOLN AND THE BREAKDOWN OF THE OLD ORDER

By Carl Sandburg

Such an epic of perplexity, transition, change is not often witnessed. In every such passage of a nation, there ought to be a character like that of Samuel. Misunderstood, misrepresented at the time; attacked from both sides; charged with not going far enough and with going too far; charged with saying too much and saying too little, he slowly, conscientiously, and honestly works out the mighty problems. He was not a founder of a new state of things like Moses; he was not a champion of the existing order of things like Elijah. He stood between the two: between the living and the dead; between the past and the present; between the old and the new; with that sympathy for each which at such a period is the best hope for any permanent solution of the questions which torment it. He has but little praise from partisans, but is the careful healer binding up the wounds of the age in spite of himself; the good surgeon knitting together the dislocated bones of the disjointed times.

stitutional patterns in several ways. Abraham Lincoln is portrayed in Selection 7-1 as a person with sympathy for the old and the new, and we suspect that he wished to make the transition from the old to the new as peaceful as possible. Yet he was fated to preside over the highest levels of violence yet seen in the history of white America. As a human being, Lincoln was not free of some elements of the old patterns, and he thereby helped the old way linger. Although he did not personally own slaves, his need for political and military support from the border states led him into relationships with those states, which, before the Emancipation Proclamation, supported the institution of slavery.

In what ways may individuals less well known than a Lincoln or a Lenin participate in economic transformation? If there is some accuracy to the idea that there are discernible patterns in the history of change in human social institutions, then we should be able to see patterns in the activities of individuals involved in social change. Individual behavior will not be random, but will fall into one of a few categories of social-change behavior, which will reflect the larger pattern of transformation of economic strategies.

Social change, then, and the ways in which people organize to participate in social change, will be part of or reflections of the larger pattern of economic transformation. The same individual might be involved in social change in several ways. Let us list and discuss the kinds of social-change activities which are implicit in the historical process of transformation of economic strategies.

Individual Compatible Change

People carry with them many roles and bits of culture from previous community forms, and can expect they will have difficulty using these old roles and cultural bits within a new form. Individuals will spontaneously and on their own initiative look for ways to change roles they are using, and bits of culture, words, ideas, or pieces of technology, in the direction of compatibility with the new economic logic. Figure 7-3 illustrates the variety of ways in which individuals participate in social change, including changing individual roles. Examples of individual role and cultural changes are:

1. Individual changes in language, for example, the rise of a series of terms like "cool," or "getting it together," which reflect a detached, self-controlled public role, compatible with a business-oriented economy.

2. Individual entrepreneurs' development of prepackaged "TV" dinners, compatible with the individuality, mobility, and emphasis on speed of a capitalist economy.

3. Students individually behaving less like apprentices and more like purchasers

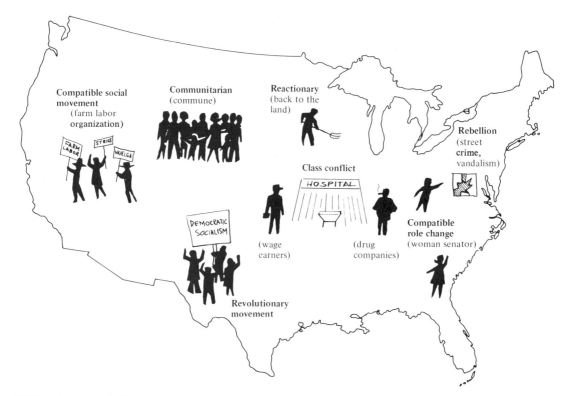

FIGURE 7-3 How individuals participate in social change. While class conflict is theorized to be the major source of social change, people react to changing economic forms in many other ways. Some of these varieties are compatible, reactionary, and revolutionary social movements; rebellion; communitarianism; and compatible role change.

of a service or product, thus changing the student role *and* the teacher role in the direction of a businesslike contract.

Thus individuals respond to a sense of inefficiency and frustration when using roles and bits of culture incompatible with the existing dominant economic logic by changing their own behavior. These individual changes may catch on and together transform larger segments of group structures and institutional patterns further in the direction of compatibility with the new dominant economic logic.

Selection 7-2 shows one woman's response to some of the inconsistencies be-

tween a bourgeois-contractual economy and the role of housewife. Mrs. Harshaw responded as an individual.

Unorganized Class Conflict

The greatest force toward social change is the pressure on institutional patterns arising out of contradiction and class conflict. This takes the form of continuous action—sometimes organized, sometimes disorganized, sometimes individual. *There is no group of "bad guys" who silently manipulate the institutions in the direction of their interests and away from the needs of the "good guys."*

Institutional patterns are shaped by the

SELECTION 7-2: Individual compatible social change. Mrs. Harshaw tries to change the role of housewife.

WOMAN OF THE HOUSE ON STRIKE—HUMANE TREATMENT

Memphis, Tenn. (AP)—Rachel Harshaw is continuing her strike against household chores. She began the work stoppage after listening to a Sunday sermon in which the minister quoted from the Bible that the man is the master of the house.

"I'm afraid that sermon stopped it," said Mrs. Harshaw, 30, mother of three children. After hearing the Mother's Day sermon, she refused to do housework, although she said she had made some concessions Wednesday.

"My demands are not met, but I did break down and pick up a few things," she said. "I've always fed the children, but I cooked breakfast this morning instead of making cereal. But I still haven't washed any clothes or made the beds.

"And I took my sign down."

The sign she had put outside the house read to passersby: "On Strike!! For shorter hours . . . one day off per year and other humane considerations. Signed: Woman of the House."

She said her husband, Jim, an insurance man, had "ignored my demands for a few days, so I put up the sign."

"The kids and I have been taking the whole thing as a joke," Harshaw said.

"In a way it's a joke," said Mrs. Harshaw, "but I'm also serious about it."

"I expect she'll give in soon," Harshaw said, before the concessions. "No I'll never clean up the place."

"I have the nicest family and husband in the world," Mrs. Harshaw said. "But when I get mad, he just takes me lightly."

More specifically, the struggle is over resources available for use, and over the ways in which resources will be used and the goals which they will be used to achieve. For example, resources such as money, legitimate access to use of violence, and knowledge (often very important knowledge) are available to those using the roles of senator, FBI director, president. These resources are used to support certain institutional patterns, and the kind of patterns preferred by those with most control over state resources will get state support. For example, fee-for-service, business-oriented health-care structures which benefit profit makers more than wage earners are likely to get state support. Whatever power wage earners have—through lobbies, congressmen, senators, voting rights—will be engaged in a struggle to direct resources toward other health-care patterns more beneficial to the interests of wage earners.

The economic-priority principle leads us to assume that it is those classes produced by contradictions within the economic structure which are the most powerful and most active. In addition we assume that there is one major contradiction within each economic logic, and the two classes produced by this contradiction will tend to be the most powerful. People will feel pushed in the direction of one or the other of these classes. People will find it hard to stay in the middle with respect to the issues which divide these two great classes. Depending on how far along are the processes of contradiction, class emergence, and class conflict, the pressures toward class-based behavior will vary from slight to strong.

Specifically, peasants and nobles may have gotten along very well in the early stages of agricultural feudalism, the nobles providing protection for the peasants' farming. However, as the contradictions in this relationship become more apparent, nobles and peasants found themselves more often in

struggle between classes and between individuals acting on the basis of class interests. Rather than reflecting the interests of one class only, institutional patterns will reflect the interests of several classes, in proportion to their power relative to one another.

conflict. In the last stages of feudalism, one was literally forced to choose sides in this conflict, no matter whether a noble loved "my peasants," or a peasant thought "our landlord is a good master."

Some class conflict is spontaneous and unorganized. The president of ITT, in trying to influence the Attorney General of the United States to stop an antitrust indictment, is engaged in class conflict. The unemployed young black man who steals increases class conflict by provoking pressures for more police control. The teacher who requires blind obedience to a "cleaned-up" version of United States history increases the "them against us" feeling of students whose experiences have taught them a different history.

Individuals on both sides seem to want peace. There is a joy in the politeness of class contact, just as some people found comfort in the feudal etiquette of the "Jim Crow" pattern between blacks and whites. It is sane to prefer peace to continuous violence, which is what class war ultimately means. But beneath the politeness the struggle persists, sometimes contained by law, often not contained by law. The Committee to Re-elect the President in 1972 operated on the prinicple that the reelection of a friend of business is more important than law.

Compatible Social Movements

A social movement is a series of group structures created as a means through which people may work together toward social change.

By *compatible social movements* we mean those social movements whose aims are the achievement of either or both of two kinds of change: (1) bringing antiquated parts of social structure and culture in line with the existing dominant logic; (2) bringing existing institutional patterns more in line with class interests.

An example of the first kind of compatible movement is women's liberation. Male-female role relations in the United States have many of the characteristics of feudal role relations. The restriction of each sex to certain kinds of tasks and cultural techniques is a *caste* relationship. Such relationships were the basis of the feudal economy. The women's movement aims to abolish these castelike distinctions. Women using movement roles believe these caste relations operate more to women's disadvantage than to men's. The women's movement also attempts to bring about the second kind of change, at least it has done so in most of its manifestations through 1973, in that it seeks to bring women into a kind of social participation that is compatible with the dominant logic of capitalist economics. That is, the movement seeks full contractual participation of individual women in the dominant institutional patterns. Selection 7-3 illustrates part of this struggle as women college students seek equal benefits from college athletic expenditures.

The trade union movement is perhaps the best example in United States history of a class-based compatible social movement. As the United States moved into an industrial economy, the bourgeois owners of industry had been freed from the old feudal restrictions on the use of property. However, the industrial work force still experienced many of the restrictions of the feudal peasantry. They did not, for example, have the right to bargain over work conditions or wage scales. Selection 7-4 illustrates working conditions in the United States just before the Civil War. The trade union movement was a response to the slavelike relationship between wage earners and profit makers, so out of place in a supposedly free economy. It was aimed at collecting working-class power and channeling it through an institutional framework. Early union organizers found, and continually had to rediscover, the need to pool re-

SELECTION 7-3: Does the woman's movement have revolutionary potential? Does it reach into every institutional pattern?

WOMEN'S MOVE FOR RIGHTS TO ATHLETIC FUNDS

By Mary Ann Durney

SF State may soon be forced to provide equal funding for men's and women's athletics.

If Senate Bill 1228, introduced in Sacramento May 12 by Senator Mervyn Dymally (D-Los Angeles) becomes law colleges which do not fund men's and women's athletics equally will receive no state funds.

Now, the Associated Students 1972–73 budget allocates $60,000 for men's athletics and $3,700 for women's.

The women's athletics, an instructionally related program, requested $10,000 in the AS 1973–74 budget but their request was cut to $4,000 by the Academic Affairs office.

Women's athletic programs include field hockey, tennis, softball, volleyball, swimming and basketball.

Objected to change

Though the AS objected to this change in its budget, the AS has no power to change the Academic Affairs budget decision on instructionally related programs. The AS is now investigating student control of student funds.

"It is time that women got their fair share of funds for athletics," said Frieda Lee, women's athletics instructor.

Women are paying expenses for traveling and lodging on intercollegiate events out of their own pockets while the men's teams expenses are paid out of the budget.

Hardship

"It is a hardship for many girls on the teams to pay their own expenses but they love the games so much they go," Lee said.

Harold Einhorn, associate vice president of academic affairs, said the reason men's athletics receives more funds than women's is historic.

"The men's athletics is receiving less now than before the strike, but it's always been that they've received more money," said Einhorn.

'Miscommunication'

He said the change in the women's athletics budget was caused by a miscommunication.

"The programs were told the budget should be in the same area of last year's, but the women's athletics misunderstood and budgeted things somewhat closer to their ambitions for all their needs," he said.

Senator Dymally hopes his bill will end the discrimination since he has found inequalities in funding "seem to be the rule rather than the exception."

"No longer will women's programs be financed out of participants' pockets or bake sales while the men's programs are funded generously out of the school's budget," he said.

SELECTION 7-4: Pre-trade union working conditions in the United States. Basis for a compatible social movement—trade unionism.

In the North are to be found all imaginable conditions that lie between the two extremes of factories and mills managed by owners who are efficient, kindly, decent, thoughtful, and factories and mills operated by hard, hopeless owners. The Hamilton Manufacturing Co. in Massachusetts issues "Public Factory Rules," proclaiming: "All persons in the employ of the Hamilton Manufacturing Company are to observe the regulations of the room where they are employed. They are not to be absent from work without the consent of the overseer, except in cases of sickness, and then they are to send word as to the cause of their absence. They are to board in one of the houses of the company and give information at the counting room where they board, when they begin, or, whenever, they change their boarding-place; and are to observe the regulations of their boarding-house. Those intending to leave the employ of the company are to give at least two weeks' notice thereof to the overseer. All persons entering into the employment of the company are considered engaged for twelve months. Those who leave sooner, or do not comply with all the regulations, will not be entitled to a regular discharge. The company will not employ any one who is habitually absent from public worship on the Sabbath, or known to be guilty of immorality.

The trade union movement is compatible with the logic of industrial capitalism. Union organizers insist on the right of workers to collectively negotiate the conditions of their work just as capitalists collectively negotiate their purchases of raw materials and their sales (Bruce Anspach/EPA Newsphoto)

sources. They had to force owners to nego-tiate a contractual relationship, one more consistent with the contractual culture grow-ing out of a capitalist economy, which al-lowed working-class people some say in the actual shaping of factory work and rules.

Trade unionism, women's liberation, black power, and the student movement of the 1960s all have in common the attempt to realize the idea of a bourgeois economic system: free negotiation of one's own place in the world. In that sense they are move-ments compatible with the central logic of the capitalist or free market economy. Selec-tion 7-5 illustrates a movement to change institutionalized patterns of religious be-havior in a direction more compatible with the mobile, contractual logic of capitalist economy.

There are many individuals, however, who use a portion of their energy in attempting to seek change *outside* the logic of the

The attempt to restore the caste relationship between blacks and whites is the basis for the Ku Klux Klan movement (Wide World Photos)

SELECTION 7-5: Compatible social movement.

CATHOLIC ORDERS SHRINKING

By George W. Cornell

New York—(AP)—A question mark hangs today over the future of the old, once thriving and powerful religious orders of Roman Catholicism. Most are shrinking. A noted American church scholar says bluntly they're "already dead."

This is the bolting thesis of Brother Gabriel Moran, a pungently articulate intellectual and leader in one of the Church's most venerable teaching orders, the Christian Brothers. He has been pressing the point for the last three years.

"We've got to face it while we still have enough concerned people left in the movement to crystallize new, living forms of community," he says. "There is still something that could be done, but it won't be true for long."

While other Church authorities cite various ailments of the religious orders, few concur with the idea that they're totally defunct, and many dismiss Brother Moran's view as mere gadfly needling of complacency.

"He makes overemphatic blatant assertions to wake people up and make them think," commented his superior in the order, Brother Aloysius Carmody, secretary-general of the 300-year-old Christian Brothers.

Nevertheless, statistically, there has been a steady shrinkage in most religious orders both for men and women for the past seven years, despite numerous changes in their structure, roles and activities.

In that period in the United States, the number of priests in religious orders has fallen from 23,021 to 16,694; the numbers of brothers has dropped from 12,539 to 9,749 and the number of nuns from 181,431 to 146,314.

Studies have projected continued declines. A product of the late Middle Ages, the orders such as the Franciscans, Dominicans and Jesuits long have been the wellspring of the Church's academic and social creativity. But their cohesive mystique has waned in modern times.

"They're slowly disintegrating," Brother Moran commented, in discussing the often indignant reactions to his conclusion that they

have become moribund. If it wasn't valid, he added, "The screams wouldn't be so loud."

"It's apparently too threatening for the institutional Church to bear, and so the Church hangs on desperately to a system that's not working," he said. "It keeps withdrawing, fighting a kind of rearguard action, with fewer and fewer left in the organizations to take the drastic action necessary."

Brother Moran, 32, a professor of theology and education and also the elected superior of the Long Island-New England province of the Christian Brothers, has sounded his warning since 1970 in lectures, articles and books.

He maintains the religous order has lost its effectiveness, can no longer accomplish its purposes, has ceased to be a viable form of organization and thus, in effect, is dead, although thousands of people still are members.

That they still remain adherents offers a continuing, but gradually disappearing means for developing new modes of community religious life that can survive in modern times, he said.

He says this will require a total dismantling of the old forms which segregate men and women in different organizations, and the development of new communities including men and women, young and old, married and single, doing away with "all castes" and involving all kinds of Christians.

To accomplish this, however, would require a basic realignment of Church authority, he notes, including a change in the concept of the priesthood itself and eventually replacement of the present geographically based parish system.

Some tentative moves in this direction already are apparent in the so-called "floating parishes," and in the widespread tendency of order priests and nuns to leave the large religious houses and live in small groups in homes or apartments.

Indications are that "this style of life will be normative for the future," says the Rev. Paul M. Boyle, president of the Conference of Major Superiors of men's orders. However, he discounts Brother Moran's idea as that of a "modern Don Quixote."

Brother Moran, a graduate of the University of New Hampshire in his native state and with a Ph.D. from the Catholic University of

America, teaches at New York Theological Seminary and also runs a mobile school called "The Alternative."

Its 10 men and 10 women participants live in communal groupings, teaching their approach to others. He says the old organizations must be scuttled and replaced with something new, "something that's more human, that builds on qualities other than geography or sexual segregation."

He envisions a Church made up of a vast variety of cells or nuclei, each perhaps of a dozen or more people, based on mutual concerns, activities and dwelling units.

"We wish to create community forms that do not yet exist," he says.

dominant economic form. We will turn next to some types of movements which do not work within the framework of the "system."

Reactionary Movements

Many individuals want the "good old days." They may have actual memories of a time when they as individuals used another economic form, or they may have been told about how their family was mistreated in the development of a new way of life. A reactionary movement is a social structure through which individuals attempt to restore the dominance of an older economic logic or some of its attendant institutional patterns.

Monarchism, the Ku Klux Klan, certain nationalist movements which seek to restore an old aristocracy (some of them called fascist) are among the reactionary movements of the recent past.

Rebellion

A movement which seeks the destruction of the dominant social order is rebellion. Rebellion is distinguished from revolution or reaction by its lack of a vision or plan for a new social order.

Rebellions are particularly common in the history of European feudalism and American slavery. The Nat Turner uprising of the 1830s is an example of a rebellion against slavery. Nat Turner, a black slave, led other slaves in an uprising against their white masters in the state of Virginia. Robin Hood and his men and the Mafia have in common that they are examples of peasant rebellions against the power of the landed aristocracy in Europe.[1] Some of the present-day street fighting and gang warfare in United States cities have features of rebellion.

Communitarian Movements

People who choose the communitarian form of social movement attempt to physically and mentally escape the dominant community form by creating a radically different form.

In our own time the "dropout" community, or commune, and the religious communitarianism of people like the Amish and Hutterite are examples. These people have in common a profound dislike of the existing social order. Their solution is the creation of a radically different way of life based on a radically different economic strategy.

These are *intentional communities*. People thoughtfully construct what they think is a better way of life and attempt to live it with others of like mind. They do not seek to lead the masses or to transform the existing social order. People who use this form of movement toward change, unlike those using revolutionary movements, usually do not seek to help the masses understand what is wrong with the existing social order or to move the masses to struggling, through increased class conflict, for a better way.

Communitarianism is an old tradition in European history. It might more appropri-

[1] E. J. Hobshawm, *Primitive Rebels* (New York: Norton, 1959).

ately be called the recurrent heresy. Thousands of people—Gnostics, Maniceans, Unitarians, Huguenots, Waldensians, Cathars—have tried to establish a "truly Christian" community in this world. In so doing, they have often run head on into the established Church and its alliances with existing governments. There appear to be contradictory tendencies in Christian thought. One tendency emphasizes a better life here, and implies a small, self-sustaining community in which each person is responsible for leading a "Christian" life. This tendency is responsible for most of the religious communitarian movements. The other aspect of Christian thought regards an established Church as the necessary intermediary between the spiritual and secular worlds, and has often been at odds with the communitarian groups. Like the history of Europe, the history of the United States is also partially the history of communitarian experiments—which attempt to make a better community, to have a vision and to live it separate from those who are hopelessly caught up in the dominant system.[2] There were several hundred intentional communities in the United States in the 1800s.

[2] Arthur Bestor, *Backwoods Utopias* (Philadelphia: University of Pennsylvania Press, 1950), and Charles Nordhoff, *The Communistic Societies of the United States* (New York: Harper, 1875). For a more extensive bibliography of intentional communities, see Richard Fairfield, *Communes, USA* (Baltimore: Penguin, 1972).

Communes have a long history in the Western world. People have dreamed for centuries of creating a more perfect small community. (Alan Winston from Editorial Photocolor Archives)

Selection 7-6 shows a recent attempt at intentional community in Brazil. This example is given as a reminder of the diversity of communitarian movements—not all are spiritual, or "hip," or political in origin.

Marx and Engels both criticized communitarian movements as utopian—by which they literally meant "nowhere." They felt if people did achieve substantial changes in their lives, and threatened the patterns of capitalist society, they would be destroyed by outsiders. They argued that people could be sure of escaping the oppressions of an exploitative economy only when *all* their fellows had escaped.

Revolutionary Movement

Another way in which individuals relate to social change is through revolutionary move-ments. A revolutionary movement is first a group structure, as are all the social movements, in which people are using roles through which they hope to achieve significant social change.

Other distinguishing features of revolutionary movements are as follows.

1. Revolutionary movements offer a blueprint for a new social order, which implies a blueprint for a new economic strategy and some idea about the new institutional patterns that the new economic strategy will involve.

2. They hold the view that the new order can only be achieved through mass action which aims at radical transformation of the existing social order.

3. They offer a plan for increasing class consciousness and class conflict, which will

The merchants who organized these markets in medieval Europe were a revolutionary class. They united to destroy the feudal caste system in a revolution that took 400 years to complete. (Culver Pictures)

SELECTION 7-6: An unusual example of a communitarian movement.

THE CITY OF GOD

At first it resembles a college campus of the placid Eisenhower years, with fresh-faced girls strolling arm in arm among brick administration buildings and barracks-like dormitories while crew-cut youths roar past in secondhand sedans. A closer look, however, reveals something surreal about this 1950's idyll, for every "collegian" sports an identification tag and each building is patrolled by armed guards. The country is Brazil and the "campus" is the self-proclaimed City of God—headquarters for Bradesco, Latin America's largest private commercial bank, and home for 1,600 of its 20,000 employees. It is also the private domain of Amador Aguiar, the bank's founder and the city's benevolent despot.

Still ruggedly handsome at 69, Aguiar now says: "There is no distinction between Bradesco and the City of God. They are one and the same."

A Presbyterian convert and unflinching Calvinist, *titio* (uncle) Aguiar has clearly impressed his philosophy and life-style upon the city's inhabitants. A huge sign over the main building entrance reads, "Only Work Produces Wealth." While Aguiar avoids imposing his brand of worship on others, attendance is mandatory at the multifaith Thanksgiving and Christmas services. Drinking and long hair are cause for dismissal; smoking and idle talk are frowned upon.

Back Seat: Godliness, however is second to Bradesco. "Banking used to be a rich man's sport," says Mario Aguiar, the founder's youngest brother and a bank director. "Here, banking is a way of life." Youngsters learn rudimentary banking concepts in the third grade. Teen-agers graduate directly from high school into the banking operations; advanced students in such areas as computers and management theory must work at Bradesco for three years or repay the company for their education. Many employees accept lower salaries than they could earn outside. "You get the feeling that what you do is noticed and appreciated," said Walter Correa Fonseca, a former janitor who is the graphics-department director. "You feel you can go as far as you want."

The system seems to work. The bank's deposits recently topped $500 million and Bradesco continues to buy up small banks to expand its network of 448 branches. Besides its commercial, investment, saving and credit banks, the Bradesco Group includes such diversified enterprises as tourism, hotels, home-building, transportation, insurance and agricultural research—and total assets exceed $700 million. Most astonishing of all, however, is that the bank's extraordinary growth is due largely to small farmers, cattle raisers and individual depositors. "It's almost as if they want to show the 'big guy' what the common man can do," observed a rival banker. And Larry Fish, loan officer at the First National Bank of Boston in Rio de Janeiro, adds, "Bradesco is in a different league altogether, a different world."

To outsiders, the most impressive aspect of that world is its mind-numbing uniformity. Aguiar has decreed that workers will be served coffee and milk at 9 o'clock every morning and coffee and bread at 3 each afternoon, and that they will brush their teeth after every meal. Bradesco's eleven board members work together in one huge room, seated at two enormous oval tables; at each place are two telephones, a pencil holder and a few pads of paper. "The people here are conditioned to be the same," says Sidnei Batista, a Telex operator who lives in nearby Osasco. "You need a card to buy at the co-op supermarket, a card to eat in the dining room. No one touches money, everything is discounted from your paycheck. The guards are on top of you all the time. They get in a frenzy if you take off your ID card and put it in your pocket."

Predictably enough, such relentless pressure to conform has produced a high turnover in the City of God. Still, the town has grown rapidly and Aguiar is now planning a whole new City of God 100 miles northwest of São Paulo with housing for 12,000 to 15,000 people. A company town on that scale might present some obstacles even to Aguiar's despotism, but Bradesco's directors aren't worried. "If employees don't adapt well, they are asked to leave," says brother Mario. "But rarely do we have to let people go. They know what they're here for."

effect the failure and radical transformation of the old order.

Violence against the existing order is not a *necessary* characteristic of a revolutionary movement. Those who have a stake in the old order often stress violence in order to undermine the importance of a movement which seeks radical economic transformation and which further seeks to do this by moving masses of people to change. It is clear that revolutions are not necessarily violent, and that there is much violence directed against social arrangements which is not revolutionary.

The author of Selection 7-7 describes attempts in Chile and Peru to change the structure of economic activity of those two countries. Do these attempts constitute revolution? The author says they do. His description reveals some of the confusion about values that occurs with consequential social

In China, a climax in the long struggle against feudalistic and capitalistic social systems occurred when the Revolutionary Army entered Peking. (Eastfoto)

SELECTION 7-7:   Attempts at revolution?

AGRARIAN REFORMS OF CHILE AND PERU

By Johnathan Kendell

Huancayo, Peru

The two most extensive agrarian reforms in the modern history of South America are taking place in Chile and Peru with radically different approaches and results.

In Chile, a 30-month-old, freely elected Marxist government has swept aside huge feudal estates and replaced them with government-controlled cooperatives that may eventually be converted into state collectives.

But the process—portrayed by the government as a class struggle—has also been plagued by waves of rural violence and illegal seizures of farms smaller than the limit set by agrarian reform laws.

There has been no attempt to enlist non-Marxist agrarian technicians and managerial people nor has an effort been made to provide small private farmers with the security that would encourage them to make new investments in their properties.

At the same time, the government-controlled cooperatives, undercapitalized and often mismanaged, have in many cases failed to meet former productivity levels.

Peru's Reform

The agrarian crisis, coupled with a rise in the purchasing power of lower-income Chileans, has resulted in severe food shortages and rampant black-marketeering in the cities, with the prospect of full-scale rationing in the months ahead.

In Peru, a left-leaning military government, which took power through a bloodless coup in 1968, has engineered an agrarian reform as far-reaching as the Chilean program, though less disruptive and dramatic.

Implementing an ideology that the generals place "between capitalism and communism," the Peruvian government has moved quickly against the rural oligarchy—that one per cent of the population that owned about 80 per cent of the arable land.

Expropriating first the wealthiest estates—the sugar plantations along the coast—the government is now extending its reform program to the farms and ranches along the Andes mountains.

The blueprint calls for the creation of cooperatives owned by employes of the former estates, and a sharing of profits with nearby impoverished peasant and Indian communities.

Anniversary Report

But the government, pursuing a cautious policy that has thus far maintained agrarian production levels, actively recruits the technicians and administrators of the old estates.

"We are not going to destroy everything that existed before and start from nothing," said Ruben Barate, director of development at Tupac Amaru, a 540,000-acre cooperative that celebrated its third anniversary this week.

"Look at the troubles the Cubans had," he added. "Look at what is happening in Chile."

The cooperative, in the high Andes some 200 miles east of Lima, was seized from the Cerro Corporation, the large United States concern that still operates the nearby mines and copper-smelting plants.

Although some of the administrators left, most stayed on with the 400 ranch hands to take control of the 175,000 sheep and 4000 cattle.

They share ownership of the vast estate with about 3000 families in 16 backward Indian communities adjoining the grazing lands.

There has not yet been any dramatic economic breakthrough for these inhabitants of the chilly, windswept Sierra. And many of them skeptically view the reform as a simple change in bosses.

As they have for centuries, these stocky descendants of the Incas live in their crude, mud-brick huts alongside unpaved paths. From the 15,000-foot slopes where their flocks graze, they can look down at the rain clouds billowing like rushing rivers through the copper-red mountain crevices.

Potent Chica

At night the men gather to drink "chica"— a mild corn brew that takes on an uncanny potency at these heights—and to sing the bittersweet "huayno," the native verse of love, work and, mainly, escape:

Tomorrow I leave you,
Mountain, Fluttering my tattered scarf;
Leaving behind the sad life
I spent by your side.

But most of them get only as far as Huancayo, the main town in the valley below. On Sundays peasants swarm into the marketplace to chatter with friends in their native Quechuan and to supplement their meager incomes by hawking their handwoven tapestries.

"It is difficult to make them understand that a revolution does not happen overnight," said Dr. Maximo Gamarra, the veterinarian who was elected by the shepherds as general manager of Tupac Amaru. "The only meaningful change for them now is silver in their pockets."

But, Gamarra explained the bulk of the profits from the cooperative has been used to repay the government for the property's mortgage and then to reinvest in more livestock, paved roads and a trout farm. Later, possibly, money may be put into a wool-spinning plant.

"Patience is something these people have never lacked," said Gamarra, who was born in a nearby Indian village. "Someday they may even have faith."

change. Calls for revolutionary change in the United States come from many directions. Selection 7-8 reveals some of the thinking of a man who describes himself as a black revolutionary. Selection 7-9 shows the frequent use of the word *revolution* in recent commencement exercises at a private American university.

Much remains to be discovered about revolutions. Lacking a clear definition, much previous work has not asked the right questions about the kinds of mass movement that have taken place throughout recorded human history. We think a conflict analysis gives hope for a clearer understanding. Conflict analysis suggests a definition which focuses our attention on factors other than violence. These other factors—contradiction, mass consciousness, workability, and coherence of the economy—might be clues to the success or failure of revolutions as attempts to resolve the serious problems created by economic failure.

At what stage in economic development do contradictions become so serious as to produce mass disaffection? What is the relationship of a revolutionary party or of revolutionary leaders to the processes of contradiction, class consciousness, and class conflict? What kinds of values or ideals seem to carry over from the old order as motivators of self-sacrifice for a better way of life for future generations? All of these are difficult questions, to be sure. But if we believe history does not stop with the present, they are the kinds of questions which must be asked and for which answers must be seriously sought.

Life-style Changes

In discussing how individuals relate to the larger patterns of social change we have focused on social movements—movements involving roles, group structures, even institutional patterns people have devised through which they can cooperate with others toward changing social structures and elements of culture.

Perhaps change does not occur in so organized a fashion.

How organized were the bourgeois, those town dwellers who devised the manufacturing-commercial economic strategy that we have come to call capitalism? Is it possible the bourgeois only developed an organized movement long after they had individually accomplished the big changes in their lives which were the basis for a new way of surviving?

SELECTION 7-8:   Example of revolutionary rhetoric.

CARMICHAEL'S NEW IDEOLOGY FOR CHANGE

Stokely Carmichael showed an audience of 500 persons last night that time has made some changes in his style and ideology.

"In 1966, 1967 and 1968, Stokely was yelling 'Go out and kill them,' " he told the crowd that gathered for his first Bay Area appearance in two years. "In 1973, such a speech would be a waste of time and we would have missed the boat."

Dressed in a tan lightweight suit, the former leader of the Student Non-Violent Coordinating Committee, black power advocate and now avowed Pan Africanist, outlined his theory of systematic and scientific revolution to the predominantly black audience at the North Peralta Community College gymnasium.

"Struggles move forward, they progress. And the form of the struggles changes," he said in a West Indian accent laced with a West African lilt.

"We must seek and create a new system through a scientific and systematic program. We must be preoccupied with building, not destroying."

He said the emphasis now was on a real change in the system: "Not reform—that's civil rights."

Blacks must stop screaming revolution and sit down to study and research what it really means, he said.

"We will begin to think as men of action and act as men of thought," Carmichael said.

Carmichael, 31, is the head of the African Peoples' Revolutionary Party which advocates a socialist system. The party, headquartered in Conakry, Guinea, where Carmichael has made his home, has been active over the past few years in underground "guerrilla" activity, which Carmichael said advances the cause of freedom for all African people.

change is usually simply a *recombination* of existing cultural and social structural elements into something slightly different. A woman who becomes a jockey, flies a plane for relaxation, writes poetry as an avocation, and says having children is for others is not changing social structure or culture. She is simply taking roles and bits of culture (for example, planes and a bachelor belief system which were formerly exclusive property of men), and combining them in a new way.

Some Americans believe that experimentation with individual life-styles can produce changes in social systems as radical as those achieved by revolutionary methods. (Mary D. Howard)

It is unclear whether experiments in changing individual life-styles ever become the basis for revolutionary change. A life-style

SELECTION 7-9: Varying uses of the term *revolution*.

'GREAT REVOLUTIONARY EFFORT NEEDED TO SAVE THE NATION'

They wrote their speeches independently and approached the subject in different ways, but there was a common thread tying together the talks given during the 82d annual Commencement and its related events.

That thread was Watergate and what the Class of 1973 might do about it.

The 2400 who received diplomas June 17 under a sunny sky heard a lot about Watergate, and not just because it was the event's first anniversary:

"Scandal . . . institutional reform . . . political disillusionment . . . Diogenes . . . cynicism . . . revolutionary effort . . . elective form of monarchy . . . countervailing forces . . . the silence of the good people."

These were a few of the key words spoken by John U. Monro, the Commencement speaker; by President Richard W. Lyman (see below); by Professor Gordon Wright, Class Day Speaker; and the Rev. John C. Bennett at the Baccalaureate service.

Monro, director of freshman studies at Miles College, Birmingham, warned the graduating seniors in an audience of 10,000 that "a great revolutionary effort" will be required to take our country back from the "men and interests" who have stolen it from us since World War II.

"All of us," he said, "face a deeply revolutionary time of trial . . . it seems clear that the next few years will not be a happy or comfortable time if we want to leave behind us a decent world for our children to live in."

He compared the coming struggle to Martin Luther King's efforts for black people: "this important black revolution went on inside our institutional structure, utilizing our institutional structure, despite the war in Vietnam, despite filibusters, despite White Citizens Councils, despite bombings, despite white moderate apathy, despite the intensive bugging and harassment of the black leadership by the FBI, despite the murder of leaders and the official killing of students and city rioters and demonstrators.

"The revolution went on because brave men and women by the hundreds and thousands committed themselves to an ideal of freedom, broke out of the mold of their daily lives, and were ready to witness with their bodies, to march in the streets, in short—to pay the classic price for their freedom."

It was, Monro said, "the kind of revolution that is at the heart of the American dream—a triumph of people over oppression."

He said "our masters are using the battle cry of 'national security'—and they are going to fool a lot of good people."

What have been and are the diversity of life-styles? Were and are there great variations in life-styles within noncapitalist economic strategies? Are life-style variations only possible when the economy is booming, because frequent life-style changes sell more clothes, cars, and other material things? Selection 7-10 describes the life-style of the "poor rich" in the United States. Under what conditions might new life-styles become the basis for social movements? Is there a connection between the "hip" life-style and organized attempts for social change in the United States? These are some of the questions raised when we examine the concept *life-style*.

Although new life-styles do not in themselves constitute social change, or necessarily lead to social change, still we wonder what the connection is between individual changes in life-style and social change.

The people of Roseto, Pennsylvania (Selection 7-11), have changed their life-style. It seems that in adopting an "American" life-style they have begun to experience some of its contradictions. Will this lead to pressure toward *social* change? Or will people stop at changing their diet and exercise patterns?

SELECTION 7-10:   Changes in life-style.

THE POOR RICH: TOUGH JOB OF MAKING IT ON $30,000 A YEAR

By David Shaw

They are in their mid-30s to late 40s now, but they were young children during the Depression, and the deprivation of those early, impressionable years has left its scars.

They are making good money, some of these Depression children—$20,000, $25,000, $30,000 a year—and they live in nice, split-level homes and drive big, late-model cars and take vacations in Hawaii and Europe and winter weekends in Palm Springs and Las Vegas.

They are not wealthy, really—no chauffeurs or private jets or $30-a-bottle wine when they eat out—but by the standards of their parents (and most of their less fortunate contemporaries) they are comfortable, well-off, seemingly without financial worries.

"That's what you think," says one such man, a $27,000-a-year executive with three children and a house filled with the material evidence of his success.

"We're the rich poor"—smiling—"or the poor rich."

Winston, an architect:

"We heard our parents bitching all the time, even after the Depression, about not being able to afford this and having to do without that, and when I started getting a good salary, my wife and I decided, by God, we didn't have to do without any more.

"We didn't get extravagant, but we spend what I make—you know, big color TV in the living room, the best stereo components in the family room, another color TV in the kids' room, good-quality clothes, all the kitchen and workshop gadgets you can think of.

"By the time I get through writing checks for the monthly credit card bills and the mortgage and taxes and all, there's nothing left.

"You look at my paycheck and inside my house and my garage and you'd think I've got it made. But I don't have any investments—no stock portfolio or real estate or bonds or anything but about $1,700 in the bank.

"I'm not set for retirement or a big disaster or anything but living day-to-day. We live well —don't get me wrong—it's just that if I got hurt bad or lost my job, like a lot of those aerospace guys, I'd have to start selling everything —fast—to pay the bills.

"It makes me feel kind of, well, trapped, insecure . . . stupid."

Browning, the poet, said it best—"A man's reach should exceed his grasp or what's a heaven for."

Leonard, an aerospace executive:

"For years, aerospace was a unique situation. When you got out of college, you had your choice of four or five good offers, all with salaries much higher than what the other graduates were starting at.

"Your raises were predictable, too. You knew pretty much what to expect every year, so you spent it before you actually got it.

"The potential of the industry seemed unlimited, and you got to feeling your potential was unlimited, too. The philosophy seemed to be 'keep reaching beyond what you have.'

"Credit is easy to come by in this bracket; that's another problem. You can borrow a month's salary on your signature; no collateral or cosigner. That's quite a temptation.

"You don't have the capital that, say, a doctor your age has, so you can't invest like he does. But, what the hell, you're living well, you figure, and the way aerospace is booming, you certainly aren't afraid of any job crisis, so you don't really worry much about accumulating a cash reserve or an investment portfolio. You're enjoying life too much.

"Then, when the crash finally comes, where are you?"

Social legislation, unionization and employe benefits have all expanded greatly since the Depression, protecting today's wage earner against many of the catastrophes confronted by his father and grandfather . . . and, often, providing him with a false sense of security.

The modern worker in this income bracket invariably has a good hospitalization policy. He has paid sick leave. He probably has a small pension coming. He may even buy some form of paycheck insurance—paying a small monthly premium to be guaranteed substantial income should injury force him to stay off work for any length of time.

Other Protections

Then there is state disability insurance and unemployment insurance and Social Security and—as a last resort—welfare. He will not wear $200 suits and drive a Porsche on that, but, at least, he will eat. And he is sure he can adapt to a lower standard of living. So why worry about saving for a rainy day? The boss and the government have umbrellas open and waiting for you already.

Jack, an engineer:

"I hear guys at work talking about their boats in the marina and their Corvettes and swimming pools. What it comes down to is they buy everything they can afford. No, not afford. They buy everything they have the cash or credit to pay for, even if they can't actually afford it.

"I guess I've had six, seven foreign sports cars in the last 10 years, I could do without them. I could move out of Palos Verdes, back to Gardena. But damn it, I've worked for my money and I feel I deserve these things.

"We wanted to go to Europe, you know, but then I got laid off. That'll have to wait awhile now, I guess. Same with the high-frequency electronic oven we wanted to get.

"Still, I was luckier than most, I got called back a couple of times, and my dad left me a little money. Now I got another good job, so I wasn't hurt too much by the layoff. You should've seen some of the other guys at TRW, though.

Financial Illusion

"With what they were making, you would've thought they could breeze through a couple or three months off, without even dipping too far into their savings.

"It didn't work out that way. They had to stop eating out and stop buying a lot of clothes and a lot of them sent the wife back to work or took part-time jobs themselves, like tending bar. They don't like it either. They're really griping."

SELECTION 7-11: Changes in life-style, and the effects of these changes.

THE AMERICANIZATION OF ROSETO

By Bill Richards

Roseto, Pa.—For the last dozen years this community of 1600 heavy-eating Italians has happily borne the title of "Miracle Town" because of its inhabitants' proclivity for cholesterol—rich food and their apparent immunity to heart attack.

Startled researchers discovered in the early 1960s that citizens of Roseto ritually sit down to meals that would send most doctors reaching for their blood-pressure gauges and electrocardiogram machines.

Yet not one person under 47 ever had a recorded heart attack. In Roseto, people seemed to eat more and live ten to 20 years longer than nearly anywhere else.

* * *

But the so-called "miracle" of Roseto is over. The town's heart-attack rate soared to three times the national average last year and the blame, according to those who have sought to explain the phenomenon, lies in the fact that residents of Roseto, for better or worse, are becoming "Americanized."

"There's no question about it," said the Rev. Genaro Leone, pastor of Our Lady of Mt. Carmel, the town's imposing Roman Catholic church. "We have joined the rat race. In the last five years our people have begun living higher than they should. This fast life just doesn't agree with us."

Father Leone noted 20 deaths last year in the small black death registry he keeps in his office safe. "Twenty years ago," the priest said sadly, "we might have had seven or eight, but no more."

* * *

Even more ominous are the heart attacks. They are beginning to strike down people in Roseto at an age that was once considered youthful here. A dozen deaths last year resulted from heart attacks, two suffered by men in their early 40s.

The residents of Roseto, 24 miles northeast of Allentown, have always been somewhat set apart from their neighbors, descendants of English and Welsh miners who came to eastern Pennsylvania during the last century to own and work quarries in what is known as the region's "slate belt."

Citizens in Roseto trace their roots to the dozen or so immigrants who came in 1882 from the small southern Italian farming villages of Roseto, Valfortore, Foggia. The Italians established themselves on a hillside and began working in the slate quarries as laborers for 50 cents a day.

They developed a local reputation for their boisterous and close-knit town life. Roseto today is still 95 per cent Italian.

The ability of the citizens of Roseto to consume huge quantities of food has become legend. Local family gatherings center around meals lasting six or more hours, and residents still boast to outsiders that their town has some of the biggest and best eaters in the United States.

Generations of meals featuring prosciutto, homemade pasta and a local favorite called "scarpetti"—green peppers fried in lard with bread dipped in a rich lard-based gravy—have had their effect on the Roseto physique, which runs toward the short and heavy side.

Despite the high cholesterol diet, the town's rate of arteriosclerotic heart disease in 1961 was only one-third of the national average of 3.59 per 1000 males and a mere one-fourth of other non-Italian towns nearby.

A medical sociologist from the University of Texas medical branch at Galveston, Dr. John G. Bruhn, led a research team to Roseto to study the phenomenon in 1961. He returned two years ago with another group of medical and social researchers for a follow-up study.

What the researchers discovered was that while the diet in Roseto had not changed, nearly everything else in the town had.

"We were stunned," said Bruhn. "There was a very obvious change under way. The men belong to country clubs and play golf. Their kids drive fancy cars and go away to college. Everyone is making and spending money as fast as they can."

* * *

The research team found that in their ten-year absence, the average family income in Roseto had jumped from $7000 to $11,300. A number of men from the town had office and managerial jobs that forced them to commute 20 to 30 miles from their homes.

Furthermore, the close family and town life also had changed dramatically, Bruhn said.

"In 1961 I never saw a Roseto family sit down to a meal where everyone wasn't at the table together," he said. "Now they run in, grab something to eat, and run out again."

The Texas researchers found that added to the former easy-going lifestyle in Roseto was the stress of earning enough to demonstrably keep up with each other.

Bruhn used the term "Americanization" to describe what has taken place in the town.

The streets of Roseto now are lined with big, expensive cars. Television antennas line the roof tops, and many of the sets are color.

Lots that stood empty for years now have costly brick and stone homes on them, and older houses show evidence of extensive remodeling.

"I think the term 'Americanization' fits us pretty well," said Roseto's mayor, Charles Angelini. "When that happens I guess you have to take the good with the bad."

* * *

Dr. Bruhn and his fellow researchers contend that the new stresses of day-to-day competition and the breakdown of the old communal life of the town, rather than its bad eating habits, have played a major part in the rising heart-attack rate.

"We have found, here and elsewhere, that many heart-attack victims are essentially loners who have nowhere else to turn when the pressure is on," said Bruhn. He contends that cholesterol, while significant, does not play the major role in heart attacks.

"In Roseto," he said, "family and community support is disappearing. Most of the men who have had heart attacks here were living under stress and really had nowhere to turn to relieve that pressure. These people have given up something to get something, and it's killing them."

One of the few truly working-class revolutions in modern history was the Bolshevik seizure of power in Russia in 1918. (Sovfoto)

SUMMARY

In this chapter we begin to answer the question, "What is pushing us from behind?" We do not think that we are isolated in a small puddle of a big history, but that there have been larger forces at work throughout history. Some of these forces are social forces—processes started by humans using particular ways of surviving.

It seems to us that the past history of human use of social tools, particularly economic strategies, continues to shape the strategies we use today. This chapter is devoted to looking at the historical process of change—the big picture, of which changes in specific social structures and cultures are a part.

In the first half of the chapter, the historical process is defined in terms of a conflict perspective. The assumptions of conflict analysis are restated. Specifically, these assumptions are that a single economic strategy dominates a time and place, that contradictions within that economic strategy produce classes and class conflict, and that class conflict is the major force shaping social institutional patterns. Conflict analysis suggests that this *is* the historical process insofar as the history of human social patterns are concerned.

Four great economic strategies have been

developed in what we know about human history. The first strategy is gathering wild foods, mainly vegetables and fruits. The second is hunting large animals. The third is sedentary agriculture, the cultivating of plants and the domesticating of animals. The fourth, machine-based, is the industrial conversion of raw materials.

The use of each of these economic strategies shapes a community form with institutional patterns and a culture unique to it. Familism, tribalism, feudalism, and capitalism are the terms used to describe the different community strategies.

Four basic social processes are at work to transform people's way of life as they specialize in the use of a particular economic strategy. One of these processes is the tendency to change patterns from older forms so that they better fit the dominant economic strategy. The second is class conflict, which arises out of contradictory relations of different people to the economic structure. The third is imperialism, the attempts by users of one economic strategy to take the resources and to transform the culture and social structure of other communities in order to harness others' labor power to their own ends. The fourth process is experimentation. Persons marginal to, displaced from, or for whom dominant community forms have become unusable experiment with new economic strategies. In time of collapse or revolutionary change within a community, some of their experiments provide the basis for a new community form.

The second half of the chapter raises the question, "How are individuals related to the historical process of change?"

Conflict analysis assumes that several kinds of social change will take place if contradiction, class, class conflict, and radical transformation are the major dimensions of social change. Several types of social change are discussed: individual compatible change, unorganized class conflict, compatible social movement, reactionary movement, rebellion, communitarian movement, and revolutionary movement.

In Chapters 8 and 9, we will show how some of the historical evidence supports a conflict analysis of tribalism and feudalism. At the same time we will indicate how the emergence and radical transformation of these community forms set "waves" in motion that are still affecting us today.

SUGGESTED READINGS

Deborah Babcox and Madeline Balkin (eds.), *Liberation: New Writings from the Women's Liberation Movement* (New York: Dell, 1971).

Richard Fairfield, *Communes, U.S.A.: A Personal Tour* (Baltimore: Penguin, 1972).

Philip S. Foner (ed.), *The Black Panthers Speak* (Philadelphia: J. B. Lippincott, 1970).

John R. Howard, *The Cutting Edge: Social Movements and Social Change in America* (Philadelphia: J. B. Lippincott, 1974).

Charles Nordhoff, *The Communistic Societies of The United States* (New York: Harper & Brothers, 1875, Dover edition, New York, 1966).

William Irwin Thompson, *At the Edge of History* (New York: Harper & Row, 1971).

Thomas Wagstaff (ed.), *Black Power: The Radical Response to White America* (Beverly Hills: Glencoe Press, 1969).

Tribalism provides roles through which different clans or extended family groups are connected. It creates a single belief system— a conventional wisdom and morality—to which all roles are directly related.

A tribal form emerges out of the hunting of large animals as the means of producing food. As the logic of this way of life develops, people using the tribal form do learn other means of subsistence. They often plant the seeds of wild grains, vegetables, and fruits and harvest them. This, however, is not sedentary agriculture such as that giving rise to feudal economies (see Chapter 9). The plots of rye, corn, or pumpkins of tribal people are moved from year to year as the people follow big game animals or domestic cattle herds. The tribes come back to the harvest after the hunt, just as they might visit a nearby grove of wild fruit trees.

The roles used by those in a tribal community—for example, warrior, hunter, vegetable gatherer, child-raiser, hide tanner—are all related directly to a set of ideas about what is good for *all* the people, ideas that are not open to negotiation. Being a good hunter does not depend on convincing customers, wives, children, or in-laws that one is a good hunter. Whether or not one is a good hunter is known directly through the beliefs about hunting which are shared by all. Linkages between beliefs and roles are stressed much more than linkages between one role and another (mother-son, for example). Roles are thus less institutionalized, and role performance is less negotiable, less open to change. There is little role conflict in the use of the tribal community form because first loyalty is to the community, not to users of other roles (son, daughter, friend, employer, father, mother). The belief system should provide the answer to any conflict, for the beliefs should be simple enough to integrate all roles and to provide answers to potential problems. Tribal communities are tight—tight because they are simple, with each role a part of a logic that is known, experienced, and agreed to by all. The logic is simple because hunting and gathering are simple ways of subsistence, with simple technologies.

In analyzing tribal social structure and culture, it is difficult to separate people from roles: Peoples' relations with others seem largely a function of their age, sex, and personality.

Tribal Culture

The most important cultural feature of tribalism is the set of ideas which gives community-wide meaning to all roles. Perhaps this will be easier to understand if we look at caste- and class-structured communities, where the moral core is less important. Caste roles are integrated through the idea of a naturally differentiated social order: that is, some people are destined to be serfs or slaves, others to be rulers. There is no idea in feudal culture that "being a peasant is good for the community"; one is a peasant because one was destined to be a peasant, and because following one's destiny is good. In the tribal community, each role is directly accountable to a set of ideas about community good— to a common morality having its roots in the mode and means of production of food. This morality is more complex than the kinship beliefs of scattered vegetable-gathering clans and small game hunters, but simpler than the caste and class cultures of agricultural and industrial economies.

The morality flows from the observability to all of the economics of survival. Once different clans are brought into relationships with each other (and how this is accom-

plished is somewhat unclear), all can see the benefits of producing more meat on a more predictable schedule, and the skills and technologies used in the process. By contrast the technologies, skills, and problems of people policing streets, doing surgery, or making cars in the United States today are largely invisible to people who do not do these things. But when experience teaches—that is, when the mode and means of production allow people to know *from their own experience* what is good for all—a universal moral code is possible. This morality is generally embellished, made symbolic, and ritualized, so that it will be easier to use, and will serve as a constant reminder of the underlying structures of tribal life. It is often expressed in the same terms that are used to explain the rhythms of animal life. In this way the culture used by tribal people reflects a logic inherent in primary dependence on hunting and mobile horticulture (plant cultivation).

Selection 8-1, a tribal prayer of native Americans of the Great Plains, shows the intense concern of the tribal person for the life of all the people within the tribe.

Figure 8-1 shows tribal social structure as a large circle within which bands, represented by individuals coming from separate tents, are linked to each other through their common linkage to a set of ideas, the moral core or conventional wisdom, represented by the central circle. The dashed lines between the individuals and the bands represent the possibility of private or secret arrangements between them, but suggest that such linkages are distinctly subordinate to the obligations of the person to the total community.

TRIBAL LIFE AND THE MORAL CORE

Some of the daily events of tribal life are best seen in the lives of native American peoples, who, as a result of their fatal encounter with European capitalism in the

SELECTION 8-1

A NATIVE AMERICAN PRAYER

Great mystery you existed
from the first.
The sky, the earth you created.
Great mystery—look upon me.
Pity me, that the people may live.
Earth, father of all, I make this offering.
Pity me. Wisest of all, I make this offering.
Pity me.
Spirit creatures of the four winds
To you I offer this pipe
That the people may live.
North—this day no other creature may
be mentioned, before the face of the North.
Let the people live.
Sunrise, no other creature may be mentioned.
May there be no adversity
that the people may live.
West, nation of thunderers
give me a good day
that the people may live.
Great mystery—you are mighty.
Pity me, that the nation may live.
Great mystery—help me with an omen
that the people may live.

SELECTION 8-2

TRIBAL LIFE AS SEEN BY A NATIVE AMERICAN IN 1870

Black Elk

HOLY MAN OF THE OGLALA SIOUX

In the moon of Making Fat (June), Sitting
Bull and Gall had a sun dance at Forest Butte,
and afterwards we went hunting again. A man
by the name of Iron Tail was with me this
time, and we were out alone. I killed a big fat
bison cow and we were butchering, when a
thunder storm was coming up. Then it began
to pour rain, and I heard a voice in the clouds
that said, "Make haste. Before the day is out
something will happen!" Of course, when I
heard this, I was excited and told Iron Tail I had
heard a voice in the clouds and that we must
hurry up and go. We left everything but the
fat of the cow and fled. When we got to the
camp of our little band, we were excited and
told the people we must flee. So they broke
camp and started. We came to Muddy Creek.
It was still raining hard and we had trouble
getting across because the horses sank in the
mud. A part of us got across, but there was an
old man with an old woman and a beautiful
daughter whose pony-drag got stuck in the
middle of the creek. Just then a big band of
Crows came charging and there were so many
of them that we could not hold them off and
we had to flee shooting back at them as they
came after us. There was a man called Brave
Wolf who did a very great deed there by the
ford that day. He was close to the pony-drag
of the two old people and the beautiful girl
when it got stuck in the mud, so he jumped off
his horse, which was a very fast bison-runner,
and made the beautiful girl get on. Then he
stood there by the two old people and fought
until all three were killed. The girl got away
on his fast horse. My cousin, Hard-to-Hit, did
a brave deed too, and died. He charged back
alone at a Crow who was shooting at a Lakota
in a bush, and he was killed. The voice in the
clouds had told the truth, and it seemed that
my power was growing stronger all the time.
When my cousin, Hard-to-Hit, was killed, it was
my duty to protect his wife, so I did; and we
got lost from our little party in the dark. It
rained all night, and my cousin's wife cried so
hard that I had to make her quit for fear some
enemy might hear her and find us. When we
reached the big camp in the morning, my relatives began mourning for my cousin, Hard-to-
Hit. They would put their arms across each
other's shoulders and wail. They did this all day
long, and I had to do it too. I went around
crying, "hownh, hownh," and saying over and
over: "My cousin—he thought so much of me
and I thought so much of him, and now he is
dead. Hownh, hownh." I liked my cousin well
enough, but I did not feel like crying all day.
This was what I had to do and it was hard
work.

form of the Caucasian invasion of America,
have been the most systematically observed
of all the peoples using tribal economies. In
some ways the tribalism of the native Americans was unique, affected as it was by the
introduction from Europe of the domesti-

cated horse and steel, but we feel the richness of the environment allowed the native Americans to develop the tribal form to the full extent of its logic.

Selection 8-2, which is a bit of the life story of Black Elk, who was a young man during the last drive to put the Sioux on reservations, tells much. It illustrates the essentials of tribal life: the hunt, and the fear of other tribes contesting the hunting grounds; the visions which are ways of grasping a little bit of the power at the center of the mysteries of life; the rituals through which both these mysteries and the

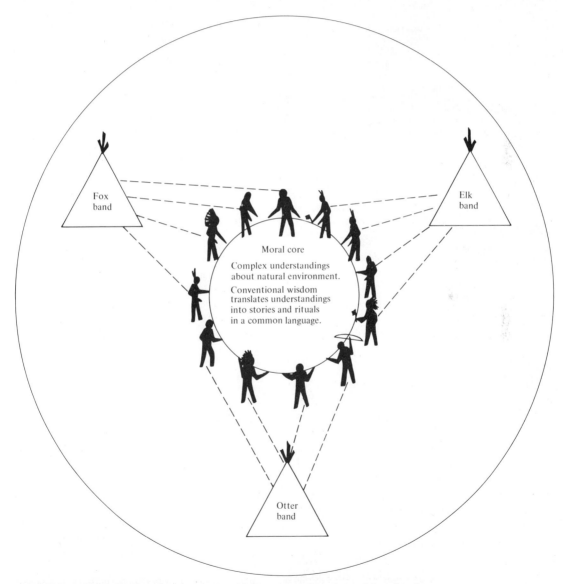

FIGURE 8-1 Tribal social structure. Kinship groups (bands) are bound together by common acceptance of a moral core. This belief system emphasizes responsibility of individuals to the tribe over responsibility to kin or other individuals.

The life of the hunter is dangerous and often lonely. A strong sense of unity with his people and with the forces which sustain animal and plant life support the hunter's life. (De Wys/EPA)

moral core are expressed and kept alive even when it is "hard work" for a fifteen-year-old boy.

The tribal form requires young men to give up their lives for members of the tribe, even those not from their own families, as in Black Elk's story. It requires them to subject their whole lives to the search for a closer relationship to those ideas which bind the community together—a search for what white Europeans have loosely translated "power." To women it meant a life of very hard work. To all native Americans it meant a very complex wisdom which might be lived or felt, but not known directly. This search occupied much of Black Elk's life; but it was a search which not all wished to pursue. Tribal logic is uniform; the people are not.

Young Sitting Bear of the Kiowa who had not had a vision said: "That's the way it is with me. Power is hard. It's hard to have and it's hard to keep. All our lives we've seen our father worrying about taking care of his power. All that it's done has been to keep him alive to old age. It's hard work for him. It doesn't make him happy. That's not the way I want it to be with me. I want my life now while I can enjoy it. I want to get what there is out of it while it can make me happy. You're different. You're like our father (speaking to his brother). You're not afraid to be old."[1]

[1] Alice Marriott, *The Ten Grandmothers* (Norman, Okla.: University of Oklahoma Press, 1945), p. 92.

The relationship between the moral core and daily life in tribal communities is exemplified in the following two cultural ideas. There was a belief among the Sioux that if the men lost their bravery, the rains would fail to come. There was another idea that if the women lost their chastity—if they committed adultery—the buffalo would disappear.[2] White Europeans, looking at the tribal community through their own cultural framework, judge these ideas "superstitious" and "primitive." Looked at through the logic of tribalism, they make a lot of sense.

The availability of food to the Sioux was the end result of a complex process which began with rain. Rain brought grass to the high plains. The grass sustained buffalo. The Sioux man, if he was brave, killed the buffalo. Killing a buffalo is a very dangerous thing to do. If the Sioux men lost their bravery, the rains might as well have failed to come, for their product—the buffalo—would have had no meaning, no existence, no social consequence for the tribe. The Sioux women had to maintain close social ties in order to work together to gather chokecherries and currants, to tan hides and sew teepee covers. If a woman were to openly commit adultery, this closeness would be destroyed by jealousy; the bonds between women of different families would be threatened. In turn, the women would be unable to maintain the necessary level of contribution to the tribal economy which would enable the men to be free to hunt. Again, the buffalo would "disappear," that is, would have no social meaning for the people. These examples are but two of a complex set of ideas relating the people to the tools of hunting, to the animals, and to the earth which sustains them.

The moral core of a tribal community attempts to describe and convey in understandable terms the life-support processes; the ecology of an area. This set of ideas must in turn be related to human social life; it must tell the people how to relate to one another in order to use the land successfully. The specific content of the moral core will differ significantly in areas which have different life-support processes—for example, coastal areas as opposed to plains areas.

Analysis of the Life of Hunting People

To analyze the life of a typical hunting people we must search for larger patterns which help us understand the separate events of daily life. For the natives of the American plains, the day-to-day events included all-male councils for making decisions, vision seeking by young men, sharing of childrearing by nonkin, periodic communal dancing, communal distribution of meat and the belongings of dead persons, communal tool and shelter making, warfare in which bravery was more important than killing, and much more. As we have said, conflict analysis predicts that the mode of production (hunting) and the tools of production (bows, arrows, spears) will shape the other parts of life. Showing how this happens is really a functional analysis, for it emphasizes that other parts of life will function to support a particular mode and means of production. Before we raise the question of how contradictions and classes might develop within tribalism to produce conflicts which further shape and ultimately disrupt the tribal way of life, let us briefly analyze how the logic of hunting shapes social structures.

Tribalism starts and sustains itself in the following way. It is obvious that in some environments, groups larger than the family will have an advantage in the struggle for survival. The problem is to fix people's loyalties to a group which includes people out-

[2] Mari Sandoz, *These Were the Sioux* (New York: Hastings House, 1961).

side the family. The solution seems to be the creation of a body of wisdom which summarizes how the group can better survive when the individual makes decisions which put community welfare before family welfare wherever there is a potential conflict between the two. The ideas will be expressed simply so that people may relate to their complexity without too much talking —"with their heart" as the Sioux said. The ideas will often be expressed in dance or through symbols, totems, feathers, beadwork, or small statues. The dancing and the objects make the ideas more real, allowing people to relate to them easily, and in turn make the community form more real.

There are four general and recurring problems in the tribal way of organizing people:

1. The problem of preventing factions from developing—preventing the community from splitting into competing groups.
2. The problem of preventing some individuals from becoming so powerful that some people might seek their favor rather than the favor of the community.
3. The problem of making the community real to the individual so that there is something larger than the family to relate to.
4. The problem of creating in the individual both general and specific responsibilities to the community.

Detailed study of tribal communities shows that the patterns of social life—the social structure, the way of doing things every day —constantly produce structures which solve these problems. Daily life is part of a very sophisticated system in which all acts are linked to the central purposes of creating and sustaining the moral core and the individual's ties to it through the roles used.

Each bit of daily life solves several of the major problems listed above at the same time. For example, let us take the task of

policing. Policing involves hurrying stragglers when the group moves, and making sure that eager young men do not jeopardize the hunt or a war party by dashing in before others are ready. Rotating the policing tasks among several people has the following advantages:

1. The people are not split into factions —those using police roles against those not using police roles.
2. It is not possible for an individual to accumulate power of the kind that comes from being a policeman all the time.
3. By seeing the community not only from the point of view of policing but also from the view of many other tasks, an individual can see the community as a whole; a full-time policemen may tend to see the community in terms of good guys–bad guys, or policemen–not policemen.
4. The responsibility of policing can be seen to result in good for the whole community, thus creating a linkage of the individual who is policing to the whole community—a sense of fulfillable responsibility to something larger than the self.

The same kind of analysis may be done with other aspects of tribal life. Dancing like other living creatures brings one closer in a nonverbal way to the truths of how those creatures live. Dancing like the bear, for example, if done with careful attention, brings one closer to how the bear lives as a hunter in the same world in which the Sioux hunt. One can then speak of getting bear "power," the sense of knowing through the dance the bear way of relatedness to earth and life. The existence of many ritual times at which a man must give away horses prevents the emergence of extremely wealthy individuals and at the same time creates occasions on which the whole community comes together in celebration of itself and its way of doing things.

There were even ways to be different, so long as these ways seemed dedicated to the celebration or renewal of the tribal morality or did not interfere with tribal life. Black Elk told of his cousin, Crazy Horse:

> [F]or he was a queer man and would go about the village without noticing people or saying anything. In his own tepee he would joke, and when he was on the warpath with a small party, he would joke to make his warriors feel good. But around the village he hardly ever noticed anybody except little children. All the Lakotas like to dance and sing; but he never joined a dance, and they say nobody ever heard him sing. But everybody liked him, and they would do anything he wanted or go anywhere he said. . . . He was a queer man. Maybe he was always part way into that world of his vision.[3]

In such ways the bits of daily life were part of a larger pattern of morality generated by the hunt and the simplicity of hunting technology.

CONTRADICTIONS, CONFLICT, AND CHANGE IN TRIBAL LIFE

Tribal life is extremely resistant to change. It does not produce a surplus that may be stored beyond a year, and hence does not produce classes with different interests in (or different shares of) surplus value. The only division in tribal life in which people stand in different relations to the mode and tools of production is that between men and women. Although sexual oppression seems (to us) a remarkable feature of most tribal life, we know of no instance in which sexual oppression made hunting impossible. However, few conflict analyses of tribal life have been made, and no one to date has reanalyzed tribal histories to look for this predictable possibility.

[3] John G. Neihardt, *Black Elk Speaks* (New York: William Morrow, 1932), p. 87.

Tribal life did center around conflict. Many tribes tried to get meat from the same herds of big game animals. In the northern American plains, the Crow, Cheyenne, Pawnee, Sioux, Shoshone, and others all chased the same animals and fought each other for the rights to hunt these animals. For the losers in intertribal warfare, hunting became a less workable way of life. The Pawnee, for example, began in the mid-1800s to rely more on squash and corn, as did the Arikaree and Mandan further north. A contradiction in tribalism is that the stronger the moral core, the more the people are bound to their own tribe and the less able they are to cooperate with others in dividing hunting grounds. The resultant warfare has two consequences: (1) the destruction of the hunting economy for some; (2) the inability to combine against outside invaders (as, for example, the Europeans).

Tribal histories also illustrate the contradictory tendency of economies to have more and more population problems as they become more successful. We have already described (Selection 4-7) the development of caste-based agricultural society in Peru as successful tribalists ran out of living room.

COLONIALISM AND TRIBALISM: ECONOMIC CONFLICT AS A DESTROYER OF COMMUNITY FORMS

Since tribal life reflects the lack of contradictory relations to surplus value, and hence lacks significant class conflict, the tribal form is often changed only through outside interference.

Many tribal peoples gave up their economies and hence their way of life only through conflict with people possessing other economies and superior power.

The history of the native Americans illustrates the great force which is economic imperialism, by which people using economies which support better organized and technically more powerful warfare destroy other economies and ways of life to gain raw materials and/or slaves and in time markets for their products. This form of conflict has as much effect, and is as powerful a shaping force on social structure and culture, as the forces of internal contradiction. Some economic imperialism reflects population contradictions in other economies. Peasants who were surplus to European feudalism invaded the hunting grounds of the native Americans. Some economic imperialism reflects attempts to suppress internal class conflict, as, for example, in the United States, where the power structure appeases a potentially volatile working class by making material comforts relatively easy to acquire. It must be remembered, however, that such comforts are too often available because the resources and labor of weaker nations have been exploited through economic coercion or force of arms.

Although economic conflict occurs wherever people use different institutional or group arrangements for solving the economic problem (for example, the Appalachian coal companies versus the Appalachian subsistence farmers), the most bitter forms of conflict arise out of the contact of people using totally different economies and community forms. The attempt to totally destroy people using another form is called *genocide*. Selection 8-3 illustrates genocide as a form of internal colonialism. Other examples abound: Bureaucratically organized West Pakistanis have committed genocide against tribally organized East Pakistanis, and Russian urbanites have attempted the extermination or dispersion of tribal minorities like the Kirghiz. We will, however, focus on white European–native American conflict because it is so well documented.

Some of the native Americans attempted to wipe out or drive away the first Europeans

they saw. According to the Norse epics, *skraelings*, probably of the Beotuk tribe, attacked and killed several members of the expedition to Newfoundland of the Norseman Thorfinn Karlsefni in about 1000 A.D.[4] Eskimo attacked the ships of Martin Frobisher in 1576.[5] The Roanoke colony in Virginia was wiped out some time between 1586 and 1590, although not without provocation.[6] It took the Spanish only fifty-six years after Columbus discovered the island Hispanola (now Haiti and the Dominican Republic) to reduce the native population from 300,000 to 500.[7] In these early contacts, the native Americans may have sensed the antipathy that their community form caused in people using a radically different community form.

The population of native Americans is estimated to have been 800,000 in the 1600s; by 1900 there were only 240,000 native Americans within the boundaries of the United States.[8] The first year after reservation confinement was complete in which the birthrate of native Americans exceeded their death rate was 1928.[9]

One of the Sioux people said: "They made us many promises, more than I can remember, but they never kept but one. They promised to take our land and they took it."[10]

Even in situations where tribalists and Europeans faced death *together*, they seemed more ready to die than to stop fighting. In one instance three Eskimo families, including

[4] Farley Mowat, *West Viking: The Ancient Norse in Greenland and North America* (Boston: Little, Brown, 1965).

[5] Samuel Eliot Morison, *The European Discovery of North America* (New York: Oxford, 1971).

[6] Morison, op. cit.

[7] Samuel Eliot Morison, *Admiral of the Ocean Sea* (Boston: Little, Brown, 1942), p. 493.

[8] Carlos B. Embry, *America's Concentration Camps* (New York: David McKay, 1956).

[9] Oliver La Farge, *As Long As the Grass Shall Grow* (New York: Alliance, 1940).

[10] Robert M. Utley, *The Last Days of the Sioux Nation* (New Haven, Conn.: Yale University Press, 1963), p. 59.

SELECTION 8-3: A feudal-tribal conflict in contemporary Africa.

AFRICA MASSACRE—THE ELIMINATION OF A TRIBAL CLASS

By Stanley Meisler

Bujumbura, Burundi—Something terrible has happened in Burundi—a chilling and systematic attempt by the government to eliminate an entire class of people. Estimates of the death toll range up to 200,000.

The enormity and horror of it all is exposed by what a visitor does not see in Bujumbura. This town on Lake Tanganyika is the capital of a country in which 85% of the population is Hutu—a short, Negroid people. Yet a visitor finds few Hutus in Bujumbura.

It is a little like entering Warsaw after World War II and finding no Jews there. A visitor would not need a tour of Auschwitz to know that something terrible had happened.

The government is run by the minority Tutsi tribe—a tall, slender Hamitic people who for centuries have acted as lords in the almost feudal society of Burundi. They struck nearly a year ago from a persistent fear of the Hutus. In fact, the government insists that all the trouble and killing were provoked by a Hutu uprising.

Fear May Be Justified

The Tutsi fear may be justified. A successful Hutu rebellion would probably decimate the Tutsis. In neighboring Rwanda, the Hutus overthrew their Tutsi lords more than a decade ago and slew thousands of them. There is always fear among the Tutsis of Burundi that the same thing could happen here.

But it would be misleading to attribute all of last year's killing to a savage frenzy of Tutsi fear. Some Hutus were killed in wild, indiscriminate killing. Others were victims of personal vendettas. But most were wiped out in a cold and calculated way by a Tutsi government that seems to have decided that it could guarantee itself power for at least another decade by eliminating all "modern" Hutus, including all potential leaders of the majority tribe.

It is this coldness that makes the events of Burundi different from the other bloodshed that has sapped Africa's strength in the last decade.

Slayings Began Last April

The killings began in late April, reached their height in May and ended, more or less, by August.

According to most sources, the government had lists of intended victims—but the lists were not exclusive, and more Hutus died than were listed.

There are stories of Hutus begging Tutsi friends to check the lists in government offices to see which Hutus were on it. One source said a Tutsi official tried to reassure the wife of a missing Hutu by showing her a government list without her husband's name on it. But he had been killed anyway.

Although many Hutus were taken away from their homes at night, a large number simply received a summons in an orderly way to report to the police at a certain time.

In Bujumbura, many victims were killed in prison. There are grisly stories about the methods of execution, all difficult to verify. But most sources agree with a diplomat who said: "They did not use many bullets."

The bodies were thrown on trucks that drove from the city to a field near the airport. In the first few days, the trucks rumbled through town in daylight. But the government later decided to try to hide what it was doing. The trucks were shifted to night runs. Under bright lights, bulldozers dug mass graves and covered them over.

There seem to have been three kinds of victims.

Lifted From Rolls

First, the government tried to kill almost every Hutu who had a government job, including Hutu soldiers. Many of the death lists were simply lifted from civil service rolls that evidently were prepared a few months earlier.

Second, the government tried to kill all Hutus who had enough wealth for potential leadership. Wealth is a relative term in Africa. Many sources say that the so-called wealthy Hutus included any who owned a shop, had a bank account or lived in a house with a corrugated iron roof instead of a thatched one.

Finally, the government tried to kill all educated Hutus. Education probably was defined differently by officials in different parts of the country. But almost all Hutu University students, many Hutu secondary school students, and perhaps half the country's Hutu teachers were killed. In one incident, six women teachers were killed in front of their students.

The categories of victims explains why a visitor can hardly see a Hutu inside Bujumbura but will see many trudging along with hoes on their shoulders on country roads.

Bujumbura, a city of 70,000, was never a Hutu city. The Tutsis who controlled the wealth and power of Burundi dominated the capital. But there were thousands of Hutus living there —those who had left their traditional peasant life in the countryside to join the modern world of the big town.

4 Million Population

These modern Hutus—all in the money economy, some educated, many in government jobs—were the prime targets.

Sometimes it is difficult for an outsider to understand how the government was able to inflict so much punishment on the Hutus in a tiny country where they make up the great bulk of its population of almost 4 million. They outnumber the Tutsis almost 6 to 1. Yet the Hutus were cowed by an army that numbered no more than 4,000 at the start of the trouble and far less after it had purged itself of Hutus.

Seventy-five thousand Hutus fled Burundi and took refuge in Zaire, Tanzania and Rwanda. But thousands more remained behind and took their punishment without much resistance.

There are stories of Hutus accepting their summonses and reporting to the police at the scheduled time even though they knew death awaited them. There are other stories of officials loading Hutus on trucks and, when the trucks were full, ordering the remaining Hutus to come back the next day. The Hutus obeyed.

One Hutu minister was overseas when the trouble erupted yet flew home to his execution. According to one story, a group of Hutus escaped only after some Europeans forced them against their will into a truck and drove them across the border.

Some observers say that even Hutus trying to escape did so halfheartedly.

"They were pathetic," said one foreigner who has worked with Hutus for many years. "They would walk down the main road to the border. If one gendarme stopped them, they would turn back."

Streak of Fatalism

Foreigners who know the Hutus well attribute their strange acquiescence to a strong streak of fatalism and an intense psychological dependence on their Tutsi lords. Much like the serfs in medieval Europe, the Hutus for centuries have given their loyalty to the Tutsis in exchange for protection. Caught in a terrifying crisis last year, most did as they were told.

The government does not deny that great killing took place last year. But it has issued a self-serving interpretation of the events.

According to an official white paper, a force of 25,000 Hutus, many led by former Congolese rebels now in exile in East Africa, attacked four sectors of Burundi on the night of April 29. Some were said to have rebelled from inside; others invaded from outside. Their aim was genocide of the Tutsi people, the report said.

It added that bands of Hutus pillaged the countryside and murdered Tutsis. The Hutus, according to the government, were armed with poisoned machetes, clubs, automatic rifles, and Molotov cocktails; they were drugged in a state of ferocious excitement and were convinced their skin was impermeable, that bullets would turn to water.

Before the Burundian army could defeat them, the government insists, the Hutu rebels had massacred 50,000 people—almost all Tutsis.

President Michel Micombero, the 33-year-old colonel who runs the military government of Burundi, has said that his army found lists of Hutu plotters on the defeated rebels. These lists were used by the government to track down and execute the plotters.

"Only the guilty have been punished," Micombero has said. "The innocent were not troubled at all."

He himself has conceded that the death toll could have reached 100,000.

The government's version of the events, however, is rejected by all foreign sources in Bujumbura.

Many foreigners are reluctant to talk with a visiting correspondent. They are afraid of expulsion.

But, reluctant or not, all foreign sources say that the government rather than seek out plotters, attempted a systematic elimination of the modern Hutus.

Many sources agree that the trouble began with some kind of Hutu uprising. But they say that the Hutu rebels killed a few thousand Tutsis at most, not 50,000. The uprising, the sources go on, became an excuse for the government onslaught against the Hutus.

A few sources, in fact, speculate that the government knew about the intended uprising but did not try to prevent it. The Tutsis wanted such an excuse, according to these sources, to begin their long-planned drive against the Hutus.

The troubles last year devastated a good deal of southern Burundi. A visitor can see much of the devastation by driving 75 miles south on the road that goes along Lake Tanganyika to the town of Nyanza Lac. It is impossible to tell, however, whether the destruction came from a Hutu uprising, fighting between Hutus and Tutsis or repression by the army.

Many homes and schools in the 30-mile stretch between the town of Rumonge and Nyanza Lac are deserted. The coffee bushes, Burundi's main crop, are overgrown and untended. In a day of driving, a visitor hardly sees a commercial truck.

Nyanza Lac itself, once an administrative center with a population of 20,000, now looks like an unused movie set for an old western. A visitor finds a Burundi flag flying on the main dirt road in the center of town but little else.

five children and two women, were cast adrift on an ice floe. They floated together from October 16, 1872, to April 30, 1873, for 1,300 miles off the west coast of Greenland through the whole of an icy arctic winter. They were near starvation most of the time. Accompanying them were eight seamen of the exploring ship *Polaris* and George Tyson, the captain, who described the following scene which took place as the eighteen people, white and brown, struggled for survival.

I ordered the seal to be taken into Joe's (an Eskimo's) hut. As he did the most toward getting the food, I thought this was right. One of the men [whites are called *men*; Eskimos are *Eskimos,* or *natives*] however took upon himself to take it into their hut. They have divided the seal to suit themselves. It seems hard on the natives who have hunted day after day in cold and storm while these men lay idle on their backs or sat in the shelter of their huts, which were mainly built by these same natives they are wronging. The men keep the largest proportion of the meat from this last seal which discourages the natives very much. Joe and Hans [the Eskimo men] say that they have very

often suffered before from the want of food, but have never been obliged to endure anything like the present experience. Considering that they are out of the hut so much more than the rest, hunting around, they ought to have a large allowance of food. I would gladly give it to them, but it would cause open mutiny among the men.[11]

The idea that people using another community form are so different, or so warlike, as to be unassimilable is used to justify extermination or genocide as a means of taking the land or resources of those people. President of the United States Ulysses S. Grant said, "We must protect the emigrants, even if it means extermination [of the Indians]."[12] Although most of Grant's generals saw themselves as simply doing a job, a tradition of masculinity, as represented by the "massacred" George A. Custer, who left

[11] E. Vale Blake (ed.), *Arctic Experiences Containing Capt. E. Tyson's Wonderful Drift on the Ice Floe, etc.* (New York: Harper, 1894); reprinted in Farley Mowat, *The Polar Passion* (Boston: Little, Brown, 1967), pp. 140–141.
[12] Henry E. Fritz, *The Movement for Indian Assimilation, 1860–1890* (Philadelphia: University of Pennsylvania Press, 1963), p. 71.

few quotations, grew up around Indian extermination. William Tecumseh Sherman, famed for his march through Georgia, presumably to free black people, said, "We must act with vindictive earnestness against the Sioux, even to their extermination, men, women, and children. Nothing less will reach to the root of the case."[13] Colonel John Gibbon said, "The remnant of this rapidly disappearing race will give us no trouble by going to war. . . ."[14]

The newspapers of the time reflect the fact that the settlers, who had more to lose than the Army, urged the military to bring the inevitable clash between two irreconcilable ways of life to a rapid conclusion. The Cheyenne, Wyoming, *Daily Leader* said in the 1870s, "The same inscrutable arbiter that decreed the downfall of Rome has pronounced the doom of extinction on the red men of America." During the same period, the Bismarck, North Dakota, *Weekly Tribune*, pronounced, "The Indians [must be] exterminated root and branch, old and young, male and female."[15] The "responsible" bureau of the United States Government, the Board of Indian Commissioners, spoke in 1879 of a Western America "whose hills are full of ores and whose valleys are waiting for diligent hands to dress and keep them in obedience with divine command."[16]

Some of these quotations have the sound of that part of conflict theory which suggests that older community forms fall of their own weight. They go beyond conflict theory in proposing that the people using those older forms must be exterminated.

Following the idea of the inevitability of Indian destruction, the native Americans were treated as a lower species. This is seen in their relationship to the law, for the law embraces and contains the community. In this case, law was a logical extension of capitalist economics; "civilized" law did not apply to native Americans. In the 1800s it was no crime to offend in any way against a native American on or off the reservation. Offenses of one native American against another were not covered by law either, although at the same time native Americans were denied the right to use their own ways of law and justice.

Finally pacified, the native American was not yet purified. It seems that it is not only the economic form which threatens those using new forms and displacing older forms, but also the supporting social structure and culture. Thus after the white Europeans had systematically stripped the native Americans of their economy, and taken away their means to make war, they set about destroying their culture. Children were taken from their parents and sent to boarding schools where they were forbidden to speak their own languages, practice their own religions, wear their own clothing, or use their own (non-"Christian") names. This cultural stripping and physical abuse of the children perfectly fits the definition of "brainwashing" supposedly first invented by communists to strip helpless white Americans of their culture. Captain Richard Pratt, director of the Carlisle school, supposedly one of the best of the "Indian" schools, summed up his aims as "the divorcement of the Indian from the worse than slavery of his old communistic systems."[17] In the same way American and British imperialism, helped by African intertribal warfare, justified the enslavement of black people for the expansion of the late feudal and early capitalist economies. In the same way black people in the United States and Africa were stripped of their culture by systematic separation of families, and denial of rights to use African family, religious, musical, artistic, and language forms, and all other African social and cultural forms.

[13] Fred M. Gans, *The Great Sioux Nation* (Minneapolis: Ross and Harmer, 1964), p. 520.
[14] Henry E. Fritz, op. cit., p. 183.
[15] Henry E. Fritz, op. cit., p. 176.
[16] Henry E. Fritz, op. cit., p. 210.

[17] Henry E. Fritz, op. cit., p. 248.

Even those native Americans who wanted wholeheartedly to embrace the new way found that they had to wait, perhaps even starve, in order to become successful whites. Only 2,589 school positions were provided for 33,000 native Americans of school age in the 1890s.[18] Agents of the United States government stole, lost, misappropriated, or simply failed to provide the beef, seeds, plows, and buildings by which native Americans could become farmers. The results of this deculturation were predictable. Native American reservation holdings in the United States decreased from 150,000,000 acres in 1855, when the reservation system was established, to 47,000,000 acres in 1933.[19] Tribal life no longer exists in its pure form on American "Indian" reservations. The remnant of some of the "Indian" nations are today struggling to create a new culture independent of white management and oppression. The development of the American Indian Movement and the events at Wounded Knee, South Dakota, in 1973 are the latest efforts in this long struggle.

Tribal life need not be romanticized. Although people have just begun to try to study the tribal form in terms of its own logic, it appears that the contradictions of tribalism were many and that many of the world's peoples have voluntarily relinquished tribalism in hopes of resolving these contradictions. Tribal life offers closeness, security, freedom (within the limits of the clearly understood tribal obligations), simplicity, and integratedness of all social life, and lacks the internal conflicts which lead to class struggle. However, tribalism seems to carry with it material poverty (few areas of the world were as rich in game as the plains of North America), suppression of women and in some instances young people, intellectual restriction, rather continuous hostility and warfare with other tribal peoples, classifica-

tion of nontribesmen as animals, and inability to extend life to the very aged, the crippled, and the chronically handicapped.

EMERGENCE OF AGRICULTURE OUT OF TRIBAL LIFE

Before we leave the native Americans to discuss feudal economies, we wish to make the connection between increasing use of agriculture and the development of class structures, since the rigid class division common to preindustrial agriculture is a precursor of the caste system used under feudalism.

Some native American peoples used quite different social structures than did the communal and democratic hunters of the Great Plains. Those who used agriculture for survival developed a stratified society with a powerful, often religiously based, elite. The Natchez, for example, a farming people of the lower Mississippi River valley, divided

The interior of a contemporary native American home on the Navajo reservation. (Pictorial Parade/EPA)

[18] Henry E. Fritz, op. cit., pp. 122ff.
[19] Oliver La Farge, op. cit.

themselves into two castes, and within the upper caste three subclasses were recognized. There were restrictions on intermarriage and retention of riches which kept the different castes in distinctly different relations to the relative abundance created by the economic system of the Natchez.[20]

The Pawnee, half way between total reliance on a hunting–mobile agriculture economy and the sedentary agriculture of the Natchez, used elements of both communal-tribal and caste social structures. Chieftainship was hereditary among the Pawnee, although it was elective for mobile tribes. There were poor commoners within the "tribe" who owned few or no horses, had small lodges, and received presents from wealthy persons. Yet at the same time the Pawnee methods of hunting, and their rituals, were much like those of their tribal neighbors—the Sioux, Cheyenne, and Crow.[21]

Tribalism survived, with its own internal logic and integrity. Through it, humanity survived. In most parts of the world tribalism gave way to other forms, most of which seemed to view the extinction of tribal life as a necessary condition of their own existence.

SUMMARY

Tribalism is a way of life which emerges out of the economic logic of hunting large animals. For the question, "How should one

human relate to another?" the answer provided by tribalism is "Through the moral core." The moral core is a complex of ideas about the natural environment and those human behaviors most likely to sustain the tribal links between separate kinship groups. Expected behavior is thus conceived in terms of the good of the entire tribe. Differences in behavior are expected by age, sex, and personality rather than by role, class, or social power.

The natives of North America developed tribalism to a high degree. They developed the institution of religion to great complexity because the morality which bound them together could best be stated symbolically through its relation to nonhuman realities.

Intertribal warfare, the emergence of social classes (as in the Maya, Inca, and other peoples), and overpopulation (as in Peru) seem to be the major internal contradictions of tribalism. Imperialism destroyed tribal life in many parts of the world. The tribal social structure of the native Americans was destroyed by the spread of both European feudalism and capitalism.

The attempt to destroy an entire people and their way of life (genocide) is a common feature of conflict between peoples using different economic logics. The history of native American-European contact is an example of the violence associated with economic imperialism.

Tribalism lay the basis for the emergence, in many parts of the world, of the logic of sedentary agriculture. Elements of tribal religion were carried over into feudal agriculture as we will see in Chapter 9.

[20] Wendell H. Oswalt, *This Land Was Theirs* (New York: Wiley, 1966), p. 478.
[21] Wendell H. Oswalt, op. cit., pp. 258–260.

SUGGESTED READINGS

Hartley Burr Alexander, *The World's Rim* (Lincoln: University of Nebraska Press, 1953).
George Dalton, *Tribal and Peasant Economics* (Garden City, N.Y.: The Natural History Press, 1967).

Peter Farb, *Man's Rise to Civilization as Shown by the Indians of North America from Primeval Times to the Industrial State* (New York: Dutton & Co., 1968).

E. Adamson Hoebel, *The Cheyenne* (New York: Holt, Rinehart and Winston, 1968).

George Hyde, *Indians of the High Plains: From the Prehistoric Period to the Coming of the Europeans* (Norman: University of Oklahoma Press, 1959).

Alice Marriott, *The Ten Grandmothers* (Norman: University of Oklahoma Press, 1945).

L. V. McWhorter, *Yellow Wolf: His Own Story* (Caldwell, Idaho: Caxton Printers Ltd., 1948).

John G. Neihardt, *Black Elk Speaks* (New York: William Morrow, 1932).

Wendell H. Oswalt, *This Land Was Theirs* (New York: John Wiley, 1966).

Marshall D. Sahlins, *Tribesmen* (Englewood Cliffs, N.J.: Prentice-Hall, 1968).

Mari Sandoz, *Crazy Horse: The Strange Man of The Oglalas* (New York: Hastings House, 1942).

Elizabeth Marshall Thomas, *The Harmless People* (New York: Vintage Books, 1965).

NINE
The Feudal Community

INTRODUCTION

Plant cultivation and animal domestication give humans for the first time the kind of surplus which allows some to do things other than work directly with the tools of production. The peasant in medieval Europe knew well the meaning of the biblical statement:

> Cursed is the ground for thy sake; in toil shalt thou eat of it all the days of thy life; thorns also and thistles shall it bring forth to thee; and thou shalt eat of the herb of the field; in the sweat of thy face shalt thou eat bread till thou return unto the ground.[1]

The Old Testament has special meaning for anyone studying the world of the medieval peasant. The Bible is the history of a people emerging from tribalism into an agricultural caste system, European feudalism is history of a people slipping back into a caste system after the breakup of the emerging capitalist community of imperial Rome.

All over the world, in places as remote from one another as China and northwest Europe, in times as separate as 5,000 years B.C. (Egypt) and the twentieth century A.D. (Vietnam) human beings have faced the same problem—the protection of the sedentary agriculturalist. The solution throughout much of the world was the creation of a caste structured community with specialized roles of warring and farming. In theory and in early practice, each caste benefits the other.

The origins of agriculture—the cultivation, breeding, and harvest of plants and animals

---

[1] Biblical curse on Adam quoted in H. S. Bennett, *Life on the English Manor: A Study of Peasant Conditions, 1150–1400* (Cambridge: Cambridge University Press, 1937).

—are a subject of dispute. Some new ideas and new archeological evidence have discredited the old theory of nomadic tribes accidentally discovering sprouts at a watering place where they had feasted the previous year and suddenly "understanding" seeds. There is evidence that in some parts of the world, the development of trading centers and small towns created a demand for large amounts of food in one place (which cannot be satisfied by wild animals, who will not remain in such busy places), and hence produced the conditions leading to experiments with seeds and animals.[2]

Whatever the origins, once people begin to plant seeds and to live in one place, they become vulnerable to attack by marauding tribesmen. This is probably one of the two or three dominant themes in all human literature; the helplessness of the farmer in the face of people who travel, who are wild,

[2] Jane Jacobs, *The Economy of Cities* (New York: Vintage, 1970), pp. 3–48.

who refuse to settle in one place and dig in the dirt. In the film *The Seven Samurai*, the director Kurosawa shows us the desperation with which the rice farmers seek the warriors who will protect them from the yearly visit of the horse-mounted bandits. Once one has chosen to plant seeds and nurture their growth in open flat regions, it is almost impossible to remain a proficient and mobile fighter.[3]

The fact that the better farmer one becomes, the worse one fights is a perfect example of how contradiction leads to class-structured relations. The impossibility of being both a good grain harvester and a mobile fighter leads to fighting specialists and farming specialists. These become *classes* because they have different relation-

[3] If this theory is correct, tribes which for cultural or geographic reasons became herders but not grain raisers would be less vulnerable, more adept at fighting, and less likely to develop a feudal system. In Europe the experience of the Swiss and the Scandinavians supports the theory.

The Samurai were a specialized warrior caste attached to the land-owning aristocracy of feudal Japan. (De Wys/EPA)

ships to the surplus value created by cultivating seeds and animals. In some places, entire tribes of less successful fighters were enslaved by more warlike people. Put to work on the land and protected by the warrior class, they became efficient farmers. This happened in the valleys of Peru, culminating in the feudal empire of the Incas. In other places, for example, the England of King Arthur's time, the division between fighters and farmers appears to have emerged within loosely allied tribal peoples.

The word *castism* is more descriptive of the basic structure of the medieval European agricultural community than *feudalism;* since the latter word is better known, however, we will use it here. Like tribalism, feudalism is a form which binds family or kinship roles into a larger system. Unlike tribalism, feudalism links together people who stand in different relations to the agricultural use of land.

In the feudal community, roles are specialized, particularly those used by men. Peasant men are excluded by birth from certain roles used by *all* males in tribal life. For example, a peasant on an English manor in 1100 A.D. did not carry weapons, could not bake bread or press wine, could not be a medicine man, and could not keep records. In a sense, he was partially freed from obligations to the larger community.

The peasant caste gave up a portion of its crops, its freedom of movement, and some yearly labor in return for protection against marauders, intercession in blood feuds (internal disputes between farmers), a primitive social welfare system (provision for widows and orphans, some help for the sick and aged), and some management of communal land (record keeping on seeds, crops, weather, etc.).

The medieval Roman Catholic church kept alive the tradition of justifying the caste structure by saying that farmers are inferior.

Saint Thomas Aquinas, a church philosopher, shows himself as being in agreement with Aristotle, himself a participant in an earlier feudalism, in the following quotation.

> [T]he division between a fighting caste and a working caste is natural and profitable; that agriculture is a necessary but illiberal occupation; and that in the best State, the tillers of the soil, if they can be just as we wish, should be slaves, robust of body, that they may well labour the earth, but deficient in understanding lest they be inventors of wiles against their masters . . . poor-spirited, *and not of the same tribe.*[4]

The peasantry probably began eventually to look physically different from the nobility. Lack of intermarriage, as well as very different kinds of lives, would have led to different physical characteristics. These would later be labeled "noble" types and "brute" types and used to justify the caste system on semiracist grounds.

DEFINITION OF FEUDALISM

Feudalism is a community form based on sedentary (living in one place) agriculture, which uses caste as a mean of relating the two important specialties of early agriculture, fighting and farming. A caste is a collection of people who all have the same relationship to the tools and mode of production. In a caste structure: people are bound to a specific economic role (and perhaps some noneconomic roles as well) for life; sons and daughters inherit the caste position of their fathers; and movement out of a caste, by marriage or otherwise, is practically

---

[4] This passage, a paraphrase from Aquinas' *Summa Theologia* in which Aquinas agrees with Aristotle, is from G. G. Coulton, *Medieval Village, Manor, and Monastery* (New York: Harper Torchbook, 1960), p. 154; italics ours.

SELECTION 9-1: The caste system still organizes some social relations in India.

THEY'D RATHER BE DEAD

New Delhi—The Indian caste system cost 78 lives when passengers on a stranded bus refused to haul themselves to safety along the same rope.

The Hindustan Times reported yesterday that a bus carrying 86 persons was trapped by flood waters Monday near the town of Alwar, about 100 miles southwest of Delhi.

Karim Khan, a tea-stall owner, went to the rescue. He waded out to the bus with a rope he had tied to a truck standing on high ground.

He asked the passengers to haul themselves along the rope to safety.

But the passengers, who belonged to two different high caste communities, refused to share the same rope and stayed in the bus.

The floodwaters rose higher and the bus was swept away, with the loss of 78 lives.

impossible. The people of one caste are related to people of another by a complex set of customs. Some of these customs prescribe economic exchange, and some prescribe the etiquette of relations between castes. Selection 9-1 is an example of the character of customary caste relations. These customs extend into every facet of life, and even into death, as this example from contemporary India reveals.

The tribalist answered the question, "How should I relate to another human?" in terms of tribal morality. The answer to the same question by a user of early agricultural community forms was given in terms of one's own caste position, the caste position of the other, and the local customs linking the two castes.

The structure of the feudal community is diagrammed in Figure 9-1. The circle symbolizes the total community—usually a single estate or manor within which lived a few hundred, or at the most a few thousand,

people. The lower half of the circle represents the peasantry, the two peasant villages within the peasant sphere indicate that there were different roles used within this caste, such as free peasant or bound peasant. The upper half of the circle represents the warrior caste, which is shown as being divided into two subcastes, the aristocracy and the clergy. More than one role existed within these subcastes in European feudalism—as, for example, knights, lords, dukes, counts, and earls in the ranks of the nobility and monks, nuns, priests, and bishops in the ranks of the clergy.

Whatever its origins, the survival of feudalism depended in the beginning on some degree of reciprocity, on a felt equality of exchange between landlord and peasant. The life of the peasant was a hard one, and it got much harder toward the end of European feudalism as the contradictions within the form began to tear it apart. But at the "height" of feudalism—let us say from 900 to 1200 A.D. in northwest Europe—both sides gained from the feudal caste system. The nobility risked their lives to protect the peasants, in return for which the peasantry gave up much of their freedom (if their ancestors ever had it). As late as the American War of Independence, the inheritors of the feudal code of chivalry, the aristocracy of Virginia, fought with one another for the chivalric honor of being the first colonists to die on Cornwallis' barricades at Yorktown.[5]

The feudal system of economic organization guaranteed to the peasants their rights to the common meadow or pasture, so necessary for the health and growth of the oxen that pulled their plows. It guaranteed their rights to the "waste" land, those swampy, hilly, or forested areas not touched by the plow. From these lands they gathered wood for their house-walls, turf for their

[5] Burke Davis, The Campaign That Won America (New York: Dial, 1970).

roofs, firewood, clay for their dams and dikes, and wild fruits and animals to supplement the grains and vegetables they grew. These rights to the land are very important to understanding the most basic part of feudal logic. No one *owned* the land in the sense we know it—in the sense of being able to sell it or do with it anything they wanted. The early caste system was based on customary *rights* of each caste to the use of the land, not

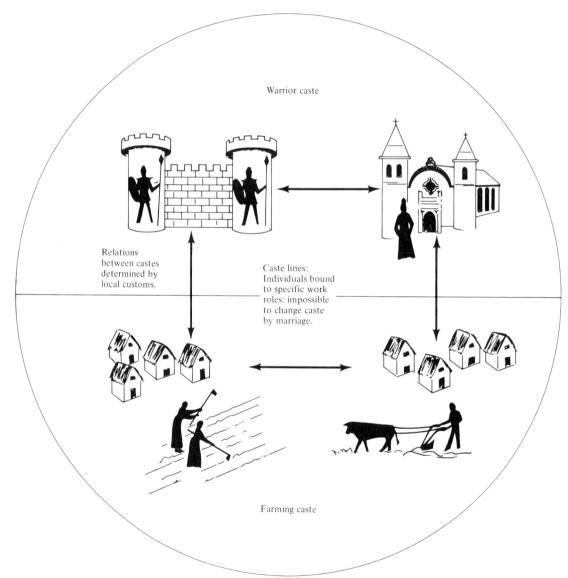

FIGURE 9-1 Feudal social structure. At least two separate castes are bound together by customary obligations. Subclasses of the warrior caste may include landed aristocracy, specialized warriors (as the Japanese Samurai), and a priesthood. The farming caste may include subclasses such as free serfs, bound serfs, and slaves.

on land ownership. The nobility had hered-itary rights to the land (although at first in En-gland and France, the grants from warrior chieftains to their fighting knights were sim-ply rights to some of the produce of land worked by free farmers). The church had rights to some of the produce of the land and was also in many places simply another landlord. The peasants also had hereditary rights to the land, rights which could be passed on to their children, usually the old-est son. As long as the community remained local and intact, exercise of these rights to the land, in a prescribed way, preserved the relationship between the castes. As we will see, the development of parallel class com-munities gave the nobility chances to make alliances elsewhere, which in turn gave them allies when they began to violate the cus-tomary rights of peasants to the land and to act as if they owned the land. Such use of the land was a signal to peasants, priests, and the emerging merchant class that the nobility were no longer following the logic which relates the form (religious symbolism, religious and ritual ceremonies, courts) to the content of the community (land use being an example of content or social struc-ture). During the breakup of the "game" of feudalism, even though the behavior of some of the players signaled that they had aban-doned the logic of feudal economics, they continued to talk as if they were playing by the old rules.

In many parts of the world, people em-braced the new form—the caste or feudal system—for the higher returns it promised. They suffered the risks also. Egypt under the Pharohs, China under the Emperors (going back to 1200 B.C.), Sparta and Athens from 600 B.C. onward, Europe from 500 to 1200 A.D., Central and South America under the Mayan priest kings and the Inca rulers are all examples of caste-based agricultural so-cieties.

Feudalism is often dismissed as a chamber of horrors. It is portrayed as a superstition-ridden, witch-persecuting, oppressive, slave-creating, ignorance-perpetuating, and war-mongering form—in short, as the worst possible form. The reality was far more complex.

A conflict perspective views economic forms as tools through which people achieve particular goals. Contradiction arises, how-ever, because certain human goals, and hence the social structures that embody or include these goals, prevent the achieve-ment of other human goals. The more suc-cessful a particular community form is in achieving some goals, the more it will fail to achieve or express other goals. In feudal-ism, people risk their lives and some kinds of freedom in return for the *possibility* of a food surplus. The farmer, living in a world in which there are tribes more mobile and warlike (because they can devote more time to war activities) than himself, must buy the possibility of raising a surplus. He does this by attaching himself and his family to the land and to a warrior caste; if captured, he accepts this relationship, and if free, he en-ters it voluntarily. He buys the possibility of food surplus at great risk, for his particular warriors may be repressive and cruel, or, worse yet, unsuccessful protectors.

The warriors risk their lives. They most surely will feel cold steel and face torture. To counteract the bitter truth, they create fabulous stories of heroes, stories which promise great rewards (in the afterlife) for those who die fighting. They create stories which make fun of farmers and their pas-sivity, so they may gird up their courage in the face of the certainty of a short life, al-most certainly ended on the point of a sword, their brains strewn around some dirty battleground and their families also put to the sword. In return the warrior has the pos-sibility of the best of women, the best of food, and slightly better living quarters, perhaps with a separate building for the animals. He certainly does not stand to gain the fabulous riches of the kind reserved for the victors of class warfare in the industrial communities.

Conflict theory sees the caste form emerging first and lasting longest where it is in closest proximity to nomadic tribes or organized banditry. How feudalism develops from its beginnings requires analysis of how the basic contradiction between the food surplus and caste oppression develops, and how the people change the form to deal with other contradictions as they emerge. Much can be done by any student, for until recently little had been done to try to use the experiences of feudalism to forward our understanding of how people respond to contradictions and the conflicts generated by them. The history books' dismissal of feudalism as the "Dark Ages" reflects the fact that most of our own patterns of life developed as reactions against or revolutionary overthrow of feudal social structures. In a way we justify our own system by claiming that feudalism was all bad—it makes *us look* that much better. In the future, perhaps, those who use the patterns which replace our own will dwell on the stupidities, oppressions, and evils of our way of doing things, while we are mute to protest that we saw few other choices open to us.

FEUDAL LIFE—A BRIEF DESCRIPTION

The description of feudal life which follows is based on materials from the history of northwest Europe, China, and Japan. Although the past tense is used, the reader should remember that feudal community forms exist today, and that remnants of feudal forms occur in places dominated by industrial economies.

One of the most important features of the feudal community was geographic isolation. The lack of roads, canals, and bridges meant there was no profit to be made in wringing the last bushel of wheat or the last ear of corn from the peasant family. The landlord could not sell it anywhere because there were no large markets. Even in preindustrial times, whenever a single ruler or class of rulers effectively bound together large areas of country with highways or water traffic, thereby creating the possibility of selling or trading surplus food, the feudal community began to use structures based on a division of labor more specialized than warrior-priest-peasant. In national communities, such as Rome and Egypt, class-structured communities emerged. Both the Roman and Egyptian empires partially preserved subject feudal communities, and when they fell, perhaps weakened by the contradictory logic of the two forms, people reverted to the use of feudalism. We would predict the longest continuous use of feudal forms in areas with the least history of successful central government.

Isolated, the peasants lived in a cluster of huts which could be made in a few hours from local materials, and destroyed as quickly. The huts were surrounded by meadow, plowed land, and forest. The lords lived in stone or timbered houses, later perhaps in castles. Peasants, priests, and warriors developed ways to secure and improve on the logic by which they all lived. For example, in the absence of accurate weights and measures, the customs defining how much each caste owed the other had to be stated in vague ways. Into this idea was built what Coulton calls "the sporting chance." Such crude measures could be manipulated, allowing a lot of room for compassion or cheating. Their use had the advantage of making the system less machinelike, less oppressive. They allowed people to relate to each other through custom, rather than overt

In Europe, Asia, and parts of Africa, feudalism created an aristocratic caste which controlled land use. Wherever this caste began to oppress the peasanty in the name of profit, empire, or kingdom, the feudal system crumbled. (De Wys/EPA)

coercion. In central Europe, the question of how far a peasant's hens might graze from his house was answered by the following traditional prescription:

> He shall stand on the ridge of his roof, shall pass his right arm under his left and grasp his hair in his right hand; then shall he take a sickle by the point in his left hand; and, as far as he can cast, so far shall his hens go; and when they go further to other folk's harm, he shall fine with three pence for every third fowl.[6]

A dispute over how much wood could be taken by a peasant from the forest of the Bishop of Strassburg was settled as follows.

> When he heweth with his axe, let him cry aloud upon the forester; and, when he loadeth

[6] G. G. Coulton, op. cit., p. 49.

his cart, let him wait; and, what with his crying at the axe work and his waiting at the lading, if he can come with his cart so far from the mark where he cut his wood that the forester (the agent of the Bishop) may not reach the cart with (a cast of) his axe with the left hand, then may the forester, if he will, follow after the cart, and thrust his right hand under his girdle, and with his left hand drag from the cart what wood he may, until he comes to the man's own toft. So far may he go; but, if he follow the man into his toft, and the peasant then turn around and smite the forester on the head, even unto death, then shall no judgment be passed upon him for that deed.[7]

Where population was growing, usable land decreasing, or crops failing, the sporting-chance mechanism could no longer be used, and the system became more obviously oppressive. In prerevolutionary China it is reported that some landlords were so stingy that they required peasants not to defecate in their fields but to walk all the way to the landlord's house so that he might use the human manure for his own fields.[8]

Within both warrior and peasant castes there was a good deal of communality through which some of the benefits and structures of tribalism were carried on. The communalism of the extended family was an important element of village social structure. Communal responsibility, for example, in the form of holding the family guilty for the wrongdoing of one of its members, supported adherence to feudal custom in Japan.[9]

Within the priestly caste, communal settlements, that is, monasteries and convents, kept alive much of the tribal morality through the idea of God's community in

[7] Ibid., p. 50.
[8] William Hinton, *Fanshen: A Documentary of Revolution in a Chinese Village* (New York: Vintage, 1966), p. 23.
[9] Matsuyo Takizawa, "Disintegration of the Old Family System," in George Dalton (ed.), *Tribal and Peasant Economies* (Garden City, N.Y.: Natural History Press, 1967), p. 350.

which each person's deeds for God contributed to the good of all, however little this morality described or applied to the world outside the walls. Because nobles and priests were interchangeable, users of church positions do not constitute a separate caste. The church was a major landlord in European feudalism; the Pope was often a successful contestant for collecting feudal power into central or kingly government. The church provided important services: it urged peace, provided arbitrators for feuds among nobles, sanctified marriage and other customs (backed them up, that is), and provided record keeping and other clerical skills. Such services, together with extensive landholding, created considerable power, and allowed some popes to play one king against another. In one instance, Pope Innocent III used Phillip Augustus of France to force John of England to return papal fiefdom to England in 1213 A.D. A bishop could appeal to the conscience of the people against a king, although not always successfully. The church, in sum, was a specialized branch of the landed aristocracy, a band of peaceful warriors.

Some degree of peasant autonomy was present in many feudal situations. The *mir* or council of the Russian feudal village was similar to the tribal council of the Sioux in the openness of its deliberations and the requirements for unanimity. The *mir* allowed villagers (peasants) to settle some questions regarding access to communal land, payment of taxes, and interfamilial disputes, and to control some aspects of the relationship to landlords. From the research on English feudalism come descriptions of communal involvement in building and maintaining the church, and collective work on the fields. Although there is some evidence that English peasants cheated one another by including small strips of others' land when plowing their own, there were many occasions in the annual work on the lord's land on which communal labor was required—plowing, hay cutting and stacking, and building and repairing fences around common pastures.[10]

Many other peasant customs and activities were survivals of tribal ways. These may have helped peasants better withstand the oppressiveness of their relations with priests and other landlords. Although peasantry is widely associated with stinginess, it is reported of Irish peasants that they gave away whatever of surplus they had. Peasant reputations for hospitality seem to reflect tribal ways. The requirement of unanimous decisions in certain manor courts reflects the tribal custom of talking for days over any decisions. The tribal wisdom was that whoever must live with a decision must help make it; it is better not to make a decision than take sides on an issue contested by two factions, thereby splitting the people. Similarly, trial by combat and the use of omens and lotteries for decision making helped to preserve communal unity in a tribal fashion by transferring the responsibility for decisions to supernatural forces or to chance. The communal gaming—"football" and other sports, some of which survive into our time—seems to have helped periodically blur status distinctions. Some orgiastic rituals, reflective of tribal ways, celebrated and made real the community by reducing the degree of individual separateness through sexual interpenetration, dance, and temporary abandonment of individual responsibilities. In these practices can be seen the harnessing of older social forms to make more acceptable the progressive triumph of the purely feudal, that is, purely caste, logic.

The peasant was not a tribal person, however. The peasant was deeply attached to a single piece of land and a single village, and owned and used his own means of produc-

[10] Bennett, op. cit., pp. 46–51.

tion. So long as it was possible to live within the customs and so long as adherence to them ensured some measure of protection, the peasant's commitment to working the earth in one place survived. The peasant's ancestor was the first to conceive of the possibility of wresting a storable food surplus from the earth, of, in a sense, making war against the earth, something which the nomadic hunter and gatherer did not think of. The bittersweet way through which the peasant maintained this new relationship to the land was by acceptance of the symbolic father—the warrior-chief, the warrior-king, the papa or pope—in the place of the father reality of the tribe. This new relationship, while it guaranteed a better material life, was at best paternalistic and full of suspicion and resentment on both sides, and at worst a degenerate slavery.

Even given the limited possibilities within the logic of feudalism, and the contradiction between food surplus and vulnerability to raid, the caste community retained its essential form for hundreds of years in northern and central Europe, Central and South America, and for thousands of years in the great river valleys of China, Egypt, and the Middle East. There is much we do not know about the internal forms of these communities. We have much to discover from the records available to us about the basic features of feudalism (land use and customs linking the castes) and much about patterns we theorize are linked to the basics—art, literature, childrearing, religious observance, decision making, warfare, and social control. More has been done, particularly by Karl Marx and his students, to apply conflict theory to European feudal forms than to feudalism elsewhere or to tribalism. Apparent exceptions to the theory, such as the Pueblos of the southwestern part of North America where people lived by sedentary agriculture for centuries within a tribal, rather than caste, form, need to be studied and theory fit to the findings.

THE DISSOLUTION OF THE FEUDAL COMMUNITY

We can analyze with more certainty the coming apart of feudalism, particularly in East Asia and northern Europe. Here feudal forms were destroyed and replaced by a literate people, and so the process could be written about. Its superficial aspects—the wars, the rebellions, the loss of heads among nobility, the slaughter of rebellious peasants —are well recorded and are served up to students either as entertainment or as quaint relics of the past which indicate how much more advanced we are. We argue that these events are interesting and understandable only as they help us construct a theory of how community forms change.

Some feudal systems disappeared through conquest by more powerful peoples. The Maya and Inca were slaughtered and themselves made feudal vassals of their Spanish conquerors. Egyptian and Middle Eastern feudalism passed into preindustrial imperialism, which constitutes a community form halfway between feudalism and capitalism which we will not attempt to analyze here.

Some feudal forms, notably the European, were destroyed from within, through the emergence of contradictions leading to the form's being unusable for certain people. The principal contradiction of feudalism is the tying together of landlord and peasant in such a way that their interests have the potential to both benefit and damage one another. The logic of a reciprocating system requires some feedback and regulatory mechanism by which the two parts that depend on one another obtain enough resources for survival. In the absence or failure of such feedback and regulation, the stronger will oppress the weaker.

Conflict theory suggests points at which there will be trouble within a feudal system, where potential contradictions exist. One example is the potential contradiction between sedentary agriculture with its fixed-size land holdings, and population growth. Where do the surplus sons and daughters of peasants and warriors go if use of land passes only to the first son?

The coming apart and transformation of the European feudal community form involved four processes, all interrelated, all having secondary effects on other parts of the social structure and culture of the time: (1) the growth of central governments; (2) the growth of populations; (3) the loss of common rights to land—the enclosure movement; and (4) creation of new roles outside the caste structure—the rise of the town dwellers, the people of the burg who, displaced from use of caste roles, created commercial or bourgeois roles.

The Growth of Central Governments

The causes of centralization of power came from both within the structure of feudalism and outside it. Competition between landholding warriors created in the nobility some of the same feeling of need for protection as that which originally created the warrior-farmer link. A life of blood feud and vengeance, added to the uncertainties of fear of invasion by strangers, was not very appealing. Warriors who aspired to kingship might gain power by playing competing landlords against one another as well as by using loyal followers, in their own courts, to ensure just and bloodless settlement of the disputes of the competitors. This was a tricky business—dispensing justice and playing both sides against one another. Many an aspiring centralizer lost his head in the process. Outside enemies, particularly those using another community form such as no-

madic tribes or emerging capitalist societies, often provided the needed stimulus for centralization of feudal power. This was the case in the creation of the Spanish nation, a kingship which united several previously autonomous provinces or imperialistic and class-stratified dukedoms against the Moors. The dukes and other independent lords united behind Ferdinand of Aragon and Isabella of Castile because these two promised success in the long struggle to rid the Iberian peninsula of the Moorish community.

Although there had been people who called themselves kings all over Europe since tribal days, few men had held real power—the ability to command the loyalty and material support of local landlords over a large area. When some men did begin to create stable central governments through the processes described above, they looked also to add church power to their own. As the only organization which could provide support for a local noble if he ventured far from home, the church had been the inheritor of Roman power. Being able to provide a service *indebts* others—that is, gives the provider power over them. Rising kings sought to make the churchly power their own, as in the case of the dispute between Henry II and his Archbishop Thomas Becket.

In the long run, there were three consequences of the rise of kings and central governments. First, central courts required bureaucrats—people who could keep records and think clearly whether they had noble ancestors or not. The demand for such skills placed a premium on learning and supported the growth of an intellectual class independent of the caste system. It is tempting to believe that once the search for knowledge burst out of the libraries of the monks it seduced kings and nobles into their own destruction—a contradiction within a contradiction. In support of this idea is a story from the court of King Louis XIV of eighteenth-century France which may or may not be true. The King and the Duke de la Valliere were discoursing on how gunpowder was made. The King's mistress, Madame Pompadour, interjected that she did not know why they bothered with questions so abstract; she herself did not know even what her rouge or her stockings were made of. The Duke de la Valliere is supposed to have replied that the answers to all these questions and many more could be found in the encyclopedia of the intellectual Monsieur Diderot, but that the King had ordered the book confiscated. The King was so fascinated that he asked that the book be circulated, having banned it without knowing it contained the answers to such useful questions.[11] It contained answers to other questions as well, for example, how to build machines which could create a power greater than loyalty to the king.

A second effect of centralization was better defense, which in turn made it possible to construct and defend roads and the commerce which could move along them. Centralization had much to do with the rise of towns and commerce.

Finally, centralization, by pacifying the countryside and providing for better organization in the towns, made the king the protector of the peasant and, insofar as it reduced the protective role of the local nobility, destroyed the original basis for the caste system while retaining the obligations of the peasantry to this system. In a sense, the success of local feudalism produced a superfeudalism, which ran against the logic of the original feudalism. A parallel process in industrial capitalist economies is the tendency toward monopolization, which frees monopoly capitalists from the restraints of competition but still binds small businessmen and unorganized workers to a structure involving the rigors of competition.

The Growth of Populations

A basic contradiction in the feudal order is the possibility of population growth. Feudal order is a fixed relationship of people to forest, marsh, and meadow, and more mouths to feed threaten this relationship. However, the more successful is the feudal form of organization in protecting farmers, the more likely is population surplus. The struggle with this contradiction can be seen all over the world. In the Japanese form of feudalism, which climaxed somewhat later than European feudalism, peasants with less than ten *koku* of land (an amount capable of producing about fifty bushels of rice in a year) were strictly prohibited from dividing their land. It was taught that "If the land should be divided up, each portion would produce so little that each son would suffer from scanty provisions and they would all be reduced (in) . . . status."[12]

The division of land produced an *outcaste* group, those sons who had no land or who had too little land to support their families. The emergence of new outcaste groups is a dangerous threat to a community based on customary relations between known and clearly defined castes. In China it is estimated that the amount of farmable land was reduced from 5.24 *mou* per capita in 1666 to 4.07 *mou* per capita in 1766. By the time of the Taiping rebellion of 1872, there had been a further reduction to 2.59 *mou* per capita. No agricultural system in which the people are tied to the land by customs and whose technology is part of these rigid customs can long survive such a reduction in its basic resource. Chinese feu-

---

[11] Alan Lloyd, *The Spanish Centuries* (New York: Doubleday, 1968), p. 249.

[12] Takizawa, op. cit., p. 353.

dalism became increasingly oppressive; and although landlords were not wealthy by European standards, they were rich relative to the near slavery of the peasants. Finally, the peasants had nothing to lose by the destruction of the system except their allegiance to the customary ways of doing things.

Russian feudalism reached its crisis in the late 1800s. For some areas in Russia there are records of the peasants' loss of land. For one district, the number of peasant households grew by 92 percent between 1881 and 1917, and during the same period the amount of farmed land increased by only 3 percent. Thus, where each homestead had an average 22.4 acres in 1881, the average was 11.8 acres in 1917.[13]

In western Europe, some peasant rebellions preceded the enormous population growth of the fifteenth century and later, but these were few and easily crushed. In the case of European feudalism, "revolution," like the French and English "revolutions," was the fight that occurred *after* feudalism was essentially destroyed; a fight between the aristocracy and their allies, who were just waking up to what they had already lost, and the bourgeoisie.

The peasants were increasingly harmed by the nearly continuous civil wars and wars of national consolidation, particularly in the fifteenth to seventeenth centuries. They got less and less of the protection which was supposed to be their end of the feudal bargain:

> Both parties fought over the peasant's fields, forced the peasant into their ranks, and blackmailed the peasant when they had gotten the upper hand.[14]

[13] *The Village of Viriatino: An Ethnographic Study of a Russian Village from before the Revolution to the Present*, translated and edited by Sula Benet (Garden City, N.Y.: Doubleday Anchor, 1970), p. 49.
[14] Coulton, op. cit., p. 105.

The cruelty practiced against the peasantry at this stage of European feudalism reflects the fact that in some places feudalism was much more oppressive than others. It is also evidence that a community form, once gotten under way, continues under great inertia. Like a ball rolling down a hill, it may begin to reveal through cracks the internal stresses and strains resulting from its crashes against obstacles, but it does not shatter until it reaches the bottom. The early peasant rebellions revealed the contradictions of the feudal form, as exemplified in a monk's quotations from eleventh-century peasant revolutionaries in the Norman part of France:

> The lords (they said) do them nought but harm; they can have no reason with them, nor no gain from their own work. Daily the peasants go with great grief, in pain and in toil; last year was ill, this year is worse; daily their cattle are taken for taxes or for services; there are so many pleas (in the manor-court) and quarrels, so many customs, old and new, that they cannot have an hour's peace. . . . Wherefore then do we let them harm us; let us shake ourselves free from their domination! We, too, are men as they; limbs we have like theirs, and our bodies are as big and we can endure as much; all that we need is only a heart. Let us bind ourselves together by oath to defend ourselves and our goods; let us hold together, and then, if they will war against us, we have one or two score peasants, able to fight against every knight of theirs.[15]

Coulton also describes, in his own words, the *Jacquerie* peasant rebellion of 1357: "Here again in Languedoc men were murdered at sight if they could not show the horny hand of toil; the atrocities committed were even worse than in Flanders and the reprisals bloody in proportion."[16]

These quotations reflect the fact that some peasants struggled against oppression, even

[15] Ibid., p. 111.
[16] Ibid., p. 129.

in the early stages of feudalism. But in the eleventh and the fourteenth centuries, either the system was relatively workable, and masses of people had not yet been displaced, or no alternate form existed to which people could flow.

External forces like plagues, which are estimated to have killed over half the peasant populations of some areas, worsened the feudal contradictions. When large areas were reduced in population in the thirteenth to fifteenth centuries, the nobility were unwilling to increase the privileges or decrease the burdens of the remaining peasantry. This contributed to a second wave of peasant rebellions, none of which were in any way successful, and most of which are probably unrecorded.[17]

Gradually, as plague became less a threat and as population grew, the contradictory inability of feudalism to survive its own success began to express itself. Whether this was obvious at the time is an intriguing question, with implications for those trying to decide if *we* have the ability to see the problems created by the successes of our own forms. At any rate, four major consequences of population growth may be listed: (1) the emergence of the free farmer, (2) the emergence of smallholders, (3) the rent system, and (4) the growth of a town labor force.

1. Where there was unorganized land available, as in northern France, kings could organize the development of those lands in order to absorb surplus population. But to attract the people there, the king or land agent of the crown had to give the new peasants freedoms of a sort they were not likely to have on traditional estates. Thus were the boundaries of caste ruptured, those left behind made envious, and a new group of mobile free farmers created.

[17] Christopher Brooke, *Structure of Medieval Society* (New York: McGraw-Hill, 1971), p. 84.

2. The surpluses of people on the estates themselves also created a new group—the *smallholders*, those who because of too-large families or late coming to the manor were left with very small pieces of land. Their existence was tenuous. They did not have as much right to the commons of the estate as did most peasants. But being a smallholder had its compensations. A smallholder was likely to have to put together many such pieces, perhaps on several manors, to survive, and thereby had to relate to several masters at once. Such simultaneous relations were more easily accomplished by contract than by custom, since the customs of different manors put conflicting demands on the smallholder and were a source of conflict between lords. Also, many of the smallholders, unable to subsist entirely on their small landholdings, began to specialize in carpentry, metalworking, blacksmithing, cloth making, baking, and barrel making. Their work laid the basis for a class of artisans who provided services for the peasant-farmer more cheaply than he could provide them for himself. These occupations and types of relationships were outside caste custom and caste etiquette.

3. Related to the emergence of smallholders was the development of the practice of substituting *paid* rents for the traditional services owed by the peasant to the landlord. For, as the population of the estate grew, the need for labor services to the landlord declined. The landlord had two options: he could reduce the labor payments from each peasant or he could demand cash payments instead of labor payments, providing there were cash markets available to the peasant. The latter was the most likely option, but once again contradictions turned this seeming advantage against the landlord. By making the peasant liable for money payments, the lord undermined all the "sporting chances" which gave flexibility and adaptability in good times and bad. The peasant either became much more heavily oppressed or was pressured to become a part of a money economy which took him outside the tight caste system of the manor in search of markets where he could sell his surplus crops or labor for money.

4. The population growth provided a ready labor force to take part in early commercial enterprises in the towns. From the estates came the workers needed to spin cloth and produce metal ware, load and unload the ships, make and repair the carts which hauled the goods, keep the records, and engage in the thousands of other small occupations out of which a new social system was being made. Some cities guaranteed freedom to any serf who could remain a certain length of time undetected by his former master. This practice reveals the conflict between old and new economies. A similar conflict can be seen in the struggle over escaped slaves between northern and southern states in the United States just before the Civil War.

Related to the emergence of a town-based labor force were two simultaneous developments: (1) the rise of a class of town- or burg-dwelling people, the bourgeoisie, who lived by producing and selling *between* rather than *within* villages, and (2) the growth of markets where the landlord could make a profit on the produce of his estates. Although the two processes are interrelated, let us look at the second separately.

The Loss of Communal Rights to the Land— the Enclosure Movement

As the landlord saw the towns growing, he saw also the growth of markets in which he could sell whatever was surplus, whatever he and his peasants did not eat or use on his estate. Without markets there had been no motivation for the landlord to demand unreasonable effort, or the last grain of wheat or pound of cheese, from the peasants; without markets, the extra food would rot. Uncoerced, the peasants related relatively willingly to the requirements of the estate. With

markets, landlords had an incentive to try and extract more and more surplus from their lands. Few landlords were so stupid as to simply take increasing amounts of food from the peasants until they could barely feed themselves. What most landlords *were* likely to do was to convert some part of the common meadowland into fenced sheep pasture. This would produce a good profit in wool and provide wage labor for some of the surplus peasants' sons who might serve as herders. It seemed, no doubt, an innocuous thing to the landlords, but the peasants saw established the precedent of the violation of custom and the taking piece by piece of the "waste" land that, within custom, they had used as their own. The enclosure movement involved more than sheep. Hillside or cleared forest might be converted into vineyards; timber and minerals might be extracted from the "waste" which in the past would have been profitless. Toward the end of the enclosure process, the land was surveyed. In many places peasants were given title to specific pieces of land, where formerly they had had rights in custom to the use of the land, but had "owned" no property. Two distinctly different ways of relating to the tools of an economy, ownership and customary rights, can be seen in conflict as a new economic strategy emerges.

Whether or not strict justice was done the peasant depended upon local circumstances and the conscience of the executing officials; it was not always possible to supply precise legal proof for property traditionally held. But in every case, the change undermined the whole peasant position. They were indeed now owners of their own farms; but they were less able than ever to maintain their own self-sufficiency. The cost of the proceeding, in some places the requirement of fencing, left them in debt; they would have to find cash to pay. When the wastes (common forest, marsh, hillsides) disappeared there disappeared also the free wood for fire or building; there would have to be cash now to buy. If there were no longer common meadows, where would the cows graze? . . . [C]ompelled to raise crops that could be offered for sale . . . confined to their own few acres and burdened with obligations, the peasants had no other recourse . . . [than to] compete on the traders' market with the old landlords whose great holdings operated with efficiency.[18]

When the peasants were "given" title to the land, they could be separated from it by purchase. Formerly, they had rights forever. In much the same way whites were able to buy land on Indian reservations once the concept of tribal landholding was broken down by insisting that individual families be given title to the land.

The beginnings of a new logic—the vision of a new community form—can be seen, in retrospect, in the twelfth century, in the fairs or episodic markets of areas like Champagne in France where merchants flocked together under protection of the counts of Champagne and Brie.[19] Buying and selling fed on each other until it seemed all were caught up in the fever. However, the landbound peasants was being destroyed, at least in their capacity as one of the basic props of the system, crushed under mounting losses in uneven competition with the large landlords and later in the markets of a thousand industrializing cities of the eighteenth century. The aristocracy were simply doing better what they had done from the beginning: managing land use. Some history books give the impression that the aristocracy developed into a class of *evil people*. From the view of conflict theory, however, most of the late feudal aristocrats were doing what any humans in their place would do given the community form they used. But the inequality in the struggle to control one's life and destiny was increasing. Within the confines of feudalism there were coming to be a few very big winners and many born losers.[20]

More than any other single factor, the conversion of the land to profit making undermined assent to the customs through which people were bound to separate statuses and separate relations to the land—to a caste system. With the interests of landlords and peasants, now mostly free farmers, so clearly opposed, only a few options were open: struggle to the destruction of one or the other status; change in interests of either or both statuses; or emergence of new ways of relating—new community forms.

THE BOURGEOIS REVOLUTION

We tend to forget that the merchant enterprisers of fourteenth- to nineteenth-century Europe helped hasten the destruction of what had once been a stable and prosperous way of life. We will next examine how a new class, the bourgeoisie, laid the basis for a new economy, at the same time destroying the old caste-feudal system—at first peacefully, later through violent revolutions.

A new set of economic roles, groups, and institutions grew up around the medieval town. A new culture and life-style was developed by the bourgeosie, the people who used this new economy. Conflict theory does not clearly indicate why this form, and not another, eventually came to be so widely used. Perhaps the theory could be made

---

[18] Oscar Handlin, "Peasant Origins," in George Dalton (ed.), *Tribal and Peasant Economies* (Garden City, N.Y.: Natural History Press, 1967), p. 474.

[19] Robert-Henri Bautier, *The Economic Development of Medieval Europe* (New York: Harcourt Brace Jovanovich, 1971), p. 110.

[20] An English lord of the seventeenth century, Sir Nicholas Throckmorton, a middling landowner, had a yearly income 800 times that of his gardener (£2400 to £3) (A. L. Rowse, *Sir Walter Raleigh* [New York: Harper, 1962], p. 289). The Marquis of Villena, fifteenth-century Spaniard, had an income 1 million times that of the average wage worker (Henry Kamen, *The Spanish Inquisition* [New York: New American Library, 1965], p. 4.)

clearer on this point through a study of alternative forms, if any, which were rejected.

One hypothesis which might derive from
conflict theory is that people will seek new
forms which will resolve the greatest number
of the most basic contradictions of the old.
In a way this is what we will suggest, although it is not a very disciplined argument,
since we are suggesting, through hindsight,
that those contradictions in feudalism resolved by the emergence of a class-structured
community form must have been the most
important ones.

It seems to us that the vision which most
pervaded the thought of those who destroyed European feudalism was the possibility of risking less to gain more. Only such
a simple and appealing vision could mobilize
people through the centuries that it took to
undo such a highly integrated community
form as feudalism. Feudalism was based on
mutual risks: the peasant tried to choose the
most powerful warrior as master in the hope
of comparable gain—one's life and relative
economic security. The warriors risked their
lives in return for food and relative riches.
At the beginnings of feudalism, this was all
that could be envisioned, all that could be
hoped for. Although risky, the form was
livable once embellished with its supporting
props and cast of players: the priest's as-
surances that God had intended those who
risked their necks to have much more than
those who worked the land; the parables
celebrating the working of the land and the
meekness of the peasantry; the peacefulness
and wholeness of life which was the fact
often enough in enough places to make
some people long for it even today. Yet the
potential contradictions within the customs
linking the two major castes worked on both
alike. As we have seen, the peasant experienced increasing oppression to the extent
that feudalism was successful in producing
a surplus and in opening long-distance commerce. The aristocracy experienced a con-

tradition resulting from increasing centralization of power. As war power was successfully accumulated by kings, lesser nobles
were forced to make choices about their
loyalty to competitors for the throne—risky
choices, choices they did not have to make
when they lived more isolated lives. Although some court favorites gained in good
measure by taking the risk, others lost all,
including their heads.

Ultimately it seems the peasant was driven
to risk more as landlessness became his
nightmare. The landlord was driven to risk
more as his survival came to depend on his
guesses as to who would survive the struggles for positions at the top of the feudal
power structure. The bourgeois vision of
commerce provided a possible livelihood for
the displaced peasant and the possibility of
a secure existence for the aristocrat who
chose to become bourgeois. In fact, today
the term *bourgeois* often brings to mind a
way of relating to others which takes minimal risks for the most assured returns—a
way without the madness of witch burnings,
insane chivalry, monstrous tortures, days devoted to pageantry and celebration of feudal
hierarchy. Bourgeois logic was built on a
philosophy of rationality; its style was expressed by the realism of Renaissance painting.

The bourgeois vision is of a world in
which power is dispersed and ordered by
contracts made between classes of artisans
and supported or guaranteed by the least
powerful state necessary to enforce these
contracts. The working out of the bourgeois
vision may yet seem nightmare to us, but to
the people of the time the vision carried the
promise of freedom from petty and large
tyranny and from random acts of cruelty and
oppression as well as the possibility of a better material life. The bourgeois form carried
the possibility, for males at least, of breaking
the chains by which the individual was
forced to relate to the world through a set

of social structural and cultural arrangements into which he was born and over which he had absolutely no control, no choice except to accept.

Additionally, the bourgeois belief system, as reflected in the constitutional writings of the English, French, and American revolutions, contained the promise of an end to the violent displacement of one community form by another. The political contract between citizen and state was supposed to ensure a flexible community form, one that could alter itself in response to emerging contradictions. Whether or not this works in practice is an important problem in the analysis of class-structured community presented in Chapter 10.

And so the people who would use this form to batter down feudal society flocked into the towns, the only place they could hope to be free of the clutches of caste. As we have said, the vision in and of itself did not require greater sacrifice. Rather, it asked that people risk *less* in order to have the possibility of gaining more over the long run. It is essentially a vision which appeals to inertia, to the tendency to seek the easiest road. Later, as the nobles saw that all those people flowing downhill as water seeking the sea were about to flood their old privileges and ways, they resisted. At that point, however, the bourgeois and their peasant allies had more than the hopeless courage of the eleventh- and twelfth-century peasants in rebellion against their masters. They fought as people armed with the feeling that they were the force destined to batter down the last obstacles to the reaching of a better world.

The towns gradually attracted the surplus sons and daughters of both major castes. At first they were not conscious of themselves as the wave of the future. They were simply trying to make a living by reducing the power of nobles and kings to interfere in commerce, the only living possible to them.

They needed income to build walls and streets, but could not require a *fixed* tax as could the lord of peasants who had hereditary rights to land which produces year in and year out. The burgesses or bourgeois town councils had to adjust the tax to the income of the individual—some paying more, some paying less. They needed a "more expeditious law [one in which] means of proof [are] more rapid and more independent of chance, and judges who were themselves acquainted with the professional occupations of those who came under their jurisdiction and could cut short their arguments by a knowledge of the case at issue."[21]

The bourgeois needed to be free of the caste requirements to stay in one place, marry within one's caste, and use only the lord's mill and bakery. They got free by building walls and by playing nobles off against each other, and in some places by making of themselves more efficient armies than those of the landed aristocracy. They needed above all enforceable contracts to guarantee commercial transactions, sales, and purchases; they needed transportation; and they needed a money system which allowed exchange over a wide area without having to haul around bulky goods for barter or trade. To accomplish this they soon had to compromise their pure vision of free local governments and lay the basis for the tendencies in capitalist economies toward rich and powerful federal governments, which they needed to build and maintain roads, support markets and fairs, coin and enforce the use of money,[22] and maintain *standing* armies, not just collections of noblemen's and peasants' sons called together on short notice. At first they supported the growing power of kings, which further undid the power of the local nobility. As early as 1115, the local

[21] Henri Pirenne, *Economic and Social History of Medieval Europe*, translated by I. E. Clegg (New York: Harcourt, Brace & World, 1937), p. 51.
[22] Pirenne (op. cit., p. 108) notes that those who refused to receive state-coined money were punished.

nobility referred to the bourgeois-controlled towns as "detestable communes."[23] Later, the bourgeois replaced kings with governments of businessmen.

So the bourgeois developed a collective vision, in conflict-theory terms a new logic. It was an abstract, but very compelling, belief system. It helped build new towns and cities, standardize law based on private property rather than custom, and create powerful central states. It brought money, an income tax, and a new sense of freedom.

There were transitional forms—ways of doing things halfway between the old and the new. Such were the guilds, associations of men of the same occupations. There were guilds of weavers, metalworkers, carpenters, stone masons—most commercial occupations of the time were organized. The existence of guilds tells us that people move slowly toward the use of new forms, adapting replicas of the old to help themselves make the transformation. The guilds had some of the protective features of castes. Sons inherited the fathers' occupations and businesses, and there was control over who could engage in what, what prices were charged, and even over new products and new ways of doing things. The guild protected the free artisan-craftsman-small businessman. Those using the guild social structural form could begin to use the new logic of competition, but they competed as a group, not as individuals.

As the guilds gave way to factories where labor was hired, the competitive feature of the bourgeois economy emerged as a powerful social force. The bourgeois social forms failed to deal with a very natural contradiction in this more competitive economy. Perhaps there was no way to guarantee that those who competed best would not destroy competition itself. Through attempts to limit competition by huge monopolistic corpora-

tions, through purchase of governments by corporations, collusion between corporations and big unions, big unions themselves emerged as the structural products of tendencies that manifested themselves in the earliest bourgeois communities.

Some of the nobility, those who could not figure out how to or did not wish to become bourgeois, resisted the destruction of the caste system. In some places in Europe, as in southern Italy and parts of Spain,[24] in many parts of Asia and Latin America, poverty-stricken versions of the caste system survive to this day. When nobility saw, usually too late, the threat posed by the rise of the bourgeois, they attacked; and the town dwellers turned from cultural revolution, the working out of a new vision, to revolutionary violence. Some of the things that make the process so fascinating, at a distance, are the variety of forms it took, the varying lengths of time it took to accomplish the dominance of capitalist economics, and the successful resistance of pockets where aristocracy and church combined. The change was bloodless in Scandinavia, where a cattle- and fish-based feudal economy got along without a powerful nobility; the change was most bloody in France where the lid was kept on longest and the castes most clearly separated. The English nobility seemed almost to aspire to become bourgeois. In Russia, where feudalism had overcome tribalism much later than in western Europe, the bourgeois revolution was delayed 250 years beyond that of England, 150 years beyond that of France. Some people were able to retain tribal forms of organization in the face of persecution, first from the feudal order, later from bourgeois police. The gypsies, whose history reveals how tenaciously a people can hold to a way of life, are described in Selection 9-2.

---

[23] Pirenne, op. cit., p. 50.

[24] See Edward Banfield, *Moral Basis of a Backward Society* (New York: The Free Press, 1958), and Julian Pitt-Rivers, *People of the Sierra* (New York: Criterion, 1955).

SELECTION 9-2: A remnant from European feudalism.

PLIGHT OF THE GYPSIES

By Ronald Harker

Who cares about gypsies? Not affluent Europe. It shows little concern for the poor and weak minority in its midst: the Rom, to give them their correct though less familiar name, whose ill-treatment, rooted in ancient prejudice, is still so common it is borne like bad weather.

An inquiry into their condition, promoted by the Minority Rights Group (MRG), an international research unit registered in Britain, finds that while Yugoslavia and Czechoslovakia care for their million Rom, the most acute intolerance is suffered by Rom within the member states of the Council of Europe.

Scattered throughout the world, outside India and Southeast Asia are nearly eight million Rom. The key to their seemingly endless persecution lies in the valuation put upon them by the non-Romani.

Suspect and Inferior

To the medieval mind, the Rom, coming from the Turkish side of Europe or beyond, and speaking an unknown tongue, were suspect and inferior. The church rejected them because it opposed fortune-telling and the practice of magic.

It was not long before they became marked as the first blacks in Europe, opposed by the pillars of medieval society, the church, the state and the guides.

The ruling classes regarded these evasive independent people, the product of migration and adaptation, as useless because they could not be easily exploited. The Rom stayed outside the feudal, and later capitalist and even socialist society, having become neither serfs nor conformist wage earners.

"Much legislation," says the report, "therefore was, and still is, designed to sweep Rom along with the dispossessed—whether sturdy beggars of 16th century England or the homeless and unemployed today—into the exploiters' sphere."

Among the inquiry's findings:

France: Has 190,000 Rom. The law discriminates against them. Those on the road are required to carry an identity card and constantly checked by police. They cannot live where they like—prefects of departments can decide where they may rest and where they may not. Everywhere throughout the department signs can be found reading, "Gypsies Forbidden."

Belgium: 14,000. The police prevent any nomadic Rom from entering the country. As in France they must carry identification cards. Families may not stay more than one day and a night at a roadside. Infant mortality is 20 per cent higher than the national average.

West Germany: 70,000. "Unable to exploit them, Germany turned the poison of race hatred upon the Rom and resorted to genocide. Thus the massacres and deportations reached their dreadful yet logical climax in the Nazi holocaust . . ."

"Today," says the report, "policy appears to be limited to confining some semi-settled families and forlorn individuals left over from the Nazi period in 40 dilapidated camps and small ghettos. Some are actually on the same sites as the wartime concentration camps. . . ."

Italy: 80,000. Only seven official camping places exist. "Police in most districts rigorously uphold local by-laws against the stationing of caravans . . ."

Spain: 500,000. Police have burned down Romani quarters. "When the tourist industry was expanding some years ago an official drive began to destroy the settlements as unsightly . . ." Huts were burned. When women protested, police shaved their heads.

Netherlands: 30,000. The Dutch have a network of properly serviced caravan sites, but the report says that government action is somewhat overshadowed by an officially-declared aim to absorb all nomadic families into urban housing and, in time, to close the sites.

Britain: 50,000. Once tried genocide, and then found it more profitable to transport Rom to its colonies. Now a 1959 law still makes it an offense for Rom to camp on a highway "without lawful authority or excuse."

A change seems at hand with the building of caravan sites, but Rom insecurity has at the same time increased because local councils have power to close down existing private sites which

Rom have bought for winter quarters—if the authority considers such sites sub-standard. "Evictions from vacant plots and slum clearance areas," says the report, accompanied by many ugly scenes and frequent violence, have become a regular feature."

A defensive action which has appeared since the report was written is a warning given by British Rom that they will report to the Race Relations Board (RRB)—a watchdog against racial discrimination—any inn-keeper who displays a sign saying "No Gypsies Served," and the board has said it will investigate any such complaint.

Communist Policies

The Communist countries of east and southeast Europe start from the premise that it is the state's duty to help underdeveloped groups, yet the Rom do not escape many of the same pressures they endure in the west and north.

USSR: 414,000. The report quotes comment from Moscow by a Romani writer, Lajko Cherenkov. "It is rare to meet a Rom in the USSR today who cannot read and write, while before the war among certain groups, for instance those in Bessarabia, nobody could.

"Most of the young generation today are finishing eighth or tenth class, and one cannot distinguish in towns between Rom and other nationalities in this respect . . . I doubt that the conservation of Romani nationality depends on nomadism and traditional occupations. They have given up these aspects of their life voluntarily . . ."

It should be added, however, that nomadism is outlawed by the Soviet Union although the law is not strictly enforced.

Poland: 53,000. Attempts to stop nomadism as a nuisance and integrate Rom began in 1952 with a policy of voluntary integration but in 1964 it turned to coercion, and within two years the Rom had ceased to wander. Complex social and health problems remained. Among housedwellers, disputes arose with Romani neighbors, and one of every seven children was found to be suffering from tuberculosis.

Hungary: 480,000. Forty percent of Rom families live in poor shacks and wooden huts in 2100 settlements, half of which have no well and two-thirds of which are without electricity. A better-placed group among Hungarian Rom are musicians. "Today," says the report, "there are perhaps 10,000 musicians with over 90 Romani orchestras playing in restaurants and hotels in Budapest alone. They have their own professional association to regulate bookings and fees."

CLASS CONSCIOUSNESS: A PARALLEL PROCESS

At this point we must face a critical question for conflict analysis. Why is it that people whose living conditions are such that an outsider observer would consider them terribly oppressed often seem content? Karl Marx said that *false class consciousness* was the force restraining the oppressed from wrecking an oppressive social structure. False consciousness includes (1) lack of awareness of the social structural origins of one's problems—blaming fate, bad luck, or oneself; (2) lack of awareness of the similar class-related problems of one's fellow humans; (3) lack of awareness of alternative social structures; and (4) lack of awareness of the power to create them. Presumably the more powerful class will do all in its power to befuddle the weaker class, using threats, rewards, and a public glorification of the small joys of the life of the lowly.

Emile Durkheim, one of the originators of modern functional analysis, reminds us that each human is born into an already organized social world. We spend the first years of our lives being taught how and why things are as they are. It would seem to take enormous effort for people, within a lifetime, to question the fundamental economic arrangements of their time, much less see clearly their own interests and class allies.

The difficulty in predicting from contradic-

In parts of Latin America, the hacienda system still organizes the lives of millions of landless farmers. Their poverty, like that of medieval European serfs, creates enormous pressures for social change. (Steve Dunwell for Editorial Photocolor Archives)

tion to class conflict lies in the subjective part of the sociological conception of power. Remember power was defined as a *relationship*. If the landlord class has many resources *relative* to the needs of the peasant class and few needs *relative to* the resources of the peasant class, then the landlord class has a great potential power advantage, and should be able, with little effort, to get the peasant class to expend great energy. Thus there is potential oppression in any unequal power situation.

Yet if we are to predict *from* contradictions producing classes of unequal power *to* class conflict we must know how one class perceives its needs and resources relative to the perceived needs and resources of the other class. Perhaps the peasant believes the priest has the resource of a reward in heaven to fit the peasant's need for salvation, while the peasant's strong back is needed by the priest or his landlord friends. Does the peasant in this case feel oppressed, or does he feel that the relationship is balanced?

The issue of class consciousness is a complex and poorly understood one. Members of dominant classes, presumably more aware

of the advantages of the class structure, often act against their own long-term interests by pursuing short-term gain. Indeed, it is the nature of contradiction that people seem blind to or powerless to concertedly act to compromise short-term goals for the preservation of social structures. A structure like feudalism, through which people seek to achieve goals of superior fighting and farming by a structure which formally relates these specialties to one another, can do a fairly good job of both but cannot produce superwarriors or superfarmers without wrecking the structure. If both groups were content to remain mediocre farmers and mediocre fighters, the structure might last much longer.

One possibility is that even without high levels of class consciousness, the more powerful class will gradually make the institutional patterns unusable for the less powerful. This seems to account for the destruction of European feudalism, Russian feudalism, and perhaps even Chinese feudalism. Revolutions in these cases seem largely to have been the work of a new class, already forced to live and use alternative structures outside the old structure. This new class (the bourgeosie in disintegrating European feudalism) may enlist the oppressed class of the old system (peasants in this case) by raising their class consciousness. Members of the old oppressed class will be potentially revolutionary to the extent they are finding the old arrangements unworkable and are in fact becoming increasingly powerless (even though they may be better off economically than they once were).

SOME PROBLEMS IN EVOLUTIONARY ANALYSIS

We hope we have shown enough of tribal and feudal life to give you an idea of the kinds of historical evidence on which we base our belief that they are fundamentally different community forms. Our view is that communities based on different land-use forms and different economic practices, and on different cultural processes relating bits of social structure to each other, will differ in many predictable ways—in religion, in politics, in warfare, in policing, in child-rearing, in medicine. They will differ also in the bits and pieces of daily life which make up these institutions, and they will differ in painting, music, sculpture, and literature. People using each form develop a different logic to provide answers to the basic question, "How shall humans relate to each other?" The specifics of life in the community should be predictable from an understanding of the logic of the economy. Our theory in summary is as follows:

I The structure of the economic base (which includes relations of people to the tools of production and the mode of production) determines the institutional structure of the community. Communities differing fundamentally in economic base will differ in social structure and culture. Some people

will be using parts of older forms or experimenting with new ones. The dominant form involves the most people and the most human energy.

II Built into each form are contradictions, bits of social structure and culture which are means to incompatible goals. The more successful people are in reaching goals through the use of one part of social structure and culture, the less successful will they or others be in reaching other goals. For example, if the achievement of freedom is structured in such a way that it is achieved only at the expense of justice, that is a contradiction. If the freedom to make much money can be achieved only by reducing other people's freedom to do the same, that is a contradiction.[25]

III If the theory is correct, it should be possible to predict group life and institutional life from a knowledge of the community form. It should be possible to predict:

A The past, what should be found in the historical records.

B The directions of change which will occur in the community *if the most important contradictions* are known. Presumably the most important contradictions are those built either into the form of social bond or into the base of economic relations.

The attempt to construct such a theory comes from a felt need to understand certain things about human social relations. Born into a community already in motion, we don't know where it started, why this particular road was chosen by our ancestors, what other roads were traveled and rejected for many reasons along the way, and where this particular road leads. We wish to know these things, and feel there are ways to find out. Whereas on a globe there are an infinite number of ways to get from one point to another by roads, we believe the choices

[25] For an analysis of this contradiction see Albert Camus, *The Rebel*, translated by Anthony Bower (New York: Vintage, 1956).

open for humans in creating economic and social structures are much more limited, and that taking some of these choices, for example, "choosing" a hunting and gathering economy, limits the possibilities even further.

Insisting that there are a limited number of possible human community forms, and that the forms have a knowability and integrity of their own, offends certain historians and to some degree all lovers of detail and uniqueness.

Although we have tried not to distort the evidence itself, in this analysis we have distorted and compressed historical sequences (for example, in England enclosure came after towns) and concentrated on those examples which support our theory. We have not mentioned the wide variations in different European feudal systems, the complex variations within castes, the freedom from caste of Swiss farmers, or the persistence of Italian city-states or communes after the fall of Rome. Nor have we dwelt on the invasions, plagues, wars, or personalities which are often used to make history seem like a story leading to a happy ending—the glorious present.

Evolutionary theories based on human history are distasteful for another reason. All of us, historians as well, might rather view history as a process leading up to our own emergence. Believing this, we might also like to believe that history will stop with us. We believe this in part accounts for the tremendous resistance to the idea that we too will experience destruction of some of our social structural and cultural tools. We think it accounts in part for the popularity of purely functional theory, which views tendencies toward integration as central and conflict-producing tendencies as relatively minor.

Another problem in developing a theory of evolutionary community change comes from knowing there are no "pure" community forms in history, that all forms are in some stage of transition, but having to believe in forms in order to build theory. A theory of biological evolution is useful in pointing out how the various species of primates developed "toward" being human. Yet the biologist knows that in reality there is no "missing link," no creature which was one instant ape, the next human. We derive much use from *theorizing* separate community forms. We *assume* tendencies which start for knowable reasons (from contradiction and conflict) and which, assuming avalanche proportions, move the forms through which humans relate toward a new logic and internal arrangement. Yet at the same time we realize that the forms are always in the process of change and are not experienced as separate by people themselves. Even in postrevolutionary Russia and China, where the most thoroughgoing transformations of social forms yet described in writing have occurred, the experiences of individuals' daily lives do not seem totally transformed.

It is often difficult to see older community forms as logics which were *right*—not just forms used because people were stupid, technologically backward, or oppressed—because of our inability to understand other logics. To some, feudalism seems like a fairy story. We keep waiting for the toadish peasants to turn into bourgeois princes, believing it was unnatural, perhaps a sign of bewitchment, for men to slave on the land for generations. Experiencing our forms as "modern," the culmination of history, we find it hard to believe that such a life could be part of a very right-seeming and natural way of doing things.

Yet we ourselves may be living with certain relics from older systems. For example, look at the caste-like relationship between male and female. The people using one of these roles are largely prohibited from using the roles of the other "caste," their roles being prescribed by birth. We assume that these role relationships are fixed and unchangeable because they reside in biology, much as St. Thomas Aquinas and Aristotle assumed caste relations to be fixed in biology. Another defining characteristic of caste is that one may not change one's caste position either through marriage or through social mobility. Men and women are encouraged to intermarry, of course, but in the past, at least, they did not change their roles in the division of labor by doing so. In fact the prohibitions against men marrying men and women marrying women (recently challenged) support the caste system because they prevent the kind of marriage which *would* threaten the traditional division of labor. Similarly, until fairly recently it was illegal for a man to become a woman or a woman to become a man. Until recently, for a man to look like a woman or a woman to look like a man was to risk the most severe censure. Serious passing was against the law except on Halloween. Minor mimicry such as long hair for men or pants for women was handled by snide remarks or, if the individual persisted, by ostracism. Now all of these supports for this relic of the caste system seem to be breaking down.

What is most to the point to the conflict theorist about this example is that no matter what replaces the old male-female caste lines, those using the new forms will find it very hard to believe there was any internal logic or any satisfaction to the old arrangement. They will be likely to see it as pure oppression.

Our theory suggests that people may be quite satisfied with arrangements which later come to look hideous. The contradictions in the arrangements themselves, or coercion applied by people using other forms, are the forces which bring change. Once change begins, people will move downhill in the direc-

tion of change, on the path of least resistance. Change is rarely a heroic struggle against the evil supporters of the old way. It is more like stumbling into a house already created by thousands of others who gave up the old ways because they had to and simply lived the only life they could.

So did the bourgeois "destroy" feudal "oppression."

SUMMARY

Feudalism is a way of life which emerges out of the economic logic of sedentary agriculture. For the question, "How should one human relate to another?" the answer provided by feudalism is "Through caste and caste customs." Feudalism is based on a relationship between farmers and warriors. Farmers are sometimes enslaved by warriors; groups of warriors and farmer specialists sometimes emerge within a tribal people. Inevitably the warrior-farmer division becomes a *caste* division. A caste is a special type of social class in which (1) people are bound to specific economic roles for life, (2) sons and daughters inherit the economic roles of their parents, and (3) movement out of a caste by marriage or individual aptitude, interest, or initiative is practically impossible. The bases of the feudal community are the local customs which specify how members of one caste shall relate to members of other castes. In feudal society the professions are the most complexly developed institutional patterns. Separate castes or subcastes emerge to deal with the special problems of a caste-based agriculture. These include professional warriors, professional priests, professional healers, professional interpreters of caste-custom.

The basic internal contradictions of feudalism are (1) the emergence of super-warriors (or kings), (2) the subsequent centralization of government, (3) after centralization, the emergence of roles outside the caste structure and especially the creation of a market economy, (4) the tendency for overpopulation.

European feudalism gave rise to capitalism, a new economic logic. A series of revolutions in the name of mercantile or bourgeois freedom destroyed European feudalism. Today, capitalist as well as socialist countries attempt to destroy feudal-life ways or to control them for their economic advantage.

In Chapter 10 we will look at the culture and social structure established by capitalism and the bourgeoisie on the ruins of European feudalism.

SUGGESTED READINGS

H. S. Bennett, *Life on the English Manor: A Study of Peasant Conditions, 1150–1400* (Cambridge, Mass.: Cambridge University Press, 1937).

Marc Bloch, *Feudal Society* (Chicago: University of Chicago Press, 1961).

G. G. Coulton, *Medieval Village, Manor and Monastery* (New York: Harper Torchbook, 1960).

G. G. Coulton, *The Medieval Scene* (London: Cambridge University Press, 1968).

Marion Gibbs, *Feudal Order* (New York: Henry Schuman, 1953).

William Hinton, *Fanshen: A Documentary of Revolution in a Chinese Village* (New York: Vintage, 1966).

E. J. Hobshawm, *Primitive Rebels* (New York: Norton, 1959).

Barrington Moore, *The Social Origins of Democracy and Dictatorship* (Baltimore: Penguin, 1967).

J. W. Nyakatura, *Anatomy of an African Kingdom: A History of Bunyoro-Kitara* (New York: Anchor, 1973).

Henri Pirenne, *Economic and Social History of Medieval Europe*, translated by I. E. Clegg (New York: Harcourt, Brace, World, 1937).

Sumner Chilton Powell, *Puritan Village* (New York: Anchor Books, 1965).

TEN
Capitalism:
The Structural and Cultural Results
of the Bourgeois Revolution

Within each community form, social relations are determined by an economic logic, the two central features of which are the means or tools of production (resource base and technology) and the relations of production (how people relate together to turn raw materials into food and shelter). In tribalism, the means of production are game animals, wild vegetation, and bows and spears. The relations of production are communal ownership of property and tribal lives supported by a conventional morality and wisdom. In feudalism, the means of production are domesticated plants and animals and rights to land. The relations of production are *customs,* basically those defining and supporting the caste obligations. In capitalism the means of production are privately owned property, particularly machines and land.

The social relations are determined by contracts that reflect the economic power of the negotiating parties and are supported by law and the police power of the state.

Throughout this chapter and the next we will use the terms *contractual* and *industrial* to refer to the economic strategy that evolved out of the bourgeois revolution. The analysis focuses primarily on industrial development in the United States. Figure 10-1 shows the social structure which emerges as people use industrial capitalist economics. The millions of specialized positions are represented by separate rooms, and the chief characteristic of these positions is constant change and addition through negotiated contracts. The use of capitalist economics produces two major social classes, the profit-managing class and the wage-earning class.

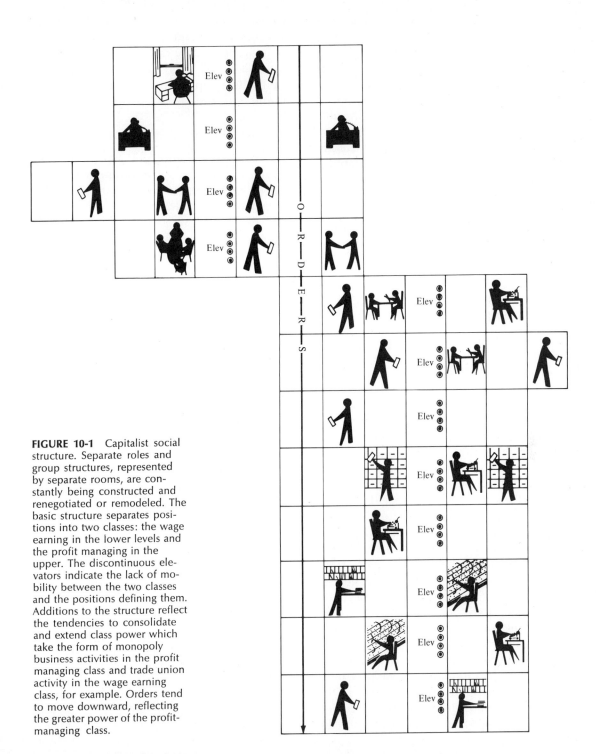

FIGURE 10-1 Capitalist social structure. Separate roles and group structures, represented by separate rooms, are constantly being constructed and renegotiated or remodeled. The basic structure separates positions into two classes: the wage earning in the lower levels and the profit managing in the upper. The discontinuous elevators indicate the lack of mobility between the two classes and the positions defining them. Additions to the structure reflect the tendencies to consolidate and extend class power which take the form of monopoly business activities in the profit managing class and trade union activity in the wage earning class, for example. Orders tend to move downward, reflecting the greater power of the profit-managing class.

The fact that the elevators in the wage-earning levels do not reach into the profit-managing levels reflects the difficulty of mobility between positions used by the two separate classes. The power difference between the classes is reflected by the fact that orders move downward, while the increase in value of products created by labor tends to move upward in the form of profit. Lateral additions to the organization of profit management take the form of monopoly, and they further unbalance the distribution of power and reduce the ability of the less powerful to negotiate the conditions of their employment, their leisure activities, and, in general, the social structures they use.

THE SOCIAL STRUCTURE AND CULTURE OF EARLY CAPITALISM

From the thirteenth to the seventeenth centuries in Europe the concentration of kingly powers, the markets, and the money systems made it possible for towndwellers to become engaged in intensive commerce. As commerce became more widespread and commercial control of the economy grew, so too did the power of the profiteers. Early in the development of commerce, the kings that had reigned over feudalism sided with the feudal lords in conflicts that developed between them and the new merchants. The old aristocracy partially destroyed itself in the various bloody wars (particularly 1650 to 1848) between members of European royal families and their allies over succession to the thrones of France, Spain, Austria, Hungary, Poland, Italy, and the states of Germany. Many wars (including the American Civil War) were caused at least in part by the conflict between the old aristocratic landowners and the emerging wealthy merchants. But the battle was one-sided; the emergence of capitalism was concentrating theretofore undreamed of wealth in the

hands of those who owned the industries. Not surprisingly, the state, as represented by the king, ultimately came to favor the benefits to be had from cooperating with the capitalists as opposed to the less rewarding promises of the landed aristocracy.

Contractual Political Institutions

The early merchants and wool spinners fought hard to get out from under the yoke of the aristocrats of the countryside. They struggled for independent town governments and for the freedoms which are taken for granted today but which were new and essential for a society based on the rule of law, or contract. They pioneered the kinds of laws summarized in the first ten amendments to the United States Constitution—the Bill of Rights. Indeed, some of these amendments have a curiously feudal sound to them —for example, freedom from being forced to quarter soldiers, freedom to bear arms, and freedom from illegal search and seizure.

Although the bourgeoisie shed their blood for these freedoms, they were already undermining them in their desire to do successful business. They wanted individual freedoms and independent local governments, but powerful central governments were to prove valuable for the unlimited expansion of trade and business. Had the emerging bourgeois class been content with limited local trade, which would have meant limits on business contracts and therefore on incomes, they could have done without powerful national governments. They might have built a society based on independent town-states.[1]

Town-state independence reemerged to some extent in the American colonies, where frontier conditions made strong central government impossible. Whatever their ambi-

[1] Parts of Europe enjoyed this kind of limited contractualism for longer periods than our compressed view of history indicates. See Daniel Waley, *The Italian City Republics* (New York: McGraw-Hill, 1969).

Continuous restructuring of social relations is important for capitalist economics since social relations must change to accommodate new business opportunities. A legislature which continuously modifies the law helps to sustain commercial expansion. (Wide World Photos)

tions, American businessmen had at first to be content with poor roads, uncertain monies, and little armed protection; hence local business and town democracy. The fifteenth-century European merchants had envisioned bigger and better things. If you wanted to sell woolen shirts, you could sell more of them if a powerful central government built roads on which you could transport your merchandise, if it kept armies which would ensure the safety of the roads and repel outside invaders, if it coined and required everyone to use a single currency, and if it used the power of the state to back up contract law as decided in the courts and legislatures.

The theme of a man making a deal with the devil has enjoyed long popularity in Western literature. The story of Faust (who promised the devil his soul for the love of Margarita) is a contractual folktale. It concerns a widespread contradiction: that often one wants something desperately enough (for Faust, Margarita's love) to disregard the enormous cost of acquiring it. In Faust's case the price was the death of Margarita and the consignment of his own soul to hell. Kings put themselves into a similar bind by supporting the bourgeois-directed rise of commerce. Bourgeois wealth helped create powerful kings. In return for giving the bourgeosie roads, markets, protection, and a national money system, the kings got taxes—wealth a million times greater than what they could wring out of their reluctant aristocrats (who in turn wrung it from peasants). It seemed a good deal for both, but the kings were soon to pay for the contradictions inherent in the relationship—they had helped create the monster which was to destroy them. Restricted by their hereditary caste ties to the aristocracy, the kings could not do everything the bourgeoisie wanted in the way of overthrowing feudal tradition in favor of commercial freedom. So the bourgeois overthrew the kings. Kings were replaced by governments of businessmen and their allies in contract, the lawyers.[2] The bourgeoisie, of course, did not go unscathed by the effects of the contradictions. By allying themselves with kings and helping to solidify centralized national governments, they necessarily forfeited some of their freedom of contract writing, thereby compromising their interest.

Government power feeds on commerce; therefore, strong governments very much want to control business ambitions. The struggle between business and government goes on to the extent that they have contradictory interests. Sometimes they combine against the consumer in capitalist societies, but within all contractual economies the truce is an uneasy one.

The contradiction between the need for big government, with its guarantees of national and international trade, and the price paid for big government in terms of limitations on business, political, religious, lifestyle, and other freedoms is a powerful part of contractual logic. It is so powerful that even those who say they want big government the least may, in the end, embrace it. The Russian Revolution of 1917 is an instructive case history.

Although Russia had not completely shed

feudalism, the Revolutionaries believed they could turn the lateness of their revolution to an advantage by profiting from the mistakes of existing contractualist (capitalist) societies. They used Karl Marx's analysis of the contradictions of capitalism as a guide. In particular, they wanted to change the tendency of contractualism to destroy itself by creating a rich class and a poor class.

However, it seems to be very difficult to resolve more than one pervasive contradiction at a time. The architects of the Russian Revolution—Lenin, Trotsky, Stalin, and others—had a choice after they seized power: They could create a decentralized democratic communism, which would resolve the tendency of contractual systems to produce big and oppressive central governments, or they could create a powerful central government, which, by building roads, enforcing a new money system, policing, and planning commerce, could use the products of industrialization to raise the poor and bring the rich down, thereby resolving a different contradiction of capitalism. They chose the latter course. Lenin died, and Stalin became the head of government. Trotsky, earlier a centralizer, began to argue that creating democratic communism was more important than centralizing nationalistic industrialization.[3] Trotsky was in the minority and was exiled. He paid the ultimate price for his heresy when he was assassinated in 1940. Stalin's argument was that even if Russia wanted a democratic communism, it could not afford it because the capitalist wolves were waiting to gobble up a democratically decentralized, less-well-industrialized Russia. This argument

---

[2] We cannot emphasize too strongly that "the rule of law" is the essence of, the same as, contractual logic—the basis of relations of production in capitalist economies.

[3] An interesting sidelight is that the first Stalin-Trotsky showdown was over the question of Stalin's suppression of minority rights in his own native province of Georgia. Lenin, who was still alive, sided with Trotsky in this issue. Stalin backed down and waited until he could get control of the Communist party to make Trotsky pay for his disagreement. Perhaps some people revere Trotsky and Lenin today as democrats (Stalin is not so regarded) because the one was exiled and murdered and the other died before having to admit the necessity of compromise.

made sense because the United States, Britain, and France had indeed mounted invasions of Russia in 1919 and had supported the White Russian counterrevolution. Trotsky (who had led the Red Army against the Whites and the foreign interventionists) and others believed that the risk of counterrevolution was less in the late 1920s and that the need for democracy was worth the risk. It is possible that by 1940, when Hitler was strong enough to invade the Soviet Union, the dilemma of democratic decentralization versus industrialization and defense might have been resolved. Unfortunately, history does not allow a single people a second chance to experiment. Some see today's China as trying the experiment the other way, with more emphasis on decentralized democratic communism. If this is so, and the theory of contradiction and conflict valid, the Chinese must proceed at the cost of whatever industrial and commercial advantages depend on strong central government. Built into the big industrial states, both socialist and capitalist, is a reliance on continuous contractual restructuring of business and on big government to support these contracts through communications technology (roads, monopolies in electricity, telephone, rails, radio, and television), police power, armies, and money. Many people bitterly regret this deal and struggle against it all their lives, but the contradiction seems central to a contractual society.

The Legal Institution

Although structures other than political institutions were transformed through the emergence of contractual capitalism (the family, education, religion, the military, communications), changes in the legal system were the most important to the early merchants themselves. If you wanted to buy wool, turn the wool into clothing, and sell the clothing far away for a profit, you would need many contracts: contracts with those who sold you the wool (on how much would be delivered and when); contracts with those who were employed to make the clothing (on wages, hours, etc.); and contracts with those to whom you wanted to sell (on when and where the product would be delivered, the quality, and the price). Each of these contracts had to be a very dependable social relationship. If any one of the other parties violated his end of the deal, you might lose your factory and your machinery, as well as your inventory of wool and clothing. If the aristocrat failed to deliver the promised wool, if the workers failed to work, or if the buyer failed to buy, you would be in big trouble. How could it be guaranteed to the others that you would live up to your contract, and to you that they would live up to theirs? The answer depended on law, backed by police power. Business people on both sides of a contract—buyer and seller—needed lawyers and judges who knew the fine points of contract law. Thus the lawyers and judges, specialists in writing and interpreting these contracts so indispensable to the new social order, were from the beginning most intimately involved with, and dependent on, the bourgeois class.

A great body of new law was written. This law was not based on custom or metaphysics or morality, at least not on a morality which assumed any good for the community other than the "good" of a contract. It was a pragmatic, practical body of law, concerned with the need of the new economy for clear and enforceable contracts, and it was as responsible as any other single factor for the high standards of living that are associated with the emergence of contractualism. It ensured precision (permitting rapid, repeatable, and calculable—or *mass*—production) as well as flexibility (allowing rapid switches to new products, new sanitary systems, and new clothing styles).

In addition to the emergence of a new body of civil (or contract) law, a new kind of courtroom developed. The courtroom became, in contractual society, an arena within which important contracts were *negotiated*. Except in the case of the most clear-cut criminal issues, such as homicide, assault, and theft, the courtroom was no longer, as it had been in the manor court, a place where an individual was called to account for violation of ancient custom. The new court was a place where those with opposing interests agreed to argue and to accept the arbitration of differences between them. Although such negotiation now may take place in relation to issues such as homosexuality and fraud, it is most prevalent in the case of civil suits—for example, when the widow of a man who was killed in a defective automobile attempts to establish a contractual obligation of the automobile manufacturer to help raise her children. Her suit is an attempt to force recognition that the purchase of an automobile is a contract in which the seller guarantees that the car is safe. The manufacturer argues that he signed no contract saying the car was safe. The issue is fought in court, where each side uses its power to persuade the court to agree with its interpretation of the contract. If the case concerns a type of contract not argued before, the decision of the judge or jury is called a *precedent*. Precedent is very important in contract law because judges do not have enough time to rehear the same contract disputes over and over again; they tend to rely on what other judges have decided in similar cases. Thus the body of contract law is constantly reshaped by new decisions. For people using contractual logic, the courtroom is the place where the most important contracts are negotiated and where legislated laws are interpreted in actual cases. This is why an analysis of law that involves the way in which lawyers and judges *behave* (as

opposed to what people say about the law) —what interests they respond to, what pressures are brought to bear on them, and the results of their interpretations of contracts— is so critical. According to conflict theory, such an analysis of the legal system forces us to reassess the law and legal processes; such a reassessment is one of the central issues in determining where industrial economies are taking us.

Money

Money lubricates contracts. If you were making wool shirts, imagine how hard it would be for you to buy wool, meet payrolls, and arrange for transportation if you had to pay with bushels of wheat, pieces of meat, or some other commodity.

In contractual society at least, business requires money. Money is a *promise* backed by the power of the national government (which drives out competing kinds of money) and by faith in the contractual system itself. Government sometimes used to back up the promise of a currency with something assumed to be desired by everyone (most often gold). Now it simply assures (1) that money will be reasonably scarce, so that a worthwhile promise today will not be worthless tomorrow and (2) that no one but itself will have the right to issue currency.

Why not just make a verbal promise? Why not just say, "You give me the wool and when I've got the shirts made, I'll give you enough shirts to pay for the wool"? One answer is that as tribal morality and feudal custom decline, people have less faith in the promises of others. In a sense, the phenomenon of decreased faith in promises is an example of how a system of logic begins to pervade other parts of social life once it gets a foothold. As the social order becomes more contractual, you are less certain about the obligations that you have to strangers

The rapid exchange of more and more goods and services is necessary for capitalist industrialization. Some of the profit from these goods is used to create more goods. (Bruce Auspach/EPA Newsphoto)

and about those which they have to you. These obligations are no longer supported by tribal morality or by unchanging, caste-based customs. This limits the people with whom you can do business on a promissory basis to your friends and relatives, surely not a very appealing prospect for an ambitious shirt manufacturer. As contracts replace custom in determining linkages between roles, promises must be replaced by something. They are replaced by money.

Another reason for not paying off in wool shirts is that your business would be limited to those who need wool shirts. In order to hire, buy from, and get transportation from —in short, to do business with—people other than those who need wool shirts, you need something that is quickly convertible into the different commodities desired and needed by all these different people. That something is money, the universal wish fulfiller.

These are the reasons for the existence of money. However, we also must analyze the effects of money. Some hypothesize that the logic of using money as the medium of contractual promises pressures us into defining all values in money terms. Try to think of other cultural and social structural changes related to the use of money.

The Decline of Older Moralities

Social relations at a particular time and in a particular place are a reflection of the logic behind the organization of work and the tools of production, a logic that creates its own particular morality. The morality of tribalism was so pervasive that the conventional wisdom defined specific role behavior in terms of the moral and the immoral— what was good or not good for the community. Feudal society was characterized by a morality that linked the individual to a particular caste and the behavior appropriate to that caste. Keeping one's place—being true to the code of one's caste—was a cornerstone of morality in the logic of feudal society.

In capitalist societies, moral behavior is measured by how well an individual accepts and lives up to many "contracts"— not all of which are written. Agreements are made between husbands and wives, parents and children, workers and employers, owners and laborers, government servants and the ruling class, and university bureaucracies and students and professors. The content of the contracts varies, and there is inevitably some disagreement over what a contract should include and what it means. Not many years ago in the United States it was assumed that the marriage contract included the obligation of the wife to stay home and raise the children. This particular contract seems to be changing as capitalism changes. It was also assumed that a woman who agreed to marry a man had never had sexual relations prior to making that agreement. Indeed, the law stipulated that discovering that one's wife was not a virgin at the time of marriage was grounds for annulling the marriage contract.

One of the characteristics of tribal (and to some extent feudal) morality was the large number of role relations that were entered into for the "good of the community" or the "good of the family." Women married men approved of by their parents and often selected by them, or they married men in their own caste because this was good for the community. Individuals did not see themselves as having the right to counteract that which was for the good of the community, even if this conflicted dramatically with their own wishes. It is helpful to speak of such community-oriented moralities as "sacred"; that is, they emphasize the unquestioning and supraindividualistic nature of many decisions.

In the case of contractual moralities the question whether a particular behavior is good for the community is not supposed to arise. Decisions do not rest on sacred values. For example, is selling cars moral behavior? Most people who live by contractual logic would consider this an absurd question. Long ago they decided that selling cars has nothing to do with morality; it is totally a matter of contract. Does it pay enough? Are the hours good? Do you deal with a good

class of people? These contractual considerations determine whether you sell cars. The only *moral* issue is whether you live up to your sales contracts.

Why does a contractual-commercial logic need a secular society, one in which specific behavior is not governed by supraindividualistic values?

The example of moneylending shows us an important reason why. In medieval Europe, lending money and charging interest (usury) was immoral because it threatened the caste structure of society. Food surpluses were small in feudal agriculture; no estate had much more than it needed to exist from one year to the next. If there was a bad year (drought, late frosts, summer hailstorms), certain estates might face a winter of starvation. It would be possible for other estates and their nobles to lend food to the starving people, but because the hungry were desperate, the lenders could charge high interest rates on their loans and could use force to collect them. Some estates would become rich and powerful at the expense of others, thus creating a hierarchy of estates and undermining the caste foundation on which feudalism rested. In the interests of preserving stable caste relations and peace, it made sense, especially for the landowners, to include usury in the realm of immoral behavior.

Within contractual economies, however, there is a need for rapid movement of capital. Lending at interest benefits both the lender, for he can make a profit from surplus that might otherwise just sit there, and the merchant, who can put the surplus or capital to work and make a profit beyond the interest he must pay to the lender. There was great pressure from the rising merchant class to take moneylending out of the category of immoral behavior and call it simply "business" or "contractual behavior." As this class gained power, it saw to it that the taint of immorality was removed from the procedure of lending money at interest. This was accomplished by redefining the term *usury*. Instead of considering the charging of any interest to be an offense against the moral code, only the charging of "excessive" interest was so considered. This process of redefinition enabled the merchant class to remold the morality of the age so that it was more consistent with its mode of production.

Another reason for the secularization of contractual society is the inflexibility of sacred morality. What is considered good for the community is a set of codes not easily forgotten, changed, or bargained over. Doing business requires flexibility. If it is a moral, sacred requirement that friends and relatives present a newly married couple with a cow, the makers of china and silverware miss out on a big market. But if the choice of a wedding gift can be secularized—if it is made a matter of personal decision, with no implications for the good or bad of the community—then more business can be done. People might even be convinced to buy the couple several presents. This process of changing the sacred matters of the past into the secular (amoral) business affairs of the present should continue if the theory of the emerging dominance of contractual logic is correct. That is, fewer and fewer specific role relations should be seen as moral or immoral; more and more things should be acceptable if both parties consent.

Removal of the designation "sacred" from the material culture (technology) opens up tremendous commercial possibilities. If a certain kind of plow has been used for 3,000 years because tilling the soil with it is part of the religious worship which holds the community together, there will not be much market for new kinds of plows. However, if the choice of plow is a matter of personal preference, with no implications for the community, many types of plows can be tried. Multiply this example by the millions of things people use, especially in industrial economies, and you have some idea of the importance to contractual logic of secularizing material culture. Almost every convenience associated with a "high standard of living" owes its existence directly to a persevering bourgeois who insisted that it was not sacrilegious to experiment with different gadgets and technologies. This bourgeois attitude laid the groundwork for, and supported the institution of, science—a complex social institution concerned precisely with narrowing the area of the sacred and expanding the area of the secular. Technologists stand by eagerly waiting to see what new bits of material culture have emerged from this *non*moral or amoral tampering with the physical world.[4]

At least two contradictions accompany this expansion of the secular. First, there is contradictory evidence regarding whether technology is intrinsically destructive. We will cover this issue in detail near the end of this chapter. Second, although the bourgeoisie is in the business of reducing the area of the sacred, it needs a morality which supports its contractual system. For example, it is moral to uphold government contracts to produce war materials, but amoral (not a moral issue) to use the products of such contracts—for example, napalm or hydrogen bombs—indiscriminately to protect business enterprises.

Much of seventeenth- and eighteenth-century European philosophical argument can be understood as an attempt to create a contractual morality. What is more interesting, however, is that the philosophers of the European Enlightenment were anticipated and helped by the Greek philosophers,

---

[4] What is important is *defining* things as nonmoral. Scientists argue that whether something like the atom bomb is moral or immoral depends on how people use it, not on the thing itself.

who were part of a social form which had also nearly evolved into contractualism 2,000 years earlier. The great emphasis the philosophers placed on reason and rationality reflects the need of contractual society for a more streamlined and abstract morality. *Reason* may be defined as the ability to find the most efficient means to a particular end; presumably it is a process unaffected by morality. However, morality or "good" in a community based on rational, reasoning, contractual behavior will be whatever is necessary to help all people be rational, reasoning, and contractual.

Among the Greek philosophers Socrates seems most modern. He argued that reason can be the guiding principle of life and that each human being must take the responsibility for finding the most rational means to live his or her own life. Other Greek philosophers explored the contradictions which still perplex the "existential" philosophers of contractual society.

> The atomist Democritus of Abdera, had written, "We know nothing in reality for the truth lies in an abyss." As to the polis, that small intense communion of Gods and men, "to a wise man, the whole earth is open; for the native land of a good soul is the whole earth." As for justice, Thrasymachus of Chalcedon, the famous sophist, was not the first to insist that justice was in the interest of the stronger, that might made right. "Rule," said Democritus, "belongs by nature to the stronger." To Protagoras's insistence that man was the measure of all things, Metrodorus of Chios added, "Everything exists which anyone perceives." As for Socrates' brave faith that knowledge differed from mere opinion, this same Metrodorus held that "None of us knows anything, not even whether we know or do not know, nor do we know whether not knowing and knowing exist, nor in general, whether there is anything or not." As to the gods, Critias . . . disposed of [them]. . . . "Then, when the laws forbade them to commit open crimes of vio-

lence and they began to do them in secret, a wise and clever man invented fear of the gods for mortals, that there might be some means of frightening the wicked, even if they do anything or say or think it in secret."
. . . [T]he sophist Antiphon handled justice with sophistication: "we revere and honor those born of noble fathers but those who are not born of noble houses we neither revere nor honor. In this we are, in our relations with one another, like barbarians, since we are all by nature born the same in every way, both barbarians and Hellenes. And it is open to all men to observe the laws of nature, which are compulsory. Similarly all of these things can be acquired by all, and in none of these things is any of us distinguished as either barbarian or Hellene. We all breathe into the air through mouth and nostrils, we all eat with hands.[5]

THE FRONTIER UNITED STATES: LAYING A CONTRACTUAL FOUNDATION

It is often alleged that the United States is so complex that it is hopeless to try to understand and explain it or to predict the directions of social and cultural change within its boundaries. We disagree totally. From the perspective of conflict theory, the United States *should* appear complex on the surface. It is dominated by a contractual logic, and from this we would predict that most of the social structure and culture is up for grabs—it *can* be renegotiated and changed, though probably not without struggle. It should seem like a circus, with new acts being created continuously and something going on in at least three rings at once. Yet conflict theory predicts that, as in the case of a circus, some stable direction is being followed behind the scenes. The direction of the social economic structures of the United States has been for many years the struggle of capitalism to displace older forms and the struggle of people to deal

[5] Stringfellow Barr, *The Will of Zeus* (Philadelphia: Lippincott, 1961), pp. 354–355.

with the contradictions inherent in capitalism and contractual logic.

Small-town America

Protected by the newness and frailty of central colonial and revolutionary government, secure in their small towns, avoiding the contradiction between free enterprise and big government, and believing they were starting fresh, early American citizens hoped to lay the foundation for a self-correcting, free (contractual) society. Actually, although they left behind some of the cynicism which characterized Europeans, who had to reconcile the new system with moral remnants of the old, they brought European contractual institutions with them.

The American small town gives us a picture of the long struggle to resolve the contradictions of capitalism. In this section on beginnings, we wish to focus attention on the small town because the first coherent statement of American contractual ideology emerged from small-town life. This ideology is still invoked by various political figures and apologists for urbanized versions of American capitalism.

Three contradictions have dominated small-town American contractualism from the beginning: (1) The rich have tended to get richer, and the poor to get poorer; (2) the machine has run wild in the garden—that is, industrialization and contractualism have seriously threatened to destroy the physical environment; and (3) secular business has tended to become immoral and in so doing, to hurt the community.

Contradictions and conflict emerge out of the use of social structure and culture and are determined by the dominant logic of the times. The goodness or badness of the people who use social structure and culture has nothing to do with the kinds of conflicts created. In fact, contradictions such as those arising from capitalism's tendency toward classes and monopolies emerged from the actions of some courageous, hopeful, good-willed American pioneers. That these contradictions still dominate the United States is evidence that the early hopefulness had an ostrichlike quality. In the next few sections we will discuss the early growth of these contradictions and show how they channeled conflict in the United States.

Some Americans are fond of believing, and their history books help them believe, that the United States was a totally coherent new society when it broke away from England. The truth of the matter is that most Americans were too busy struggling to survive in their mortal combat with the native Americans and the new land to figure out a *new* society. They transplanted European contractualism as it then existed, without major modifications. They were selective, but they selected from only one source.

There was nonetheless a strong impulse to abandon contractualism in the colonies in the 1600s.[6] The major attempt to abandon contractualism was in the form of what Page Smith calls "covenanted" communities, a form used primarily in the 1700s and 1800s. These were communities made up of members of a single church who had signed a covenant together to live out all their social institutions within the framework of a single religious idea. Many early New England and Ohio valley small towns used this form. Neither class structures nor separate institutional patterns for rich and poor arose, either because of intense sharing or because groups not getting their fair share could and did break off to form new covenants. In the covenanted community, deviants were rehabilitated rather than punished by having to "pay a debt to society." Decisions were made by a meeting of the entire church and

[6] Page Smith, *As a City upon a Hill: The Town in American History* (New York: Knopf, 1966), p. 73.

were unanimous. There was very little room for contracting in such a community. The outlines of life were given by some variation of communal Christianity, as distinct from the hierarchical version on which Saint Paul built the church of Rome. The specific day-to-day arrangements for farming, parceling land, making and distributing goods, and educating the young were dictated by this vision and by the inspired communal decision making of the covenanted individuals. The communitarian solution, as an alternative to contractual life is still with us. Christian covenanted communities have been and are being created continuously. Hutterites, Mennonites, and Amish are widely accepted communitarian groups. "Hippie" Christians and various guru-following sects try the same thing, although they have yet to achieve respectability. Despite the number of attempts, however, the communitarian form itself failed in its competition with contractualism to dominate the new nation. Quakers and Congregationalists retain the structure of the old covenanted church and have a distrust of bureaucracy and of hierarchies of priests and preachers; they retain an emphasis on consensual decision making,

but they make their livelihood in the world of business and enjoy their profits. Many hope to have the best of both worlds, the world of business and the world of the commune. They wish fervently for the profits and material well-being promised by the other. Even Henry David Thoreau, who wrote of the virtues of a solitary life spent communing with nature, returned to town to chop wood, discuss philosophy, and sell his writing.

Two well-known prophets of, and apologists for, the small-town solution to capitalist contradictions were Thomas Jefferson and Abraham Lincoln. Jefferson believed that the landowning farmer would keep America free through his own independence and attachment to the land. He believed that the farmer, and the small-town businessman who supplied his needs, could coexist in stable harmony; that industry and the countryside could be made harmonious within a small-town framework; and that there was a religious principle which united all these parts of American society. Lincoln believed that if big business could be restrained, the American ideal could survive. Each person could start as a worker, either in farm or machine labor, and could save enough to become his

The dominant place of business activity in small town life is reflected in the importance of its main street and its commercial buildings. (De Wys/EPA)

own employer as a small farmer or small businessman. He believed that the clash of interests between profit-managing and wage-earning classes would be resolved in the United States. When each person was both a worker and an owner, the conflicting principles of profit and work would be solved inside the heads of human beings rather than through class warfare. Karl Marx more accurately predicted that this class, which both owns and works with the tools of production (small farmers, shopkeepers, independent artisans, and service people), would be driven either into the ranks of wage earners or into the bourgeois class. Lincoln's hopeful solution was prevented by the onrush of capitalist logic—the fact that in competition there are few limits short of driving independent competitors out of business.

The small-town residents often divided rapidly into a class of those who owned the major business enterprises and their professional peers, on the one hand, and wage earners, on the other. As Page Smith has shown, small businesses failed more often than they succeeded. But the class structure remained intact.

Selection 10-1 describes the extent to which young people have left American small towns. The report suggests that small-town economies have lost the chance to create a different form of capitalism. Since they must compete with city-based corporations, small-town businesses cannot succeed to the extent of providing jobs for the young.

The Rich Get Richer and the Poor Get Poorer

Just as highly successful feudalism in the form of rival superwarriors, or kings, tended to destroy feudalism, highly successful contracting tends to destroy capitalism. Unless prevented from doing so by some noncontractual morality, more powerful individuals or groups will structure their contracts in

such a way that they will get more and others will get less. Rich individuals, families, and groups will become richer, and poor individuals, families, and groups will become poorer until the situation is such that most people are unable to control (contract for) their own lives.

Since the amount of contractual power (material resources, knowledge, legitimacy) is limited and since being successful in writing one contract increases one's chance of success with the next one, capital and power can be accumulated only until they are all used up. Players of *Monopoly*—the real estate game invented in the 1930s—realize that the aim of the game is to end it. One person wins, and the others go broke.

Four options—each complex, with many varieties—become open as this destructive tendency emerges in contractualism:

1. Less successful businessmen can band together to increase collectively their contract-writing power. Wage earners (who may include in their ranks people who fail in business) may also form groups, or unions, as a counterforce to the power of monopolists.

2. Contractualists themselves can accept limits on their right to use power in writing contracts. Most people talk as if they accept this, favoring laws against monopolistic practices in business and stiff inheritance taxes. Most business *behavior* indicates that these limits must be imposed by someone else, and preferably on someone else's business and inherited fortune. It took a major depression and a very bright economist, John Maynard Keynes, to point out to capitalists that if they got very rich by making a profit on what they made and if other people got very poor because they did not have the power to write contracts for good wages or the money to pay for college educations for their children, then soon the poor would not be able to pay the rich to buy back the goods they (as workers) produced, and the

SELECTION 10-1: Effects of movement away from small-town America.

THE FOLKS LEFT BEHIND WHEN THE YOUNG MOVE AWAY

TED SELL

Pratt, Kansas—Towns like this are shaded gray, where widowhood is a natural state, where drug stores do a large business in aspirin for arthritis relief.

They are towns dominated by the elderly—the result of the flight to the cities 30 years ago and more.

The bustle of the 1920s and '30s, when such towns represented a far larger share of America's population and economic activity, has been replaced by the quiet of courthouse benches where graying men recall when the blacksmith shop closed.

The courthouse often needs paint, and old ladies debate whether they will live long enough to justify major home repairs.

Tom, in his 70s, looked through the cafe window to where a chill Kansas wind made patterns with the rain on the neat, brick-paved street.

"Me and Mama," he said, "we talked about buying a place in Florida, but when we sold out we didn't get as much as we thought and Mama was sick and she's buried here now and all my friends that's left is around here. So I'm staying."

This man is one of the 1135 persons past the age of 65 in Pratt's total population of 6736. And Pratt typifies a sociological phenomenon of America today: the concentration of what the U.S. Census Bureau calls "older people" in small towns.

Towns of 10,000 and fewer account for 12.2 per cent of the U.S. population. But they have 26.8 per cent of the citizens older than 65.

Why are places named Pratt, Belleville or Monroe havens for the aged?

Simply stated, it is because the young have moved away.

The number of persons beyond the age of 65 in the United States has more than doubled since 1930. But more significantly, the proportion of older persons has nearly doubled—from 5.4 per cent to 9.8 per cent of the population.

What that means is that older persons are a far more visible segment of the population, especially in small towns.

This phenomenon makes small-town America almost a different country.

A four state survey revealed that few older persons in small towns seriously entertain the idea of leaving, even though the big medical centers—a major consideration—are in the cities, and even though it is the cities that have elaborate programs for older residents.

Why do they stay?

First, most older persons in small towns treasure their friendships even as the number of friends dwindles.

Second, most older persons cite lower prices in smaller towns.

Third, virtually all of these people are impressed with the safety of small towns, the lack of crime.

Fourth, most talk about the convenience of getting around on foot, of being able to walk a few blocks to stores or doctors.

Art Wilson Jr., manager of the Pratt Chamber of Commerce, estimated that 35 per cent of the town's adult population is 65 or older—if the enrollment at the Pratt Community College is ignored.

Wilson noted that much of the town leadership is young—under 36. But the large population of older people, he said, means that much of Pratt is "nonproductive, and at the same time requires more services than the young productive citizens."

His estimate took account of the other phenomenon of small-town America: By and large, towns of 5000 to 10,000 are towns of children and the elderly, with few in between.

There is no shortage of children in such towns. Parks bulge. Every schoolyard has small boys playing basketball.

But the towns seem to be light in the 18-to-50 bracket.

Family size in such towns tends to be larger than in the cities. Those persons in the 18-to-50 year age bracket who do remain in their home towns continue to produce children to populate the schools.

In many towns, the best-kept structure is the funeral home.

In the 65 or-older bracket, 34 per cent "depart" every decade, according to the Census Bureau.

"We provide a real service," an Iowa mortician said, "and it's because we know everyone in the family. There's something really satisfying about having the family come around later and thank you for a nice service."

The fact that the market potential is greater in a town with 20 per cent elderly, the mortician said, is balanced by the fact that funeral prices are lower in small cities.

Hence, a dominant influence in the towns of the old is the bleak burying grounds outside of town, away from the water supply.

The cemeteries are starkly utilitarian and the prairie winds whine against artless marble headpieces that record the names and life dates of persons who, for the most part, died young or aged. There are so few in between.

rich would not be making much money anymore.

3. The rich of course do not like a resolution of this dilemma which imposes restrictions on their power; one solution is to do away with capitalism by imposing a totalitarian system in which decisions on prices, what to buy, where to live, what kind of work to do, and the right to contract for wages are all taken away from the masses of people. A dictatorship of the powerful (the rich, the experts, the brutal, or some combination of the three) is the result. This option was tried in Nazi Germany.

4. A fourth option is to expand resources continuously through more efficient technology. Wages *and* profits may increase at the same time if resources become constantly cheaper. This may result in a static class structure, with the rich getting very rich but the workers feeling less oppressed because their wages have increased. It is widely

Thorstein Veblen pointed out that conspicuous consumption in the form of elaborate clothing and expensive forms of entertainment resulted from the lack of moral limits on the acquisition of money. (Pictorial Parade/EPA)

believed that this situation exists in the United States today. The extent to which it represents a solution to the contradictory tendency of capitalist contractualism to destroy itself suggests several important kinds of study for all students of social life in the United States. First, are resources becoming cheaper? The "energy crisis" suggests that basic resources are in fact becoming more expensive relative to wages. Second, does the technology of cheaper resources also produce a more oppressive work environment and more oppressive police technologies? Third, does the power of workers to control their own lives relative to the managers actually decline even as their standard of living rises? Some recent studies of workers in western European nations show that a rising sense of powerlessness in the wage-earning class accompanied the spectacular economic growth there from 1945 to 1974.

These are the options. As we shall see, it is a critical sociological task to evaluate the degree to which contractual social orders are moving in the direction of one or another of these options.

In the 1800s monopoly capitalism was imposed on America's small towns from the outside. Page Smith points out that the philosophy of rugged individualism grew up in the cities as a rationalization for playing a hard game of contract. Markets were big enough and sufficiently unaffected by area-wide disasters such as crop failure so that businessmen could afford to foreclose mortgages, charge high interest rates, sell shoddy merchandise, and employ labor at slave wages under slave conditions without losing the markets, while at the same time proclaiming "survival of the fittest" (rugged individualism) as an economic philosophy. Gradually, some farsighted capitalists in the small towns came to realize that by joining forces with big-city capital, someone who had real ambition and did not care how his fellow townsmen felt about him could play this hard game of contract with its high rewards. Small-town industrial tycoons and class structures were born. The entrepreneur could borrow enough capital from city bankers to make him independent of local crop failures, and he could get city help in marketing his product over a wide area so as to be free of the fluctuations of local markets and the expectations of his neighbors that he be nice to them. He could import cheap labor (usually members of a recently migrated group) in order to hold down labor costs. The cheap labor provided a new bottom for the class structure, and the entrepreneur provided a new top. The surprised townspeople found themselves arrayed at many points in between. Wherever this process went on, the face of an emerging dominant form—a purely contractual community—could be seen. Thus did the vision of Lincoln and Jefferson become a pie in the sky as the logic of contractualism overwhelmed the dream.

The Machine Tears Up the Garden

Thomas Jefferson believed the United States could bring industry together with agriculture in perfect harmony. Although, by the early 1800s, the evils of industrial capitalism were evident in the horrors of European factories and workers' slums, Jefferson and other United States towndwellers believed that their free, undespoiled countryside; their prosperous, landowning farming class; and their factories could all benefit one another.

Machine and garden were to be brought together by laissez faire (not, as popularly supposed, "let alone") capitalism, together with cheap land on the Western frontier, which would produce a stable, prosperous, land-loving middle class that would dominate national politics. The members of this middle class would resolve the contradiction between profit making and wage earning by being themselves both owners and workers —small businessmen, independent farmers, and professionals. Since they would be tied to a local place because of the necessity of working with the local tools of production, they would also have an interest in preserving local natural resources.

Laissez faire capitalism, especially as practiced in the United States, fulfilled the struggle for freedom of the bourgeois merchants begun in Italy, France, and England in the eleventh century. In America there was no ancient aristocracy to tie up land and restrict the development of commerce through ancient rights and powers supported by legislatures and courts. United States capitalism was a series of structural arrangements through which freedom of commercial enterprise was encouraged. Free enterprise meant the presence of court and police support of commercial contracts, legal structures which allowed the creation of corporate entities not bound by the laws applying to individuals, a federally supported banking system and the money to supply it, and tariff laws which protected local products from foreign competition. The structures *not* created were of equal importance. There were no legal restrictions on employer-employee contracts, and hence nothing but the relative power of the two parties determined wages and working conditions. There were no legal restrictions on success; that is, there was no definition of too much success, and there were no restrictions on accumulation of capital or ownership of factories. The legal restrictions on the public effects of "free" enterprise were so limited as to be nonexistent. That is, there was no body of law which specified restriction of practices that had detrimental effects on the social structure (for example, restrictions on business practices which were inflationary or depressionary or which pauperized workers) or on natural resources and the physical environment such as restrictions on business practices which ruined rivers, destroyed public forest land and rangeland, or was harmful to wildlife.

There was a very human willingness to believe that in the "new" world we could have our resources and pursue our business goals too. It was clear to very few that without some struggle to resolve the contradictions between machine and garden, the one would destroy the other. In fact, today much of the countryside and its resources have been devastated, and the independent farmers who were to resolve the contradiction (according to Jefferson and Lincoln) have been driven off the land. Most of the capital and the means of production are in the hands of a few. Paradoxically, we persist in believing that we can have both machine and garden. Some of our unwillingness to face the physical problems of cities reflects a feeling that machines will take care of themselves. The belief that machines will also solve the problems of the environment shows how persistent is the unwillingness to confront the contradiction between the two.[7]

Creating an Amoral Morality

In essence, contractualism says that the private good is the measure of virtue against which social arrangements should be compared. Yet if contractualism itself is to survive, it must be raised to a public good which is more important than private rights or interests. It is not surprising that many people preferred to fall back on older moralities rather than solve this dilemma.

Even though they are frightened by some of the implications of a purely contractual morality, most United States citizens do not

[7] For a study of these contradictory beliefs and their place in United States history, see Leo Marx, *The Machine in the Garden* (New York: Oxford, 1964).

go in for careful study of the degree to which their lives, the institutional patterns they use, and what they believe support contractual morality. For example, in one study, a large majority of people who were showed the Bill of Rights without a title described it as a subversive document.[8]

Some very simple resolutions of the contradiction between contractualism and morality designed to promote the public good have been proposed, most of which are only variations of the theme that "might makes right." Mark Twain, Sinclair Lewis, and others made a living satirizing the view that morality is whatever a smart businessman can get away with. A more recent version (proposed by Charles Wilson, one-time president of General Motors, when he was Secretary of Defense of the United States) was, "What's good for General Motors is good for the United States." There are many other examples of propositions equating self-interest with community interest. Almost every new group, subculture, or way of life attempts to equate its own interests with those of the country and, if it is powerful enough, to impose its morality on others.

The tendency to expect "moral" behavior of others, and to abide by contractual rule only for oneself began to produce increasing conflict as the small-town mix of tribal-feudal-contractual morality gave way before the spread of totally contractual arrangements. The rich argue that the poor have a moral obligation to get off welfare but that the tax loopholes and business subsidies available to the wealthy are purely contractual matters. This feeds the cynicism of those who have trouble making free contracts— the aged, the poor, the young, and the racial and ethnic minorities. Real conflicts of in-

terest exist between these groups. Covering them with a double-standard morality adds fury to the conflicts springing from contradiction.

Contractual Structures and "Bigness"

Three contradictions which seem very much a part of contractual logic have been described.

1. Successful contract writing seems to destroy contractualism by driving many out of the contractual framework. The rich get richer and the poor get poorer. Within the dominant patterns through which economic activity is institutionalized, this tendency leads to monopoly dominance by a few giant corporations.

2. Contractualism seems contradictory to a public morality which would see environmental preservation as one of the chief goals toward which behavior should be aimed. Contractualism itself will be the only agreed-upon public good, and if contracts harm the community, so be it. Where contracts have paid enough, wilderness has been despoiled, resources depleted, the independent farmer bought or forced off his land, the small community starved, and the water and air befouled. In short, there seems to be a contradiction between contractualism and preservation of the environment; the more contractualism there is, the more environment is despoiled.

3. Contractual society seems characterized by large amounts of hypocrisy (attempts to get others to behave morally while oneself behaves contractually), conflicts over morality, and attempts by the powerful or the fanatic to impose moral behavior by force.

Conflict theory proposes that the use of contractual logic itself produces these conflicts and the problems that go with them; that a contractually oriented people must

[8] The recent one-man (one-woman too?), one-vote decision of the Supreme Court is an example of contractual morality written into law.

continually struggle with these problems; and that a very important question is, "What are people doing to resolve these contradictions?" Are present compromises effective; or are dominant institutional patterns becoming less usable for masses of people? In the next chapter we will describe the conflicts arising out of these contradictions.

There remains a further problem of contractual capitalism, which we will call "the problem of the flush toilet."[9] Is it possible for something to be good when taken in small doses, but poisonous in large doses? The flush toilet is no doubt good when used on a small scale. However, no one envisioned a world in which several million people might simultaneously flush their toilets during a station break in a televised moonshot or at half time during a professional football game. It is important to ask whether there are other effects of masses of people using a contractual system. There are some who argue that masses of people can use a contractual logic only within something very much like a police state. This would certainly be a contradiction, namely, that a logic originally designed to promote and safeguard individual freedom should produce totalitarian dictatorship or, perhaps worse, a dictatorship of giant organizations. The study of resource exhaustion leads some to conclude that people must be denied the right to demand more and more goods and services even though they can afford to pay for them. In Selection 10-2 the implication of a steady supply of goods and services is that someone must control that supply since free market control will lead to resource exhaustion.

9 Robert H. Dreisbach said that the "water-seal toilet is the next most wasteful invention of civilization after the automobile [in *Handbook of the San Francisco Region, Environment Studies* (Palo Alto, Calif.: 1969, p. 534]. Dreisbach points out that the flush toilet requires 5 gallons of potable water per day for survival, while a human being requires only 1/3 gallon.

The argument goes that the bureaucracies, which are the efficient medium for contract writing (like the medium which nourishes bacteria in petrie dish), come to have a life of their own. Like individual contractors, they begin to try to control their environment by linking up with other bureaucracies through corporate mergers, joining of government bureaus, or "cooperation" between police departments. These mergers are always for worthy purposes. For example, all water-control projects may be brought under one giant federal bureaucracy in order to "promote conservation of water"; "ensure efficient allocation of water to industrial, agricultural, and private uses"; etc. The result for individual farmers and private users, however, is that for practical (behavioral) purposes, they have lost all control over the water they use. Now if social economic arrangements come to be made up of thousands of such giant bureaucracies, individuals ultimately lose to these giants all power to contract their own existence.[10] Selection 10-3 reports on a conference at which people from rural areas describe the extent to which they have lost control over rural land and hence control over their lives.

Analyzing the degree to which bigness is inherent in contractual logic—the degree to which bigness prevents individual contract

10 A generation of us who were nourished on movies about totalitarianism—the anti-Nazi and anti-Japanese movies of World War II and the anti-Communist movies of the late forties and early fifties—are most sensitive to this. We were taught that totalitarian societies are characterized by night police raids; tapped telephones; the rewriting of history; official lies about present government and corporate policy; the planting of evidence (narcotics, falsified documents, stolen goods) in order to incriminate those whose opinions are unacceptable; plainclothes policemen who shoot people in the back and claim self-defense as a motive; laws requiring that citizens carry identity papers and cards; political leaders who attack scapegoat groups in order to avoid talking about real issues and problems; leaders who rant, scream, and become angry so that the masses will identify with their anger; and, finally, attacks on weaker nations in the name of some abstract cause, such as "saving the world from capitalism."

Resource exhaustion and bourgeois culture.

WHEN OUR RESOURCES RUN OUT

It has been called Hubbert's Pimple—a simple line on a graph that goes up from zero and then crashes back down to zero.

It can be labeled oil, coal, uranium, copper, lead, or any of a vast number of this planet's exhaustible resources.

What it means is that the so-called work ethic is doomed—as well as the idea that a person can get interest on his money by putting it in a bank savings deposit.

At least, that's the interpretation given by the man the pimple is named after, M. King Hubbert.

The line shows the eventual depletion of many of the things our economy requires—at least, according to M. King Hubbert, if the economy continues in its present form.

Hubbert, 69, the man the pimple is named after, is one of the most sought-after lecturers in the nation in this ecology-conscious, energy-crisis-ridden age.

He is currently a Regents Professor of Geophysics at the University of California at Berkeley on leave from his official position as staff research geophysicist at the U.S. Geological Survey in Washington, D.C.

For the past 20 years he has been speaking before any audience that would listen, telling them our culture is built upon an impossible premise: economic growth.

Seventeen years ago, for instance, he told a gathering of oil company executives that by 1973 the rate of increase in oil production would begin going down for the first time in the industry's history.

"They didn't want to believe it," he said. "When told they had used up just one-fourth of the world's oil in 100 years, they thought that meant we have 300 years to go before running out."

It doesn't work that way, he said. Most of the oil used so far was consumed in the past decade or so and, at current rates of increasing consumption, all the oil that can be economically drilled will be used up in a relatively few more years.

Hubbert puts the date at about the year 2000 —27 years from now.

"Well, they panicked," he said in an interview in his Berkeley office the other day, "and their solution was to decide there is a lot more undiscovered oil than they previously estimated."

As it turned out, says Hubbert, the peak in oil discovery and the rate of increase in production actually occurred two years ago.

As a man who worked for Shell Oil Co. for 20 years, discovering oil, and a man who perfected the theoretical techniques that turned oil discovery into a precise science, Hubbert's word is now accepted.

And, since almost the whole country is talking about recycling, curtailing growth, conserving energy and cutting out waste these days, Hubbert has ceased being a maverick and is now regarded as a leading expert on what's wrong with the country's way of doing things.

"We can't go on growing forever," he said: "people are finally coming to accept that.

"The question," he said, "is what do we do about it. Since our present culture is unsuited to a steady-state situation, how do we make the transition to non-growth without catastrophe?"

He claims to know the answer—and he doesn't see the problem as an energy crisis. If oil and gas run out, uranium can supply energy for many years. If that runs out, fusion is possible; ultimately, the sun's rays could be trapped to supply enormous power. But what will run out, says Hubbert, are the exhaustible resources, mostly metals, on which a technological culture depends.

The implication of all this, he said, is that mankind as a whole will soon (by the end of the century, he thinks) have to settle for a constant, steady supply of goods and services being produced each year.

That means, he said, with only a few exceptions industries will not be able to consume materials faster than they can be reclaimed.

In short, he thinks almost everything will have to be recycled.

And, since the amount of goods that money will buy cannot increase, "interest rates will have to be zero."

"If the amount of money goes up, and what it buys doesn't, nobody is better off," he said. "Inflation would exactly equal interest, canceling out the whole point of having interest in the first place."

On top of that, he said, "we may have to get away from the idea that whoever eats, must work."

The reason, he said, is that for the most part machines are more efficient than men. Hand labor cannot be competitive.

Yet, if everyone worked in automated factories and industries, production would be so astronomically high that resources would be depleted at an enormous rate—not to mention the problem of finding a market for the products.

Some work will remain, he said, and service industries will take up some of the slack, "but we'll just have to get used to the idea of immense leisure time. Maybe some people won't work at all, or everyone will be on a ten-hour work week, or something, but it can't stay the way it is."

Hubbert's hope is that the change can occur peacefully—but he says it also is possible that the world economy will fall apart and lead to a transition period of chaos and suffering before "things settle down."

SELECTION 10-3: The exclusion of rural people from control over basic institutional patterns.

RURAL MEN SING OUT FOR LAND REFORM

LYNN LUDLOW

The delegate from North Dakota amused himself in the lobby by revising Woody Guthrie's hopeful lyrics to a song that became enormously popular because, like so many songs, it wasn't really so.

"This land is *their* land," he sang. "This land is *their* land—from the redwood forests, to the New York island. . . ."

On this note ended the First National Conference on Land Reform, which brought more than 400 delegates from 38 states to swap stories here about everything from strip-mining to conglomerates, from timber rights to absentee syndicates that harvest tax benefits.

The four-day conference at the San Fran-

ciscan Hotel was organized by the Center for Rural Studies here.

Absentee Ownership

It ended yesterday in a spate of resolutions aimed at absentee land ownership, "exploitation of rural labor," help for family farms and justice for "non-white groups in America . . . unjustly stripped of their historic claims to land."

It was a mixed batch of dirt farmers, graduate students, lobbyists, environmentalists, professors, pamphleteers, consumerists and public interest lawyers. When ex-Sen. Fred Harris of Oklahoma spoke to them about his "new populism," they stood up to applaud him, but it wasn't a political gathering.

Most delegates came with particular complaints about particular issues, mostly complex. Here are some of them:

Strip-mining

"Many parts of Appalachia (he pronounced it "apple-at-cha") have become a wasteland due to the irresponsibilty of corporations who were 'developing' our land."—Paul Kaufman, West Virginia attorney for Appalachian Research and Defense Fund.

Rural Lot-sales Subdividing

"Although not as dramatic in appearance as strip-mining or some water reclamation projects, its effects are, in the long run, equally destructive and irreversible . . . they play on the greed of "the gullible and the discontent of the urban wage slave."—Harvey Mudd, Central Clearing House, Santa Fe, N.M.

Syndicates

"Absentee capital in the farming industry can survive on less profit (because of tax benefits) and really compete unfairly . . . and drive out the farmer for whom farming is a way of life." —Charles Davenport, law professor, University of California, Davis.

Federal Land

"The era of giveaways (in cheap mineral, timber and grazing rights to corporations) is still with us."—Michael McCloskey, executive director, Sierra Club.

Family Farms

"The trouble is the government, while issuing policy statements praising the family farm, is doing more than any other institution in America to destroy it."—Roger Blobaum, economic consultant, Iowa.

Technology in Farming

"We're putting in five calories of energy (in the form of oil, gas, fertilizer, processing, pesticides, machinery production) for every one calorie of food produced."—Michael Perelman, professor, Chico State University

Agribigness

"The result of conglomerate entry into agriculture is that the single-activity farmer must compete against producers who not only corner the market through vertical integration (ownership of land, crops, processing and marketing) but produce at a loss, deriving the benefit not from profits on the sale of agricultural production but rather from tax gains and land speculation."—Sheldon Green, National Coalition for Land Reform, San Francisco.

Indian Land

"The fundamental issue is one of control . . . Too much power is in the hands of federal administrators; the situation hasn't changed much since those days when the superintendents ran the reservations like dictators."—Kirke Kickingbird, Kiowa Tribe, attorney for Institute for Development of Indian Law.

writing—is critical to understanding nations dominated by contractual logic. However, very little systematic research on this has been done (for reasons mentioned above).

There are some, notably Alvin Toffler, writing in *Future Shock*,[11] who believe that totalitarian bigness will be destroyed by the triumph of pure contractualism. Toffler argues that when contractualism really takes hold, bureaucracies will become temporary structures, continually being contracted out

[11] Alvin Toffler, *Future Shock* (New York: Random House, 1970).

of existence. How this magical transformation of such a well-entrenched structural pattern is to occur is not made clear. Others, such as George Orwell in *1984*, see the end product of the logic of contractualism and state intervention in this economy as the creation of a superstate which controls every facet of every person's life, brooking no disagreement with what is centrally defined as "good."

Conflict analysis spotlights problem areas in contemporary social relations as no other type of analysis does. Conflict theory suggests that any particular historical period is best understood by studying the contradiction and the logic of the dominant economic form and its attendant social relations.

In this chapter we have focused on the contradiction and logic inherent in the capitalist economic form that emerged in Europe and was transported to the United States as well as much of the rest of the world, including that 70 percent which was at one time a colony of one of Europe's capitalist nations or a neocolony under the influence of Europe, America, Japan, or the Soviet Union.

Since the turn of the century a new economic form, with its own logic and unique pattern of social relations, has emerged: socialism. Socialist revolutions have been dramatic attempts to resolve some of the basic contradictions in bourgeois capitalism. The central structural reform in socialism is transfer of the ownership of the most important tools of production from private hands to the state. The aim of Socialism is to give the workers and peasants (the masses) control over the use of profit—the surplus value, or capital—produced by transforming raw materials into goods and services. Some revolutions in the name of socialism, such as that in the Soviet Union, have resulted in the replacement of one set of profit managers by another. The essence of bourgeois capitalism—contractual control over profit and industrial technology—does *not* inevitably change fundamentally simply as a result of replacing capitalist economic forms with socialist ones.

Recognizing this, the Chinese revolution, which in 1948 succeeded in replacing the feudal-capitalist system that had theretofore prevailed, attempted to institutionalize an economic form and a logic which placed complete control over the productive processes and the profits in the hands of "people's committees" of workers and peasants. It is too early to know how successful this attempt to permanently resolve the conflicts and replace the basic features of capitalism will be. But the reality of attempts to replace capitalism with other economic forms (including monopoly capitalist systems and multinational corporations) cannot be ignored as potent forces shaping the future as well as the present.

In the next chapter we turn our attention to the *effects* of the contradictions in capitalist economies on the people living in the United States. Is this a nation of winners and losers? Have we created a nation in which people no longer behave morally toward one another? Have we created a nation in which we destroy the land that gives us life as rapidly as we write contracts? Have we created a nation in which the goals of efficiency and quality in contract writing produce a totalitarian, bureaucratic police state?

Summary

A revolutionary new social structure replaced feudalism through Europe from 1500 to 1918. This was a new form of economics, which structured economic relations between individuals on the basis of private ownership of property; few limits on the sale of property, goods, and services; and private control of profits on these sales. This was bourgeois (or capitalist) economics, and it generated a whole set of new institutional and cultural patterns. These included (1) the contract as the answer to the fundamental question of how one individual should relate to another; (2) political institutions that removed restraints on much individual behavior and heavily represented other interests important to the bourgeois, or profit-managing, class; (3) legal institutions that relied on cases and precedents rather than metaphysical, moral, or natural bases for law; and (4) reliance on money as an important means of facilitating contract writing.

American ideology as represented in the writings of Jefferson and Lincoln hoped for a flexible and classless society. In the American small town and its literature is found a pervasive belief that anyone who tried hard could become wealthy. However, even in small towns a small, self-perpetuating, profit-managing elite came to control both political and economic life.

Several contradictory tendencies began to emerge as Americans used capitalist economic structures in both city and town.

First, contractualism allowed successful profit managers to expand their power with few limits. This led to the creation of a national, self-perpetuating power elite, partially through creation of monopoly. The end result has been a reduction in the power of the wage-earning class to compete as well as contract for control of nonbusiness aspects of their lives.

Second, in the absence of noncontractual limits on business activity, industries began to do serious damage to the physical environment and to deplete resources. By using their enormous political power, industrial capitalists are able to resist imposing these costs of doing business against profit.

Third, no clear statement of a contractual morality has emerged and gained institutional support.

Fourth, just as individuals in the profit-managing class tend to increase the amount of wealth they control, so do the organizations they control tend to increase in size. The most successful contractors become larger, while the unsuccessful organizations are disbanded. Bigness of organizations, business, government, and service tends to further reduce the degree to which the individual can control his or her life.

Other peoples have tried, with varying degrees of success, to resolve some of these contradictions by creating industrial economies, segments of which are owned by the government (socialism) or by the people who use them (communism).

SUGGESTED READINGS

Alexis de Toqueville, *The Old Regime and the French Revolution* (New York: Anchor Books, 1955).

Helen Merrill Lynd and Robert Lynd, *Middletown* (New York: Harcourt, 1937).

Page Smith, *As A City Upon a Hill: The Town in American History* (New York: Knopf, 1966).

ELEVEN
Contradictions and Conflicts

The "American" dream is as noble as any ever dreamed, if by noble we mean hopeful. The mercantilist philosophers who wrote the United States Constitution and Declaration of Independence envisioned and tried to structure a society that would be all that humans had seemed to struggle toward throughout history. It would provide security and challenge, wisdom and practicality, beauty and strength, freedom and justice. The social structure itself would allow those who desired it to become rich, but the poor would be secure and would remain poor only if they lacked motivation or were mentally deficient. The independent farmer was to be made secure, thereby providing a stable mass which would not be torn by the split between owners and producers. Science and technology were to be used for the social good, and the wilderness was to be tamed, if not conquered. People believed they could have a moral society while individuals were free to contract whatever life they wished so long as hurt was done to no one. Like children who, given three wishes, make the last one a wish to have a hundred more wishes, the framers of the Constitution added a political system whereby any unforeseen problems could be resolved by compromise through a representative legislature. The founding fathers shared with Karl Marx the idea that an end to the cycle of contradiction and class conflict could be built into social structure. On paper, their scheme is certainly an ingenious and hopeful one.

A sociologist must insist on asking, "What happened after the talk?" Did people's behavior fit the plan? Was Eden flawed by evil capitalists, by riff-raff foreigners and labor agitators, by cynical politicians? We think not. The design itself contained contradictions, as does any which seeks contradictory goals. The problems people have had in the United States seem, in retrospect, predictable from an analysis of the contradictions inherent in its positive social and economic forms.

CONFLICTS BETWEEN THE INS AND THE OUTS

Racial and Other Exclusions

There was never a single society dominated by contractual logic. Yet the contractual design assumed that everyone would play the contractual game. Perhaps it was blindness, perhaps wishful thinking, to ignore those who from the beginning were not allowed to contract *their* place in the geographical United States: women, the native Americans and the black slaves. Why the status of black and red people, yellow and brown (who were also accepted as noncontracting inferiors), is so critical can be seen clearly through conflict analysis. Their exclusion is a living denial of contractual logic. If contractual logic is to do all that was and is claimed for it, it must be good for all people. If some people are denied the right to contract (for noncontractual reasons, namely so that their helplessness can be exploited), the political and business leaders of the country, and the millions who benefit from the exclusion, are revealed as hypocrites.

Racist beliefs and racist institutions support the exclusion of people of color and represent a denial of any claims of equality under the contractual system. When put into institutional form (exclusion from jobs, police discrimination, educational discrimination) racism exposes the United States as a place in which the legally powerful (that is, those with state support) brutalize the weak. Contractualism where all have equal rights to

make contracts has never been tried in the United States. A measurable decline in racism would partially gauge the degree to which the United States is becoming a single contractual society.

For different reasons, other groups have been slow to become full-time users of contractual social relations and logic. Each instance of a group using noncontractual forms is evidence that the founding fathers stated a theory of how a contractual society might be ordered to a people not yet ready to fully accept contractual logic. Thus we must analyze not only the emergence of inherent contradictions in contractualism but also the degree to which people are still using older forms and the resulting conflicts between the different forms.[1]

Measures of institutionalized racial exclusion are measures of conflict between people partially using logics other than contractualism. Measures of sexism, professionalism, ruralism, and ethnocentrism are to some degree measures of the same thing. In each of these there are advantages to people using the older forms, but the older forms are incompatible with and antagonistic toward contractual logic. Those using the older forms are under pressure to change. The pressure to change and the resistance against change are seen, for example, in conflicts between men and women over women's rights and between organized medicine and collections of patients over socialized medicine.

Sexual Exclusion

We have analyzed sexism as a form of caste relationship. In this view, males and females both find advantages in conforming to a noncontractual division of labor (one in

---

[1] "Older" does not mean "inferior." A theory of evolutionary dominant social logics implies no judgment that what is new is better than what is old. The new may solve old problems, but in doing so creates new ones. It is a matter of opinion whether the old or new problems are to be preferred.

which the duties of neither are open to negotiation) and the idea that the marriage bond is a moral obligation. This type of caste system is under enormous pressure today because many women believe the system is exploitative and unfair. Selection 7-3, page 139, described one of the obvious sexual exclusions at any American college—the unequal amounts of money spent on men's and women's athletic programs.

Professional Exclusion

Professionalism grows also out of feudal institutions and has great potential benefits for both the professional and the client. Pro-

fessionalism is a social arrangement whereby the practitioners of highly specialized skills (medicine, law, education, research) agree to provide their skills to others in return for the right to regulate *their own* behavior rather than have it regulated by contract with consumers and courts. The benefits should be obvious. The professionals, knowing what is good technique and what is not, should demand higher standards of themselves than would nonprofessional regulators such as judges, juries, bureaucrats, or consumers. Grateful for the freedom they receive to determine their own work, they should in turn train themselves to give the best and

The bureacratized factory system of production replaced the mass of self-employed craftsmen and farmers upon whom Jefferson and Lincoln placed their hopes for a classless society. (Pictorial Parade/EPA)

most ethical service possible and to act morally—that is, for the good of the community —in order to retain the confidence of their clients. This confidence is the basis on which they retain the right to self-regulation. "Socialized medicine" has been regularly denounced in the United States because it is believed that doctors paid salaries by a governmental insurance agency will be under legal pressure, supervised by nonprofessional bureaucrats, to deliver the cheapest rather than the highest-quality medical care. These arguments deserve serious study. Do doctors, lawyers, teachers, and researchers who must contract their services, either to state agencies or to groups of individuals, become less devoted to the truth, to what is good for the client and the community? Whatever the answer, there are strong pressures in contractual society to break down the professions and make them more easy to assimilate into contractual, particularly bureaucratic, structures.

At the same time, as shown in Selection 11-1, the surprise with which journalists describe a "selfless doctor" reveals how far most professionals have moved away from the ethic for which they are granted self-regulation and toward contractual relations with their clients. At the same time, many types of bureaucrats want to call themselves professionals in order to upgrade their "image" (a good image can be used as leverage to get better contracts). People using police, mortician, business manager and executive, real-estate agent, and other roles insist on calling themselves professional. Will these pressures work toward breaking down professional morality and toward making professionals simply highly trained bureaucrats whose responsibilities are defined more by contract than by loyalty to professional moral and ethical standards? It is easy to be moral in a professional sense in a society in which the interests of the client are also the interests of the community. In a place dominated by contractual logic—where there is little agreement, except vague generalities, on what is good for all people—there is no easy way for the professional to figure out what the moral behavior *is* in return for which the community has given the power to self-regulate. Should a psychiatrist inform the police if a patient has threatened to shoot someone? Should a psychiatrist tell the court that a client has confessed to a crime in the interests of sparing the community from the individual? Psychiatrists in a California murder case revealed that their client had confessed to a murder, although he pleaded innocent in the trial and was convicted only on circumstantial evidence. The psychiatrists also "inadvertantly" revealed where the murder weapons could be found, although the weapons had not been found when their client was convicted.[2]

Should a lawyer retained by a corporation to help it violate the spirit or the letter of federal antipollution legislation act professionally (that is, for the good of the community) or contractually (that is, for the good of the client)? There is much conflict between nonprofessional role users and professionals, as witness, for example, the harassment of teachers, or the declining prestige of physicians and lawyers. It appears that as contractualism spreads, conflict between contractualists and professionals increases, and the professions as self-governing bodies of moral entrepreneurs may disappear.

Rural Exclusion

Ruralism refers to a tendency of people living on the farms and in small towns to use noncontractual social forms. Recent studies of small towns stress the degree to which rural and small-town people are tied into the national economy, watch national television,

---

[2] *San Francisco Chronicle*, February 2, 1972.

SELECTION 11-1: Professionalism as a Noncontractual Means of Relating to Others.

SELFLESS DOCTOR REVEALED— AT FUNERAL

The identity of a selfless doctor described two years ago in the Bulletin of the San Francisco Medical Society was revealed yesterday.

The doctor's devotion was reported in the June, 1971, Bulletin in a letter from Dr. David Leigh Rodgers.

The letter read, in part:

"Last night I was called to see a physician in an ICU (intensive care unit). He had vomited two quarts of blood and passed out an hour earlier, and he was a bit shocky still.

"After looking him over I retired with the residents to a neutral corner . . .

"When we returned to the ICU, there was the physician—pale as a ghost, still in shock, blood going in one arm and a blood pressure cuff on the other and a gastric tube disappearing into his nose.

"And what else was going on? The Lord can take me now if what I say is not true. He was dictating notes to his wife about who to call and what to do about his patients.

"There is nothing on earth I can think of that would make most mortals think about themselves so much as puking up two quarts of their own life's blood. Yet there he was, carefully outlining what should be done about someone else."

The letter was read yesterday at memorial services for Dr. Thomas J. Mannell, 44. Dr. Mannell recovered from the severe hemorrhage he suffered in 1971, but he died Sunday when his car went out of control in West Marin and crashed into a tree.

Tiny Christ Episcopal Church in Sausalito was crammed beyond capacity by friends and relatives of Dr. Mannell, who practiced in San Francisco and lived with his wife and four children in Sausalito.

tional society.[3] All of this may be true, but much of the evidence is based on talk rather than behavior. Rural and small-town United States citizens may talk like big-city people, but the most important question from the viewpoint of conflict theory is, "To what degree is their *behavior* contractually determined?" It is instructive to note the deep perplexity that small-town people feel regarding the issues which bother people in big cities. Street crime, antiwar protests, and class and racial oppression are treated by smalltowners as manufactured rather than real issues. This is why it is so easy for the smalltowner to dismiss many of these issues as "commie plots." Their experience does not include the same problems, and they assume other people's experiences do not *really* include economic exploitation, political blackmail, racial oppression, or police violence. In those small towns which survive as independent economic entities, particularly farming and ranching communities, these conflicts do not exist to the degree they do in the cities. Limited markets and vestiges of community morality still restrict exploitation of the poor by the rich. In many places the contradiction between the machine and the garden does not exist simply because no one has yet wanted to place industry there. This further reduces the likelihood of economic exploitation, a rigid class structure, racism, and police and managerial violence. Customs that are part of an older morality are often retained—for example, neighbors carrying in a dinner to a family who has suffered a death, one person helping another person repair machinery, and other obligations undertaken for the community rather than for short-term gain. If there *is* a small-town morality, a noncontractual morality visible in behavior, we may

[3] Arthur J. Vidich and Joseph Bensman, *Small Town in Mass Society* (Princeton, N.J.: Princeton University Press, 1958).

have attitudes similar to those of urbanites, and travel widely—in short, the degree to which they are fully integrated into a nayet have a long way to go before we pass the era of rural–big-city conflict. A much closer look at small-town behavior is needed to tell us. To some degree the cities and suburbs are inhabited by small-towners unprepared for and unwilling to assume responsibility for keeping a contractual system running. Populist revolts against contractualism have been and may still be linked to antibigness, anticontractualism, and racism where this gives political advantage. At the same time, there are signs that a kind of colonial exploitation of rural areas is increasing. Appalachia is an area where coal mining companies have stripped or dug away a resource. Using the connivance of local elites, keeping labor disorganized, and feeling no responsibility to the people as a mass (all techniques of colonialism the world over), the coal companies have kept Appalachia impoverished, while the profits from the areas' resources have made residents of Chicago, Philadelphia, and New York rich. This internal colonialism seems to be increasing. The building of giant coal- or gas-burning electric plants and atomic reactors, oil-shale strip mining, and water diversion now promise (under the slogan "energy crisis") to devastate large parts of Western America

as well. The people in places where these energy producers are at work will have little say over the loss of natural resources and will get little financial return for the disruption of their way of life.

Ethnic Exclusion

America was supposed to "melt" people into the new system. Many assume that this has taken place—that the United States is a functionally integrated society and that people coping with immigration through using their own cultures and social structures are assimilated until proved otherwise. Such a view provides little critical analysis of the conflicts generated by these different national backgrounds, this *ethnicity*. Recent interest in minority problems has spurred reassessments of ethnic behavior, some of which have found distinct cultural and social structural patterns persisting into fifth and sixth generations in such supposedly assimilated national groups as the Irish, Italians, and Polish.[4] Whatever the degree of cultural separatism, two forms of conflict are related

[4] Nathan Glazer and Daniel P. Moynihan, *Beyond the Melting Pot: The Negroes, Puerto Ricans, Jews, Italians, and Irish of New York City* (Cambridge, Mass.: MIT Press, 1963).

Under the guise of an "energy crisis," coal and oil companies have won government support for continued exploitation of rural resources and continued survival of their corporations through consumer reliance on fossil fuel energy. (Alain Heler from Editorial Photocolor Archives)

to it: that resulting from hatred of out-groups, or ethnocentrism, and that resulting from ethnic favoritism which subverts contractual logic.

Ethnocentrism is the belief that one's own group's way of doing things (*our* culture and *our* social structure) is right and other ways are not only wrong but threatening. This kind of conflict cannot be mediated or resolved contractually. The values are not contractable and hence not compromisable. Many studies of racist beliefs (as distinct from institutional racism, that is, racist practices built into group structures) have discovered that this type of racism has two sources: (1) the attempt to justify oppression, particularly castism and slavery; and (2) the fear that others believe differently because they are biologically different and therefore the beliefs are uncompromisable (the two parties cannot contract together).[5]

Persistent loyalty to ethnic subcultures also subverts contractual logic and contracted obligations. Ethnic loyalty allows people who have climbed the social ladder to dispense political favors and jobs to their "own" people without reference to contractual qualifications, such as experience, degrees, skills, and aptitude. These practices tend to harden class lines and to convince those on the bottom that contractual logic is a fake. From their perspective, "It's not what you know but who you know."

Self-Exclusion: Stop the World; I Want to Get Off

In theory it should be possible to agree to live noncontractually. However, "dropouts," whether religious groups such as the Hutterites and Amish or generational groups, such as "hippies," have always experienced conflict. Perhaps those who get the best of most contracts they write would like to see every-

one forced to live contractually. The U.S. Bureau of Indian Affairs has for 100 years vacillated between the policy of allowing native Americans to exist as tribal units rather than contracting individuals and the policy of forcing them out of tribalism by any means necessary. Small-towners may soon find that they want out of a system which allows the Department of Interior and large oil companies to contract for underground explosions of atomic devices. Ground-level structural damage is freely admitted by the corporations, which rationalize that the amount of oil released by the explosions will be worth it. Local residents do not have the power to alter such contracts, which are made between the corporations and the federal government. People displaced by construction of freeways, dams, urban "renewal," and missile sites are powerless to retain their own homes. However, faced with underground big bomb blasts and coal-burning electric generating plants which pollute entire states, large numbers of people may begin to question how well their "rights" are guaranteed by a contractual system; they may demand to be allowed to drop out.

Rural people, hippie communes, Indian tribes, members of ethnic cultures advocating separation—such groups raise two interesting questions. (1) Should contractualism contain within it the right to opt for noncontractualism, to drop out? (2) Is the collective contract displacing the individual contract, and what will be the long-term consequences if it does?

CLASS CONSCIOUSNESS AND COLLECTIVE CONTRACTS

The kinds of conflict generated by people being excluded under capitalism and by the contradictions in contractual logic itself become conflicts between large classes of people rather than between individuals. One of the most frequently used ways to reduce

---

[5] A summary of these studies is found in Paul F. Secord and Carl W. Backman, *Social Psychology* (New York: McGraw-Hill, 1964), pp. 429–30.

oppression between social classes is for the weaker to become conscious of their oppression and combine their individual power. The collective *consciousness* of class, class conflict, and class oppression does not come automatically from the experience of social conflict. The trade union movement in the United States is organized around the working class but excludes large segments of the American labor force. Does this reflect lack of class consciousness, limited oppression, a false sense of potential advancement, economic affluence partially based on use of other countries' resources, or a combination of these factors? Much analysis remains to be done of how class consciousness emerges (see Chapter 9, page 192).

There does seem to be a tendency to join with others to write collective contracts. Purchasers of prepaid health insurance, and members of special interest groups (Black Muslims, district political coalitions, conservation organizations, church members, in fact, people using almost any large, formally organized structure), increasingly expect to use their collective muscle to deal contractually with their social environment.

A parallel phenomenon is the increasing use of class action law suits. These are requests that a court of law place a limit on the behavior of an individual or a collection of individuals with regard to their relationship to an entire class of other individuals. For example, the court may be asked to find that an oil refinery is violating its contractual obligations by polluting air. Even though no single individual is hurt enough to be heard in court, a large number of individuals living nearby are together hurt enough to require the judge to consider the oil refinery in violation of the law. Does this movement toward collective negotiation signal a fundamental change in the structure of classes? For example, is "consumers versus technocrats" the most important clash of

interests in advanced capitalist *and* advanced socialist economies? Even those accused of being mentally ill and the dying have advocates for the extension to them as classes of the right to contract to seek or not seek help as can be seen in Selections 11-2 and 11-3. We could expect that many people formerly excluded from contractual ways of organizing their lives would try to seek collectively the power to do so.

CONTRACTUAL CONFLICT AND CONTRADICTIONS

Some forms of conflict resulting from the use of contractual logic spring from the exclusion of groups of individuals from the use of the contractual form. Other major conflicts grow out of contradictions in the economic structure. Conflict theory proposes the following sequence of events which grows out of the use of contractual logic.

1. Successful contract writers tend to monopolize and control production of products, which leads to their ability to monopolize income and all purchasable resources. Several things result from this monopolization.

2. As the economic pie gets larger, the powerful increase their share of income and power relative to the weak, which in turn leads to control of public policy, and oppression of the weak through agents of social control such as the schools, the police, the courts, the prisons, and the mental institutions.

3. All these processes together should increase class conflict as the weak are more and more squeezed out of the system, more and more prevented from writing contracts through lack of power to negotiate.

A measure of the extent to which these things are happening in the United States is a measure of the breakdown of the contrac-

SELECTION 11-2: A psychiatrist describes exclusion of the "mentally ill" from the right to contract for the basics of life.

A CIVIL RIGHTS FIGHT FOR THE MENTALLY ILL

MILDRED HAMILTON

"All we ask is that people who are mentally ill be treated at least as well as people accused of crimes," said civil rights champion George J. Alexander, a co-founder of the American Association for the Abolition of Involuntary Mental Hospitalization, Inc.

Alexander, who is also dean of the University of Santa Clara School of Law, talked yesterday about the growth and acceptance of the AAAIMH, which will hold its second annual meeting tomorrow on the Santa Clara campus.

Psychiatrists, lawyers, stockholders, writers, representatives of many branches of rights' movements will participate in the all-day session, free and open to the public, at 206 Daly Science Building.

A major speaker will be Dr. Thomas Szasz, professor of Psychiatry, State University of New York, AAAIMH co-founder and outspoken critic of his profession and of mental hospitals.

"Our aim is to abolish all involuntary mental hospitalization," said the law school dean, who dates his involvement to acting as Dr. Szasz' attorney. "His strong stand against coercive psychiatry was received badly originally by his colleagues and there was pressure to muzzle him 10 years ago.

"I think and hope that day is over. Our organization is drawing a broad-based membership. Civil liberty groups are taking up the cause and we anticipate a Supreme Court ruling similar to that on designating special treatment of children unconstitutional."

Dean Alexander, 42, who came to Santa Clara two years ago after a distinguished career in the East, believes society can exist without locked door institutions that are not jails. "Great Britain does, and these mental institutions are beginning to be phased out in California."

People who offend society by breaking the law can and should be punished, he said. "However, the great dividing point is whether we punish people for something they have done or whether we punish them on the basis of somebody's prediction about what they might do.

"Psychiatrists," he said, emphasizing the point by bringing his coffee cup down on his desk top, "are not equipped to predict. They are trained in healing instead of in predicting. And there is a tremendous pressure on them to overcommit. Just labeling a person as mentally ill in most cases is a massive deprivation of his civil rights."

Belief that most mental institutions provide incarceration rather than treatment permeates the AAAIMH writings and comments of its leaders.

"It is a sham to use medical terms in connection with this imprisonment," said Dean Alexander.

"People with emotional problems should be free to seek help whenever and wherever they wish—or not to seek help. Is there really any reason to make a decision for them in our society, which is based on individual freedom? A parallel is the man who needs an operation. He has the right to make the decision to have it or not to have it."

The law school dean, who with his attorney wife has done extensive research and writing on mentally disabled and the law, called coercive psychiatry "more a barrier to treatment than the manner of treating."

"Now when a person asks for help it may mean that he becomes ensnared in the system. He could be locked up, lose his liberty and his property as normal adjuncts of seeking help. And we won't even mention the possible side effects that a certain Missouri senator might talk about," he said in reference to Thomas Eagleton, dropped as Democratic vice-presidential nominee after revealing his mental health treatment.

"When we can assure people of treatment without this danger of punishment, more people with emotional problems will seek aid."

tual system as it has been used in this country. In the next section we present observations of the kind one must make if one is to try honestly and objectively to determine how

SELECTION 11-3: Extensions of contractual logic.

DYING WITH DIGNITY: A GOD GIVEN RIGHT

LOUIS CASSELS

In the Declaration of Independence, America's founding fathers affirmed the belief that every human person is endowed by God with inalienable rights to life, liberty and the pursuit of happiness.

Had they foreseen the capacities of modern medicine, they might have added a fourth basic human right: the right to die with dignity.

Dying is a universal human experience. Like all other experiences, it has content and quality. It can be done bravely or cravenly; reluctantly or with serene acceptance. It can take place in the warmly supportive setting of a home and a family, or in the coldly impersonal atmosphere of an institution.

Time was—and not so long ago, at that—when most people died in their own beds, surrounded by their loved ones, in full knowledge that their time had come.

Today, death is more likely to occur in a hospital or nursing home. The patient, if conscious, is surrounded during most of his waking hours by professional personnel who all too often feel it is part of their duty to "keep up the spirits" of the dying by deceiving them about the gravity of their condition.

Many patients are denied any knowledge of the approach of death because they are in a comatose condition for weeks, months or even years before their hearts finally stop beating. Run enough tubes from the patient's body to modern medical gadgetry and he can be kept technically alive long after he has ceased to think, feel, understand or interact as a sentient human person.

Dr. Melvin J. Krant, a physician who heads Boston's Equinox Institute, says people who die in institutions have "little opportunity to be assisted in working out meaningful details of the dying experience."

The whole focus of institutional attention is on keeping the patient technically alive as long as possible instead of respecting his right to die with dignity. All too often, says Krant, a dying person is treated in an institution "as a leper, rather than as a man or woman reaching the end of a personal life."

Krant believes several things must be done to restore the possibility of a dignified dying experience.

First, he urged that both children and adults be "educated for death" by schools and churches. They should be helped to face the inevitability and "naturalness" of death as something that will happen sooner or later to everyone they love—and to themselves.

Second, health insurance regulations need to be changed so that families are not under tremendous financial pressure to put a gravely ill relative in a hospital or extended care facility. This would reopen the option of dying at home in one's own bed, a method of departure for which many people have a stronger preference.

Third, Krant says, we need to "review and explore the meaning of control of one's dying." By this, he does not necessarily mean people should be encouraged to end their own lives by suicide, or that terminally ill people be ushered out by deliberate medical execution.

Since most people move slowly into death, their right to "control" their dying experience really means that they are allowed to retain power of decision "over those few remaining choices and options" which may determine how long they'll linger or where they'll die.

All major Christian and Jewish bodies uphold Krant's contention that there is no moral reason why any person should be compelled to undergo extraordinary medical measures rather than peacefully accept a natural death.

But most doctors are imbued with the idea they should never stop fighting to maintain technical life—no matter how hopeless or costly the battle may be, or how the patient or his family may feel about the matter. Thus contemporary society often robs people of the right to control their own dying and thus to die with dignity.

far these theorized processes have gone and are going. In the paragraphs immediately below, we show through example how they emerged in the United States.

What Happens If There Is More Money?

Is the amount of resources available to people using a contractual logic fixed, or is it constantly increasing? If the pie gets bigger all the time, there are three possibilities: (1) the rich take all the increase while the poor remain poor or perhaps get poorer; (2) the rich get richer but the poor get richer also; (3) the rich get poorer and the poor get richer—that is, the poor take the majority of the increases in resources. The last outcome would indicate that contractualism is working well. It would indicate recognition that increases in resources reflect increases in productivity which are the result of the efforts of the many, not of the few. It would indicate a social mobility, and a spreading of the power to write successful contracts. It would be accepted that at any one time, some people will be somewhat better off than others, but that this is a temporary, not a fixed, condition. Analysis of the size of the pie, the size of yearly productivity increases, and the distribution of the income resulting from these productivity increases is therefore crucial in assessing how well contractualism is working.[6]

Early in United States history it became apparent that the very rich were taking most of the productivity increase resulting from the application of machine technology to production of goods and services. The union movement tried unsuccessfully to increase the share going to some (a minority) of the workers. From the early 1930s to the 1960s the relative share of the economic pie going to upper- and lower-income groups remained virtually unchanged. It appears that in the decade of the 1960s the upper groups actually increased their relative share, and some of the lower groups actually lost purchasing power (see Chapter 17).

[6] The pie may be getting bigger, but this raises the question, "Is it getting bigger because the rich are stealing from other countries?" Such a process might help keep internal conflict down and keep the contractual game going here for the short run at the risk of destroying it in the long run, through conflict with other countries that do not like being robbed or through the creation of the militaristic state needed to keep fighting wars all over the world.

Social Power and Better Contracts

There are forms of power other than money: knowledge, possession of the tools of coercion, possession of legitimacy (occupancy of offices with prestige), and emotional resources (the ability to satisfy the emotional needs of others).

Power is a measure of a relationship between roles, classes, or individuals. Traditionally in sociology the tendency of the rich to have power advantages has been measured through studies of occupational mobility—the ability of sons to move up an occupational prestige ladder relative to their fathers. This view of social power assumes that the job one holds is an adequate measure of one's power to contract. It ignores the fact that such power includes much more than occupational prestige. How much scarce knowledge does an individual possess, how much control has he or she over the activities of government, what control is exercised over the tools of coercion (that is, over police and military activities), and what control over money? You cannot see *power* relations by comparing the incomes of the rich with the incomes of the poor. Even the money power alone of the rich is much greater than that measured by their income. Much money power is gained by manipulation of stocks and bonds and by such corporate privileges as use of corporate credit cards, airplanes, cars, equipment, homes, medical facilities, insurance programs, vacation retreats, recreational facilities, telephones, sauna baths, psychiatrists, and so on.

An analysis of the power structure in the United States and the question of to what degree it is rigidifying (people becoming more and more fixed in the relative power they have to write contracts for jobs, homes, education, and leisure, and a greater tendency for people to be fixed in the power structure, high or low, by their birth) requires much more than simple measures of occupational mobility. A new generation of soci-ologists is just beginning the task of cata-loging power differences.[7]

The Great Depression of the 1930s probably did more than any other single event to raise the question in the United States of whether the country was inevitably to be dominated by an aristocracy based on inherited wealth. For the first time, many people questioned the idea that anyone could improve their ability to contract a better life in direct proportion to how hard they worked.

Social Power and Unequal Control of One's Life

Politics is the making of decisions by groups of people about how scarce resources shall be distributed. In theory, democracy involv-ing full enfranchisement means that each voting person has equal control in making crucial decisions. These decisions include the amount of taxes to be paid, whether one shall be drafted or go to war, whether high-ways and suburbs shall be built (and the many other ways one's taxes will be used), how contracts will be enforced, and how rights will be guaranteed. Another view is that individual voting power alone cannot ensure life control, but that people are all users of some group structures (PTA, unions, business associations) which do give them equal power because these collectives exert equal pressure on those who make the de-cisions. A third view is that whether indi-viduals exert voting pressure or groups exert lobbying pressure, the important decisions will be made by the economic class with the most power. The decisions will be made to the advantage of the powerful and often to

[7] The most thorough recent treatment, Ferdinand Lund-berg's *The Rich and the Super Rich* (New York: Bantam, 1968) was written by a financial writer. C. Wright Mills, *The Power Elite* (New York: Oxford, 1956) remains a classic description of the process, although the supporting documentation is not as extensive as Lundberg's.

the disadvantage of those whose needs are greater and whose resources are fewer.

People in the United States suspected fairly early that the rich could buy the gov-ernment and therefore subvert the contrac-tualist doctrine of equal voting power. The late 1800s were a time of scandalous pur-chase of governors, senators, congressmen, and government bureaucrats by the so-called robber barons, the great financiers and spec-ulators of the day. In the 1920s the admin-istration of President Warren Harding was known for the corruption of government officials by corporate interests. This suspicion approaches certainty in light of the complex events surrounding the 1972 presidential election. There has long been suspicion that the ability of people to freely contract is limited by the control of political policy making by the powerful.

In addition to ensuring freedom from eco-nomic slavery, the contractual economic sys-tem is supposed to promote efficient use of resources. According to capitalist theory, people transfer resources in a free market from those who use them badly to those who use them efficiently by not buying bad products and by not voting for officials who waste public resources. However, the ten-dency of the powerful to control large areas of governmental contract writing interferes with this process. Large areas of policy mak-ing on the use of resources have been totally removed from the contractual system. Cer-tainly no single consumer or purchaser, no single voter, has any effect on pollution policy, foreign policy, or certain areas of domestic policy. Even organized groups of consumers and voters have found they lack power relative to business elites in shifting resources away from groups that appear to be using them unwisely. In the Marxian version of conflict analysis, this process has a double effect, the sum of which is de-scribed by the word *alienation*. An analysis

THE PARKS THAT EXCLUDE POOR

"The state park system basically caters to the upper or middle income families and not the poor," state Parks Director William Penn Mott Jr. says.

But Mott added that the department is "trying to overcome this deficiency."

Mott's comments came during a news conference on the deck of the historic schooner C. A. Thayer at the Maritime State Historic Park at the foot of Hyde Street in San Francisco.

The conference was called by Mott and Theme Events Ltd., a nonprofit corporation that wants to stage a fair in the park in July and August. During the event, it is proposed to raise the admission fee to the park from 75 cents for adults and 25 cents for children to $2.50 and $1.

Newsmen had asked Mott whether the higher fees would prevent poor families from attending the park.

of the use of profits by capitalist managers (and perhaps socialist bureaucrats as well) is important to the understanding of alienation.

If demand for goods remains equal, the selling price of a good is largely determined by three factors: the cost of labor, the cost of raw materials, and overhead costs (replacing worn-out tools, buildings, etc.). Profit equals selling price minus labor, overhead, and raw-material costs. Profit is the value added to the raw material by labor as it is converted to something people can use. Labor includes the work done at a punch press drilling holes in a sheet of steel to make it a car door, work done by secretaries to make sure the door gets shipped to an assembly point, and work done by advertising writers to make people want the car badly enough to pay a high price for it. The

important question for Marx is, What is *done* with this value that all the workers have added to what was originally a piece of iron ore in the ground? What is done with profit? Some profit will be reinvested in research or in new machinery to increase productivity of workers. But Marx predicted that large amounts of this profit would be spent making life easy for those who owned the tools and thus controlled profit (through laws on private property, inheritance, etc.). More important, much of the profit would be spent to shape institutional patterns (education, foreign policy, art, literature, etc.) toward support of increased profit making and toward other interests of the profit-controlling class. Selection 11-4 shows how far this institution-shaping process goes in excluding the poor from tax-supported, publicly owned parks.

These uses of profit affect the workers who created the surplus value in two ways. First, the workers are alienated from control of that which they created in the first place. Marxist conflict theory predicts that this will create psychological states of helplessness and apathy, and reduce class consciousness and the capacity to organize. Second, the use of profit in this way results in using worker-created value power (profit) to support institutional patterns which often go against the interests of workers. This kind of analysis would explain the Vietnam War, for example, as one justified by a foreign policy designed to support profitable markets and increase access to cheap raw materials in Asia, with the fighting done by a conscript army whose patterns of drafting take the sons of workers while leaving the sons of profit makers at home (in college, or with psychiatric assertions of "unfitness").

This double alienation of workers from the products of their labor is a critical area of study for conflict analysis. Are workers willing to exchange the power of surplus value, which might be used to make their work meaningful and to control the work itself, for job security and increased consuming of TV, recreation, and other devices to make family life palatable? Do the masses of workers experience poor patterns of education, health care, and resource planning as the result of letting the profit-controlling class exercise most power in shaping these institutional patterns? These questions need very serious study if we are to sense how near or how far we are from the end of the American dream of a "free" society. Some of the systematic observations for analysis of these issues have been done by Irving Howe, Robert Blauner, Ely Chinoy, and Michael Crozier.[8]

In summary, conflict analysis predicts that the masses of people will gradually lose control over their own lives. This occurs to the extent that industrial technology and the power of those who control distribution of profits do two things: (1) split the workers from each other[9] and produce a sense of powerlessness resulting *from the structure of work itself;* and (2) produce dominant institutional patterns that do not solve working-class problems, but in fact make them worse.

Social Power and Police and Court Oppression

Contractual logic implies and requires the rule of law. A successful contractual system must have fair enactment of law and fair

practices of arrest, charging, trial, and sentencing. If the law is biased toward the powerful and against the powerless, then the contractual system is in trouble. The law, and therefore the logic behind it, will be seen as a sham, a fraud, a hypocrisy. Further, those who are oppressed will be driven outside the contractual system; they will increasingly lack power to make contracts involving their own lives. Thus, when analyzing the present health of the contractual system, it is important to look at all aspects of the application of law. The question is, "Does the law discriminate against the less powerful?"

In a study done in the 1930s, Edwin Sutherland showed that 90 percent of the seventy largest corporations in the United States were habitual criminals. Were these corporations to be treated like individual habitual criminals, they would either be executed or imprisoned for life.[10] Apparently corporations are treated more leniently than individuals when they violate the law.

Conflict over the definitions of deviance and the pinpointing of deviants extends far beyond the struggle over criminal law. There are also continuous attempts to extend criminal law to include "moral" behavior. Crimes with victims (murder, rape, robbery, fraud, embezzlement) fit contractual logic quite well. One or more persons have been treated unfairly—a relationship has been carried out by force, trickery, or stealth rather than by contract. However, people are also arrested, charged, and convicted for crimes without victims: drunkenness, prostitution, gambling, use or sale of addictive drugs, homosexuality, nudity in public, or acting "crazy." In each of these behaviors, "society" is assumed to be the victim. Yet in a contractual com-

[8] See Irving Howe (ed.), *The World of the Blue Collar Worker* (New York: Quadrangle, 1972); Robert Blauner, *Alienation and Freedom* (Chicago: University of Chicago Press, 1964); Ely Chinoy, *Automobile Workers and the American Dream;* Michael Crozier, *The World of the Office Worker* (Chicago: University of Chicago Press, 1971).

[9] Industrial technology splits the working class by producing a hierarchy of specialists. A computer programmer and a drill-press operator live in separate worlds. As a result of living in these different worlds, and the great differences in wages, the programmer and the blue-collar worker are more aware of the differences between themselves than of the differences in economic power between all wage earners and those who control profits.

[10] Edwin H. Sutherland, "The Crime of Corporations," from Albert Cohen, Albert Lindesmith, and Karl Schuessler (eds.), *The Sutherland Papers* (Bloomington, Ind.: Indiana University Press, 1956). A total of 980 adverse decisions were rendered against the seventy, an average of fourteen per corporation. Ninety-eight percent were recidivists, that is, had two or more convictions.

munity the only morality which should be relevant involves behavior which supports free, faithful, and honest contract writing. It seems that more powerful groups are tempted to force less powerful groups to copy and thereby sanctify their (middle- and upper-strata) behavior.

In fact it is likely that the attempt to impose morality harms the community much more than any of the behaviors described as "crimes without victims." Prosecution of working-class sexual behavior, gambling, drinking, or drug taking hurts the community in three ways. First, through lawmaking and law enforcement, the middle and upper strata intensify class conflict, deny contractual morality, and drive people outside the system (often into prisons or asylums). Second, the strong attack against working-class behavior prevents the less powerful from defining middle-strata behavior as criminal; business activities may harm the community, but they are not defined as illegal. Third, the attempted suppression of these behaviors creates underground organizations which will deliver the illegal services. Where there is demand for illegal services—prostitutes, gambling, non-middle-strata drugs—there will be a supplier. Because competition to supply illegal markets will necessarily be violent, taking place, as it must, outside the law, it is to the advantage of police and citizens if the supplier is organized. Organized crime is precisely the supplier that can guarantee that the illegal services demanded will be supplied quietly and with a minimum of mess and damage to a community's reputation. The community pays a high price for making the leisure-time activities of the less powerful illegal.

MEASURES OF CLASS CONFLICT

So far in this chapter we have told the story of the emergence of two kinds of conflict in the United States: (1) the conflict between in groups, those included in the contractual system, and out groups, those excluded from contract writing, either by force or by choice; and (2) that conflict which emerges out of the contradictions inherent in contractualism itself. Three examples of the second type of conflict are: (1) the powerful in conflict with the less powerful over who shall benefit from increases in productivity in the economy; (2) the powerful in conflict with the less powerful over determination of government policy; and (3) the powerful in conflict with the less powerful over definitions of deviant behavior and over control of police and court behavior.

However, we need measures of the intensity of conflict generated by the three areas of contradiction between private and public interests so characteristic of contractual society. In the conflict view, these are as follows:

I. Class rigidity and class conflict, in order to test the degree to which contractualism is destroyed by concentrations of power
II. Industrial conflict, with measures of destruction of the physical environment, in order to test the degree to which contractualism is incapable or capable of sustaining a favorable physical environment
III. Ideological conflict as a measure of the degree to which
A. The powerful attempt to impose their morality on the weaker
B. The degree to which a class-free contractual morality exists

Although the facts or observations we present are chosen to prove a point—namely, that the conflict perspective increases our understanding of and ability to predict United States social life—the verdict is not unanimous. The conflict and oppression predicted do in fact exist. But the totally monopolistic society is not a police state for most of its citizens, nor has individual freedom totally disappeared. This is why the study of *trends* is so important. Are conflict and op-pression increasing or decreasing?

Class Rigidity, Class Conflict, Class Consciousness

Although, as we noted above, the measures of occupation, income, and education used in many studies to define social strata do not perfectly reflect contract-writing power, they are the most widely used measures we have.

In general, as the great migration to cities tapered off in the 1920s (the black migra-tion to the cities came later), the possibility of moving up the income ladder in the United States hit a plateau. Between 1920 and 1960 the possibility of moving up the ladder neither increased nor decreased; since 1960 it has decreased slightly.[11]

Data on social mobility in the United States are farily accessible. The United States census regularly asks people what they do for a living and what their income and edu-cation are. Some people are asked what their fathers did, which allows us to see if sons are doing better than their fathers. However, census data usually overestimate mobility because (1) they underreport the least mobile (the down-and-out who cannot be found to be questioned), and (2) when reporting on the middle strata they focus on the male occupation and income even in situations where wives' occupations and in-comes may significantly increase family con-tract-writing power.

Are the well-off increasing their power? Are the poor slipping back? Is the country becoming polarized between a jet-set elite of corporate, military, and government man-agers and a mass of tax-burdened people with a houseful of broken-down gadgets? It

takes many kinds of observations to begin to answer such questions. Table 11-1, which tabulates mobility of black males and white males by comparing the jobs of civilian men aged twenty-five to sixty-four years in March 1962 with the jobs of their fathers, is a start. The data show the following:

1. Some upward mobility for white males. For example, 21.3 percent of the sons of white lower-strata manual workers moved into higher white-collar jobs, while only 36 percent remained stationery at lower manual levels.

2. Very little upward mobility for black males. For example, only 8 percent of the sons of black lower-strata manual workers moved into higher white-collar jobs, while 61 percent of the sons of black lower-strata manual workers remained at the same occu-pational level as their fathers.

3. Very little downward mobility for whites. For example, 11.9 percent of the sons of white-collar workers were working at the lower-strata manual level in 1962, while 54.3 percent of the sons of white collar workers had remained at the same level as their fathers.

4. Very great downward mobility for black males. For example, 53 percent of the sons of black higher-level white-collar work-ers were working at the lower-strata manual level in 1962, while only 10 percent of the sons of black higher white-collar workers stayed at the same level as their fathers.

Further data needed to begin to assess class rigidity are: (1) comparisons of inter-generation mobility in the past to see if the rates of social mobility for whites and/or blacks have changed; and (2) measures of the contract-writing power at the various in-come and occupation levels in the society.

Meanwhile, even more work needs to be done to see if and how the rigidities in the class structure, the tendency for the rich to get richer and the poor poorer, translate into class consciousness and class conflict.

[11] A large part of the "upward mobility" of the 1800s and early 1900s was the result of movement from the farm into blue-collar or manual labor. It is not clear how much this move improves social power, or if it does so at all.

TABLE 11-1 Mobility from Father's Occupation to 1962 Occupation (Percentage Distributions), by Race for Civilian Men Twenty-five to Sixty-four Years Old, March 1962.

	1962 Occupation[1]							
Race and father's occupation	Higher white collar	Lower white collar	Higher manual	Lower manual	Farm	Not in experienced civilian labor force	Percent	Number (000)
Negro								
Higher white collar	10.4	9.7	19.4	53.0	0.0	7.5	100.0	134
Lower white collar	14.5	9.1	6.0	69.1	0.0	7.3	100.0	55
Higher manual	8.8	6.8	11.2	64.1	2.8	6.4	100.0	251
Lower manual	8.0	7.0	11.5	63.2	1.8	8.4	100.0	973
Farm	3.1	3.0	6.4	59.8	16.2	11.6	100.0	1,389
Not reported	2.4	6.5	11.1	65.9	3.1	11.1	100.0	712
Total, percent	5.2	5.4	9.5	62.2	7.7	10.0	100.0	——
Total, number	182	190	334	2,184	272	352	——	3,514
Non-Negro								
Higher white collar	54.3	15.4	11.5	11.9	1.3	5.6	100.0	5,836
Lower white collar	45.1	18.3	13.5	14.6	1.5	7.1	100.0	2,652
Higher manual	28.1	11.8	27.9	24.0	1.0	7.3	100.0	6,512
Lower manual	21.1	11.5	22.5	36.0	1.7	6.9	100.0	8,798
Farm	16.5	7.0	19.8	28.8	20.4	7.5	100.0	9,991
Not reported	26.0	10.3	21.0	32.5	3.9	6.4	100.0	2,666
Total, percent	28.6	11.3	20.2	26.2	6.8	6.9	100.0	——
Total, number	10,414	4,130	7,359	9,560	2,475	2,517	——	36,455

SOURCE: U.S. Department of Health, Education, and Welfare, *Toward a Social Report*, 1970, p. 24.

This would suggest the need for the following kinds of observations:

1. How aware are people of other people's mobility? Do they blame mobility or the lack of it on themselves? It has long been argued that one of the "strengths" of the contractual system is that people are led to believe that failure to control one's own life is a result of stupid contract writing rather than the result of unequal distribution of power.

2. Is the working class deprived relative to the rich, but well off by its own standards? Is the working class getting enough of a share of an expanding pie to be happy, even though a small number of rich people are taking the largest part? Answering this question requires measuring power other than income, for perhaps the working-class situa-

tion has improved through such things as subsidized housing loans, freeways, larger investment in public welfare programs, medical insurance for the aged and indigent, and negotiated fringe benefits for organized labor, including medical, life, and income insurance. The working-class position may have improved enough to reduce class consciousness and class conflict, even though the position of the managers who control profit distribution has improved much more.

It would be useful to dig out observations on who has gotten what proportions of the increased goods and services resulting from improved productivity over the past twenty or thirty years. This would be a crucial observation. The philosophy which justifies the contractual system says that if people work harder or use machines better, they will produce more goods and be better off than before. It is claimed that power inequalities and tendencies toward new caste systems or totalitarian elitism will thus be minimized. If, as Marx predicted, the rich grab the greater share not only of present productivity,[12] but also of whatever new productivity comes along, contractualism breaks down. In other words, if the rich expropriate the money resulting from better work, faster work, or more efficient work (in the name of whatever good cause—defense, reinvestment, increasing the number of jobs, etc.), class structure cannot become *less* rigid (except by working-class expropriation of the rich through taxes or revolution). Further, this expropriation results in a powerful thrust toward the destruction of the contractual system by removing from the working class one of the few means it has for improving its contract-writing position.

There are other important indicators of trends in class rigidity and class conflict. Four of these are:

1. Bigness, the destruction of small business and small farming, which has a tendency to concentrate wealth and reduce opportunities for individuals to improve their contract-writing power;[13]
2. Unequal returns from education;
3. "Structural" unemployment, the tendency of unemployment to be concentrated among the weak rather than to be randomly distributed; and
4. Unequal treatment under the law.

Bigness Some have declared the battle to preserve individual contract writing in the

[12] Productivity is the amount of goods and services, usually measured in dollars, produced by the average worker per unit of time. There has been an average annual increase in productivity of 2.3 to 3.0 percent in the United States for the past thirty years or more.
[13] This reduces that large class on which Jefferson and Lincoln pinned their hopes—those who both own and work the tools of production. Marx called them the *petit-bourgeois.*

economic sphere already lost, and good riddance. Who wants to go back to the days of slave wages and child labor? They cheerfully admit there are only three contract writers in the economic structure—big government, big labor, and big business—but they say that affiliation with any one of these three guarantees that people will get their contracts (for economic life) written *for* them. Indeed, only one out of ten new jobs during the 1950s was in the business-labor sector. Government produced 90 percent of the new jobs. Government ensures job security and a contractually guaranteed piece of the pie.

Although some see big-group contract writing as a solution to the kinds of contradictions which have emerged in the United States, there are problems. For example, such a solution relegates to second-class citizenship all those not protected by unions, big business, or a government job. The aged, the retired, the young, those in business for themselves on a small scale, craftsmen, artists, inventors, and scholars (as distinct from teacher-bureaucrats) become outcasts from the contractual system. Further, it is not clear that the big three have equal power; very large numbers of working people are not in industries in which organized labor has the power to contract wages and working conditions. In other industries, labor leaders do not fight very hard for workers' interests. There is also good evidence that government is used by big business to oppose labor interests; government systematically spends much more money on those kinds of projects which involve middle- and upper-strata time rather than working-class time. Defense spending, space spending, and research spending all benefit the profit-controlling class far more than the wage-earning class. Finally, it is not clear if the economic segment of society can be dominated by *group* contracting while the other segments of life remain in the province of *individual* contract writing. Group contract writing seems almost like a new community form. George Orwell's book *1984* portrays a society in which *all* aspects of life are governed by an interlocked government-business-labor syndicate, headed by a symbolic but all-powerful Big Brother. Already in the United States some of the distinctions between the "bigs" are blurred. Are college teachers bureaucrats or independently contracting professional scholars and educators? Are physicians professionals or employees of the government? Are subsidized farmers, railroads, aerospace companies, and communications media any less a part of government, any less on welfare, than the poor mother filling out her aid-to-dependent-children forms? Measures of the degree to which big government, big business, and big labor penetrate noneconomic areas are extremely important to the evaluation of the status of the contractual system.

Some figures on the penetration of bigness into the family farm, supposedly part of the foundation of the contractual system, may give an idea of how success is destroying one part of contractualism. According to testimony given to the Senate Subcommittee on Migratory Labor:[14] (1) more than 2,000 American small farmers go out of business every week; (2) 19 percent of all farm families live below generally acknowledged poverty levels; and (3) in order to compete (that is, not be destroyed in competition), the small farmer today needs an initial 400,000 dollar investment in land and equipment. Government subsidies, which go in much larger amounts to the large corporate farms, allow these large farms to drive prices so low that the small farmer must have the same kinds of expensive machinery as the large farms to produce food at competitive

prices. In effect, the federal government takes from the working class in order to pay big farmers to drive small farmers out of business. Twenty-nine corporations control 23 percent of California's farmland. Forty-five corporations own 61 percent of the state's "prime" crop land. Tenneco Corporation owns 345,000 acres of land in Kern County, California; in 1969 it made profits of 91 million dollars, paid no income taxes on these profits, and accepted 13 million dollars in subsidies from the government. The 1902 Reclamation Act, which stipulates that the federal government should supply no irrigation water from federal projects to farms larger than 160 acres (320 acres for husband and wife) is not enforced; its enforcement has been successfully opposed by the U.S. Department of the Interior, together with the U.S. Bureau of Reclamation and the big farm corporations. If it were enforced, the government would no longer be able to subsidize big corporate farms in their drive to eliminate small farmers. Incidentally, lower food prices and better food are not the results of a system of big corporation farms. Nutritionists have testified that the mass production of food by giant farm corporations usually results in less nutritious foods containing higher amounts of poisons required to make giant-sized fields into the ecological deserts needed to grow single crops over large areas.

Students are invited to make the same sorts of inquiries into the state of small business in their own communities or across the nation and to analyze the relationship between the failure of small farming and small business opportunities and the failure of the contractual system.

Unequal returns from education In theory, education produces the knowledge required to ensure that people act in their own best interests as voters, consumers,

[14] *San Francisco Chronicle*, San Francisco, Calif., Jan. 11–13, 1972.

business people, and in all other areas of contract writing. It is very difficult to assess how well education does this, since the dominant educational institutional pattern is one through which people try to do many other things. (This is partly a result of class, racial, and ethnic conflict over the goals of education.)

Schools are expected to maintain discipline, keep young people off the streets and out of competition with adults for limited numbers of jobs, and provide technicians for corporate interests (which specialization may actually hurt an individual's ability to write better contracts in many areas of life). They also give people an idealized version of the contractual system, which may actually interfere with their ability to write contracts by blinding them to the need to objectively analyze the system and their position in it. If schools fail to equalize contract-writing power, contractualism is being badly hurt, for schools are one of the few institutions in society specifically charged with seeing that contract-writing power is equalized.

At present the only observations which tell us how schools affect contract-writing

power are studies of the money returns from education, that is, how much each added year of schooling adds to yearly or monthly income. However, children of poor parents get less money return from the *same amount* of education. This shows that the educational institution is failing to support the contractual system and failing to help resolve the contradictory tendency of powerful contract writers to write others out of the system.

We need much more detailed information on this subject. The limited data we have (see Table 11-2) suggest the following.

1. Whites get much larger returns from education than nonwhites: for example, a suburban white gets $32.80 per week more in income from completing high school, while a central-city poverty-area nonwhite gets $8.83 per week extra from putting the same number of years into getting a high school diploma.

2. Within racial groups (if we assume a higher proportion of working-class people in central cities and a higher proportion of profit controllers in the suburbs) working-class youth of both races get a much lower dollar return from both high school and col-

TABLE 11-2 Income Returns to Time Invested in Education by Race and Urban Location, March 1966.

Region	Whites			Nonwhites		
	Incremental return to high school	Incremental return to college	Cumulative effect*	Incremental return to high school	Incremental return to college	Cumulative effect*
Central-city poverty areas	$24.88	$36.48	$61.36	$8.83	$33.03	$41.86
Rest of central city	$ 9.16	$51.62	$76.30	0**	$53.50	$53.50
Suburban ring	$32.80	$65.32	$98.12	0***	$38.87	$38.87

* Sum of all individual "steps" in the step-function regression models.
** 79 percent of the observations in this cell displayed maximal schooling of 12 years.
*** 85 percent of the observations in this cell displayed maximal schooling of 12 years.
SOURCE: David Gordon, *Problems in Political Economy: An Urban Perspective* (Lexington, Mass.: D. C. Heath, 1971), p. 189. Author's calculations from the 1966 *Survey of Economic Opportunity.*

lege than do non-working-class youth. For a white youth from the central city the cumulative effect of high school and college education is an additional $61.36 per week; for a suburban youth the same education adds $98.12 to weekly income. Education *does* increase contract-writing ability, at least as it is crudely measured by increases in income. Yet class discrimination and racism make education less useful for those who most need to improve their contract-writing power if the system is to work.

"Structural" unemployment   Both apologists for and critics of capitalism agree that unemployment is one of the unavoidable costs of the system. People using tribal and caste economies are so bound into an unchanging division of labor as to avoid being sometimes thrown out of work, but even in caste society, surplus sons and daughters of peasants do not fare so well. In socialist economies, unemployment has been reduced close to zero.

Unemployment is inevitable under capitalism given the necessity for keeping a flexible labor force that can be induced: (1) to move when productive shifts take place and (2) to work at low-paid, undesirable jobs (e.g., coal mining, house cleaning, trash collecting, and street cleaning) as the only alternative to being unemployed. All of this, of course, functions to keep labor costs down and profits up.

In theory, unemployment under capitalism should be distributed randomly through the working population. The executives of frisbee companies whose products sell poorly should also be thrown out of work until they can find new opportunities for their executive talents, just as the manual laborer in the same companies should be unemployed until his or her manual skills can be fit to some new product.

The fact is, however, that some groups seem rarely, if ever, to experience unem-

ployment; other groups seem rarely, if ever, to find work. This phenomenon is called *structural unemployment*, for it is the relationship to the social structure which seems to determine which groups will be unemployed. In other words, the economic base of the social structure is organized in such a way as to deny work within the dominant economy to some people for most of their lives.

If this is what is happening, it is part of the same terrible contradiction inherent in previous systems—namely, that their very strength was also their fatal weakness. The strength of contractualism results in the increase of commerce, and especially the efficiency of commerce. Machine commerce is the ultimate in efficiency. Yet with machines, the rich, big government, and big labor can get along without the very poor. In fact, rather than reducing the money power of the rich as a means of lowering demand on goods, thereby reducing inflation, or spreading government jobs among the poor (interrelated ways of both lowering unemployment and reducing inflation), the powerful may cynically adopt economic policies aimed at increasing unemployment (price and wage controls without controls on profit) in order to reduce inflation at the expense of workers.

Structural or partial employment has been well known to the least powerful members of the working class in recent years. Reduction of unskilled job opportunities and failure of skill-improvement programs, coupled with sexism and racism, have made every major United States city a place where the dance from one form of unemployment compensation to another goes on for years. White working-class unemployment rates are twice those of all other whites. Since 1945 the black unemployment rate has been twice that of all whites. And the unemployment of women is hidden behind sexist accounting policies which do not "see" the women who want to work but cannot find jobs. Other structural unemployment may be related to age (early retirement and keeping young people out of the labor force) and geographical area. Those areas which are dominated by single industries (often through the connivance of big business and big government, for example, southern California and Texas aerospace) periodically experience very high rates of unemployment. Sometimes this regional structural unemployment reaches into the middle-income levels, as in the late 1960s in areas dominated by aerospace corporations, but typically the working classes and particularly working-class minority people are hit hardest.

David Gordon sees structural unemployment as resulting from the creation of a dual labor market in the United States.[15] He says that since the amount skilled clerical work adds to the value of a good or service can no longer be accurately measured (if it ever could), employers recruit and pay wages on such vaguely defined criteria as "dependability." Most employers find race, age, and sex to be easy to use as criteria for hiring, believing these reflect "dependability." The result is that the black, the young, and women get low-paying, part-time work if hired at all, thus creating a dual labor market that draws from (1) the primary labor pool, those with jobs carrying the promise of career advancement, or a feeling of security promoted by a sense of identification with a company or government bureaucracy; and (2) the secondary labor pool, those who can find only low-paying or part-time work, carrying no possibility of advancement (and often carrying the certainty of frequent "layoffs" as business conditions change). This process splits the working class, for people using roles in one labor market do not iden-

tify with people using roles in the other. This inhibits working-class organization, and makes it difficult to deal with the problems of unemployment, poverty, and control over work conditions. The existence of a pool of insecure workers benefits employers. The wages they pay will not reflect worker productivity but will be very low, reflecting the inability of these disorganized workers to demand wages proportional to their productivity. If profit managers do not conspire to keep people insecure, excluded from secure work, and unskilled, they surely do not do much to improve the situation. From this analysis one can conclude that, short of revolutionary change in economic structure, only when the young, racial-ethnic minorities, and women realize that their problems are the same can they overcome the present organizational weakness in the struggle to protect the interests of wage earners.

Struggle over who is deviant In Chicago, working-class people in general and black working-class people in particular are the more frequent victims of crimes against both property and person. This is revealed by a study of five Chicago neighborhoods by the National Advisory Commission on Civil Disorders, 1968 (Table 11-3). A study done in the 1960s in the eastern United States indicates that working-class people are disproportionately the victims of all forms of business fraud, from shoddy merchandise through loan-sharking practices.[16]

A more critical question (although perhaps not to the victims) is whether all people in the United States receive equal treatment before the law. Although there is no single large-scale study of the degree of discrimination against the powerless in court, one national study of the handling of grand larceny and felonious assault cases does compare

[15] David M. Gordon, *Problems in Political Economy* (Lexington, Mass.: Heath, 1971), pp. 60–68.

[16] David Caplovitz, *The Poor Pay More* (New York: Glencoe Free Press, 1963).

TABLE 11-3 Incidence of Index Crime and Patrolmen Assignments per 100,000 Residents in Five Chicago Police Districts, 1965.*

	High-income white	Low-middle-income white	Mixed white	Very low black	Very low black
Index crimes against persons	80	440	338	1,615	2,820
Index crimes against property	1,038	1,750	2,080	2,508	2,630
Patrolmen assigned	93	133	115	243	291

* Report of the National Advisory Commission on Civil Disorders, 1968.

"indigents" with "nonindigents." An "indigent" is defined for this study as a person who is unable to afford a lawyer. Bear in mind that until the rendering of recent Supreme Court decisions, most courts were under no pressure to provide legal counsel for those unable to pay for a lawyer. The present study compares treatment of indigent and nonindigent individuals on several aspects of treatment by the state and federal courts including: receipt of preliminary hearing, receipt of bail, length of wait for trial, determination of guilt, and sentence. Thirty-four percent of indigents brought before state courts on assault charges did not get preliminary hearings, while only 21 percent of nonindigents did not get a preliminary hearing. Seventy-five percent of all indigent suspects in state larceny and felony assault cases remained in jail before trial (which means unearned punishment and inability to prepare for trial), while 69 percent of nonindigent larceny and 79 percent of nonindigent assault cases raised bail and got out of jail. On the other hand, indigents had shorter waits for trial than nonindigents, which may reflect less time put in on the case by court-appointed lawyers. About 90 percent of all indigents studied were found guilty compared to 80 percent of all nonindigents. The indigent were less likely to be recommended for probation and less likely to be granted probation or suspended

sentences. Federal court data showed that for those without a prior record: 25 percent of the indigent were not recommended for probation compared to 16 percent of the nonindigent; and 23 percent of the indigent did not receive suspended sentences or probation compared to 15 percent of the nonindigent. The same study found discrimination based on youth, race, and sex, three other definers of relative powerlessness. Youth were more likely to be found guilty but received shorter sentences for the same offense. Black people (the only nonwhite group studied) were less discriminated against than poor whites, but were much less likely to receive a jury trial in assault cases. Women were found to be less discriminated against than men in every category of court action.[17]

Statistics on conviction of criminal deviance are quite clear: lower-strata people are disproportionately convicted of assault, larceny, burglary, rape, and homicide. These convictions carry prison sentences, especially for second offenses. The estimated yearly cost to society of these crimes is $1,415,000,000.[18]

[17] Stuart S. Nagel, "The Tipped Scales of American Justice," *Transactions*, May-June, 1966. The data are based on a 1963 study by the American Bar Association of a balanced sample of 194 counties in 50 states; there were a total of 11,258 cases for the state data and a total of 36,265 cases in all.
[18] *Crime in the United States*, The President's Commission on Law Enforcement and the Administration of Justice, 1967.

The population of United States prisons is almost exclusively working-class whites, blacks, and other individuals of color or ethnic minority status. Prison riots often reflect prisoners' own analyses of their situation as resulting from political processes defining crime, arrest, and sentencing. (United Press International)

Middle- and upper-strata people are disproportionately convicted of commercial theft, embezzlement, fraud, forgery, and driving under the influence of alcohol, and the yearly cost is estimated at $5,668,000,000. (This amount does not include the loss people suffer as a result of undetected illegal business practices.) These convictions carry fines rather than prison sentences, fines which are often seen as a cost of business. Middle- and upper-strata crimes cost more, but are punished less. Corporate crime is hardly punished at all.

Two questions remain:

1. Is there class injustice in the treatment of persons suspected of crime? Are working-strata people more likely to be apprehended, arrested, charged, brought to trial, convicted, and sentenced than middle- and upper-strata individuals who *commit the same offense?* Are they more likely to serve time or pay fines? We invite you to search out data which would answer this question. Selection 11-5 relates findings from studies of sentencing practices in New York.

2. Is there class injustice in definitions of behavior as criminal? Are larceny, burglary, rape, and assault more heavily punished because they are a greater threat to the contractual system than are fraud, embezzlement, forgery, and commercial theft? In other words, it may be that people are not punished for their class background so much as for the fact that when they set out to cheat, they cheat in a way which threatens the system. A person who assaults, shoots, burglarizes, rapes, or holds you up does not allow you a chance to make a deal, which is the essence of contractualism. Presumably this person is more feared, and therefore punished more, no matter what the class background and even though the amounts of money stolen are small and individuals rather than large groups are hurt. The millionaire who defrauds us by selling us shoddy television sets and cars, or steals our tax money by bribing the government to give defense contracts, is not punished so heavily as the street thief. He stole large amounts, but he did it contractually, and there was presumably a chance to make a deal, or catch him first, had we been smart enough. It is recognized that a certain amount of trickery, fraud, psychological manipulation, and bluff are inherent in the idea of contract. "Let the buyer beware" is supposed to alert us to this. This is an inter-

SELECTION 11-5: Observations supporting a conflict analysis of criminal justice institutional patterns in the United States.

THE UNEVEN HAND OF JUSTICE

LESLIE OELSNER

New York—Jack Greenberg took $15 from the postoffice; on sentencing day last May in Manhattan federal court, he drew six months in jail. Howard Lazell "misapplied" $150,000 from a bank; on his sentencing day, the same month in the same courthouse, he drew probation.

Such are the contradictions in the sentencing system here, in both federal and state courts. A study by the New York Times found a host of such contradictions, a host of differences in sentencing which reflected differences in the defendant's finances, in his race, in geography, in the judge's personality.

Defendants charged with the same crimes get widely disparate sentences. Crimes which tend to be committed by the poor get tougher sentences than crimes which tend to be committed by the well-to-do. Sentences for serious offenses sometimes show no hint of seriousness.

"Lawless"

The problem of sentence disparities has increased as judges have been given more and more discretion; it has gotten to the point where many in the courts call sentencing "chaotic" and federal Judge Marvin E. Frankel, an acknowledged expert on the subject, calls it "lawless."

The Times found that the sentencing system includes such elements as these:

• Stiffer sentences for defendants with assigned counsel than for defendants with private counsel. According to a report by the administrative office of the United States courts for federal fiscal year 1969, defendants with assigned counsel—those who could not afford private counsel—were sentenced more than twice as severely as defendants with private or no counsel.

A new study by the Vera Institute of Justice of courts in the Bronx indicates a similar pattern in the state courts.

• Stiffer sentences for blacks than for whites.

The Federal Bureau of Prisons records of inmates sentenced to federal prisons in fiscal 1970 show that the average sentence of whites was 41.9 months; for blacks, 57.5 months. Whites convicted of income tax evasion were committed for an average of 12.8 months; blacks, 28.6 months. In some cases the average for whites was 61.1 months; blacks, 81.1.

• Stiffer sentences for those who are convicted after trial than those who plead guilty ahead of time and thus save the state the expense of trying them. In the state courts this difference is simply accepted and is a major consideration in plea negotiations between defense and prosecution; in the federal system, with better record keeping, there are even statistics to prove it.

In fiscal 1969, the administrative office of the U.S. courts reports, those who were convicted after trial were sentenced more than twice as severely as those who pleaded guilty ahead of time.

Differences in sentences between those convicted in New York City's local courts and those convicted for the same crimes upstate, with the upstaters getting the tougher sentences.

• Differences in sentences between those convicted in the federal court in Manhattan and those convicted in the federal court in Brooklyn, with those from Brooklyn averaging longer terms.

"The Unloved"

• Disagreement between judges as to whether the disparities are justified or not, with some, such as Chief Judge David N. Edelstein of Manhattan federal court, saying the problem is not serious, and others, such as Judge Frankel in the same court, taking the opposite stance.

"There's a traditional difference in sentences for different types of crimes, and it tends to discriminate against the uneducated, unloved, social reject," says United States Attorney Whitney North Seymour Jr.

"The guy who steals packages from the back of the truck is going to get four years," he says. "And the guy who steals $45,000 is going to get three months."

The difference is more than the traditional distinction made between violent and nonviolent crime. The difference now, by Seymour's reckoning, is between "common crimes."

"A conviction is still a conviction even if there is a suspended sentence," says Judge Edelstein. "He stands before the court and community for all his life as a convicted defendant . . . a suspended sentence is a sentence."

Yet Seymour rejects such reasoning.

Matter of Identification

"Is it really hard to accept the fact that a poor black also can lose his job, also can lose his family's respect?" asked Seymour. "It's that argument really that shows dramatically the fact that the present system of criminal justice can identify with that kind of defendant (the businessman) but not with that poor black school drop-out."

The modern theory of sentencing is to fit the punishment to the criminal as to the crime (as opposed to the old-fashioned rule of fitting it merely to the crime), thus necessitating at least some disparity.

But the Times found that disparities crop up over and over in the city's courts which are not entirely explicable on the grounds of difference between the crimes or the criminals: the explication lies elsewhere.

No Guidelines

The crucial factor, to many observers, is that sentences are determined by individual men with differing backgrounds and differing theories—and with no precise guidelines.

For while the general purposes of sentencing are well known—to rehabilitate the criminal, protect society, deter crime and create respect for the law—there are no rules spelling out how these purposes are to be achieved.

"The basic evil of sentencing is its lawlessness," says Judge Frankel, author of a forthcoming booklet on the subject. "There's too little law and too much discretion. There aren't enough rules of general application that tell everyone where he stands. The defendant, the judge."

Those who believe that punishment is a proper function of sentencing can logically be expected to be tougher than those who agree with district attorney Burton B. Roberts, a candidate for the State Supreme Court, that "the word 'punishment' shouldn't be used at all," and that the purposes of sentencing should be limited to protecting society, deterring crime and rehabilitating the criminal.

esting hypothesis, but the question remains, "Which hurts contractualism more, noncontractual crime or criminal contracting?"

Conflict over Industrial Despoilation of Environment

Both capitalist and socialist theoreticians share the idea than an industrial economic structure will produce the liberation which they assume humans have sought in a 5-million-year struggle to be free of the wants and needs imposed by nature—in other words, to be free of the necessity to work hard and long in order to simply survive.

Only in the past ten years have numbers of people in both capitalist and socialist countries begun seriously to assess how much we are hurting ourselves by the means we have taken to liberate ourselves from nature and from hard work. In some "under-developed" parts of the world there has been serious discussion among admittedly well-fed elites about whether their countries ought to be allowed to industrialize. They fear the high costs from environmental destruction and population explosion due to the falling death rates. However, it is our impression that wherever the masses of people have had the chance, they have chosen industrial-contractualist social structures. The immediate benefits are obvious—a better chance to survive as individuals, a better chance to see one's children survive, a more materially rich life. Costs can be charged to later generations, or ignored in the belief that "It's none of my business" or "Science will save us."

Earlier we showed how industrialization, at least in its early stages, worsens class conflict, and how it is a process nearly everywhere accompanied by planned attempts to destroy people holding on to tribal or feudal systems. Here we wish to hint at some of the kinds of conflicts that have emerged out of the contradiction between contractualism and the adaptation of the human species to the physical environment. The question then is, "Does a system which produces comfortable individual adaptations to the physical environment (*individual* conveniences like cars, refrigerators, disposals, flush toilets, airplanes) inevitably destroy that environment, thereby destroying the economic structure of which these conveniences are a product?"[19] Put another way, is some individual inconvenience necessary for the survival of human communities in nature? This is a very large question, but the most recent belief is that contractual systems of both socialist and capitalist varieties can destroy themselves by destroying the capacity of earth to support life. We do not refer to the development of hydrogen fusion weapons, which could presumably destroy life by thermonuclear warfare, but to the day-to-day working of contractual industrial societies.

Life on earth is supported by three basic processes:

1. Cyclical processes by which nutrients are continually reused by all forms of life. As oxygen is produced by plants and breathed by animals; carbon dioxide is given off after the oxygen is used; and the plants take the carbon dioxide and produce oxygen once again. In addition to the oxygen cycle, there are the carbon cycle, the nitrogen cycle, the sulphur cycle, the phosphorus cycle, and many others. Each is equally important because a chain is only as strong as its weakest link; a system collapses when the necessary element or nutrient in shortest supply is gone.

2. The inflow of energy from the sun and the conversion of solar energy into plants, which in turn provide usable energy for animals, including human beings.

3. The growth and stable maintenance of populations, including populations of plants, animals, and insects, all of which support each other in the exchange of nutrients and energy and thereby indirectly support human life.

Contractual industrialism creates very real direct threats to nutrient cycling, to energy input and transfer processes, and to stability of plant and animal populations. Corporations and individuals contracting for corporate and individual gains, pleasures, and comforts produce smog, water pollution, pesticide pollution, thermal pollution, destruction of plant and animal species, and land pollution. These are all serious dangers to life itself because of their threat to nutrient cycles and to stable populations. Smog also disrupts the input of sunlight, although there is disagreement about how much additional smog would be needed to have a real effect on energy input and hence on climate and plant growth.

How does the contradiction between contractualism and the quality of the physical environment generate conflicts? Since we are concerned with conflict between human beings, particularly with structured conflict, we will not discuss the ways in which the environment fights back. Many "natural disasters," such as floods, landslides, and forest fires, are the results of individually contracted uses of land which create the conditions causing the disaster.

The preservation argument is that resource use should be controlled by noncontractual processes, that keeping land "undeveloped"

---

[19] There are other possible costs which have not as yet produced significant conflict. One is described by the concept of population erosion advanced by biologists to explain why communities of simple organisms exposed to a relatively harsh environment survive longer than communities of organisms exposed to a relatively mild environment. Apparently some conditions conducive to individual survival threaten species survival (Roscoe Spencer, "Individual and Species: Biological Survival," *The Humanist*, vol. 3, 1958, pp. 155–161). Another possibility is that population growth increases group conflict in humans much as it does in caged rats.

is important both to human psychic needs[20] and to the survival of other species that form a part of the chain of life on which we depend. The contractual side of the argument is that "progress" means increasing control of nature and that the rights of individuals to do with property whatever they can afford are more important and more real than "environmental" rights.

These two viewpoints bring organized collections of people into conflict. Timber-cutting corporations may be told they can no longer use certain trees, or may be prohibited from clear-cutting (cutting everything at once) on public land. Because the companies can no longer cut as much timber, they lay off workers. Workers become enraged at "environmentalists," blaming them for the loss of their jobs. All the residents of a small Colorado town are forced to move because the Army Corps of Engineers builds a dam which will flood their town. Their protests are unavailing because the Corps, focused on the single goal of flood control, feels a "controlled" river is more important than the town. Sheep and cattle growers are enraged by government regulations against killing coyotes, mountain lions, and eagles. They write letters asking if the "bleeding heart" types in the city will not also pass laws to protect sewer and tenement rats so that when country people come to the city they can enjoy seeing "wild life." Projects which benefit the few—for example, the Glen Canyon dam of the Colorado River, which mainly benefits corporation farms in Arizona—may violate public law (by allowing backup waters to undercut Rainbow Natural Bridge), but Congress is unwilling to go

[20] Although not everyone hikes in the wilderness, the preservationists feel that just knowing the wilderness is there promotes a feeling of freedom which cannot be otherwise had. To understand this, imagine how you would feel if you knew bears, lions, birds, elephants, giraffes, and other wild things no longer existed anywhere free. How would you feel if you knew there was nowhere you could go to be free of crowds of humans?

against commercial interests by enforcing the law against violation of national parks and monuments. Smog, noise, destruction of open land, pollution of public waters so that they cannot be used for recreation—these are all concentrated in and around cities, making the already burdened lives of ghetto dwellers more difficult. All result from the right of individuals, corporations, and government bureaus to use whatever power they have to contract for whatever uses of the earth they desire. They result from the indifference generated by the contractual system toward the statement and enforcement of public values, values which transcend private or group interests. They also result from the very real contradiction between industrialization and preservation. This conflict is *within* the structures through which public interest is hopefully achieved rather than between public and private interests. Even in socialist economies, where private economic interests are presumably subordinated to public interests, there is failure to successfully pursue preservation goals.

These conflicts may appear far removed from the lives of many United States citizens. Preservationalism has been called a fad by some and denounced by leftists for taking our attention away from the "real" issues. Eighty percent of United States citizens live in metropolitan regions and experience some of the worst aspects of environmental degradation, but citydwellers appear to become hardened by the gradualness with which environmental quality worsens. They appear willing to accept anything that makes individual lives seem more comfortable in the short run. The phenomenon raises again the very real question of class consciousness and collective problem solving. Why do people not see and act on the contradictions which seem so real to sociological analysis? Selection 11-6 clearly shows the worldwide

SELECTION 11-6: Impact of industrialization on the environment of Mexico City.

MEXICO CITY SMOG: AN ENVIRONMENTAL NIGHTMARE

ALLAN RIDING

Mexico City—The unbalanced nature of Mexico's economic development since World War II is probably most responsible for Mexico City's deep social crisis. The concentration of resources in the industrial sector adversely affected agriculture so that millions of peasants were forced to migrate to urban centers in search of work.

Today, Greater Mexico City has a population of over 11 million, a six-fold rise in 30 years. Other cities such as Monterrey, Guadalajara and Puebla, have experienced similar phenomena.

30 Million

The rapid increase in the size of Mexico City makes it thoroughly unmanageable and increasingly difficult to live in. The only grim compensation today is that it will be worse tomorrow: the city's population is expected to reach 30 million by the end of the century.

Visitors to Mexico City first notice the air pollution. Arriving by air, they can see an ominous brown mist hovering over the Valley of Mexico; by car, the transition is more gradual as they slowly drive ever-deeper into the smog bowl.

Soon, they complain of itchy eyes or sore throats and occasionally they suffer serious respiratory problems. But for the locals, the pollution is no better. Increasingly, the wealthy inhabitants of the city are moving their homes further from the city center, into the hills and mountains that surround the capital.

The causes of the air pollution are multiple. Some 17,000 factories of varying size are concentrated around Mexico City, pouring tons of filth into the atmosphere daily. Many of these plants are government-owned, including one of the worst culprits, the PEMEX oil refinery at Aztcapozalco, which pumps sulphurous fumes into the urban zone whenever a Northerly blows.

Cars, Buses

Then there are perhaps one million vehicles in Mexico City, many of which are so old that black exhaust smoke is unavoidable. Again, the state-owned buses are among the worst culprits, although the poor quality of the petroleum used is probably more responsible.

In the slum districts, known here as "lost cities," heating and cooking is done with dirty fuel, while garbage is dumped on wasteland then burned when the stench becomes unbearable.

At certain times of the year, high winds around the dried-up Lake Texcoco whip the dust storms that engulf the center of the city and send passers-by spluttering into shop doors.

Poison Fumes

Finally, the geographic position of the Mexican capital makes everything worse. Mexico City stands at 7500 feet (2250 meters), surrounded by volcanoes and mountains, an almost perfect bowl within which poisonous fumes are trapped. The normal cloud level of 8000 feet prevents the pollution from escaping; and the frequent sun provokes a lethal photo-chemical reaction in the pollution.

The government has launched a campaign to make Mexico City a more habitable place. Last year, a tough anti-pollution law was adopted which would fine owners of vehicles or factories producing visible emissions.

But the problem is too vast for a quick solution: after almost a year, the Under-Secretary for the Environment, Sr. Francisco Vizcaino Murray, said that only 5700 of the 17,000 factories around Mexico City were complying with the law. And in case of smoke-producing vehicles, many owners complain that transit policemen are merely using the law as another excuse to extort a bribe or "bite" from the drivers.

Nevertheless, the government claims that industrial pollution has fallen by 35 per cent in the past year. And while the air is not noticeably cleaner for pedestrians, the snow-capped volcanoes outside the capital were visible more frequently in 1972 than in 1971.

Other forms of pollution, however, are direct products of the vastness, the over-population and the poverty of Mexico City which cannot be altered with ease. And of course, the poor districts of town are the worst affected.

For example, the capital is chronically short of water despite the rainy season when its drainage system immediately proves itself inadequate. Many parts of town have neither running water nor proper drainage, ideal conditions for the spread of disease.

Due to the city's rapid growth, there is also a serious lack of housing and a good proportion of the population must live in over-crowded conditions or in shacks made of mud or cartons and covered with corrugated iron. A National Housing Institute was recently created by the government with the aim of attacking this crisis. But it will take several years before any impression can be made on the problem.

Traffic Disaster

For the wealthier classes, the housing shortage is manifested in the high cost of accommodation—more expensive than London and perhaps equivalent to Washington, D.C. And even these residential districts occasionally suffer water shortages and black-outs.

Nor do traffic jams discriminate between rich and poor. Despite the construction of a 400 million dollar underground system two years ago, the totally-inadequate transport system obliges drivers to bring their cars into the city center. Since the capital's streets were probably made for one-quarter of today's vehicles, the results are daily disastrous.

On the outskirts of Mexico City, the government has begun constructing a series of "new towns" of 250,000 inhabitants in order to reduce pressure on the capital. But they are more likely to accommodate new migrants to the urban zone rather than absorb the slum dwellers from the city.

The city's main problem remains its size and its continuing growth rate of 5.7 per cent per annum (compared with 0.5 per cent for London and 1.5 per cent for Paris). The municipal authorities and facilities simply cannot cope with this human mass and they fell further behind last year.

The only solution is for the city's growth to slow down and its municipal services to increase rapidly. But the present momentum is so great that a population of close to 20 million is inevitable before a balance-point is reached.

dimensions of the disproportionate burden of industrial pollution borne by the poor.

These contradictions are important. Although perhaps overstated, the threat to life-support processes is real: no science that we now have, except that which directly harnesses solar energy, promises any basic solution to environmental degradation. Yet oil and coal companies have persuaded the United States government to spend billions of dollars to continue the use of their ever-more costly (both in money and pollution) energy sources. The amount spent on solar energy development is very small. The contradiction between a contractual technology and a preserved environment produces a complex class conflict situation. Presently the contradictory tendency of industrial economies to increase individual well-being while destroying life-support processes has

not generated clear-cut classes. Individuals continue to hope to compromise these goals, or to somehow achieve both, *within the dominant contractual structure*. However, some individuals identify more strongly with the preservationist goal, usually those who have already experienced an affluent life-style. This leads to a complicated conflict situation in which profit controllers can play off working-class people against preservationists.

We pointed out how individual technology and the related dual labor market tends to stratify wage earners and reduce class consciousness. Rarely do situations arise which make clear the common problem of wage earners—their lack of control over the surplus value they produce. Neocolonial wars like that in Vietnam and environmental destruction are two issues which have recently affected all strata within the wage-earning class in much the same way. Large numbers of people have for the first time been led further and further in the process of questioning the costs of contractualism. Conflict over the value of the environment leads to critical analysis of the system itself more than does conflict over issues like income or rich and poor and conflict over who is deviant, since it is hard to find individual scapegoats for the contradictory tendency of contractualism to destroy the environment.

As we have suggested, should those in the secondary labor market (blacks, the young people, and women) combine with preservationists around a vision of a more equitable but less rapacious economic strategy, they would create a powerful force for revolutionary change.

Conflict over Morality

In a sense each specific contradiction in any community form produces moral conflict. For example, the tendency of the rich to get richer at the expense of the poor, a contradiction within the contractual form, produces conflict between rich and poor over scarce resources. But it also produces conflict over what is good for the community, that is, *moral* conflict. Some argue that the possibility of getting rich is good for all because it provides an incentive for people to work hard. Others argue that it is bad for people to be able to get rich because it produces large numbers of people who are driven outside the dominant logic (the poor) and who hate it. Similarly the tendency to degrade the environment produces not only conflict over resources and their use, but over what is for the good of all. Some say it is good for people to be free to do as they wish with their land, their cars, and their flush toilets. Others say this freedom is bad, unless severely limited, because it destroys

the physical processes which support life. Thus the conflict between timber cutters and preservationists generates cultural conflict, conflict over beliefs about what is good for the community as a whole.

A second major type of moral conflict is the conflict over whether there *ought* to be a purely contractual system. Contractualism, like any other community form, requires that people behave in ways that are good for its survival. A contractual system must have at least the following moral principles:

1. It is good for all people that each individual be free to contract his or her life.

2. Whatever is necessary to ensure that contracts are written without coercion is for the good of all.

3. Law must ensure that these free and uncoerced contracts do not harm others.

4. It is important that people live up to contracts.

Like any other morality, the principles of contractualism must be expressable and capable of being symbolized, understandable, and supportable. They must fit people's life experience. People must find the contractual morality believable in their own lives and situations, and the social structure and culture they use must make it easy to live up to.

There is a question about the degree to which the contractual morality (1) has been coherently stated; (2) is widely symbolized and celebrated; and (3) is supported by other institutional patterns, particularly those specializing in morality—the religious and educational institutions.

If anything, the privileged classes seem to have fought to preserve an older morality which emphasizes the importance of being meek, passive, and nonaggressive, expecting reward in another world rather than through present contracts; deferring to one's betters (the fact that many church organizations are structured hierarchically supports this); and

Religious institutions contain both the ideas held over from tribal and caste forms as well as those that create a morality that supports and celebrates contractual capitalism. (Bruce Auspach/EPA Newsphoto)

avoiding conflict at all cost. All of these bits of behavior which are held up to people as moral (for the good of all) are consistent with a caste system and inconsistent with a contractual system.

Two questions then are important about conflict over a contractual morality: (1) Do the privileged groups benefit from a publicly proclaimed and institutionally supported caste morality (is public morality the opiate of the masses, as Marx claimed)? (2) Are there signs of the emergence of a truly contractual morality?

We have practically no well-organized data with which to answer these questions now, but we will offer a few unsystematic observations.

In the area of conflict over contractual morality, it is crucial to observe behavior rather than just talk. Talk may tell you what people *think* they must say in order to better their chances to write good contracts. Only behavior can tell you what people do for the good of the "all," that is, for their fellow human beings, as distinct from what they do for their individual benefit. Public officials

often urge others to act out the old morality (that is, to cheerfully, quietly, and thankfully keep your place) while they themselves act in a fashion which is not only immoral by the standards of their talk but immoral by the standards of contractual morality as well. They act aggressively to accumulate power, which they use in their own interests, giving the lie to their talk about "the decent (silent), hard-working (no pushy unionists), god-fearing (willing to be cheated now for a payoff later) American citizen." The Watergate scandal and the political demise of Spiro Agnew and Richard Nixon have coincidentally revealed that many high public officials violate criminal law, take bribes, and fail to pay taxes. This behavior violates the contracts which bind them to impartial and lawful use of their offices.

We thus have two kinds of moral conflict which are separate from the moral issues involved in rich versus poor and industry versus environment: (1) conflict between adherents of caste morality for others and contractual morality for themselves and those who get worked over by this double standard; (2) conflict between those who would rather use a caste morality, and not let a contractual morality emerge at all, and those who support contractualism. Erich Fromm suggested that people are afraid to be free and will "escape from freedom" to tyranny and oppress those who want freedom.[21] One of the most important tasks for sociology should be to bare these double standards and the conflict they cause and at the same time to assess the degree to which a contractual morality is built into the institutional and cultural patterns used in the contemporary world.

To further complicate matters, some people seem to reject both the old or caste morality (as expressed in traditional religious institutions and professions) *and* the new contractual morality. Organized tribalism (hippie communes, group marriages), Westernized versions of Eastern mysticism (sufi communes, zen communes, guru worship), modernized versions of European mysticism (devil worship), and philosophies which are amoral, (that is, which suggest that the "common good" does not exist, or that humans have little control over events and cannot act morally) all seem to reject both caste and contractual morality. It is possible that these are not moralities in the sense that they have little effect on people's behavior but much effect on their talk. Only people's behavior will tell us the extent to which users of these forms are in conflict with users of older moralities, or with both caste and contractual morality.

Combined Effects of Contradiction: The Mass Media as Example

Our analysis of the effects of industrialization in the United States has assumed that a contractual logic and bourgeois culture was the

[21] Erich Fromm, *Escape from Freedom* (New York: Holt, Rhinehart and Winston, 1941).

cause of and existed simultaneously with industrialization. The reasoning behind this assumption reduces to the need of individuals to have more freedom than in agricultural feudalism, where people are tied to the land—freedom to leave the land, to leave families, and to think about new machines, new products, and new ways of doing things. The contradictions within contractual logic were analyzed separately. However, they do affect each other.

An example of the interacting effects of contractual-industrial social forces can be seen in the way the mass media of communication, particularly television, are used in the United States. Machine technologies create the possibility of coordinating human work on an enormous scale. The telephone, the assembly line, rapid transportation, standardized parts can all be used through bureaucratic work structures to coordinate the work of thousands of people over vast distances. The work of a clerk in the supermarket is coordinated with the work of farmers, slaughterhouse workers, food packagers, and package makers. This technical capacity to support big organizations has two important effects. First, enormous losses are possible because enormous investments are made in raw materials, wages, and equipment long before products are sold to consumers. Second, production is so efficient that many more goods are produced than workers could reasonably be expected to buy given existing wage patterns.

The mass media are used to partially solve both these problems. Through mass media, of which television is the most effective, demand for products can be manipulated and managed. Control of what people will buy is, predictably, achieved by appeals to fears of loneliness, sexual deprivation, or anxiety about social prestige. By creating insatiable demand for specific products, profit makers increase the likelihood that their long-range investments will be profitable. The desire for these products (automobiles, all-electric kitchens, respectable drugs) is further stimulated by educational patterns which communicate the same messages to schoolchildren. High school home economics courses, rather than teaching students how to survive independently of the system, inculcate the need for the gadgets, foods, and house adornments that go with the middle-strata life-style shown in TV commercials. Auto mechanics courses, rather than teaching how to build one's own transportation, teach how to service the product sold on TV. The deluge of messages seen on commercial and even "noncommercial" television all continue this dependency. In both present-day socialist and capitalist economies, wage earners are thus doubly penalized and doubly stratified. They are penalized in loss of control over the surplus value received as wages. They are stratified and separated from consciousness of common interests both by technical stratification and by the varying degrees of alienation and inferiority they feel depending on how far short they fall of the unreachable goals held out by advertising.

Although this is a superficial analysis in that it lacks supporting systematic observations, it suggests a variety of needed studies. For example, we might begin by analyzing television programs in terms of what they present as the "good life."

THE MYTH AND THE REALITY

There is perhaps a deeper contradiction which helps us summarize the problems of the contractual system itself: the contradiction between pride in the system and the logic of change built into the very idea of contract. Throughout the history of human social structure and cultures, we assume that those have longest endured which generated the most pride and satisfaction in their particular place, their way of life, and their physical appearance. In fact, place (nationalism), way of life (ethnocentrism), and skin color (racism) are three of the most basic supports of early contractual, feudal, and tribal structures. Yet people using a purely contractual system are committed to being open-ended. The old forms of pride may have helped people struggle to keep the things they liked about contractualism (as American and Soviet nationalism could both be mobilized to make the world safe for their different versions of "democracy" in World War II). But these old sources of pride are under assault everywhere. Nationalisms break down as separatist groups demand the right to contract their own ethnocentrism or nationalism. The behavior of French Canadians, Irish Protestants, American blacks, American Indians, and Kirghiz Russians seems to be an expression of the desire that national boundaries be fluid. Deserters and draft dodgers were said to be so prevalent because the Vietnam war was so unpopular. Perhaps, however, people are becoming increasingly unwilling to be mobilized for any *national* wars. Others want to contract individualized life-styles, thereby assaulting the ethnocentrism on which community pride was once based. Of course, if enough people contract out, there is no longer a mainstream, no longer an "ethnic" source of identity and pride in the dominant cultural or community form. Others wish to break down racial boundaries, and boundaries on how one looks. Racial intermarriage and refusal to look one's age, sex, or race, or refusal to look like people are "supposed to look" who use certain jobs or social positions—all these are assaults on the physical symbols of familiarity in social relations. Paradoxically, at the same time that people's behavior indicates less and less commitment to the contractual form itself, people's talk seems to become strictly prideful.

Part of the dominant United States culture is supposed to be a love of public humility. We are careful not to act like conquerors when we conquer, and we avoid badges, titles of nobility, and in general looking high and mighty. We seem to think we have thereby wisely been the first people in history to avoid the trap the Greeks described when they spoke of how often pride of the mighty goes before a fall. We may discover that the trap is unavoidable.

Many Americans are committed, particularly in business, to the idea that our system is open to change. The "democratic process," after all, implies the idea that if people so desire, they can buy any product they wish. Also implied is the idea that we can get rid of democracy, abandon technology, and establish moon worship as the national religion if we choose. Curiously enough, however, no public figures and very few private individuals ever seriously question the system itself. Not only do they not question whether it is an intrinsically good tool or a useless one, they do not generally even ask how well it is working. The public version is that the system is basically sound. Problems are either the fault of individuals (put those welfare recipients to work) or will be fixed sooner or later (some counsel just waiting, others counsel spending a little more money). Attempts to seriously analyze the system are not often found in public discussions occurring in legislatures, newspapers, television, or schools. The message gets across very effectively to everyone that change would be a very bad thing, much as people used to get the idea quite clearly from the lack of discussion of sex in the family that sex was a very bad thing.

Now this is clearly a contradiction of

major magnitude. The philosophers of contractualism saw the chief strength of the system to be its flexibility, its ability to change, to respond to and to resolve the conflicts generated by its contradictions. Yet without serious analysis of these contradictions and conflicts it is difficult to imagine how the system can flexibly respond to them.

We fool ourselves by looking not at the system (which is what sociology should do, if no other discipline) but by looking at individuals. For example, polls taken since 1949 show that United States citizens are not only generally satisfied with their work, income, and housing, but are becoming more satisfied. Here are the figures:[22]

	% satisfied	
	1949	1969
Work	69	88
Income	50	67
Housing	67	80

These are measure of satisfaction with some important kinds of contracts that people write. But we sadly mislead ourselves if we believe these figures tell us all that is important to know about how the *system* is doing.

Perhaps blind pride in the system is necessary for people to work together in order to keep it going. If that is true, it is a foregone conclusion that systems will have to be violently transformed, for people will not seriously study the social tools they are using until after they are destroyed. If we assume that whatever problems we see are the result of individuals (criminals, deviants, perverts, crazy people, people with evil intentions, commies), other systems (the international communist, communist-Jewish, Jewish, intellectual, or capitalist conspiracy) or the result

[22] Richard M. Scammon and Ben J. Wattenberg, *The Real Majority* (New York: Coward-McCann, 1970). Material taken from Gallup poll.

of human nature, we will never study the system itself for solutions to our problems. It is as if one went to fix one's car with a theory which required one to look for the causes of its not running in the driver, in the air above or the dirt below, or in other cars parked nearby, or just threw up one's hands and said, "It is the nature of cars not to work."

SUMMARY

This chapter has extended the conflict theory of the evolution of community forms into the present. We have showed how some important events in the United States, both past and present, can be explained within a class-conflict framework.

We showed how people living in the United States came to be dominated, although not totally organized around, a contractual logic. We presented data which supported the idea that conflict in the United States, indeed in any society dominated by contractual logic, is inherent in the contradictions within contractual logic. We suggested the kinds of observations that are needed to further test this theory. These are observations on the displacement of older forms of social relations by contractual relations and observations on class conflict and disintegration arising from contradictions within a contractual-capitalist strategy.

We described conflicts of three types, reflecting three basic contradictions in contractual industrialism: (1) the tendency of the rich to get richer and the poor to get poorer, and the contractual system to become a new kind of caste system; (2) the tendency of contractualism to destroy the environment; and (3) the tendency of contractualism to destroy the institutional supports of a truly contractual morality. The conflicts resulting from these contradictions are: (1) class conflict, as evidenced by lack of mobility of

people from one class to another, unequal application of criminal justice, destruction of weak (but not inefficient) economic groups, creating a dual labor market and unemployment; (2) conflict between those espousing the public value of preserving the environment and those wishing to pursue private interests with respect to the use of land, air, and water; (3) conflict between those using older moralities or double-standard moralities and those trying to develop a truly contractual morality.

The idea behind this chapter is that the study of society requires the analysis of contradictions and conflict inherent in the logic by which that society is organized. Such an analysis does not mean finding one perfect solution to the contradictions of a particular social form, nor does it claim that all human behavior is predictable from a knowledge of the contradictions and conflicts inherent in a particular form.

As we have suggested, a comparison of the Soviet Union and the United States using conflict theory would show that while choosing to ensure greater equality of contract writing by limiting people's freedom to contract and thereby partially resolving the contradictory tendency of the rich to get rich at the expense of the poor, the Soviets have not thereby resolved all the contradictions of contractualism. Further, an objective look at people in the Soviet Union, as in the United States, will reveal human beings doing many other things besides using the dominant social arrangements.

Before moving on to a more detailed analysis of the elements of industrial economies, we want to suggest that although serious analysis of present-day social life may require some loss of pride in the dominant system, this may be offset by a gain in respect for the people who attempt to make social arrangements work in spite of the contradictions with which they must struggle.

SUGGESTED READINGS

William Sheridan Allen, *The Nazi Seizure of Power: The Experience of a Single German Town, 1930–1935* (Chicago: Quadrangle, 1965).

Richard C. Edwards, Michael Reich, and Thomas Weisskopf (eds.), *The Capitalist System: A Radical Analysis of American Society* (Englewood Cliffs, N.J.: Prentice-Hall, 1972).

K. William Kapp, *Social Costs of Private Enterprise* (New York: Schocken, 1971).

Robert S. Lynd and Helen Merrell Lynd, *Middletown: A Study in American Culture* (New York: Harcourt Brace, 1929).

Bernard Sternsher (ed.), *Hitting Home: The Great Depression in Town and Country* (Chicago: Quadrangle, 1970).

Maurice Zeitlin (ed.), *American Society, Inc.: Studies of the Social Structure and Political Economy of the United States* (Chicago: Markham, 1970).

PART FOUR

SOCIAL RELATIONS IN THE MODERN ERA

In the chapters on tribalism, feudalism, and capitalism we analyzed segments of human history from a conflict perspective. We argued that the rise of new economic logics, and new contradictions, classes, and class conflicts, is a coherent and powerful force shaping human social relations.

In this part, specific aspects of the industrial-contractual economic logic will be examined. Attention will be focused on the United States and the capitalist industrialism which dominates there. Although socialist economies are not analyzed, we have implied throughout that more-or-less free contracts either between individuals or collectivities are the basis of industrial economies the world over. From this perspective, people using either socialist or capitalist economic structures must deal with the contradictions inherent in contractual logic. Thus we would expect similar problems to confront the people of both the Soviet Union and the United States, although they may describe themselves as using very different systems.

Among the most important effects of contractual logic is the contradictory tendency to concentrate in the hands of a few the power to decide the distribution of surplus value (or profit, as it is called in the United States). From power concentration flows a variety of problems for both the power wielders and the masses.

Chapter 12 analyzes in detail the concentration of power in the United States. Particular attention is paid to the effects on lawmaking and policy making in governmental bureaucracies, whether federal, state, or local. One of the major creations of bourgeois social structure is the state. The state, unlike the personal rule of feudalism, legitimates the use of violence in the name of a whole people. Violence that is legitimate is done in the name of the rule of law or contract and presumably in the interests of protecting the whole of the people whom the state serves. We have analyzed the state as emerging primarily to meet the aims of bourgeois commerce. An obvious extension of this analysis is to ask if the military arm of the state serves primarily class rather than national interests. In Chapter 13, such an analysis is applied to the military institution in the United States. One important consequence of power concentration is the use of state power (ultimately the use of armies and threat or use of war) to support the interests of the powerful (more profits) in other parts of the world—that is, *imperialism*. Chapter 14, "Imperialism and Industrialization," focuses on United States foreign policy. Events over the past thirty years have shown that imperialism also flows from economies with

state control of surplus value (socialism) and even from the more powerful underdeveloped, but developing, economies.

Chapter 15 analyzes one of the basic blueprints used in contractual-
industrial economies to order human relations—bureaucracy. Bureaucracy
tends to concentrate power. Bureaucracy's use spreads, partly as a defensive measure, into attempts to solve noneconomic problems—health;
care for the aged, sick, and dependent; education; even religion.
C. Wright Mills pointed out in his book *The Power Elite*[1] the tendency
toward convergence of interests among those using the top positions in
different bureaucratic hierarchies. That is, leaders of military, government,
and business bureaucracies tend to support each other's interests, indeed
to have many interests in common. Thus is created a contractual power
elite, one with quite different characteristics from feudal court nobility.
The analysis of bureaucracy is another way to get at an analysis of the
force created by the contradictory tendency toward power concentration
where contractual-industrial logic is used. This force cuts across and
tends to transform a variety of institutional patterns. Indeed, to bureaucratize and thereby give legal support to a particular way of solving a
problem—for example, providing welfare for dependent children—is to
give that pattern dominance and permanence.

Concentration of power has a profound influence on that cluster of
group structures through which people are apprehended, arrested,
charged with crime, convicted, imprisoned, and paroled—"the criminal
justice institution." Chapter 16, "Deviant Behavior and Social Control,"
emphasizes that within contractual-industrial logic, *who* is deviant and
to what degree is a matter settled in terms of bargaining power. In other
words, we can expect continuous negotiation over the definition of lawful
versus criminal behavior. In Chapter 16 statistics and case histories are
used to begin an analysis of the effects of power concentration on the
way individual or collective behavior is judged "deviant." That this is also
important in socialist economies, and that both the Soviet Union and the
United States produce similar types of "deviants," can be seen through
examining a long list of personal stories smuggled out of the Soviet Union.
The accounts of Andrei Amalrik and Aleksandr Solzhenitsyn are among
the most recent.[2]

Finally, we must consider the effects of power concentration on *individuals*. This effect is most easily measured by money income. Chapter 17
examines the trends in income inequality in the United States. Are we
moving further toward the ideal of an equal distribution of money power
—toward equal power to control life situations? Money power includes
not only income but also controllable wealth, such as stocks, bonds, and
real estate, which, in capitalist economies, all increase the ability to

[1] C. Wright Mills, *Power Elite* (New York: Oxford, 1959).
[2] Andrei Amalrik, *Involuntary Journey to Siberia* (New York: Harcourt Brace Jovanovich, 1970).
Aleksandr Solzhenitsyn, *The Gulag Archipeligo* (New York: Harper & Row, 1974).

control life situations. In this chapter, then, we return to an analysis of how social forces affect individual lives. This rests on the humanist assumption that society is for people. The basic question raised by conflict analysis starting from that assumption is, "Given that there are structured solutions to human problems, for whom and how well do these solutions work?"

TWELVE
Power

In the 1960s many Americans began to recognize what some social scientists had been saying for many years: if we are to understand the world we live in, we must understand power. Theorists with as differing orientations as Karl Marx, Max Weber, Gaetano Mosca, and Vilfredo Pareto long ago recognized the importance of power in social relations and devoted a substantial proportion of their energies to its study.

What brought the importance of power into sharp relief for the American public was a series of incidents, events, and social perceptions that changed the perspective within which "society" in general and America in particular was viewed. In the 1960s many Americans came to believe (rightly or wrongly) that:

The United States was deeply involved in a war (in Vietnam) that was strongly opposed by large numbers of the population.

The President had the power to authorize massive warfare without the consent of Congress or anyone else.

"Secret" governmental agencies (such as the CIA) operated largely unnoticed but determined the course of events for millions of people through the support of secret armies and activities designed to influence and control foreign governments.

Political conventions which nominate candidates for office are controlled by forces other than rank-and-file party members.

The assassination of several leading American political and religious leaders may have been engineered by powerful groups inside and outside the government.

The group structures that make up the executive branch of the federal government and the people who use these structures are tools for the personal ambitions and beliefs of the President.

Widespread violations of criminal law (burglary, breaking and entering, violent provocation, illegal wiretapping, planting, or destroying evidence in criminal cases) characterize the way that Presidential cronies in this and perhaps previous administrations use the power of government.

Government is controlled by and for the wealthy. (This view is now held more widely than at any time since the beginnings of the Great Depression.)

The powerlessness of women in political and economic institutions is a major reason for their continuing exploitation.

Government programs to eliminate poverty are virtually voided in their effectiveness by the power of the state bureaucracy to subvert and alter the principles of the program.

The police are blatant oppressors of the interests, rights, and wishes of large sections of the population.

These views, some of which are doubtless accurate portrayals of what was taking place and some of which are undoubtedly only partial truths, forced a reassessment of the role of power in social relations. The fact that significant numbers of people began to see the world, and especially the United States, in these terms was sufficient to ensure that social science inquiry would also revive and extend its interest in the study of power.

In the debate that followed and the research that buttressed the debate, we find a division, once again, between the functional and conflict perspectives, with each view leading to quite different conclusions about where power lies and how much power different groups have. The functional view that was prevalent for many years prior to the 1960s assumes a *pluralistic* model of power; the conflict view assumes an *elitist* model.

THE PLURALIST-ELITIST CONTROVERSY

The pluralist model sees power in the modern industrial society as diffused. Some pluralists acknowledge that there are, in all societies, small groups of people who control much of the wealth, but they contend that competition between different economic interests (for example, small and big business interests, rural and urban interests) leads to a diffusion of power rather than to its concentration. The pluralists also argue that people in business focus largely on the problems of their own particular profit-loss margins, and are thus kept from making any concerted effort to protect their class interests. The pluralists claim, in fact, that business people are often bitter enemies of one another.

The elitist model argues that the control of the means of producing and distributing the material resources of a country rests in the hands of a relatively small number of persons who own or at least control the industrial, manufacturing, and financial institutions. The elitist starting point for the analysis of power in America, for example, is as follows.

America is a capitalist society, that is, an economic system where the major portion of economic activity is conducted on the basis of private ownership and control of the means of production and financial institutions and the private appropriation of economic surplus. Preserving capitalism has been the primary goal of *the most articulate and politically powerful sector of the economic elite* during the twentieth century because it is inextricably tied to the maintenance of class privilege, [that is] a disproportionate share of world and national wealth and its translation into power, status and increased life chances for the members of the economic elite and their progeny.[1]

In this theoretical argument between pluralist and elitist the role of the government is crucial. Pluralist analysis views the government as largely a value-neutral organ in which competing interests (business-labor, urban-rural, big business–small business) vie for favors. From the pluralists' view, the outcome will be a reasonable (i.e., functionally useful) compromise that is ultimately in the interests of the masses of people. In this model, the power of the masses to elect and presumably control the political leaders of the nation is seen as the principal mechanism by which power remains diffused.

Elite analysis argues that governments (whether national or local) are unduly influenced, if not completely controlled, by those classes that control the productive and financial institutions of the nation. The dependence of the politicians on economic elites for such things as the financial support of their campaigns ensures that those who run and are elected to political office will mainly represent the viewpoint and interests of the economic elites.

In evaluating the relative merits of these theories, we will concentrate on their empirical validity; that is, we will look at their ability to account for the operation of power both historically and in contemporary society.

POWER IN LATE FEUDAL ENGLAND

In Chapter 9 we reconstructed the history of early agricultural economies as creating a pressure toward specialized warrior and peasant classes, which later become rigid castes. This pressure was stronger where food surpluses were largest. In contrast to func-

[1] Bachrach, Peter, and Baratz, Morton, *Power and Poverty: Theory and Practice* (New York: Oxford University Press, 1970).

tional analysts, we argued the existence of contradictions—tendencies toward class conflict—and disruption of the logic of feudalism. In its beginnings, we can expect contractual business activity to take place between groups of entrepreneurs and artisans with relatively equal power. As the logic develops, however, we expect contradictions to create two classes, an increasingly powerful business elite and an increasingly weakened wage-earning class. The nation-state, a contractual government, emerged out of this power-diffuse situation in late feudal England.

The process of forming the nation-state began in England when William the Conqueror declared himself king of all England in 1066. The land he had conquered was at the time divided into eight separate kingdoms, each resting on a feudal economic base with church and landowner sharing legal, political, moral, and coercive power over the people. From 1066 on there emerged a series of violent as well as nonviolent struggles for power between the Crown of England (the descendants of William the Conqueror), the Church, and the feudal landowners. There was indeed a pluralistic power structure in England from 1066 until at least the sixteenth or seventeenth century.

In the fourteenth and fifteenth centuries a new force entered the struggle for power—the bourgeosie, the makers of commerce. At first the new form of economic relation flourished in the Mediterranean countries of Europe (Spain, Portugal, and Italy), but it quickly diffused to other nations as well. Over the next few centuries commerce, trade, and, somewhat later, the process of industrialization destroyed a feudal England, already weakened by contradictions in the relations between landed nobility and peasantry. In its place rose a capitalist industrial state.

During the transition from feudalism to capitalism, England continued to be wrenched by struggles between competing groups of elites. At first the government sided with the Church and the feudal landlords in opposition to the emerging men of commerce and trade. The emergence of commerce, trade, and industry posed a real economic threat to the feudal landowners and the Church by reducing the dependence of the masses on feudal landlords for their livelihood.

Feudalism was based largely on the legal binding of people (serfs) to the land. This class was totally dependent on their master's land for survival. But with commerce came cities and the availability of ways of converting labor to goods other than being a serf. Thus, some laborers began leaving the country for the city. The landowners were already suffering a labor shortage because of the plague that had swept England in the fourteenth century and killed 50 percent of the population, and they sought assistance from the state. At this point the state sided with the landed aristocracy and passed laws prohibiting people from leaving their homes to seek employment elsewhere.

The development of commerce, trade, and industry, however, was not to be stopped by such measures. In time, the cities grew, and a far greater surplus of goods was provided by the commercial and industrial sectors of the economy than had ever been possible under feudalism.

The struggle between the new classes who controlled the nation's productive process in the cities and the old ruling aristocracy continued until the seventeenth and eighteenth centuries, when the state ultimately settled the fate of the landed aristocracy by aligning itself with those who controlled the industrial, commercial, and financial sectors of the economy. In some cases the landed aris-

tocracy joined the emerging capitalists and provided titles and dignity in exchange for capital. Others remained aloof and in time lost their control of economic surplus and their position of power.

This period of English history and its counterpart in America, where the struggle was raging between the northeastern industrializing states and the southern feudal states (culminating, of course, in the Civil War), was then truly a period aptly characterized as one of pluralistic powers.

But the pluralistic nature of power in England and America rapidly changed after industrialization. The state came to represent, and for a time to be practically indistinguishable from, the owners of the industries and the financiers who controlled the flow of money. This was the era of the robber barons, in which capitalism was given every opportunity—legal or illegal—to develop by the state, the church, and virtually every other institution in America.

During this period the applicability of the pluralist model breaks down completely. An accurate account of the distribution and functioning of power, both within the industrial nations and between industrialized and nonindustrialized nations, at this historical juncture must stress the role of an upper class of capitalists who controlled the means of production and the sources of power. To the extent that any struggle for power existed, it was limited to a struggle between very unequal adversaries: an unorganized labor force, almost totally dependent on industry for its livelihood, and capitalists, who controlled the industries and the coercive forces of the state. The only real struggles were battles for domination within the ruling class, but even here the struggle was bounded by agreement not to attack the capitalistic structure of the economy. Thus the internal battles of the bourgeosie *never threatened their power as a class.* Class loyalty became so great that some did not attack the system which promised such riches even after they had lost their businesses.

In order to discover whether the pluralist or the elitist analysis is appropriate for understanding contemporary industrial economies, we must turn to the empirical data gathered by social scientists.

The pluralist model finds its strongest support in studies that focus on the operation of power in small communities. The political scientist Robert Dahl is a staunch advocate of the pluralist model of power as a consequence of his study of power in New Haven, Connecticut. Dahl's research established that the upper class of New Haven was not a "ruling elite" because on those issues that were most important to the community the upper class did not get involved in the decision-making process at all.

Recently, two other political scientists, Peter Bachrach and Morton Baratz, have shown that Dahl and other pluralist theorists have failed to adequately define the "most important" issues in the life of a community. Obviously, by selecting some issues as most important while ignoring others, it is possible to show support for either a pluralist or an elitist model. More importantly, Bachrach and Baratz point out that Dahl and the pluralist theorists fail to take into account what they call the "mobilization of bias" in the decision-making process. Specifically, the persons who are in positions to make political decisions may reflect the interests of the upper classes so completely that actual participation by the upper strata is unnecessary. In other words, the consequences of decisions may tell us more about the power structure of a society than does an analysis of who actively gets into the decision-making process. With this in mind, Bachrach and Baratz studied specific decisions made in Baltimore, Maryland—decisions that in fact would affect the interests of the upper class of Baltimore—and they found that both in actual involvement and through the mobilization of bias the upper class of Baltimore had its interests protected by those making decisions in the government.

With regard to national government, the pluralist model suggests that the competitive struggle between different interest groups leads to a diffusion of power such that no class or group receives a disproportionate share of decisions to their advantage. The elitist model argues that the advantage held by the upper strata means that most if not all decisions made by the state are made to favor upper-strata interests.

A complete answer to the argument would, of course, necessitate knowing all the intricacies of decision making, which in all likelihood will never be available to social scientists. As Watergate has shown, much decision making is purposely hidden, and we are unlikely to know about the pressures brought upon congressmen and executives as they make decisions and vote upon various bills and proposals. We can, however, look at the consequences of the decisions made. Do they, in the end, favor one class rather more than another, or do they favor different classes? And, secondly, we can look at the class background of people who hold the key positions of power in the state. If we find that the decisions made favor the upper class at the expense of other classes, and if we find that those who influence and control the decisions are themselves from the upper class, then we have strong evidence in support of the elitist model. Conversely, if we find that decisions favor different classes and that the decision makers have different class backgrounds, then we have found strong evidence in support of the pluralist model.

POWER IN AMERICA: THE CONSEQUENCES

One of the most important functions of the state in modern society is the dual function of collecting money through taxes and redistributing that money through government spending. A test (but not the only one, of course) of the relative utility of the pluralist and elitist model is provided by asking who pays the taxes and who benefits most from the government's spending of tax money. Again we will use the United States as our principal example, but there is evidence that what is true in America is also true in most other modern industrial nations.

In 1970 the United States government collected a total of 198.6 billion dollars in taxes. Almost half of these taxes ($90.4 billion) came from personal income taxes. Of these taxes, 75 percent were paid by people who earned less than $10,000 a year. Thus, despite the fact that the official tax rate is much higher for higher-income groups, the fact is that the bulk of income taxes are paid by middle- and lower-income groups. As we pointed out earlier, many of the wealthiest people in the United States pay little or no taxes; and the average income tax paid by those with incomes over $10,000 a year is in fact no higher than the taxes paid by those who earn under $10,000 a year. When all forms of taxation are considered, one finds the distribution of tax rates shown in Table 12-1. Furthermore, the total amount of revenue lost to just *federal* government through tax loopholes for the rich has been estimated to be at least 50 billion dollars per year. According to functional analysis, this money is not "lost." The loopholes supposedly benefit all Americans by encouraging people to invest in business activity. This in turn should create more jobs, wages, goods, and services. Economists disagree on how much these deductions "multiply" into new jobs.

TABLE 12-1   Distribution of Tax Rates, 1972

Money income levels	Overall tax rate percentage
Under $2,000	50.0
$2,000–$2,999	34.6
$4,000–$5,999	31.0
$6,000–$7,999	30.1
$8,000–$9,999	29.2
$10,000–$14,999	29.8
$15,000–$24,999	30.0
$25,000–$49,999	32.8
Over $50,000	45.0

SOURCE: Thomas Bodenheimer, "The Poverty of the State," *Monthly Review*, vol. 24, no. 6, November, 1972, p. 15.

Some of it goes directly to make life easier for the rich; some goes back to profits whose allocation is decided by the elite. No scientific analysis has ever been made to reduce these loopholes by the amount they fail to contribute to economic growth. This fact in itself supports the usefulness of the elitist model in helping us understand government tax policy.

Of the nonpersonal income taxes collected by the state, corporation taxes and employment and payroll taxes account for about 35 percent. Employment and payroll taxes are paid equally by employer and employee; corporation taxes are largely passed on to the consumer through the price of the product. Thus, in effect, it is the mass of wage earners who pay the bulk of federal taxes. The same is true of state and local taxes, even though there is supposedly a much higher tax on the wealthier members of a community.

The facts that the wealthy avoid paying a disproportionate share of taxes and that the tax structure is largely a matter of taking income from the lower strata supports the elitist interpretation of the power structure in the United States rather than the pluralist view.

But what happens to the money once it is in the hands of the state? How does the government redistribute the resources it has collected? If the pluralist model is correct, the government should redistribute its received income in ways that favor all social classes more or less equally according to their numbers in the population. If the elitist model is correct, we should find that incomes received by the federal government are spent primarily for the benefit of the profit-controlling class and only incidentally for the benefit of the wage-earning class.

In a breakdown of federal expenditures for 1970, over 50 percent of the total expenditures either went for national security or related expenses (such as interest on public debt, which is itself largely a result of expenditures on national security in earlier days). Furthermore, we should note that interest on the public debt is paid primarily to large financial institutions and corporations holding public bonds.

These expenditures for "national security" are mainly outlays made by the federal government to large corporations for the construction of equipment or the production of services. The largest single item in the budget of the Department of Defense is "procurement." In 1962, 62 percent of the Department of Defense budget was spent on contracts, mostly with civilian contractors. Of these contracts, the majority are sent to a handful of the country's top industrial corporations. Between 1940 and 1944, 43 percent of the contracts for supplies went to the 10 largest corporations in the United States; 67 percent went to the largest 100 corporations.[2] According to Senator Hubert Humphrey, in 1963 twenty-four companies received 70 percent of the entire defense expenditures.[3]

[2] G. William Domhoff, *Who Rules America* (New York: Oxford, 1959), p. 121.
[3] Tristram Coffin, *The Passion of the Hawks* (New York: Macmillan, 1964), p. 159.

Expenditures for health, education, and welfare, which would conceivably benefit the lower- and middle-income groups rather more than the upper, accounted for only 32 percent of the total federal budget. We do not know to what extent this expenditure represents a real benefit for the wage-earning class; but the research done by Bachrach and Baratz, as well as recent research by Handler and Hollingsworth, make it clear that much if not most of these monies end up being subsidies for local and national business interests, and little of it goes toward improving the relative economic position of the lower socioeconomic strata.

Even such apparently lower-income-oriented programs as farm price supports and agricultural research are in effect subsidies for large businesses. Agricultural benefits accrue mainly to large farmers or large farm-owning corporations, which in many cases are subsidiaries of big financial institutions such as the Bank of America. Indeed, it is probably not too far from the truth to say that only the 4 percent of the federal expenditures that went for veteran's benefits in 1970 represents a redistribution of income that clearly benefits the lower economic strata rather than the upper.

The federal government also exerts its power in the interests of large corporations by a variety of subsidies, loan guarantees, and hidden support. The most obvious subsidy occurs when a large industry is in financial difficulty and the government provides loan guarantees to save the corporation from bankruptcy. A recent example was Lockheed Aircraft, one of the world's five largest corporations, which was on the verge of bankruptcy. Banks would not loan the corporation any more money unless the federal government would guarantee the loan. Congress and the President approved such a guarantee and provided the funds necessary to keep this privately owned corporation from bankruptcy without, incidentally, making any conditions such as those typically demanded of welfare recipients at the lower end of the social class structure.

Hidden support in a variety of forms is also critical in the use of state power to benefit the upper strata. "Foreign aid" is doubtless one of the more important government subsidies to large industry. Senator Frank Church, in voting against the foreign aid program, made the point succinctly: "There is abundant evidence that our foreign aid program is much less philanthropic than we have cared to portray. Indeed, the figures suggest that it is patently self-serving." Former Agency for International Development Director William Gaud disclosed that "93 percent of AID funds are spent in the United States for products supplied as part of foreign aid programs."[4]

Another example of a hidden subsidy is the little-known Overseas Investment Program, which is totally financed by the federal government and pays premiums on insurance to Lloyds of London (in 1971, the premium was two hundred and fifty million dollars) to insure American businesses overseas against being expropriated. Thus, if the Chilean government expropriates the copper mines of American business, the losses (or at least part of them) are made up by insurance funds that come from tax monies.

The state also determines who shall be permitted to engage in a variety of occupations, businesses, and "public services." In making these decisions, it exercises power over the lives and minds of people that is unparalleled in human history.

Take, for example, the distribution of government handouts—what lawyer Charles Reich has called "the new property." The federal government makes decisions which allocate property worth millions of dollars:

a television license, a radio station franchise, the right to drill for oil, a contract to build an airplane. In each of these instances the recipient holds a legal contract from the government. Since the franchise for a television station is a virtual monopoly, the recipient stands not only to become wealthy but also to exert substantial influence over the minds and tastes of the people. When television franchises became available, the government could have allocated them to groups representing the whole range of conflicting political, economic, and social interests in America today. But they did not. The franchises went instead to the already powerful and economically affluent: the three major radio networks (NBC, CBS, and ABC) received the bulk of the most attractive and most lucrative stations. In cities where franchises went to companies other than the major radio networks, they were given to people who already owned the newspaper or radio stations, or to groups which were part of the major corporate and business interests in the community. The poor, the black, the chicano, the radical, the intellectual communities were thereby preemptorily eliminated from access to the mass media, and control was maintained by those who already had large amounts of power. Nationally and locally, the elites became wealthier and more powerful.

The airwaves which can carry radio and television messages are limited in number partly in reflection of present limits to radio and television technology.[5] Thus the government, in granting TV licenses, grants a monopoly over the use of air. If there is anything which is owned by everyone or by no one, air must be that thing. Yet an increasingly small number of large corporations "owns" the air used to transmit messages.

[4] Both quotes from Frank Church, "Why I Voted No," *The New Republic*, Nov. 13, 1971, p. 15.

[5] If there is a TV tuner which can receive an infinite number of stations, its invention has not been announced by the Federal Communications Commission.

The story is told over and over. The large farmer benefits from farming subsidies while the small farmer finds it increasingly difficult to compete—*not* with the large farmer as such but with government-subsidized corporations that control and manage monopolistic farming enterprises. When people owning small businesses cannot survive in the competitive market (more often than not because of competition with large corporations), they go bankrupt and their lives are possibly ruined. But when the Penn Central Railroad or Lockheed Aircraft or Boeing gets into financial difficulties, the government provides funds to save it. Direct loans and loans from banks over which the government has control (banks from which government agencies recruit their executives) provide a major source of support for the powerful, while those outside the realm of the elites must operate within a "free enterprise" system. Where bank loans are not used, government contracts suffice. These contracts ostensibly go to the company that promises, by way of bidding, to produce the best product at the lowest price. In fact, it goes to the company that has the most political muscle. When Boeing Aircraft receives a contract from the government, the senators from the state of Washington announce it as a personal victory for them. And indeed it is a victory—for them and for Boeing's lobbyists. Aircraft companies, motor manufacturers, and every other major industry hire retired high-ranking military and government personnel *not* because of their skills as administrators but because of their contacts (power) in the Defense Department. For the same reason, the banking industry and the major banking corporations (Chase Manhattan and the Bank of America, for example) hire former members of the federal agencies that "regulate" banking.

In the face of the persistent tendency for the state to favor the interests of large industries rather than small, corporations rather than individuals, and the capital class rather than the wage earner, it is not surprising that sociologist T. B. Bottomore has concluded:

> [I]f power is really so widely dispersed [as the pluralist theory suggests], how are we to account for the fact that the owners of property —the upper class in Marx's sense—still predominate so remarkably in government and administration, and in other *elite* positions; or that there has been so little redistribution of wealth and income, in spite of the strenuous and sustained effort of the labor movement to bring it about: Is it not reasonable to conclude . . . that notwithstanding political democracy, and despite the limited conflicts of interest which occur between *elite* groups in different spheres, the upper class in capitalist societies is still a distinctive and largely self-perpetuating social group, and still occupies the vital positions of power: Its power may be less commanding, and it is certainly less arrogantly exercised, than in an earlier period, because it encounters an organized opposition and the test of elections, and because other classes have gained a limited access to the *elites:* but the power which it has retained enables it to defend successfully its most important economic interests.[6]

The extent to which money power has become concentrated as a result of the political processes favoring large corporations can be seen in descriptions of corporate wealth. Selection 12-1 describes the enormous wealth of IBM.

IS THE UPPER STRATA A GOVERNING CLASS?

To what extent do people in the upper strata actively engage in the political decision-making process to ensure that their interests are protected? The answer to that question

[6] Bottomore, T. B., *Elites and Society* (New York: Basic Books, 1965).

SELECTION 12-1: The money power of IBM.

$4 BILLION IN CASH JUST SITTING AROUND

MILTON MOSKOWITZ

How would you like to have nearly $4 billion in cash sitting around and not know what to do with it?

That is the problem confronting International Business Machines Corp., the dominant factor in the world computer industry.

IBM's embarrassment of riches was pointed up recently by Business Week, the weekly McGraw-Hill magazine for businessmen. Business Week reported that IBM's cash hoard has now reached $3.8 billion, which means the computer manufacturer may have passed both General Motors and Exxon as the corporation with the largest amount of liquid assets.

IBM's piggybank bulges because the company "manufactures" money as fast as one of its computers spews out information. Its treasury has doubled in size during the past five years.

In previous times this wouldn't have caused any problems. As a company increased its earnings, it simply passed on the gains to the owners. But the corporate world is no longer so simple.

IBM has been paying out higher dividends to its shareholders. However, it is subject, along with other corporations, to government guidelines which have restricted dividend increases to 4 per cent. IBM's profits have increased much faster than that—they went up 23 per cent last year—and so the company has had to bank the difference.

IBM seems to be a company that attracts money just by breathing. Two examples:

Foreign investment controls which were relaxed only last month have limited the company's overseas investments to 40 per cent of the net profit derived from each country. IBM felt it needed more and so it went overseas to borrow $500 million in long-term debt. And the cash that wasn't needed immediately went into the bank, further inflating the liquid assets.

IBM sells stock to its employees, not to raise capital but to encourage ownership. That brought in $325 million in 1973.

How big is a $3.8 billion cash bundle? Well, as Business Week pointed out, it's about equal to the treasury reserves of Belgium or Saudia Arabia before the oil embargo. It's also larger than the assets of all commercial banks.

What does IBM do with its cash? Well, it loans it to you by investing primarily in short-term U.S. government bonds, notes and bills. This money-lending operation netted IBM interest income of $270 million last year. That alone would be enough to rank IBM as one of the 50 largest profit makers in U.S. industry.

This incredible cash flow stems from IBM's powerful grip on the fastest-growing market (information processing) in the world. Over the past 20 years, its share of the domestic computer market has ranged from 66 to 74 per cent. Its share of the world market is estimated at 60 per cent.

No other industry in this country is so dominated by one company. No non-IBM company has ever held more than 10 per cent of the computer market except for Univac in the very early days of the industry.

The top four companies—IBM, Sperry Rand (Univac), Honeywell and Control Data—now control 85 per cent of the market.

Two electronic giants—RCA and General Electric—abandoned their computer manufacturing operations rather than fight IBM.

And so IBM continues to be inundated with money. Why can't we have such problems?

takes us to the very heart of the conflicting views held by pluralist and elitist theorists. For regardless of the *use* of power, which, as we have seen, favors the upper-strata owners of economic resources, the question remains: Do the upper strata achieve their ends by active participation or by the simple use of a government organized so that upper-strata interests automatically come first? As capitalist-industrialist technology becomes more complex, much of the nation's political attention focuses on keeping the machines running and trying to solve problems created by machine technology. The solution of these problems and support of research into new technology (aerospace and atomic power are examples which absorb billions of tax dollars) seem always to benefit those who own the machines more than those who do not. Plans for income maintenance, or a leave of absence every seven years, or even for a more humane work environment get little legislative attention, and the interests of wage earners seem not to be regarded when Congress or state legislatures do take up these issues.

Studies of the social backgrounds of persons in the legislative, executive, and judicial branches of the federal government make it very clear that these persons are disproportionately chosen from the upper strata. For example, from 1947 to 1957, 58 percent of the Democrats in the United States Senate were the sons of business and professional men and only 5 percent were the sons of wage earners. This is the party that is ostensibly the most "working class" oriented party in America. One-fifth of the members of the Senate and House are millionaires and the majority of those who are not millionaires are from upper-strata families or in professions that serve the upper strata, such as the law.

Presidential nominees are almost exclusively from either upper-strata families (recently, President Kennedy and President Roosevelt) or are politicians who have been financed by and worked for the profit controllers as either lawyers or political "friends" or both. The same thing is true of appointments to the Supreme Court, which are traditionally reserved for upper-strata lawyers. Thus, in all three major branches of government, upper-class affiliation is an important ingredient for success. The profit-managing class may not completely control these institutions, but it is clear that they are disproportionately represented.

Two students of power in America, E. Digby Baltzell and G. William Domhoff have provided a great deal of evidence which establishes the existence of a small group of Eastern aristocrats who intermarry, go to the same private schools and universities, are members of the same select clubs, take their vacations in the same places, and run the major industrial and financial institutions of America. From his study *Who Rules America*, Domhoff concludes that there is a governing class in America "made up of rich business-

Analysis of elite influence suggests that presidential nominees must be persons approved by corporate leaders. One of the impeachment charges against President Nixon was that in return for campaign contributions he raised dairy product prices. (Editorial Photocolor Archives)

men and their descendants, who interact at private schools, exclusive summer resorts and similar institutions." These families are mostly the descendants of the industrialists and financiers who emerged victorious in the struggle for control of America's industry in the nineteenth century. Many of the names are well known to everyone; the Rockefellers, Mellons, Carnegies, Cabots, Kennedys, and Lodges are but a few of the more visible.

Establishing the existence of an interacting, self-conscious, and cohesive capital or profit-managing class is, however, only the first step. To establish that this class is also a governing or "ruling" class requires showing that they control and influence decisions which are in their interests and opposed to the interests of others, that is, determining whether the capital class is disproportionately represented in key cases of decision making.

Pooling of resources among corporations or associations of the rich allows members of the profit managing class to increase their collective money and political power. Often, as in the case of a physicians association's investment in drug companies (Selection 12-2), profit making may come before the interests of the clients and consumers when those supposed to protect consumer interests (as are physicians) join hands with those whose main interest is to make a profit.

As we will show in Chapter 14, a cornerstone of the modern industrial nation is the exploitation of other nations' natural resources and the control of foreign markets for selling the goods produced by the industrial nations. The avenue by which this is accomplished is a government's foreign policy. It follows, therefore, that one area of considerable importance to those who control America's means of production is America's foreign policy. It also follows that if the capital class is a governing class, its

members will regard foreign policy as a key area for active involvement.

The foreign policy of the United States has been and still is largely in the hands of the capital-class business and financial aristocracy. This control stems from domination of government agencies by representatives of this class, influence gained by controlling the principal nongovernment foreign-policy boards, and control of charitable foundations that create and instigate the foreign-policy objectives of the capital class.

Domination of Government Agencies

Several government units have roles in forming and shaping America's foreign policy: the National Security Council, the Department of State, the Department of Defense, and specially appointed Presidential and agency committees. Who has the key positions that determine the output of these agencies of power? With rare exceptions, the heads of Defense, State, and the National Security Council have been leading members of the upper-class aristocracy or are persons who were managers of the business interests of that social class. Domhoff points out that[7]:

[T]he heads of State, Defense, and Treasury during the postwar years have been almost without exception members of the power elite. For example, Robert Lovett of Brown Brothers, Harriman served as Secretary of Defense, as did Charles E. Wilson of General Motors, Neil McElroy of Procter and Gamble, Thomas S. Gates, Jr., of Drexel & Co. (in 1961 he became president of Morgan Guaranty Trust) and Robert McNamara of Ford Motor. Treasury Secretaries have included John Snyder of the First National Bank of St. Louis, George Humphrey of M. A. Hanna Company, Robert Anderson of the W. T. Waggoner oil estate, and C. Douglas Dillion of Dillon, Read; heads of

[7] Domhoff, G. William, Higher Circles (New York: Random House, 1970.)

SELECTION 12-2: Interconnected Resources of Physicians and Pharmaceutical Companies. Do drug prescriptions benefit patients, or physicians and drug companies?

AMA PURCHASES OF DRUG STOCKS OKd

New York—Trustees of the American Medical Association have ruled that three AMA-owned investment portfolios, valued at more than $22 million, are free to acquire securities of drug companies.

The decision was made public here yesterday by AMA officials in the wake of a recent disclosure that another AMA-controlled fund already contains about $10 million worth of stocks in firms that manufacture pharmaceuticals.

The AMA's own principles of medical ethics urge physicians not to invest in companies related to medicine or the "health care industry."

Policy

But a spokesman for the association insisted yesterday there is no conflict of interest at all in the AMA's investment policy.

The AMA, whose annual budget runs to about $33 million, controls four separate funds. All are managed by outside investment counseling firms.

The largest of the four is the Members' Retirement Fund, which is valued at about $135 million and owns about $10 million in drug firm stocks.

According to Samuel P. Miller, AMA director of finance, this fund was restricted from acquiring pharmaceutical company stocks until last November. At that time, Miller said, he decided the restriction was pointless, and the fund's managers bought drug firm stocks because they are currently rated high for both growth and income.

Funds

At the AMA's annual convention here this week the Board of Trustees decided that three other funds should be unencumbered too.

With a go-ahead from the association's Judicial Council the Trustees voted to permit its investment managers to buy drug company stocks and also considered authorizing the purchase of tobacco company securities. The AMA, like all medical organizations, strongly opposes cigarette smoking as a major cause of cancer.

The three funds now freed of investment restrictions are: AMA reserves, totaling $7 million in stocks; an employee retirement fund of about $10 million, and the AMA Education and Research Foundation fund of about $5 million.

AMA officials insist this new freedom to participate in a "well-recognized growth segment of the economy" does not mean the AMA will curtail its activities reviewing and criticizing new prescription drugs.

The organization publishes a wide-ranging critical drug review called AMA Drug Evaluations, and a new edition of this volume is due in August.

State have included John Foster Dulles of Sullivan and Cromwell, Dean Rusk of the Rockefeller Foundation, Dean Acheson of Covington and Burling, General George C. Marshall, and Boston aristocrat Christian Herter. It is possible to be more specific by looking at the composition of the NSC when it was studied by journalists during the Truman, Eisenhower and Kennedy administrations.

When John Fischer of *Harper's Magazine* wrote of Mr. Truman's Politburo as "the most powerful and least publicized of all government agencies," it included in addition to Acheson, Marshall, and Snyder the following

wealthy leaders: Averell Harriman of Brown Brothers, Harriman; Charles E. Wilson of General Electric; and Stuart Symington of Emerson Electric. The Secretary of the NSC was a big businessman from St. Louis, Sidney Souers. His assistant was James Lay, a former employee of utilities companies, whom Souers had met during World War II. Others present for NSC meetings were Alben Barkley, vice president; General Walter Bedell Smith, Director of the CIA; and General Omar Bradley, Chairman of the Joint Chiefs of Staff.

When *U.S. News and World Report* ran a story in 1956 on "How Ike Makes the Big Decisions," the following were regularly a part of the NSC in addition to Dulles, Humphrey and Charles E. Wilson:

Richard Nixon, Vice President, who was selected and financed for a political career by top corporate executives in Southern California.

Arthur S. Fleming, a lawyer, who was formerly president of Ohio Wesleyan University.

Percival Brundage, a partner in Price, Waterhouse & Company.

Allen Dulles, a former partner in the large corporate law firm of Sullivan and Cromwell.

Lewis Strauss, investment banker and personal financial advisor to the Rockefellers.

William H. Jackson, a lawyer who managed the investment firm of John Hay Whitney, as well as sitting on the boards of Great Northern Paper and Bankers Trust.

Dillon Anderson, a Houston Corporation lawyer who was the President's Special Assistant for National Security Affairs.

Harold Stassen, former governor of Minnesota and former president of the University of Pennsylvania.

Admiral Arthur W. Redford, Chairman of the Joint Chiefs of Staff.

McGeorge Bundy, the aristocrat who managed the NSC for President Kennedy, played a leading role in foreign affairs throughout the 1960s until he left government service to become president of the Ford Foundation. His staff included Walt Rostow of the MIT Center for International Studies, Harvard economist Carl Kaysen, Michael Forrestal (son of the former Secretary of Defense who was also a one-time president of Dillon, Read), and Robert Komer (a government official).

The following were members of the executive committee of the NSC which met regularly over a period of two weeks to determine American reactions during the Cuban missile crisis of 1962.

Lyndon Johnson, Vice President, representative of Texas oil interests.

Dean Rusk, a former president of the Rockefeller Foundation.

Robert McNamara, a former president of Ford Motor.

Robert F. Kennedy, a multimillionaire from Boston.

C. Douglas Dillion, a former president of Dillon, Read.

Roswell Gilpatric, a corporation lawyer from New York.

McGeorge Bundy, a Boston aristocrat who was formerly dean at Harvard.

Adlai Stevenson, a corporation lawyer from Chicago.

John McCone, a multimillionaire industrialist from Los Angeles.

Dean Acheson, a corporation lawyer and former Secretary of State.

Robert Lovett, an investment banker with Brown Brothers, Harriman.

General Maxwell Taylor, a Presidential adviser and former chairman of the Mexican Light and Power Company, Ltd.

Major General Marshall S. Carter, Deputy Director of the CIA.

George Ball, a Washington corporation lawyer, later to become a partner in Lehman Brothers.

Edwin M. Martin, a State Department official specializing in Latin America.

Llewellyn Thompson, a foreign-service officer.

Theodore C. Sorensen, Presidential speechwriter and adviser.

The same general pattern is also found in special policy committees appointed by the President and by various government agencies. When President Johnson appointed a "task force on violence" following the murder of Robert Kennedy, the upper class was well represented and those businesses most likely to be affected by the outcome of such a task force were best represented. The commission itself was headed by the brother of a former president of the United States. The two lawyers who were primarily responsible for the research and writing of the commission both worked for law firms that represented the two leading television and

Members of powerful governmental policymaking committees are chosen almost exclusively from those people of the same powerful class who sit as directors of the most powerful corporations in the United States. (Editorial Photocolor Archives)

radio networks of the country. Given the possibility that widespread violence might be linked to television programming policies, it was obviously important that the television industry have firm control of the commission. In effect they did have such control, which was gained by placing their representatives in key positions. Studies of other special committees and government advisory groups show similar control by upper-strata interests.[8]

Non-governmental Foreign-policy Makers

Nongovernmental agencies are also critically important to the foreign-policy output of the nation. By defining the issues and gathering information to support certain views, these agencies feed in the perspectives and data on which the policy makers rely.

The Council on Foreign Relations, which is ostensibly a nonpartisan group interested in foreign affairs, is doubtless the most influential nongovernmental body. It is, in fact, a highly partisan representative of the interests of America's upper class. The Council

[8] Domhoff, *The Higher Circles*, pp. 134–135.

is financed by Chase Manhattan Bank, Continental Can Company, Ford Motors, Bankers Trust, Cities Service, Gulf, General Motors, and a host of other leading American corporations whose profits depend heavily on the control and exploitation of other nations. Further, the people who actually run the Council on Foreign Relations are themselves members of the American capital class. In the 1960s nearly 50 percent of the 1,400 members of the Council were listed in the Social Register, which is evidence of their aristocratic origins.[9]

SUMMARY

Two theories of power have been examined: the pluralist theory, which grows out of the functional perspective, and the elitist theory, which grows out of the conflict perspective. The question we asked is, "Which type of analysis leads us farther toward understanding the kinds of problems we think important?" If you wish to understand how diverse peoples have managed to live in the United States under a government dominated by business for 200 years, a pluralist analysis

[9] Ibid., p. 116.

might suggest useful places to make observations and useful explanations. However, if you think it important to know why the United States gets into wars, why one-fourth to one-third of its citizens live in poverty, and why racial violence occurs, an elitist analysis provides far better explanations and leads in more useful directions in stimulating further understanding.

Close examination of the operation of power on the federal level reveals that in America at least the upper strata is an active and largely successful wielder of power. The government functions mainly by taxing the middle and lower strata in order to support the interests and activities of the largest business and financial institutions of the country. Further, representatives of the profit managers are actively engaged in politics and in shaping government policy in ways that make it inevitable that the interests of the upper strata will receive first priority in the decision-making process.

Although we will not dwell in detail on the issue here, it is apparently the case that although America may be an extreme case of domination by an upper-strata elite, it is not alone. Even those nations that have had socalist governments for many years have found it difficult to curtail the power of the upper strata. Sweden, for example, has had a democratically elected socialist party since the early 1930s, yet the distribution of wealth has not changed substantially during this forty-year period. Indeed, the wealthiest man in the world today is not American but Swedish. There is some evidence that even the Soviet Union has not found it possible to avert the emergence of a ruling elite who benefit disproportionately from their control of the state machinery that in turn controls the means of production in Russian society.

SUGGESTED READINGS

C. Wright Mills, *The Power Elite* (New York: Oxford University Press, 1956).

Robert Dahl, *Who Governs? Democracy and Power in an American City* (New Haven, Conn.: Yale University Press, 1961).

Gabriel Kolko, *The Roots of American Foreign Policy: An Analysis of Power and Purpose* (Boston: Beacon Press, 1969).

Peter Bachrach and Morton Baratz, *Power and Poverty* (New York: Oxford University Press, 1970).

G. William Domhoff, *Who Rules America?* (Englewood Cliffs, N.J.: A Spectrum Book, Prentice-Hall, 1967).

————, *The Higher Circles* (New York: Random House, 1970).

Senator Frank Church, "Why I Voted No," *The New Republic*, November 13, 1971.

THIRTEEN
The Military in America

Although the military is a central institutional pattern in America that affects every individual either directly or indirectly, there is a great lack of widespread public knowledge about the military and an equally great lack of concern on the part of academic social scientists who are concerned with a critical analysis of American society. This systematic oversight may be explained in part by the historic lack of a strong military tradition in the United States. Whatever its origin, this lack of knowledge and concern serves to distort the current reality, both in the United States and in the world at large. This chapter examines the historical background of the American military, its development since World War II, its relation to the American power structure and American social stratification, and certain new developments that

are the result of the Vietnam War and the protest movements of the sixties.

THE HISTORICAL TRADITION

The historical roots of the American military are best summarized by Charles H. Coates and Roland J. Pellegrin, both of whom served in the Army before they became academic sociologists. (Coates, by the way, retired from the army with the rank of colonel; he is also a West Point graduate.)

Americans like to think of themselves as peace lovers, and to contrast their nation with more warlike ones. The historical record reveals, however, that since the early colonization of the continent we have engaged rather consistently in warfare of one kind or other. Prior to securing independence, the American colonists participated in the local and global conflicts in which England was perennially engaged. As an independent nation, we conducted major warfare against England, Mexico, and Spain in the nineteenth century. The same century saw our Civil War and repeated military engagements with the Indians. In the twentieth century, of course, our participation in warfare has been even more extensive. An examination of the historical record reveals that we have participated in every major global conflict since 1689.

Perhaps we should characterize ourselves as unmilitary rather than peace-loving. A truly peace-loving nation undoubtedly would have avoided much of the warfare in which we have been involved. On the other hand, we have not made systematic preparations in advance of these past conflicts, as would befit an aggressive or militaristic nation. It is in this sense that we can be considered unmilitary or unmilitaristic.[1]

The above quotation stresses the fact that the United States has a long tradition of warfare, but a relatively minor tradition of militarism. This seeming paradox is partly explained in the following comment by Coates and Pellegrin:

Such forms of militarism as have existed historically in the United States have arisen mainly in connection with efforts to expand the territory and influence of the nation. The development of the doctrine of "Manifest Destiny" in the early nineteenth century, and our adventures in imperialism later in that century and the turn of the present one, embroiled us in military exploits which stimulated militaristic tendencies.[2]

Coates and Pellegrin quite correctly cite the territorial expansion of the United States

beyond its continental borders as the primary cause of the growth of a militaristic tradition. That the United States did not have a strong military tradition for the greater part of its history can best be explained by the fact that it was a wide-open land surrounded by two oceans and weak nations, and was therefore not vulnerable to constant attack. While naval power was always given consideration by American governments, a large standing army and defense budget were considered unnecessary. Ideologically, the founding fathers and subsequent national leaders were fearful of large military establishments as threats to democracy and individualism.

Most of the expansion of the United States across the North American continent was accomplished without the aid of massive arms. The Louisiana Purchase, the acquisition of Florida, and the purchase of the Oregon Territory are examples of this. When arms were used, they were employed against relatively weak enemies such as the Spanish, the Mexicans, and the Indians. Furthermore, the organization of the armed forces in those days mitigated against the development of a strong military establishment. Most of the military forces that did exist were in the form of decentralized state militias rather than a centralized federal army. American frontiersmen were themselves armed and played a significant part in the destruction of native American culture, especially after the Army had penned the Indians onto reservations. C. Wright Mills pointed out that:

The small regular army was supplemented by state militias and formed into The U.S. Volunteers, the commanders of these troops being appointed by governors of the states. In this quite unprofessional situation, regular army men could be and often were jumped to generalship in The Volunteers. Politics—which is also to say civilian control—reigned supreme.

[1] Charles H. Coates and Roland J. Pellegrin, *Military Sociology: A Study of American Military Institutions and Military Life* (University Park, Md.: Social Science Press, 1965), p. 22.
[2] Ibid., p. 41.

At any given time, there were few generals, and the rank of colonel was often even the height of the West Pointer's aspiration.[3]

Although the expansion of the United States across the North American continent did not engender the development of large standing armies and centralized military power, it was an expression of a deeply rooted agrarian capitalism which manifested itself in land hunger, land speculation, and the rapid settlement of people on the newly acquired land. The thrust of this changed with the end of the Civil War, a bloody, costly, four-year war which terminated with the victory of northern industrial capitalism over southern agrarian feudalism. This victory meant that no longer would it be sufficient for people to settle on newly acquired land and develop an agricultural base. Rather, the new expansion was imperialistic in the modern sense: the American industrial system needed new markets to sell its ever-increasing industrial production and mechanized agricultural production. With the increasing accumulation of capital, new areas had to be opened for investment. Thus the *basis* for expansion changed with the development of industrialism in the United States, but expansion was a crucial part of this industrialization.

As with the expansion of agrarian capitalism, the expansion engendered by industrial capitalism was accomplished, at least until the end of World War II, with relatively little militarism. The goals of expansion of markets, export of capital, and obtaining necessary raw materials could be met without the policy of colonization as it was practiced by the European powers. Indeed, as Gareth Stedman Jones points out, there was great hostility on the part of businessmen and politicians to such a policy of colonization:

> There was opposition to territorial expansion in noncontiguous areas. It was argued that colonialism of this kind would lead to the dangers that had brought down the Roman Empire—through the necessity of large standing armies and an increasingly strong military caste. But there was no disagreement about the wisdom of informal methods of domination.[4]

The imperialistic expansion of the United States has taken place primarily in Latin America and Asia. This penetration initially took place without the development of large standing armies, although naval power was a significant factor. Certainly there were military considerations. Secretary of State Seward, while recognizing the problems of militarism, thought that it was necessary for the United States to have complete control over Alaska, Hawaii, and the Panama Canal if the United States was to dominate the Pacific.[5] Also, the Spanish-American War was an outbreak of nationalism and militarism which furthered American hegemony over the Caribbean and increased American influence in the Pacific. The primary method of economic expansion, however, was not military occupation. In South America, the United States had traditionally prevented further European encroachment through the Monroe Doctrine. Latin American countries were tied to the United States through tariff concessions, trade benefits, the exploitation of natural resources through the application of American capital, and the threat of intervention if the host country did not live up to American expectations. A classic example of

---

[3] C. Wright Mills, *The Power Elite* (New York: Oxford, 1959), p. 175.

[4] Gareth Stedman Jones, "The Specificity of U.S. Imperialism," *New Left Review*, vol. 60, March, April, 1970, p. 74.

[5] Ibid., p. 72.

such intervention was the invasion of Cuba by the United States marines in 1917 after a Cuban revolt. Among the six demands placed upon any new Cuban government was "amenability to suggestions which might be made to [the Cuban President] by the American Legation," and "a thorough acquaintance with the desires of the United States government."[6] These policies, however, did not require massive military power.

Insofar as American penetration into Asia is concerned, the United States initially followed an even less militaristic policy. Our policy is best summarized in the following quote from Jones:

> The Secretary of State in 1899 issued a demand for equal access and fair treatment for U.S. economic power in China. A further note asserted America's direct interest in maintaining the territorial and administrative integrity of that country. These Open Door notes were America's characteristic contribution to the practice of Imperialism. It was not akin to British imperial policy in the period. London's version of the policy acknowledged spheres of interest whereas the U.S. demanded abso-

lute equality of treatment. Convinced of the necessity to expand and yet wanting to avoid the pitfalls of a formal colonial empire (with the consequent necessity of war against rivals), the U.S.A. employed the strategy of the Open Door to exploit its growing economic power.[7]

World War I saw the mobilization of American military might on a scale that was unique in American history. In comparison to previous American military efforts, the American military effort in the first World War was a highly centralized activity, which can best be construed as a response to an emergency situation. This is especially true when viewed from the perspective of America's goal in the world. The United States feared Germany both as a threat to American hegemony over Latin America and as a threat to the existing imperial world order of Great Britain, France, and Japan. With the victory of the allies, the United States hoped to increase its commercial penetration of Latin America and Asia by expanding policies that it had already championed—"the open door, the freedom of the seas, the prohibition of territorial

---

[6] Ibid., p. 79.

[7] Ibid., p. 81.

United States military power has been used sparingly to maintain markets and resource bases in other countries. Threats to the economic domination of Latin America have led to military intervention (as in this photograph, taken in the Dominican Republic in 1967) and to United States involvement in revolts by Latin American military leaders against democratic governments. (Pictorial Parade/EPA)

changes except in accordance with the wishes of the inhabitants, compromises between advanced powers and underdeveloped territories that ensured the economic expansion of the former, and a political system of control which would be dominated by the United States, Great Britain, France, and Japan."[8] Thus, the war aims of the United States were consistent with a low military profile. It was anticipated that allied victory in World War I would allow the United States to gain increasing access into the already existing colonial and imperial empires while keeping Latin America as its private reserve.

Thus, throughout the periods discussed above, including World War I, the United States succeeded in expanding its markets, exporting capital, and gaining access to raw materials without the use of massive military establishments.

This whole picture changed drastically, however, after World War II. World War II witnessed the collapse of the old European colonial empires. This occurred because of the tremendous expenditure of manpower and resources by the European powers during the war and because of the increased development of anticolonial and revolutionary movements in the colonized lands of Africa and Asia. The United States found itself pitted against these revolutionary movements and supported the colonial powers— for example, France, in Indochina. These anticolonial movements had the blessing of the Soviet Union; the United States defended its position in terms of anticommunism and as the defender of democracy and freedom. The United States found itself at the end of the war occupying most of Western Europe and all of Japan. It saw itself pitted against revolutionary communism and Soviet power in Europe. The threat of communist takeovers in Europe, as well as the collapse of the colonial empires, put the United States in the position of the defender of Western capitalism. This situation made it mandatory for the United States to maintain its military posture throughout the world; it took on the role of acting as the world's policeman. The United States could no longer count on the European powers, mainly Great Britain and France, to supply the military umbrella over the colonized world in which the United States could profitably trade and invest. This meant the end of informal domination in Asia and Africa for the United States; from this point on, it has had to supply the military power itself.

A careful analysis of American military power throughout the world in the postwar period would take us too far afield. Since we are primarily concerned with the impact of the military on American institutional patterns, we will focus on another aspect of the growth in American militarism after World War II, namely, the economic ramifications of militarism in the United States. Many influential Americans considered the Great Depression to be partly the result of underconsumption and the lack of opportunities for new investment. They recognized that the Depression did not really come to an end until the enormous spending for armaments began during the early war years. During the war, they saw the American economy boom, both in terms of production and profits, as a result of military expenditures. Military production ended underconsumption and opened new opportunities for investment. There was a general fear, especially on the part of government economists, that disarmament after the war would bring about another depression. While there was a reduction in military expenditures after the war, the depression did not occur, primarily because of consumer demands stored up

[8] Ibid., p. 83.

during the war in the form of savings and because of foreign-aid programs such as the Marshall Plan which stimulated demand for American goods. Nevertheless, military expenditures never declined to prewar rates, and they did serve as a tremendous stimulus for the economy. Military spending continues to be a significant part of the American economy. Its importance is discussed by John Kenneth Galbraith:

> In the decade of the thirties, expenditures for national defense (excluding those for veterans and interest) amounted to between 10 and 15 percent of the administrative budget. In the first half of the sixties they were between 55 and 60 percent. This reflected an increase in the annual outlay from about three-quarters of a billion dollars at the beginning of the thirties and a little over a billion in 1939 to a little over $50 billion in 1965.
>
> If a large public sector of the economy, supported by personal and corporate income taxation, is the fulcrum for the regulation of demand, plainly military expenditures are the pivot on which the fulcrum rests. . . .[9]

Galbraith stresses the importance of military expenditures as a means of regulating demand in the economy. Since there is no other segment of the American economy that performs this function, the military establishment has become a dominant part of the economy. The following quotation from Coates and Pellegrin indicates the magnitude of the economic power of the United States military.

> Some idea of the role of the military establishment in the economy can be gained by taking note of the assets it has acquired. The value of military holdings is almost beyond comprehension. As of June 30, 1962, the real and personal property of the Department of Defense was given as approximately $164.8 billion. . . . This figure, fabulous as it seems, is widely regarded as underestimating by far the actual value of military assets. Much of the present holdings is not listed at current value. Some have estimated that the assets of the military establishment may total at least $200 billion.
>
> It is when we compare military assets with those of mammoth civilian enterprises that we get some perspective on the magnitude of military holdings and operations. In September, 1958, Dudley C. Sharp, Assistant Secretary of the Air Force, stated in an address that the net assets of the Air Force were in excess of $70 billion. He pointed out that the holdings of this branch of the armed forces exceeded in worth the combined value of the 55 largest industrial corporations in the United States. Included, of course, were such giant concerns as DuPont, General Motors, Standard Oil of New Jersey, U.S. Steel, and the Ford Motor Company.[10]

Gone are the days of the decentralized American military that was characteristic of nineteenth-century America. No longer are the militia and an armed citizenry the bulwark of American defense. No longer can an army be outfitted with carbines, horses, blankets, rations, and uniforms. Now the military is at the center of the American economy itself.

Before we analyze the relationship between the military establishment and the American economy any further, it is worthwhile to place the growth of American militarism in the context of America's new role as world policeman. While we have been looking primarily at the dollar amounts spent on the military, a great deal of insight can be gained by looking at the number of United States forces abroad and the location of United States military installations. This information is summarized in Table 13-1. These military forces are located in 340 installations abroad in 32 countries. Having

[9] John Kenneth Galbraith, *The New Industrial State* (New York: Signet, 1968), pp. 238–239.

[10] Coates, op. cit., pp. 85–88.

taken on the responsibility of defending Europe from the Soviet Union and maintaining the status quo in the "Third World" countries, the United States is truly a global power.

TABLE 13-1 United States Military Forces Abroad, as of September, 1969

Asia and Pacific	
Korea	56,000
Okinawa	45,000
Japan	40,000
Philippines	30,000
South Vietnam	508,000
Thailand	49,000
Nationalist China	10,000
Total	738,000
Latin America	
Panama Canal Zone, Guantanamo (Cuba), Puerto Rico	23,000
Other	1,000
Total	24,000
North America	
Canada, Greenland, Iceland	10,000
Western Europe	
West Germany	228,000
Other Nato countries	82,000
Spain	10,000
Total	320,000
Middle East and Africa	10,000
United States Fleets	
Western Pacific, Vietnam	95,000
Mediterranean	25,000
Total	120,000
Grand total	1,222,000

SOURCE: Congressional Quarterly Service, *Global Defense: U.S. Military Commitments Abroad,* Washington, 1969, p. 38.

Having looked at the magnitude of American military expenditures and the deployment of the military throughout the world, we are now in a better position to examine the unique quality of the relation of the military to the economy. A quantitative analysis of the role of the military in its function as a lever of demand in the economy and as a field for profitable investment misses the more subtle aspects of the effects of military expenditure. The special quality that makes military spending different from other types of spending is the importance of planning

and technological innovation in the production of military goods. Galbraith states this aspect of military expenditures very clearly:

[The] Department of Defense supports, as noted, the most highly developed planning in the industrial system. It provides contracts of long duration, calling for large investment of capital in areas of advanced technology. There is no risk of price fluctuations. There is full protection against any change in requirements, i.e., any change in demand. Should a contract be canceled the firm is protected on the investment it has made. For no other products can the technostructure plan with such certainty and assurance.[11]

While any type of expenditure could serve to bolster the lagging demand of advanced American capitalism, and while many kinds of expenditures could serve as a field for investment, military spending is unique in that it underwrites the development of advanced innovations in technology. The high cost and risks that would accrue even to the largest and most monopolistic firms are absent when it comes to the military establishment. Military spending has served as the bedrock of certainty in an economy that still has vestiges of competition and is still dependent on consumer markets. The importance of planning and technology in military procurements, and a great deal of the ideological support for it, can be understood in the context of the following statement:

There can be no question regarding the crucial importance of promoting military technology in the nuclear era. Any power that lags significantly behind in military technology, no matter how large its military budget or how efficiently it allocates its resources, is likely to be at the mercy of a more progressive enemy. Both weapons and systems for delivering them have gone through several revolutions in the few years since the end of the Second World

[11] Galbraith, op. cit., p. 317.

War. Individual bombs are now 1,000 times as powerful as those dropped on Hiroshima and Nagasaki. . . . Breakthroughs in missile technology are continually threatening the whole offensive or defensive apparatus of one side or the other. Keeping ahead in the technological race is not in itself a guarantee of security in these circumstances; it remains essential to incorporate the technology in operational hardware ("forces in being") and to deploy them and use them with skill and intelligence. But no amount of production, skill, and intelligent use can compensate for significant technological inferiority. . . .[12]

The vast expenditure of resources on advanced military technology are closely linked with corporate economic power in the United States. Coates and Pellegrin point out that:

Military personnel costs make up slightly over one-fourth of Department of Defense expenditures. . . . The largest single item in the budget is not salaries for personnel, but procurement (32.0 percent in 1964). In 1962, $29,255,000,000 (or 62.5 percent) of the Department of Defense budget of $46,815,000,000 were spent on military contracts, mostly with civilian organizations. Most of this money (89.4 percent) went to business firms in the United States. An additional 4.9 percent went for work outside the United States; 3.9 percent for intragovernmental purchases; and 1.7 percent to educational and nonprofit institutions.[13]

Since World War II, the Defense Department's expenditures for procurement have gone to a relatively few large corporations. G. William Domhoff points out that "between 1940 and 1944, 33 percent of the supply contracts went to the top 10 corporations, 67 percent to the top 100 corporations."[14]

A statement by Hubert Humphrey quoted by Tristram Coffin demonstrates that the situation had not changed in 1963:

Twenty-four companies accounted for 70 percent of the entire defense expenditures. Of almost 22 billion dollars in defense spending about 16 billion went to 24 companies. There were four companies each receiving over 1 billion dollars in defense sales. . . . We have transferred to some of these industrial and technological giants great power and influence over the development of weapons systems. The continued concentration of economic power and the loss of the government's decision-making power over aspects of defense policy are trends which should worry us.[15]

The above quotations bring us to a turning point in our discussion. Thus far, we have examined the historical background of the American military, its development since World War II, and its significance in the American economy. We are now in a position to examine the tremendous interdependence between the corporate structure of the United States and military spending in greater detail.

The control of the military can best be demonstrated by studying the personnel that head the major policy-making bodies of the federal government. The National Security Council, for example, is supposedly in charge of formulating military-diplomatic-intelligence policies; the actual operations of the National Security Council depend to a great extent on Presidential prerogative. It is made up of the President, Vice President, Secretaries of State and Defense, the head of the Office of Defense Mobilization, and whoever else the President wants to bring in. The Secretary of the Treasury has often been included in this group. In Chapter 12, page 278, we listed the members of the National

---

[12] Charles J. Hitch and Roland N. McKean, *The Economics of Defense in the Nuclear Age* (Cambridge, Mass.: Harvard University Press, 1967), pp. 243–244.

[13] Coates, op. cit., p. 90.

[14] G. William Domhoff, *Who Rules America?* (Englewood Cliffs, N.J.: Spectrum, 1967), p. 121.

[15] Tristram Coffin, *The Passion of the Hawks* (New York: Macmillan, 1964), p. 159.

Security Council in the Truman, Eisenhower, and Kennedy Administrations,[16] demonstrating the preponderance of corporate executives on the NSC. Domhoff has provided information on the Defense Department and on the State Department that indicates that the backgrounds of the heads of these departments is similar to those on the National Security Council.[17] That these policy and advisory bodies are made up of business leaders and upper-strata members is indicative of the power of industrial and financial interests. No one would make the claim that these men form a monolithic group that never has internal disagreements. The point that must be stressed is the apparent power they wield in policy formation that relates to the military. That these men have such important and prestigious governmental positions demonstrates the significant interlocking of corporate and governmental power.

While the predominance of top corporate officials at the highest echelons of the federal government is a dramatic example of the fusion of corporate and government interests in general, it is the tip of the iceberg as far as the relationship between corporations and the military is concerned. As the military grows, so does its need for more commodities. As the corporate sector grows, it is capable of supplying the military with ever more sophisticated armaments. With the growing complexity of military technology, the relationship between the military proper and the corporations that serve it becomes increasingly close. The military itself may plan a new weapons system, for example. The sophistication of modern weapons systems requires close and sustained interaction between the military and the firms that are producing the weapons system. Often, a

corporation with plans for a new weapon will use all its contacts in the Pentagon to win acceptance of the weapon by the military. This close interaction between the military and the corporate world has led to an increased transfer of personnel between the military and the corporations. Many former generals and admirals, along with lower-echelon officers, have taken positions in corporations. Their familiarity with military operations, as well as their connections, have enhanced the cooperation between the military services and the corporations.

In addition to these informal ties, many formal ties have developed. The growth of military associations is a prime example of this. Domhoff quotes Jack Raymond in this context:

> The special interest groups that best epitomize the military-industrial complex are the organizations of military service supporters, such as the Association of the United States Army, the Air Force Association, and the Navy League. . . . The members are active, reserve, and retired members of the Armed Forces, defense contractors, community leaders, and supporters. The organizations are financed by membership fees and sums from contractors who pay for exhibits at conventions, subscribe to various dinner meetings and rallies, and place advertisements in the official publications.[18]

The military associations are very influential lobbyists for military appropriation bills in Congress. Many congressmen refer to their publications as sources of information on new weapons. These associations are especially significant in that they represent a conscious organization of the military and the corporations, who have seen fit to work together in formal ways and for particular purposes.

[16] G. William Domhoff, *The Higher Circles: The Governing Class in America* (New York: Vintage, 1971), pp. 130–132.

[17] Domhoff, *Who Rules America?*, op. cit., p. 117

[18] Jack Raymond, *Power at the Pentagon* (New York: Harper and Row, 1964), p. 122.

We have seen that there is a convergence of corporate personnel and military personnel at every significant level of decision making and planning that involves military procurement and policy; the highest levels of policy making are dominated by upper-echelon business leaders. One should not get the impression, however, that these men crassly and openly pursue their corporate interests on these policy-making bodies. Rather, there is a marked tendency for them to equate the national interest, national security, and world peace with the goals of increased military preparedness and policies of anticommunism and containment. In seeing the United States as threatened by the Soviet Union, China, and anti-imperialist revolutions, they develop an essentially military definition of reality. Certainly this view is shared by large segments of the American population, including organized labor, which knows that military production creates jobs. At least in this regard, it is useful to keep in mind the importance of worldwide expansion for the growing American economic system. All groups who share in the benefits of this system, or who think that they are benefiting from it, will be in basic agreement with policy decisions which maintain this system.

What of the social composition of the military—the social class and ethnic, religious, and regional backgrounds of military officers? In studying these factors, it must be kept in mind that the armed services represent a relatively closed society, with its own caste system, legal system, transportation networks, life-style, and even economic organization. The military has a great deal of control over the socialization process of those who enter its ranks; their attitudes and outlooks are determined to a great extent by this socialization process and by the segregation of the military from the civilian world. With this in mind, it is still instructive to see which groups in the society have access to the high-status, better-paid, and more responsible positions in the armed services.

Morris Janowitz, a University of Chicago sociologist, has done a great deal of work on the sociology of the military and has studied in detail the social origins of military leaders. There is a wealth of information on the military in his book *The Professional Soldier: A Social and Political Portrait*. In discussing the social origins of military leaders, Janowitz states the following:

> It was assumed that, instead of a representative social background, the American military would have many of the characteristics of the business and political elite. They would be heavily recruited from native-born, Anglo-Saxon, and upper social stratum parentage. Upper social stratum would not mean the most elite business families, but rather the prosperous, the professional, and the upper middle class.[19]

With this as an introduction, Janowitz goes on to detail the social origins of the military leadership. Table 13-2 shows his findings regarding nativity.[20] It is not surprising that the military leadership is recruited overwhelmingly from native Americans; this pattern of native-born military leadership is true throughout the world. Janowitz also found

TABLE 13-2   Military Leaders, 1910–1950: Native Born versus Foreign Born

	Army, %	Navy, %	Air Force, %	Total, %
Native-born	99	97	97	98
Foreign-born	1	3	3	2
Number	295	361	105	761

[19] Morris Janowitz, *The Professional Soldier: A Social and Political Portrait* (New York: Glencoe Free Press, 1964), p. 81.
[20] Ibid., p. 82.

that there was a preponderance of leaders who had a rural background as opposed to an urban background. In 1950, 66 percent of the Army leadership and 70 percent of the Air Force leadership had a rural background.[21] It is also clear that as far as regional backgrounds are concerned, the South is generally overrepresented. In 1950, 56 percent of Army leaders and 44 percent of Navy leaders had southern origins.[22]

While place of birth and regional background of the military leadership are of interest, the most important aspect of the background of military leaders for our purposes is social stratum. Janowitz has found that while American military leaders have traditionally come from the more privileged strata, there has been an infusion of lower-middle-strata personnel into military leadership positions in recent times (see Table 13-3).[23] From Janowitz's data, it is clear that the upper stratum has become increasingly less represented in the military leadership, while the upper-middle stratum, with the exception of the Air Force, now dominates. The lower-middle stratum has made increas-

ing inroads into the military leadership, as has the upper-lower, although its percentage is still small. As for the occupational classes from which the military leadership is drawn, the business, professional, and managerial classes are most highly represented.[24] In terms of religious denominations, the vast majority of military leaders come from Protestant backgrounds, with Episcopalian and other traditionalist denominations greatly overrepresented.[25] Coates and Pellegrin point out that in 1962 black officers accounted for 3.2 percent of the officers in the Army, 0.24 percent in the Navy, 1.24 percent in the Air Force, and 0.21 percent in the Marine Corps.[26] Janowitz concludes that "the military elite has been drawn from an old-family, Anglo Saxon, Protestant, rural, upper middle-class professional background."[27]

The trend toward greater representation of lower-middle-strata and, less significantly, upper-lower-strata individuals in the military leadership is best explained by two factors. First, many of the leadership positions that have been created as a result of the growth in size of the military since World War II have not been filled, for whatever reasons, by the upper stratum. These positions have been filled by people from the lower-middle stratum. Second, as the military has become more technologically oriented, it has had to draw on people who have the requisite technological skills. The importance of education and performance on tests has become increasingly important in selecting military personnel. This has made it possible for lower-middle-strata individuals to compete for openings in the expanding military technostructure. Thus, both the growth of the military and the technological changes that

TABLE 13-3 Military Leadership, 1910–1950: Trends in Social Origin

	Army, 1910–1920, %	Army, 1935, %	Army, 1950, %	Navy, 1950, %	Air Force 1950, %
Upper	26	8	3	4	—
Upper-middle	66	68	47	57	30
Lower-middle	8	23	45	34	62
Upper-lower	0	1	4	5	8
Lower-lower	0	0	1	0	0
Number	38	49	140	162	60

[21] Ibid., p. 86.
[22] Ibid., p. 89.
[23] Ibid., p. 90.

[24] Ibid., p. 91.
[25] Ibid., p. 99.
[26] Coates, op. cit., p. 264.
[27] Janowitz, op. cit., p. 100.

have occurred in it have made it relatively more open to individuals from lower socio-economic strata.

There is another, ominous, side to the picture of white upper-middle overrepresentation in the military elite and nonwhite lower-strata underrepresentation. Albert J. Mayer and Thomas Ford Hoult did a study of social stratification and combat survival for men from Detroit, Michigan, during the Korean War. They begin their study by stating:

Casualties suffered by Detroit men during the Korean war indicate that certain aspects of American social stratification are harsh realities which can mean a matter of life and death to those involved.[28]

Mayer and Hoult used the following sampling procedure in determining the effects of social stratification on casualty rates:

First, all city census tracts were categorized in terms of median income, and then casualty rates were determined for each of the eight levels delineated. Second, a 5 percent sample of housing by blocks was utilized in determining casualty rates per 10,000 occupied dwelling units for 13 average-value-of-home categories. The sample was drawn by recording in an appropriate home value category the number of occupied dwelling units in every twentieth block in the city, beginning with block number one in tract number one as recorded in 1950 census block statistics for Detroit. The number of dwelling units appearing in each category was then multiplied by 20 to obtain an estimate of the number in each of the average-value-of-home categories.[29]

Some of their findings are tabulated in Tables 13-4 to 13-6.[30]

[28] Albert J. Mayer, and Thomas F. Hoult, "Social Stratification and Combat Survival," *Social Forces*, vol. 34, December, 1955, p. 155.
[29] Ibid., pp. 155–156.
[30] Ibid., pp. 157–158.

The data show a clear pattern. As income becomes higher, the casualty rate becomes lower. As the average value of homes increases, the casualty rate tends to decline. The casualty rate for nonwhites is almost

TABLE 13-4 Korean War Casualty Rate per 10,000 Occupied Dwelling Units, by Median Income of Census Tract, Detroit, Michigan

Median income	Casualty rate per 10,000 occupied dwelling units
Under 2,500	14.6
2,500–2,999	10.8
3,000–3,499	9.1
3,500–3,999	8.6
4,000–4,499	7.5
4,500–4,999	6.6
5,000–5,499	5.8
5,500 and over	4.6

TABLE 13-5 Korean War Casualty Rate per 10,000 Occupied Dwelling Units, by Average Value of Home, Detroit, Michigan

Economic level as given by average value of home	Rate per 10,000 occupied dwelling units
Under 4,000	16.4
4,000–4,999	15.5
5,000–5,999	13.1
6,000–6,999	15.1
7,000–7,999	9.2
8,000–8,999	5.3
9,000–9,999	5.3
10,000–10,999	5.4
11,000–11,999	7.2
12,000–12,999	5.7
13,000–13,999	6.1
14,000–14,999	6.7
15,000 and over	4.3
Total rate	8.4

TABLE 13-6 Korean War Casualty Rate per 10,000 Occupied Dwelling Units, by Value of Home and Race, Detroit, Michigan

| Value of home | Rates by race and by value of home | | |
	White rates by value of home	Nonwhite rates by value of home	Total rates by value of home
Under 8,000	11.5	16.8	12.4
8,000–14,999	5.4	7.7	5.6
15,000 and over	4.3	—	4.3
Total rate	7.7	13.3	8.4

twice as high as the rate for whites; even in economically comparable areas, the casualty rate of nonwhites is markedly higher than that for whites. The study by Mayer and Hoult demonstrates that social stratification was highly significant in determining the fate of members of the military during the Korean War. In general, we can say the upper strata tend to become military leaders while the lower strata serve as cannon fodder.

We are now in a position to take a brief look at new developments in the military which are a result of the Vietnam war and the protest movement of the sixties. The Vietnam war, which grew out of America's support of the French effort to prevent a revolution in Vietnam, has been a unique episode in American history. The United States became directly involved in the hostilities in Vietnam after the French terminated their own counterrevolutionary efforts. American participation in the war has been long, costly in both lives and resources, ill-defined insofar as pronounced goals, and unsuccessful. The war engendered a mass antiwar movement that Charles C. Moskos, Jr., has characterized as follows:

It is fair to assert that the original opposition to the war in Vietnam began with this country's intellectual and academic community. The

antiwar movement has since come to encompass a diverse constituency including, variously, college students, some Establishment spokesmen, black militants, eminent professionals, and suburban housewives. Moreover, as the opposition to the specifics of the war increased, the very legitimacy of military service has itself been impugned. Intellectuals and student radicals, in particular, have vociferously turned upon the military on a number of fronts. Illustrative of this passion are the harassment of military recruiters on campuses, the efforts to remove the ROTC from college curriculum, and the frontal challenge of the ties between major universities and military research. More broadly, the entire framework of America's military policies has come under critical scrutiny.[31]

The antiwar movement must be placed in the context of American military history. The emergence of a powerful military establishment and permanent, large, standing armies during peacetime dates back only to the end of World War II. The Vietnam war, as an expression of this newly established military structure, has caused many Americans to question the very basis of that structure; the antiwar movement has ushered in a reexamination of the military establishment. Several legislators, such as Senator George McGovern, have pointed out that while resources have been lavished on the military, American cities have progressively decayed, poverty has continued for masses of the American population, the environment has deteriorated, and the system of medical care has reached a state of crisis. The population of the United States has become increasingly polarized. Antiwar spokesmen have criticized not just the war in Vietnam but the entire post-World War II military establishment. Senator Mansfield has introduced leg-

[31] Charles C. Moskos, Jr., *The American Enlisted Man: The Rank and File in Today's Military* (New York: Russell Sage Foundation, 1970), pp. 178–179.

islation in the Senate that will greatly reduce the American military presence in Europe.

Internally, the armed services have not been immune to the effects of the Vietnam war. Moskos points to the following examples of this development:

At one level, activities directed toward military personnel entailed distribution of antiwar pamphlets to servicemen, and setting up coffee houses near military installations where off-duty servicemen could be engaged in political conversation. The movement against the war in Vietnam also brought forth a whole genre of protest newspapers—the "GI underground" press aimed at the enlisted ranks of the military. At least forty such newspapers have been surreptitiously published on or near military posts, one apparently from within the confines of the Pentagon itself. Steps were taken in 1969 to establish a "GI Press Service" to service these newspapers.

More significant, there were direct efforts to organize GIs within the military organization itself. The most notable of such activities is the Trotskyist-influenced American Servicemen's Union (ASU) founded in 1967. Headed by former Private Andrew Strapp, the ASU program includes the election of officers by enlisted men, collective bargaining for servicemen, and the right to refuse illegal and immoral orders—such as fighting in Vietnam. The ASU regularly publishes a well-edited newspaper, *The Bond*, which though grossly overstating the level of internal military strife, nevertheless reports incidents that rarely see print in the standard press. In 1969 the ASU claimed an enlisted membership of 5,000 with representation on all major military posts.[32]

It is clear that antiwar sentiments have directly affected the military. In addition to activities within the United States, there is an active movement in western Europe that has distributed literature and made attempts to encourage servicemen to desert; they go

so far as to assist deserters.[33] Moskos states that

By early 1969 American deserters in foreign countries numbered about 800, the principle sanctuary being Sweden. . . . The desertion figures for the Vietnam period, however, must be put into perspective. The 1967–1968 desertion rates in the armed forces were less than those of the World War II years and only slightly higher than during the Korean conflict.[34]

The civil rights movement and other more militant black liberation movements have also had a significant effect on the military. While Moskos points out that the majority of blacks in the armed services think that conditions in the military compare favorably to conditions in civilian life, he points out that incidents with racial overtones have been increasing in recent years. He gives two examples of such racial flare-ups:

Two of the most dramatic occurred in the summer of 1968. Over 250 black prisoners took part in a race riot in the Long Binh stockade outside of Saigon. The stockade was not brought under complete military control for close to a month. At about the same time in the United States, 43 black soldiers at Fort Hood, Texas, refused to leave as part of the force assigned to guard the Democratic Convention. The soldiers feared that they might be used to combat Chicago blacks. That black soldiers may find that they owe higher fealty to the black community than to the United States Army is a possibility that haunts commanders.[35]

There have been many racial incidents at Army bases in Germany, and the Army has had to send trouble-shooters to Army installations to try to resolve these difficulties

---

[32] Ibid., pp. 157–158.

[33] Ibid., p. 159.
[34] Ibid., p. 160.
[35] Ibid., p. 128.

by increasing understanding between black and white servicemen. An example of this racial tension was reported in the *Los Angeles Times* on November 21, 1971.

> Trouble had been brewing for months and came to a head in a pitched battle in the mess hall July 18.
>
> A black, Pvt. Lareon Dixon, of Oklahoma City, was arrested on suspicion of inciting the brawl. The next day, there was a protest demonstration which ended with 53 men refusing a direct order from Lt. Col. David W. Partin, 39, the commanding officer, to break it up.
>
> The facts that charges against Dixon were later dropped for lack of evidence and that a white soldier was arrested and convicted are of little importance now. What will be remembered about the case is that 29 of 53 refused to take company punishment and chose courts-martial.[36]

This incident, which began in Darmstadt, Germany, grew to involve the ACLU and the NAACP. Washington intervened in the case and ultimately it was General Michael S. Davison, the Army's commander in Europe, who finally lifted the charges against the group. The *Times* reporter points out that while "rap" sessions which were instituted to relieve racial animosity at Darmstadt may have kept tensions down, they also disrupted the usual structure of officer leadership and may have helped to pave the way for the solidarity of the "Darmstadt 53." In any event, it is clear that racial problems are seriously threatening the established military organization.

SUMMARY

Before World War II the American military establishment was relatively weak and de-

centralized. (World War I is best viewed as a strong response to an emergency situation.) United States expansion across the North American continent and, when the economy became more fully industrialized, American penetration into foreign markets in order to sell products, gain access to raw materials, and invest capital was accomplished using some military power but depended, for the most part, on the established colonial empires of the European powers. The United States wanted the economic benefits of imperialism without the disadvantages inherent in possessing a large colonial empire.

This situation changed drastically after World War II. With the demise of the west European colonial empires, the threat of Soviet power, the spread of world revolution throughout less-developed nations, and the ascendancy of American military power, the United States took on the responsibilities of checking Soviet power, defending western Europe, and preventing socialist or anti-American revolution. This means that American military power would henceforth have to be maintained at a high level throughout the world.

Along with its direct military functions, the military establishment has taken on a central role in the American economy. It has become a regulator of demand, as well as a prime source of profitable investment in technologically sophisticated equipment. Throughout this development, there has been an increasingly strong interaction among military leaders, high-level corporate executives, and government officials. Often, the same individual shifts from one role in the military-industrial complex to another. Thus, not only is the military at the heart of the economy but, as a result, is also tightly bound to the American power structure and to the maintenance of imperialism and world industrialization.

[36] Joe Alex Morris, Jr., "U.S. Army in Germany: Vexing Racial Picture," *Los Angeles Times*, vol. XC, Nov. 21, 1971, section G, p. 1.

SUGGESTED READINGS

Charles H. Coates, and Roland J. Pellegrin, *Military Sociology: A Study of American Military Institutions and Military Life* (University Park, Md.: The Social Science Press, 1965).

Tristram Coffin, *The Passion of the Hawks: Militarism in Modern America* (New York: The Macmillan Company, 1964).

Congressional Quarterly Service, *Global Defense: U.S. Military Commitments Abroad*, September, 1969, Washington, D.C.

G. William Domhoff, *The Higher Circles: The Governing Class in America* (New York, Vintage Books, Random House, 1971).

————, *Who Rules America?* (Englewood Cliffs, N.J.: A Spectrum Book, Prentice-Hall, Inc., 1967).

John Kenneth Galbraith, *The New Industrial State* (New York: A Signet Book, The New American Library, Inc., 1968).

Charles J. Hitch, and Roland N. McKean, *The Economics of Defense in the Nuclear Age* (Cambridge: Harvard University Press, 1967).

Morris Janowitz, *The Professional Soldier: A Social and Political Portrait* (New York: The Free Press of Glencoe, 1964).

Gareth Stedman Jones, "The Specificity of U.S. Imperialism," *New Left Review*, 60 (March, April, 1970), pp. 59–86.

Albert J. Mayer, and Thomas F. Hoult, "Social Stratification and Combat Survival," *Social Forces*, 34 (December, 1955), pp. 155–159.

C. Wright Mills, *The Power Elite* (New York: Oxford University Press, 1959).

Joe Alex Morris, Jr., "U.S. Army in Germany: Vexing Racial Picture," *Los Angeles Times*, vol. XC (November 21, 1971), Section G, pp. 1–3.

Charles C. Moskos, Jr., *The American Enlisted Man: The Rank and File in Today's Military* (New York: Russell Sage Foundation, 1970).

FOURTEEN
Imperialism and Industrialization

From the thirteenth to the sixteenth centuries, the bourgeois revolution was slowly taking place in Europe. The first signs of a new set of economic, political, and social relations began quietly with the emergence of trading and commerce between nations. Italy, Spain, and Portugal were at the center of this emergent form as they captured the monopoly of trade and commerce.

By the fifteenth and sixteenth centuries what began as trade and commerce among a small class of entrepreneurs had altered the class structure of most European societies to such an extent that feudalism had been replaced by capitalism. Most European nations were locked in competition with one another for the control and exploitation of new resources and markets. Spain established the pattern of control over foreign countries with its conquest of the native Americans in what is now Latin America. England pri-

marily, but also France, Germany, Portugal, Belgium, the Netherlands, and other European nations, conquered, colonized, and exploited both the natural and human resources of North America, much of Asia and Oceania, and virtually all of the vast continent of Africa. Through this process, which depended heavily on maintaining a powerful naval fleet, a minority representing roughly 30 percent of the world's population came to comprise a *metropolis* which dominated the economic, political, and social life of the remainder of the world, which thus became an exploited, largely powerless, *satellite* containing the majority (approximately 70 percent) of the world's people.[1]

[1] This distinction was elaborated by both Adam Smith, *The Wealth of Nations*, and Karl Marx, *Capital*, volumes 1 to 3. More recently it has been elaborated by Paul Baran, *The Political Economy of Growth*, and by Andre Gunder-Frank, *Capitalism and Underdevelopment of Latin America* (New York: Monthly Review, 1967).

BEGINNINGS OF THE INDUSTRIAL REVOLUTION

Gradually commerce and trade were supplemented in Europe by the emergence of manufacturing. No longer were people bound to the land and to the certainty that they would be able to achieve no better material life than their grandfathers. Entrepreneurs—freed from the intellectual shackles of caste customs and encouraged by growing numbers of men available to work in towns —envisioned harnessing labor to new machinery on a scale never before imagined. By the eighteenth century the industrial revolution was well under way. A critical ingredient in the success of this revolution was the exploitation and use of natural resources from the satellite areas of the world. As the industrial nations in the metropolis of Europe produced more and more goods from their industrial processes, the satellite nations served increasingly as a market.

To protect "their" resources and markets, the European metropolis frequently found it necessary to fight battles and even wars against groups in the metropolis or against one another. One example is the "opium wars" in which England forced China to permit England to sell opium in China. The opium was raised in India and had been introduced to China by the East India Company as a commodity which could be traded for Chinese silks, pottery, and other products which could then be profitably marketed in Europe. The Chinese monarchy opposed the trading in opium, both because its introduction reduced revenues in English currency, on which the Chinese government had become dependent, and because some Chinese leaders felt that opium was harmful to the people. England successfully fought against the Chinese and forced the government to allow British merchants to distribute opium in China, where its use became widespread

and was not curtailed until the Communist revolution in 1948.

In *The Wealth of Nations*, Adam Smith accurately anticipated the following consequence of uneven industrial development.

> A trading and manufacturing country naturally purchases with a small part of its manufactured produce a great part of the crude produce of other countries: while, on the contrary, a country without trade and manufacturers is generally obliged to purchase, at the expense of a great part of its crude produce, a very small part of the manufactured produce of other countries. . . . [T]he inhabitants of the one must always enjoy a much greater quantity of subsistence than what their own lands could afford. The inhabitants of the other must enjoy a smaller quantity.[2]

[2] Adam Smith, *The Wealth of Nations.*

Oil prospecting in Libya. The benefits from whatever oil was found went largely to European and American petroleum corporations, their consumers, and the wealthy elite in Libya. (Pictorial Parade/EPA)

It is a conservative guess that at one time over 80 percent of the world's total available resources were being used principally for the benefit of less than 20 percent of the world's population. In 1970 around 75 percent of the resources were being used for 20 percent of the population. Whatever the truth—and, of course, specific estimates are at best only educated guesses—the important point is that the industrial process has concentrated the wealth of the world in the hands of a few nations. The economist Andre Gunder-Frank summarized this process as follows.

[I]t is this exploitative relation which in chainlike fashion extends the capitalist link between the capitalist world and national metropolises to the regional centers (part of whose surplus they appropriate), and from these to local centers, and so on to large landowners or merchants who expropriate surplus from small peasants as tenants, and sometimes even from these latter to landless laborers exploited by them in turn. At each step along the way the relatively few capitalists above exercise monopoly power over the many below, expropriating some or all of their economic surplus and to the extent that they are not expropriated in turn by the still fewer above them, appropriating it for their own use. Thus, at each point, the international, national and local capitalist system generates economic development for the few and underdevelopment for the many.[3]

The form of domination of the nonindustrialized countries varies considerably.[4] The most blatant domination occurred when the industrialized nations of Europe colonized vast territories of the world, first by the conquest or seizure of land followed by the transfer of large populations from the industrialized nations to the nonindustrialized territories. England, France, and Spain followed this procedure in bringing North and South America into the orbit of European trade, as did England in East and South Africa.[5] In the second form of expansion, administrative colonialism, or what is sometimes called *indirect rule*, the colonizing nation provides a small contingency of their own nationals who, through coercion, bribery, and propaganda, recruit people from the existing populations to administer the colony for the benefit of the colonizing nation.[6] England pursued this policy in India, Nigeria, and most of West Africa. Later, the United States followed this pattern to establish domination over Cuba, Guatemala, the Philippines, Liberia, Nicaragua, and, more recently, Okinawa, South Korea, and South Vietnam.

The last of the expansionist policies that effectively establishes and maintains the metropolis-satellite relationship is *the imperialism of free trade*. Bringing a nonindustrialized nation into a trade relationship with an industrialized nation inevitably produces domination of the nonindustrialized by the industrialized. Even without resorting to force, the rich nation can exploit the poorer one. "Free trade," lacking any morality other than attempting to ensure that people live up to their contracts, places no real limits on this exploitation. Indeed, racist beliefs about the inherent inferiority of exploited peoples have encouraged exploiters to be unusually frank in expressing the "rightness" of their exploitations.

In 1974 the United States exerted its power to maintain economic and political control over less-developed nations. (See Selection 14-1.) The degree to which the United States government and American business interests

[3] Andre Gunder-Frank, op. cit., pp. 7–8.
[4] William Appelman Williams, *The Great Evasion*, part I (Chicago: Quadrangle, 1964).

[5] Robert B. Seidman, *Law and Development*, University of Wisconsin, mimeographed, 1971.
[6] Michael Crowder, *The Story of Nigeria* (Ibadan, Nigeria: University of Ibadan Press, 1968).

C.I.A. CHIEF TELLS HOUSE OF $8-MILLION CAMPAIGN AGAINST ALLENDE IN '70–73

By Seymour M. Hersh

Washington—The director of the Central Intelligence Agency has told Congress that the Nixon Administration authorized more than $8-million for covert activities by the agency in Chile between 1970 and 1973 to make it impossible for President Salvador Allende Gossens to govern.

The goal of the clandestine C.I.A. activities, the director, William E. Colby, testified at a top-secret hearing last April, was to "destabilize" the Marxist Government of President Allende, who was elected in 1970.

The Allende Government was overthrown in a violent coup d'état last Sept. 11 in which the President died. The military junta that seized power say he committed suicide but his supporters maintain that he was slain by the soldiers who attacked the presidential palace in Santiago.

Intervention in '64

In his House testimony, Mr. Colby also disclosed that the Central Intelligence Agency first intervened against Dr. Allende in 1964, when he was a presidential candidate running against Eduardo Frei Montalva of the Christian Democratic party, which had the support of the United States.

The agency's operations, Mr. Colby testified, were considered a test of the technique of using heavy cash payments to bring down a government viewed as antagonistic toward the United States. However, there have been many allegations that the C.I.A. was involved in similar activities in other countries before the election of Dr. Allende.

Mr. Colby also maintained that all of the agency's operations against the Allende Government were approved in advance by the 40 Committee in Washington, a secret high-level intelligence panel headed by Secretary of State Kissinger. The 40 Committee was set up by

President Kennedy in an attempt to provide Administration control over C.I.A. activities after Cuban exiles trained and equipped by the agency failed in their invasion of Cuba in 1961.

A Special Hearing

Details of the agency's involvement in Chile were first provided by Mr. Colby to the House Armed Services Subcommittee of Intelligence, headed by Representative Lucien N. Nedzi, Democrat of Michigan, at a special one-day hearing last April 22. The testimony was later made available to Representative Michael J. Harrington, a liberal Massachusetts Democrat who has long been a critic of the C.I.A. Harrington wrote other members of Congress six weeks ago to protest both the agency's clandestine activities and the failure of the Nixon Administration to acknowledge them despite repeated inquiries from Congress. A copy of a confidential seven-page letter sent by Mr. Harrington to Representative Thomas E. Morgan, chairman of the House Foreign Affairs Committee, was made available to The New York Times.

The testimony of Mr. Colby indicates that high officials in the State Department and White House repeatedly and deliberately misled the public and the Congress about the extent of United States involvement in the internal affairs of Chile during the three-year government of Dr. Allende.

Shortly after Dr. Allende won a plurality in the presidential elections in September, 1970, high Chilean officials told newsmen, as a dispatch in The New York Times reported then, that the "United States lacks political, economic or military leverage to change the course of events in Chile, even if the Administration wished to do so."

However, Mr. Colby testified that $500,000 was secretly authorized by the 40 Committee in 1970 to help the anti-Allende forces. Another $500,000 had been provided to the same forces in 1969, Mr. Colby said.

Bribe Attempt Reported

Mr. Allende's victory was ratified by the Chilean Congress in October, 1970, and the State Department later declared that the Administration had "firmly rejected" any attempt to block his inauguration.

But Mr. Colby testified that $350,000 had been authorized by the 40 Committee in an unsuccessful effort to bribe members of the Chilean Congress. The bribe was part of a much more complicated scheme intended to overturn the results of the election, Mr. Colby testified, but the over-all plan, although initially approved by the 40 Committee, was later rejected as unworkable.

While the Central Intelligence Agency was conducting these clandestine operations, there were reductions in United States foreign-aid grants to Chile in development bank loans and in lines of credit from American commercial banks. Commodity credits for vitally needed grain purchases also were restricted.

United States officials have declared that there was no over-all Administration program designed to limit economic aid to the Allende Government, but critics have noted that large-scale loans and aid are now going to Chile.

President Allende repeatedly complained about what he told the United Nations in December, 1972, was "large-scale external pressure to cut us off from the world, to strangle our economy and paralyze trade and to deprive us of access to sources of international financing."

Colby Declines Comment

Mr. Colby acknowledged in a brief telephone conversation this week that he had testified before the Nedzi intelligence subcommittee about the C.I.A.'s involvement in Chile, but he refused to comment on the Harrington letter.

Mr. Nedzi, contacted in Munich, West Germany, where he is on an inspection trip with other members of the House Armed Services Committee, also declined to comment.

Mr. Harrington noted in his letter that he had been permitted to read the 48-page transcript of Mr. Colby's testimony two times, apparently without taking notes. "My memory must serve here as the only source for the substance of the testimony," he wrote.

A number of high-ranking Government officials subsequently confirmed the details of the C.I.A.'s involvement as summarized by the Massachusetts Representative, a liberal who has long been a critic of the agency's policies.

Companies' Help Rejected

In 1964, Mr. Colby testified, some American corporations in Chile volunteered to serve as conduits for anti-Allende funds, but the proposal was rejected. A similar proposal in 1970 led to a widely publicized Senate hearing last year.

The C.I.A. director also said that after Dr. Allende's election, $5-million was authorized by the 40 Committee for more "destabilization" efforts in 1971, 1972 and 1973. An additional $1.5-million was provided to aid anti-Allende candidates in municipal elections last year.

Some of these funds, Mr. Colby testified, were provided to an unidentified influential anti-Allende newspaper in Santiago.

In his summary of the Colby testimony, Mr. Harrington noted that "funding was provided to individuals, political parties, and media outlets in Chile, through channels in other countries in both Latin America and Europe."

"Mr. Colby's description of these operations was direct, though not to the point of identifying actual contacts and conduits," Mr. Harrington added.

One fully informed official, told of The New York Times's intention to publish an account of the clandestine C.I.A. activities in Chile, declared, "This thing calls for balanced reporting to put the blame where it should be laid."

"The agency didn't do anything without the knowledge and consent of the 40 committee," he said, pointedly adding that the committee was headed by Mr. Kissinger, who was then serving as President Richard M. Nixon's National Security Adviser.

Secrecy Called Necessary

Another Government official similarly defended the C.I.A.'s role in funneling funds into Chile and the agency's subsequent denials of any such activities. "You have a straight out policy that the United States conducts covert action on an officially authorized basis," he said. "If you do such things, obviously you're not going to say anything about it."

"On this kind of covert action," the official added, "it's up to those asked to do it to do it secretly."

Mr. Kissinger, although fully informed of

The Times's account through an aide, did not respond.

A number of officials whose information about such activities has been accurate in the past declared in interviews this week that there was a sharp split between some State Department officials and Mr. Kissinger over the 40 Committee's Chile policy.

Kissinger's Comment

In his only public comment on the Allende coup, Mr. Kissinger told the Senate Foreign Relations Committee last year: "The C.I.A. had nothing to do with the coup, to the best of my knowledge and belief, and I only put in that qualification in case some madman appears down there who without instructions talked to somebody. I have absolutely no reason to suppose it."

In his July 18, 1974, letter to Representative Morgan, Mr. Harrington quoted Mr. Colby as testifying that the 40 Committee authorized an expenditure of $1-million for "further political destabilization" activities in August, 1973, one month before the military junta seized control in Santiago.

"The full plan authorized in August was called off when the military coup occurred less than one month later," Mr. Harrington wrote. He added, however that Mr. Colby had testified that $34,000 of the funds had been spent—including a payment of $25,000 to one person to buy a radio station.

A specific request earlier in the summer of 1973 for $50,000 to support a nationwide truckers' strike that was crippling the Chilean Government was turned down by the 40 Committee, Mr. Harrington further quoted Mr. Colby as testifying.

A Difference of Opinion

"In the period before the coup," one official said, "there was a pretty firm view on the part of the 40 Committee—which is Kissinger and nobody else—that the Allende Government was bound to come to destruction and had to be thoroughly discredited."

"The State Department supported this, but in a different way," the official recalled. "It wanted to stretch out any clandestine activities to permit the regime to come to a political end.

"The argument was between those who wanted to use force and end it quickly rather than to play it out. Henry was on the side of the former—he was for considerable obstruction."

All of the officials interviewed emphasized that the Central Intelligence Agency was not authorized to play any direct role in the coup that overthrew Dr. Allende. It was also noted that most of the subsequent denials of agency involvement in the internal affairs of Chile were made in the context of a direct United States role in the overthrow.

"On most of those you have to look at the language very carefully," one official said of the denials.

Shortly after President Allende's overthrow there were unconfirmed reports that the trucker's strike, which was a key element in the social chaos that preceded the coup, had been financed, at least in part, by the C.I.A.

At a closed hearing on Chile before a House Foreign Affairs subcommittee last October, Mr. Colby refused to rule out the possibility that some anti-Allende demonstrations in Chile may have been assisted through subsidiaries of United States corporations in Brazil or other Latin-American countries.

He was sharply questioned about that possibility by Mr. Harrington, who emerged during Congressional debate as a leading critic of the Administration's Chilean policies.

Representative Harrington, reached yesterday at his Massachusetts office, refused to discuss his letter to Mr. Morgan, which he termed confidential. Nor would he discuss other aspects of the possible American involvement in the fall of President Allende.

In his letter, Mr. Harrington complained about the "inherent limitations facing members of Congress in uncovering the facts of covert activities such as those in Chile."

He also expressed dismay that the Administration had authorized the covert expenditure of $1-million in August, 1973, "without any apparent deterrent being posed by the recently completed hearings into I.T.T. [International Telephone & Telegraph] involvement in Chile and the Senate Watergate committee's disclosure of C.I.A. activities related to Watergate."

A Senate Foreign Relations subcommittee concluded hearings last April into what I.T.T. officials acknowledged was an attempt to contribute $1-million to the United States Government for use by the Central Intelligence Agency to create economic chaos in Chile. Testimony showed that the offer was rejected after discussions that apparently involved Mr. Kissinger and Richard M. Helms, then director of the agency.

A number of high State Department officials testified under oath at those hearings that the United States was not making any attempts to interfere with Chile's internal politics.

Edward M. Korry, former Ambassador to Chile, declared: "The United States did not seek to pressure, subvert, influence a single member of the Chilean Congress at any time in the entire four years of my stay. No hard line toward Chile was carried out at any time."

Charles A. Meyer, former Assistant Secretary of State for Latin-American Affairs, similarly testified that the United States scrupulously adhered to a policy of nonintervention. "We bought no votes, we funded no candidates, we promoted no coups," he said.

Senator Frank Church, Democrat of Idaho, who is chairman of the Subcommittee on Multinational Corporations, could not be reached for comment. The subcommittee's chief counsel, Jerome I. Levinson, expressed anger today on hearing of Mr. Colby's testimony. "For me," he said, "the fundamental issue now is who makes foreign policy in a democracy and by what standards and by what criteria?"

Mr. Levinson said that the subcommittee had been "deliberately deceived" during its public hearings last year.

In his letter to Mr. Morgan, Mr. Harrington said that he had turned to the Foreign Affairs Committee chairman "as a last resort, having despaired of the likelihood of anything productive occurring as a result of the avenues I have already pursued."

Mr. Harrington noted that the subcommittee on Inter-American Affairs had held five hearings on human rights in Chile since the junta came to power, with testimony from only one State Department witness with full knowledge of the clandestine C.I.A. activity.

And that witness, Harry W. Shlaudeman, a Deputy Assistant Secretary of State for Inter-American Affairs, refused to testify about agency activities, Mr. Harrington wrote.

He urged Mr. Morgan to call for a full-scale public investigation of the Nixon Administration's involvement in Chile. Mr. Morgan could not be reached for comment, nor could it be learned whether he had responded to Mr. Harrington's letter.

The Foreign Affairs Committee will begin sessions next week on the Administration's foreign military-aid requests, committee aides said. Amendments have been offered calling for the halving and for the complete elimination of the Administration's request for more than $20-million in military aid and training for Chile.

can maintain control over another country is illustrated by what happened in Chile after Salvador Allende was elected President of that country.

Allende ran for office as a Marxist-Socialist who opposed the domination of the Chilean economy by large American corporations, such as International Telephone and Telegraph, copper-mining operations, and oil companies. Shortly after his election to the Presidency, Allende began to fulfill his campaign promises by nationalizing many of the leading industries, including the copper mines which the United States depended on for large amounts of its copper resources.

On the eve of Allende's election, the presi-

dent of I.T.T. (International Telephone and Telegraph) contacted the United States Central Intelligence Agency (C.I.A.) and offered to provide a million dollars for clandestine operations aimed at overthrowing Allende's duly elected government. Although the offer was turned down, a much more thorough campaign backed by government funds was inaugurated.

As head of a special advisory group that gave directions to the C.I.A., Henry Kissinger, who was at this time a special adviser to President Richard Nixon, directed the C.I.A. to spend $8 million in an effort to undermine and ultimately overthrow Allende's regime. The $8 million was in effect the equivalent of $40 million since the deal was transacted on the black market. The influx of such a huge sum of money was bound to have dire consequences for the recently established Chilean government. The money was used to pay off members of middle-class labor unions to strike and boycott the government and to pay newspapers and political opponents of Allende.

These payments were made in accordance with the directives of Washington's 40 Committee. Supposedly the watchdog of C.I.A. activities, this committee is composed of five members headed by Henry Kissinger, former Harvard professor and Nobel Peace Prize winner. It was Kissinger who directed the payment of these monies that undoubtedly contributed to the right-wing military coup which forcefully overthrew Allende's elected government.

When Kissinger was questioned about the justification for intervening in Chile's internal affairs, he claimed it was the right thing to do because Chile would have become a "one-party state." The implication was that the United States got involved in order to protect a democratic government, but the United States is concerned whenever a foreign government's policies are inimical to the economic interests of American business. The one-party state under a military dictatorship which replaced Allende and invited American business back to Chile has not had to suffer, as Allende did, from covert antigovernment tactics.

Indeed, one could well argue that American foreign policy and intelligence activities have clearly favored dictatorships such as those in Spain, Haiti, Greece, and South Vietnam as long as the regimes made the countries safe for American business interests.

Today, use of foreign "aid," capital investment, loans, and, of course, war (or "police actions") provide the major means of continued domination and exploitation of nonindustrialized nations. The capital that flows from the industrialized nations carries with it strings and conditions that eventually produce more capital *outflow* back to the industrialized nations than there is capital coming in. Pierre Jallee, in his study of capital flows between the underdeveloped and developed countries, calculated that the total drain on the underdeveloped countries by the developed capitalist countries came to 12 billion dollars in the one-year period of 1964 to 1965, that is, 1.5 times the total volume of aid. This figure does not include the enormous value which is added to irreplaceable raw materials in industrial processing, a potential source of wealth forever lost to the underdeveloped countries when their resources are exported to developed nations.[7] The "energy crisis" has forced a look into the details of United States corporate involvement in exploitation of resources overseas, particularly petroleum. There is mounting evidence of collusion between supposedly competing companies (with the U.S. Department of Justice a knowledgeable bystander) to fix prices they pay for crude oil, exhaust oil fields as rapidly as possible, and engage in wasteful but speedy types of petroleum production. This process which favors multinational corporate giants in turn increases the degree of monopoly in domestic oil production, refining, and marketing. Monopoly in turn makes possible the creation of "shortages" and, ultimately, higher (noncompetitive) prices to consumers, as described in Selection 14-2.

The prevailing mythology about the relationship between industrialized and nonindustrialized societies is, of course, quite different from what we have described. The industrialized nations claim that they are

[7] *The Third World in World Economy,* Modern Reader, 1969, p. 117.

SELECTION 14-2: Analysis of effects of corporate power on gasoline supplies.

FTC REPORT FUEL SHORTAGE

G. DAVID WALLACE

Washington—The petroleum shortage is the product of anticompetitive practices fostered by government regulations and manipulated by the major oil companies to protect their profits, a study by the staff of the Federal Trade Commission says.

"In the many levels in which they interrelate, the major oil companies demonstrate a clear preference for avoiding competition through mutual cooperation and the use of exclusionary practices," the study said.

The oil companies "have behaved in a similar fashion as would a classical monopolist: they have attempted to increase profits by restricting output."

The only effective competition to survive has come from independent gasoline stations, said the study, although it estimated that 1200 independent stations closed in the first five months of this year.

"What has happened here is that the majors have used the shortage as an occasion to attempt to debilitate, if not eradicate, the independent marketing sector."

If the majors' attempt "is at all successful in diminishing the market shares of independents, the consumer will pay dearly," the study said.

The study is the result of nearly two years of work. The staff obtained answers to detailed questionnaires on relationships between the majors and independents. Attorneys and economists searched the files of more than 50 unidentified cooperating companies. Federal and state regulators provided data. Executives of major oil companies have been called before nonpublic hearings.

The study was intensified at the request of Congress and presented to the five-member commission last Monday. The commission has not taken any action nor made the document public, but the Associated Press obtained a copy from sources outside the FTC.

Also under study by the commissioners is a still-unreleased legal analysis of possible ac-

tions aimed at spurring competition in the industry.

Industry sources have said the analysis recommends a concerted, antitrust attack on the biggest companies, control over pipelines, refining operations and marketing.

The report noted that Arco, Exxon, Gulf, Mobil, Texaco, Shell, Standard Oil Co. of California and Standard Oil Co. of Indiana—the "Big Eight"—as of 1970 held 64 percent of the nation's proved crude oil reserves, accounted for 58 percent of the crude refining capacity and sold 55 percent of the gasoline.

"The petroleum refining industry is the pivotal point in the petroleum industry," the study said.

A shortage of refining capacity has been cited as the root cause of present fuel shortages. The FTC staff argued that the refinery level is where industry cooperation and government policies have granted the most power to the 18 major companies.

Even the recent lifting of import quotas by President Nixon won't be likely to attract refinery competition, the study said. "Just as the federal government first restricted imports and then removed them, they may be restored at a moment's notice."

The study also cited a system called prorationing used by the states of Texas, Louisiana, Oklahoma, New Mexico and Kansas to regulate production.

"Prorationing has been exploited by the majors to raise crude prices above their competitive level and results in a major misallocation of the economy's resources."

Cooperation

There are independent refiners, but most are located inland, making it difficult to obtain foreign crude oil. And many cannot process high-sulphur imported oil.

The staff found that during the period of the most intensive study, 1967 through 1971, the independent refiners had little trouble getting supplies, turning to the majors for half of their crude oil.

But the independents have been running far below capacity during the current shortages because they haven't been able to get crude oil.

Here, the staff said, the independents bump into several phases of cooperation among the majors: cooperation in joint bidding on leases and crude purchases from independent drillers, cooperation in pipeline operations and cooperation in crude exchanges.

The exclusion of independent refiners from crude supplies has been crucial to the plight of the independent gasoline stations, the staff said, since 90 percent of the gasoline from independent refiners went to the cut-rate retailers in 1971.

Imposed Shortages

"The data clearly indicate that the eight largest firms have dealt only nominally with independent marketers. Several have testified in investigative hearings they will not sell to independents, regardless of price."

The study also noted that although the Big Eight wouldn't sell to the independents, smaller integrated producers provided the independents with 46 percent of their gasoline in the period 1967 through 1971.

"Therefore, although the eight largest majors do not sell to independent marketers, they can impose shortages upon independent sellers by reducing sales to smaller majors."

The FTC said the independents have apparently been able to offer cheap prices by cutting out frills like credit cards and mechanics and concentrating on pumping gasoline.

"Cartel"

The majors are starting to change their marketing strategy to intimidate independents, said the study, closing large numbers of unprofitable stations and opening off-brand discount operations.

"The industry operates much like a cartel with 15 to 20 integrated firms being the beneficiaries of much federal and state policy," said the study.

"The government has established a climate which encourages cooperative and exclusionary behavior by these firms.

"These policies have all contributed to the current gasoline shortage. The major integrated oil companies are, however, taking advantage of the present shortage to drive the only visible long-term source of price competition, the independent marketer, out of market after market."

One obvious barrier to new refinery entrants is the estimated $250 million cost of a new refinery, the staff reported. It said there has been no new entrant in the refining field since 1950.

But the study said that even if a potential new refiner could raise the money, he'd shy away.

One reason cited was the federal oil depletion allowance, which provides a tax credit for a proportion of profits earned on crude oil. The purpose was to encourage oil exploration.

But the FTC staff said that because the allowance makes crude oil profits the least taxable of any phase of the majors' operations, the majors claim that most—if not all—their profits come on crude oil.

Through this simple bookkeeping operation, "it pays to raise crude prices up to a point where refinery profits have been reduced to zero," the staff said.

giving their resources, in the form of loans and outright gifts, to the nonindustrialized nations. In the annual discussion of the United States budget it is inevitable that some congressman or senator will make points with his constituency by arguing against the "lavish foreign giveaway programs." These programs are, in fact, not giveaways at all but investments that bring a very high return. Measuring the amount of money spent by industrialized nations in nonindustrialized nations and comparing this with the amount of capital taken back from the nonindustrialized nations makes this very clear. Foreign aid seems to be a mechanism by which the industrialized nations purchase the goodwill and support of elites in the nonindustrialized nations in order to expropriate their labor and resources. Furthermore, foreign aid is largely in the form of loans which must be repaid at interest. The receiving country may pay its debts by purchasing goods and services from the lending country; by shipping such goods on ships owned by the lending country; or by spending the aid on specific projects, such as the building of highways or railways that will serve the foreign corporations of the lending country which are based in the receiving country. Underdeveloped countries spend most of their needed capital simply paying back such "aid."

The Joint Brazil-United States Economic Commission estimated that between 1939 and 1952 the United States withdrew from Brazil *sixty-one* times as much capital as it invested in the country. In 1960 the United States received 1,300 million dollars in capital from all underdeveloped countries and returned to them a total of only 200 million dollars in foreign aid, military aid, and the like. For the period 1956–1961 statistics compiled from Department of Commerce data show that the capital coming into the United States from underdeveloped countries was 147 percent greater than the capital being sent to those countries.[8]

The nature of the relationship between the industrial and nonindustrial nations is easily grasped when we realize that the level of affluence enjoyed in the industrial nations is possible only because of the raw materials and the export markets provided by the nonindustrialized nations.

RAW MATERIALS[9]

Until the twentieth century the United States exported more raw materials than it imported. By 1930, however, the United

[8] Andre Gunder-Frank, op. cit., p. 163.

[9] The statistics in this and the following two sections are taken from the following sources: Gabriel Kolko, *The Roots of American Foreign Policy* (Boston: Beacon, 1969); Reginald H. Green and Ann Seidman, *Unity or Poverty?* (London: Penguin, 1968); Doris Lessing, *Going Home* (London: Panther, 1957); Pierre Jallee, *The Third World in World Economy* (New York: Monthly Review, 1969); Harry Magdoff, *The Age of Imperialism* (New York: Monthly Review, 1969); Stephen Hymer, "The Internationalization of Capital," *Journal of Economic Issues*, vol. 6, no. 1, 1972, pp. 1–21.

States was importing 5 percent of its copper, 9 percent of its lead, and 4 percent of its zinc. By 1960 the United States was importing 32 percent of the iron ore consumed by American industry, 98 percent of bauxite (aluminum), 35 percent of lead, and 60 percent of zinc. In 1956 the United States imported at least 80 percent of thirty-nine necessary commodities. As a Senate report stated in 1954, "To a very dangerous extent, the vital security of the Nation" would be in "serious jeopardy" if the mineral-rich nations of the nonindustrialized world were to cut off their supplies of natural resources to the United States and other industrialized nations. The following items are revealing of the scope and importance of the nonindustrialized nations to the industrialized:

From 1956 to 1960 the United States imported over 50 percent of its required metals and over 55 percent of its wool.

From 1913 to 1965 the share of the nonindustrialized world's contribution to the world's natural resources output went from 3 to 37 percent of the iron ore; 15 to 65 percent of the petroleum; 21 to 69 percent of the bauxite (aluminum).

The United States' share of world oil output fell from 61 percent in 1931 to 29 percent in 1964.

In 1960 over half the United States' iron ore imports came from Venezuela and three other Latin American countries.

Over half the world's known deposits of manganese, an essential ingredient in the production of steel; are in Russia and China. Most of the other 50 percent of the world's known reserves are in South Africa, Gabon, Brazil, and India.

South Africa and Rhodesia account for nearly all of the world's known chromium reserves.

Cuba and New Caledonia have over half the world's nickel reserves.

Chile, Northern Rhodesia, Zambia, the Congo, and Peru have over two-thirds of the copper reserves of the world outside the United States.

China has three times and Guayana about six times the American reserves of bauxite.

Malaysia, Indonesia, and Thailand have two-thirds of the world's tin reserves, with Bolivia and the Congo possessing most of the balance.

Foreign-owned firms, particularly British and American, dominate the economies of Zambia and Rhodesia.

The United States–owned Gulf Oil Company has exclusive rights to oil exploration in the Portuguese colonies of Africa, particularly in Mozambique and Angola.

British, German, and United States companies supply 40 percent of Mozambique and Angola's imports.

The United States is the world's largest importer of Angolan coffee.

In 1960, the Congo (Kinshasa) was producing two-thirds of the world's cobalt, 90 percent of the industrial diamonds, 70 percent of the commercial diamonds, and 10 percent of the copper.

In the mid-fifties 25 percent of the Congo's exports went to the United States, 25 percent to Belgium; 14 percent to France, 20 percent to other European nations, and 8 percent to Britain.

AGRICULTURAL RESOURCES

Great Britain depends upon its former colonies in the nonindustrialized world for the

Copper bars being unloaded in the United States. The availability of cheap mineral resources from nonindustrial nations is one of the supports of American "prosperity." (United Press International)

bulk of its agriculture. These nations produce agricultural goods at a price considerably below that which could be had from domestic production or purchased from other industrialized nations. This was a key factor in permitting Great Britain to greatly increase its industrial specialization before and after World War II.

The United States is primarily an exporter of agricultural products, and its relationship to the underdeveloped world is thus better understood in terms of markets (discussed below). However, for certain commodities, such as coffee, cocoa, bananas, and ground nuts, the United States is either completely or largely dependent upon the nonindustrialized world.

MARKETS, PROFITS, AND LABOR

An ongoing problem for the industrialized nations is the creation and maintenance of markets for the products they increasingly overproduce. Over the last fifty years, the nonindustrial nations have played a crucial role in providing these markets. At the same time, the nonindustrialized world has found its markets for products (other than raw materials) declining. From 1950 to 1960 the nonindustrialized nations' share in world exports declined from 31 to 19 percent. Most of this decline was a consequence of increasing exportation by European industrialized nations—especially those in the European Economic Community. "It can be seen that during these ten years the unit value of the exports of the developed capitalist countries grew by 7 percent, while it fell by 8 percent for the Third World." The deterioration of the terms of trade from their point of view cost the underdeveloped countries some 4.3 billion dollars in 1965.[10]

The United States accounts for over 20 percent of the world's export trade, a sig-

[10] Pierre Jallee, op. cit., pp. 72 and 75.

nificant part of which is in agricultural products. The United States exported 6.9 billion dollars worth of agricultural products in 1966, as compared with 2.9 billion dollars worth in 1950. Note the following:

In 1964 the extended value of foreign markets absorbing United States exports came to two-fifths of the total value of American internal production of agricultural goods, manufactured goods, and minerals.

The former colonies of Africa, Asia, Oceania, and South America account for the consumption of more than one-third of American exports and a similar proportion of direct American capital investment.

Profits are considerably higher in overseas investments. United States companies' profits on South African investments approach 25 percent, whereas 6 to 12 percent is a more normal profit margin for investments within the United States.

In 1950 earnings on foreign investments represented about 10 percent of all after-tax profits; by 1964 foreign sources of earnings accounted for about 22 percent of these profits.

From 1955 to 1965 the manufacturing industries increased their overseas sales by 110 percent while the increase in domestic sales was only 50 percent.

American firms employ directly from 5 to 7 million people in foreign countries and a growing but unknown number indirectly through contracting, licensing, and so forth. By comparison, the total employment of the 500 largest American firms is 13 or 14 million people. Many large corporations have 40 percent of their labor force outside the United States.

The 100 largest corporations in the United States own 55 percent of total net capital assets of all corporations. Thus, although the 10,000 largest corporations may have only a small interest in foreign markets and resources, the fact that the 100 largest corporations have a strong interest in them gives these corporations a disproportionate influence on American foreign policy and American political forms.

The profit margin for investments overseas, especially in less developed nations, is much greater than the profit margin for industrial and capital investment within the United States. In 1969 the rate of earnings on United States investment in underdeveloped countries was 18.7 percent as opposed to 8.3 percent for investment in developed countries. The rate of earnings in the underdeveloped countries was up from 14.0 percent in 1959, while the rate of earnings on investment in developed countries had declined from 9.0. In 1958 Standard Oil of New Jersey had two-thirds of its assets in North America, but only one-third of its profits came from this area. Jersey Standard's foreign profits were *twice* as high as its domestic profits, with only half the investment.[11] Table 14-1 shows the relationship between assets and profits for this corporation in 1958. By regions of the world, it had 114 companies in the United States and Canada, 77 in Europe, 43 in Latin America, 14 in Asia, 9 in Africa, and 18 elsewhere.

TABLE 14-1 Assets and Profits of Standard Oil of New Jersey by Area of The World, 1958

Country	Assets, %	Profits, %
United States and Canada	67	34
Latin America	20	39
Eastern hemisphere	13	27

SOURCE: Paul A. Baran and Paul M. Sweezy, *Monopoly Capital: An Essay on the American Economic and Social Order* (New York Monthly Review, 1966), p. 193.

It is important to realize that despite the worldwide investment and assets pattern of

[11] Foreign earning data from Thomas E. Weisskopf, "United States Foreign Private Investment: An Empirical Survey," in Edwards, Reich, and Weisskopf (eds.), *The Capitalist System*, 1972, p. 431.

corporations in the capitalist world, these corporations do *not* tend to export capital. Thus, the often-heard argument that the nonindustrialized world needs foreign capital seems to ignore the fact that, if future performance can be judged by past experience, foreign corporations will not be willing to make such capital investment. Apart from a small export of capital initially, Jersey Standard, for example, has relied solely upon the profits from its foreign companies for the extension of its manufacturing holdings.

In fact, it seems true not only that foreign investment will be from profits made within the country in which the initial small investment was made; but that it will be made only after incredibly *high* percentages of profits have been removed. Doris Lessing reports that officials of copper mining companies in Northern Rhodesia told her that the annual profits of the copper mines are about 125,000,000 dollars, of which *over half* leaves the country as profit for the parent corporations (in this case the Rhodesian Selection Trust, which is American owned, and the Anglo–American–De Beers, which is South African and British owned). The annual wage bill for African labor in this profitable enterprise is less than 15 million dollars. M. D. Banghart, vice president of the Newmont Mining Corporation, which has extensive investment in South Africa, noted that his company could make an average profit of 27 percent on investments in South Africa, but only about half that profit on investments in the United States.[12]

All of this makes it clear that it is to the industrial world's advantage to keep the less developed countries dependent upon it and to keep them underdeveloped (nonindustrialized). This is managed through forming coalitions with local elites who implement and maintain the policies which benefit the

[12] Green and Seidman, op. cit., p. 101.

industrial nations, controlling and influencing internal politics to ensure that political leadership is in the hands of compliant local government officials, and manipulating foreign aid to support friendly governments and punish hostile ones. The pattern of influencing and controlling the national destinies of less-developed nations is frequently referred to as *neocolonialism.*

The neocolonialism of today maintains the gulf between the industrialized metropolis and the nonindustrialized satellite nations. In this sense the situation remains much the same as it has been for the last 500 years. In a sense the system has created what is perhaps the newest basic economic strategy: a vast, flexible feudalism in which the lower castes are the masses of people in the nonindustrial nations and the landlords are the affluent, even the poor, in the industrial nations.

The enormous power differences thus developed between the industrial metropolis and the satellite nations are reflected in the fact that the largest United States corporations are much richer than many entire nations. Selection 14-3 compares United States corporations' annual sales volume with the gross national product of nations. Changes have nonetheless occurred in the past decade or two, and more can be expected. Many former colonies or neocolonies have more or less broken the chains that bound them to the capitalist economic system. Not surprisingly, those nations that have broken off have generally improved the standard of living for their people at a much more rapid rate than have those nations that have remained part of the world economy of capitalism. Cuba, for example, is the only nation in Latin America to have achieved the goals set for all Latin American countries by the Alliance for Progress. China has developed rapidly and uniformly since the 1948 revolution and has virtually eliminated the almost total economic and political control to which imperialist nations such as England, Japan, and the United States had subjected it in the preceding 400 years.

In Africa the situation is less clear. Attempts at independence from the capitalist economic system have been rare and not terribly dramatic. Tanzania and Zambia have both tried to develop a form of "African socialism" which has depended on trade and political relations with Western capitalist nations. So too have Algeria, Libya, Egypt, and Guinea. More important, perhaps, are the liberation movements in Mozambique, Guinea, Bissau, and Angola, which have recently succeeded in forcing the Portuguese to give these nations at least partial independence, thus ending the last European colonies in Africa. The white colonies of South Africa and Rhodesia remain, and of course economic and political control by European countries is all-pervasive throughout Africa. The form of colonialism has changed, but many of the most important economic and social consequences have not.

In general, the *trend* since World War II has been toward the increasing independence of former colonies from domination, exploitation, and subjugation. However, historical processes are slow (remember, it took 400 years for capitalism to replace feudalism), and the fact remains that most peoples of the world remain under the thumb of Western (both capitalist and socialist) imperialism and control. Some former imperial powers, such as Spain and Portugal, have themselves become virtual satellites of Europe's metropolis. The *net* gain (in terms of numbers of people) is perhaps in the direction of more independence, but the race is still very close.

America's position in the metropolis-satellite structure of the contemporary world is particularly relevant to understanding the current scene. As the most technologically

SELECTION 14-3: The power of large corporations compared with nations.

THE ROLE OF THE GIANTS IN WORLD ECONOMY

MILTON MOSKOWITZ

General Motors is losing ground to Switzerland but it's still comfortably ahead of Venezuela, Finland and Iran.

Ford Motor has spurted ahead to pass Indonesia, Austria and Turkey—and it's now pressing Denmark.

Hitachi has come from nowhere to beat out Morocco.

IBM, in a great leap forward, has passed Peru, Israel, Thailand, Taiwan, Malaysia and Ireland.

This is no fantasy, but ranking tables prepared by the Library of Congress for a Senate committee investigating the role of giant corporations in the world economy.

According to some academic pundits and some science fiction writers, the giant multinational corporations will rule the world in another 50 years, doing business at a volume of $100 billion and $200 billion a year.

The tables done by the Library of Congress lend validity to this forecast. They rank the 100 largest entities in the world—countries and companies—for the years 1960, 1965 and 1970. The companies are interspersed with the countries to show their huge clout.

Each country was ranked by its gross national product, a measure of output. Each company was ranked by its annual sales volume.

It's clear that the business corporations are gaining on the countries. In 1960, the top-100 list consisted of 59 countries and 41 companies; in 1965, the composition changed to 58 countries and 43 companies; by 1970, there were 49 countries on the list—and 51 companies.

The United States and the Soviet Union headed the roster for all three periods. The major changes in the top-level rankings were the rise of Japan and the decline of Britain. In 1960, Japan ranked seventh and Britain fourth. Today, Japan ranks third and Britain seventh.

With sales of $18.8 billion in 1970, General Motors ranked 24th, just behind Switzerland, which had a GNP of $20.6 billion. In 1960, GM ranked 16th in the world but the only reason it lost so much ground is that 1970 was a strike year.

GM's sales are now about $30 billion, which would place it 20th, below the Netherlands but ahead of Belgium.

The 1970 standings, after GM, read:

25. Yugoslavia. 26. Pakistan. 27. South Africa. 28. AT&T. 29. Standard Oil of New Jersey (now Exxon). 30. Denmark. 31. Ford.

The first non-U.S. company to appear on the list is Royal Dutch Shell—it ranked 36th with sales of $10.8 billion, sandwiched between Norway and Venezuela, where it has extensive investments.

Sears, Roebuck landed in 41st place, between the Philippines and Greece, but it easily outsold Turkey, Chile, Colombia.

IBM, the computer maker, was the most sensational climber. It moved during the decade from 92nd to 47th place, right behind Chile but ahead of Mobile Oil and Colombia.

In 1960, there were no Japanese companies on the list. Now there are two—Nippon Steel (70th) and Hitachi (83rd). Also in 1960, there were no German companies on the list. Now there are six—Volkswagen (64th), Siemens (86th), Farbwerke Hoechst (89th), Daimler-Benz (91st), August Thyssen-Hutte (93rd) and BASF (95th).

Displaced from the list during the decade were Nigeria, Algeria, International Harvester, Ghana, North American Aviation, Lockheed, General Dynamics and Iraq.

advanced society and the leader of world capitalism, America has enjoyed unprecedented affluence. In recent years, however, America's perch at the top of the capitalist marketplace has become less secure. A recent analysis by Gabriel Kolko provides evidence that if America did not maintain its present control over large portions of the world (South America, Mexico, the Caribbean, parts of Asia, and parts of Africa), world economic power would shift to Japan and western Europe.[13] America must maintain satellite countries that are forced to buy American products at American prices while providing resources for America's industries. It has been through America's foreign policy that the metropolis-satellite relationship has been maintained. At the same time, a united front against resource exploitation, such as that exhibited by the Arab nations, can severely disturb the economies of the industrial nations. Conflict analysis would predict the use of violence by the industrial nations to reduce Arab unity, perhaps to colonize the oil sources.

AMERICAN FOREIGN POLICY

As we noted in Chapter 13, American foreign policy is created and controlled by those who benefit most from the relationship between the metropolis and the satellites. Analysis of the social class background of top government decision makers shows that American foreign policy is determined by men who come from the largest corporations, banks, investment houses, and Wall Street law firms. William Appleman Williams describes American foreign policy as follows:

[E]xpansion of the marketplace is directly and explicitly relevant to an understanding of American foreign relations. It offers, to begin with, a good many insights into the major periods of American diplomacy. The first of these began in the middle of the eighteenth century and culminated in the 1820s. The increasing British efforts after 1750 to control and limit the existing American marketplace, its further agrarian expansion westward, and its increasing share in international trade, led

to a confrontation with the colonists that lies at the heart of the American Revolution.

Similar British attempts to restrict American territorial expansion after independence had been won, and to set limits upon America's international trade . . . promoted and accelerated and intensified the nationalism which led to the War of 1812. And the American push into Florida, and into the trans-Mississippi region, was obviously expansionist in origin and purpose. The vision of a great trade with South America and Asia, while not as central to these movements as the concern for land, was nevertheless a significant part of the continuing pressure to expand the marketplace that culminated in the Trans-Continental Treaty of 1819 with Spain. . . . The drive to dispossess the natives of their land, and the campaign to remove all restrictions on trade with the various tribes, combined to drive the Indians further westward while, at the same time, subverting any efforts to integrate them as full citizens into the white men's society and weakening their ability to resist further encroachments. . . .

The general drive to expand the marketplace during . . . the late nineteenth century provided the primary energy for the American economic move outward into Europe, Africa, Latin America and Asia. That expansion has been sustained and intensified in the twentieth century. Nobody but Americans thrust world power upon the United States. It came as a direct result of this determined push into the world marketplace. John D. Rockefeller's comment on the policy of Standard Oil typifies the attitude of both centuries. "Dependent solely upon local business," he explained in 1899, "we should have failed years ago. We were forced to extend our markets and to seek for export trade."

America's increasing opposition to Germany and Italy began not with the attacks on Czechoslovakia or Poland, but in connection with basic (German-Italian) economic policy . . . as early as 1933, and in response to German penetration of Latin-American economic affairs. . . .

---

[13] Gabriel Kolko, *The Roots of American Foreign Policy: An Analysis of Power and Purpose*, op. cit. See also G. William Domhoff, *The Higher Circles: The Governing Class in America* (New York: Vintage, 1971).

Antagonism toward the Soviet Union involved the same issues in an even more central and unqualified manner. The struggle, which was begun in 1917 and 1918, involved an outright rejection by the Soviets of the cardinal principles of the capitalist marketplace. . . .[14]

Since 1900 the United States has engaged in a series of wars with the principal aim of protecting America's overseas markets and the established metropolis-satellite relationship. It is also in competition with Russia for satellites (since World War II) that the United States has engaged in the cold war arms race and a series of "small" wars—particularly Korea and Vietnam.

We have said that one principal mechanism of control within a satellite country is through a local elite who support the existing metropolis-satellite relationship. The industrial nation can use all its resources to establish and maintain those elites who comply with its wishes; military aid which builds up the available forces of the established elite is a most important technique for perpetuating the status quo as well as being profitable to United States arms manufacturers. In his study of Chile, Andre Gunder-Frank characterized a worldwide pattern when he noted that the "metropolis-satellite structure" led "the most powerful interest groups of the Chilean metropolis to support an economic structure and policies which maintained the exploitation . . . [because] they were thereby able to continue their exploitation of the people in the Chilean periphery. . . ."[15]

BREAKING NEOCOLONIALISM

Once a nonindustrialized nation becomes a satellite of an industrialized metropolis, the relationship is extremely difficult to change. Nonindustrialized satellites have grown de-

pendent upon the metropolis for the small amount of capital that is available, and to break the control of the metropolis would mean an immediate reduction in the general standard of living. The metropolis controls all or most of the resources in the satellite country. If these resources are eliminated from the nation's productive processes, there will necessarily be a decline in productivity and a slowing of economic development. Furthermore, the pressures that can be exerted by the industrialized nations make breaking the established relationship even more costly. When Ghana attempted to move out of the orbit of neocolonialism established by the British government, Great Britain was able to drop the world price of cocoa—thereby undermining Ghana's economy. Since Ghana's main export was cocoa, the British countermove was devastating and led eventually to the replacement of the independent government with one more congenial to British business interests.

To conceive of nonindustrialized nations as forming a "Third World" suggests (and inevitably leads to explicit theories) that the nonindustrialized nations form a social unit that has developed independent of the industrialized nations and is independent of them today. This suggests that the nonindustrialized nations have not industrialized because of characteristics which they share and which the industrialized nations do not have, or have outgrown. As Pierre Jallee writes:

To accept too easily the term [Third World], to introduce it into ordinary language, means to introduce insidiously the idea that the group of countries about which we have spoken constitutes a particular entity, a world in itself, in regard to which the theories and reasoning applied to the group of capitalist (industrialized) countries should be revised, adapted, and more or less adulterated.[16]

[14] William Appelman Williams, op. cit., pp. 32–35; 45–46.
[15] Andre Gunder-Frank, op. cit., p. 95.

[16] Pierre Jallee, "Third World: Which Third World?" *Revolution*, vol. 1, no. 7 (English edition).

If we accept the term "Third World," we seem to be reasoning that the "first" world —the industrialized world—got that way by itself, and not by exploiting three-fourths of the less-developed world.

A similar situation holds for the frequently made observation that nonindustrialized nations are "dual societies." In this argument, nonindustrial people are divided into a small, industrialized, Westernized, "modern" population, which is centered in the cities, and a large, rural, nonindustrialized, traditional society that is agrarian. As we pointed out earlier, however, the significance of this fact is that such an arrangement allows the elites of these countries to live in the style of their peers in the industrial metropolis, supported by the resources supplied by the rural area. As Gunder-Frank noted:

Those people in the underdeveloped countries who were not or are not at any one time incorporated into the capitalist system's market as visibly direct sellers of labor or buyers of products are not for all that unintegrated into, isolated from or marginal to the capitalist system. Theirs is another fate which is a no less necessary result of the essential internal contradiction of the capitalist system. . . . They have witnessed the capitalist system produce its sometimes sudden, sometimes slow, but always inevitable world, national and regional shifts in supply and demand for their former output of spices, sugar, cocoa, coffee, tea, rubber, gold, silver, copper, tin and other raw materials, and of industrial goods as well, which for months, years, decades, or even centuries transform whole populations of once independent producers or dependent workers into the "floating" or "marginal" bare or non-subsistence populations of the capitalist system's ubiquitous underdeveloped rural and urban slums and ghettos.[17]

In fact, as Selection 14-3 suggests, some

[17] Andre Gunder-Frank, Latin America: Underdevelopment or Revolution (New York: Monthly Review), 1969; excerpted from pp. 225–229.

multinational corporations are today so powerful that they may seek profits in several countries even in the face of political opposition. Using such terms as third world or dual society leads us to develop theories of development which border on the ludicrous. Two theories of development deriving from the functional perspective of seeing nonindustrialized nations as the Third World are illustrative.

Achievement Motivation and National Development

If we view nonindustrialized societies as part of a third world, we might ask, as has one theorist, "What is it about the individual psyche of populations that differentiates industrialized populations from nonindustrialized populations?" From such a perspective comes David McClelland's theory of achievement motivation.

In its most general terms, the hypothesis states that a society with a generally high level of achievement will produce more rapid economic development.[18]

McClelland's theory of economic development is based on the assumption that "it is values, motives or psychological forces that determine ultimately the rate of economic and social development."[19] With a swipe of the pen McClelland has provided a theory of development which implicitly denies the importance of 400 years (or more) of history. According to this theory, the enslavement of Africa is not connected with Africa's failure to industrialize; the economic dependency of Latin America created, fostered, and maintained by the United States is not relevant to economic development; the in-

[18] David McClelland, The Achieving Society, p. 205, and "Motivational Patterns in Southeast Asia with Special Reference to the Chinese Case," Journal of Social Issues, vol. 29, no. 1, January, 1963, p. 17.
[19] Ibid., pp. 224–225.

dustrialized nations' successful exploitation of satellite areas has nothing to do with development. All one need know is that nonindustrialized nations lack the proper amount of "achievement motivation." Had they had a sufficient amount, presumably, the slave-

ships of England, France, and America would have never been able to ply the waters of Africa. Yet strangely, it was the high achievement motivation of some African tribes (from McClelland's perspective) that made them slave traders while others were slaves. Such a perspective also implies what is not true: that underdeveloped nations have always been that way. In fact, of course, many currently nonindustrialized societies were at one time highly developed and in many cases dominated a good part of the world as a result of their superior technology much as the West does today. Their underdevelopment was created by western expansionism and imperialism, not by a lack of "achievement motivation."

To extract the fruits of their labor through pillage, slavery, forced labor, free labor, raw materials, or through monopoly trade—no less today than in the times of Cortez and Pizarro in Mexico and Peru, Clive in India, Rhodes in Africa, the "Open Door" in China—the metropolis destroyed and/or totally transformed the earlier viable social and economic systems of these societies, incorporated them into the metropolitan dominated worldwide capitalist system, and converted them into sources for

What it means to be marginal to the economies created by capitalist and socialist imperialism can be seen in the lives of people living in the suburbs of Caracas, Venezuela. (Mary D. Howard)

SELECTION 14-4: Size and complexity of a large multinational corporation.

THE SHADOWY WORLD OF ITT

Washington—From World War II contracts with the Nazis to trade negotiations with Russia, British journalist Anthony Sampson puts the spotlight on the shadowy world of a giant multinational conglomerate in a new book, "The Sovereign State of ITT."

Drawing on a rare volume of ITT office memos and government documents, the author goes beyond already headlined disclosures of alleged ITT use of the Central Intelligence Agency in an unsuccessful effort to block the election of President Salvador Allende in Chile in 1970, and the lobbying of Vice President Agnew and other high-placed friends to avoid an anti-trust action in 1971.

International Telephone & Telegraph Corp., is depicted as an empire with a wide variety of business interests in 70 countries, conducting its own foreign diplomacy, relying on its own communications and spy network and motivated solely by a relentless thirst for profits.

Harold S. Geneen, who became ITT president in 1959, is pictured as the monarch and commander-in-chief of an army of 400,000 employes, reigning from castles in New York and Brussels and taking his court of highly paid vice presidents with him on frequent travels throughout his domain.

But at the same time, when it suits a purpose, ITT is shown to claim local autonomy for its subsidiaries and foreign enterprises.

The book, published by Stein and Day, goes on sale July 30.

In the last decade, Geneen has transformed ITT from a group of scattered telephone companies into the world's 11th largest multinational conglomerate, buying up hundreds of large and small disconnected businesses.

The author of the book, Sampson, long-time staff member of The London Observer concludes, however, that many of Geneen's policies resemble those of an earlier era:

During World War II, ITT kept in touch with its German companies and the Axis powers through interlocked affiliates in Argentina, Switzerland and Spain, at the same time making submarine detectors for Allied convoys.

"Thus while ITT Focke Wulf planes were bombing Allied ships and ITT lines were passing information to German submarines, ITT direction finders were saving other ships from torpedoes."

Wartime ITT letters, cables and telephone conversations were monitored by the State Department and the Federal Communications Commission, but ITT was never prosecuted.

An anti-trust complaint against both ITT and A.T.&T. was drafted in the Justice Department in 1946, but was never signed.

An espionage trial of three ITT employees in Hungary in 1949 disclosed ITT pursuing its own foreign policy trying to detach Hungary from the Communist block, while at the same time courting favor with the Communists.

ITT hit the front pages in 1972 with the leak to columnist Jack Anderson of a memo from ITT lobbyist Dita Beard linking a $400,000 pledge for the Republican convention to ITT efforts to avert divestiture of the $2 billion Hartford Insurance Companies in anti-trust litigation.

Sampson reviews the 1972 Senate hearings and disclosure of additional ITT letters and memos revealing a massive lobbying campaign to persuade Richard W. McLaren, then Justice Department anti-trust chief, to settle on ITT terms. ITT ended up keeping the Hartford group but divesting itself of other properties.

One letter from ITT vice president Ned Gerrity thanked Vice President Agnew for "your assistance."

Geneen himself was shown to have talked to Secretary of Commerce Maurice H. Stans, Treasury Secretary David M. Kennedy and his successor, John B. Connally; Paul W. Mc-Cracken, chairman of the Council of Economic Advisers; Peter G. Peterson, White House economic adviser, and four other members of the White House staff, Arthur F. Burns, Charles W. Colson, John D. Ehrlichman, and Peter Flanigan.

Other ITT officials approached then-Attorney General John N. Mitchell and his deputy, Richard G. Kleindienst.

The author traces the intensity of the Hartford merger lobbying effort to an earlier failure. Justice Department intervention thwarted ITT's attempt to add ABC to its empire in 1966 and 1967.

its own metropolitan capital accumulation and development. . . . [The people in these societies] have, as in India, seen imperialism destroy the organization, handicrafts, industry and trade as well as the livelihood they derived from these. . . . The resulting fate for these conquered, transformed, or newly established societies was and remains their decapitalization, structurally generated unproductiveness, ever increasing poverty for the masses—in a word, their underdevelopment.

Underdevelopment, far from being due to any supposed "isolation" of the majority of the world's people from modern capitalist expansion, or even to any continued feudal relations and wars, is the result of the integral incorporation of these people into the fully integrated but contradictory capitalist system which has long since embraced them all.[20]

Pattern Variables and Underdevelopment

Following the theoretical perspective of Talcot Parsons, Bert Hoselitz has argued that nonindustrialized societies differ from industrialized societies in terms of widely held values about how to relate to others.

Stripped of its tautological aspects (which would negate the theory's testability), the theory suggests that nonindustrialized societies are that way because they deserve it. The argument is that success in nonindustrialized societies depends on "connections," whereas in industrialized societies it depends on ability. The argument is also made that it is precisely because industrialized societies have always emphasized merit rather than, say, kinship ties that they industrialized.

The falsity of this argument is apparent if one looks either at the presumed meritocracy structure in industrialized societies or the presumed kinship criteria in nonindustrialized societies.

One of the "miracles" of economic development in the last seventy-five years has been Japan. Yet this has been accomplished,

as most observers agree, by utilizing kinship criteria. For example, factories are organized around the principle of hiring entire families rather than individuals. One is employed, in other words, because of his kinship ties, not because of his own abilities or aspirations.[21] Selection 14-4 describes one of the ways in which kinship and family ties are encouraged in Japanese factories.

Kinship, ethnic, or friendship criteria also abound in Europe and the United States—among the working classes as well as among the elites.[22] The children of the wealthy inherit wealth and power in industrialized societies regardless of their ability. The best education in industrialized societies goes to the children of the wealthy, not to the most intelligent or most deserving. Power and wealth perpetuate themselves within all economic systems and in proportion to the amounts of surplus value generated by that system. In this sense, all societies are *particularistic*, a term Hoselitz uses to describe connections based on kin, class, or ethnic connection. To argue that industrialized societies are less particularistic than nonindustrialized societies is ridiculous. The use of relatives, friends, and classmates in United States government, for example, is widespread.

Roosevelt's and Kennedy's brain trusts co-opted all sorts of American social scientists. Harvard historian Arthur Schlesinger, Jr.'s aid to the development of underdeveloped countries has so far consisted in writing the now famous White Paper on Cuba which was intended to justify the coming invasion of that country at the Bay of Pigs. He later admitted lying about the invasion in the "national interest." Stanford economist Eugene Staley wrote

[20] Andre Gunder-Frank, op. cit., pp. 24–48.

[21] James Abegglen, *The Japanese Factory* (Glencoe, New York: Free Press, 1958).
[22] David Granier, *The European Executive* (Garden City, N.Y.: Doubleday, 1962); Ferdinand Zweig, *The British Worker* (London: Penguin, 1962), and *The Worker in an Affluent Society* (London: Heinemann, 1962); Raymond Williams, *Culture and Society* (London: Penguin, 1961).

SELECTION 14-5: The mixture of family and bureaucratic institutional patterns in Japan.

BOY MEETS CO-WORKER

Japan—Like many Japanese executives, the heads of Mitsubishi like to consider their workers one big happy family. The combine's 260,000 employees are scattered among 27 member firms that make everything from diodes to diapers, but they can sing the company song, vacation at company resorts and enroll in Mitsubishi-sponsored haiku-writing and flower-arranging courses. Yet for years Mitsubishi executives have stewed over an insult to the ideal of togetherness: some 80,000 Mitsubishi workers are unmarried.

After a year of investigation, a top-level executive committee is now offering a combination of technology and tradition to close the gap. Mitsubishi's giant IBM system/370 Model 165 computer has been put to work making matches. For 8,000 yen (about $30) a Mitsubishi worker can get the names of as many as ten employees of the opposite sex best matched to his or her own talents, traits and concept of an ideal mate. Eight courtship counselors, most of them wives of Mitsubishi executives, guide candidates in making final selections. "Mitsubishi boys and girls spend a lot of time and money in search of their future husband or wife," says Hiroyuki Ito, a former Mitsubishi insurance executive who heads the mating effort. "We aim to cut that unnecessary wandering to a minimum."

Some 260 employees have taken advantage of the service since it began two months ago, and a dozen couples are in initial stages of courtship. So far there have been no weddings. Arranged marriages represent a persistent tradition in Japan—one recent study estimated that 20% of matches in Tokyo are still put together by parents—but company counselors insist that they exert no pressure on employees to marry their print-out partners. Mitsubishi executives do admit that they value such intramural mergers. Says Ito: "When the wife shares the same corporate frame of reference with her husband, she can only understand him more and help achieve for him a higher degree of performance and efficiency as an employee."

The Future of Underdeveloped Countries and then planned it in the renowned Staley-[General Maxwell] Taylor Plan to put 15 million Vietnamese in the concentration camps they euphemistically christened "strategic hamlets." Since the failure of that effort at development planning, MIT economic historian Walt Whitman Rostow has escalated the effort by writing *The Stages of Economic Growth: A Noncommunist Manifesto.* He wrote of these stages at the CIA-financed Center for International Studies on the Charles River and has been operationalizing them on the Potomac as President Kennedy's Director of Policy and Planning in the State Department and President Johnson's chief adviser on Vietnam. It is on behalf of Vietnamese economic growth that Rostow has become the principal architect of escalation, from napalming the South to bombing the North, and beyond. Then, doubtless due to universalistic particularism and achieved ascription, Eugene Rostow moves from professing international law at Yale University to practicing it at his brother's side in Washington. Meanwhile, after performing his role as Dean of Humanities at Harvard University, McGeorge Bundy becomes W. W. Rostow's superior in Washington and goes on television to explain to the misguided and incredulous why this economic development theory and policy is humanitarian (after which he goes on to direct the Ford Foundation and its influence on education and research). In the light of the manifest and institutionalized role-summation and diffuseness of these deans of humane scholarship and professors of applied social science, the clandestine direction of Project Camelot by the Department of Defense and the financing of the United States National Student Association by the CIA pale into the shadows.[23]

More dramatic is the finding by Floyd Hunter in his study of "Ivydale" that some of the most influential men in the community were a group of college classmates who had from college days worked to put

[23] Andre Gunder-Frank, *Underdevelopment or Revolution,* op. cit., p. 28.

one another into positions of power.[24] When one of the clique became president of the university, he appointed others to posts of leadership. The criteria may be different in the United States than in Liberia (friendship rather than family), but they are no less particularistic.

SUMMARY

One of the most important characteristics of the world today is the fact that most of the world's people live on the edge of starvation, caught by poverty, while a small minority of the world lives in affluence. If we are to understand the world we live in, we must understand why this is so.

Functional perspectives attempt to explain underdevelopment as a state resulting from inherent characteristics of the nonindustrialized societies, without regard to their relationship to industrialized societies. This is like trying to explain poverty without looking at the economy.

Looking at the world as divided into two parts—an industrialized metropolis and a periphery of nonindustrialized satellites—is the starting point for understanding the contemporary relationship among nations of the world. This division, which has its roots in the historical processes of industrialization, shapes the lives of people and the behavior of nations everywhere. It is one of the funda-

mental features of the social structure of the modern world.

The rapacious expansionism of the European nations in the fourteenth, fifteenth, and sixteenth centuries was a result of a search for markets and resources to enhance the wealth of those nations. The discovery of less industrialized worlds where warfare was less efficiently carried out permitted them to establish profitable colonies.

The future is undertandable only if we take into account the multinational character of inequality. The less-developed nations of the world are on the verge of revolution against the developed nations in an effort to reduce the current inequality between themselves and those who control the means of world production. As of this writing, wars are taking place against colonial or neo-colonial powers in Mozambique, Guinea, Vietnam, Ethiopia, the Cameroons, Rhodesia, South Africa, and Northern Ireland. In recent years there have been similar confrontations —with greater and lesser degrees of success —in Cuba, Hungary, Poland, Czechoslavakia, China, and Thailand, to mention only a few.

The history of the next century will undoubtedly continue to reflect the conflicts resulting from the basic patterns of inequality that exist between different nations of the world. Most of the conflicts—revolutions, civil wars, and international warfare—will involve nations of the industrialized world fighting against nations of the less-developed world.

[24] Floyd Hunter, The Big Rich and The Little Rich, pp. 31–44.

SUGGESTED READINGS

Andre Gunder-Frank, *Capitalism and Underdevelopment in Latin America* (New York: Monthly Review Press, 1967).

————, *Latin America: Underdevelopment or Revolution* (New York: Monthly Review Press, 1969).

Gabriel Kolko, *The Roots of American Foreign Policy* (Boston: Beacon Press, 1969).

Reginald Green and Ann Seidman, *Unity or Poverty?* (London: Penguin Books, 1968).

William J. Pomeroy, *American Neo-Colonialism: Its Emergence in the Philippines and Asia* (New York: International Publishers, 1970).

William Appelman Williams, *The Great Evasion* (Chicago: Quadrangle Books, 1964).

Doris Lessing, *Going Home* (London: Panther Modern Library, 1957).

Paul A. Baran, *The Political Economy of Growth.*

————, *Aid as Imperialism* (New York: Monthly Review Press, 1957).

FIFTEEN
Bureaucratism

The Bureaucracy! Red Tape! More often, the G–– D––– Bureaucracy! Whether dealing with government agencies, schools, retail stores, or gasoline stations one is confronted by a background of bureaucracy that organizes the work, and even the life-style, of the bellboy, the teacher, the foreman, the clerk, or the official. A bureaucratic organizational form may be used to achieve such diverse ends as making war, worshipping God, organizing workers, socializing children, or distributing illegal goods and services.

What is this thing that is so much a part of our lives? Why does it have the shape it does? How much control does it have over our lives, and what does that control portend for the future? How can we understand, cope with, and change bureaucracy?

In preceding analyses of elements of social relations in the contemporary United States we have said that power differences between classes are the shapers of political decisions, and that existing foreign-policy decisions enrich the profit-controlling class and reduce domestic discontent by pillaging the resources of less-developed countries for use in the United States. In this chapter we analyze the basic social form, or cultural blueprint, through which power differences are rigidified and solidified—bureaucracy.

The breakup of feudalism, the bourgeois revolution, and the emergence of capitalism were accompanied by the emergence of bureaucratism as a logical extension of the emergent economic and political relations. The rationalization of social relations into events that should be contained within rules administered by hierarchically structured positions within organizations became the dominant mode of organization. Officials, managers, and clerks came to dominate the life conditions of everyone.

People organized bureaucratically may work for years to achieve goals justified only by higher-level bureaucrats and hired technicians whose pyramided power leaves them largely unanswerable to their clients. In the case described in Selection 15-1, the clients are taxpayers.

One of the first social scientists to see the incredible importance bureaucy would play in the lives of contemporary people was Max Weber. Others—Karl Marx, Frederick Engels, and Emile Durkheim, to mention only a few —saw the importance of bureaucracy, but Weber's analysis is so outstanding that it is a primary source for anyone doing sociological analysis of bureaucrats.

Max Weber on Bureaucracy

Weber's analysis of bureaucracy begins with a distinction among three types of authority: charismatic, traditional, and rational. *Charismatic authority* is that whose "legitimacy" depends on the ability of an individual to mobilize support for his leadership by virtue of his or her own personal characteristics.

Traditional authority exists where "legitimacy is claimed for it and believed in on the basis of the sanctity of the order [God's law] and/or the attendant powers of control as they have been handed down from the past. . . ."[1] It is an authority which persists because the weight of tradition supports its legitimacy. The authority of the male over the female in family (and other) social relations is an example of traditional authority. "Traditional authority thus draws its legitimacy not from reason or abstract rule but from its roots in the belief that it is ancient,

that it has inherent and unassailable wisdom. . . ."[2]

The ideological foundation upon which the bureaucratic form is constructed is *rational authority*. The claim to legitimacy of rational authority lies in its presumed objectivity, that is, the fact that the authority derives from rules rather than from personal loyalty or personal obligation. The fact that bureaucracies may not in reality operate "rationally" is not an issue. The issue is that bureaucracies pretend to derive their authority from the application of universal standards by which all decisions and people are judged. In the Weberian analysis, our legal system epitomizes the appeal to this kind of authority.

In Weber's conceptualization the law represents "rational" authority because its legitimacy rests on the existence of a set of rules which govern decisions. Now it may be the case that these rules favor one class over another, that they are misapplied consistently so that some people and some classes are constantly subjected to penal sanctions while other people and other classes violate the rules with impunity. The actual operation of the system may in every way violate the premise on which the system is constructed. But if the system's claim to legitimacy is that it abides by rules (is governed by "laws," not by "men") then it represents an appeal to rational authority.

Rational authority in the modern world is best seen in bureaucratic structures. According to Weber, "modern officialdom, or bureaucracy, functions in the following way:

1. There is the principle of fixed and official jurisdictional areas, which are generally ordered by rules, that is, by laws or administrative regulations. . . .

2. The principles of office hierarchy and

---

[1] Max Weber, *The Theory of Social and Economic Organization* (Glencoe, Ill.: Free Press, 1947), p. 341.

[2] Robert A. Nisbet, *The Sociological Tradition* (London: Heinemann, 1967), p. 142.

SELECTION 15-1: Bureaucracy and expenditure of tax money.

THOSE FLYING FOLLIES OF THE ATOMIC AGE

H. PETER METZGER

New York—Predictably, the breakdown of checks and balances allowed the Atomic Energy Commission to indulge in unrestrained technical frivolities without precedent since the building of the Pyramids—because, charged with promotion as it was, and given a blank check by Congress, the AEC was able to coast along quite some way on our childlike awe of the miraculous achievement of the Manhattan Project.

Money had brought us one miracle—why not more?

High priests of religion ran the affairs of men in the days when no limits existed over man's belief in magic. It took the new priests of science and technology, whose bewitching power could be more readily demonstrated, to capture the imaginations of men and thus emasculate the old priesthood forever.

Until very recently, the scientist and the engineer enjoyed a position of infallibility in men's minds unequaled since the power of the church before Galileo.

Accordingly, even the sky was no limit, as the AEC found not only its legitimate programs but even its hare-brained schemes rolling in research millions.

Soon billions would be thrown away on schemes so foolish they should never have gotten on the drawing boards, much less off. It wasn't until some spectacular failures that some AEC scientists and even Congress finally learned that the atom had its limitations after all.

By all odds, the all-time worst idea was Pluto. That program was so bad it was actually canceled.

The military potential of the nuclear reactor was recognized even before the "atomic pile" had successfully sustained a nuclear chain reaction. The nuclear alternative's chief advantage is its ability to provide power for long periods of time without refueling.

Its military disadvantages have to do with its limited portability due to the great weight of the shielding required to protect its operators from atomic radiation.

Another great disadvantage, although more important to the public than to the military, is the enormous hazard posed by the release of huge quantities of radioactivity in the event of the destruction of the nuclear reactor in combat or through accidental collisions.

All things considered, the nuclear reactor is singularly suited to naval vessels and particularly the submarine. Nuclear power has provided the real advantage of decreasing the vulnerability of naval vessels in a way not possible by conventional means.

At the same time, naval nuclear power has not subjected our nation to greater risks from atomic radiation than the benefits (extra military security) provided by going nuclear. Accordingly, the Naval Reactor Program was a great success.

But that question is fundamental to all nuclear technology: Suppose we can build the nuclear alternative, will it really be better than the conventional method already in use, considering the extra risk?

That question has rarely, if ever, been addressed honestly by the AEC before it embarked on a new nuclear adventure. Invariably, when risk-benefit analyses are made of new atomic schemes, every assumption concerning the nuclear alternative is extravagantly optimistic, while developments in the conventional method already in use are assumed to remain static during the decade or so it might take to develop its atomic equivalent.

Probably the best example of bad decision-making in this connection is the flying nuclear reactor. An idea as formidable in its destructive portent and as insane (from the point of view of the risks that society must take in order to receive the benefits promised) as was Pluto is hard (though not impossible) to find.

Described by the AEC as "a nuclear ramjet propulsion system supersonic low altitude missile," Pluto was a nuclear edition of the pilotless V-1 German "buzz-bomb" of World War II. It had an atomic jet engine and carried a nuclear warhead up front.

Independent of refueling stops, this flying atomic bomb was to cruise at very low altitudes (to avoid detection by enemy radar) and at very high speeds (faster than sound) all the way to its target across the world. . . .

It might be expected that a great lesson was

learned from the nuclear-airplane fiasco: that not only must the nuclear alternative be better than conventionally available techniques in order to be worthwhile, but, considering the greatly increased risks involved, it must confer advantages absolutely unavailable elsewhere.

But even if the ANP could be made to work, its advantages are available elsewhere. The best that could be said is that the nuclear jet engine would avoid inflight refueling, hardly an advantage great enough to counterbalance the tremendous risks involved.

Remarkably enough, the lesson was not learned at all. The Air Force is now engaged in a new examination of nuclear aircraft propulsion, and today the National Aeronautics and Space Administration spends a quarter of a million dollars each year on "in-house" nuclear-airplane studies, but concedes the "difficult task of overcrowding the subjective response of the public toward nuclear-powered airplanes."

Perhaps most difficult to believe is that in 1971 the Navy actually awarded a new contract to Lockheed Aircraft to develop concepts to modify the giant C-5A airplane into a nuclear-powered seaplane.

All 47 of these airplanes were grounded by the Air Force in late 1971 after an engine "spun to the ground" when the pilot applied full power during a pre-takeoff check.

It developed later that cracks were found in the engine mount of at least one other C-5A, which had only 500 hours of flight time.

Consider how fortunate we are that the Navy's program for a nuclear-powered C-5A had not progressed very far in 1971, for in the dropping off of engines, it is far better to clean up gasoline than atomic fallout.

of levels of graded authority mean a firmly ordered system of super- and subordination in which there is a supervision of the lower offices by the higher ones. . . .

3. The management of the modern office is based upon written documents ("the files"). . . .

4. Office management . . . usually presupposes thorough and expert training. . . .

5. When the office is fully developed, official activity demands the full working capacity of the official, irrespective of the fact that his obligatory time in the bureau may be firmly delimited. . . .

6. The management of the office follows general rules, which are more or less stable, more or less exhaustive, and which can be learned. Knowledge of these rules represents a special technical learning which the officials possess.[3]

The most profound implication of Weber's theory of bureaucracy is that bureaucracy is the endpoint of a historical process toward increasing rationalization of authority and indeed of all facets of culture and society—from businesses and schools to art, music, education, and even personal feeling. The change is not necessarily something to be desired. Weber saw bureaucracy as replacing the arbitrary authority practiced by tyrants, but he also envisioned the emergence of a bureaucratic despotism characterized by an indifference to individuals that could be more devastating to the development of human fulfillment than the despotism of kings. The tyranny of bureaucracy emerges because in the end bureaucracy begins to protect itself for its own ends. "Thus the hospital reaches the point of serving, not human illness primarily, but the hospital; the university, the church and the labor union all become dominated, through processes of rationalization, by their intrinsic organizational goals. . . ."[4] Weber's analysis was indeed prophetic.

As we have emphasized before, one test of whether our understanding has grown through using a particular perspective is whether it allows us to see things that might otherwise have escaped our attention. Judging from the widespread use of Weber's model, one would suspect that social scientists have found the perspective useful. Indeed, we can see how the Weberian per-

[3] H. H. Gerth and C. Wright Mills, *From Max Weber* (New York: Oxford University Press, 1946), p. 1.
[4] R. A. Nisbet, Ibid., p. 147.

Among the defining characteristics of the bureaucratic form of organizing human work are (1) narrowly specialized jobs and (2) written records that define these jobs and record decisions made and actions taken. (Daniel S. Brody from Editorial Photocolor Archives)

spective can enrich analysis if we use it to analyze the relationship between the police and organized crime in America.

To some extent, organized crime exists and, usually, thrives in every city in the United States as well as in cities in most of those areas of the underdeveloped world where the United States government has strong influence. This is not to say that there is some superpowerful worldwide organization headed by a "godfather" and run along feudal lines of authority, backed by its own standing army. The best available evidence indicates that each city has its own independent crime cabal composed of racketeers, prominent businessmen, lawyers, politicians, and law enforcement officials who run prostitution, theft rings, gambling, drug distribution, and other illegal activities.[5] In every case one finds that the police and sheriff's departments that are formally charged with the responsibility of enforcing laws against

gambling, prostitution, drug distribution, and the like are in fact cooperating with and even organizing the traffic in these criminal activities. Preposterous as this may seem, the situation is in fact quite understandable if we look at it in terms provided by the analysis of bureaucracy which we have just presented. The simple fact is that by cooperating with and managing criminal activities law enforcement agencies are able to reach the goals of the bureaucracy that comprises the law enforcement organization as a whole. To understand this let us look briefly at the position of law enforcement agencies in America.

On the one hand, law enforcement agencies are obligated to enforce the law, albeit with discretion. On the other hand, considerable disagreement exists over whether or not some acts, such as gambling, prostitution, homosexuality, and drug use, should be subject to legal sanction at all. Furthermore, law enforcement agencies are not independent of politics and politics is not independent of those who control the means of production. Thus the ruling class and to some extent even the wage-earning class can bring considerable pressure to bear on

    [5] William J. Chambliss, "Vice, Corruption, Bureaucracy, and Power," *Wisconsin Law Review*, Winter 1972. (Also available in reprint from MSS Publications, 655 Madison Ave., New York.) Donald R. Cressey, *Theft of the Nation* (New York: Harper & Row, 1969). James Q. Wilson, *The Police and the Community* (Baltimore: Johns Hopkins University, 1972).

law enforcement agencies to "overlook" or "temper" the enforcement of laws against themselves. There are in fact two camps: some influential persons insist that all laws be enforced rigorously, while others insist that some laws, especially vice laws, be loosely enforced.

The fact that law enforcement agencies operate bureaucratically allows us to use Weber's analysis to understand what might otherwise be difficult to comprehend. Law enforcement agencies, like other bureaucracies, have adopted procedures and practices which protect the organization. The goal of preserving the bureaucracy has taken precedence over the "mission" of enforcing the law. As it happens, the "best" strategy for the law enforcement bureaucracy to adopt, the one which achieves organizational goals best, is one of active participation in the rackets. Why this is so will become clearer as we proceed.

Given that some people with power demand access to vice and others with power demand its suppression, the law enforcement solution must be one that *apparently* does both. If the enforcement agencies can appear to do both, then their organization is less likely to be "reformed" or otherwise attacked. If the police or sheriff's department can give those who want their community free of vice the impression that this is the case while simultaneously providing the vices for those who want them, then the bureaucratic problem of organizational survival is solved.

Law enforcement agencies restrict vice operations to those sections of the city where the people are either themselves active participants in the vices or politically powerless and unable to make their opposition to the existence of the vices heard. This means that drug distribution, prostitution, loansharking, gambling, bookmaking, etc., take place primarily in the working-class sections of the city. Since those middle- and upper-class persons most opposed to the presence of vice rarely if ever venture into the city's slums and ghettos, they remain unaware that vice is rampant, and those members of the community who seek such pastimes can be easily steered to the appropriate sections.

So long as the vices remain invisible to those who want the laws enforced but available to those who do not, the police dilemma is resolved. However, the permanent resolution of this dilemma cannot be had simply by agreeing to let people run the vices in certain areas of the city. The existence of such activities as gambling and prostitution mean an ever-present threat of violence.

Because the services and goods involved in such activities are illegal, competition for them need not even pretend to follow the laws which govern legal business competition. Rather than drive out competitors through such means as monopoly pricing, those breaking the law may take a more direct route—that of physical violence. This violence makes a stink: people who may like gambling, drugs, and prostitution get upset at murder and assault. Also, people who lose large sums of money gambling often become violent, and people who desperately need a "fix" to sustain their drug addiction will sometimes steal or even kill to get it. Prostitutes are often physically assaulted by customers. And high-interest loans, as well as gambling debts, cannot be collected by court order since the debts are illegal in the first place. Finally, persons who are privy to the existence of the vices can threaten the status quo by bringing the prevalence of vice to the awareness of those influential people who oppose it.

For all these reasons, the police must go farther than mere tolerance, or limiting institutionalized vice to certain areas of the city, in order to avoid attack on police work and police organization. They must actively involve themselves in the organization and management of vice operations. In the end, law enforcement agencies become partners in the enterprise—sharing in the profits (which are incredibly high), making decisions on investment of capital, and enforcing the illegal and extralegal rules necessary to keep the enterprise functioning smoothly. All of these activities ultimately inhibit, if they do not destroy, the ability of the law enforcement agencies to control other types of crime and to serve as an "impartial" enforcer of the law. But organizationally the goals of the bureaucracy are met, and this is the governing principle of bureaucratic organization.

A similar analysis could easily be done on universities. Students are given numbers, IBMed, processed, funneled here and there, forced to take this course or that one, and generally used by the bureaucracy to meet bureaucratic goals of keeping administrative and faculty roles intact and turning out a quota of technical degrees that will satisfy the legislature. The true goal of universities —education—is subordinate to the organizational goals of the bureaucracy.

It is imperative to bear in mind that bureaucracy does not function independently of economic structure and power and power-related differences of society. Bureaucracy is a convenient form for efficient centralization of power. As was clear from the analysis of the law enforcement agencies, those who control the economy are in the last analysis the source of control over law enforcement bureaucracy. So too with universities. The reason the university must process rather than educate students is because people who control the dominant political and economic structures demand processing. Processing produces people who will take their proper place in the labor force—docile technicians who will use the low-echelon bureaucratic roles. Education produces people who might want to change the existing social relations.

Whither Bureaucratism?

Conflict analysis states that every economic strategy—be it feudalism, industrial capitalism, or industrial socialism—has within it the seeds of its own destruction. The inherent contradictions of feudalism were the source of feudalism's demise. The inherent contradictions of industrial capitalism are likewise forcing profound changes which will ultimately destroy it. Whether bureaucratism, a cultural child of the bourgeois revolution, is itself the next economic strategy is a question requiring extensive analysis. Just as capitalism grew out of the artisan extensions of feudalism to become an economic strategy in its own right, so bureaucratism may be in the process of becoming an economic strategy. Certainly the world view of the bureaucrat has little of the risk-taking, innovative, market-extending attitude of the early capitalists. Also, by limiting individual responsibility to narrowly defined jobs, bureaucratic structures leave working people free during nonwork hours, and often mentally free even during work hours. This sense of noninvolvement in work is a powerful force, at least in the United States. It partially makes up for the meaninglessness of much of the specialized, trivial work accompanying industrialization. It blinds masses of people to the social consequences of their work; for example, most employees of napalm manufacturers could not be sure *their* chemicals destroyed children in Vietnam even if they cared what happened to what they helped make. In short, bureaucracy is a painkiller— not necessarily the evil drug implied by some conspiracy-oriented conflict theorists, but a potion representing freedom from personal responsibility.

There is, however, a fundamental contradiction in the bureaucratic form when it pervades so many social relations: the goals of the bureaucracy are achieved at the expense of the interests of the people the bureaucracy is supposed to serve. Those who must deal with the bureaucracy as employees or clients or customers become alienated from the organizational form, and scream loudly against red tape and the G–– d––– bureaucrats. The alienation may smoulder for a lifetime, and even through generations, but in time it will create a new consciousness— new conflicts and in the end demands for change—which cannot be subverted, channeled into profitable directions, or suppressed. In the end the fact that bureaucracy does not serve the interests of those it processes will bring forth conflict between those at the top of the bureaucratic ladders, who benefit most, and those at the bottom or those excluded altogether from the use of bureaucratic roles. The bureaucratic form will have to change or be destroyed.

We are only now seeing the first waves of this process. The university students in the late sixties who took over administration buildings did so not simply because this was the center of power on the campus but because this represented the hub of the bureaucratic wheel. The Bank of America was burned by University of California students not just because it was "the biggest damned capitalist thing around" but also because it was the most bureaucratically structured organization in the immediate area.

In some bureaucracies in the capitalist world the problems are recognized and attempts are made to break down some of the role specializations and authority hierarchies characteristic of the form. Selection 15-2 is an advertisement in which the Saab automobile manufacturing company proudly describes its efforts in this direction.

The Soviet Union's attempt to build socialism is floundering under the burdens of an immense, inflexible bureaucracy. The failure to build a democratic socialism in the Soviet Union is certainly partly attributable to contradictions inherent in bureaucracy, just as the student rebellion in the United States and elsewhere is partly attributable to a reaction against bureaucracy.

In the 1960s China underwent a profoundly important "self-cleansing" in an effort to restore to "the people" control over their own

Those who are unemployed are familiar with long lines, endless forms, and people— using bureaucratic roles—who can only deal with specialized segments of their clients' problems. (Andrew Sacks from Editorial Photocolor Archives)

SELECTION 15-2: An attempt to solve the problem of bureaucratic (assembly-line) alienation.

Bored people build bad cars. That's why we're doing away with the assembly line.

Working on an assembly line is monotonous. And boring. And after a while, some people begin not to care about their jobs anymore. So the quality of the product often suffers.

That's why, at Saab, we're replacing the assembly line with assembly teams. Groups

of just three or four people who are responsible for a particular assembly process from start to finish.

Each team makes its own decisions about who does what and when. And each team member can even do the entire assembly singlehandedly. The result: people are more involved. They care more. So there's less absenteeism, less turnover. And we have more experienced people on the job.

We're building our new 2-liter engines this way. And the doors to our Saab 99. And we're planning to use this same system to build other parts of our car as well.

It's a slower, more costly system, but we realize that the best machines and materials in the world don't mean a thing, if the person building the car doesn't care.

Saab. It's what a car should be.

There are more than 300 Saab dealers nationwide. For the name and address of the one nearest you call 800-243-6000 toll free. In Connecticut, call 1-800-882-6500.

destiny by reducing the trend toward increasing bureaucratism.[6] By taking over the universities, the students purged the bureaucrats and entrenched elites; by taking over government offices and factories the workers did the same. It remains to be seen whether this experiment in attempting to control the bureaucratic tendencies of modern states was a permanent solution or only a temporary halting of the bureaucratic process. Perhaps the cultural revolution in China was merely the tool of competing bureaucratic elites using students and the image of Mao to achieve their own ends. Perhaps, as Mao Tse-tung has suggested, the only permanent solution to bureaucratism is permanent revolution where periodically the masses step forward and oust those who have gained power and authority in the bureaucracies. Perhaps a more lasting, less painful solution is possible. In any event, what we are clearly witnessing today is the emergence of widespread dissatisfaction with the bureaucratism that has enveloped our lives. When and how this dissatisfaction will be translated into action that will change the present social relations is a question to which we do not have any immediate answer.

[6] William Hinton, *Fanshen* (New York: Monthly Review, 1966).

SUMMARY

Max Weber's analysis of bureaucracy emphasized the historical development of bureaucracy and the inevitable tendency of bureaucracies to develop internal goals which become ends in themselves. We illustrated how this tendency can be used to provide insight into the operation of bureaucracies by examining the way law enforcement agencies solve the problem of organized crime.

It is our thesis that the contradiction between survival of specific bureaucratic organizations and the increasing powerlessness of most people using the bureaucratic form will ultimately destroy the bureaucracy or at least alter it so substantially that it will become a new social form. Perhaps this process will be like the organized conflict that occurred in China, or perhaps some other form will emerge. In any event it is clear that we are at the threshold of some significant changes of and challenges to bureaucratism, changes and challenges which promise to deepen the contradictions inherent in modern social forms.

SUGGESTED READINGS

Loren Baritz, *The Servants of Power* (Middletown, Conn.: Wesleyan University Press, 1960).

Peter M. Blau and W. Richard Scott, *Formal Organizations* (San Francisco: Chandler, 1962).

Harry Braverman, "Labor and Monopoly Capital: The Degradation of Work in the Twentieth Century," *Monthly Review*, vol. 26, no. 3, July-August 1974, pp. 1–134.

Henry Jacoby, *The Bureaucratization of the World* (Berkeley: University of California Press, 1973).

Gyorgy Lukacs, *History and Class Consciousness* (Cambridge, Mass.: M.I.T. Press, 1971).

SIXTEEN
Deviant Behavior and Social Control

INTRODUCTION

Traditional functional analysis treats those fined or sentenced to jail as *deviants*. In the popular view, those arrested, and charged with and convicted of crimes, are deviants—criminals or insane people on the outside of society.

Conflict analysis suggests that arrest and conviction are as much a part of the economic and political power struggle as are taxes, foreign relations, and the bureaucratic organization of work. It suggests that the lives of arrested persons—beyond the roles of "criminal"—will reveal a common powerlessness. Powerlessness, rather than personality type deprived" environment, or a "broken' .ume, will be the most important common characteristic of those jailed. In

short, the laws defining deviance, and the process of arrest, charge, arraignment, plea bargaining, conviction, sentence, and release are all better understood if analyzed as part of a power struggle originating in economic contradictions generating competing class struggle.

Psychological and social psychological analysis assumes that the law, courts, and arresting agencies reflect a popular consensus on right and wrong. Violations of law are explained as resulting from ineffective or improper childrearing and its effects on personality in psychological analysis. Social psychological analysis emphasizes such environmental factors as schools and delinquent subcultures.

Functional analysis explains violations of law as resulting from: (1) ineffective social structures (families or schools) leading to collections of failures who create deviant subcultures aimed at getting what individuals need but are denied; (2) in-migration of people whose ideas about right and wrong differ from the majority. A subtle possibility connected with this analysis is that both kinds of people may be doing society a favor (that is, may be functional) by serving as negative examples or by providing illegal but wanted services.

Conflict analysis assumes disagreement about right and wrong among many classes (not just majority and minority). The law, arresting agencies, and courts will always reflect the relative powers of these contending classes. All aspects of the legal system, from lawmaking to assignment of prison term, will reflect the fact that the different classes are treated differently.

DEFINING DEVIANT BEHAVIOR

What makes behavior deviant? When Ashland Oil Company secretly contributed 100 thousand dollars to Richard Nixon's reelection campaign, was that act deviant? When Union Oil Company secretly contributed huge sums of money to a campaign to defeat a bill before the California voters to spend a small amount of the revenue from gasoline taxes on an exploration of the possibility of having rapid-transit systems in California's major cities,[1] was that deviant? Was it deviant for the automobile industry to purchase Los Angeles' only rapid transit system and slowly phase it out, thus increasing the city's dependence on the automobile?[2]

The tax assessor in Gary, Indiana, for years sold favorable tax assessments to large businesses in return for secret campaign contri-

butions,[3] and the prosecuting attorney in Seattle, Washington, allowed gambling to flourish in the city so long as he received his share of the profits.[4] Joey, a man in his thirties, kills people for hire,[5] and Harry King is a professional safe cracker who spends most of his time stealing from banks and grocery stores so he can buy 200 dollar suits and spend money lavishly in Las Vegas.[6] Are these people deviant?

The vice-presidents of General Electric, Allis Chalmers, Westinghouse, and assorted other electrical companies conspired for many years to fix prices on everything from five-cent bolts to billion-dollar generators.[7] Were they deviant? Every city in the United States has hordes of homeless men who work irregularly, drink frequently, and are arrested continuously, and who account for much of the law enforcement effort in our cities. Are they deviant?

Sociologists in the functionalist tradition have usually tried to answer this question by classifying deviant acts according to their seriousness. They assume that there exists a set of norms or values—ideas about what is right and wrong, what is good and bad—which are generally ascribed to by almost everyone "in the society." Emile Durkheim said that one could isolate a set of ideas that existed in "all healthy consciousnesses in the society" and talk of crime as those acts which were in violation of these beliefs.[8]

Pursuing the logic implied by an assumption of a set of norms on which there is con-

---

[1] J. Allen Whitt, unpublished Master's thesis, University of California, Santa Barbara, 1973.

[2] See excerpt in Fig. 1.1 from Peter Barnes' "So-So Rapid Transit," *The New Republic*, September 1, 1973, pp. 18–20.

[3] George Crile, "A Tax Assessor Has Many Friends," *Harper's*, November, 1972, pp. 102–111.

[4] William J. Chambliss, "Vice, Corruption, Bureaucracy, and Power," *Wisconsin Law Review*, Winter, 1972.

[5] Joey, *Killer: The Autobiography of a Mafia Hit-Man* (New York: Playboy Press, 1973).

[6] Harry King, *Box Man: A Professional Thief's Journey*, (as told to and edited by William J. Chambliss) (New York: Harper and Row, 1972).

[7] Richard Austin Smith, "The Incredible Electric Conspiracy," *Fortune*, April, 1961.

[8] Emile Durkheim, *The Division of Labor in Society* (Glencoe, N.Y.: Free Press, 1960).

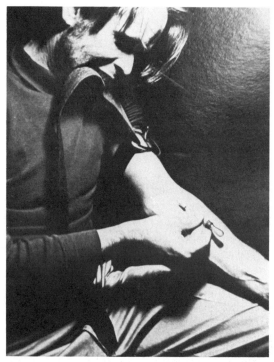

This person, rather than a person using alcohol to get high or a corporation president who cheats consumers of millions of dollars through price-fixing, is more likely to be considered and treated as a criminal in the United States today. (De Wys/EPA)

sensus, sociologists then typically spoke of "degrees of deviance" and developed various definitions of kinds of deviance accordingly. Thus, William Graham Sumner suggested that we could distinguish among "folkways," "mores," and "laws"[9]—folkways being norms which cover relatively mundane acts, such as whether to eat peas with a fork or knife, which side of the table a guest should sit at, etc., and laws being norms that are more strongly held and that apply to more important matters such as childrearing or property rights.

The first problem with starting with the assumption that there are areas of widespread consensus is that the assumption itself

[9] William Graham Sumner, *Folkways* (New York: Dover, 1959).

seems incorrect. Industrial economies generate social classes and varieties of social experience which lead to an infinite variety of "folkways, mores, and attitudes toward law"; consensus is hard to find. The vice-presidents of General Electric were well aware that they were violating the law but they believed, judging from their expressed opinions at their trial, that what they were doing was nonetheless right and just. When the staff surrounding President Nixon approved the entry of the Democratic headquarters, they were aware of the illegality of their acts, but they nonetheless felt that what they were doing was right. So, too, the professional thief who makes his living opening safes, the corrupt police captain or sheriff, and the professional killer all justify their behavior as right and proper. Furthermore, they live with other people who share their normative beliefs.

The functional perspective on deviance also misses an appreciation of the fact that political and economic forces shape our changing definitions of deviation and hence "create" classes of deviants. Historical analyses of particular deviant classes make this quite clear.

As children we were all exposed to the glamor and excitement of pirates. Typically "criminals of the sea" were depicted as either gallant heroes seeking adventure or bloodthirsty villains acting on their violent, greedy impulses. In fact, of course, they were neither. Piracy emerged out of the policies of Spain during the early colonial period. Spain was deeply involved in establishing colonies in Latin America. The peoples of the Caribbean Islands, however, made poor colonial subjects; they rebelled against their colonial masters and frequently died rather than succumb. One of the islands in the Caribbean, Santa Domingo, was finally abandoned by the Spanish after unsuccessful efforts at colonization but not before most of the inhabitants had been killed by Spanish soldiers. The slaughter of the humans allowed the cattle on the island to multiply rapidly, and in time the few remaining natives of Santa Domingo were blessed with a great abundance of cattle which they killed and cured into dried beef. Ships from England, France, and Spain began stopping at Santo Domingo and trading for the dried beef. The captains of these ships became known as *buccaneers* (after the French word for "one who smokes meat"). The Spanish government, however, opposed this trade because it interfered with their control of the area and their economic interests. They called the beef traders criminals and began attacking their ships. In response the buccaneers armed themselves and fought back, and in retaliation attacked and looted Spanish ships as well as the enclaves of Spanish towns along the coast of Latin America. Thus was born piracy, whose roots did not lie in the psychological makeup of the pirates or in conflicting values held by them. Pirates and the Spanish government shared the same desire to profit from trade and commerce. The government, however, had control of the ideological forces of the time and was thus able to brand its Island competitors criminals.

Examples illustrating the point are legion. Vagrancy laws in England emerged, shifted focus, and were changed in response to changing needs for labor by the ruling classes of England from the fourteenth to the twentieth centuries.[10]

The history of the institutionalization of those called "mentally ill" is an equally enlightening example of how the state creates deviant classes.[11] Foucault has shown how people once thought to be odd and at times

even saintly were gradually seen as dangerous and a threat to the community's well-being. Foucault shows by careful historical analysis how this transformation came about as a result of changes in seemingly unrelated factors. As the frequency of leprosy declined in Europe, the need for leprosoriums to isolate lepers from the community at large declined. But the physical structures for housing the lepers and the labor force used in those institutions remained intact. The people formerly regarded as odd were declared "mentally ill," and came to replace lepers in those institutions. In this way an entire problem of "deviance" was, in a sense created.

More recently we can see how the change in laws regarding the use of "dangerous drugs" from heroin to marijuana has been affected by the powerful. The federal government and various law enforcement agencies have created an atmosphere in which what, prior to 1900, was seen as a matter of a private citizens' rightful discretion has come to be defined as criminal in the most pejorative sense of the word.[12]

What, then, does it mean to say that an act is "deviant"? All it can mean sociologically is that some groups have the power to define the behavior of other people or groups as deviant. This is not to say, of course, that there is never anything resembling consensus. Most everyone in Norway may agree that to beat one's children senseless is wrong. But the fact remains that the only way such an act (child beating) becomes defined as deviant is through the ability of one group to impose that definition on others. Were the appellation "deviant" limited only to those things around which

[10] William J. Chambliss, "A Sociological Analysis of the Law of Vagrancy," *Social Problems*, Summer, 1964, pp. 67–77.
[11] Michael Foucault, *Madness and Civilization* (New York: Pantheon, 1965).

[12] See especially Alfred R. Lindesmith, *The Addict and the Law* (Bloomington, Ind.: Indiana University Press, 1965); Howard S. Becker, *Outsiders: Studies in the Sociology of Deviance* (Glencoe, N.Y.: Free Press, 1963); William J. Chambliss, "The State, The Law, and The Definition of Behavior as Criminal or Delinquent," in Daniel Glaser (ed.), *Handbook of Criminology* (Chicago: Rand McNally, 1974).

there was consensus or near consensus, then the study of deviance would have a homogeneity which is desperately lacking. As it is, we are struck with an endless array of acts defined by somebody or other as "deviant," and it is one sociological task to somehow develop coherent explanations and descriptions of this vast conglomeration of human actions.

A start toward unraveling the difficulties connected with the variations in definitions of deviance is an analysis of *how* some groups are able to have their particular conception of what is deviant accepted as the "official" stance—that is, defined by law as criminal. Obviously this touches only a small segment of what is normally regarded as deviant behavior but it nonetheless covers an extremely important segment. In America it covers, for example, not only acts like stealing, assault, embezzlement, and murder, but such things as public drunkenness, homosexuality, drug use, nude swimming, people under sixteen talking back to their parents, and being in a place without being able to account satisfactorily for one's presence. Given this very wide net, it is likely that whatever we discover from studying crime will apply more generally to deviant acts which are not incorporated in the criminal law as well.

HOW DO ACTS GET DEFINED AS CRIMINAL?

Writing from the perspective of functionalism Emile Durkheim specified several characteristics of acts which were defined as criminal. As mentioned above, Durkheim suggested that criminal acts are those that are offensive to "all healthy consciousnesses." Durkheim also suggested that criminal acts are acts that are not only offensive, but very strongly so.[13]

[13] Durkheim, op. cit.

Unfortunately, this rather rosy perspective on the law does not stand up very well under careful investigation. Indeed, a review of the available data from researches into the origins of the law indicates that very few laws reflect any kind of "community consensus" of what is wrong. Most of the laws passed reflect the interests of either the ruling class or some interest group that is able to marshal sufficient power to have its particular morality written into law.

The laws regarding theft—something about which most people assume there has always been consensus—were, in fact, developed in England during a time when the emerging class of merchants and traders were able to convince the lawmakers of the importance of protecting the merchant and trader's property from people who worked for them or who might try to appropriate their property.[14] And, as we have seen, the laws of vagrancy developed first to allow the ruling class of landowners to keep the farmworkers from leaving their land, and were later invoked to protect the ruling class of merchants from having "rogues and vagabonds" wandering the streets and highways where the merchants were transporting their goods. Even laws governing murder and rape emerged only when those acts became a threat to the ruling class of a feudal English society; so long as those acts threatened only the serfs and peasants they were settled on a very personal basis without interference from the state.

CAUSAL THEORIES OF CRIME

Some people argue, of course, that even though the emergence of criminal laws may be explained in political terms, the fact remains that given the prescriptions on behavior contained in the criminal law some

[14] Jerome Hall, *Theft, Law and Society* (Indianapolis: Bobbs-Merrill, 1952).

people commit illegal acts and others do not—that is, some people are criminals and some are not. The sociologist has only to answer why this is so. The fact is, however, that criminal law is so broad and criminality so widespread that virtually everyone in the United States commits crimes. Thus if we want to explain why some people commit crimes and others do not, we are really committed to the development of a general theory of human behavior. This is a perfectly reasonable quest, but it hardly leaves any unique place for the study of deviant behavior.

A more reasonable approach, arising out of the conviction that deviance is an area worthy of inquiry in its own right, is to recognize the political nature of deviance and to study the political processes by which acts are defined as deviant (what we have done above) and how some people come to be regarded as having committed those acts. The study of crime is *not* then the study of the "causes" of criminal behavior, but the study of the activities of those political, legal, and social groups that define and label people criminal.

A recently published study comparing middle- and lower-class gangs of high school youth provides an example of how looking at deviant behavior from the conflict perspective provides insights normally missed by functional analysis. Selection 16-1 is a summary of this study.

CRIME AND THE CONFLICT PERSPECTIVE

Seeing crime from the perspective of power places it squarely within the theoretical logic of the conflict perspective. The definitions of crime and deviance in a particular society develop out of the conflicts between different social classes and groups. The general principle for explaining crime from the conflict perspective is that certain acts and individuals will be labeled criminal when it is in the interests of the ruling class to so label. Most often this suggests an economic base: when the economic interests of the ruling class are threatened, the deviant label is most likely to be applied. Other factors, of course, are at work—for example, the ruling class or some segment of the ruling class may attempt to impose its own sense of morality on the entire population—but the economic motive will be the most important.

Examples are easy to come by. In the Soviet Union it has apparently become quite commonplace to use the label "mentally ill" as an excuse for incarcerating people who openly disagree with the policies and practices of the Soviet government, thus effectively removing them from a position where their criticisms might be heard.

Union organizers were labeled as criminal, arrested, beaten, sent to prison, and generally punished by the law enforcement agencies in the early days of unions in the United States. Later such measures were used on groups of students demonstrating against war or protesting the policies of the universities where they were enrolled. The laws protecting private property all reflect the interests of the ruling class in protecting the major source of its privileged position. Obviously an economic system dependent upon the private accumulation of wealth depends on protection of the individual's rights to use that wealth to purchase, control, and use commodities in any way he or she sees fit. The point isn't that the laws protecting private property are "right" or "wrong," but that they are laws which reflect the interests of those with the most property at the expense of the interests of those with the least. For example, protecting your car from being stolen is not in the interests of those classes who do not have a car but who would find one very useful or enjoyable.

In fact, of course, most law enforcement

SELECTION 16-1

THE SAINTS AND THE ROUGHNECKS

WILLIAM J. CHAMBLISS

Eight promising young men—children of good, stable, white upper-middle-class families, active in school affairs, good precollege students— were some of the most delinquent boys at Hanibal high school. While community residents and parents knew that these boys occasionally sowed a few wild oats, they were totally unaware that sowing wild oats completely occupied the daily routine of these young men. The Saints were constantly occupied with truancy, drinking, wild driving, petty theft, and vandalism. Yet not one was officially arrested for any misdeed during the two years I observed them.

This record was particularly surprising in light of my observations during the same two years of another gang of Hanibal high school students, six lower-class white boys known as the Roughnecks. The Roughnecks were constantly in trouble with police and community even though their rate of delinquency was about equal with that of the Saints. What was the cause of this disparity? The result? The following consideration of the activities, social class, and community perceptions of both gangs may provide some answers.

The Saints from Monday to Friday

The Saints' principal daily concern was with getting out of school as early as possible. The boys managed to get out of school with minimum danger that they would be accused of playing hookey through an elaborate procedure for obtaining "legitimate" release from class. The most common procedure was for one boy to obtain the release of another by fabricating a meeting of some committee, program or recognized club. Charles might raise his hand in his 9:00 chemistry class and ask to be excused—a euphemism for going to the bathroom. Charles would go to Ed's math class and inform the teacher that Ed was needed for a 9:30 rehearsal of the drama club play. The math teacher would recognize Ed and Charles as "good students" involved in numerous school activities and would permit Ed to leave at 9:30.

Charles would return to his class, and Ed would go to Tom's English class to obtain his release. Tom would engineer Charles' escape. The strategy would continue until as many of the Saints as possible were freed. After a stealthy trip to the car (which had been parked in a strategic spot), the boys were off for a day of fun.

Over the two years I observed the Saints, this pattern was repeated nearly every day. There were variations on the theme, but in one form or another, the boys used this procedure for getting out of class and then off the school grounds. Rarely did all eight of the Saints manage to leave school at the same time. The average number avoiding school on the days I observed them was five.

Having escaped from the concrete corridors the boys usually went either to a pool hall on the other (lower-class) side of town or to a cafe in the suburbs. Both places were out of the way of people the boys were likely to know (family or school officials), and both provided a source of entertainment. The pool hall entertainment was the generally rough atmosphere, the occasional hustler, the sometimes drunk proprietor, and, of course, the game of pool. The cafe's entertainment was provided by the owner. The boys would "accidentally" knock a glass on the floor or spill cola on the counter— not all the time, but enough to be sporting. They would also bend spoons, put salt in sugar bowls and generally tease whoever was working in the cafe. The owner had opened the cafe recently and was dependent on the boys' business which was, in fact, substantial since between the horsing around and the teasing they bought food and drinks.

The Saints on Weekends

On weekends the automobile was even more critical than during the week, for on weekends the Saints went to Big Town—a large city with a population of over a million 25 miles from Hanibal. Every Friday and Saturday night most of the Saints would meet between 8:00 and 8:30 and would go into Big Town. Big Town activities included drinking heavily in taverns or nightclubs, driving drunkenly through the streets, and committing acts of vandalism and playing pranks.

By midnight on Fridays and Saturdays the Saints were usually thoroughly high, and one or two of them were often so drunk they had to be carried to the cars. Then the boys drove around town, calling obscenities to women and girls; occasionally trying (unsuccessfully so far as I could tell) to pick girls up; and driving recklessly through red lights and at high speeds with their lights out. Occasionally they played "chicken." One boy would climb out the back window of the car and across the roof to the driver's side of the car while the car was moving at high speed (between 40 and 50 miles an hour); then the driver would move over and the boy who had just crawled across the car roof would take the driver's seat.

Searching for "fair game" for a prank was the boys' principal activity after they left the tavern. The boys would drive alongside a foot patrolman and ask direction to some street. If the policeman leaned on the car in the course of answering the question, the driver would speed away, causing him to lose his balance. The Saints were careful to play this prank only in an area where they were not going to spend much time and where they could quickly disappear around a corner to avoid having their license plate number taken.

Construction sites and road repair areas were the special province of the Saints' mischief. A soon-to-be-repaired hole in the road inevitably invited the Saints to remove lanterns and wooden barricades and put them in the car, leaving the hole unprotected. The boys would find a safe vantage point and wait for an unsuspecting motorist to drive into the hole. Often, though not always the boys would go up to the motorist and commiserate with him about the dreadful way the city protected its citizenry.

Leaving the scene of the open hole and the motorist, the boys would then go searching for an appropriate place to erect the stolen barricade. An "appropriate place" was often a spot on a highway near a curve in the road where the barricade would not be seen by an oncoming motorist. The boys would wait to watch an unsuspecting motorist attempt to stop and (usually) crash into the wooden barricade. With saintly bearing the boys might offer help and understanding.

A stolen lantern might well find its way onto the back of a police car or hang from a street lamp. Once a lantern served as a prop for a reenactment of the "midnight ride of Paul Revere" until the "play," which was taking place

at 2:00 A.M. in the center of a main street of Big Town, was interrupted by a police car several blocks away. The boys ran, leaving the lantern on the street, and managed to avoid being apprehended.

Abandoned houses, especially if they were located in out-of-the-way places, were fair game for destruction and spontaneous vandalism. The boys would break windows, remove furniture to the yard and tear it apart, urinate on the walls, and scrawl obscenities inside.

Through all the pranks, drinking, and reckless driving the boys managed miraculously to avoid being stopped by police. Only twice in two years was I aware that they had been stopped by a Big City policeman. Once was for speeding (which they did every time they drove whether they were drunk or sober), and the driver managed to convince the policeman that it was simply an error. The second time they were stopped they had just left a nightclub and were walking through an alley. Aaron stopped to urinate and the boys began making obscene remarks. A foot patrolman came into the alley, lectured the boys and sent them home. Before the boys got to the car, they began talking in a loud voice again. The policeman, who had followed them down the alley, arrested this boy for disturbing the peace and took him to the police station where the other Saints gathered. After paying a $5.00 fine, and with the assurance that there would be no permanent record of the arrest, the boy was released.

The boys had a spirit of frivolity and fun about their escapades. They did not view what they were engaged in as "delinquency," though it surely was by any reasonable definition of that word. They simply viewed themselves as having a little fun and who, they would ask, was really hurt by it? The answer had to be no one, although this fact remains one of the most difficult things to explain about the gang's behavior. Unlikely though it seems, in two years of drinking, driving, carousing, and vandalism no one was seriously injured as a result of the Saints' activities.

The Saints in School

The Saints were highly successful in school. The average grade for the group was "B," with two of the boys having close to a straight "A" average. Almost all of the boys were popular and many of them held offices in the school. One of the boys was vice-president of the student body one year. Six of the boys played on athletic teams.

At the end of their senior year, the student body selected ten seniors for special recognition as the "school wheels"; four of ten were Saints. Teachers and school officials saw no problem with any of these boys and anticipated that they would all "make something of themselves."

How the boys managed to maintain this impression is surprising in view of their actual behavior while in school. Their technique for covering truancy was so successful that teachers did not even realize that the boys were absent from school much of the time. Occasionally, of course, the system would backfire and then the boy was on his own. A boy who was caught would be most contrite, and would plead guilty and ask for mercy. He inevitably got the mercy he sought.

Cheating on examinations was rampant, even to the point of orally communicating answers to exams as well as looking at one another's papers. Since none of the group studied, and since they were primarily dependent on one another for help, it is surprising that grades were so high. Teachers contributed to the deception in their admitted inclination to give these boys (and presumably others like them) the benefit of the doubt. When asked how the boys did in school, and when pressed on specific examinations, teachers might admit that they were disappointed in John's performance, but would quickly add that they "knew that he was capable of doing better," so John was given a higher grade than he had actually earned. How often this happened is impossible to know. During the time that I observed the group, I never saw any of the boys take homework home. Teachers may have been "understanding" very regularly.

One exception to the gang's generally good performance was Jerry, who had a "C" average in his junior year, experienced disaster the next year, and failed to graduate. Jerry had always been a little more nonchalant than the others about the liberties he took in school. Rather than wait for someone to come get him from class, he would offer his own excuse and leave. Although he probably did not miss any more classes than most of the others in the group, he did not take the requisite pain to cover his absences. Jerry was the only Saint whom I ever heard talk back to a teacher. Although teachers often called him a "cut-up" or a "smart kid," they never referred to him as a troublemaker or as a kid headed for trouble. It seems likely, then, that Jerry's failure his senior year and his mediocre performance his junior year were consequences of his not playing the game the proper way (possibly because he was disturbed by his parents' divorce). His teachers regarded him as "immature" and not quite ready to get out of high school.

The Police and the Saints

The local police saw the Saints as good boys who were among the leaders of the youth in the community. Rarely, the boys might be stopped in town for speeding or for running a stop sign. When this happened the boys were always polite, contrite, and pled for mercy. As in school, they received the mercy they asked for. None ever received a ticket or was taken into the precinct by the local police.

The situation in Big City, where the boys engaged in most of their delinquency, was only slightly different. The police there did not know the boys at all, although occasionally the boys were stopped by a patrolman. Once they were caught taking a lantern from a construction site. Another time they were stopped for running a stop sign, and on several occasions they were stopped for speeding. Their behavior was as before: contrite, polite, and penitent. The urban police, like the local police, accepted their demeanor as sincere. More important, the urban police were convinced that these were good boys just out for a lark.

The Roughnecks

Hanibal townspeople never perceived the Saints' high level of delinquency. The Saints were good boys who just went in for an occasional prank. After all, they were well dressed, well mannered, and had nice cars. The Roughnecks were a different story. Although the two gangs of boys were the same age, and both groups engaged in an equal amount of wild-oat sowing, everyone agreed that the not-so-well-dressed, not-so-well-mannered, not-so-rich boys were heading for trouble. Townspeople would say, "You can see the gang members at the drugstore, night after night, leaning against the storefront (sometimes drunk) or slouching around inside buying cokes, reading magazines, and probably stealing old Mr. Wall blind. When they are outside and girls walk by, even respectable girls, these boys make suggestive remarks. Sometimes their remarks are downright lewd."

From the community's viewpoint, the real indication that these kids were in for trouble was that they were constantly involved with the police. Some of them had been picked up for stealing, mostly small stuff, of course, "but still it's stealing small stuff that leads to big time crimes." "Too bad," people said. "Too bad that these boys couldn't behave like the other kids in town; stay out of trouble, be polite to adults, and look to their future."

The community's impression of the degree to which this group of six boys (ranging in age from sixteen to nineteen) engaged in delinquency was somewhat distorted. In some ways the gang was more delinquent that the community thought; in other ways they were less.

The fighting activities of the group were fairly readily and accurately perceived by almost everyone. At least once a month, the boys would get into some sort of fight, although most fights were scraps between members of the group or involved only one member of the group and some peripheral hanger-on. Only three times in the period of observation did the group fight together: once against a gang from across town, once against two blacks and once against a group of boys from another school. For the first two fights the group went out "looking for trouble"—and they found it both times. The third fight followed a football game and began spontaneously with an argument on the football field between one of the Roughnecks and a member of the opposition's football team.

Jack had a particular propensity for fighting and was involved in most of the brawls. He was a prime mover of the escalation of arguments into fights.

More serious than fighting, had the community been aware of it, was theft. Although almost everyone was aware that the boys occasionally stole things, they did not realize the extent of the activity. Petty stealing was a frequent event for the Roughnecks. Sometimes they stole as a group and coordinated their efforts; other times they stole in pairs. Rarely did they steal alone.

The thefts ranged from very small things like paperback books, comics, and ballpoint pens to expensive items like watches. The nature of the thefts varied from time to time. The gang would go through a period of systematically shoplifting items from automobiles or school lockers. Types of thievery varied with the whim of the gang. Some forms of thievery were more profitable than others, but all thefts were for profit, not just thrills.

Roughnecks siphoned gasoline from cars as often as they had access to an automobile, which was not very often. Unlike the Saints, who owned their own cars, the Roughnecks would have to borrow their parents' cars, an event which occurred only eight or nine times a year. The boys claimed to have stolen cars for joy rides from time to time.

Ron committed the most serious of the group's offenses. With an unidentified associate the boy attempted to burglarize a gasoline station. Although this station had been robbed twice previously in the same month, Ron denied any involvement in either of the other thefts. When Ron and his accomplice approached the station, the owner was hiding in the bushes beside the station. He fired both barrels of a double-barreled shotgun at the boys. Ron was severely injured; the other boy ran away and was never caught. Though he remained in critical condition for several months, Ron finally recovered and served six months of the following year in reform school. Upon release from reform school, Ron was put back a grade in school, and began running around with a different gang of boys. The Roughnecks considered the new gang less delinquent than themselves, and during the following year Ron had no more trouble with the police.

The Roughnecks, then, engaged mainly in three types of delinquency: theft, drinking, and fighting. Although community members perceived that this gang of kids was delinquent, they mistakenly believed that their illegal activities were primarily drinking, fighting, and being a nuisance to passersby. Drinking was limited among the gang members, although it did occur, and theft was much more prevalent than anyone realized.

Drinking would doubtless have been more prevalent had the boys had ready access to liquor. Since they rarely had automobiles at their disposal, they could not travel very far, and the bars in town would not serve them. Most of the boys had little money, and this, too, inhibited their purchase of alcohol. Their major source of liquor was a local drunk who would buy them a fifth if they would give him enough extra to buy himself a pint of whiskey or a bottle of wine.

The community's perception of drinking as prevalent stemmed from the fact that it was the most obvious delinquency the boys engaged in. When one of the boys had been drinking, even a casual observer seeing him on the corner would suspect that he was high.

There was a high level of mutual distrust and dislike between the Roughnecks and the police. The boys felt very strongly that the police were unfair and corrupt. Some evidence existed that the boys were correct in their perception.

The main source of the boys' dislike for the police undoubtedly stemmed from the fact that the police would sporadically harass the group. From the standpoint of the boys, these acts of occasional enforcement of the law were whimsical and uncalled for. It made no sense to them, for example, that the police would come to the corner occasionally and threaten them with arrest for loitering when the night before the boys had been out siphoning gasoline from cars and the police had been nowhere in sight. To the boys, the police were stupid on the one hand, for not being where they should have been and catching the boys in a serious offense, and unfair on the other hand, for trumping up "loitering" charges against them.

From the viewpoint of the police, the situation was quite different. They knew, with all the confidence necessary to be a policeman, that these boys were engaged in criminal activities. They knew this partly from occasionally catching them, mostly from circumstantial evidence ("the boys were around when those tires were slashed"), and partly because the police shared the view of the community in general that this was a bad bunch of boys. The best the police could hope to do was to be sensitive to the fact that these boys were engaged in illegal acts and arrest them whenever there was some evidence that they had been involved. Whether or not the boys had in fact committed a particular act in a particular way was not especially important. The police had a broader view: their job was to stamp out these kids' crimes; the tactics were not as important as the end result.

Over the period that the group was under observation, each member was arrested at least once. Several of the boys were arrested a number of times and spent at least one night in jail. While most were never taken to court, two of the boys were sentenced to six months' incarceration in boys' schools.

The Roughnecks in School

The Roughnecks' behavior in school was not particularly disruptive. During school hours they did not all hang around together, but tended instead to spend most of their time with one or two other members of the gang who were their special buddies. Although every member of the gang attempted to avoid school as much as possible, they were not particularly successful and most of them attended school with surprising regularity. They considered school a burden—something to be gotten through with a minimum of conflict. If they were "bugged" by a particular teacher, it could lead to trouble. One of the boys, Al, once threatened to beat up a teacher and, according to the other boys, the teacher hid under a desk to escape him.

Teachers saw the boys the way the general community did, as heading for trouble, as being uninterested in making something of themselves. Some were also seen as being incapable of meeting the academic standards of the school. Most of the teachers expressed concern for this group of boys and were willing to pass them despite poor performance, in the belief that failing them would only aggravate the problem.

The group of boys had a grade point average just slightly above "C." No one in the group failed either grade, and no one had better than a "C" average. They were very consistent in their achievement or, at least, the teachers were consistent in their perception of the boys' achievement.

Two of the boys were good football players. Herb was acknowledged to be the best player in the school and Jack was almost as good. Both boys were criticized for their failure to abide by training rules, for refusing to come to practice as often as they should, and for not playing their best during practice. What they lacked in sportsmanship they made up for in skill, apparently, and played every game no matter how poorly they had performed in practice or how many practice sessions they had missed.

Two Questions

Why did the community, the school and the police react to the Saints as though they were good, upstanding, nondelinquent youths with bright futures but to the Roughnecks as though they were tough young criminals who were headed for trouble? Why did the Roughnecks and the Saints in fact have quite different careers after high school—careers which, by and large, lived up to the expectations of the community?

The most obvious explanation for the differences in the community's and law enforcement agencies' reactions to the two gangs is that one group of boys was "more delinquent" than the other. Which group *was* more delinquent? The answer to this question will determine in part how we explain the differential responses to these groups by the members of the community and, particularly, by law enforcement and school officials.

In sheer number of illegal acts, the Saints were the more delinquent. They were truant from school for at least part of the day almost every day of the week. In addition, their drinking and vandalism occurred with surprising regularity. The Roughnecks, in contrast, engaged sporadically in delinquent episodes. While these episodes were frequent, they certainly did not occur on a daily or even a weekly basis.

The difference in frequency of offenses was probably caused by the Roughnecks' inability to obtain liquor and to manipulate legitimate excuses from school. Since the Roughnecks had less money than the Saints, and teachers carefully supervised their school activities, the Roughnecks' hearts may have been as black as the Saints', but their misdeeds were not nearly as frequent.

There are really no clear-cut criteria by which to measure qualitative differences in antisocial behavior. The most important dimension of the difference is generally referred to as the "seriousness" of the offenses.

If seriousness encompasses the relative economic costs of delinquent acts, then some assessment can be made. The Roughnecks probably stole an average of about $5.00 worth of goods a week. Some weeks the figure was considerably higher, but these times must be balanced against long periods when almost nothing was stolen.

The Saints were more continuously engaged in delinquency but their acts were not for the most part costly to property. Only their vandalism and occasional theft of gasoline would so qualify. Perhaps once or twice a month they would siphon a tankful of gas. The other costly items were street signs, construction lanterns and the like. All of these acts combined probably did not quite average $5.00 a week, partly because much of the stolen equipment was abandoned and presumably could be recovered. The difference in cost of stolen property between the two groups was trivial, but the Roughnecks probably had a slightly more expensive set of activities than did the Saints.

Another meaning of seriousness is the potential threat of physical harm to members of the community and to the boys themselves. The Roughnecks were more prone to physical violence; they not only welcomed an opportunity to fight; they went seeking it. In addition, they fought among themselves frequently. Although the fighting never included deadly weapons, it was still a menace, however minor, to the physical safety of those involved.

The Saints never fought. They avoided physical conflict both inside and outside the group. At the same time, though, the Saints frequently endangered their own and other people's lives. They did so almost every time they drove a car, especially if they had been drinking. Sober, their driving was risky; under the influence of alcohol it was horrendous. In addition, the Saints endangered the lives of others with their pranks. Street excavations left unmarked were a very serious hazard.

Evaluating the relative seriousness of the two gangs' activities is difficult. The community reacted as though the behavior of the Roughnecks was a problem, and they reacted as though the behavior of the Saints was not. But the members of the community were ignorant of the array of delinquent acts that characterized the Saints' behavior. Although concerned citizens were unaware of much of the Roughnecks' behavior as well, they were much better informed about the Roughnecks' involvement in delinquency than they were about the Saints'.

Visibility

Differential treatment of the two gangs resulted in part because one gang was infinitely more visible than the other. This differential visibilty was a direct function of the economic standing of the families. The Saints had access to automobiles and were able to remove themselves from the sight of the community. In as routine a decision as to where to go to have a milkshake after school, the Saints stayed away from the mainstream of community life. Lacking transportation, the Roughnecks could not make it to the edge of town. The center of town was the only practical place for them to meet since their homes were scattered throughout the town and any noncentral meeting place put an undue hardship on some members. Through necessity the Roughnecks congregated in a crowded area where everyone in the community passed frequently, including teachers and law enforcement officers. They could easily see the Roughnecks hanging around the drugstore.

The Roughnecks, of course, made themselves even more visible by making remarks to passersby and by occasionally getting into fights on the corner. Meanwhile, just as regularly, the Saints were either at the cafe on one edge of town or in the pool hall at the other edge of town. Without any particular realization that they were making themselves inconspicuous, the Saints were able to hide their time-wasting. Not only were they removed from the mainstream of traffic, but they were almost always inside a building.

On their escapades the Saints were also relatively invisible, since they left Hanibal and traveled to Big City. Here, too, they were mobile, roaming the city, rarely going to the same area twice.

Demeanor

To the notion of visibility must be added the difference in the responses of group members to outside intervention with their activities. If one of the Saints was fronted with an accusing policeman, even if he felt he was truly innocent of a wrongdoing, his demeanor was apologetic and penitent. A Roughneck's attitude was almost the polar opposite. When confronted with a threatening adult authority, even one who tried to be pleasant, the Roughneck's hostility and disdain were clearly observable. Sometimes he might attempt to put up a veneer of respect, but it was thin and was not accepted as sincere by the authority.

School was no different from the community at large. The Saints could manipulate the system by feigning compliance with the school norms. The availability of cars at school meant that once free from the immediate sight of the teacher, the boys could disappear rapidly. And this escape was well enough planned that no administrator or teacher was nearby when the boys left. A Roughneck who wished to escape for a few hours was in a bind. If it were possible to get free from class, downtown was still a mile away, and even if he arrived there, he was still very visible. Truancy for the Roughnecks meant almost certain detection, while the Saints enjoyed almost complete immunity from sanctions.

Bias

Community members were not aware of the transgressions of the Saints. Even if the Saints had been less discreet, their favorite delinquencies would have been perceived as less serious than those of the Roughnecks.

In the eyes of the police and school officials, a boy who drinks in an alley and stands intoxicated on the street corner is committing a more serious offense than is a boy who drinks to inebriation in a nightclub or a tavern and drives around afterwards in a car. Similarly, a boys who steals a wallet from a store will be viewed as having committed a more serious offense than a boy who steals a lantern from a construction site.

Perceptual bias also operates with respect to the demeanor of the boys in the two groups when they are confronted by adults. It is not simply that adults dislike the posture affected by boys of the Roughneck ilk; more important is the conviction that the posture adopted by the Roughnecks is an indication of their devotion and commitment to deviance as a way of life. The posture becomes a cue, just as the type of the offense is a cue, to the degree to which the known transgressions are indicators of the youths' potential for other problems.

Visibility, demeanor and bias are surface variables which explain the day-to-day operations of the police. Why do these surface variables operate as they do? Why did the police choose to disregard the Saints' delinquencies while breathing down the backs of the Roughnecks?

The answer lies in the class structure of American society and the control of legal institutions by those at the top of the class structure. Obviously, no representative of the upper class drew up the operational chart for the police which led them to look in the ghettos and on streetcorners—which led them to see the demeanor of lower-class youth as troublesome and that of upper-middle-class youth as tolerable. Rather, the procedures simply developed from experience—experience with irate and influential upper-middle-class parents insisting that their son's vandalism was simply a prank and his drunkenness only a momentary "sowing of wild oats"—experience with cooperative or indifferent, powerless, lower-class parents who acquiesced to the laws' definition of their son's behavior.

Adult Careers of the Saints and the Roughnecks

The community's confidence in the potential of the Saints and the Roughnecks apparently was justified. If anything, the community-members underestimated the degree to which these youngsters would turn out "good" or "bad."

Seven of the eight members of the Saints went on to college immediately after high school. Five of the boys graduated from college in four years. The sixth one finished college after two years in the army, and the seventh spent four years in the air force before returning to college and receiving a B.A. degree. Of these seven college graduates, three went on for advanced degrees. One finished law school and is now active in state politics, one finished medical school and is practicing near Hanibal, and one boy is now working for a Ph.D. The other four college graduates entered submanagerial, managerial or executive training positions with larger firms.

The only Saint who did not complete college was Jerry. Jerry had failed to graduate from high school with the other Saints. During his second senior year, after the other Saints had gone on to college, Jerry began to hang around with what several teachers described as a "rough crowd"—the gang that was heir apparent to the Roughnecks. At the end of his second senior year, when he did graduate from high school, Jerry took a job as a used-car salesman, got married, and quickly had a child. Although he

made several abortive attempts to go to college by attending night school, when I last saw him (ten years after high school) Jerry was unemployed and had been living on unemployment for almost a year. His wife worked as a waitress.

Some of the Roughnecks have lived up to community expectations. A number of them were headed for trouble. A few were not.

Jack and Herb were the athletes among the Roughnecks and their athletic prowess paid off handsomely. Both boys received unsolicited athletic scholarships to college. After Herb received his scholarship (near the end of his senior year), he apparently did an about-face. His demeanor became very similar to that of the Saints. Although he remained a member in good standing of the Roughnecks, he stopped participating in most activities and did not hang on the corner as often.

Jack did not change. If anything, he became more prone to fighting. He even made excuses for accepting the scholarship. He told the other gang members that the school had guaranteed him a "C" average if he would come to play football—an idea that seems far-fetched, even in this day of highly competitive recruiting.

During the summer after graduation from high school, Jack attempted suicide by jumping from a tall building. The jump would certainly have killed most people trying it, but Jack survived. He entered college in the fall and played four years of football. He and Herb graduated in four years, and both are teaching and coaching in high schools. They are married and have stable families. If anything, Jack appears to have a more prestigious position in the community than does Herb, though both are well respected and secure in their positions.

Two of the boys never finished high school. Tommy left at the end of his junior year and went to another state. That summer he was arrested and placed on probation on a manslaughter charge. Three years later he was arrested for murder; he pleaded guilty to second degree murder and is serving a 30-year sentence in the state penitentiary.

Al, the other boy who did not finish high school, also left the state in his senior year. He is serving a life sentence in a state penitentiary for first degree murder.

Wes is a small-time gambler. He finished high school and "bummed around." After several years he made contact with a bookmaker who employed him as a runner. Later he acquired his own area and has been working it ever since. His position among the bookmakers is almost identical to the position he had in the gang; he is always around but no one is really aware of him. He makes no trouble and he does not get into any. Steady, reliable, capable of keeping his mouth closed, he plays the game by the rules, even though the game is an illegal one.

That leaves only Ron. Some of his former friends reported that they had heard he was "driving a truck up north," but no one could provide any concrete information.

Reinforcement

The community responded to the Roughnecks as boys in trouble, and the boys agreed with that perception. Their pattern of deviancy was reinforced, and breaking away from it became increasingly unlikely. Once the boys acquired an image of themselves as deviants, they selected new friends who affirmed that self-image. As that self-conception became more firmly entrenched, they also became willing to try new and more extreme deviances. With their growing alienation came freer expression of disrespect and hostility for representatives of the legitimate society. This disrespect increased the community's negativism, perpetuating the entire process of commitment to deviance. Lack of a commitment to deviance works the same way. In either case, the process will perpetuate itself unless some events (like a scholarship to college or a sudden failure) external to the established relationship intervenes. For two of the Roughnecks (Herb and Jack), receiving college athletic scholarships created new relations and culminated in a break with the established pattern of deviance. In the case of one of the Saints (Jerry), his parents' divorce and his failing to graduate from high school changed some of his other relations. Being held back in school for a year and losing his place among the Saints had sufficient impact on Jerry to alter his self-image and virtually to assure that he would not go on to college as his peers did. Although the experiments of life can rarely be reversed, it seems likely in view of the behavior of the other boys who did not enjoy this special treatment by the school that Jerry, too, would have "become something" had he graduated as anticipated. For Herb and Jack outside intervention worked to their advantage; for Jerry it was his undoing.

Selective perception and labeling—finding, processing, and punishing some kinds of criminality and not others—means that visible, poor, nonmobile, outspoken, undiplomatic "tough" kids will be noticed, whether their actions are seriously delinquent or not. Other kids, who have established a reputation for being bright (even though underachieving), disciplined, and involved in respectable activities, who are mobile and monied, will be invisible when they deviate from sanctioned activities. They'll sow their wild oats—perhaps even wider and thicker than their lower-class cohorts—but they won't be noticed. When it's time to leave adolescence most will follow the expected path, settling into the ways of the middle class, remembering fondly the delinquent but unnoticed fling of their youth. The Roughnecks and others like them may turn around, too. It is more likely that their noticeable deviance will have been so reinforced by police and community that their lives will be effectively channeled into careers consistent with their adolescent background.

effort is *not* devoted to the direct protection of private property, life, or limb. In fact, the police may be regarded as a "reserve army" which stands ready to protect the interests of the ruling class when the conflicts that are inherent in a class society break into open rebellion as they inevitably do from time to time. Thus the reserve army is there when unions try to force the owners of the means of production to pay higher wages or give better working conditions, when the poor attempt to take over the control of the stores in their neighborhoods, or when students demonstrate against government policy.

This reserve army becomes increasingly powerful as police agencies across the country get computer connections with one

THE CHILL OF MISTAKEN RAIDS

One night two months ago, a group of armed men burst into homes in Middle America and brought terror to two families.

The men were narcotics agents, and they had made a mistake. Their error put Collinsville, Ill., in headlines and touched off a storm of indignation.

• In January, William Pine was awakened by his daughter's screams as armed men broke through the front and back doors of his Winthrop, Mass., home. He was pushed against a window with guns pointed at his head before state police realized they had the wrong house.

• Heyward H. Dryer, 22, was shot and killed Oct. 2, 1969, in his Whittier, Calif., apartment when a narcotics agent who had broken into the wrong apartment on the floor above fired a shot through the floor.

• On May 18, an off-duty Texas Department of Public Safety officer was shot to death in a raid on a Houston apartment after an informer mistakenly identified him to narcotics agents as having sold ampetamine pills.

Also, a grand jury in Eureka, Calif. indicted a federal narcotics agent in the death of a man who fled from his cabin when agents descended on it by helicopters.

In a "wrong-house" raid in Norfolk, Va., a patrolman was killed when a housewife fired through her front door. Other mistake raids occurred in Oakland, Phoenix and Atlanta.

Federal spokesmen recall no dismissals of agents for abuses on raids.

The Nixon Administration has declared "all-out global war on the drug menace." State and local enforcement has been stepped up, partly through the efforts of the Office of Drug Abuse Law Enforcement (DALE) which was set up in the Justice Department in January 1971 to carry the federal attack on drugs, particularly heroin, down to the street level.

This campaign has resulted in record numbers of search or arrest warrants and put record numbers of drug traffickers and record amounts of illegal drugs out of circulation.

But civil liberties groups and persons in the enforcement field charge that legal restrictions or operating safeguards have in some cases been ignored.

Herbert Giglotto, 29, and his wife, Louise, 28, were asleep in their Collinsville home on April 23 when a crash and some screaming awakened them.

"I take about three steps out of bed, and I see these hippies with guns. I told my wife, 'We're dead,' " Giglotto said.

Giglotto says he and his wife were knocked down across their bed and handcuffed. He was threatened with death at gunpoint as the men shouted obscenities at them. One agent flashed a gold badge, which Mrs. Giglotto only glimpsed.

When the men realized their mistake, they left without apology or explanation, Giglotto said.

Donald Askew, 40, and his wife, Virginia, 37, had just sat down to dinner that night in Collinsville when armed men began to kick their door in. Askew told his son to run for his life.

Again there were threats and no apologies before the men left, Askew said.

The Bureau of Narcotics and Dangerous Drugs agents who participated in the raids under DALE's auspices were suspended, according to Special Asst. Atty. Gen. Myles Ambrose.

DALE's legal officer, Robert Richardson, said in Washington that the men were suspended with pay.

Since the Collinsville incident, Ambrose has reminded DALE's 41 area offices to be more careful.

The law allows agents to enter a home without a warrant if they have probable cause to believe they can catch someone violating the law.

BNDD, which has 1,320 agents in the United States, gives its trainees 10 weeks training in fundamentals.

DALE, composed of about 100 lawyers working with agents and a special federal grand jury in each of its cities, "has no opportunity to train, or retrain, agents assigned to it," Richardson said.

DALE has 465 federal agents, half from BNDD and the rest from other federal agencies, and more than 400 local or state law enforcement officers on assignment to it.

A $900,000 settlement was reached in a suit over the killing in Whittier, and state and local officers involved drew suspensions.

In the Houston raid, the officers have not been suspended, but a grand jury is investigating.

SELECTION 16-3: Potential for error in technology of crime detection.

COMPUTER, CITY GOOF— HE'S JAILED

Bill O'Brien

The Police computer and the local municipal court clerk's office have collaborated again to jail a completely innocent man.

Paul Kruisbrink, 30, said today he is seeking an attorney to represent him when he joins the swelling ranks of miffed citizens suing the city for false imprisonments.

The Pleasanton real estate salesman spent five hours in the Concord City Jail last June 3 as a result of a San Francisco traffic warrant that never should have existed.

His variety of trouble began last March 26 when he ran a red light at 17th and Harrison Streets here. He misread the $19.50 demand for bail as merely $9.50 on the citation he signed for the arresting policeman.

Kruisbrink first mailed in a check for $9.50.

The court clerk's office informed him he was $10 shy. So Kruisbrink mailed in an additional $10. He assumed the citation was settled.

On June 3, in Concord with his wife and two small children, he was cited for making an illegal crossing of a yellow line.

The arresting officer made the routine radio request for a check of the Police Information Network Computer (PIN) for a determination of whether Kruisbrink was wanted for any past parking or traffic violation.

PIN reported that the $19.50 red light infraction had advanced to warrant stage and now demanded a bail of $55.50, which Kruisbrink did not have at the moment.

He spent five hours behind bars, protesting his innocence, while his wife drove to Pleasanton, borrowed the required bail from a neighbor, and drove back to Concord.

"It was embarrassing to be arrested out on the street with your family like that," recalled Kruisbrink today.

The real estate salesman was given June 18 as a court date for him to protest his being served with the warrant he had paid in the citation stage.

Kruisbrink reported to the Hall of Justice here but could find himself on no court calendar. In desperation he went to the traffic court clerk's office where a female employee rummaged through a small box of receipts kept beneath a counter.

Finally, according to Kruisbrink, the young woman conceded: "Yes, we made a mistake— you'll get your money back."

another ostensibly, for example, to fight the "drug" problem. Dossiers on private citizens are established and traded back and forth between police agencies. Individuals are increasingly subject to harassment and intimidation as overzealous and often mistaken use of police power becomes increasingly frequent. Selections 16-2 and 16-3 are case histories reflecting the thin line between a reserve army and a police state.

It is also necessary that the reserve army appear to have an ongoing function of fighting "crime" and not merely a function of suppressing change. Furthermore, if they are

to be effective in time of need they must have had some actual practice "in the field" —the field being the ghettos and slums of the large cities. Here police spend endless hours looking for drunks, vagrants, poker and crap games, family quarrels, and drug transactions. By pursuing the ghetto "criminals," the police ensure that they will be regarded as crime fighters, even though they do not, in fact, threaten the status quo. They do not look for drunks, family quarrels, or poker games in upper-class suburbs. Indeed, they organize themselves so as to avoid being aware that such things go on. If police departments were limited to enforcing only those laws that represented "important breaches of norms generally agreed upon in the community," the number of police could be reduced by 80 percent. But if that were done, it would be impossible to control the occasionally violent and peaceful mass uprisings generated by the inequalities in wealth, power, and prestige that characterize the economic structures of capitalist societies.

Who, then, is deviant? The answer is that those classes are deviant who can be so labeled by the passage of laws and the enforcement of laws in the interests of the ruling classes of a society. *Crime* and *deviance* are politically determined phenomena which are inevitably shaped by conflicts among social classes inherent in a system characterized by unequal distribution of resources.

SUMMARY

In this chapter, deviance is examined from a conflict perspective.

Deviance is an appropriate term for functionalist analysis. Functional analysis of crime, for example, starts with the assumption of widespread agreement on what constitutes right and wrong. This agreement is assumed to be reflected in criminal law, and laws will be passed to punish what is agreed to be seriously wrong behavior. Thus one can speak of criminal deviants, those who violate laws supported by the vast majority.

A conflict perspective starts from the testable assumption that in capitalist industrial nations there is little agreement on right and wrong. From this, an analysis of crime is developed which suggests that behavior defined as illegal, arrests for illegal behavior, and sentencing practices will all reflect the relative power of social classes.

The police will be the focus of pressures from social classes to differentially enforce the law to favor one class over another. They will also be under pressure to serve as a reserve army in the class struggle. The more powerful class will be able to use police to suppress peaceful or violent mass moves that are against its interests.

SUGGESTED READINGS

Daniel Bell, "Crime as an American Way of Life" (Indianapolis: Bobbs-Merrill, Reprints in Sociology).

William J. Chambliss, "Vice, Corruption, Bureaucracy, and Power," *Wisconsin Law Review*, Winter 1972. (Also available in reprint from MSS Publications, 655 Madison Ave., New York.)

Joey, *Killer: The Autobiography of a Mafia Hit-Man* (New York: Pocket Books, 1973).

Harry King, *Box Man: A Professional Thief's Journey* (as told to and edited by William J. Chambliss) (New York: Harper and Row, 1972).

Alfred W. McCoy, *The Politics of Heroin in Southeast Asia* (New York: Harper and Row, 1972).

Richard Quinney, *Critique of Legal Order* (Boston: Little, Brown, 1974).

Robert N. Winter-Berger, *The Washington Payoff* (New York: Dell, 1972).

SEVENTEEN
Social Inequality:
The Sources of Conflict and Change

INTRODUCTION

In previous chapters we considered certain elements of contemporary industrial life: the military, power, imperialism, bureaucratism, and the legal system. This chapter is concerned with the relationship of the individual to the massive forces unleashed by industrialization. This subject may be analyzed in many ways. Traditional texts emphasize the social psychology of contemporary "society"; analysis is done of the effects of social organization on the organization of people's personalities or life-styles. Various examples of "adjustment" or "maladjustment" are isolated and studied.

Conflict analysis focuses attention not on personalities but on the ability of particular individuals to control their own lives. This ability is assumed to depend on a given person's relationship to the technology and organization of production of the economy. Social inequality reflects the differences in individual power that result from contemporary industrial organization.

Throughout we have emphasized that social conflict underlies all human social relations. We have also stressed that an understanding of the conflicts, or contradictions, inherent in the structure of social relations of a particular historical era is the key to understanding human behavior. In this, the concluding chapter of our book, we turn to the causes and consequences of *social inequality*, that aspect of social relations in modern times which most affects people's lives, and the dialectics of social conflict and social change.

* This chapter was written in collaboration with Paul Stevenson.

FUNCTIONAL THEORIES OF SOCIAL INEQUALITY

Karl Marx, the "father of communism" and creator of one of the world's major economic and sociological schools of thought, predicted that one day men would live in a "classless" society where people would not be categorized and divided by the kind of work they did, by varying degrees of access to knowledge, or by differences in wealth. He described life in this society somewhat poetically as being a place "where nobody has one exclusive sphere of activity but each can become accomplished in any branch he wishes, production as a whole is regulated by society, thus making it possible for me to do one thing today and another tomorrow, to hunt in the morning, fish in the afternoon, rear cattle in the evening, criticize after dinner, in accordance with my inclination, without ever becoming hunter, fisherman, shepherd or critic."[1]

While such a state of affairs is possible, it is clear that it never has been the prevailing situation throughout the history of man. Indeed, one of the most persistent facets of human behavior is the fact that people have organized social relations around a division of labor. No place has ever been discovered where people did not specialize to some extent. Among nonindustrialized peoples, the most common types of labor are hunting, fishing, farming, fighting, trading, food gathering, and housekeeping. Most people engage in one or another of these activities at all times. But the men who plant the food do not also hunt, and those who hunt usually do not farm. In farming communities, specialization is even more evident.

As technology advances, and division of labor becomes more widespread, differences in social standing increase. Some people are able to obtain a greater share of the wealth by virtue of their particular work, and are hence able to control others and to make them do what they want them to. Among all industrialized peoples, along with the division of labor has come the division of resources and, in a word, *inequality*.

The functionalist perspective for studying the question of social inequality has its roots in the view expressed by the Greek philosopher Aristotle. Aristotle argued that there was a natural relationship between the elite and the masses. "From the hour of their birth, some are marked out for subjection, and some for command."[2] Aristotle believed that the relationship between "master" and "slave" grew up naturally because the slave was incapable of making his own decisions and would die without the master's guidance; the master, in turn, needed the slave's strength, manual labor, and bravery. Master and slave, ruler and ruled, elite and masses thus lived in a state of mutual protection and benefit. As we saw in Chapter 9, in early feudal economies peasant and warrior were related to one another in a way that provided mutual benefit for both. As feudalism disintegrated, however, the "mutual benefit" argument became a mere rationalization. The equalitarian beliefs espoused in bourgeois revolutionary rhetoric like the United States Declaration of Independence also gave way, in time, to rationalizations of class differences.

The "Necessity" Argument

In the early 1900s the sociologist William Graham Sumner expressed eloquently one type of rationalization for inequality:

> Competition is a law of nature. Nature is entirely neutral; she submits to him who most energetically and resolutely assails her. She grants her awards to the fittest, therefore, without regard to other considerations of any kind. Such is the system of nature. If we do not like

[1] Karl Marx, *The Communist Manifesto*. Marx's most important single work on capitalism is *Das Capital*, volumes 1 to 3 (New York: International, 1967).

[2] Aristotle, *Ethics* (New York: Dutton, 1950), p. 4.

it, and if we try to amend it, there is only one way in which we can do it. We can take from the better and give to the worse. . . . Let it be understood that we cannot go outside the alternative: liberty, inequality, survival of the fittest; non-liberty, equality, survival of the unfittest. The former carries society forward and favours all its best members; the latter carries society downwards and favours all its worst members.[3]

[3] William Graham Sumner, *The Challenge of Facts and Other Essays* (New Haven: Yale University Press, 1913), p. 25.

These views have led to more sophisticated analyses of social inequality. The facile observation that master and slave benefit mutually from their relationship is hardly enough to explain industrial class differences. It became necessary to ask, as Kingsley Davis and Wilbert Moore did, why it is that social inequality exists among all contemporary peoples. Because of the widespread existence of inequality Davis and Moore concluded that inequality was somehow necessary for "society." They therefore

Food stamps have replaced the bread lines of the 1930s. Inflation and monopolization have decreased the working person's purchasing power. (Editorial Photocolor Archives)

tried to explain the "universal necessity which calls forth [inequality] in any social systems"[4] as follows:

> Society must somehow distribute its members in social positions and induce them to perform the duties of these positions. [Society] must thus concern itself with motivation at two different levels: to instill in the proper individuals the desire to fill certain positions, and, once in these positions, the desire to perform the duties attached to them.[5]

Social inequality motivates members of society to fill positions and to work hard after filling.

> Social inequality is thus an unconsciously evolved device by which societies insure that the most important positions are conscientiously filled by the most qualified persons. . . .
> [T]hose positions convey the best reward and hence have the highest rank, which (a) have the greatest importance for the society and (b) require the greatest training or talent.[6]

Politicians, writers, and people in general have, of course, long been arguing that social inequality comes about because people who have the most talent are "naturally" rewarded more because they contribute more. What Davis and Moore added to this commonsense argument is the idea that the prevailing inequality must exist in order to motivate people to work hard to fill the positions at the top.

Put another way, the argument is that social inequality is functional for society because it motivates people to work hard in order to achieve and retain difficult jobs which require the use of talents which not all men possess.

How well does this theory meet the requirements that any theory must meet if it is to be useful: generality, testability, and empirical validity?

The Davis-Moore theory qualifies well as a general theory. It analyzes the fact of social inequality in a manner which permits us to account for a vast array of social phenomena across a large span of time and space.

The theory's testability is not, however, so immediately clear. How testable a theory is depends on how some of the key concepts in the theory are defined. For example, the idea that some positions in every society are more "important" than others is a key concept in the Davis-Moore theory. If "importance" is defined in terms of the *rewards* received by those who occupy the most important positions, then the theory is not testable; it is tautological. That is, it simply says that: (1) the most important positions in a society are those that receive the greatest rewards, and (2) the positions that receive the greatest rewards are the most important in the society. No matter what data are presented, the theory remains true *by definition*. It is therefore not testable.

As matter of fact, any theory may be rendered untestable by defining key concepts in ways that make the theory true by definition. It is possible to avoid this pitfall by making definitions independent of the things that are proposed as explanation. Thus, the functional theory of social inequality as articulated by Davis and Moore is testable if we define the most important positions as those that must be filled in order for a given people to survive within the institutional framework they are using.

We turn, then, to a consideration of the theory's empirical validity. That is, how well does the theory fit the facts of social inequality? To answer this we must look at

[4] Kingsley Davis and Wilbert Moore, "Some Principles of Stratification," *American Sociological Review*, vol. 10, 1945, pp. 242–249. See also Kingsley Davis, "A Conceptual Analysis of Stratification," *American Sociological Review*, vol. 7, June, 1942, pp. 309–321, and *Human Society* (New York: Macmillan, 1949).
[5] Davis and Moore, op. cit., p. 242.
[6] Ibid., pp. 243–244.

inequality in a number of different places and in different historical periods.

In his study of a town he calls "Ivydale" the sociologist Floyd Hunter came to the conclusion that one of the most rewarded positions in Ivydale (that is, one of the positions that led to the greatest wealth, power, prestige, and privilege in the community) was one of the *least* important to the functioning of the community. Hunter says:

> Let us speak for a moment of the man considered by his neighbors to be one of the wealthiest individuals in the community. We speak of Fritz Rinston, who made a great deal of money managing a firm that wrote radio jingles. . . . In analyzing Fritz Rinston's fortune and its community function, we could only conclude that during the period that his services and that of his company were in demand, the amounts paid to him greatly exceeded the amounts he was required to return to others for community services rendered to him. We are not at all persuaded that Rinston is any more intelligent or clever than hundreds of other persons in the community. We are of the opinion that the requirements of radio sponsors for amusing jingles were great, and that they were willing to pay large sums for the product put out by Rinston's outfit, but we are not convinced that the result was more worthy of higher rates of pay than those offered a good teacher of English literature, with whom we were acquainted, who worked during the whole period as hard as Rinston and who earned considerably less. . . . The things that Mr. Rinston had to do to acquire his favorable book balances do not seem, in retrospect, extraordinarily arduous or especially creative.
>
> We further noted that Fritz Rinston no longer uses his talents in the market-place, yet, this is no bar to his use of past credits accrued to his accounts. The teacher of English literature, with a young family, on the contrary, is still hard at work and in debt.[7]

[7] Floyd Hunter, *The Big Rich and the Little Rich* (New York: Doubleday, 1965), pp. 9–10.

By contrast, the least rewarded positions are often the ones without which the day-to-day problems of people simply cannot be solved. For example, in England during 1970 the sewerage workers went out on strike. Overnight the major sources of drinking water for millions of people became polluted, fish died by the hundreds of thousands, and diseases began spreading rapidly as sewage backed up, causing widespread infection. The "functional importance" of the sewerage workers was made readily apparent to everyone. Yet these workers were striking to achieve a raise in their minimum pay from 30 to 40 dollars a week. (This in a country where an actress, whose principal contribution to the social order is displaying her large breasts on film, was robbed of 1 million dollars worth of jewels the same week that the sewerage workers struck.) Yet the top executives of large corporations who earn 3 and 4 thousand dollars a week could go on strike and the consequences would not be so widely felt. Indeed, when the London School of Economics was closed for six weeks because of student political activities, no fish died, no disease spread and nobody's water was polluted. Some even argued that one kind of pollution—that of the youth's minds—was *stopped* for this period. Yet professors are paid high salaries and enjoy great prestige and even, occasionally, considerable power.

Also in England, as in the United States, the independent farmers and farm workers who provide what is surely the most essential commodity are among the worst paid, as Selection 17-1 shows. An analysis of the farm workers' plight reveals they are not paid in relation to their "marginal productivity" (the economists' term for workers' contributions to the lowering of production costs). Like other marginal workers, they are paid in proportion to their collective weakness.

SELECTION 17-1: Farm workers in England remain at the bottom of the income scale.

LOW-PAID FARM WORKERS

RICHARD EDER

Studham, England—There are only a few ornaments in the living room of George Brown's cottage: A set of china foxhounds, a studded fox-head on the wall and a goldfish swimming murkily in a globe of water. The water is terribly cold.

"This term 'freeze,'" said Brown, who was wearing thick flannel under his overalls. "To us farm workers it is really a freeze."

He had come in from the fields at lunchtime, bringing the gray Buckinghamshire weather with him. A small heap of coals was laid in the grate—the cottage's only heating apart from the kitchen stove—but it would not be lit until evening.

Coal costs $36 the half-ton and Brown, who brings home $45 working a 52-hour week, tries to make his half-ton last three or four months.

He is one of 200,000 hired farm workers, among the lowest paid in Britain. It is in the cold farm cottages of Norfolk and Devon, of Buckinghamshire and the North Country, that the wage freeze, adopted earlier this month as part of Prime Minister Edward Heath's effort to bring inflation under control, takes its most literal shape.

"Used to the cold?" demanded Bob James, who works on a vast Hertfordshire farming estate. "With what we're paid we've got to be used to it. But that doesn't mean we don't feel it."

Brown, a Yorkshireman who has the Northerner's explosive articulateness, said: "Here you have the agricultural worker, loyal to his job, loyal to his employer, keen to take care of his animals, finally getting a decent rise and the government takes it away."

An activist in the agricultural workers union, he is impatient with his fellows' lack of militancy. "Here you have it"—he hit the wall with his fist and his accent grew broader—"our bugbear, the tied cottage."

The union, in the strongest union country in Europe, counts fewer than half the land workers among its ranks. It does not attempt major strikes even though its members' pay is far below the national average. And though workers are leaving the land, they are not leaving as quickly as might be expected.

One of the strongest among a number of reasons for this relatively passive reaction to difficult conditions, is the semifeudal arrangement by which the worker lives in a house—a "tied cottage"—that is his only as long as his farmer employs him. In a tight housing market, the word "eviction" still has a compelling 19th-century fearfulness in the countryside.

"We have a roast once a month," Brown said. "For breakfast we'll have a couple of poached eggs and sometimes a bit of bacon. For lunch potatoes, some green stuff and maybe a pudding. At night we have bread and tea."

"We eat worse than we did five years ago," he went on. "The prices just go up and up. You don't buy clothes. You try to cut some of your pleasures. I used to smoke—gave that up. Sometimes we buy a gallon of petrol for the van and ride around a bit."

It is food prices—many of which are not covered by the freeze—that worry farm workers most. English farms are increasingly industrial operations, and though in some areas the worker may get some free potatoes or a little milk, he must buy virtually all his food in town.

A bit of land is usually available for a vegetable garden, but since the farm worker puts in 15 or 20 hours a week in overtime to stretch his wage, he has little time or energy for it.

The three-month ban on raises—which may be extended to five months—hits the agricultural workers with a peculiar immediacy. Just at the time it went through they had won an $8 increase in their minimum wage, the biggest they had ever received—to $46 for a basic 42-hour week, effective next month.

Large cities everywhere come to a virtual standstill, and are made almost uninhabitable, when such workers as streetcar conductors, taxi drivers, and street cleaners or rubbish collectors refuse to do their job. Yet these jobs, which require particular talents and training (if nothing else it requires considerable training in alienation to be able to retain one's self-esteem while working at such poorly regarded and rewarded jobs) are given the lowest rewards of any in society. Other positions, which are highly rewarded and presumably demand greater talent and sacrifice, can go unfilled for long periods of time and there is little effect on how well people's problems are solved. When Columbia University in New York was shut down by student demonstrations there was hardly a ripple of inconvenience or loss of heartbeat in the city. Or when "Broadway Joe" Namath, who is paid more for throwing an egg-shaped, air-filled piece of leather for one hour than the average garbage collector makes in an entire year, fails to throw for a day—or even forever—there is no threat whatsoever to America's well-being. Athletes and entertainers are among the highest paid people in America; yet their occupations are among the most expendable. They are also occupations for which there is a huge supply of talent which can easily be tapped whenever desired.

Further, occupations that are highly regarded in one place may not share the same position in other places. People using physician roles are among the most highly paid people in America; the functionalist would therefore assume that these occupations are among the most important. In Britain, however, doctors are paid far less money, even taking into account the lower standard of living in Britain than in the United States. Surely it does not make sense that the medical doctor is less important to British people than to Americans.

By pointing out that many functionally crucial jobs (e.g., sewerage workers and rubbish collectors) are rewarded very poorly, we have seriously undermined the functionalist hypothesis that social inequality is necessary in order to motivate people to perform "functionally important" jobs.

Further refutation of the functionalist position is provided in a study by Richard Schwartz of two kibbutzim in Israel.[8] In these two communities Schwartz found several positions that are essential if the communities are to continue as they are. In one community (Orah) Schwartz considered the essential positions to be those of routine workers; in the second community (Tamim), the functionally important roles were those of the decision makers. He notes that "each position, whether or not the 'most important' in the society, is important in that failure adequately to fill it results in dissatisfaction for the members and a threat to the survival of the settlement." Contrary to what would be expected from a functional analysis of inequality, these communities do *not* find it necessary to create economic inequality in order to motivate people to fill these jobs.

In Orah routine jobs are made sufficiently attractive to motivate people to occupy them through such things as rotating the routine tasks done, providing outside work that requires nonroutine actions, and constantly attempting, through mechanization, to reduce the amount of routine work necessary to the community's survival. None of these features of the organization of work includes an unequal distribution of rewards.

Deferred Gratification

A corollary of the argument saying that inequality is necessary states that since the more prestigious and more rewarding positions require more training, "society" must build into the socialization process a willingness in some of its members to "defer gratification" before they become economically and socially independent. People will be motivated to make this sacrifice only if the carrot at the end of the stick is juicier than the one to be had immediately. In other words, people can be induced to go to col-

[8] Richard Schwartz, "Functional Alternatives to Inequality," *American Sociological Review*, vol. 20, August, 1955, pp. 424–430.

lege or to seek specialized technological training only if the positions open to them when they complete their training bring greater wealth, power, prestige, and privileges. Going to a university is "deferring gratification."

It is difficult to see how anyone who has even walked through a university campus in America, Europe, Asia, or Africa could take such a view seriously. Can it be reasonably argued that college students would really rather be working in a coal mine or the assembly line of a factory with their lower-strata peers than attending college? The youths who attend college and universities do so quite comfortably. In most countries the people who attend the universities have a higher standard of living than their wage-earning peers—through the income status of their parents and through loans, grants, and scholarships. It is nonsense to say that students living in comfortable apartments or dormitories, with access to automobiles and a life of considerable leisure, are deferring gratification. There would doubtless be no shortage of eager applicants for universites or colleges even if the jobs that one qualified for at the conclusion of the education were no more rewarding than those available without it.

It is even arguable that the bulk of the university-trained students have not learned any skills that are particularly useful even in the dominant institutional patterns. Most graduates of universities must be completely trained for their jobs after they leave college or university (excepting, of course, that minority of students who specialize in engineering or natural science). The training seen as so necessary in functional analysis is for the most part redundant and superfluous.

Personal Sacrifice

Another functionalist argument for the necessity of inequality is that those jobs that receive the greatest rewards are the most de-

manding of personal sacrifice, which is why they must be rewarded more highly. While this may be true of some jobs, it is certainly not true of others. The laborer who works next to noisy machinery and therefore becomes partially deaf by the age of forty has made every bit as much of a personal sacrifice as the business executive who must pamper his ulcer. The beggar who stands in the rain, snow, and sleet for long hours is every bit as hard-pressed, albeit in a different way, as the professor who faces students.[9] The laborer who operates a jackhammer all day is making as great a sacrifice, if not a greater one, as the judge who sentences him to jail if he gets too drunk. The sacrifice made by the coal miners of the Appalachian mountains whose income is scarcely above the starvation level has been described by Harry Caudill.

> [C]oal companies are permitted to treat coal lands as practically valueless until the coal is actually mined. This tax cheating keeps the tax base at rock bottom, depriving mining communities of schools, so that the average West Virginian miner has completed only 8.8 years in the classroom. His lack of education drives him into the pits and keeps him there. And in the mines death stalks him at every turn. The chances are one in six he will be seriously injured in a given year, one in 240 that he will be killed. And if his bones are not crushed by blundering machines or falling slate from the roof, it is a practical certainty that in ten or twelve years his throat and lungs will fill with a fine dust consisting of particles of coal, slate and silica, and by age fifty or fifty-five he will be a wheezing, coughing human derelict whose miseries medical science cannot relieve even for a single moment by day or night until he reaches his grave.[10]

In contrast, the life of the "super rich" in industrial nations is often a life of leisure,

[9] Samuel Wallace, *Skid Row as a Way of Life* (New York: Free Press, 1966).
[10] Harry M. Caudill, "The Appalachian Tragedy," *New York Review of Books*, November 19, 1970, p. 19.

play, and travel. At worst the challenges, tribulations, and personal sacrifices involved in occupying the most rewarded positions are no greater than the sacrifices of the coal miners or the factory workers.

THE CONFLICT THEORY OF INEQUALITY

Karl Marx's analysis of social inequality still stands as the most fully developed conflict model available. Marx's starting point is the assumption that inequality can only be understood if we first look at social relations *holistically*. Any element of a set of social relations can be understood only if we can relate that element to the whole. The whole is more than simply the sum of its separate parts.

For the sake of analysis Marx begins with the observation that in order for human beings to survive they must provide for themselves the basic necessities of food, shelter, and clothing. Humans supply these basic necessities through a struggle with nature. Humans labor together in this struggle, and must be reasonably successful before they can engage in philosophical, re-

ligious, or political pursuits. A societal superstructure of values, beliefs, and political and cultural institutions is built upon an economic base, or substructure, which consists of the natural resources, technology, and human labor available, brought together in a particular means of production. In a sense, the distinction between substructure and superstructure is an abstraction, since, in reality, the two are quite interrelated and often indistinguishable. Marx did not argue that no interaction took place between the two and that in no case has the determining sequence run from superstructure to substructure. In simple terms, the astute social analyst must try to understand what is going on in the economic base, even though such an understanding may be quite incomplete or inadequate. No social analyst can afford to limit his or her investigation of society to the superstructure, a limitation so often made by most sociologists today.

According to Marx, a person's place in the hierarchical ordering of society is dependent upon the social relations of production and property relations. Property relations are simply distinctions between owners and con-

The rewards of money power in most industrial nations include an access to food, travel, and recreation that is denied the masses of people. (Editorial Photocolor Archives)

trollers of the means of production and non-owners and noncontrollers. The social relations of production refer to the manner in which technology and the processes of production are organized and the authoritative ordering of production which prevails. Who oversees whom? What are the rights and responsibilities, the duties and rewards "that govern the interaction of all individuals involved in organized productive activity"? These concepts are the basis of a Marxian discussion of class.

Capitalism may be briefly defined as an economic system in which the commanding heights of the economy are owned and controlled by a few while the vast majority must sell their labor power to the few in return for a living income. Resources are allocated according to the profit principle. The workers give up control of the productive processes and the resultant products. The owners dispose of products as they see fit; they have first claim to the income resulting from any sale of products and distribute such money as they so desire. There have been some modifications in this model of capitalism over time; these are important, but they have not changed the essentials of the model.[11] Thus today countries such as the United States, Britain, Canada, Australia, France, Germany, Sweden, Japan, and so on are clearly capitalist.

In capitalist countries there is then, according to Marx, division of people into two major classes—the owners and the nonowners, the capitalists and the workers. This provides a solid basis for an unequal distribution of income, wealth, and power.

Unfortunately, Marx did not live to complete his chapter on classes in Capital, although all of his work is permeated by class analysis. The fact that one has to work at

arriving at an adequate understanding of Marx's analysis of classes has been the basis of much misunderstanding of Marx on this matter. By using Marx's method rigorously, however, and by carefully reading his major works, it is possible to arrive at a rather good comprehension of his treatment of the subject.[12]

Marx wrote at many levels of abstraction. At a high level of abstraction, he would deal with but a few variables, holding others constant. By so doing he was able to isolate the essentials of a mode of production and arrive at many useful insights and understandings. However, he clearly was aware that such a high level of abstraction is, in some sense, a distortion of social reality. Thus he would move to more concrete levels, introducing more variables, to make his analysis more complex and more realistic.

Marx used this approach in his analysis of social classes. He began his class analysis of the capitalist mode of production at a rather high level of abstraction, isolating but two classes—the bourgeoisie and the proletariat. He then moved to more concrete analyses by introducing discussion of intermediate strata and classes. That he was clearly aware of the rise of a "new middle class," for example, is clear from a reading of Capital and has been underlined in an important essay by Martin Nicolaus.[13] Thus, the Marxian analysis of the class structure of capitalism is not an oversimplified one, as critics sometimes claim, but rather a complex and full one.

Since the workers under capitalism are not in control of the work process, i.e., they do not determine what product will be produced, what will be done with it after it is produced, or the conditions under which it

[11] These changes include the rise of unions, the monopolization process, and the involvement of the state in the economy.

[12] Theotonio Dos Santos, "The Concept of Social Classes," Science & Society, vol. 34, no. 2, pp. 166–193.
[13] Martin Nicolaus, "Proletariat and Middle Class in Marx: Hegelian Choreography and Capitalist Dialectic," in James Weinstein and David Eakins (eds.), For a New America (New York: Vintage, 1970).

will be produced, they are separated or alienated from their product. Thus, the workers have "no intrinsic interest in either [their] direct activities or their goal, and motivation must then take the form of working for the extrinsic incentive of wages."[14] For these wages to be effective "considerable inequality (and therefore considerable reward for working properly) must exist."[15] We thus have a beginning of a comprehension of inequality *between* classes (owners and non-owners) and among strata *within* classes (wage and salary differentials among workers). There is also the beginning of an understanding of the possibilities of conflict as the owners appropriate the products of the workers, making the owners' relationship to the workers exploitative and antagonistic. Owners not appropriating the surplus find their businesses not able to compete with those who do, and go out of business. Further conflict is generated when the development of the productive economic forces to their fullest is incompatible with the existing class structure. Here the possibility of revolution comes to the fore.

Two other aspects of Marx's political-economic thought are worth noting at this point. First, he saw that capitalism was moving toward monopoly: the concentration and centralization of industrial enterprises. Second, he viewed capitalism as a far-reaching, global system. The importance of these two elements of his thought will become clear in what follows.

TRENDS IN SOCIAL INEQUALITY

The functional and conflict perspectives come to quite contradictory conclusions on the question of changes in the amount of social inequality that will come as people move through the process of industrialization. In the nineteenth century leading sociologists of the functionalist school such as Emile Durkheim, Alexis de Tocqueville, and Frédéric Le Play saw social inequality as declining due to the extension of the vote to all classes. Tocqueville spoke eloquently for this view when he argued:

> The gradual development of the principle of equality is a providential fact . . . as there is no longer a race of poor men, so there is no longer a race of rich men; the latter spring up daily from the multitude and relapse into it again. Hence, they do not form a distinct class.[16]

Modern-day functionalists have also expressed the view that social inequality is declining. Reinhard Bendix and S. M. Lipset argued not long ago that in the United States "the proportion of the national income received by the lower strata has increased."[17]

The conflict perspective has invariably argued just the opposite. Early conflict theorists such as Mosca and Pareto expected social inequality to remain a "providential fact" (providential to those in power) due to the ability of those in control of the political and economic structures to maintain their privileged positions. Marx argued that the history of industrial societies would show an "increasing proletarianization" wherein the privileged positions of the ruling class would cause the working class to become increasingly desperate, leading, ultimately, to a working-class revolution.

---

[14] Richard C. Edwards, Arthur MacEwan et al., "A Radical Approach to Economics," in David M. Gordon (ed.), *Problems in Political Economy: An Urban Perspective* (Lexington, Mass.: Heath, 1971), p. 16.
[15] Ibid.

[16] Alexis de Tocqueville, *Democracy in America*, vol. I (New York: Harper & Row, 1966), p. 6. For a discussion of these various writers see Robert A. Nisbet, *The Sociological Tradition* (New York: Basic Books, 1966).
[17] Seymour Martin Lipset and Reinhard Bendix, *Social Mobility in Industrial Society* (Berkeley, Calif.: University of California Press, 1959), p. 5.

Once again we must ask; "Which view fits most closely with the extant empirical data on trends of social inequality in industrial societies?"

Inequalities between Classes

The vast majority of the population in capitalist countries does not own or control the means of production, distribution, and exchange. This contention has been empirically documented. Robert Lampman has shown that in 1953, 1 percent of adult Americans owned 76 percent of all privately held corporate stock in the United States,[18] an increase of 15.5 percent from 1922. Only about 15 percent of the American populace owned any corporate stock, with much of that being but small holdings. The corresponding Canadian figure is only 14 percent owning any stock, with a similar concentration in the hands of a few.[19] In Sweden over 90 percent of the economy is privately owned, with the ownership being even more concentrated than in the United States.[20]

The distribution of wealth in the United States is similarly unequal. For example, in 1962 the top 1 percent of the population owned some 31 percent of all of the wealth, and the top 20 percent owned 76 percent of all the wealth.[21] G. William Domhoff has demonstrated that 1 percent of the American populace effectively controls the major corporations, the political parties and governmental institutions, the mass media, and so on.[22] This upper class can clearly be called a "ruling class."

In a study published in 1962 Gabriel Kolko demonstrated that income distribution in America had changed very little since the turn of the century; the federal government's "progressive" income tax had done little to alter the pattern. More recent studies by Gordon, Budd, and Ackerman, et al., have confirmed Kolko's earlier study as well as showing no distributive change up to 1969.[23] The data are presented in Tables 17-1 and 17-2.

Selections 17-2 and 17-3 use 1970 census data to show that the income is concentrated even more than had been previously suspected. The work of Budd and Gordon (cited above), and Bodenheimer,[24] also demonstrates that government tax policies have only marginal effects upon equalizing income distribution. Much of the income of the poorer groups, in fact, goes toward paying taxes, while the relative, and in some cases absolute, burden of upper-income groups is noticeably less.

In spite of the propaganda concerning America's affluence in the 1960s, there was an absolute decline in real income over the 1960–1968 period and only a slight increase in real income for the 1960–1969 period for many groups of Americans. The Canadian

[18] Robert J. Lampman, "The Share of Top Wealth-Holders in National Wealth, 1922–1956," in Maurice Zeitlin (ed.), American Society, Inc. (Chicago: Markham, 1970), p. 104.
[19] Statistics Canada, Incomes, Assets and Indebtedness of Families in Canada, 1969 (Ottawa: Queen's Printer, 1973).
[20] Perry Anderson, "Problems of Socialist Strategy," in Perry Anderson and Robin Blackburn (eds.), Towards Socialism (London: Collins, 1965), p. 232; Jean Meynand and Susan Sidjanski, L'Europe des Affaires (Paris: Payot, 1967), p. 179; C. Hermansson, Monopol och Storfinans and Konsentration och Storforetag (Stockholm: Arbetarkultursforlag, 1962 and 1959); and Dr. Holger Heide, Die langfristige Wirtschaftsplanung in Schweden (Tubingen: J.C.B. Mohr, 1965).
[21] Frank Ackerman et al., "The Extent of Income Inequality in the United States," in Richard C. Edwards, Michael Reich, and Thomas E. Weisskopf (eds.), The Capitalist System (Englewood Cliffs, N.J.: Prentice-Hall, 1972). p. 211.

[22] G. William Domhoff, Who Rules America? (Englewood Cliffs, N.J.: Prentice-Hall, 1967).
[23] Gabriel Kolko, Wealth and Power in America (New York: Praeger, 1962); David M. Gordon, "Trends in Poverty: Editor's Supplement," and "Recent Evidence of Government Impact: Editor's Supplement," both in David M. Gordon (ed.), Problems in Political Economy: An Urban Perspective (Lexington, Mass.: Heath, 1970), pp. 237–244 and pp. 260–262; Edward C. Budd, "Inequality in Income and Taxes," in M. Zeitlin (ed.), American Society, Inc. (Chicago: Markham, 1970), pp. 143–150; and Ackerman et al., op. cit., pp. 207–218.
[24] Thomas Bodenheimer, "The Poverty of the State," Monthly Review, vol. 24, no. 6, pp. 7–18.

SELECTION 17-2: Actual control of wealth is hard to measure. Studies of income distribution, however, show high concentrations of income. Studies of control of capital (wealth) show even greater inequality.

AT THE SUMMIT OF THE AFFLUENT UNITED STATES SOCIETY

WILLIAM CHAPMAN

Washington—There are many more truly affluent Americans than is thought and collectively they have a much higher proportion of the nation's total income than most Americans realize.

These are the conclusions of two U.S. Census Bureau experts who today presented an analysis showing how handsomely the upper-upper class is compensated when all of their income—cash and otherwise—is considered.

For example, they said that only about 200,000 American families appeared to be in the top bracket—$50,000 and over—in 1968, based on a Census Bureau survey that covered only the money income reported in sample interviews.

But actually, about 900,000 families were in that class when their total income was added up.

Futhermore, the people in the top bracket seemed to receive only 1.8 percent of the national income when the 1968 survey was completed.

But they really accounted for 11 percent of the total income in the country when everything else was totaled up, the analysts concluded.

It all adds up to a greater concentration of real income in the upper layers of American society.

"When you take into account incomes not reported to the census, and all the other factors, it's clear that incomes are more unequally distributed than it would appear at first," Herman P. Miller summed up in a recent interview.

Mr. Miller, chief of the Census Bureau's population division, and an assistant, Roger A. Herriot, presented their calculations today at a meeting in New York of the National Industrial Conference Board.

They said that the 1968 census survey, which forms the basis of many income studies of the United States, turned up a total of $543 billion. To that, they added a number of other income sources, such as realized capital gains and retained corporate earnings. They also found that, compared with income statistics furnished by the Office of Business Economics and based on tax returns, there was $76 billion unreported to the Census Bureau's interviewers.

They came up, finally, with a total income of $805 billion and a substantially different picture of how incomes are allocated among Americans of different classes.

While the rich seemed to be richer, the middle classes seemed not to fare so well, comparatively.

For instance, families in the $10,000-to-$15,000 bracket had about 30 percent of the national income when money alone was the yardstick.

But they had just 20 percent of the national share when "total income" was computed.

Under the conventional survey taken by the Census Bureau, the top 5 percent of the families received about 17 percent of the national total. But when the adjustments were made to portray "total income" of the nation, they appeared to receive 22 percent of the total. Meanwhile, the middle fifth of the population had about 16 percent under both analyses.

SELECTION 17-3: Trends in inequality of income distribution.

RICH HOUSEHOLDS "GETTING RICHER"

Washington—American households headed by women and by nonwhites are poorer than those headed by men and by whites. Also, rich households are getting richer.

These were among points contained in the latest statistics on household income released yesterday by the Commerce Department.

The median income of households in the United States in 1972 was $9,700, up 7.4 percent from 1971 when the median was $9,030. The median is not the average but means that half the households got more money and half got less.

The real gain in median money income was listed as 4 percent because consumer prices rose 3.4 percent during 1971.

The average income for the 11.2 percent of households which were nonwhite was $7,793 in 1972, and the average household income for the 88.8 percent of households which were white was $11,725.

The statistics showed that 22.6 percent of all American households were headed by women, and the average income for these households was $5,673. The average income of the male-headed households was $12,920.

The 4.2 percent farm households had an average income of $9,629 per household while non-farm households had an average income of $11,359.

Nearly 20 percent of all U.S. households are headed by persons 65 or more years old and the average income of these households was $6,330.

The richest 5 percent of American households accounted for 17 percent of the 1972 aggregate income. In 1967, this bracket amassed 16.1 percent of the aggregate household wealth.

situation was even worse; the decline in real income started almost immediately after World War II, in spite of a rising per capita gross national product.[25]

What then was the basis for American affluence in the postwar period if for much of that time real income declined for the middle- and lower-income groups? As Richard Parker has so clearly demonstrated, many purchases were made as a result of the development of credit buying or deficit spending.[26] Tanzer writes, "More than 10 percent of the families who earn under $7,500

per year (45 percent of the entire population) have to devote more than 20 percent of their income to debt repayment. . . ."[27] The debts of middle- and upper-income groups, and various governmental levels, have risen since World War II, particularly during the 1960s. Although these debts have contributed to economic growth, they have the long-run effect of weakening the foundations of the American economy.[28]

The inequalities in stock ownership, industrial power (centralization and concentration), wealth ownership, and income distribution which currently exist in the industrialized corporate capitalist system of the United States are present in highly similar form in the other developed capitalist countries. Thus, for example, the economies of Great Britain, Sweden, Canada, and Denmark all show similar persistent inequities.[29] The underdeveloped capitalist economies exhibit even greater inequalities.[30] State socialist economies, such as Yugoslavia, which are moving in the direction of a capitalistic market economy, show increasing industrial and income inequalities while state socialist

[25] Table 17-2 is calculated from Budd, op. cit., and Ackerman et al., op. cit. The Canadian case is examined by Leo Johnson in his "Incomes, Disparity, and Impoverishment in Canada Since World War II" (Toronto: Hogtown Press, 1973).

[26] Richard Parker, *The Myth of the Middle Class* (New York: Harper and Row, 1969)

[27] Michael Tanzer, *The Sick Society: An Economic Examination* (New York: Holt, Rinehart, Winston, 1971), p. 193; Richard Parker, op. cit.

[28] Tanzer, op. cit., pp. 188–210; Paul M. Sweezy and Harry Magdorff, *The Dynamics of United States Capitalism* (New York: Modern Reader, 1972), pp. 7–30, 180–196.

[29] For Great Britain see H. Frankel, *Capitalist Society and Modern Sociology* (London: Lawrence and Wishart, 1970); Richard M. Titmuss, *Income Distribution and Social Change* (London: Allen and Unwin, 1962). For Sweden see reference 20 of this text; Sten Johansson, *The 1968 Survey of Levels of Living in Sweden* (Stockholm: Ministry of the Interior, 1968); and Paul Stevenson, "Monopoly Capital and Inequalities in Sweden," *The Insurgent Sociologist*, vol. v, no. 1, Fall, 1974. For Canada see Statistics Canada, *Income Distributions by Size in Canada* (Ottawa: Information Canada, 1972); and Ian Adams et al., *The Real Poverty Report* (Edmonton: Hurtig, 1972). For Denmark see Jacques Hersh, " 'Welfare State' and Social Conflict," *Monthly Review*, vol. 22, no. 6, pp. 29–43, and the *Statistical Yearbook* (Copenhagen: Det Statistike Department, 1964).

[30] Thomas E. Weisskopf, "Capitalism and Underdevelopment in the Modern World," in Richard C. Edwards, Michael Rich, and Thomas E. Weisskoph (eds.), The Capitalist System (Englewood Cliffs, N.J.: Prentice-Hall, 1972), pp. 442–458.

TABLE 17-1   Distribution of Before-tax Family Income, 1929–1969

	1929	1935	1941	1947	1950	1956	1960	1969
Poorest fifth	3.5	4.1	4.1	5.0	4.5	5.0	4.9	5.6
Second fifth	9.0	9.2	9.5	11.8	12.0	12.4	12.0	12.3
Middle fifth	13.8	14.1	15.3	17.0	17.4	17.8	17.6	17.6
Fourth fifth	19.3	20.9	22.3	23.1	23.5	23.7	23.6	23.4
Richest fifth	54.4	51.7	48.8	43.0	42.6	41.2	42.0	43.5*
Richest 5 percent	30.0	26.5	24.0	17.2	17.0	16.3	16.8	14.7†

* Includes capital-gains income, as in other years.
† Excludes capital-gains income.
SOURCE: Gabriel Kolko, *Wealth and Power in America* (New York: Praeger, 1962).

economies holding firm to centralized planning have shown tendencies toward greater regional and class equality.[31]

Poverty

The persistence of economic inequalities in capitalist economies is underpinned by the persistence of substantial numbers of people living in various degrees of poverty both

within a particular capitalist nation and, when capitalism is viewed as an all-encompassing political-economic system, in the world at large.

Herbert Gans has recently argued that poverty is a necessary component of capitalist economies for the following reasons.[32]

First, the existence of poverty makes sure that "dirty work" is done. Every economy has such work: physically dirty or dangerous, temporary, dead-end and underpaid, undignified, and menial jobs. These jobs can be filled by

[31] Howard M. Wachtel, "Workers' Management and Interindustry Wage Differentials in Yugoslavia," *Journal of Political Economy*, vol. 80, no. 3, part I, May-June, 1972, pp. 540–560; and I. S. Koropeckyj, "Equalization of Regional Development in Socialist Countries: An Empirical Study," *Economic Development and Cultural Change*, vol. 21, no. 1, October, 1972, pp. 68–85.

[32] Herbert J. Gans, "The Positive Functions of Poverty," *American Journal of Sociology*, vol. 78, no. 3, September, 1972, pp. 275–289.

TABLE 17-2   The Average Real Income of Various Groups (Family Units) During the 1960s

(Mean Income of Docile in 1960 Dollars)

Decile year	1960	1965	1966	1967	1968	1969
Lowest	$ 1,200	$ 1,116	$ 1,001	$ 1,118	$ 1,029	$ 1,296
Second	2,440	2,270	2,185	2,147	2,219	2,496
Third	3,630	3,377	3,340	3,441	3,468	3,864
Fourth	4,930	4,585	4,550	4,690	4,735	5,256
Fifth	6,110	5,683	5,706	5,896	6,027	6,292
Sixth	7,310	6,799	6,800	7,119	7,259	7,616
Seventh	8,590	7,990	7,963	8,422	8,594	9,008
Eighth	10,200	9,486	9,365	9,909	10,073	10,648
Ninth	12,710	11,822	11,275	12,109	12,130	12,976
Highest	22,320	20,758	21,405	21,076	22,729	23,762
Average	7,940	7,385	7,353		7,837	8,336

SOURCE: These figures were calculated from the annual *Survey of Consumer Finance*, The University of Michigan, Ann Arbor, Michigan, and through the use of The Consumer Price Index published by the U.S. Department of Commerce in its annual *United States Statistical Yearbook*.

paying higher wages than for "clean" work, or by requiring people who have no other choice to do the dirty work and at low wages. In America, poverty functions to provide a low-wage labor pool that is willing—or rather unable to be unwilling—to perform dirty work at low cost.

Second, the poor subsidize, directly and indirectly, many activities that benefit the affluent. For one thing, they have long supported both the consumption and investment activities of the private economy by virtue of the low wages which they receive. . . . A French writer quoted by T. H. Marshall pointed out that "to assure and maintain the propensities of our industries, it is necessary that the workers should never acquire wealth."

Third, poverty creates jobs for a number of occupations and professions which serve the poor, or shield the rest of the population from them. . . . Penology would be miniscule without the poor, as would the police. . . .

Fourth, the poor buy goods which others do not want and thus prolong their economic usefulness, such as day-old bread, fruit and vegetables which would otherwise have to be thrown out, secondhand clothes, and deteriorating automobiles and buildings. They also provide incomes for doctors, lawyers, teachers, and others who are too old, poorly trained or incompetent to attract more affluent clients.

Fifth, the poor can be identified and punished as alleged or real deviants in order to uphold the legitimacy of dominant norms.

Sixth, another group of poor, described as deserving because they are disabled or suffering from bad luck, provide the rest of the population with different emotional satisfactions; they evoke compassion, pity and charity. . . .

Seventh, . . . the poor offer affluent people vicarious participation in the uninhibited sexual, alcoholic, and narcotic behavior in which many poor are alleged to indulge. . . .

Eighth, . . . the poor function as a reliable and relatively permanent measuring rod for status comparison, particularly for the working class, which must find and maintain status distinctions between itself and the poor. . . .

Ninth, the poor also assist in the upward mobility of the nonpoor. . . . By being denied educational opportunities or being stereotyped as stupid or unteachable, the poor thus enable others to obtain the better jobs. Also, an unknown number of people have moved themselves or their children up in the socioeconomic hierarchy through the incomes earned from the provision of goods and services in the slums.

Tenth, . . . the aristocracy uses the poor to justify their own existence as a privileged class by doing charitable deeds for the poor.

Eleventh, the poor provide the labor (cheaply) which constructs the monuments of a historical period which give it its claim to uniqueness: such as bridges, buildings, and in an earlier era the Pyramids, Greek Temples, etc.

Twelfth, the poor create a culture which the more affluent can occupy themselves enjoying or collecting such as jazz music, archaeological artifacts, peasant art and American Indian rugs.

Thirteenth, the poor serve as symbolic and real constituents for numerous groups dependent upon disaffection such as radical political groups, fundamentalist religious sects.

Gans' argument, which is consistent with the Marxian conflict model, finds substantial support in the fact of persistent poverty throughout capitalist nations. The term *poverty* must be taken, of course, in context. A group or individual income may increase absolutely over a period of years but may decline relative to other groups' or individuals' rate of increase.

The standards by which poverty is usually judged are absolute. Thus, if a group's basic needs for food, shelter, clothing, and health care are satisfied, then they are probably not at poverty level. In 1964 the United States Council of Economic Advisors arrived at a minimum low-cost budget for a family of four. The figure was based upon an earlier Department of Agriculture study made in

1955 which showed that 35 percent of the expenditures of low-income families went toward food; the size of the total budget was calculated by the Council of Economic Advisors by multiplying the usual food allowance by three. As a result a minimum budget of 3,955 dollars was arrived at for a nonfarm family. This figure was *higher* than the amount welfare agencies were providing for families on public assistance. For this reason the Council adopted a "more realistic" poverty line of 3,000 dollars for families and 1,500 dollars for individuals. In 1962 it was found that 20 percent of the American populace was living in poverty.[33] By 1970 this "absolute minimum" budget had been raised to 3,800 dollars for families, a figure which supposedly took the rising cost of living into account. About 11 percent of the American populace were still living in poverty by this standard.

The difficulty with the 1970 standard stems from the fact that the minimum budget was still based on a multiple of three, i.e., three times the minimal dietary costs. During this period, however, the costs of clothing, shelter, and health care rose faster than the cost of food. (It wasn't until about 1972 that food prices started to rise as quickly.) Thus, a more reasonable multiple would probably have been four. Using such a multiple in 1968 one would arrive at a minimal budget of 4,548 dollars for a family of four. Using that poverty line, we can say that 37.5 million Americans, or 19 percent of the population, were living in poverty.[34] In short, a more realistic poverty line indicates that the decline of poverty in the United States from 1962 to 1968 was much less than what official government proclamations (based on

their definitions) would lead us to believe, the real decline being but 1 percent.

The U.S. Department of Labor has calculated what it calls a "modest but adequate" family budget, based upon the following life-style.

> Clothes are replaced over a period of two to four years and furniture over a longer period. Transportation is by used-car unless the city has a well-developed public transportation system. There is no hired help for the wife in her housekeeping chores. The recreation allowance permits only a movie every two or three weeks. The education category covers day-to-day school expenses such as book fees and materials—it does not provide for money to be put away for college or any kind of post-high school training. The entire budget in fact makes no provision for savings of any kind to meet future major expenses. . . . This budget also makes no provision for legal assistance. . . . the medical category is quite generous—fifteen visits to the doctor for the entire family and one hospital stay per year.[35]

With this minimal living standard as a guide, the minimal family budget was some 9,100 dollars in the period 1966–1967.[36] There were 59.4 percent of American families *below* that line at that time. In 1967 the budget line was raised to 9,800 dollars.[37] Allowing for 5 percent inflation per year, the 1971 line would be 10,800 dollars. About 55 percent of American urban families were at or below that line in 1971.[38]

The number of people living in poverty goes up dramatically during economic recession. At all times in capitalist economies except during major wars poverty is a fact of life for from 20 to 30 percent of the popu-

[33] Clair Wilcox, "The Measurement of Poverty," in M. Zeitlin (ed.), *American Society, Inc.* (Chicago: Markham, 1970), pp. 154–155.

[34] David M. Gordon, "Trends in Poverty: Editor's Supplement," in David M. Gordon (ed.), *Problems in Political Economy: An Urban Perspective* (Lexington, Mass.: Heath, 1971), pp. 238–240.

[35] Donald Light, "Income Distribution: The First Stage in the Consideration of Poverty," in Milton Mankoff (ed.), *The Poverty of Progress: The Political Economy of American Social Problems* (New York: Holt, Rinehart, Winston, 1972), p. 186.

[36] Ibid., p. 187.

[37] Ackerman et al., op. cit., p. 212.

[38] *New York Times*, August 20, 1972, p. 1.

lation. Significantly, this is a *very* conservative measure based as it is on the government's own definition of poverty.

Racism and Sexism

Inequality is not distributed randomly through the population, nor is poverty and powerlessness reserved for those who lack the innate ability to survive in a competitive economic system. Rather, certain groups are systematically excluded from equal participation in the competition.

As Gans pointed out and as we noted in Chapter 11, a marginal labor pool keeps labor costs down. Exclusion of black people or others of color from certain jobs makes them liable to unemployment and hence more likely forced to accept temporary low-paying jobs. High rates of unemployment for black people have been reported since the first United States Census.

The largest group to be systematically excluded in capitalist economies is women. Exclusion of women from work and other roles, together with attendant stereotypes and prejudices, is called *sexism*. Sexism in the United States involves women working for the maintenance of the existing social patterns without any real control over their lives. It is based fundamentally on the traditional treatment of women as wards and servants of men.[39] Women, in their economically and socially dependent position as housewives and mothers, represent a reserve labor force which can be used when needed (as during World War II when women worked in the factories and in construction) but which is kept from competing for scarce jobs when job opportunities are reduced. The economist John Kenneth Galbraith has summarized the importance of a subjugated class of women to the economic system as follows:

The conversion of women into a crypto-servant class was an economic accomplishment of the first importance. Menial employed servants were available only to a minority of the pre-industrial population; the servant-wife is available, democratically, to almost the entire present male population. . . . The value of the services of the housewife has been variously calculated, somewhat impressionistically, at roughly one-fourth the total Gross National Product. The average housewife has been estimated (at 1970 wages rates for equivalent employment) to do about $257 worth of work a week or some $13,364 a year.[40]

Linda Majka has neatly summarized the current state of women in a capitalist economic system.

Sexism in the United States involves work for the society without power in society and the treatment of women as wards of men. Women are a reserve force of part-time superexploited workers. They earn less than men given equal education. They are the least organized, least skilled, most transient, last hired, first fired group in the labor force. This experience prevails in spite of the fact that over half of the women in the labor force work to survive and are the sole supporters of their families. There is a strikingly low participation of women in public life, which also reflects the small proportion of women in the professions in general and especially small numbers at the top. Male supremacist attitudes and institutionalizations extend beyond the sphere of production and completely define women's place in society. Denied the status and power originating in the productive sphere, women are stereotyped as dependent and inferior in all spheres. The results are at best paternalism and at worst tyrannical restriction. Thus denied full autonomy, women live *through others* as extensions of the self, in order to substitute for a life of action and activity.[41]

[39] Linda Majka made this point in her Ph.D. dissertation, University of California, Santa Barbara, 1973.

[40] John Kenneth Galbraith, "Economy of The American Housewife," *Atlantic*, vol. 232, no. 2, August, 1973, pp. 78–83.

[41] Majka, op. cit.

Table 17-3 shows the 1969 pattern of income inequality among men, women, blacks, and whites, inequalities which have, of course, persisted throughout recent United States history.[42]

TABLE 17-3 Median Incomes by Sex and Race, 1969 Workers with Year-round, Full-time Jobs

	Male	Female
Black	$5,900	$4,100
White	$9,000	$5,200

SOURCE: U.S. Bureau of the Census, *Current Population Reports*, ser. P-60, no. 70, Washington, p. 5. Quoted in Ackerman et al., op. cit.

Taxation and Economic Inequality

The failure of economic inequality to change substantially in the United States reflects at least in part a failure of the income tax system to effectively reduce the incomes of the upper-strata groups. Although much is made of the high taxes paid by the economically most privileged classes, in fact the evasion of taxes is more the rule than the exception for the privileged.[43] While the official tax rate for those earning over 100,000 dollars a year is over 70 percent, the actual amount of taxes paid by this group is well below 30 percent. That average is only slightly higher than the average paid by most middle-income taxpayers. In 1959 fifteen persons with incomes in the top 1 percent of the population—incomes ranging from 1 million to 28 million dollars a year—*paid no federal taxes at all*.[44] The fact is that most of the tax revenue of federal and state governments comes from the middle- or lower-income taxpayer who cannot afford or does not know how to employ someone to save him from paying taxes.

[42] Richard C. Edwards, Michael Reich, and Thomas E. Weisskopf (eds.), *The Capitalist System*, op. cit., "Editor's Introduction," pp. 288–290 and pp. 324–325.
[43] Philip Stern, *The Great Treasury Raid* (New York: Random House, 1964).
[44] Gerhard Lenski, *Power and Privilege: A Theory of Social Stratification* (New York: McGraw-Hill, 1966), p. 321.

The official tax rate in the United States supposedly means that up to 90 percent of the income of the wealthiest stratum will be collected in taxes. In fact, however, the percentage of income paid in taxes for this group is far below 90 percent. Those earning over 5 million dollars a year (a higher income, one might add, than the total gross national product of some small countries) pay on the average less than 25 percent of their income in taxes.

The situation with regard to inheritance taxes is similar. Although the general view held by the public (and perpetuated by politicians and other members of the ruling class) is that most of a man's inheritance is eaten away by taxes, figures show that while the official rate for inheritance taxes on estates of 20 million dollars and over is almost 70 percent, the actual taxes on estates of this size average less than 16 percent of the value of the estates.[45]

The point is that decisions about whether or not inequality is being reduced cannot depend on listening to the rhetoric of politicians or the myths of the people; they must depend on analysis of what is actually taking place. And, in industrialized nations throughout the world, what is taking place is that the ruling classes—the elites, that is, those who hold political and economic power—are able to perpetuate their position and their privileges despite professed ideological belief in the value of an equalitarian society. As Gerhard Lenski has said:

[T]he rhetoric of politicians is frequently egalitarian in character, but the legislation more often aristocratic. . . . See, for example, the Democratic Congressman who said, "Ways and Means is the strangest of all the House committees—and the hardest to understand. Judging by the voting records of its members on the floor of the House, the liberals *ought* to have darn near a working majority. But their

[45] Ibid., pp. 342–343.

public voting records and their 'operating' records in the committee, behind closed doors, are two different things."[46]

Recent disclosures that Ronald Reagan paid no California income tax in the years 1970 and 1971 and that Richard Nixon's federal tax payment for 1973 was $400,000 less than it should have been reflect growing awareness of the most visible tax inequities. But no publicity has been given to analysis of 1970 census data showing low-income groups paying more in income tax than they receive in welfare and other government benefits. Legislative action, when it comes, seems to aim at getting equality of ability to cheat on income tax for upper-income groups rather than to seriously use income tax as a device to reduce inequities in the tax structure.

Economic Inequality in Other Industrial Nations

Comparable resistance to any substantial redistribution of wealth is also apparent in other industrialized democracies. An examination by John Strachey in 1956 of the distribution of wealth in Great Britain found that from 1911 to 1939 10 percent of the total population received 50 percent of the total income while the remaining 90 percent of the population shared the other 50 percent. From 1939 to 1951 there was a slight redistribution of income in favor of the wage earners, but this trend has probably been reversed since then. Strachey concludes, "All this is evidence that capitalism has in fact an innate tendency to extreme and ever-growing inequality."[47]

These conclusions, based as they are on incomes reported to the tax office, no doubt underestimate the real inequality. The means to hide real income, to take advantage of untaxable capital investments, to benefit from insurance programs, etc., are possessed almost entirely by the wealthy. Taking such things into account, Richard Titmuss, in his 1962 analysis of income distribution in Great Britain, came to the following conclusion:

> There is more than a hint from a number of studies that income inequality has been increasing since 1949 while the ownership of wealth . . . has probably become still more unequal, and, in terms of family ownership, possibly strikingly more unequal, in recent years.[48]

Since the 1930s the Swedish government has practiced a deliberate policy of trying to reduce social inequality. While the disparities between the very rich and the very poor have indeed been somewhat reduced, the fact remains that the Swedish have not succeeded in eliminating a fairly large economic elite that lives by a far higher standard than anyone else.[49]

The situation in socialist countries is somewhat less clear, since we lack the systematic studies that would enable us to make an objective analysis. The best available evidence indicates that in the Soviet Union there remains a substantial difference in the income of the average working man and the income of those political bureaucrats and communist party members who are the leading government officials.

According to one analyst, the highest incomes in the U.S.S.R. are 300 times as high as the lowest incomes and 100 times as high as the middle incomes.[50] These differences suggest that income inequality in the U.S.S.R. is far greater than might be expected. (In the

[46] Ibid., p. 342, 343n.
[47] John Strachey, *Contemporary Capitalism* (London: Gollancz, 1956).
[48] Richard M. Titmuss, *Income Distribution and Social Change* (London: Allen and Unwin, 1962).
[49] Perry Anderson, "Sweden: Mr. Crosland's Dreamland," *New Left Review*, January-February, 1961, Appendices 4–12, and "Sweden II: Study in Socio-Democracy," *New Left Review*, March-June, 1961, pp. 34–35.
[50] Milovan Djilas, *The New Class: An Analysis of the Communist System* (New York: Praeger, 1957).

United States the highest incomes are 11,000 times as great as the lowest incomes and 7,000 times as high as the medium incomes.)[51]

Inequality, then, is one of the facts of life of modern industrial nations. Although the extent of inequality varies dependings on government policies, the *existence* of considerable inequality is indisputable. Given the fact of inequality, who benefits most from its presence?

To answer this question we turn to a consideration of social mobility in industrial societies. We want to see who ends up at the top, who ends up at the bottom, and who remains at various points in between.

MOBILITY

How Much Mobility Is There?

The term *social mobility* refers to a change in status which may be movement up, down, or sideways. When an impoverished rural population moves into the slums of the urban complex and changes its occupations from those of poor tenant farmers to sporadically employed unskilled laborers, we speak of sideways or *horizontal mobility*. If someone or some group of people move from positions of low esteem and low pay to positions of higher esteem and pay, this is obviously *upward mobility*. *Downward mobility* occurs when people receive lower incomes or prestige than they had previously.

Considered in this general way, mobility has certainly existed in all industrial societies. When industrialization occurs, large segments of the population must shift from one occupational category (usually farming) to occupational categories which go along with industrialization (such as working in a factory). What is *not* necessarily a part of industrialization is general upward mobility.

[51] Lenski, op. cit., pp. 312–313.

The most commonly used measure of mobility is a comparison of the occupation of males in one generation with the occupations of their fathers. Thus if 20 percent of the male population holds jobs of lower status than did their fathers, we say that 20 percent of the population has been downwardly mobile.

Using this measure of mobility, Lipset and Bendix compared the mobility rates of a number of industrial societies.[52] In general what they found was that about 70 percent of the population in the nations studied was stationary. In the 30 percent of the population that was mobile, there was a slight tendency for persons to be more often upwardly than downwardly mobile. But this tendency was *not* true in all countries. It is clear that the conclusion frequently voiced that upward social mobility is a prominent feature of industrialized (and particularly American) nations is unsupported by the facts. In addition, the failure to measure women's mobility, except by inference from their husband's mobility, grossly over-estimates upward mobility.

Occupational Mobility

Much of the mobility that has occurred in the United States can be explained generally as a result of technological changes. As the country has industrialized, there has been an expansion of the professional and technical sectors of the labor force, and the clerical and service sectors, and a decline in the farming sectors. From a study done by Peter Blau and Otis Duncan in 1967 we can see that farmers and farmworkers become blue-collar workers generally, while some people from blue-collar backgrounds shifted into

[52] Seymour Martin Lipset and Reinhard Bendix, *Social Mobility in Industrial Society* (Berkeley: University of California Press, 1959); see also Peter Blau and Otis Dudley Duncan, *The American Occupational Structure* (New York: Wiley, 1967).

white-collar occupations.[53] For males, at least, the percentage of blue-collar workers has remained essentially unchanged since 1900.[54]

The mobility that does occur is over rather short distances in the occupational hierarchy. Blau and Duncan write, "Short-distance movements exceed long-distance ones. . . . In general, the closer two occupations are to one another in the status hierarchy, the greater is the flow of manpower between them."[55] It is important to note that the lives of blue-collar and white-collar workers are increasingly similar. Gordon writes, "Official Census data reveal that income in some occupations is distributed *more unequally* than in the economy as a whole, and that the number of workers employed in such occupations is growing."[56] Gordon also notes that job insecurity is experienced by both white- and blue-collar workers.

> Comparing 1959 and 1970, two years in which the aggregate unemployment rates were nearly comparable, one finds that the percentage of the unemployment in white-collar occupations increased by 50 percent—from 21.8 percent to 32.0 percent—while the white-collar share of total employment grew by only 10 percent.[57]

Mobility studies done from the functionalist perspective, such as Blau and Duncan's, are almost totally concerned with mobility with regard to occupation and not with mobility between classes. Such a focus leads Blau and Duncan to make a grievous error. After attempting to measure the degree of

upward mobility from the blue-collar category into the elite occupations of industrialized capitalist countries,[58] they conclude that there is more upward mobility in the United States than in other advanced capitalist countries. "It is the underprivileged class of manual sons that has exceptional chances for mobility in this country. There is a grain of truth in the Horatio Alger myth.[59]

Examining their data and methodology closely, one arrives at a very different conclusion. In the first instance, there is not really "exceptional" mobility, since only about 10 percent of people from blue-collar backgrounds in the United States move up into Blau and Duncan's elite. Second, and most important, Blau and Duncan define the American "elite" so broadly that it is surprising that there is not *more* movement into it. Their definition of *elite* includes teachers, social welfare workers, nurses, clergymen, accountants, public administrators, and so on. The question that must be asked is, "Is moving from being the son of a steelworker to being a teacher or welfare worker really that much of an upward move?" It seems to us that a more significant move, and one more appropriately a test of the Horatio Alger myth, would be for the son of a blue-collar worker to enter into that 1.6 percent of the population which owns 82.2 percent of all privately held stock in the United States, or into that 0.5 percent of the populace (identified by Domhoff as the "upper class")[60] which effectively controls the major economic, political, and cultural institutions in America. Shifts of this magnitude are very, very rare and in no way characteristic of mobility in the United States.

As we showed in Table 11-1 (page 239), downward mobility is five times more likely

---

[53] Peter Blau and Otis Dudley Duncan, *The American Occupational Structure* (New York: Wiley, 1967), pp. 418–423.

[54] Richard Hamilton, *Class and Politics in the United States* (New York: Wiley, 1972), pp. 156–159; Albert Szymanski, "Trends in the American Working Class," *Socialist Revolution*, vol. 2, no. 4, pp. 101–122.

[55] Blau and Duncan, op. cit., pp. 36–37.

[56] David M. Gordon, "From Steam Whistles to Coffee Breaks," *Dissent*, vol. 19, no. 1, Winter, 1972, p. 198.

[57] Ibid., p. 199.

[58] Blau and Duncan, op. cit., pp. 433–435.

[59] Blau and Duncan, ibid., p. 435.

[60] G. William Domhoff, *The Higher Circles* (New York: Random House, 1970); F. Lundberg, *The Rich and The Super-Rich* (New York: Bantam, 1968).

for black sons of higher white-collar workers than for white. Downward mobility for the class of people in the secondary labor pool (women, blacks, Chicanos, orientals, and native Americans) serves both to make them available for low-paid, dirty work and to make wage-earning white males feel thankful for what security they have.

Some time ago C. Wright Mills reviewed all the studies which identified the social-class background of America's chief corporate executives. He found that only "12 percent are sons of wage workers or of lower white-collar employees."[61] Extrapolating from these findings shows that only about 0.005 percent of people from blue-collar backgrounds become top corporate executives— hardly much support for the Horatio Alger, Blau-Duncan myth.

Finally, the finding by Blau and Duncan of greater upward mobility for the United States in comparison with other industrialized capitalist countries is dependent on their broader definition of elite in the United States case as opposed to the other nations. Thus, with regard to the cross-cultural data they present, we find that the more broadly defined is the elite the greater is the upward mobility into it.

Thus we must conclude that although the transition from feudal to industrial economies opened different avenues of mobility for a short period of time, the recent history of industrialized nations has been characterized by the existence of relatively static elite groups that receive only a trickle of new blood from below. Even in the early 1900s most of the owners and managers of industry came from old established and professional families.[62] The studies of Philadelphia's business elite and the Eastern "Protestant establishment" by E. Digby Balt-

zell have shown how the elite business and professional groups in America form a closed class, a place in which must be inherited.[63] The relatively few people who do break into the elite groups from other social-class backgrounds come mainly from strata immediately below the elite groups, not from the wage-earning class. Furthermore, as Baltzell also shows, new membership is restricted to those who are Protestant and attend the "correct" Eastern schools. In his work *Classes in Modern Society*, T. B. Bottomore emphasizes this point by saying:

> The long-range movement from the manual strata into the elites . . . has not been very considerable at any time during the present century. Miller has shown that even in the first decade of the century successful business men had not generally risen from the lower strata of society, but had come for the most part from old, established families in the business and professional strata. Similarly, a very thorough study of social classes in Philadelphia has revealed that the leading positions in the economic system are occupied predominantly by individuals from the established upper class families.[64]

EDUCATION AND INEQUALITY

The dominant educational process in advanced industrial nations is an institutional pattern which operates to perpetuate and maintain the system of inequality. In the United States, pupils are supposed to be judged on "merit," and advanced according to their "ability" as determined by performance in the classroom and IQ test scores. In reality, the educational system prepares the sons and daughters of the lower strata to accept their future in lower-strata positions while middle- and upper-strata sons and daughters are shown the road to middle-

---

[61] C. Wright Mills, *The Power Elite* (New York: Oxford University Press, 1956), pp. 127–128.
[62] Ibid.

[63] E. Digby Baltzell, *An American Business Aristocracy* (New York: Collier, 1962).
[64] T. B. Bottomore, *Classes in Modern Society* (London: Allen and Unwin, 1965).

and upper-strata jobs. The daughters of all social strata are cajoled, coerced, or manipulated into accepting the inferior status of housekeepers and mothers who will participate slightly or not at all in the economy or the political process. In short, the educational system perpetuates the social class and caste system by sifting and screening people psychologically and socially into those categories which "fit" the established class structure. As Martin Carnoy puts it:

Children are taught to respond to certain rewards and punishments, to learn the criteria for success and failure, and to be highly sensitive to their "record," that vague, never-seen file which follows them—constantly growing thicker—throughout their lives. The values and culture transmitted in the schools largely reflect the ideology of the upper echelons of the hierarchy. Today's school is the result of an elite rule that has distorted the role of the schools from the nineteenth century until now.[65]

The use of IQ as a basis for making this process of channeling appear "objective" and "fair" is an excellent illustration of how the barbarism of class conditioning can be made to appear legitimate. In Weber's terms, this is the "rational authority" by which the structure is legitimized.

With the exception of a few extremists, social scientists no longer defend the position that IQ tests are able to cut through the consequences of environment and tap some basic intellectual capacity.[66] Even the extremists end by accepting the tautological

nature of IQ testing, that is, that "IQ is what IQ tests measure." What *do* IQ tests measure, if not innate ability? Mainly they measure the socioeconomic status of the respondent. The tests invariably contain questions about objects and items familiar to middle- and upper-strata children but likely to be alien to children from the lower strata. For example, an item on an IQ test widely used in elementary schools asks the child, "What color are rubies?" Obviously, a middle- or upper-strata child is much more likely to be familiar with rubies and their color than a lower-strata child.

Even more revealing is the following question from the Stanford-Binet IQ test. For example, a child is asked to compare pictures of two women and tell the tester "which one is prettier." Not surprisingly, the "right" answer is the neat, respectable, middle-strata woman. Identifying her as "prettier" makes one more intelligent. Children are also asked to explain "why it is better to give money to a charity than to a beggar." Any sensitive and *intelligent* working-class child might well question the assumption that it is better to give to a charity than to a beggar.

All such items discriminate heavily against children from low-income families. To suppose that tests with questions like these somehow measure "intelligence" is absolutely absurd. Yet it is on the basis of just such test results that the educational psychologist Arthur Jensen has seriously proposed that there are inherited intelligence differences between blacks and whites which make the blacks less capable of being educated. And it is on the basis of this fallacious reasoning that Richard Hernstein has proposed that the Census Bureau routinely collect data on IQ which could then be used as a basis of instituting policy designed to limit population growth in certain parts of the United States.

[65] Martin Carnoy (ed.), *Schooling in Corporate Society* (New York: McKay, 1972), p. 2. See also Christopher Jencks et al., *Inequality: A Reassessment of the Effect of Family and Schooling in America* (New York: Basic Books, 1972).
[66] Arthur Jensen, "How Much Can We Boost I.Q. and Scholastic Achievement," *Harvard Educational Review*, vol. 39, no. 1, pp. 1–123. For criticisms of Jensen's work see Jerome Kagan, "Inadequate Evidence and Illogical Conclusions," *Harvard Educational Review*, vol. 39, no. 2, pp. 126–129; J. M. Hunt, "Has Compensatory Education Failed? Has It Been Attempted?" *Harvard Educational Review*, vol. 39, no. 2, pp. 130–152.

Were the consequences of these tests insignificant, the tests would simply be laughable. Unfortunately, the IQ test is a major source of information fed into the educational system used to channel children into different tracks and ultimately to keep them in the social class of their origin. The IQ test, like the school system as a whole, fails to select the "most talented" students in any way save to accept as a given fact that the offspring of the upper strata are the most talented and those of the lower strata the least. It is a self-perpetuating class system justified by an elaborate facade of objective evaluation and testing. But in the end it is no more than a rationalized (but not necessarily rationally intelligent) system for maintaining a class-structured capitalist society.

A recent analysis by economists Samuel Bowles and Herbert Gintis compared the relative importance of IQ and class status in determining jobs held after leaving school.[67] Their research makes it very clear that social-stratum background is a good predictor of job status after leaving school but IQ reflects only social-stratum background. Bowles and Gintis go on to argue that the necessity of filling positions of unequal income and status causes the elite strata to use IQ tests as a mechanism for channeling lower-strata people into lower-strata jobs. This perpetuation of inequality hits hardest at women and minorities.

But IQ tests are not the sole basis for moving pupils into their inherited class positions. The constant perpetuation of those values and ideals which are congenial to the lifestyle of the middle- or upper-strata child but

[67] Samuel Bowles and Herbert Gintis, "IQ in the U.S. Class Structure," *Social Policy*, vol. 3, nos. 4 and 5, November-December, 1972, January-February, 1973. See also Samuel Bowles, "Schooling and Inequality from Generation to Generation," *Journal of Political Economy*, vol. 80, no. 3, part II (supplement), May-June, 1972; Richard Gintis, "Education, Technology, and the Characteristics of Worker Productivity," *American Economic Review*, May 1971, vol. 61, pp. 266–279; Samuel Bowles, "Getting Nowhere: Programmed Class Stagnation," *Society*, vol. 9, no. 8, 1972.

incongenial to the life conditions of the lower-strata child results in a sometimes subtle, sometimes not so subtle, isolation and ridicule of lower-strata youth. This process closes the doors of success to the low-income child while rewarding the middle- or upper-income youth for adhering to middle-strata standards.

The teacher, a rather large buxom woman in her early forties, was seated behind her desk when the first graders began drifting in for that first day of school. Many of the students appeared genuinely nervous over their new position in life. Others seemed to have their butterfly stomachs under control. One of the first to enter was a primly dressed, pony tailed blonde who entered the room with a smile and a "good morning" to the teacher. She moved immediately to a seat in the front row, sat demurely down tucking her dress under her legs, folded her hands, and waited with eyes fixed in the general direction of the teacher.

Shortly after the bell rang, a disheveled boy with clean but worn clothes entered the room. He looked around with a scowl; observed the scene somewhat critically. His movements were fluid to the point of being arrogant. His hair was slightly uncombed and his demeanor spoke a total lack of being impressed with the scene. He moved rather noisily to the second row from the back, sat down abruptly while looking over the other students, and slouched belligerently in his chair. All eyes turned to him as he walked in "tardy" but the student's eyes moved back to watch the teacher in time to see a very deep frown cross her face. For those that missed her disapproval of this youth's behavior there was a brief but controlled anger expressed in a short statement she made about the importance of being on time and coming to school looking tidy.[68]

Of course it was not inevitable that the middle-strata girl would be tidy and neat and

[68] William J. Chambliss, "Field Notes, Classroom Observations," 1966.

the lower-strata boy would be unkempt. But given the facts that the girl was a second child in a family whose mother did not work, while the boy was the fourth of five children in a family where the mother went to work an hour before school started, the odds were against the boy's meeting the approved standards of punctuality and tidiness. And the approval of one demeanor and disapproval of the other is the beginning of a lengthy process by which lower-strata youth are encouraged to "accept their position" in a class-structured society.

Malcolm X reported a similar, though somewhat more dramatic, experience in school[69]:

> Somehow, I happened to be alone in the classroom with Mr. Ostrowski, my English teacher. He was a tall, rather reddish white man and he had a thick mustache. I had gotten some of my best marks under him, and he had always made me feel that he liked me. He was, as I have mentioned, a natural-born "advisor," about what you ought to read, to do, or think —about any and everything. We used to make unkind jokes about him: why was he teaching in Mason instead of somewhere else, getting for himself some of the "success in life" that he kept telling us how to get?
>
> I know that he probably meant well in what he happened to advise me that day. I doubt that he meant any harm. It was just in his nature as an American white man. I was one of his top students, one of the school's top students—but all he could see for me was the kind of future "in your place" that almost all white people see for black people.
>
> He told me, "Malcolm, you ought to be thinking about a career. Have you been giving it thought?"
>
> The truth is, I hadn't. I never have figured out why I told him, "Well, yes, sir, I've been thinking I'd like to be a lawyer." Lansing certainly had no Negro lawyers—or doctors either —in those days, to hold up an image I might

> have aspired to. All I really knew for certain was that a lawyer didn't wash dishes, as I was doing.
>
> Mr. Ostrowski looked surprised, I remember, and leaned back in his chair and clasped his hands behind his head. He kind of half-smiled and said, "Malcolm, one of life's first needs is for us to be realistic. Don't misunderstand me, now. We all like you, you know that. But you've got to be realistic about being a nigger. A lawyer—that's no realistic goal for a nigger. You need to think about something you *can* be. You're good with your hands— making things. Everybody admires your carpentry shop work. Why don't you plan on carpentry? People like you as a person—you'd get all kinds of work.
>
> The more I thought afterwards about what he said, the more uneasy it made me. It just kept treading around in my mind.
>
> What made it really begin to disturb me was Mr. Ostrowski's advice to others in my class— all of them white. Most of them had told him they were planning to become farmers. But those who wanted to strike out on their own, to try something new, he had encouraged. Some, mostly girls, wanted to be teachers. A few wanted other professions, such as one boy who wanted to become a county agent; another, a veterinarian; and one girl wanted to be a nurse. They all reported that Mr. Ostrowski had encouraged what they had wanted. Yet nearly none of them had earned marks equal to mine.

Counseling, grades, IQ tests, college board exams, and an incredible array of informal observations and reactions are all part of an educational process that perpetuates inequality and ensures a labor force that will fill all those jobs and tasks that are essential to the American political economy. Students who "succeed" in high school get into the best universities. In the case of the most elite of the elite universities it is commonplace for entrants to have attended one of a limited number of extremely expensive "prep" schools whose sole purpose is to

[69] Malcolm X, *The Autobiography of Malcolm X* (New York: Grove, 1967).

train the students in the art of passing the entrance and first-year examinations at the university of their choice. Junior colleges and state colleges are available for those who cannot join the "top 10 percent" who make it into the prestigious universities. And of course the jobs available on graduation are determined largely by the prestige or "ranking" of the university the student attends.

There are, of course, those who escape all this channeling. Very rarely, a son or daughter of an elite family fails to accept or assume his or her "natural" place at the top of the class system. More often, though still rarely, a child of the streets will rise to the heights of the elite. But these are exceptions which are tied closely to the labor demands of the economy at a particular point in its historical development. In hard times, that is, when the economy is not expanding, mobility declines precipitously. Those jobs that are available at the top are reduced in number, and the children of the elite are sufficient in number to fill them.

Previous attempts to break the educational cycle that perpetuates the inheritance of class standing have not been terribly successful. The control and influence of the upper classes on those who do the educating virtually ensure that the children of the upper classes will have the greatest opportunity to obtain class-compatible positions. China recently abolished all entrance requirements for university admission, and students are now being chosen by their work groups in the cities or by local groups of farmers in rural villages. We have no idea how well this new program will succeed in its intention, which is to make the university open to those who want to learn regardless of class background. This new pattern is described in Selection 17-4. We do know, however, that the experiment has yielded evidence that students chosen by criteria other than previous performance or entrance ex-

aminations do as well if not better than those chosen by the presumably objective measure of examinations.

THE MAINTENANCE AND REPRODUCTION OF INEQUALITY

Occupational roles in countries dominated by capitalistic economic patterns can be classified according to the degree of independence one has at his or her place of work. For some there is relative autonomy while for others there is a high degree of discipline and direct control. Thus some jobs require a significant degree of self-direction and internal discipline, and others require obedience, predictability, and the willingness to subject oneself to external controls. Different personality attributes are associated with the satisfactory performance of these differing occupational roles.

Psychologists tell us that many important personality attributes (such as motivation, perseverence, docility, dominance, flexibility, tact, manner of speech, modes of dress, etc.) are developed at a young age in the context of the family and further developed and reinforced in other institutions that are part of the socialization process, such as the schools. These personality attributes tend to vary by social class.

That different social classes develop varying personality traits which are passed on to their children has been suggested in the research of Melvin Kohn.[70] Furthermore, Kohn has shown that class-related similarities and differences in personality type occur in countries other than the United States.[71] Kohn concludes, "The close relationship between fathers' occupational experiences and

[70] Melvin L. Kohn, "Social Class and Parent-Child Relationships: An Interpretation," *American Journal of Sociology*, vol. 68, 1963, pp. 471–480.
[71] Leonard I. Pearlin and Melvin L. Kohn, "Social Class, Occupation, and Parental Values: A Cross-National Study," in Charles Anderson (ed.), *Sociological Essays and Research: Introductory Readings* (Hometown, Ill.: Dorsey, 1970), pp. 290–310.

SELECTION 17-4: Attempts to reverse inequality by open university admissions.

CHINESE UNIVERSITIES DROP ENTRANCE EXAMINATIONS

LEE LESCAZE

Hongkong—As they reopen for technical classes after a four-year hiatus, China's universities have abandoned entrance examinations in favour of admitting students selected by their peers.

The new enrolment policy makes it possible for workers, peasants, and soldiers to join more conventionally qualified youths as university students. It is a result of Mao Tse-tung's cultural revolution and a logical product of his long-held conviction that the way for China to overcome her backwardness is by raising all men simultaneously, rather than by the Western route of building on a society's best minds, which creates a privileged leadership class.

Some of the places in the universities are allocated to each province, and within a province to the counties, the farm communes, and the industrial centres. When the Tachai production brigade, a team in Shansi province whose achievements are constantly held up as a model for other communes, was told that it could send a student to Peking's Tsinghua University, it immediately called a meeting of the farmers.

At the meeting, according to a recent New China news agency report, the peasants noted that the revisionist educational policies of the disgraced Chief of State, Liu Shao-chi, "prevented poor and lower-middle peasants from entering institutions of higher learning."

At the end of their discussions, they unanimously chose the brigade's bookkeeper, who was also a leading Communist Party member, to be their first student at Tsinghua University —China's most famous school of engineering. The choice of a man with experience in the Communist Party is apparently not unusual. The same New China news agency report said that most of the worker-peasant-soldier students now entering the universities are members of the party or the Communist Youth League.

Hard Work

The criterion for choosing students is that they be pacesetters in the three great revolutionary movements. These are "class struggle" or political action, "struggle for production" or hard work, and "struggle for scientific experiment," which means technical ability.

Often the newly chosen students are sent to college with gifts that will serve to remind them of their proletarian origins.

Each worker-student selected from the Taching oilfield, was given a set of the selected works of Mao Tse-tung and a spade before leaving for the university.

However, in spite of such reminders, some of the students forget their proletarian heritage, the report said. It described a young woman studying at the electrical engineering department of Tsinghua University, who was about to go to town one day, when she noticed that her clothes had become stained with oil. She worried that people would notice the stains. Her worry only lasted a moment, however, for she remembered that in the past she had often gone to speak with the people of her village while her clothes were drenched with sweat and covered with mud from her farm labours.

She studied Chairman Mao's teachings on hard struggle and realised that "it was not her clothes that were dirty but her ideology that was becoming soiled."

China's aim, according to official articles, is the creation of "Socialist" universities which will only be realised after "profound social revolution" ends the "thousands of years" during which schools "were designed to train successors for the landlord class and the bourgeoisie."

The Peking leadership has, throughout recent years, expressed repeatedly its concern about whether the new generations of Chinese, who did not experience the exploitations of pre-Communist China and did not fight in the revolution, will continue along the Maoist line or abandon building communism—as China believes the Soviet Union has done.

Memory

To keep alive the memory of what China was like before the Communists took power, older people tell stories of their early years to students. In the universities, some of the elderly worker-peasant-soldier students are appointed teachers to lecture on the hardships they suffered under capitalism.

Education in the early years of Communist rule is dismissed in recent articles as having been little improvement over the pre-Communist system. One example given recently was that only 170 students from worker families in Shanghai were enrolled by Tsinghua University from 1959 to 1963, while 330 children of "Shanghai capitalists" were admitted. It took the cultural revolution, during which universities were closed for four years, to bring about the necessary educational changes, Peking's official statements make clear.

their values for their children indicate that fathers are simply preparing their children for occupational life to come. . . . Fathers come to value these characteristics in their own right and not simply as means to occupational goals."[72]

The varying personality attributes are reinforced in the schools. Schools in different neighborhoods hold up different personality traits as desirable, and try to shape their students' aspirations, self-images, and self-confidence. Teachers, guidance counselors, and school administrators ordinarily encourage students to develop aspirations and expectations in line with their social-class background. Research has also showed that teacher expectations, based on a supposed knowledge of class background and/or "potential," shape students' performances. Robert Rosenthal and Lenore Jacobson, for example, showed that two groups of students of similar ability but labeled differently, that is, high potential versus ordinary, were treated differently by their teachers. The high-potential group did what their teachers expected—they performed above average—and the supposedly ordinary group performed at the average level.[73]

Thus the educational system in many ways operates to distribute academic credentials unevenly, and to reward only certain kinds of behavior. This in turn leads to an unequal distribution of economic rewards.

THE STRATIFIED LABOR MARKET

Another aspect of the perpetuation and reproduction of economic inequality in a capitalist-type economy has been labeled the "dual labor market theory." Reich, Gordon, and Edwards define labor-market segmentation "as the historical process whereby political-economic forces encourage the division of the labor market into separate submarkets, or segments, distinguished by different labor market characteristics and behavioral rules."[74] There are, for example, white-collar and blue-collar occupations, upper-middle and working-strata jobs, occupations in monopoly and competitive industries.

The owners of capital try to reinvest in those areas which promise the greatest return. Certain corporate enterprises surge ahead, while others, if they continue to exist at all, remain at a lower level. There are only a thousand or so giant corporations in America while there are hundreds of thousands of small businesses. "The result of uneven development between industries has been the creation of an extensive working poor population. In 1968 over ten million workers—one in five private nonsupervisory employees—earned less than $1.60 an hour in the United States."[75] There is, in fact, a high correlation between the industry a worker is employed in and his or her take-home pay. Those working in highly tech-

[72] Ibid., p. 310.
[73] Robert Rosenthal and Lenore F. Jacobson, *Pygmalion in the Classroom* (New York: Holt, Rinehart, Winston, 1968), pp. 61–97.

[74] Michael Reich, David M. Gordon, and Richard C. Edwards, "A Theory of Labor Market Segmentation," *American Economic Review*, vol. 63, May, 1973, p. 359.
[75] Barry Bluestone, "Economic Crises and the Law of Uneven Development," *Politics and Society*, Fall, 1972, pp. 68–69.

nologized and monopolized industries have a higher take-home pay.[76]

Employers try to stratify all parts of the labor market in order to maintain their control. For example, the monopoly sector tends to have employees who are male, white, and in the twenty-five- to fifty-year-old age bracket. The competitive, or "secondary," sector tends to fill its positions with non-white workers, young people, and women. According to Howard Wachtel, they do this for three reasons: "first, [the] ease with which employers can identify these groups; second, the resignation of these groups to their jobs in the secondary sector; and third, the advantages this provides in dividing workers along racist, sexist, and age lines—prejudices deeply engrained in American society."[77] The driving force in an economy so structured is the quest for profit and corporate growth. Although lip service may be given to humanitarian values, one would not expect to find support given to efforts to reduce poverty, chronic unemployment, or even stratification in the working class because all of these conditions favor high profits and corporate growth. Selections 17-5 and 17-6 describe the obstacles that block the attempts of the poor to create other ways of getting education and legal assistance.

Some of the more important elements or variables contributing to the perpetuation of economic inequality are: parental income, parental wealth, parental occupation, parental position in the hierarchy of work relations, parental education, level of schooling, the segmented labor market. We would argue that these variables, along with sex and racial

differentials, are the major elements for explaining different incomes.

Parental income may not contribute directly to one's income but it has major indirect effects through environmental factors and education. In other words, money enables one to purchase clothes, homes (neighborhoods), cultural effects (books, entertainment, etc.), friends, higher levels of schooling, and so on. All these contribute to the development of one's personal attributes (manners, appearance, degree of self-confidence, etc.). These, in turn, have a determining effect upon one's occupation and income. Parental wealth does much the same, and often has a direct effect upon income through inheritance.[78] Parental position in the hierarchy of working relations has a *direct* effect on income, as well as an indirect effect on personality, level of schooling, and occupation. Many such direct and indirect effects of the various variables can be identified.

INEQUALITIES AMONG NATIONS

Capitalism has passed through a number of different stages—from a competitive stage in the United States and Britain to a monopoly form characteristic of contemporary industrial capitalism in general.[79] In the competitive stage the individual firm grew by reducing costs, increasing supplies, underselling rivals, and hence realizing larger profits. As some firms prospered and grew, other firms fell by the wayside. The average firm became so large that it had to consider the effect that its own production was having upon the market price. These firms began

[76] Ibid.; see also H. M. Wachtel and C. Betsy, "Employment at Low Wages," *Review of Economics and Statistics,* vol. 54, 1972, pp. 121–129.

[77] Howard M. Wachtel, "Capitalism and Poverty in America: Paradox or Contradiction?" *American Economic Review,* vol. 62, May, 1972, p. 190.

[78] For the importance of inheritance in maintaining economic inequality see John A. Brittain, "Research on the Transmission of Material Wealth," *American Economic Review,* vol. 63, May, 1973, pp. 335–345.

[79] We use *monopoly* here in the Baran and Sweezy sense which includes *oligopoly.* See Paul Baran and Paul M. Sweezy, *Monopoly Capital* (New York: Modern Reader, 1966).

SELECTION 17-5: Grass-roots attempts to create new institutional patterns do not get much support from federal government.

THE POSTAL STREET ACADEMY IS BROKE

RON MOSKOWITZ

The Postal Street Academy, which has turned 300 hard core dropouts into high school graduates in the past three years, is out of money and may go out of existence.

Federal financing of the project ended on June 30 and movers came yesterday to repossess the furniture from the school at 1441 Van Ness Avenue.

That left the school's building an empty shell and demoralized the 15-member staff, which has agreed to stay on without pay until new funds can be found.

So far the federal government has given the school about $1 million in grants. Maurice James, director of the academy, said he has applied for new federal financing but will not know if he can get it until September.

The school, which has 180 students enrolled, got its name from its original fund source, the Post Office, which established the academy to turn dropouts into trained postal workers.

When that financing ceased after a year, the school got new money from the U.S. Department of Health, Education and Welfare to continue its operations a second year.

But again the money ran out and the school was—under pressure from many politicians and civic leaders—paid for a third year by the U.S. Department of Labor. But that one-year contract ended June 30.

James said he could not understand why the federal officials didn't leave the furniture for two more months because it is not needed by other agencies and will only go into storage in a warehouse.

But a spokesman for the Department of Labor here said the school cannot legally use the furniture once its contract with the government is over.

James said the academy will hold a series of benefits throughout the summer to help the school keep going until fall.

By fall, James hopes to have a new grant—this time from the Department of Justice, because 70 per cent of his students are either on probation or parole.

"The Post Office has agreed to help us with the rent and we are asking corporations and politicians for donations so we can at least keep our building and program together until then," James said.

Labor Department officials said the grant was not renewed because it was not one of the programs recommended by the Mayor's Manpower Planning Committee. Besides, it was understood from the beginning the grant would be for one year only, they added.

James said the Mayor's committee did not include his program because it is more academic than vocational in nature.

Students, he said, learn basic communications skills, with emphasis on English. When students get eighth grade proficiency in English, they are given civics, history, math, drama, biology, typing and further training in reading. Then they get a high school equivalency diploma after eight months, he said.

James said that since the program started three and one-half years ago, the school has graduated about 300 students, some 200 of whom have either found steady jobs or decided to further their education elsewhere.

SELECTION 17-6: Class conflict revealed in attempts to destroy alternate or parallel institutionalized attempts to solve working-class problems.

WAR ON THE POOR?

The California Rural Legal Assistance program is a rare government enterprise: a poverty program that actually works too well. The 40-lawyer operation—federally funded through the Office of Economic Opportunity—provides legal services for more than 550,000 poor farm workers, most of whom would otherwise have no access whatever to counsel or the courts. In its four stormy years, the agency has won a stunning 80 per cent of its cases—a record that prompted OEO to increase its grant this year by $205,000 to $1.9 million. But CRLA has won some powerful political enemies in the process. A fortnight ago, under a provision of the law that allows a state to veto Federal poverty funds, Gov. Ronald Reagan struck down the OEO grant—and thus put it squarely to the White House to override the veto or kill the program once and for all.

Promising a privately financed alternative to CRLA, Reagan charged the agency with "gross and deliberate violation of OEO regulations" and "failure to represent the true legal needs of the poor"—charges that grew out of an investigation conducted by California's state poverty director Lewis K. Uhler. Uhler, a former member of the John Birch Society, sent out a letter to 3,000 attorneys and judges around the state inviting complaints about CRLA's operations and "standards of legal ethics"—and assuring that replies could remain anonymous. Among the complaints Uhler termed "alarming": that one CRLA attorney had used four-letter words in front of high-school students and that another had counseled strikers from the United Farm Workers Organizing Committee.

to limit their supplies so as to be able to set prices at a point which would yield the greatest profit. Not to do so would mean an inability on the part of the firm to keep pace with its rivals. Thus did the monopolization process begin. Its consequences have been duly noted by Sweezy:

> Given these possibilities and constraints, the result is an irresistible drive on the part of the monopolistic firm to move outside of and beyond its historical field of operation, to penetrate new industries and new markets. Thus the typical production unit in modern developed capitalism is a giant corporation, which is both conglomerate (operating in many industries) and multinational (operating in many countries).[80]

Capitalism has been "international" ever since its beginnings. This internationalism has taken a number of different forms—first

[80] Paul M. Sweezy, *Modern Capitalism and Other Essays* (New York: Modern Reader, 1972), p. 8.

the mercantile, next the laissez faire, and now the monopolistic. International capitalism is a system of interrelated parts and elements, many of which have been consistently in sharp conflict with other parts. In short, the larger number of exploited countries have clashed with the smaller number of dominant countries. Nothing that happens in one part can be understood if it is considered apart from the system as a whole.

The spread of capitalism throughout the globe produced economically developed and economically underdeveloped spheres. The economically developed nations have been concentrated in North America (excluding Mexico), Europe, and Japan, and the economically underdeveloped nations have been centered in continental Asia, Africa, and Latin America. Capitalism has also generated regions of underdevelopment within the developing, industrialized metropoles, and small pockets of development within the underdeveloped, nonindustrialized peripheries.

The underdeveloped regions, or *satellites*, have been and remain characterized by an emphasis on raw material production with a dependence upon one or a handful of raw material exports. The corporate concerns of these underdeveloped countries are increasingly controlled by foreign investors through multinational corporations which gear their activities to the benefit of the corporation as a whole rather than toward the priorities of the country in which they have located themselves.

The economic surplus generated by the satellite is expropriated and appropriated by the metropolis (the industrial sector), often through the corporate enterprise.[81] The economic surplus is channeled up the hier-

[81] This term was developed by Paul Baran in his *The Political Economy of Growth* (New York: Prometheus, 1960). It is that part of surplus value which is being accumulated, i.e., not being consumed by the capitalist class.

archal chain with each level helping itself to a portion; hence each level develops at the expense of the lower level(s). Stavenhagen writes:

> [T]he developed areas of the underdeveloped countries operate like a pumping mechanism, drawing from their backward, underdeveloped *hinterland* the very elements that make for their own development.[82]

Within the underdeveloped countries as a whole, the local elites, who served the colonial powers in the past, now serve the multinational concerns which control most of the power and wealth. What local capitalist enterprises have managed to develop on their own have been or are being squeezed out by the larger multinational corporations which control world capitalist markets. The powerful military and governmental apparatuses available to such corporations have maintained an environment favorable to the interests of the multinational corporations. A favorable environment includes the removal of obstacles impeding the penetration of national markets by corporate concerns, and the prevention of the rise of forces opposed to such penetration and domination.

The inequalities among nations are well known and need little documentation here.[83] A few figures will be listed simply to remind the reader of the extent of this inequality. In 1965, for instance, the average per capita income (in United States dollars) for the rich, nonsocialist countries[84] was 2,040 dollars, and the average for the poor, nonsocialist countries was 167 dollars.[85] The average rate of economic growth for the rich, nonsocialist countries over the 1950 to 1967 period was 3.0 percent as compared with 2.2 percent for the poor, nonsocialist countries.[86] The economic gap is great and it is widening.

The widening economic gap between the rich and poor nonsocialist countries can be attributed, to a large extent, to the economic exploitation of the poor countries by the rich countries. Most people realize that the United States has greatly profited from its foreign direct investment[87]; figures regarding the minimal extent of this profit making are presented in Table 17-4. Here we can see that the United States has received in income payments (profits, dividends, etc.) 26.2 billion dollars more than it has invested in Latin American and other, largely nondeveloped countries. Petras and Frank, among others, have shown that such figures are *underestimates*.[88] Furthermore, the Canadian data are misleading, since the United States has been operating at a net gain rather than a net loss since 1960.

The French economist Pierre Jalée has copiously documented the drain upon all poor countries by all rich countries. He writes:

> [T]he World Bank evaluated income transferred from the developing countries in 1964 at more than four billion dollars (sic) and at about five billion for 1965, southern Europe excluded. Since in the course of those two years, the

[82] R. Stavenhagen, "Seven Fallacies about Latin America," in James Petras and Maurice Zeitlin (eds.), *Latin America: Reform or Revolution?* (Greenwich, Conn.: Fawcett, 1968), p. 16.

[83] Pierre Jalée, *The Pillage of the Third World* (New York: Modern Reader, 1968), and *The Third World in World Economy* (New York: Modern Reader, 1969). See also Robin Jenkins, *Exploitation* (London: Paladin, 1971), and Thomas E. Weisskopf, "Capitalism, Underdevelopment and the Future of the Poor Countries," *Review of Radical Political Economics*, vol. 4, no. 1, pp. 1–35.

[84] By *nonsocialist* we mean economies not claimed to be organized along Marxist-Leninist lines.

[85] Thomas E. Weisskopf, "Capitalism, Underdevelopment and the Future of the Poor Countries," *Review of Radical Political Economics*, vol. 4, no. 1, pp. 1–35.

[86] Ibid.

[87] For example, see Linda Majka, "The Military Industrial Complex Reconsidered," unpublished M.A. thesis, Department of Sociology, University of California, Santa Barbara, 1973.

[88] Andre Gunder-Frank, *Latin America: Underdevelopment or Revolution* (New York: Modern Reader, 1969), pp. 50–52; James Petras, *Politics and Social Structure in Latin America* (New York: Modern Reader, 1970), pp. 234–235.

TABLE 17-4　Income from Direct Investments 1950 to 1970
(Billions of Dollars)

	Europe	Canada	Latin America	Other
Flow from United States	15.5	10.6	6.0	9.5
Income	10.4	10.0	17.1	24.6
United States net gain	−5.1	−0.6	+11.1	+15.1

SOURCE: From Linda Majka, "The Military Industrial Complex Reconsidered," Unpublished M.A. thesis, University of California, Santa Barbara, 1973.

influx of fresh capital in the form of direct private investments equalled only 970 and 1,360 million dollars respectively, there was a net deficit of 3½ billion dollars annually for the countries in question, namely the Third World.[89]

Jalée also notes the deficit the less-developed countries experience when trading with the rich countries. The overall trade deficit for less-developed countries varied between 1.2 and 1.8 billion dollars over the 1964–1966 period. These figures indicate a *trend* pointing to a continuing overall increase in the deficit over time.[90]

The foreign aid which the rich, capitalist nations. Foreign aid is largely in loan form tries does nothing to alleviate the capital drain experienced by the underdeveloped nations. Foreign aid is largely in loan form and must be repaid with interest. There are also conditions for receiving such aid, including the following:

1. The aid received is to be used to purchase the products of the lending nation.
2. The shipping of such goods is to take place on the shipping lines of the nation lending the money.
3. The aid lent is to be used to serve the businesses of the lending nation which operate in the country receiving the aid.

[89] Pierre Jalée, *Imperialism in the Seventies* (New York: Third Press, 1972), pp. 72–73.
[90] Ibid., p. 73

Thus the aid is designed to further the status quo in the borrowing countries—a status quo through which the rich nations profit. The result is that foreign aid is negatively correlated with the economic growth rates of the nondeveloped countries (the more the aid the less the growth), and the public debt of these countries grows rapidly.[91]

The rich, capitalist nations have become increasingly dependent upon the poor countries for much of their natural resources. There are at least two reasons for this dependence. First of all, the rich countries may never have had the resources. Second, rich countries may have depleted those resources which are cheaply and easily extractable. In 1968, North America, with less than 9 percent of the world's population, consumed 67.5 percent of the world's consumption of natural and imported gases, 38.6 percent of the world's consumption of liquid fuel, and 37.5 percent of the world's consumption of total energy. In the same year, the United States, with 6 percent of the world's population, consumed 26 percent of the world's

[91] For a thorough examination of the role of foreign "aid" see T. Hayter's *Aid as Imperialism* (Middlesex, Eng.: Pelican, 1971). For studies relating foreign aid to economic growth, see, for examples, W. Gordon, "Has Foreign Aid been Overstated? International Aid and Development," *Inter-American Economic Affairs*, vol. 21, 1968, pp. 3–18; K. G. Griffin and J. L. Enos, "Foreign Assistance: Objectives and Consequences," *Economic Development and Cultural Change*, vol. 18, 1970, pp. 313–327; Paul Stevenson, "External Economic Variables Influencing the Economic Growth Rate of Seven Major Latin American Nations," *Canadian Review of Sociology and Anthropology*, vol. 9, no. 4, 1972, pp. 347–356.

consumption of steel, 42 percent of the world's consumption of rubber, 35 percent of the world's consumption of tin, and 26 percent of the world's consumption of fertilizer.[92]

Given the effects of these rates of consumption on world resource levels, on air and water pollution which crosses national boundaries, and on the life-support cycle, it becomes clear that it is more accurate to speak of overdeveloped nations rather than developed and undeveloped nations. The promises held out by the overdeveloped nations that they will produce some scientific magic (cheap nuclear power, new high-protein foods) seem more and more empty as the years go by.

Jalée has noted the extent of the dependence of the rich countries upon the resources of the underdeveloped nations:

> In the case of steel manufacture, the [rich] countries today are not only dependent on the Third World for iron ore to meet at least one-third of their needs—and this dependence is increasing rapidly—but they are almost totally dependent upon foreign sources for those ever more indispensable materials, manganese and chromium, and they import more than three-quarters of their cobalt requirements. As for metallurgy, aluminum has become a basic metal and the [rich] countries can only satisfy their needs for it from the foreign countries that supply nearly three-quarters of these requirements. The [rich] countries also depend on foreign sources for two-fifths of their copper and virtually all their tin. In all these areas, the countries of the Third World are either the exclusive source (cobalt, copper) or they predominate overwhelmingly (manganese, chromium, aluminum, tin) when competitive

supplies are traded to the [rich] countries by socialist countries.[93]

Further Comments on Regional Inequality

We have already noted how metropolis regions pump out the economic surplus of satellites *within* national boundaries or states. This relationship goes far toward explaining regional inequities within developed and underdeveloped capitalist nations. There are, of course, other contributing factors. Mandel has noted that profit rates vary from area to area, with high-profit regions receiving more investment and thus development.[94] The former editor of the *American Economic Review*, John Gurley, writes:

> Private profit-making requires efficiency. To be efficient, a business firm builds on the best . . . it locates where the most profits can be made —next to other factories that can give it low-cost access to supplies, or near markets where it can sell its products—even though a great social good might be served by locating in a depressed, poverty-ridden area. For the same reason, a banker extends loans to those who are already successful, or to those with the best prospects.[95]

In summary, then, the economic inequalities among nations and among regions within nations are rooted in the normal operations of the capitalist mode of production. We can now turn our attention to the inequalities between industries.

INEQUALITIES BETWEEN INDUSTRIES

It appears to be an economic law of capitalism that industries become concentrated and centralized, with the less competitive

[92] Frank Ackerman, H. Birnbaum, J. Wetzler, and A. Zimbalist, "The Extent of Income Inequality in the United States," in Richard C. Edwards, Michael Reich, and Thomas E. Weisskopf (eds.), *The Capitalist System: A Radical Analysis of American Society* (Englewood Cliffs, N.J.: Prentice-Hall, 1972), p. 208.

[93] Jalée, *Imperialism in the Seventies*, op. cit., pp. 43–44.
[94] Ernest Mandel, "Capitalism and Regional Disparities," pamphlet (Toronto: Hogtown Press, 1972).
[95] John Gurley, "Capitalism: The Root of the Problem," in Tom Christoffel, David Finkelhor, and Dan Gilbarg (eds.), *Up Against the American Myth* (New York: Holt, Rinehart, Winston, 1970), p. 53.

falling by the wayside while the remaining firms grab the markets that are left behind. This monopolization process has occurred in every capitalist country no matter what the situation with regard to acceptance or rejection of such things as cartels, antitrust legislation, etc.[96]

The empirical result of this process for the United States has been noted by Bluestone.

> In 1968 the one hundred largest corporations had a greater share of manufacturing assets than did the two hundred largest in 1950, and the two hundred largest in 1968 controlled a share equal to that held by the thousand largest in 1941. By 1969 these two hundred firms controlled two-thirds of all manufacturing assets. The remaining one-third was split among literally hundreds of thousands of smaller firms.[97]

Bluestone further notes that this growing concentration of wealth and economic power is a result of the internal growth of the most profitable firms, which allows them either to gobble up the smaller firms, or to continue growing while the other firms struggle to keep alive.

CONCLUSION

Inequality is an inevitable consequence of capitalism—inequality among classes and strata within capitalist countries and inequality among nations. That this inequality can be understood from the conflict perspective, and is only muddled by a functional analysis, has been the major argument in this chapter.

America, and most of the capitalist world, is in a state of dire economic crisis. Energy resources are diminishing, unemployment is rampant, and inequalities are growing. Persistent inequality is a major source of social conflict and a fundamental cause of social change. As inequalities in wealth, standard of living, power, and life chances increase, so too does the pressure for change. The institutions that attempt to reduce the impact of inequality—for example, in the law, by defining class conflict as "deviance," and in the educational system, by defining lower-strata children as "uneducable" or "hypertense"—are under increasing pressure. Internal rebellions, increasing criminality, and an increased consciousness of the institutional source of "personal" problems are manifestations of the economic crisis. Internationally, the nations that control and exploit most of the world's resources are being pressed to either redistribute the world's wealth or go to war to protect their privileged positions. Going to war, however, consumes a nation's manpower and causes further conflicts and discontent. Thus it is that the momentum toward change stems from contradictions built into the very logic of the economic form. And so it is that we can expect to see the historical process of conflict and change that we have surveyed in this introduction to sociology continue into the future.

[96] Ernest Mandel, *Marxist Economic Theory*, vol. II (New York: Modern Reader, 1970), pp. 393–440. For a different interpretation from a radical perspective see Gabriel Kolko, *The Triumph of Conservatism* (Chicago: Quadrangle, 1963).

[97] Barry Bluestone, "Economic Crises and the Law of Uneven Development," *Politics and Society*, Fall, 1972, pp. 67–68.

SUGGESTED READINGS

Robert Alford, "The Political Economy of Health Care," MSS Modular Publications, Reprint no. 96.

Harry Caudill, *Night Comes to the Cumberlands* (Boston: Little, Brown, 1967).

Noam Chomsky, "The Fallacy of Richard Hernstein's I.Q.," MSS Modular Reprint no. 682.

Thomas B. Cottle, *Time's Children* (Boston: Little, Brown, 1971).

Herbert Coles, "Life in Appalachia: The Case of Hugh McCaslin," MSS Modular Publications, Reprint no. R726.

Herbert Gans, "The Positive Functions of Poverty," MSS Modular Publications, Reprint no. R76.

Andre Gunder-Frank, "The Development of Underdevelopment," MSS Modular Publications, Reprint no. R208.

Karl Marx, "The So-called Primitive Accumulation," MSS Modular Publications, Reprint no. R629.

Richard Parker, *The Myth of the Middle Class* (New York: Harper & Row, 1972).

Richard Rubenstein, *Rebels in Eden* (Boston: Little, Brown, 1970).

William Ryan, *Blaming the Victim* (New York: Pantheon Books, 1971).

George Vesey, *One Sunset a Week* (New York: Saturday Review Press, 1974).

NAME INDEX

SUBJECT INDEX